Chinese Fund for the Humanities and Social Sciences

China's Private Economy: Institution Innovations and Development

Li Wei'an et al.

Translated by Liu Xingyun, Wang Yujin

Paths International Ltd

中国财经出版传媒集团
经济科学出版社
Economic Science Press

Abstract

Based on Institutional Economics, Evolutionary Economics, Comparative Institutional Analysis and Management Theory, tracking the institutional innovation during the development of private economy, the book constructs a common analytical framework for studies on institutional innovation and development of private economy. Firstly, the book analyses the process and mechanism of private economy's evolution, and abstracts a more common pattern of private economy's evolution that is featured by interaction between multiple forces and push of both government and the private and breaks the limitation of regional pattern. Secondly, the book makes a deep analysis of some key problems faced by private economy, explores the innovational mechanism in entrepreneurial behavior, financing choice, equity arrangement and governance optimization, and internationalization of private firms. Lastly, the book evaluates the developing status of private economy and private firms, and gives some advice on institutional innovation and development of private economy.

This book contains three parts with eight chapters. The first part is *Theoretical analysis on private economy evolution and innovation*, which contains two chapters of *Institutional change and organizational evolution in the development of private economy* and *Dynamic process of private economy institution innovation.* The second part is *Development barrier and institution innovations of private enterprises*, which contains four chapters of *Entrepreneurial behaviour and entrepreneur environment of private enterprises*, *Analysis on financing obstacles for private enterprises*, *Governance issue in the growth of private enterprises* and *Institutional environment in international development process of private enterprises.* The third part is *Evaluation and countermeasure of private economy and enterprise development*, which contains two chapters of *Evaluation on the governance of private listed companies* and *Policy suggestions on institution innovation and development of private economy.* The basic contents of each chapter are as follows:

Chapter 1: *Institutional change and organizational evolution in the development of private economy.* Based on a review over twenty years' development of private economy and organization evolution, from the prospective of ideology preference, Local government behavior, historical path dependence, institution complementation and productivity competition between economic organizations, this chapter analyzes the mechanism of institution transition and organization evolution during the development of private economy. After comparing different regional developing patterns of private economy, the book abstracts a common evolution model of mutual interaction, infiltration, competition and substitution among private economy, State-owned Enterprise reform and foreign capital infiltration.

Chapter 2: *Dynamic process of private economy institution innovations.* Using the dynamic model in economics, starting with two key factors: technology progress and information asymmetry that restrict the development of private economy, this chapter analyze the evolving mechanism of institution innovation of private economy, and gets some important conclusions. 1. From the prospective of optimal technology progress rate, this chapter finds that strengthening patent protection has less effect on social welfare when invention cost is higher. 2. Through analyzing the relationship between optimal patent system and the dynamic efficiency of private economy, this chapter finds that both the optimal patent length and width are limited. 3. Through an endogenous economic growth model, this chapter finds that the asymmetry of quality information will not only cause the market of private economy to shrink, but also depress the pricing of knowledge product, decrease R&D investment, and eventually block a country's knowledge growth.

Chapter 3: *Entrepreneurial behaviour and entrepreneur environment of private enterprises.* Firstly, this chapter makes a deep investigation on entrepreneurial rationality, exposits the process and key factors of entrepreneurial activities, changes the traditional cognition that the success of starting an undertaking is decided by entrepreneur's gift. Secondly, this chapter points out that start-up environment is different from investment environment, and start-up policy is also different from policy for small and medium sized firms, suggesting that what the government should emphasize is not investment environment, but start-up environment. Finally, based on the essence of matching entrepreneurs with opportunities, this chapter proposes to build mutual interaction between entrepreneurs and opportunities, which overcomes research lines that used to emphasize only on the identifying and grasping of opportunities by entrepreneurs and analyses the evolution of China's entrepreneurs from an interactive relationship.

Chapter 4: *Analysis on financing obstacles for private enterprises.* This chapter first sums up the institutional factors into three aspects: national economy influence, local government power and marketization level, and then constructs a new theoretical framework explaining the difference of private economic development patterns in different regions, makes a systematical analysis on how endowment difference and institution rent change affect the financing choice of private firms, makes an empirical research on financing amount and structure of private firms, and concludes: 1. Institution evolution pattern determines the developing pattern of private economy. Different combinations of historical starting and dynamic evolving path lead to various developing patterns in different regions, and thus result in corresponding finance patterns. 2. Institution rent decides the financing choice of private firms. 3. Private firms face both aggregate and structural contradiction, and the latter is greater than the former.

Chapter 5: *Governance issue in the growth of private enterprises.* This chapter studies the inflexion point of governance during the development of private firms, the principal-agent relationship and transfer of control rights inside family firms, the influence of human resource on governance etc. Conclusions are: 1. Family governance has some rationality at certain stage, but will become obstruction with further development of private firms and thus should develop towards open family firms. 2. To make the best use of the separation of two rights, government should strengthen legal protection of private property, and family firms should consummate internal audit and control mechanism, prevent the opportunism of managers, and establish effective incentive mechanism so as to make the interest of managers is in line with that of family firms. 3. The level of diversification of ownership equity and control right transfer is higher for private firms at a mature stage than for those at an earlier stage of development.

Chapter 6: *Institutional environment in international development process of private enterprises.* Following the classical paradigm of "Structure-Behavior-Performance" in industrial organization theory, this chapter first analyzes the relationship between export behavioral characteristics and performance. Then, from the prospective of international division of labor and value chain, this chapter analyzes the typical market dislocation problem in the export of private firms. Conclusions are:

1. The horizontal difference between export products of private firms is low. 2. The products' vertical difference is not high. 3. Market structure of low centralization leads to private firms' lack of market power in export market. 4. The comparative benefit derived from international division of labor and trade is not only decided by the optimization of export product structure at technology level, but also decided by the institution innovation of export firms at organization level.

Chapter 7: *Evaluation on the governance of private listed companies.* This chapter constructs a governance index of private listed firms from four dimensions-board of directors, ownership equity structure, incentive and restriction for the management and information disclosure, and finds there exist the following governance problems in private listed firms: (1) Group control is the crux that leads ultimate controlling shareholder to take encroachment behavior. (2) Board of directors is characterized by large shareholder control. (3) Compensation for the management is low, and the management's shareholding is non-linearly related with firm performance. (4) The governance of board of supervisors needs to improve. (5) The zeal for information disclosure and the independence of audit opinion are improving, and the independent director system plays an important role on improving the information disclosure of listed firms.

Chapter 8: *Policy suggestions on institution innovation and development of private economy.* This chapter is mainly a summary of the above seven chapters' conclusions and policy suggestions on prompting the institution innovation and development of private economy.

Preface

The historical development of private economy in China is reflected by a process of continuous institution innovation. It is in line with of the nature of Chinese economy, including marketization and internationalization. As a leading force of Chinese economic development for the past 20 years, private economy has come to an important strategic pass where we can achieve breakthroughs under the process of restructuring the state-owned economy and entering into overseas-funded enterprises and opportunities.

How can we evaluate the contributions made by private economy during the process of 30 years of rapid reconstruction of China's economy? Under what kind of environment and institution has the current private economy and all of its organizations realized the constant developments? What kind of demands for the changing institution will be proposed during the change of new politics, economy, law and society? How can we understand private enterprises and the dynamic development through institution innovations under the conditions of asymmetric information and increasingly rapid technical change? How to better understand entrepreneurship, entrepreneurial behaviour and its characteristics, which are important sources for the promotion of private economy's rapid development to propose a policy proposal on improving entrepreneurial environment for private enterprises? In aspect of financing choke point that hinders the rapid development forprivate economy all the time, what role has the folk finance played on earth? Under the situation of increasing and expanding scale and the business scope of enterprises, what developmental obstacles will be encountered by traditional family-based governance mode of private enterprises? How can we understand the breakthroughs in governance structure and mechanisms? How can private enterprises conduct the internationalized process of their business under the shock of economic globalization; How we propose the corresponding policy and suggestions aimed at problems in the development of private economy in order to make it stable.

Attempting to address these questions, it is important to 1) adopt institutional economics, evolutionary economics, comparative institutional analysis and management science as a theoretical basis; 2) take institution innovations in the development of private economy as the principal line, basing on the overall framework of constructing and analysing institution innovations and development research of private economy. This book begins by summarizing private economy development mode with multiple interactions and up-and-down promotion, which can surpass the boundary of the region and has a more universal meaning through the analysis on historical process and mechanism of the evolution of private economy system. Secondly, through the analysis on key issues that private enterprises face during their development, this book will explore the mechanisms of institution innovations for private enterprises in areas of entrepreneurship and entrepreneurial behaviour, selection of financing channels and methods, optimal design of ownership arrangement and governance mechanisms, and way of international development. Finally, through the evaluation and analysis of the development conditions of private economy and enterprises, this book will propose policy recommendations for perfecting innovation and development of private economy system, while trying to provide a reference for innovation and development of private economy to promote scientific development and the construction of a harmonious society.

This book contains three parts with eight chapters. The first part is *Theoretical analysis on private economy evolution and institution innovations*, which contains two chapters of *Institutional change and organizational evolution in the development of private economy* and *Dynamic process of private economy institution innovations.* The second part is *Development barrier and institution innovations of private enterprises*, which contains four chapters of *Entrepreneurial behaviour and entrepreneur environment ofprivate enterprises*, *Analysis on financing obstacles for private enterprises*, *Governance issue in the growth of private enterprises* and *Institutional environment in international development process of private enterprises.* The third part is *Evaluation and countermeasure of private economy and enterprise development*, which contains two chapters of *Evaluation on the governance of private listed companies* and *Policy suggestions on institution innovation and development of private economy.*

The compilation of this book is facilitated through the strong support of officials in the Ministry of Education and funded under projects of the *Research on the Issues of Innovation and Development of Chinese Private Economy System* (Project Grant No. 03JZD0018) for PSS of the Ministry of Education. This book integrates and synthesizes excellent scientific researches from several institutions such as Business School of Nankai University, Corporate Governance Research Center of Nankai University, Institute of Economics of Zhejiang University, Private Economy Research Center of Zhejiang University and the Information Center of the Development and Research Center of the State Council. The outline of this book is compiled by Li Wei'an, who is the Chief Expert of the research group, and is in charge of editing. Other chapter contributors include Li Wei'an, Jin Xiangrong, Cheng Xiusheng, Zhang Yuli, Yang Bin, Deng Hongtu, Wu Lidong, Pan Shiyuan, Zhu Xiwei, Yuan Qinghong, Li Ya, Zhang Yaowei, An Xiang, Wang Hui, Wang Shiquan, Wu Desheng and Zhang Fengxiang. In addition, researchers, postgraduate and doctoral candidates from various listed institutions, from home and abroad, have made significant contributions to the publication of this book. We would like to express our sincere thanks and gratitude for their contributions and hard work.

Li Wei'an

Contents

Part Ⅰ Theoretical Analysis on Private Economy Evolution and Institution Innovation

Part Ⅱ Development Barrier and Institution Innovation of Private Enterprise

Part Ⅲ Evaluation and Countermeasure of Private Economy and Enterprise Development

Part Ⅰ

Theoretical Analysis on Private Economy Evolution and Institution Innovation

Chapter 1

Institutional Change and Organizational Evolution in the Development of Private Economy

The development of China's private economy is a process of continuous institution innovations. It is important to investigate the types of organizational and environmental factors that have shaped China's private economy, and its political, economic, legal and social contexts. With these factors in consideration, this chapter establishes the evolution model of the "multi-interactive mechanism to achieve superior to subordinate system" with universal meaning. In addition to reviewing the development of China's private economy during the past 20 years, this chapter explores important concepts including local government ideological preferences, productivity competition, system complementarities and corporate governance. Furthermore, this chapter compares the difference between regional characteristics of developed models and the relations (interactive, penetrative, competitive and alternative) among private, state-owned and foreign companies. Overall, the goal of this chapter is to explain the institutional changes and evolution of China's private economy. These factors provide the theoretical basis for the study of regional specialties and the convergence trend of the private economy development, revealing the possible institutional arrangements of compatible mechanisms which the local government created for the development of the private economy.

1.1 Emergence and evolution mechanism of private economy

1.1.1 Definition of private economy

Private economy is the general form of enterprises under a market-based economy, which is also prevalent in Western developed countries. With the rapid development of China's economy and the marketization process, private economy has gradually become more prominent. Although the term "private economy" is used more frequently, there is no clear definition at the moment. Because of differences in its interpretations, it is associated with non-standard policy making, administration and statistical caliber, which can cause unnecessary confusion.

This book argues that the so-called private economy is an economic activity based on individual entrepreneurship, which regards the private economic development as the main body, including various forms of ownership (e. g. private economy refers to the private economy and private capital holding economy, the state-owned holding, collective holding①, Hong Kong, Macao and Taiwan investment economies and foreign investment economy are not included). Its basic characteristics are private investment, meaning that the private company or individuals bear the risk of economic activities. The strong driving force of its development is the inherent wealth requirements and the entrepreneurial vision and motivation of developers.

Private economy is a diversified concept that consists of mixed economy with specific historical background. During the transition process, it changed from the traditional planned economic system under the intensive publicization to the market economy. Thus the concept of "private economy" acts as the general designation of the above economic composition, which is conducive to our theoretical research, policy development and macro management and other aspects of works.

1.1.2 Mechanism of private economy: social transformation, ideology and institutional change

The process and results of institutional change and social transformation are considered "historical", and not just based on the process towards economic efficiency. It encompasses the establishment of unconventional concepts that are compatible with the market economy, as well as the establishment of ideologies and belief systems that that characterize civil society. Therefore, social transformation is always in the core and key position in the process of institutional change.

---

① Collective economy (collective and collective holding) has achieved privatization through two reforms, the investment and asset management form of the existing small amount of collective enterprises are similar to the nature of "double state-owned", but also not included in private economy.

Although many in China have different views on how to reform the country and economy, they share a consensus in two respects: (1) China's reform is a market-oriented reform, and (2) that this market-oriented reform regards the continuous growing of private economy as its main carrier. However, it is still important to consider China's economic and political reform from a historical perspective, as well as to have a discussion about the empirical data associated with China's reform.

The year 1979 is when China's reform drastically took place. Why did people seem to be so strong for traditional socialist ideology preference before, while they continue to replace the old ideology preference with the new ones, namely that how did it occur such a big difference before and after this significant ideological preference①? Before 1979, the Chinese commune system was implemented in the rural areas, but the system was gradually disintegrated afterwards and was replaced by the household contract responsibility system. Although the household contract responsibility system provides for the collective nature of land ownership, a single farmer is still considered to be its main business unit, which is similar to the property ownership structure of the private ownership of land of the traditional, family-based smallholder economy. Although the land is still owned by the collective, the autonomy of production and management are fully owned by farmers. Thus, although peasants own the majority of the right to use the land, the collective has the ultimate disposition right in the legal sense, which makes farmers' land property very incomplete as a result. In turn, the implementation of the contract responsibility system means that private economy has expanded, developed, and grown in China's rural areas in a legitimate way. It is predicted that this trend will eventually spread to the urban cities, and the city's privatization process also starts from city's collective economy. In the middle and late 1980s, with the gradual realization of reform measures such as decentralization, contracting, profit tax and shareholding system, the privatization process of small and medium-sized state-owned enterprises has begun.

The development of private economy or the process of privatization has become an important part of China's economic and social transformation. People have continuously strengthened the belief that they should adhere to reform through the improvement of the efficiency brought about by the development of private economy.

---

① A more detailed description of the differences in this ideology and its transformation is found in Deng Hongtu, "Evolutionary Interpretation of China's Institutional Change in the Transition Period", Social Sciences in China, No. 5, 2004.

This process also provides legitimate political resources for the reform and the theoretical resources of "mastering the masses".

Through the theoretical interpretation of this historical process, we see that the transformation of ideas and even ideology, and the (people's) worship of economic efficiency have constituted a logical structure (mechanism) of mutual explanation (annotation), mutual inspection and even mutual reinforcement with social transformation together. This logical structure, which has been repeatedly emphasized by academics and politicians, has become a very popular theory of reform today. Through the economic vitality and efficiency improvement released by the private economy, many have shown that the market orientation of reform is feasible and legitimate. What's more, by means of the economic growth brought by economic efficiency improvement, some have also explained the rationality and legitimacy of the new ideology. However, social transformation has consequences. Privatization not only brings the objective results of efficiency improvement, but also brings "employment difficulties" caused by "downsizing efficiency". The industrialization of medicals, public health and education has made the working class bear an unprecedented mental burden and economic burden, and the distribution of income is clearly "tilted"① towards capital, power and special status in the society. These phenomena make us open to reform economic and social policy, while implementing the principle of social justice in essence as the historical basis for social transformation. In this way, the examination of institutional change or social transformation cannot be evaluated solely on efficiency principles or simply efficiency standards, but should use the principles of social justice to carry out the necessary "historical review". It is, therefore, important to ask whether the economic efficiency is improved after the institutional change, whether the ideology of society is in line with the basic preferences of the public, whether the use of public power conforms to the fundamental interests of people, and whether the "group demarcation" of public rights and private rights meet the efficiency standards and public regulations? Reflections and answers to all these questions will deepen our

---

① Research has shown that China's Gini coefficient has reached 0.48. What's worse, a large number of "interest groups" which monopolize social resources and public rights have emerged in China. See also Lang Xianping: "China's Gini coefficient has increased to 0.5: where will China go." Zhang Ruoyu: "Deterrence of interest groups to erode social justice", recorded in Shanxi Daily, August 17, 2006; Jiang Yong: "Deterrence of the expansion of economy interests," recorded in Lookout, No. 40, 2006.

understanding of the origin and evolution of China's private economy.

In Chinese economic system before 1979, the commune members have a clear and shared "collective nature" both in organization and the way of labor. The income between members and cadres cannot be separated by the political and economic system in the structure of income distribution. Members are at the leadership level in politics, and cadres periodically travel to rural areas for inspection in order to understand the situation of people there and implement the ruling party's specific deployment of agricultural development. However, the people's commune system makes it difficult for farmers to get rid of the shackles of land, and there is no freedom of personal choice. The "non-retractable" of the right to participate in labor and income distribution rights make the "team-based, three-level-based" commune system difficult to produce direct economic stimulus for individuals, thus reducing the productivity of labor to a certain extent①. However, the commune system also produced another effect, that is, to make industry, agriculture, commerce, academics and army combined as a whole. Through the condensation of political organization and economic organization, scattered farmers join to engage in large-scale irrigation and water conservancy construction. In addition, the high degree of political and economic mobilization of the commune system has allowed the rural cooperative medical care to proceed smoothly, which has effectively reduced the damage to the health of the farmers and reduced the mortality rate of infants, thus prolonging the life expectancy of people. This achievement astounded the World Health Organization, so that socialist China once became a global model.

The implementation of contract responsibility system is equivalent to declaring the disintegration of the people's commune system, making the establishment of other institutions in this system, such as rural cooperative medical organizations also intangibly disintegrated. Of course, the contract responsibility system has stimulated the enthusiasm of peasants, and the freedom of choice is greater, which allows the peasants the possibility of flocking to the city and other industries. While this historical process is revealed as positive, the disintegration of the rural people's commune system has also led to a significant decline in the political mobilization and economic mobilization of the ruling party or the grassroots government in rural areas. As a result, the rural infrastructure can only be "used but not constructed" for a long

① Lin Yifu, "Agricultural Production Association's Withdrawing Right, Cost and Laziness: A Reply"; Lin Yifu, "On the System, Technology and China's Agricultural Development", Peking University Press, 2000, pp. 211 – 233.

period of time. In addition, due to the lack of collective action capacity, peasants' individual management mode makes them face two aspects of pressure: one is the market pressure, and a single farmer has essentially no ability to negotiate with the market, so he is virtually powerless within the confines of the market. Another aspect is the pressure of officials with whom a single farmer almost has no negotiation ability to negotiate. This has to do with due to administrative bureaucracies, and the inability to resist the politics and economic conditions which were brought on by various "exorbitant taxes" by administrative institutions at all levels from villages, towns and counties.

Therefore, from the perspective of rural areas, any reform measures have a historical duality, as people attempt to break through various constraints of the people's commune era, and get rid of the "three rural dilemmas" brought by the institutional transformation, as is the case with the urban reform. Although the manifestation is different from that of rural areas, the decline in workers' political status is almost synonymous with their expansion of economic freedom of choice, with a "historical duality" as well. In any case, China's economic transformation in general should receive a positive evaluation, because the non-state economy has received an unprecedented development after the disintegration of the rural people's commune system, which allows China to sustain economic growth. However, we cannot ignore the fact that workers and peasants suddenly become "the disadvantaged" in political vocabulary with the growth of economy, while the constitution defines them as owners of society and has stressed that the "workers ' and peasants' alliance" is the foundation of socialism. If we do not introduce the standards of political justice and instead blindly follow the efficiency principles of neo-classical economics, we will be trapped in an institutional or constitutional legitimacy dilemma. The lasting conflict between the actual disadvantaged and the "masters" status conferred by the constitution will not only confront us with theoretical dilemmas, but will also deprive us of the courage and power to challenge it.

This section first provides the basic definition of social transformation and institutional change. On this basis, this section argues that the factors such as social justice, institutional spirit and public power are logically consistent with the institutional system, and the former is the core of the latter. In this way, institutional change or social transformation is the reunification of reshaping the systematical spirit, changing the concept and ideology and improving efficiency under the norms and regulation of the principles of social justice. From this perspective, we find that there are fatal flaws in the reform logic of "efficiency first and public attention".

The philosophy of utilitarianism and efficiency are thought to be superior to the principle of social justice, so that the public and individual's right to development has become an "excuse" to reform policy, but this will lead to inherent tension and disorder of social relations. Although the principles of social justice are originated from the reasonable demands of different interest groups and the interest interaction of all social members in the process of historical evolution, its manifestation is only an abstract, spiritual, and conceptualized logical system. Thus, it must carry and manifest by means of specific social rules and public orders. Therefore, public power, the organizational structure and the private property rights should consist of moral and ethical standards established by the social justice principles and the corresponding efficiency standards. The social transformation caused by their changes is considered reasonable and credible, which can then withstand historical and logical tests. By studying historical facts of the evolution of China's private economy, we can then arrive at this conclusion.

1.1.3 Diversity of the evolution of private economy system: divergence in ideological preferences, local government's policy and institutional evolution

This section uses historical data to describe and analyze the "historical logic starting point" of the reform of state-owned economy, the evolution of non-state-owned economy, the nature of public ownership economy, the "systematical complementarity", the "mutual embedding" of state-owned economy, and the non-state-owned economy, as described by the evolution of the private economy. This evolution is a based on the process of transition and institutional innovation trajectory which allowed for the development of the private economy.

In academia, scholars have established a number of theoretical frameworks to explain China's institutional change process. The first research framework often divides the Chinese economy into two pieces: one is called the stock economy, mainly composed of the traditional collective economy and the state-owned economy; another is the non-state-owned economy, such as individual economy, private economy and incremental economy composed of township enterprises. This research framework argues that China has not carried out a package of rapid privatization reforms, but rather gradually completed the marketization process from the incremental reforms[1]. Fan Gang noted that economic reform will bring interest adjustment. Because of the existence of the interest relationship, the reform cost is divided into two forms: the implementation cost and the (interest) friction cost. Led by incremental reforms and followed by stock reforms, it will be easier to coordinate the various interests in order to realize the "Pareto improvement" of the reform process[2].

The second research framework is put forward by Yang Ruilong[3] and Zhang Weiying[4]. Based on the decentralization of the central and local, they argue that decentralization will cause regional competition that will make the local government and businesses to organized together with the fear of corruption in which the central government will make business operators obtain the remaining control and claim right, causing the government gradually to withdraw from the enterprise, to complete the privatization of state-owned economy, and the market economy system will be established.

Zhou Ye'an[5] put forward the evolution of institutional changes. He argues that the analytical framework of the compulsory institutional change[6] and the induced institutional change[7] cannot fully reveal the whole figure of the institutional change. The former ignores the spontaneous innovation behavior of members in society, and the latter neglects the possible role of the government[8]. In his view, China's reform

---

① Lin Yifu, Cai Fang, Li Zhou, "China's Miracle: Development Strategy and Economic Reform", SDX Joint Publishing (Shang hai) Co. Ltd. , 1994, pp. 20 - 60.

② Fan Gang, "The Political and Economic Analysis of Progressive Reform", Shanghai Far East Publishers, 1996, pp. 64 - 90; Fan Gang: "On the Reform Process", contained in "Reform, Opening up and Growth", SDX Joint Publishing (Shanghai) Co. Ltd. , 1991; Fan Gang: "Two Reform Costs and Two Reforms", Economic Research Journal, No. 1, 1993.

③ Yang Ruilong, "The Three-stage Theory of China's Institutional Changes", Economic Research Journal, No. 1, 1998.

④ Zhang Weiying, "Regional Competition and Privatization", China Center for Economic Research of Peking University, No. 20, 1999.

⑤ Zhou Ye'an, "The Evolution of China's Institutional Change", Economic Research Journal, No. 5, 2000.

⑥ Lin Yifu, "On the Economic Theory of Institutional Change: Induced Institutional Changes and Compulsory Institutional Changes", "Property Rights and Institutional Changes—A School of Property Rights and the New Institutional School Translation", SDX Joint Publishing (Shanghai) Co. Ltd. , 1994.

⑦ V. W. Rutter, "Induced Institutional Change Theory", "Property Rights and Institutional Changes—A School of Property Rights and the New Institutional School Translation", SDX Joint Publishing (Shanghai) Co. Ltd. , 1994, pp. 327 - 370.

⑧ We believe that Zhou Ye'an's comments on these two forms of change may not be correct; Rutter emphasizes the demand for institutional change, while Lin Yifu emphasizes its supply side, but it cannot prove that Rutter and Lin Yifu must ignore the other factors of institutional change. However, Zhou Ye'an's "problem consciousness" is enlightening.

process is intertwined with the dual order evolution path in which the government can choose external rules and social members choose the internal rules; the conflict and coordination between the two rules function throughout the process of institutional change. In the process, the central government plays more of a judge's role, and local governments are more engaged in institutional entrepreneurship. The result is that the government gradually withdraws from the field of institutional innovation, but the territory of internal rule of civil innovation is gradually expanded. At the same time, Zhou Ye'an also analyzed the economic consequences of local government competition caused by local decentralization. He argued that competition among local governments did not necessarily lead to benign economic growth. Protective strategies and predatory strategies may be selected, which can lead to industry isomorphism, and interregional transaction costs will increase①. However, Zhang Weiying argues that the industry isomorphism and redundant construction are exactly a viable path and the necessary costs of privatization and marketization.

The above researches have portrayed the transition of China's economic system to a considerable extent. But the problem is that incremental reforms cannot be carried out without stocks, that is, state-owned economy. Incremental reform and stock reform are essentially complementary. In addition, although the decentralization between the central and local allow for the privatization of private economy, an intermediary transformation mechanism is needed in order to make this historical condition play its role. "Decentralization" as argued by Zhang Weiying and Yang Ruilong failed to examine the process of the transformation mechanism from the details, and their theoretical model did not consider the "systematical complementarity" between the state-owned and the private economy. Although Zhou's theoretical frame takes into account the coordination and conflict between the government and members of society, internal and external rules, it is too general and abstract to explain the process of institutional change in China. The assumption is that the government provides external rules, social members create internal rules, and the two rules conflict and coordinate with each other. However, it is unclear why Wenzhou's model is based on private innovation "system" and Southern Jiangsu model is based on community governments to provide rules will appear in the process of China's economic transition. Of course, both Zhang Weiying's "central, local

① ZhouYe'an, "Local Government Competition and Economic Growth", Journal of Renmin University of China, No. 1, 2003.

decentralization" and Zhou Ye'an's "evolution of internal and external rules" cannot be adequate to explain this process.

As for the literature① that solely solves the mystery of Chinese township enterprises or the mystery of China's economic growth, it provides a unique perspective on how the institutional structure of Chinese community economic organizations evolves and how the management mechanism is improved, it cannot reveal the trajectory of change for how the township enterprises generate and develop from a historical perspective. In addition, these studies cannot get rid of the limitations of property theory and transaction cost theory, so they cannot theoretically explain why "evolutionary bifurcation"② will appear in economic organizations and economic systems of different regions in China in the given similar macroeconomic conditions and political constraints circumstances. Therefore, it is necessary to construct a new analytical framework to reveal the basic path of organizational evolution and institutional change of private economy in different regions of China.

This section argues that the local government's ideological preferences will determine its private economic policies and thus affect the formation of expectations of private enterprises for the future. The productivity competition and institution complementarity between state-owned enterprises and private enterprises will together shape the "system complementarity" of a particular region, leading to the selection of different corporate governance structures by private enterprises in different regions. In addition, the marginal efficiency comparison of state capital and private capital in different regions will lead to differences in the rate at which different local governments "correct their traditional ideology preferences", and further determine the differences in private economic policies, which make the evolution of private economy in different regions bifurcate. Under the constraints of historical conditions in different regions, local governments that are more completely free from traditional

---

① Feng Qu, "Reform of Township Enterprises Looking from the Fund-raising Mechanism: A Case Study of the Dynamics of Institutional Change", Reform, No. 5, 2000; Feng Qu and Zhang Tao, "Authority, Authority Organization and Efficiency—Review on the Way of Economic Transition", World Economic Papers, No. 5, 2002; Li Daokui, "The Fuzzy Theory of Property Rights in the Economic Transition", Economic Research Journal, No. 4, 1995; OiJ., Fiscal Reform and the Economic Foundation of Local State Corporatism in China, World Politics, Vol. 45, No. 1; Chang & Wang, The Nature of Township Village Enterprise, Journal of Comparative Economics, 1994, 19, pp. 434 – 452; Che & Qian, Insecure Property Rights and Government Ownership of Firms, Quarterly Journal of Economics, 1998.

② Sun Zao and Lu Zhengwei, From Government to Enterprises: Reviews on Research Literature of China's Private Enterprises, Economic Research Journal, No. 4, 2003.

ideology preferences will enable private enterprises to gain faster access to the relative efficiency of the organization, so that the private economy can enter a process of continuous organizational innovation, which is the origin of the Wenzhou model; those local governments who are slowly getting rid of the traditional ideology preferences will participate in the process of enterprise evolution in the form of grassroots political power, thus generating township enterprises with fuzzy property rights structure (i. e. the origin of the Southern Jiangsu model). Those local governments that adhere to traditional ideology preferences pay more attention to the effect of state-owned enterprise reform on economic growth, and thus cannot provide a reasonable policy environment for the development of private economy, which makes the private enterprises lack the stable expectation and prevent the private economy from having the comparative advantage on efficiency compared to state-owned economy. This is the development status of private economy in the middle and western regions. Finally, the productivity competition and institutional complementarity will be "organized" into the "dynamic mechanism" of private economic evolution and state-owned economic reform, which will induce different types of economic organizations to continuously improve the governance structure and maximize their profitability goal. Under the influence of comparative efficiency, the evolution of different regional economic organizations and the institutional change trajectory will converge, which makes the community structure of Southern Jiangsu model eventually transform into the ownership structure of Wenzhou model.

1. The evolution of private economy: a theoretical explanation

In relevant literature, the "historical logic starting point" is also called the "initial condition" or "historical origin" of the transition economy. Lin Yifu and Yao Yang define the "initial condition"① as the basis for the rural industries, the proportions of state-owned industries and the structure. Wang Limin believes that a variety of initial conditions should be fully considered, including political, economic and cultural aspects. For example, central and local decentralization is the "political initial condition" faced with China's economic reform. The labor force is concentrated in the agricultural economy, and the decentralized system under the partition of the organization is the "economic initial conditions" faced with the initial reform.

① Lin Yifu and Yao Yang, "Industrialization in the East Asian Miracle", "Reflections on the Wonder of East Asia", China Renmin University Press, 2003, pp. 103 – 138.

Advocating frugality, and economic transactions with relationship as the knot constitute the "cultural initial conditions"① . Therefore, China's progressive reform has an efficient comparative advantage compared to the former Soviet Union's radical reform.

Unlike the previous study, the "historical logic starting point" discussed in this part has the following three meanings:

First, it is equivalent to the "initial condition" or "historical origin"② as defined by Lin Yifu, Yao Yang and Zhou Qiren.

Second, the "historical logic starting point" has the methodological significance of economic analysis. The "historical logic starting point" can not only influence the choice of economic subjects as an external constraint, but also can infiltrate inside the "behavior motive" of economic subjects as an internal constraint by means of ideology, culture and customs, to influence and determine the expected utility function and behavior choice of the participants (such as enterprises or local government).

Third, the "historical logic starting point" first acts as a realistic constraint, but given the constraints, economic actors will cause differences③ in response pattern due to their cultural background and geographical differences.

Thus, different "historical logic starting points" can lead to different preferred structure and economic response patterns, which will ultimately affect the contract choice of economic actors, and induce people in different regions to choose different, heterogeneous organizational forms under the real constraints. In this part, different preference structures and economic behavioral response patterns are embodied in both the ideology preferences of local governments and the expected objective functions of state and private enterprises.

---

① Wang Limin, "The Initial Conditions of the Transition Economy", Shanghai Journal of Economics, No. 9, 2003.

② Zhou Qiren, "China's Rural Reform: Changes in State and Ownership Relations—A Review of the History of Economic System Changes", Social Sciences Quarterly (Hong Kong), No. 8 (3), 1994; Chen Jianbo, "Property System of the People's Commune—A System Analysis of the Property System which is Strictly Restricted by Non-exclusive", Economic Research Journal, No. 1, 1994; Chen Jianbo, "Institutional Change and Rural informal System", Economic Research Journal, No. 1, 2000; Zheng Hongliang, "A Study on China's Township Enterprises' Behavior Objectives and Behaviors", Management World, No. 6, 1998.

③ China is divided into coastal areas, the mainland, eastern areas and western areas. The transport convenience and the per capita land area of provinces are different, and people's preference function is also very different.

As for a government in action, ideology not only has the "metaphysical" philosophical meaning, but also a utilitarian economic concept[1] integrating "teleology" and "causal law". The government chooses a policy to be "purposeful", while choosing a certain policy and waiving another policy are related to the "historical cause" (such as the historical logic starting point) and the "reality" (such as the real constraint). The ideology of local governments depends on the ratio of state capital and private capital to the efficiency produced by their respective marginal outputs. Different types of capital and its marginal output efficiency will determine the local government's ideological preferences and the resulting policy orientation and policy itself. For example, if the local private capital accounts for a larger proportion in the total social capital, its marginal output rate is higher than that of state-owned capital, then the local government will tend to provide a more relaxed policy environment for the development of private economy. It is the same on the contrary. The reason why policy preferences and ideological preferences are linked is that the local government has indeed faced the problem of "socialism" or "capitalism" in the transition period, market orientation, or planning orientation dilemma.

In general, the efficiency advantage of private economy in production and operation will put pressure on state-owned enterprises to promote the transformation of state-owned enterprises. The advantages of state-owned economy in technology, financing and investment will promote private enterprises to continuously optimize the governance structure, strengthen the competitive advantage, which is the productivity competition process. The "spillover effect" of state-owned economy in technology, capital and human capital provides a favorable external environment for the development of private economy. Private economy creates the necessary prerequisites in tax, employment and industrial structure adjustment for downsizing staff, improving efficiency and achieving the transformation of the state-owned enterprises, which is the system complementarity process. "Productivity competition" and "system complementarity" will form a dynamic mechanism of the development of private economy and institutional innovation, so that "corporate governance" has become the inevitable choice for the development of private economy. The proportion and industry distribution of state-owned economy and private economy in different regions will lead to the "system complementary form" with regional differences, which will make the "development model" of private economy in different regions different from each

---

① Mises, Human Action: A Treatise on Economics, Fox & Wilkes, San Franciso, 1996, pp. 23 - 29.

other. Finally, productivity competition and system complementarity will make the economic system of different regions "converge" in a similar trajectory and then show the homogeneous ownership structure and property structure. Therefore, whether it is the Wenzhou model, or the Southern Jiangsu model, or the economic development model of the middle region, they will show a convergence effect to some degree.

Based on this, it is necessary to construct a new analytical framework to reveal the basic path of organizational evolution and institutional change of private economy in different regions. It should be said that this study provides a systematic theoretical explanation for why China's institutional changes in different regions will encounter "path difference" and how to achieve "institutional evolution convergence" compared with similar researches.

However, the formation of "system complementary characteristics" in different regions is closely related to the local government's ideological preferences and its correction rate. This important problem is not paid much attention and effectively analyzed in the mainstream literature.

2. Local government ideology preferences and endogeneity of policy①

The vast majority of researchers, and even many public figures, think that ideology is given "parameters" and is exogenous. However, in this section, we explain that ideology is endogenous, and governmental decision-making depends on the government's ideological preferences. Thus, it is also endogenous②. In mainstream economics literature, these two views compete with each other.

North argues that neoclassical individual rational assumptions make it difficult to show that large groups do act in the absence of significant returns to compensate

① After the publication of the "simplified version" of this chapter (recorded in Social Sciences in China, No. 5, 2004), we saw similar papers of Zhang Qi and Liu Mingxing discussing ideology (2004). Their research field was more open and they studied cross-national data. It proves empirically that there is an inherent relationship between ideology and the strength and breadth of government intervention in economic activities. See also Zhang Qi & Liu Mingxing: "Ideology and Government Intervention".

② What we stress here is that the policies implemented by policymakers are depend on their policy preferences, which directly depend on the ideological preferences of these decision makers. But people want to know is not the policy the result of the balance of various interests? Why do government ideological preferences prevail in the promulgation and implementation of policies? Is not the policy the result of the game of interests between all parties? The answer to these question will be made in the fourth part of this chapter. Here only emphasize the statistical characteristics of policy decisions. One issue that must be noticed is that, for a transition economy, the disadvantaged groups, though numerous, are not popular because they are not politically or publicly decisive. This issue must be illustrated by the characteristics of the political structure of a particular period in China.

individuals for large sums of money, so that the real personal efficiency function is much more complex than the simple assumption that is present in the neoclassical theory. Thus, if there is no clear theory on ideology or theory on knowledge sociology in a broader sense, there will be a great gap in explaining the capacity of the current resource allocation or historical change (in economics). North argues that ideology can give members a sense of loyalty to the group, can reduce the group members' "free rider" behavior, and, what's more, it can provide the country with the legitimacy of implementing governance. Thus, an empirical ideological theory is essential to analyze the role of an independent judiciary in influencing the allocation of resources, but an empirical ideological theory① is needed to explain the long-term reform.

However, it is obvious that North has no clear and consistent "consideration" on how to integrate ideology into personal rational hypothesis of neoclassical economics. He distinguishes the control of technology, population, ownership and government on resource, the decisive influence of relative price changes on human behavior, and its key role on the efficiency of resource allocation from ideology, or distinguishes the decisive influence of cognitive patterns on human behavior from its important role on resource allocation efficiency strictly. In this way, he actually agrees that ideology is exogenous.

Through studying the propensity of the Republican and Democrats' political choice in the Congress and the White House, Edward J. Lopez & Carlos D. Ramircz emphasized the endogeneity of ideology. They argue that the ideology of political parties is technically better than that of individual ideologies, because the latter's life cycle is limited, while the former is relatively long enough to facilitate long-term observation. Party ideology is the "agent" of the legislator's ideology. The preferences of politicians' ideology were initially drawn to the part of political parties' preferences that is suited to their wishes and preferences.

For example, the Republican Party would attract more people who are ideologically more conservative in terms of their perspective on inequality, and the candidates of those legislators will also be bound by the party program of the Party. These Party programs are, to a considerable extent, a disciplinary constraint on behavior and an effective incentive for voters. These incentives include not only shared resources, mutual vote, but also loyalty to political parties as a personal reputation. It

---

① Douglas C. North, "The Structure and Change of Economic History", The Commercial Press, 1992, pp. 46 – 59.

is neither for the client's desire, nor for the disciplinary constraints of political parties, but to be a long-term career, so that they cannot violate the preferences of his party, or cannot be inconsistent with his party's ideology. As a result, legislators and ideology of political parties have a high degree of relevance. The important question is that when the members of the party change, the ideology of the party will change as the proportion of the member changes. This shows that ideology is endogenous.

Poole & Rosenthal (1997) argues that the large-scale change in party ideology stems from the "structural proportional effect" in which members change, and if the structural proportions of party members change greatly, then the political ideology of the party will also change greatly. But the change in party ideology has nothing to do with the change of its members in the ideological position. The key is whether the proportion of people holding a position and belief in a political party is dominant. With the preferences and beliefs of independent decisions, the newly joined legislators do not need to share the preferences of the original legislators (in ideology). For example, if a new large number of young Republican members happen to be very conservative, then we can predict that the party will be conservative in the future for a long time until another wave of less conservative young members join the party. Thus, for political parties, its ideological changes will be cyclical①.

Historical facts show that there is a structural causal relationship between the factors that determine the efficiency of resource allocation, such as changes in ideology and relative prices, technological change, and so on. The more you can examine this point from the long history, the more you can prove the correctness of this argument. "Physiocracy" has become an important concept of governance in ancient China, the key lies in the fact that the benefits of commercial activities and agricultural activities are difficult to rely on their spontaneous profit-seeking activities to achieve a stable Nash equilibrium solution. It is difficult to monitor business activities, and the state lacks a matching means of effective taxation on long-range trades. For the sake of national security and the resolution of the financial crisis, the Chinese government will inevitably make "physiocracy" ideology and national will②.

---

① Edward J. Lopez and Carlos D. Ramirez (2000), "Is Political Ideology Endogenous? Evidence from the Business cycle". Poole and Rosenthal (1997), Edward J. Lopez and Carlos D. Ramirez (2000). Poole and Rosenthal (1997), "Congress: A Political-Economic History of Roll Call Voting", New York, NY: Oxford University Press.

② Deng Hongtu, "History of the Official Business: An Economic Analysis", China Economic Quarterly, Volume II, No. 3, 2003.

China's 30 years of institutional change history has shown that the ideological preferences are endogenous. The following discussion illustrates how the relative changes in prices affect local government's ideological preferences and local governments' policies (that is, the marginal financial contribution of different types of economic organizations to local governments, and the relative importance and change of total fiscal contribution). They will show that, to a considerable extent, the local government's ideological preferences and their policies are endogenous, and we can even say that not only the policy is the result of choice, but further the decisive factor in determining how policy preferences are formed is the result of choice.

3. Local governments' ideology preference and policy preference①

Chinese politics is characterized by a "head responsibility system". For government agencies, the "head" includes party secretary and top executive head (such as county magistrate, mayor and governor). The party secretary and chief executive have a functional division of labor, and the former mainly focuses on ideology, while the later focuses on the overall work of the government, especially economic work. In theory, the party secretary can "lead" the top executive head at a crucial moment. In this way, the party system has the following compositions:

(1) Party secretary and his supporters;

(2) Executive head and his supporters;

(3) All the other executives, except the party secretary and chief executive and their respective supporters, are in the middle state, neither vividly supporting the party secretary, nor clearly supporting the executive head. Their daily responsibility is to deal with daily tasks to complete the duties corresponding to the job functions. However, experience shows that members of the government in the "middle state" also have political preferences related to whether the party secretary or executive head is dominant in any political conflict.

Therefore, the game of internal members of the government has actually become a profit distribution process between the party secretary and chief executive and their respective supporters. When the party secretary prevails, the other members of the government in the middle will prefer the party secretary's policy agenda, for the

---

① This section does not "modelling" any relevant discussions. The preparation of contents stems from Professor Yao Yang's useful comments. We only discuss theoretically that the government will form a common time preference on ideology as a whole, that is, the government members will be homogeneous, and thus the policy choice will logically tend to be "homogeneous".

reason that they have greater promotion opportunities or other benefits in this way. When the executive head prevails, the government members in the "middle state" will make another choice.

Two entrepreneurs will be introduced: one is the manager of the state-owned enterprise; the other is the manager of the private enterprise. And it is assumed that there is no "entry barrier" to the entrepreneur who is about to enter the area within the jurisdiction of a specific local government, but each entrepreneur engaged in business activities in the area can feel the local government's "policy preference", so they can decide whether to stay, or continue to operate in this area.

In fact, we can discuss the game of local government members and their local governments as the game between a whole and the entrepreneurs, in order to arrive at the basic conclusions about the characteristics of local government's behavior.

First, suppose there are two participants: the party secretary and his supporters, executive head and his supporters. Assume that they have two strategies to choose from: conservative and reform, where conservatism is to adhere to the traditional socialist beliefs, ideologically committed to safeguard the interests of state-owned enterprises, so the policy that does not harm the development of private economy but also the development of state-owned enterprises at the same time is implemented. The reform here refers to both the maintenance of the legal status of the state-owned economy, and the strong support for the development of private economy.

In fact, under our assumptions, the government better choose "reform" rather "conservatism", because the "reform" program will allow private enterprises to engage in business activities in this area, so that the government can get more tax as a whole.

Second, if the government takes the "reform" strategy, it is better for private enterprises to stay to continue to operate better than to give up the business activities in the area, because it is expected to invest in this early, there must be precipitation costs, it will be difficult for them to recover precipitation costs if they choose giving up, and they will lost the "reform bonus" at the same time. On the contrary, if the government adopts a conservative "strategy", the firm faces two choices, either to leave or continue to operate. However, factors that determine whether private enterprises choose to "leave" or "continue to operate" depends on the private enterprises' expected benefits and comparison on these two programs, but also the "lobbying" ability of private entrepreneurs to the government and the time preference for government policy expectations.

However, we can conclude that the government's policy preference is a key factor in the game between the government and private entrepreneurs, and the government policy preference depends on how much tax the private enterprise can bring to the government. Generally speaking, outside state-owned enterprises, it is better for private economy (enterprises) to exist than absent, and the reason is that the private economy is the source of taxation outside the state-owned enterprises.

Our conclusion is that the repeated game between government members and government and private entrepreneurs will deflect the government's "transcendental" ideology, and eventually they will adopt policies that favor the development of private enterprises. Therefore, in general, the internal members of the government in the repeated game will give birth to "homogeneous ideology preferences", and will eventually take homogeneous development policies to promote the development of private economy.

4. Local government's ideology preference and regional economic institutional change

First of all, this section only studies government behavior, and the purpose is to understand the role of the government in the evolution process of China's private economy development. This section constructs the efficiency function of the government by introducing concepts such as ideology preferences.

This section demonstrates that ideological preferences determine the government's policy preferences and thus influence the change path of the economic system. The discussion here does not take into account the efficiency function of a single enterprise and its choice. As for a government in action, "ideology" is not just a "metaphysical" philosophical meaning, but also a utilitarian concept① of economics integrating the "teleology" and "causal law". The government chooses a policy to be "purposeful", but choosing a certain policy over another policy is related to the "historical cause" (such as the "historical logic starting point"②) and the "reality" (such as the real constraint). The ideology of local governments depends on the ratio of state capital and private capital to which they face and the efficiency compared to their respective marginal outputs. The reason why policy preferences and ideological

---

① Mises, Human Action: A Treatise on Economics, Fox & Wilkes, San Franciso, 1996, pp. 23 – 29.

② Deng Hongtu, Economics Interpretation of Organization, Organization Evolution and Institutional Change, Nankai Economic Studies, No. 1, 2003; Relatively Rational Research, Research of Institutional Economics, No. 1, 2003.

preferences are linked is due to local government's influence from "socialism" or "capitalism" in the transition period, as well as "market orientated", or "plan-orientated".

Assuming an economic society has three participants: government, state-owned enterprises and private enterprises, then it can be expected that the organizational evolution of the economic society and institutional changes depend on the following factors:

First, governmental preferences (including ideology preferences) and policies;

Second, it is the productivity competition and institutional complementarity between private enterprises and state-owned enterprises. The result of a productivity competition is that a more competitive corporate governance structure will replace another relatively inefficient corporate governance structure. The latter must be contracted under the pressure of the productivity competition to obtain heterogeneous capacity, thus occupying the minimum market share① required to achieve greater than or equal to zero profit. In addition, if the organizational evolution of the private economy is compatible with that of the state-owned economy, and form an inherently consistent system, then this results in an "institutional complementarity" between the two types of economic organizations.

The second factor is mentioned in this section, but a more detailed discussion will take place in the third section.

There are three variables that characterize the efficiency function of the local government: taxation (depending on state-owned enterprise income Y_g and private enterprise income Y_s), ideological preference (the ratio of private capital and state-owned capital, K_s/K_g) and non-material income (political status, social status and psychological satisfaction, denoted by A). Political status, social status will be described as "material income", and psychological satisfaction can also be described with "material income". The reason why ideology preferences are expressed in K_s/K_g is that for local government officials, the proportion of state-owned capital means whether the socialist public ownership is dominant in a long period of time. K_s/K_g has a very rich political connotation for government officials with traditional socialist complexes, and K_s/K_g can have another meaningful explanation for those who are open-minded, that is, K_s/K_g is the indicator for whether the market economy system

① The market share can be defined as the "market share threshold". If the enterprises can not reach this threshold, it is difficult for them to survive or their profit is negative.

is perfect[1].

Assume that g_1, g_2, g_3 are local government officials' preferences (coefficient) for leisure $(1 - e_m)$, tax $A\ (Y_g + Y_s)$, traditional socialist ideology complex (K_s/K_g) and political, economic and social status (A), $g_1 > 0$, $g_2 > 0$, $g_3 > 0$, and $g_1 + g_2 + g_3 = 1$. $A = e_m p$, on behalf of the authority of local government officials, p on behalf of the local government officials' potential. The higher the potential, the higher the authority, and the greater the impact on business activities, the more able to achieve more power rent. But the authority is also related to whether officials are willing to play a sufficient impact, that is, the degree of effort (e_m)[2].

In addition, for local governments it can be assumed that it faces a super enterprise consisting of state-owned enterprises and private enterprises. For a super enterprise, its production function can be defined as:

$$Y_{super} = (K_g + K_s)^{\beta}(L_g + L_s)^{(1-\beta)} \qquad (1)$$

Here, β and $(1 - \beta)$ are the marginal contribution rates of capital and labor to the super enterprise's income (Y_{super})[3]. In the subject set out in this section, it may be argued that:

$$Y_g + Y_s = Y_{super} \qquad (2)$$

Accordingly, the local government's efficiency function can be written as:

$$\max_{e_m, K_g, K_s} V_c = g_1 \ln(1 - e_m) + g_2 \ln[Pe_m(K_g + K_s)^{\beta}(L_g + L_s)^{1-\beta}] + g_3 \ln(K_s/K_g) \qquad (3)$$

Calculate the (first order) partial derivative of K_g in formula (3):

$$\frac{g_2\beta}{K_g + K_s} = \frac{g_3}{K_g} \qquad (4)$$

It is certain that K_g and K_s are two determinable quantities (or "constant quantities") in a specific period, so that $K_g/(K_g + K_s) = C$ (constant), so formula (4) can be re-expressed as:

$$Cg_2\beta = g_3 \qquad (5)$$

---

① It is necessary to point out that K_s/K_g is not "ideology" itself, but merely an "economic magnitude" that indicates ideology and its "deflection index". This will be briefly discussed below.

② The "potential index" (p) of this chapter follows Feng Qu and Zhang Tao: "Authoritative, Authoritative Organization and Efficiency—A Review of the Economic Transition Path", World Economic Papers, No. 5, 2002. However, the problem consciousness and reason of this chapter are different from Feng Qu et al. This chapter defines the ideology preferences and forms the basic elements of this chapter model together with the mathematical expression of the productivity competition and the system complementarity introduced later.

③ In fact, according to the assumption that an economic society only has two enterprises, namely, state-owned enterprise and private enterprise, therefore, the actual Y_{super} in the article can be considered national income.

The economic meaning of formula (5) is that the ideology preference of the local government (g_3) is influenced by the marginal contribution rate of the capital (β) and the tax preference coefficient (g_2), and β and g_2 determine g_3 in the way of multiple. Observations show that the local government has the "impulse" of financial expansion, and always wants to attract taxes and rent. Given the g_2 unchanged①, the local government's ideological preferences are determined by β, which is the contribution of capital to output in the region's economy as a whole.

It can be seen from formula (3) that β represents the contribution of total capital to output, but because the total capital includes state-owned capital and private capital, the result is that the economic meaning expressed by formula (5) is more complicated, there are two cases that must be noted:

(1) Given the same technology, the total amount of capital including private capital and state-owned capital is constant, and it is determined by total output and uneven savings rates. If the state-owned capital expands, private capital is reduced; on the contrary, if the private capital expands, state-owned capital is shrinking. It is expected that (ultimately) the size of the state-owned capital and private capital is their respective marginal output rate, denoted by ε_1 and ε_2 respectively.

(2) If the technology is innovated and improved in a specific period of time, then the state-owned capital and private capital will continue to produce "incremental" under the stimulation of technological innovation, respectively expressed by ΔK_g and ΔK_s. The degree of optimization of the organizational structure or governance structure (or the degree of adaptation to the market) determines the organization's utilization or innovation ability of (patent) technology. Thus, the marginal rate of return or capital growth of different types of economic organizations is different. Economic organizations with comparative efficiency advantages (ultimately) will have a higher capital growth rate, that is, if $\varepsilon_2 > \varepsilon_1$, there will be $\dot{K}_s > \dot{K}_g$②.

Based on the above discussion, this section gives the following theorem:

Theorem 1: Under the traditional economic system, $K_s \approx 0$, the local government's ideological preference g_3 is related only to the rate of return of state-owned capital β. g_3 and β will form a regular "preference" relationship, that is, the greater the K_g, the more stable the public ownership, the more the local government

---

① Although the local government has the "impulse" to attract more tax, the tax rate and tax base remain unchanged in a certain period of time, Therefore, it is reasonable to assume that g_2 is stable.

② Note: $\dot{K} = dK / dt$. If the growth rate of private capital has been more than the growth rate of state-owned capital, then it may surpass the total amount of state-owned capital.

has the ideological preference. In turn, rigid ideological preferences will make the local government tend to maintain the total amount of K_g through policy and to ensure that K_g is an absolute advantage in total capital.

Theorem 2: Given the policy impact, technological change and market competition pressure, if there is a new heterogeneous economic organization and leads to higher capital marginal efficiency, the "ideological steady state" the former ownership of economic structure corresponding to will be gradually broken. But ideology will only have a "lagging response" to technological change and market competition pressure. The rate of change in ideology depends on the magnitude of the marginal efficiency of the capital of different types of economic organization and the total comparability. Expressed with formula as follows①:

$$I = (\varepsilon_2 - \varepsilon_1)^{\alpha}\left(\frac{\sum K_g}{\sum K_s}\right)^{1-\alpha} \qquad (0 < \alpha < 1) \qquad (6)$$

From theorem 1 and 2, the following conclusions can be drawn:

Inference 1 : The ideology of local government is formed in the "historical logic starting point" or "initial condition" that it faces. If it is faced with a large number of state-owned enterprises with large-scale, its tax or rental sources are more dependent on these state-owned enterprises. And as long as the marginal efficiency of private capital and the marginal efficiency of state-owned capital (i. e. $(\varepsilon_2 - \varepsilon_1)$) are not large enough, then its ideological preferences will continue to converge on the traditional capital structure or form of ownership. If the capital marginal efficiency of private enterprises is much higher than the marginal efficiency of state-owned capital, even if the private capital is less than the state-owned capital in the total amount, as long as the local government's marginal rent from private enterprises is higher than the marginal rent of state-owned enterprises, the local government will gradually revise its ideological preferences and will gradually go away from the original capital structure or ownership form and converge to the ideological preference regarding private capital as the main body②.

Inference 2 : local governments' policy depends on its idcological preferences, and the traditional ideology preferences will make local governments choose to expand

① Ideology, expressed by I.

② The marginal efficiency and marginal contributions of state-owned and non-state-owned capital are different, or their trends are different, at least in the beginning and the middle of the transition. In the end, the marginal efficiency of state-owned and non-state-owned capital will converge, but that is already state-owned and non-state-owned capital equilibrium. This issue is related to the distribution of the industry, which needs special discussion.

the policy of state-owned capital in the total amount, although this policy will lead to a decline in the efficiency of state capital. The revised ideological preferences will make local governments tend to choose more policies to develop private economy, although this policy will lead to the decline in the proportion and total amount of state-owned capital.

Now, we can clearly and succinctly describe formula (5): if the state-owned capital is dominant in the total amount compared with private capital, the "marginal efficiency difference" of state-owned capital and private capital is not significant, the total amount of tax or rent drawn by a local government from state-owned enterprises can meet its general needs, the local government tends to be "conservative", that is, to maintain the traditional ideology preferences.

At this point, β will be more on behalf of the contribution of state-owned capital. On the other hand, if the difference in the capital marginal efficiency between private enterprises and state-owned enterprises is significant due to historical reasons, such as population and land tensions, and the tax or rent drew by the local government from the state-owned enterprises cannot meet its general needs, then the local government tends to reform, that is, deviating from the "steady state" of the original ideology①. At this point, β will be more on behalf of the contribution of private capital. As a result, the local government's ideological preferences will be gradually revised, which will affect its policies. In the transition period, the difference of institutional change path in different regions is the result of this policy.

Figure 1 - 1 shows that when the rate of change in the "difference" of the marginal contribution rate of non-state-owned capital and state-owned capital (right vertical axis) increases as the proportion (horizontal axis) of non-state-owned capital increase in the total capital, the local government's ideological preference on private economy (left vertical axis) is also growing. At this point, the local government tends to provide policies to promote the development of private economy, which corresponds to the following three stages:

First, the OM stage: at this point, non-state capital only accounts for a small share, so the local government is not interested in developing the private economy;

---

① National Bureau of Statistics: "China Industry Economy Statistics", China Statistics Press, 1987; Statistical Bureau of Jiangsu Province: "Jiangsu Statistical Yearbook in 1983", 1984, pp. 102 - 109. Statistical Bureau of Shandong Province: "Shandong Statistical Yearbook in 1983", 1984, pp. 122 - 133; State Administration of Taxation: "China Taxation Yearbook", China Taxation Publishing House, 2000, pp. 791 - 799. These data prove that the regional distribution of state-owned capital and non-state-owned capital affects the taxation structure around the country and indirectly proves that this kind of distribution affects regional policies.

Second, the MT stage: the marginal contribution rate and capital amount of private capital increase (the second derivative value of the right vertical axis is greater than zero in Figure 1 – 1), the local government will clearly establish the policy to promote the development of private economy;

Third, the TR stage: the marginal contribution rate of private capital slows down (the second derivative value of the right vertical axis is smaller than zero in Figure 1 – 1), the local government's policies to develop private economy tend to be mature, and the share of private capita is in an advantageous position at this time. The marginal contribution rate of state-owned capital and non-state capital tends to be equal until point R, the local government's policy for private economy will be replaced by the industrial policy.

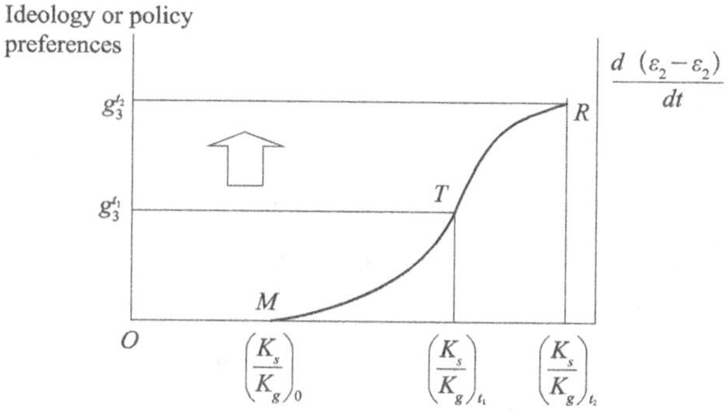

Figure 1 – 1 The ratio of state-owned capital to private capital, marginal efficiency of capital and ideology preferences of local government

5. "Bifurcation of paths" in evolution and institutional change of economic organizations in different regions: systematical complementary and "multiple equilibrium"

(1) Basic assumptions.

In order to simplify the analysis, suppose there is a super enterprise consisting of state-owned enterprises and private enterprises. In this way, the elements of state-owned enterprises and private enterprises, including human capital and material capital investment, can be seen as the investment of the same enterprise, and their respective output can also be seen as two different outputs from the same enterprise. The revenue function of the super enterprise can be expressed as①:

① It is worth noting that formula (7) and formula (3) are different; the latter expresses the output function, and the former expresses the income function.

$$\underset{i_s, i_g, K, K_{g_s}}{\text{Max}} \ R = R[\ln(\eta_s K_s + \eta_g K_g)^{\beta}(\eta_s i_s + \eta_g i_g)^{1-\beta}]$$

$$s.t.\ 0 < \eta_g < 1, 0 < \eta_s < 1 \tag{7}$$

Here, the meaning of β is the same as β in formula (1) and (3). Formula (7) replaces L_s, L_g with i_s, i_g, the reason is that this emphasizes the contribution of human capital to output. Such a replacement does not affect the nature of the problem. η_s and η_g are the transaction efficiency (or organizational efficiency) of state-owned enterprises and private enterprises, which are used to express the competitiveness of certain organizations. If $\eta_s > \eta_g$, which means that private economic organizations have a competitive advantage compared with state-owned economic organizations; on the contrary, it means that state-owned enterprises have higher organizational efficiency than private enterprises. ($\eta_s i_s + \eta_g i_g$), ($\eta_s K_s + \eta_g K_g$) indicates that there is a "systematical complementarity" in human and material capital between state-owned and private enterprises. Formula (1) and (7) have shown that the "system complementarity" of element inputs leads to a super enterprise not only to provide normal returns but also to provide "complementary benefits". "Systematical complementarity" in this model can be understood as "the complementarity between human capital and material capital"①.

In order to make the discussion relatively simple, we assume that state-owned enterprises and private enterprises share 1/2 ②of the total income of the super enterprise. Thus, the profits (or rents) of private enterprises, state-owned enterprises and local governments are:

$$\pi_s = \frac{1}{2}R(\cdot) - i_s - K_s - \frac{1}{2}\theta_s p e_m R(\cdot) \text{ ③} \tag{8}$$

$$\pi_g = \frac{1}{2}R(\cdot) - i_g - K_g - \frac{1}{2}\theta_g p e_m R(\cdot) \tag{9}$$

$$\pi_c = \frac{1}{2}(\theta_s + \theta_g) p e_m R(\cdot) - e_m \tag{10}$$

θ_s and θ_g are the capacity indices that the local government draws the "rent" from

---

① This does not mention the "systematical substitution" caused by the "productivity competition" of state-owned enterprises and private enterprises, but in essence this is the same problem, depending on the efficiency ratio of the two and the total amount (physical capital and human capital).

② The distribution ratio 1/2 is only "a subjective set" to simplify the discussion, which will not affect the analysis logic of this chapter.

③ ($\cdot$) after R in equation (8), (9) and (10) represents $\ln(\eta_s k_s + \eta_g k_g)^{\beta}(\eta_s i_s + \eta_g i_g)^{1-\beta}$ in equation (10), see equation (11) and (12).

private and state-owned enterprises, which reflects taxes or "rent" tax rate or "rent rate" that the local government draws from different types of enterprises are different. Obviously, $\theta_s + \theta_g = 1$. For the sake of brevity, $\gamma_i = \theta_i pe_m$ $(i = s,\ g)$ representsthe tax rate or rent rate of state-owned enterprises $(i = g)$ and private enterprises $(i = s)$.

(2) Discussion.

In order to understand the marginal contribution of human capital and material capital of state-owned and non-state-owned enterprises to the total income of super enterprises in the form of "systematical complementarity", we calculate the first-order partial derivative of i_s, i_g, K_s and K_g in formula (8).

$$\frac{\partial R(\cdot)}{\partial i_s} = \frac{\partial R(\cdot)}{\partial K_s} = \frac{2}{1 - r_s} \tag{11}$$

$$\frac{\partial R(\cdot)}{\partial i_g} = \frac{\partial R(\cdot)}{\partial K_g} = \frac{2}{1 - r_g} \tag{12}$$

Then, calculate the second-order partial derivative of i_s and i_g in formula (7) and put in the relevant conclusions expressed by formula (11), we can get①:

$$\frac{\partial^2 R}{\partial i_s \partial i_g} = \frac{\eta_g}{(1 - \beta)(1 - \gamma_s)\eta_s} \tag{13}$$

The following formula can be obtained using the same method:

$$\frac{\partial^2 R}{\partial K_g \partial K_s} = \frac{\eta_g}{\beta(1 - \gamma_s)\eta_s} \tag{14}$$

The economic meaning of formula (13) and (14) is that given the constant β and γ_s, the second-order partial derivative of the super enterprise's total income between i_s and i_g, between K_s and K_g is greater than zero, which means that there is a certain degree of complementarity between i_s and i_g, K_s and K_g. The second-order partial derivative and η_g constitute a proportional relationship with η_g, which means that private enterprises will be limited by the "productivity competition" of state capital and private capital in terms of the complementarity of human capital and material

---

① In fact, the formula listed in text should be: $\frac{\partial^2 R}{\partial i_s \partial i_g} = \frac{2\frac{\eta_g}{\eta_s}\eta_g}{(i_s + \frac{\eta_g}{g_s} i_g)(1 - \beta)(1 - \gamma_s)\eta_s}$. But in order to intuitively explain the problem, the author of this chapter especially makes a simplified treatment. The reasons are as follows: first, i_s and i_g are the human capital of private enterprises and state-owned enterprises, which is "constant" in a certain period; second, the η_g/η_s in the molecule is 1 times larger than η_g/η_s in the denominator, and the degree of change is doubled. Therefore, it can be simplified to equation (13). So can the equation (14).

capital.

According to formula (7), we can see that under the condition of $K_s + K_g = 1$, $i_s + i_g = 1$ (in the case of no big economic total amount), there is:

$$\eta_g = \eta_s \tag{15}$$

This means that the local government at this time will not have a special preference for the non-state-owned economy, and will not give special support on policy. It can be inferred from formula (11) and (12):

$$\frac{\partial R(\cdot)}{\partial i_s} = \frac{\partial R(\cdot)}{\partial K_s} = \frac{\partial R(\cdot)}{\partial i_g} = \frac{\partial R(\cdot)}{\partial K_g} = \frac{2}{1 - r_g} = \frac{2}{1 - r_s}$$

Accordingly:

$$\gamma_g = \gamma_s \tag{16}$$

It means that the tax revenue from state-owned and non-state-owned economy depends on the ICOR (incremental capital output ratio) of human and material capital. If the organizational effectiveness of the private economy is better than that of state-owned economy, that is $\eta_s > \eta_g$, then for a long run, there will be $\gamma_s > \gamma_g$, which will definitely influence the policy preferences of local government. Directly, $\eta_s > \eta_g$ indicates that the "competition degree" between the private and state-owned economy should exceed their "degree of system complementation". As an organization, if the "transaction efficiency" of private economy is better than that of state-owned economy, the rate of capital accumulation of private economy is higher than the rate of capital accumulation of state-owned economy, which will result in a "change" in the ideological preference of local government, according to the analysis in (formula 15), so the policies encouraging the development of private economy are promoted. If $\eta_s \gg \eta_g$ ("$\gg$" means the private economy, as an organization or contract structure, its transaction efficiency is better than that of state-owned economy, and this trend is irreversible), the ideological preferences of the local government will veer to policies of large-scale privatization, and this forces the state-owned economy to exercise equity diversification reform.

According to formula (16), if $\eta_s = \eta_g$, it means, theoretically, the contribution margin ratio of tax revenue and rent of private economy and state-owned economy to local government is equal (that is $\gamma_s = \gamma_g$), the local government will treat the private economy and state-owned economy equally; if $\eta_s > \eta_g$, $\gamma_s > \gamma_g$, it indicates that the local government will be in favor of the private economy; if $\eta_g > \eta_s$, $\gamma_s > \gamma_g$, it suggests that the local government will incline to the state-owned economy.

Furthermore, the next section introduces the equilibrium conditions. Make formula (13) equal to formula (14), then, $\beta = 1/2$①, it is the "equilibrium conditions of system complementariness" of human and material capital. If $0 < \beta < 1/2$, it indicates that the development of private economy is at the stage that the expansion of material capital is much needed, it requires more "system complementariness" of material capital, that is, the private economy must obtain more raw material, second-hand equipment and credit support from the state-owned economy, and the expansion of material capital is more important than that of human capital; if $1/2 < \beta < 1$, it shows that the private economy development is on the way form the extended expansion of material capital to a intension-type human capital expansion. Provided the technique is unchanged and the local policies are "constant", $\beta = 1/2$ is a stable equilibrium point, because if the private economy develops too fast, it will be constrained by the local government's ideological preference, "policy restraint" and the following financing constraints and human capital constraints, as a result, the private economy has to develop towards the steady state ($\beta = 1/2$). But, if the ideological preferences of local government changes and it exerts continuous technological innovation, as well as the transaction efficiency of the private economy is better than that of the state-owned economy, so "an equilibrium condition of system complementariness" (the opposite is "an equilibrium condition of system competition") will change, and a new "equilibrium condition of system complementariness" which the private economy takes advantage over creates②. But Figure1 – 2 indicates that, β is affected by the ideological preferences of the local government and it determines the evolutional path of private economy. As is put forward previously, β has an abundant and deep economical connotation, which represents the material capital marginal ratio of super enterprises, as well as the nature of material capital, that is whose material capital. "Whose material capital marginal ratio" will become a logic evidence, historically and practically amend its traditional ideological preferences. Combining Figure 1 – 1, Figure 1 – 2 and formula (5), and theorem 1 and 2, deduction 1 and 2, it is clear that β is closely connected with the capital marginal ratio of private economy and state-owned economy (which is ε_2 and

---

① $\beta = 1/2$ is related with the previous assumption, and it aims to simplify the discussion. Note that the result is of theoretical significance, and indeed, β is not equal to 1/2.

② It is worth noting that when discussing the value of β, it is necessary to examine η_s and η_g, and the relationship between them.

ε_1 respectively). If the private economy is dominant in the overall economy, then the capital marginal ratio of overall economy β will approach closely ε_1. At the same time, β has an internal logic relationship with η_s and η_g, if $\eta_s > \eta_g$, then the expansion rate of private economy will be faster than that of state-owned capital, and β will to a large extent transform into the capital marginal efficiency of private economy (ε_1), it enables the formula (5) and formula (11) - (16) to clearly disclose the meaning of economic policies.

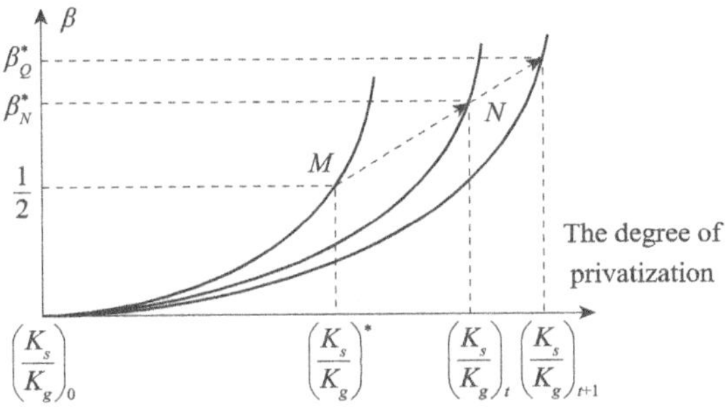

Figure 1 - 2 Equilibrium state: the change of β and the degree of privatization

In sum, assume that the local government is sensitive to the change of β, which indicates that the lag time of ideological preferences is shortened dramatically. In the economic environment which is based on the government's loose policies in the private economy, the local market is more open and therefore, the " system complementariness" of the private economy and state-owned economy rapidly surpasses the stable point (see the point where $\beta = 1/2$ in Figure 1 - 2) and reach point N where township enterprises are flourishing (similar to the pattern in southern Suzhou province) or point Q where the private economy stays (similar to the Wenzhou pattern).

The analysis of this section reaches the following theoretical and political conclusions: for the transition economy, the local government and the power utilization are very important; the ideological preferences of the local government decide the private economy policy. The evolution trajectory of a local private economy is different from that of another place; the key lies in different ideological preferences of local government. So the policy is different, which makes the evolution of the private economy divergent. The key factor determining the bifurcation of path lies in whether the marginal efficiency of state-owned and private capital is equal in different places. If equal, the private capital (including human and material capital) does not constitute a comparative advantage. But the difference between them influences and determines the local government's ideological preference and then decides the policy. This makes the evolution of private economy in different path at the same time.

6. Experience evidence

The previous sections provided an overview of the evolution of the private economy in Zhejiang and Jiangsu province. We believe that it is the different origins of history and logic that lead to the difference of capital distribution and ownership structure in state-owned and private economy (including township enterprises) in these regions. Therefore, the capital marginal efficiency of these different types of economic organizations and the transaction efficiency of the organization show significant differences, which leads to the competition of productivity; on the other hand, "system complementariness" among different types of economic organizations. Together, they determine the difference of "system complementariness" in different regions, which makes distinct local government have different "reactions" in revising their ideological preferences: the faster the response, the more the local government tends to "reform", the more proactive and active the choice of preferential development of the private economy policies; otherwise, the slower the response of local governments, objectively, it will delay the timing of reform, and ideological preferences will appear "lag", so that its policy cannot meet the needs of private economy development in time.

For Jiangsu's township enterprises, we can find the historical and logical origin and the transformation of the local government's ideological preferences are critical to the development of non-state-owned economy. In the 1970s, a large number of commune and brigade enterprises appeared in the rural area of Jiangsu province, the local grassroots government was the owner of these enterprises①. When it was 1980s, China began to implement the contract system of responsibility linked to production,

---

① Statistical Bureau of Jiangsu Province: "Jiangsu Statistical Yearbook in 1983", June 1984, pp. 100. Statistical Bureau of Shandong Province: "Shandong Statistical Yearbook in 1983", August 1984, pp. 123. Pan Wei: "Peasants and Market", The Commercial Press, 2003, pp. 99. The statistics show that the commune and brigade enterprises in Jiangsu are not only better than those in Shandong which are well developed, but also in leading position among the whole country. Therefore, it is easy to understand that the boom of township enterprises from the 1980s to the mid-1990s is the determinant of the development of local economy in Jiangsu province. The contract structure which is called fuzzy property right by economists has a "historical cause", in fact, the political and ideological preferences of the local government has played an important role.

the commune and brigade enterprises played an important role in the local government's tax revenue, labor employment and raising farmer's income①. Undoubtedly, the positive influence on the employment exerted by the commune and brigade enterprises and the irreplaceable contribution to the local fiscal revenue②, the local government's ideology tends to collective ownership of the economy, and regarding the policy, it will strongly advocate the transformation of the commune and brigade enterprises into township enterprises with collective property, farmers do not become self-employed individual famer because of the contract system. The grassroots government processes power and can integrate resources and offer loan credit. Therefore, the township enterprises can develop rapidly under the financial restraint③. The power capital of the grassroots government and the human capital of the owner of township enterprises can tie together and form a special "fuzzy property right structure", which supported the rapid development of most local economy in Jiangsu in the mid-1980s and 1990s. It is obvious that the "fuzzy property right structure" is the result of rural enterprises adapting to the imperfect market under the condition of two historical heritages, namely, the grassroots power (political heritage) and the commune and brigade enterprises (economical heritage), the degree of privatization is less than the Zhejiang-Wenzhou pattern we'll discuss below, so it can be represented as point N in Figure 1 -2.

For Zhejiang and other places, the contradictions are very prominent, which makes people living in the region develop a special business culture. Because of the flexibility of the private economy mechanism and the ability to adapt to the market, the marginal efficiency of the material capital of the private enterprises is higher than that of the state-owned capital under the condition of shortage economy in the 1980s. The transaction efficiency of the organization is obviously superior to the state-owned enterprises, and the low portion of state-owned capital in Zhejiang, compared to the private economy capital, the total contribution of state-owned capital is not a decisive advantage, which makes the local government prefer to develop private economy and

---

① Pan Wei: "Peasants and Market", The Commercial Press, 2003, pp. 102 - 103.

② Statistical Bureau of Jiangsu Province: "Jiangsu Statistical Yearbook in 1983", 1984, pp. 102.

③ "China Statistical Yearbook in 1996", China Statistics Press, 1996, pp. 140 - 141. The statistics show that the "total" (measured by the investment of fixed asset) of collective economy in Jiangsu, Zhejiang and other provinces has surpassed the state-owned economy until the early 1990s. The total amount of collective economy and other types of economy in Guangdong have exceeded the state-owned economy. It is hard to imagine that the government will not support the economic organization politically and financially when considering a certain type of economic quantity and the fiscal revenue of the local government.

revitalize the local industry in terms of ideology and policy choices. Because the local government revises its ideology preference earlier, so it makes the development environment of the private economy more advantageous than other places, and it creates the condition for the Zhejiang private economy to realize the continuous organization innovation. In addition, a loose policy environment and economic environment are prone to endogenous entrepreneurial groups, which will greatly increase the frequency of technological and organizational innovation. The Wenzhou pattern is the common result of the local government revising the ideological preference and the independent innovation of private economy. Obviously, the degree of privatization of such an organization equilibrium model is higher than that of fuzzy property rights, so it can be expressed in the point Q in Figure 1 – 2.

In fact, point N is the "intermediate state" of point M and point Q. If the market economy system improves, the "fuzzy property right structure" of township enterprises will bear more entrust-agent cost than private economy with clear property rights. Its organizational transaction efficiency is not as good as the latter, therefore, under the pressure of productivity competition, it will further improve the property tight structure or the corporate governance structure, so that the point N will become unstable, and the result is the township enterprises would be further privatized, from point N to point Q. This is exactly the reason why the township enterprises of Jiangsu Province carry on the property right reform in the late half of the 1990s.

Most of the private economy in the central region or the northeast old industrial base are at the point M, because the capital marginal efficiency of these areas is low, and the majority of GDP (gross domestic product) is created by state-owned capital. Because the organization efficiency of the private capital and state-owned capital is close to each other, and the local government lacks the incentive to develop the private economy, thus the "ideological preference lag" comes into being①, which makes these regions to be a "development trap" of the private economy (such as point M in Figure 1 – 2). But, as the market economy improves, the trans-regional flow of capital elements and human capital will make the local government with the lag of ideological preferences turn to adopt the policy of developing private economy. In an easing environment, the private economy will obtain a high organization efficiency, and the private capital marginal efficiency will also raise, which will force the local

① "The lag of ideological preference": it indicates that the local government is confined to the traditional ideology and cannot issue the policies for the private economy timely.

governments of central provinces to realize the reversal of ideological preference, and create more incentives for the private economy development. Therefore, it is necessary to adjust the ideological preference of the local government, improve the transaction efficiency of the private enterprises and raise the marginal efficiency of private capital to get rid of the development traps of the private economy.

7. Measurement

(1) Theoretical explanation of measurement model.

This section holds that the ideology is the selective result of local government, and the ideological preference of the local government is determined by the regional ownership structure, as well as the fiscal contribution and marginal contribution of different types of economic organizations in this framework. Therefore, with regard to policies, the local government in favor of traditional socialism ownership structure will introduce a series of policies that benefit the state-owned economy, and those that prefer the "revised" socialism ownership structure will introduce a series of policies to benefit the private economy.

This section attempts to build a measurement model to test the logical structure developed above and the rationality of the viewpoints above. According to the foregoing analysis, the local government's ideological preference will eventually be embodied in the policy, and the result of the policy is "cumulative effect of policy", that is, after a period of change in economic structure, the result will affect the type of ownership and the distribution of economic organizations in the industry. More importantly, it will ultimately be reflected in the financial contribution of different types of economic organizations. The reasons why this section holds this view are that:

First, many areas, such as the old industrial base in the northeast, concentrated their investment activities in infrastructure and heavy industry in the 1950s, observations have shown that, until 1990s, the situation has not changed much, and it is easy for us to make a judgment of the region's ideological preferences. Thus, even a more rigorous economic analysis does not seem to be involved in determining the underlying causes of the local government's ideological preferences. This deep reason cannot be simply interpreted as the established historical constraint, although "historical constraint" and "ideological rigidity" do play a very paramount role. However, it is important to explain why the ideological preference in the region has been rigid. Or, we should provide evidence that there is no "deflection" or "revision" of "ideological preference" in the region.

Second, different distribution of ownership structure and different types of economic organizations in different regions in 1996 is the result of "historical accumulation" of economic system reform and the process of change in the beginning of 1978. This process makes different regions present the "path (evolution) bifurcation" of institutional change, and the ideological preference of local governments in some regions has been "deflected", while the ideological preference of some local governments has been rigid. The fundamental reason is that the historical accumulation effect of reform in different regions is different, and the cumulative effect of reform is embodied in the ownership structure and the distribution of various economic organizations in different regions in the 1996. In order to identify the "institutional nature" of these distinct economic organizations, it is necessary to cite the financial contribution and proportion of various types of economic organizations in different regions of the year.

Based on the two reasons above, we select 1996 as the data sample year. This is because the reform began in 1978 and continued until 1996, lastly nearly 20 years. Since the ideological preference in different regions has different characteristics, we believe that the data of 1996 has statistical and economic significance. After 1996, the local governments strongly feel the "competitive pressure" from the relatively developed regions. Because the township enterprises had already transformed, the "imitation effect" and "learning effect" appear in the policy, and the lagging regions and developed regions have shown a "convergent" trend in policies.

The basic measurement model is as below:

$$\left(\frac{K_s}{K_g}\right)_{1996} = C + \alpha_1 \mathrm{REGION}_{1996} + \alpha_2 \mathrm{LAND}_{1996} + \alpha_3\left(\frac{\mathrm{GDP}_i}{\sum \mathrm{GDP}}\right)_{1996} + \alpha_4\left(\frac{MF_g}{MF_s}\right)_{1996} + \varepsilon \tag{17}$$

In equation (17), C and ε is the intercept and error term respectively, the subscript 1996 represents the year. It is necessary to reemphasize that the main reason for choosing 1996 as the year of study is that the Asian financial crisis of 1997, as an important exogenous variable, has a serious impact on the Chinese economy. Therefore, the change of local government ideology and the decision process and conduction mechanism of policy adjustment are more complex, from central government to local government, and they will exert more intervention in economy, because all levels of government will take more account of the country's economic and financial security in the decision-making process. Its ideological preference will tend to "maintain the macroeconomy stable". In addition, as noted above, around 1997, the township enterprises in Jiangsu province were in the "critical condition" of enterprise restructuring due to the "historical cumulative effect" of economic structure evolution. Moreover, as time goes on, the role of ideology in government intervention may fall, as the new generation of rulers replaces the old generation and the government intervention cost rises①. According to the theoretical expectation, the estimated coefficient α_1 of the geographical location and per capita arable land of each province should be positive, and the α_2 should be negative. The per capita arable land could measure the "the degree of tension between people and land" in certain area, especially in the comparison of different provinces. For example, the uniqueness of commercial culture emerges from different provinces. For example, the community members of Zhejiang province are more motivated to engage in commercial activities than community members in Liaoning province, because the former has less per capita land than the latter. In addition, the geographical location of the different provinces exerts great effects on the local government's ideological preference, because the transaction cost of interregional trade in the inland area is higher than that of the same trade in the coastal region. This also means that in the provinces with more per capita arable land, the local government's ideological preference is less prone to deflection. We expect that, when $|\alpha_2| > |\alpha_1|$, the per capita arable land has a greater impact on ideological preference than geographical location.

Theoretically, if we fully understand the mechanism of ideological formation, then we can clearly evaluate and judge the decisive influence of ideological preferences on the process of policy making. There are two indicators that can influence the ideological preference of local government: one is the ratio of per capita GDP in this region to per capita GDP around the nation; the other is the portion of marginal contribution of private economy to fiscal revenue and the portion of marginal contribution of state-owned economy to fiscal revenue. These two indicators measure the competitive pressure between regions and the competitive pressure of different types of economic organizations in the same region respectively. The former will induce the local government to form an institutional learning effect, that is, the backward regions are commonly motivated to carry out a continuous "institutional study" from advanced regions. When the former realizes that the advanced region

① Zhang Qi and Liu Mingxing's paper have also discussed this issue (2004).

makes great progress in their economy through the growth of private economy, then the local government may revise the previous ideological "preferences", and turn to enact policies to support the development of the private economy. But, whether the policies have the continuity of time and consistency of political logic is depended on whether the marginal contribution of private economy to the local fiscal revenue is greater than the marginal contribution of the state-owned economy to the local fiscal revenue. In the comparison of different types of economic organizations, those with more efficient economic organizations will be "favored" by local governments. We can anticipate that $\alpha_3 > 0$, $\alpha_4 < 0$, and it is statistically significant.

Clearly, the factors that determine the ideological preferences include geographical location, the per capita area, the proportion of marginal contributions to fiscal revenue by different types of economic organizations, and the ratio of per capita GDP to the country's per capita GDP. Then, the ideological preference and these factors form some kind of "reciprocal effect mechanism"; but the per capita land area and the geographical location are given, which can be defined as "exogenous" "economic parameters". Therefore, the ideological preference embodied in the policy preference will become the "policy variable" that decides the development of different types of economic organization, although it is indirect to the actual economic performance. With this in mind, we can understand deeply the "political economy basis" of local policy preference.

(2) The results of measurement and its explanation.

We employ the related statistical data of 30 provinces and municipalities directly under the central government and autonomous regions in 1996, and we select the per capita arable land (RJGD), the ratio of per capita GDP in each province to national per capita GDP (GG), the state-owned economy's contribution to the fiscal revenue (RGR), and the virtual variables which reflect the geographical differences, W, M, E, HKTW, of which, W represents the western region; M represents the central region; E is eastern region, and HKTW represents Hong Kong SAR. and Taiwan Province. The interpreted variable is the ratio of private economy to state-owned economy, HSHG.

We use EVEIWS 3.1 econometric software to conduct the analysis. First of all, we test the data instability, through the unit root test, and find that only RGR passes the instability test, and others are unstable variables. After the first order difference, we find that DGG, DRJGD and DHSHK all pass the test, and they are first order unstable variables. The related analysis, the cause test and co-integration test are well-supported by our previous theoretical models. Furthermore, the regression equation I shows that the DHSHK and RGR have a negative correlation with a confidence level of 5%. This shows that the greater the contribution of state-owned economy to fiscal revenue, the more the local government prefers the non-private economy (state-owned economy), which is consistent with our theoretical analysis. The E and HKTW, as geographical virtual variables, pass the significance test (confidence level is 5%), and they have a clear positive correlation. In addition, W, the virtual variable of eastern part and M, the virtual variable of central part fail to pass the significance test. This indicates that in eastern coastal regions, Hong Kong SAR. and Taiwan Province, the local government prefer the private economy, that is to say, the developed regions always prefer the private economy. This is consistent with our theoretical analysis. In the process of regression, we find that DHSHK and DGG have a significant positive correlation with a significance test less than the confidence level of 5% (the regression equation II shows that the developed regions prefer the private economy), which is also consistent with our theoretical analysis. In the process of regression, we find that the per capita arable land index fails to pass the 10% confidence level of the significant test, but if we put the confidence level appropriately wider, the index can pass the significant test which the confidence level is 13%. In general, the result of the econometric analysis in the Table 1 – 1 supports our previous theoretical analysis.

Table 1 – 1 Regression equation results

Explanatory variable DHSHG	Regression equation I		Regression equation II	
Explanatory variable	Correlation coefficient	Probability	Correlation coefficient	Probability
HKTW	3. 134882	0. 0325		
E	1. 775881	0. 0195		
RGR	-1. 558323	0. 0453		
DGG			0. 935824	0. 0407
C	-1. 657089	0. 0060	0. 029760	0. 9372
R-squared	0. 444254	-0. 026812	0. 146170	-0. 026812
AdjustedR-squared	0. 377565	2. 137324	0. 114546	2. 137324
D. W	2. 284196	0. 001851	2. 650004	0. 040678

8. Conclusions

Unlike the literatures that emphasize decisive influence of property rights, culture and technological changes on the evolution of the private economy, this section analyzes the local government's ideological preferences. The ideological preferences decide the local government's policies in the private economy, as the ideology is not simply equated with belief, region or moral ethic system, it is essentially influenced by the "comparative organization efficiency" of private capital and state-owned capital, or the "comparative marginal efficiency" of private capital and state-owned capital. Whether the ideological preference can be revised in time and induce the local government to choose the policy of developing private economy, it depends on the absolute total amount and relative amount of the state-owned economy and private economy in a certain region.

It is the combination of historical and logic development, along with the productivity competition between state-owned enterprises and private enterprises, the institutional complementation between state-owned and private capital, that has given rise to different evolution trajectories in different private economy. The productivity competition, institutional changes and the local government's ideological preferences jointly determine the remarkable difference of the "system complementary characteristic" in different regions, which makes the Wenzhou pattern of Zhejiang province, the Southern Suzhou pattern of Suzhou province, and the Pearl River delta pattern in Guangdong province start their respective bifurcation evolution trajectory at the beginning. The evolution of this pluralistic private economy will converge to the equilibrium point in different position in their development stage. But under the effect of the pressure of the productivity competition and the system complementation of state-owned and private economy, these different evolution paths will eventually approximate or converge to the "optimal equilibrium point". For economic analysts, however, it is important to see the difference in evolution and discover the mysteries that give rise to these differences.

This section contends that, under the constraint of historical conditions in different regions, the local government that has completely abandoned the traditional ideological preference to then accommodate the private enterprises to obtain the comparative efficiency advantage of the organization quickly. As a result, the private economy operates as an independent organization innovation, which is the origin of the Wenzhou pattern; those who slowly abandon traditional ideological preference will take part in the process of enterprise evolution in the form of grass-root power, thus the township enterprises with an unclear property right structure will arise, which is the origin of southern Suzhou province pattern. Local governments that adhere to the traditional ideological preference emphasize the effect of state-owned enterprise reform on economic growth. Therefore, it cannot provide a reasonable policy environment for the development of the private economy, which makes the private enterprises lack the stable expectation, so the private economy is unable to have an effective advantage over the state-owned economy in a large scale. This is the exact situation of the development of private economy in central and western part.

1.2 Motivation of the evolution of private economy organization: productivity competition and institutional complementariness

This section discusses the determinants of economic growth in the transitional period. It is well known that since 1978 China's economy has maintained a high growth rate. As Kuznets says, a rapid rate of economic restructuring, including shifts from agriculture to industry to services, is a feature of economic growth. This process involves urbanization, the shift from household workshop to employment relations, and the growing role of formal education. Furthermore, Kuznets believes that the growth of the modern economy is closely related to the foreign trade, technological progress and the government's strategic positioning (1973, 1981)① . For a transition economy, the role of government is very prominent. Under the traditional planned economy, the distribution of the means of production depends on the government's plan, and the distribution of the labor force is realized by the administrative order of the government personnel department, even the supply of consumption goods is controlled by the government. In order to realize the transition planned economy to market economy, the role of government is still critical and it cannot be ignored. The market economy is a new institution, which requires various economic subjects to freely choose the form of trade or contract, and to make decision to seek profits. Therefore, an institutional structure can systematically keep each economy under a series of trading activities in a freeway, which is also proactive and fair②. This institutional structure also has the nature of public goods. In theory, public goods can be generated by the profit-seeking subjects in the process of profit-driven transaction or game, but form the historical experience, the process of spontaneous evolution is too "long". Therefore, the transition country or the emerging country (government) can

---

① Robert J Barrow and Havel Sala I Martin, He Hui and Liu Mingxing, trans. *Economic Growth*, China Social Sciences Press, 2000, P5.

② For the occident, the market economy is self-evident. To China, while it is in the process of economic transition, the market economy is an epoch-making event.

directly absorb the experience of the developed markets, and offer all kinds of basic institutional arrangements.

Given many "historical constraints" to the planned economy, the construction of new institutional arrangements has three different "paths":

First, for the "Genesis" path, even if the banks, public enterprises and others achieve wholly the "privatization goal" overnight, the inevitable result is that the market economy system is regarded as fundamentally economic and social system and makes effect. This is the transition path of Soviet Union (Russia). The philosophical basis of this transitional path is that "people cannot cross the same river by two times."

Second, it is clear that reform is a process based on a set of complete privatization. However, it cannot show that the behavior of economic entity is immediately "market reaction", that is, the formation expectations of economic subject and the judgment for market still needs to pass "learning process". In addition, individuals also gradually understand, absorb and comprehend the knowledge about the market economy system. The imperfections of information and knowledge make institutional arrangements only progressive and adaptive. Social transformation can only meet the adaptive efficiency standards, but it cannot be based on efficiency standards. The meaning is that the constraints of ideological constraints and knowledge shortages and the conversion costs of ideology will lead to that there are many intermediate states or transitional states in the process of transition. The formation of system is "marginal", "dynamic adaptability" and "trial and error". But in theory, "transition" implies that institutional change always carries out convergence or approximation towards the optimal system of security①.

Third, natural evolution is based on a track or process, that is, there is not a transcendental reform target in theory, but "laissez faire" as the body between autonomous institutional arrangements by game or endogenous growing. But in fact, for a transitional economy, the process of transition from planning to market and the deregulation of government are the result of a "system design". Only can enterprises become the main body of market and the members of enterprises can realize the transformation from "unit man" to "economic man" by relaxing control first. Therefore, the simple process of natural evolution is almost nonexistent in the course

① The so-called optimal institutional arrangements are nothing more than "institutional arrangements" that enable a variety of resources to have Pareto efficiency.

of transition.

This shows that, from the general theoretical logic, if we want to measure the determinants of economic growth, we must examine the role of government for transition economy. For example, Genesis means that the government chooses to be "God"; while the transitional institutional arrangement means that the government carries out bargaining with various economic subjects, and finally they mutually choose a kind of contractual institutional arrangements (structure) by taking into account the interests of all parties; the so-called natural evolution process also has government factors. Because the government is also the main beneficiary, it enters into the game of rights and power with other economic entities together (common). Thus, "dynamic adaptability" or "trial and error" is a kind of "natural characteristic" manifested in the process of the game of each subject, which shows that the "intermediate institutional arrangement" and the "natural evolution state" of system are essentially equivalent.

To examine the role of government, we must examine the institutional effects of economic growth. Although when we discuss the institutional arrangements of economic growth, we can list many intermediate institutional arrangements①, such as price dual system, exchange rate dual system, township enterprises with fuzzy property rights, financial contract system, etc. However, in examining the institutional effects of economic growth, it is necessary to transform the contribution of intermediate institutional arrangement to economic growth into the economic analysis variable that can describe, define and even measure or carry out normative research in order to explore the practical impact of transitional institutional arrangements on economic growth. In this section, we call all institutional arrangements that have both market orientation and some characteristics of traditional planned economic system as "intermediate institutional arrangements" and the social economic system with intermediate institutional arrangements is called as the economic system of binary (institutional) structure.

The analysis structure or logic of this section is that "historical logic starting point" affects and determines the reform dimension of state-owned economy and the "evolution track" of private economy; the result of competitive pressure of "productivity competition" in the system or organization induces the starting and

---

① Many scholars argue that the intermediate system arrangements are regarded as "transitional institutional arrangement". This chapter argues that these two claims can be mixed. This chapter adopts the term "intermediate institutional arrangement" and is inspired by Prof. Zhou Bing, Institute of Economic Research, Nankai University.

improvement of state-owned enterprise reform, which ultimately lets the organization evolution of various forms to take refuge in efficiency standards. In addition, from 1949 to 1977, through the industrial accumulation of prioritizing capital growth and the long-term investment, improvement, consolidation and development in various types of infrastructure, China's rural and urban reform have their own determined object and historical premise. The other economic organizations, 5 non-collective and non-state-owned economies have been the historical conditions of constantly developing and growing or "historical logic starting point". From the perspective of history, the reform of state-owned enterprises provides objectively "institutional resources" for the development of non-state-owned economy. Therefore, the evolution of privatization or private economy is the result for state-owned and non-state-owned economy (each other) to carry out productivity competition and system complementary. The evolution of any kind of economic organization is not unidirectional. They both have competitive relationship and complementary relationship, and "institutional complementary" and "mutual block humanity" eventually shape a variety of organization forms and let them appear "regional"①.

In fact, since 1978, although the planned economy has an absolutely dominant position in the initial stage of reform, it has a number of characteristics of market orientation which occurs once the government authorities give the state enterprises a certain degree of autonomy and profitability. For example, under the stimulation of profit seeking motivation, the enterprise leader will adjust the organizational form of production within the enterprise as soon as possible and try to find more opportunities to retain more profits. If the enterprise property rights are a group of residual control and residual claims, the enterprise will retain more profits. This does not mean that the distribution of property rights have been in effect, which means that people begin to break through the state-owned enterprise property in practice, and ideas and ownership must be highly concentrated in the country's ideological shackles in practice and ideas. An enterprise reform aimed at decentralization and entitlement will inevitably lead to the reorganization of residual control and claim right for enterprises. This shows that the property rights' (oriented) reform of state-owned enterprise is inherently endogenous and institutional after obtaining (and giving) corresponding production and operating autonomy. The following will demonstrate that it is the

① Deng Hongtu, "The Interpretation of Evolution for Chinese Institutional Change during the Period of Transition: Taking the Evolution Process of China's Private Economy as an Example", "Social Sciences in China", No. 5, 2004.

"historical constraint" established by the logical starting point of the transitional state of property right reform.

From the research point of view, "the logical starting point of history" not only shows that the initial conditions or related constraints in various economic organizations in economic transition, but it also means that the mainstream ideology or traditional custom will affect the expected benefits (functions) and contract selection of economic entities. It puts the influence of ideology, culture and values on the behavior of individuals or organizations into the analytic field of economics and constitutes the decisive factor in the whole analytic framework. Therefore, the "historical logic starting point" is an important research perspective and "analysis basis" in this part.

It is easy for researcher to "see the trees but not the forest" if we only investigate the evolution "track" of some specific (economic) organization in the period of transition. Because the evolution of one form of economic organization constitutes the "economic environment" or "exogenous variable" in the evolution of some other economic organizations. Different types of economic organizations always "interactively" provide necessary conditions to rely on or obstacles that must be overcome for the evolution of relevant economic organizations. Finally, the "superior productivity structure" will always let the evolution process of some type of economic organization occupy the upper hand. Therefore, the organization evolution (inevitable) has two sides, which seem to contradict each other at the same time, and include the two seemingly contradictory contradictions between the productivity competition and the institutional complementary between different types of economic organizations①.

In this part, in the process of transition, the analysis of "organization evolution" and "historical logic starting point" is to provide a historical case study that is related to organization evolution causes; the discussion on the "productivity competition" between various organization forms is trying to lead to make in-depth analysis for the "first driving force" and subsequent "sustained power" of organization form evolution; the research on system complementarity reflects that we try to explore the "institutional relevance" contained in the evolution process of various forms of organization and reveal these correlations as much as possible. We believe that the so-

---

① Deng Hongtu, "Relatively rational research", Research of institutional economics, No. 1, 2003; "The economic interpretation of organization, organizational evolution and institutional changes", Nankai Economic Studies, No. 1, 2003; "The reconstruction for the economic analysis of historical materialism methodology: the paradigm crisis and paradigm transformation of mainstream economics", Tianjin Social Sciences, No. 5, 2004. Readers are also asked to refer to the contents of chapters one and two in this book.

called transition characteristics are precisely contained in the "productivity competition" and "system complementarity" of different organization forms in the co-evolution.

In the fourth part of this study, we will make the econometric analysis for the organizational motivations of economic growth, and the final conclusion will give the general conclusion of this part.

1.2.1 Transit and "historical logic starting point": brief description of economic history①

1. Public will (preference) and "heavy chemical industry" path

According to the logic of Hayek, Popper and Arrow②, social organizations, economic organizations and even the state do not seem to have "will" and "preferences". Because personal preferences cannot be summed up in terms of culture, faith and belief, people with common historical, experiences and shared natural conditions③ must "intersect" in the way of thinking, perceptions of reality and the basic value judgments. At the same time, because of the externalities of individual behavior, people with the same historical and natural conditions will undoubtedly have common interests. The historical evolution can be seen as a n people game in the extension of time and space. There are political and economic organizations among the n people; there are not only formal authority departments, but they also have the informal social groups (non-public authority department); there is both units and individuals. In this kind of multi-organization and multi-person game, the practice, social customs, order, the phase of culture, ethics and moral social choice will become the "common knowledge" of game participants. The so-called common knowledge, that is, as we all know, everyone knows that others know and so on. If each participant has the same, similar or related "common knowledge", an

① As for the influence of historical logic starting point on the reform and institutional change, the author involves in both the third and fourth chapters of this book. This chapter discusses this question again, which is intended to show that, first of all, this question holds an important and pivotal position in the analytical paradigm of this book; secondly, in this chapter, the author attempts to give a new formulation for this problem.

② Hayek: "The Principles of Free Order", Beijing Joint Publishing, 2001. Popper: "The Theory of Historicism Poverty", China Social Sciences Press, 2001; "Open Society and Its Enemies", China Social Sciences Press, 2002.

③ Natural conditions, that is, resource endowments.

organization, a group or a political party will exhibit similar common (public) preferences" with the "personal preference" of organization, group or party member. Therefore, the "common will" of organizations, groups and political parties will be established. In the game of n people, "discourse game" is also a "necessary means" for the strategy interaction of participants. "The power of saying" of different economic and political organizations describes their own preferences and wills as the "public will" that has a sense of justice of the whole society. Finally, the "mainstream discourse" accepted by the public must be the "discourse" that embodies the will and preference of strong groups①. Preference is not only endogenous and stable, but it also is exogenous, contextual and variable②.

Based on this, the state and the government will have the existed historical and logical basis. In this case, the state, economic and social organizations will undoubtedly have their will and preferences, and the internal members of state or group will share the unanimous ideologies and belief systems. This proves that the construction of rationality is a factor that cannot be ignored in the process of deciding the change of social system. This is important, because it provides the logical basis for analyzing the relationship between government actions and economic growth. From 1949 to 1976, the development of China's economy coincides with political and strategic preferences in the era of Mao Zedong. In the era of Mao Zedong, regime and state system, ideology (political beliefs or beliefs), industrial economic base, opening up, political and economic organization (including state-owned enterprises, collective enterprises, also including rural people's communes and collective enterprise), class structure (level) and the cooperative medical system that almost covers the entire rural and other aspects provide extremely rich "historical heritage"③ since the beginning of reform and opening up in 1978. They constitute mutually China institutional change or the "historical logic starting point" of social transformation and

---

① Common knowledge is not only the "external constraint" of public discourse, social transformation, institutional change, or participant's game, but it also constantly changes with the participants' strategic interaction. When the social revolution arrives, "common knowledge" may change structurally and fundamentally.

② Samuel Bowles, "Microeconomics: Behavior, Institution and Evolution" (Chinese Edition), China Renmin University Press, 2006, pp. 72 – 73.

③ Perhaps some feel that this kind of historical heritage is not the "product" that is provided by heritage provider and that is highly consistent with "subjective" and purpose, and maybe even it is possible that the subjective choice of later is very different. My answer is that this is not the core of problem, and we only objectively and neutrally examine the influence of "historical heritage" on the trajectory of future institutional change.

(to a considerable extent) shape and determine the unique Chinese-style reform path (track)①.

Before and after the economic reform in 1978, Chinese enterprises were mainly collectively owned enterprises based on public ownership (see Figure 1-3). The reasons for the formation of this dual (public ownership) economic structure can be attributed to the ideology that the ruling party pursues and the choice for the socialist ideal and the way of realization in order to fully demonstrate the institutional superiority of socialism "justice, grant and prosperity". Even more crucially, it can be attributed to the strong will of the ruling Communist Party of China to reform itself from a typical small-scale peasant economy to an independent industrial economy, so as to shorten the economic gap, political gap and cultural gap between China and other modern and powerful industrialized countries. To this end, the ruling party must formulate and implement the "industrial priority growth strategy", develop heavy industry at great prices, construct and improve various types of infrastructures including industry, agriculture and transportation.

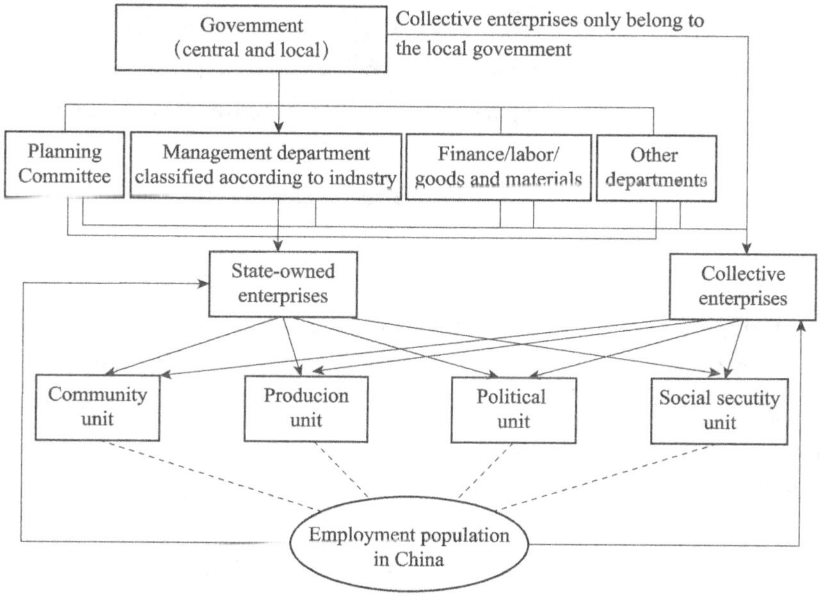

Figure 1-3 "Historical logic starting point" of China's economic system transition from micro perspective

① Deng Hongtu and Li Ya, "The Interpretation of Economic History for China's Institutional Change during the Period of Transition: the Institutional Predicament and the Endogeneity of reform", Nankai Economic Studies, No. 2, 2004.

The "catch-up strategy" put forward by Lin Yifu is the reason why ruling party implement "state control" and "planned economy". But the author wants to emphasize that the "catch-up strategy" is also decided by political ideal and political belief to a certain extent. The strategies of planned economy and national economic control are consistent with the historical and logical judgment of classical Marxism-Leninism for capitalism and imperialism. In their writings, they assert that the free market mechanism is difficult to solve all sorts of contradictions that exist naturally and are difficult to reconcile between the planning that capitalist social production requires and the disorder of decentralization for the production of micro enterprises. Once this kind of contradiction intensifies, it will cause the economic crisis. And this kind of economic crisis is considered as the "chronic illness" which the capitalist system itself is difficult to solve. Therefore, Marx and Lenin argued that only adopting the planning method can we ensure the effective use of social resources so as to avoid the cyclical crisis of capitalism. The establishment of socialist belief and political ideals or belief is closely related to these theoretical logics of Marx and Lenin. Naturally, because of "proposition" or "truth" that Marx and Lenin to which many of their followers subscribe, the ruling parties of socialists have purposely organized, a priori, a planned economy. This shows that the "planned economy" of ruling party first is regarded as the superiority of socialism to get theoretically demonstration, while the "catch-up strategy" is the means that logical starting from reality should adopt or choose to prove the superiority of socialist system. Of course, if we want to achieve "catch-up strategy", we must strengthen the "planning system". Tremendous pressure of logical self-consistent ideological constraints and industrialization and national security aspects will force the ruling party to use the means of planned economy to "crowd out" people's consumption fund, to oppress people's consumption desire in order to carry out large investment for heavy industry and military industry by adopting the means for the "scissors difference" of industrial and agricultural products (see Figure 1 - 4). For example, in 1966 - 1971, only the investment that plans for the "third front" accounted for 50% - 60% of total budgets. This result is conducive to the completion of country's industrialization in the short term and strengthening the "hard power" of country to ensure national security and long-term development. In fact, the total industrial output value in 1949 accounted for only 30% of total GDP, while the corresponding index is 80% in 1977. Therefore, from the social production capacity and the total value of industrial and agricultural output perspective, China had been the "industrial country" that was dominated by industry in 1977. Some scholars believe that the presented performance differences of Chinese economy and Russian economy after the reform can be mainly explained the differences in the economic structure before the reform. In their views, China is basically an agricultural country before the reform, and the Soviet Union is the highly industrialized city state. In the state economy, the workers are highly subsidized. Therefore, in the Russian reform, urban employment workers are not likely to leave the state economy to other departments like peasants, even if other economics have higher productivity. The situation in China is just the opposite (Sax and Hu Yongtai, 1994, referring to Zhang Jun, 2006, 14). This statement is not enough to summarize the "essence" of Chinese institutional change, and the reason is that: first, as stated above, in fact, China has been an "industrial country" in the structure of total output value; Second, after the reform, the output value, annual growth rate and absorbed labor quantity of Chinese state-owned enterprises have been growing in 1977 – 1996 in the past 20 years (Zhang Jun, 2006, 15; The comprehensive Department of the National Bureau of statistics, 1990; 2000; 2005); Third, the key point is that many documents ignore an important aspect, that is, when discussing the problem of institutional change in China, there is no historical logic starting point, the political mobilization of ruling party, the development of social enterprise before the reform and opening up. Moreover, the raising international political and economic consequences of China's diplomatic action began in 1969 had profound impact on the path of reform since 1978①.

In general, the history of Chinese industry from 1949 to 1977 is the "the history of practice" of classic socialist planned economy, which stimulates each other's

① However, Sax and Hu Yongtai's literature (1994) also implied the influence of population structure on China's reform track. If it is not from the output value and the contribution of GNP (or GDP) growth but from the population structure point of view, China still can be regarded as an agricultural country, which also explains the fact that China's industrialization before the reform is not accompanied by the cities. Before the reform, industrialization mainly concentrated in the areas of infrastructure which is a very capital-intensive industry, and part of the foundation for modernization of a country. Based on China's population and growing infrastructure, most of China's economic growth in the reform is caused by the population migration and the changes from the agricultural economy to the industrial economy. Therefore, the contribution of economic growth before reform lies in the independence and integrity of chemical industry. One of the great contributions of reform and opening up lies in the opening of domestic labor market, which allows farmers in the rural marginal output to be able to accept the lowest possible wage to state-owned enterprises, private enterprises and foreign enterprises. This is the important source of China's economic growth which will be studied in greater detail in the subsequent sections

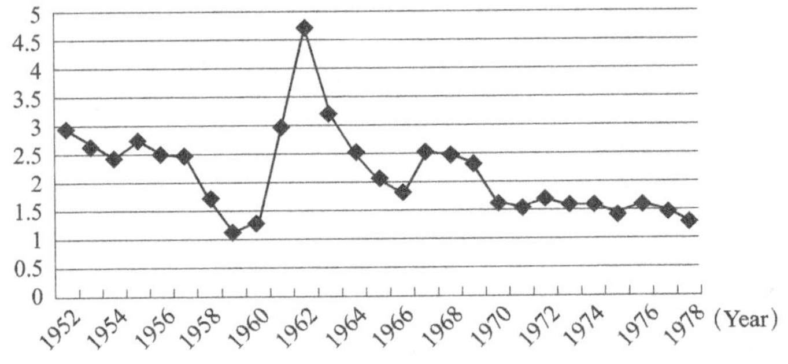

Figure 1 – 4 Trend chart of consumption/accumulation from 1952 to 1978

Note: The proportion of consumption/accumulation had been on the rise during 1954 – 1955, 1959 – 1962, 1966 – 1967, 1972 – 1973 and 1975 – 1976. During these periods, this proportion grew faster in 1959 – 1962. Each period is associated with some particular political background. In 1955, the first "Five Year" plan was waiting for large-scale implementation and promotion; In 1959 – 1962, it was coincided with the Chinese economy in the most difficult period; In 1972 to 1973, the communist Party of China held the tenth Congress, which decided to adjust politic and economy; in 1975, the ruling party made efforts to rectify the national economy, and the president Mao Zedong proposed that "the national economy must be carried up". In 1976, Premier Zhou Enlai, Chairman Zhu De and Chairman Mao Zedong passed away one by one. The consumption here mainly refers to household consumption, which excludes government consumption. The accumulation here includes both the formation of fixed capital and the increase of inventories.

Source: "The Compilation of Statistical Data for New China in Fifty Years", China Statistics Press, 1999.

"demand" and "desire" to meet each other's needs as much as possible in an unusual way. When the two are inconsistent, it indicates that the economic crisis has emerged. One reason for this inconsistency may arise from the structural or institutional problems encountered by both the industrialized and planned economic systems themselves; another reason is that the "political cycle" resulting from changes in personal choice of political leaders and their influence on the economic operation mechanism. However, the policy changes in the political leaders are related to the economic pressures that the internal political and economic institutions bear, and the changes in the external international environment are related to the impact of industrialization in China. On the basis of the intricacies and role of these intricacies, China was first politically independent on the basis of the history of semi-colonial and semi-feudal conversions for one hundred years, and then China carries out national construction in a unique way. By 1977, it has generally established independent modern industrial system and national economic system. All of these not only are the historical starting point of our reform, but they also have become the objective or goal of our reform.

2. Historical logical starting point or "historical heritage"

The success of economic reform and the growth of the Chinese economy have an immense literature. Much of the literature regards the achieved sustained economic growth in China for nearly 30 years as opening up, such as joining WTO, the accumulation of technology and human capital, organization transformation and innovation etc., but they ignore the "historical preparation" of "institutional antecedents" for the reform and opening up. If there is no such "historical preparation", China's reform path will be another way. The Shang Yang reform in the history of China is successful, but Wang Anshi's reform ended in failure. Since the late Qing Dynasty in China, the reform has been also ups and downs and full of hardships, and ultimately it was difficult to get rid of the plight of repeated defeats. The longitudinal comparison of history will give us very valuable revelation, that is, a successful reform must have political and economic "institutional antecedents". In other words, in the "historical logic starting point" of reform, we must have a set of sustainable leadership authority and strong ruling ability, strong political will, simple and clear belief system, logical self-consistent ideology and reform subject that is difficult to deal with (including ruling group) and the interests groups that reform measures propose defining challenge and other power structures and constitutional structures that combine politic, economy, society and culture①.

The reform in our country begins in the countryside. The disintegration of people communes has influenced the collective economy of villages and societies to form as a unit. Farmers can freely control the working time and decide the specific production and management contents according to different climate and seasonal conditions. Of course, due to the collective ownership nature of land, the small peasant economy after the disintegration of communes is not exactly the same as the small peasant economy in history, and the land cannot flow freely. Therefore, in addition to local government (such as township government, administrative village), any family could not merge the land and become the operators of land monopoly. The implementation of commune disintegration and contract responsibility system enables the peasants to obtain a part of land property rights, so that the production

① The "constitutional structure" used here is in a general sense, which is different from the western democratic constitutional (the separation of powers, representative democracy and multi-party rotation). The "constitutional structure" here refers to the "unity" of the rule of law under the framework of party politics and constitution.

management of regarding household as the unit had several private properties. In this sense, rural reform is the first step in the transformation of China's private economic system.

With regard to the commune system of rural people, Huang Zongzhi provides a fairly general "interpretation":

"For the state power of Ming and Qing Dynasties, the rural economy is mainly the object of taxation, while the peasants are mainly a source of tax revenue. In addition to taxation, the state power has little interference with agriculture and peasant life. However, the new regime is far more than a tax collector: it intends to control the business of countryside and grasps the economic decisions of each household. In order to achieve these goals, the new regime not only extends its tentacles vertically to the countryside, but they also extend power horizontally, especially around the rural economy. The three key steps of this revolution planning are land reform, the three food grain (country implements grain production, ordering and marketing)[①] and production collectivization. Through these movements, the old political and economic system based on the decentralized and self-supporting smallholder farms was replaced by party state system that has huge system based on collectivization and planned economy (Huang Zongzhi, 2000)."

Originally, the collective economy of planned economy and people commune was relatively subversive and "negated" in the history of the traditional, typical small-scale peasant economy. But in 1979, through the implementation of household contract responsibility system, under the condition of the land still retaining the nature of collective ownership, "three all-based, team-based" commune system disintegrates. From the formal point of view, this is the small-scale production and management model to replace the collective production and management mode of commune. This is the "negative" from the former to the latter. The disintegration of the rural people communes is the "historical logic starting point" in which the Chinese private economy and private property system rise again. However, despite the people communes "withdraws from the stage of history" under the strong demand of ruling party's reform line. The left "historical legacy" still plays "unique" role in China's economic and political system changes since the reform and opening up, so that the institutional change of our private economy shows the "transition path" of privatization

① Huang Zongzhi: "Smallholder families and rural development in the Yangtze River Delta", Zhonghua Book Company, 2000, pp. 167.

that is different from the former socialist countries in Eastern Europe. We can break the "historical logic starting point" of reform into the following four factors:

(1) Political mobilization capability.

The "political mobilization ability" of the ruling party is the "historical logic starting point" for the smooth development of reform and opening up. Huang Zongzhi believes that the land reform and the improvement of tax rates make national regime unprecedented deep natural village in terms of the relationship between regime and village. The old state regime, gentry or landlord, the triangular relationship of peasant was replaced by the new state power and the bilateral relations of peasant. Purchasing, marketing and production "three policies" not only absorb the entire small farm economy into the national plan. In fact, it has strongly pushed farmers into the collective economy. Collectivization makes the party and government power organs more vertical and deep to the grass-roots level of society, and every peasant directly feels the power of state. The situation is very different from that of the Ming and Qing Dynasties. At that time, the emperors and officials were separate from the daily life of countryside. In fact, since 1978, the beginning of bringing order out of chaos is developed and completed by political mobilization. Then in 1979, it starts officially the rural economic system reform. It also persuades the rural cadres and the masses to believe that the "scattered operations, co-production contract" of regarding family as the unit is an ideal rural broad road to socialism through political mobilization (such as public opinion, political preaching, etc.) persuasion. In the 1930s, Mao Zedong proposed to establish branches in the company, and this set of political means to use the political way to pure military forces in the 1950s was used in rural areas and cities. The ruling party thus completed the rural collectivization and the socialist transformation of urban industry and commerce. Therefore, they establish a set of the industrial system of independent national economy regarding city as the center and the people commune system based on countryside. Although this kind of political mobilization often regards sacrificing efficiency as the cost, it lets the ruling party win unprecedented political authority and high-strength social governance capacity. The ruling party can usually put the central government's strategy, intent and even political ideas into continuing to implement through the most basic rural or the branch secretary of factory①.

① This intensive political mobilization capability enabled the ruling party to concentrate its national financial resources on investment and construction in the energy industry, processing industry, equipment industry, defense industry and infrastructure in 1977.

Hence, "the reform" process seemed to be "antinomies". On the one hand, through the CCP organizations at all levels the central government generated powerful political mobilization capability, employing the Mao Zedong Thought and the Ideology of Communism to unify the will of the masses of all classes[①], which greatly reduced the government's administrative cost and the implementation cost of the policy and allowed the ruling party's line, guiding principles and policies to be approximately implemented even in a situation that was constantly changing. Until 1978, it has been two years since Chairman Mao Zedong passed away. The ruling party began, prepared and proceeded to reform and open to the outside world which applied the political resources created by the Mao era by the grass-root party organizations' persuasion, demonstration, education even some compulsory measures, changing the collective operation mode formed in 1957 into "responsibility system" of running factories with contractual management and the organizational form or mode of production of small family or small-scale peasant economy, that is, "land allocation to households". It used the way of mass participation and experienced the process of introduction, implementation and promotion, which provided the farmer with corresponding rights to use, arrange, plan for management objectives and select which crop to grow. However, it also raised other problems. For example, that the farmers had the freedom to select and conduct autonomous management objectively had an impact on the powerful political mobilization capability of the ruling party as the connection of farms in the decentralized operation mode wasn't as close as the people's commune, making it impossible for the local governments and Party branches to mobilize those peasant households who had obtained fully autonomous rights on time and space by collective organization such as the production brigade and production team. As a result, the political mobilization capability of the governing party was weakened rather than be enhanced. If the ruling party couldn't realize the "innovative transformation" in response to such changes on the grass-root organizations in rural areas, its political mobilization capability and available political resources would be greatly discounted. Inevitably, the rural economic reform was launched in 1978 through the political resources created by the Mao Zedong era. Though the marginal value of such resources would decrease gradually as the ruling

① We must note that in the late 1970s Deng Xiaoping repeatedly emphasized to understand the Mao Zedong Thought in a integrate and correct way: it aimed to insure the unity of the ruling party as well as the basic value of the general system of socialist political beliefs.

party constantly loosened administrative control over agricultural operations so that the farmer enabled to use economic rationality to choose their production and operation activities. Still, it is important to not underestimate the positive impact of the "legacy" of the ruling party left in Mao era which stuck to the Mao Zedong Thought as belief and faith on the reform and opening up. Since the lasting reform of the political and economic system consisted of political tension and conflict, the unification of the initial ideology and faith was indispensable; it cushioned the conflicts between politics and the society caused by the inevitable differentiation of interests from reform and opening up. The Mao's political mobilization approach and the Mao Zedong Thought allowed China's reform not to " confront " the "counterattack" by the "interest group" which would do great harm to any reform as in history. Hence, China could throw itself into the reform and opening process in an "economic" and more affordable way. The rural reform brought pressure to cities, which also generated a great number of surplus rural labors and they flooded into cities, producing plentiful labor resources for state-owned enterprises in cities. As a consequence, it was a shock to the labor-intensive industry.

For one thing, the state-owned enterprises in the face of such cheap labor resources, was bound to change the long-standing wage quota system and labor employment system, increasingly pursuing the allocation rights for input factors and autonomous rights for production and management; for another, the collective economy and individual economy that were independent of the state-owned one also enabled to freely hire migrant workers who were free from land and thus gained new opportunities for development in labor-intensive industries. "This" was the beginning of the evolution of China's private economy. The reform "antinomies" contains such (reform) logics, namely reform starts from powerful political mobilization while its ideal result or objective only can be obtained at the cost of continuously reducing this political mobilization capability (see Figure 1 – 5).

(2) Commune and brigade enterprises.

The commune and brigade enterprise was the "institution antecedent" for the township enterprises rose in the 1980s and reached a high point in historical significance in the mid-90s. After 1996, township enterprises began to turn into joint-stock or joint-stock cooperative enterprises, realizing the separation of enterprise from administration of the rural grass-roots government. The blossom of the township enterprises in China was deemed as the huge achievement of the reform and opening up as well as a practicable path for realizing the agricultural industrialization.

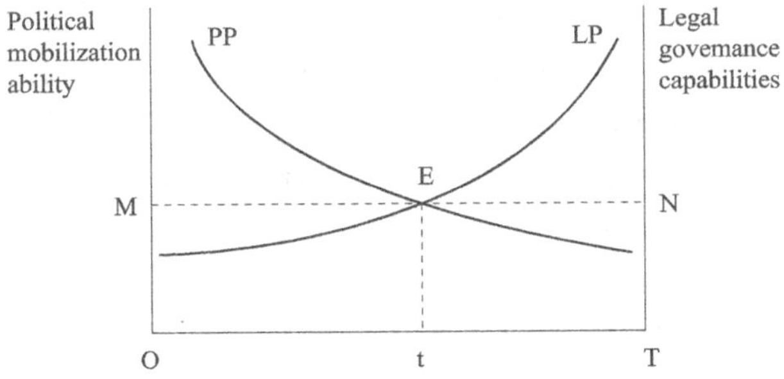

Figure 1 –5 Evolution tendency of political mobilization capability and rule of law capacity in history

Note: PP represents the political mobilization capability of the ruling party; LP represents the rule of law capacity in a transferring society. The basic meaning of this graph is that with the deepening of the reform and opening up process, marketization and privatization will reduce the ruling party's " traditional " political mobilization capability at the grassroots level, but it can strengthen the legal governance capability of society and ultimately both stand in a "compromise" state.

Before 1949, China was a poor agricultural country. After the founding of People's Republic of China, home sideline industry grew vigorously. By 1954, about 10 million peasants were partially involved in industrial production with an output value of 2. 2 billion Yuan. Compared at a comparable price of 1957, the output value of 1949 was only 1. 16 billion Yuan.

During 1955 and 1957, the agriculture stood in a climax period of cooperative transformation; many regions over-emphasized the importance of agriculture and lagged the development of sideline industry. In 1957, the output value of rural sideline production was only 2. 29 billion Yuan, accounting for 4. 3% of the total agricultural value. The people's Commune Movement began in 1958 provided a theoretical support and practice opportunity for commune-run enterprises. In December 10, 1958 the sixth Plenary Session of the 8th Central Committee of the CPC stressed that the people's commune must develop industries in a large scale, combining the handicraft industry with machinery industry, making full use of the local steel, local machine tools and other native materials, equipment and approaches to gradually turn the local industries into international ones from small scale to a large one, from low level to a high one, step by step narrowing the gap between urban and rural areas. The transferring an appropriate proportion of labor force from agriculture to industry helped to speed up the country's industrialization process.

The people's commune factory was a very critical system choice for Mao Zedong and CPC. It is a political, economic, cultural and social organization that integrates "workers, peasants, businessmen, academics and soldiers" whose aims were, from the perspective of Mao Zedong era: first was to consolidate the dictatorship of the proletariat; the second was to facilitate the distinction of urban and rural areas in respect of the household registration system so as to provide system guarantee for the smooth operation of the planned economic system; third was to take the commune as "important medium" to promote rural industrialization, and ultimately narrow the difference between urban and rural areas. Therefore, the institutional arrangements of the people's communes and the corresponding political mobilization had led to the unprecedented development of commune enterprises, although the "exaggeration" of the Great Leap Forward in industrialization from 1957 to 1959 led to a large area of agricultural production reduction and serious ecological consequences, which objectively had a negative impact on the development of commune enterprises. Nevertheless, from 1966 to 1976, the Chinese commune enterprises still achieved favorable results under the huge pressure of population growth①.

The commune enterprises mainly focused on the modernization of agriculture based on rural resources, taking the need for agricultural development and agricultural mechanization as the "main driving force". On the one hand, it could supplement the shortage of national plans to provide the necessary fertilizers, agricultural cement and various forms of mechanical maintenance services for rural areas; on the other hand, the close relations with city or state-owned enterprises allowed commune enterprises to make good use of state-owned enterprises' disused machines or textile equipment (such as Jiangsu province, Shanghai, etc.). With the help of technical cadres in state-owned enterprises, it had developed the spinning factories, silk factories, socks factories, agricultural machinery factories, printing plants, metal products factories; at last, through the contract with the state-owned enterprises to undertake its fractional processing and those with unreasonable input-output ratio, it developed the commune-run enterprises that integrated handicraft industry and modern industry in one (Huang

① The discussion on commune enterprises in this chapter (including data sources) mainly refers to Cong Shuhai and Zhang Yan's book: "The Economic Development History of New China (1949 - 1998)", Shanghai University of Finance and Economics Press, pp. 242 - 246, 279 - 286.

Zongzhi, 2000)[1]. Historical materials show that the county, commune and even grass-roots government of big production brigade made a good use of the market gap (that is, many state-owned enterprises only cared about production without setting up commercial sales outlets), "supply and demand shortage" caused by the planned economic system, as well as the ruling party's eagerness to solve the surplus labor issues and implement the policy resources of the industrialization, it developed a series of considerable commune enterprises. During the period of 1965 to 1979, the number of small-scale commune enterprises increased by 45,000 and the number raised up to 106,000 by 1976. In the early 1970s, half of the cement output of China and nearly all the agricultural cements, as well as half of the chemical fertilizer output were produced by small-scale enterprises. In 1972, commune enterprises contributed to nearly 50% of the industry output value of machinery and building materials[2].

Huang Zongzhi emphasizes that the success of household economy, private economy and free market system in Wenzhou makes it normal for people to ignore the historical contribution of commune enterprises and collective economy to Chinese industrialization. The unique aspect of China's rural development neither lies in the "bottom-up" mode of the British or Wenzhou-style nor in the "top-down" model of China's industrialization and modern urbanization from 1840 to 1949. Rather, it lies in the active role played by the production brigade, commune-rank of collective organizations and grass-roots political power. Before 1996, collective industries were actually the main industrial organization body of the Yangtze River Delta and most of China's rural areas. It was this kind of production organization that drove the industrialization of most rural areas in the 1970s and 1980s, making it distinguish from that of the countries in the third world (Huang Zongzhi, 2000). Apparently, the determination of the unique nature of China's ownership, the "historical conditions" of the Maoist era and the post-Mao Zedong era, the development of commune enterprises as well as the subsequent prosperity and evolution of the private economy led by the township enterprises are the "historical logic starting point" that we are looking for (see Figure 1-6, Figure 1-7).

---

① Through the discussion of the industrial development of Hua Yangqiao commune, Huang Zongzhi draws a typical Chinese-characterized rural industrial development process.

② The data came from Cong Shuhai and Zhang Yan's book: "The Economic Development History of New China (1949-1998)", Shanghai University of Finance and Economics Press, pp. 246.

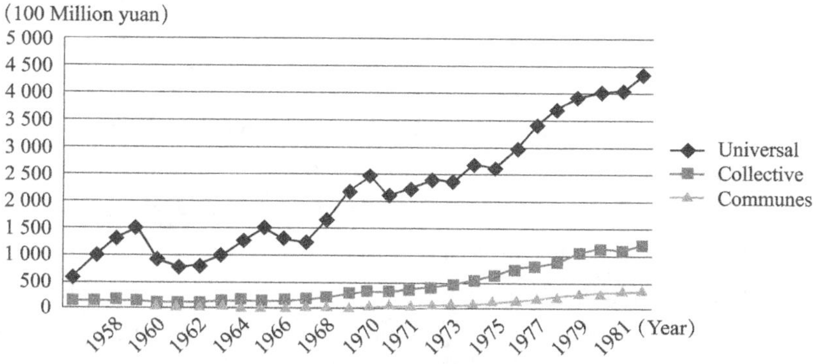

Figure 1 – 6　Trend of total industrial output value of different types of ownership enterprises (1957 – 1982)

Note: The industrial output value of 1957 – 1971 was calculated at the constant price of 1957; the industrial output value from 1971 to 1980 was calculated at the constant price of 1970; the industrial output value from 1981 to 1982 was calculated at the constant price of 1980. The variation trend of the data in Figure 1 – 7 is limited to before 1982, and afterwards until the mid-90s of the 20th century, the data of development of commune enterprises (township enterprises) cannot be shown. However, just at that time China's township enterprises developed rapidly, which drew great attention from academia and political field. Figure 1 – 6 shows that since 1969 China's collective enterprises, including commune enterprises have been developing stable.

Source: "China Statistical Yearbook", China Statistics Press, 1983, pp. 214 – 215.

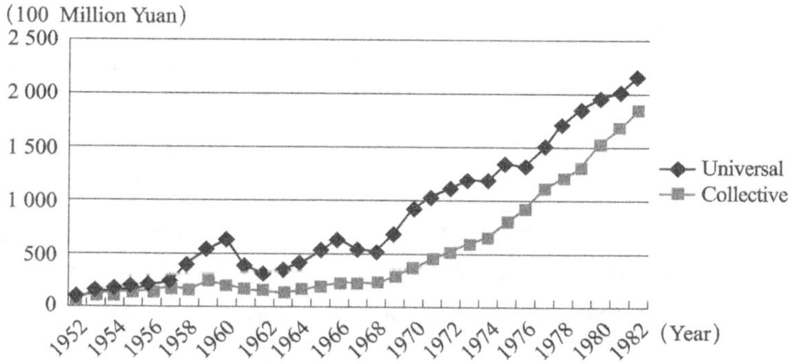

Figure 1 – 7　Trends of total industrial output index (1952 – 1982)

Note: The figure shows the change in the gross domestic product (GDP) of the whole population and the collective ownership index. The trend is 100% in 1952, and then the total industrial output value over the years is calculated. This chart shows the growth collective enterprises (including social enterprises) since 1969 have seen rapid development, rather than the wave-shape development of the whole enterprise. In 1970 – 1982, the development trend of collectively-owned enterprises appeared to be more "fierce" than the development trend of the enterprises owned by the whole population.

Source: "China Statistical Yearbook", China Statistics Press, 1983, p. 216.

From the 1970s to the mid-1980s, it can be argued that the development of the collective economy ranks among the top of the country, such as Shandong, Zhejiang, Jiangsu and Guangdong. The ratio of the industrial output value of the whole enterprise and the collective enterprise is much lower than the national average, and it is precisely in such places that the economic growth rate is much higher than the level of the rest of the country. In the fourth chapter, the author traces the origins of institutional evolutions in the different regions. In areas where the state-owned economy is more concentrated, taxation, labor and employment of local governments and the improvement of people's living standards are more dependent on the state-owned economy. This means that the local government in the formulation of policies will take more measures to protect the interests of the state-owned economy. On the contrary, in the areas where the proportion of state-owned economy is not high and the non-state-owned economy is relatively developed, such as Jiangsu and Zhejiang, (government) tax sources, employment opportunities and even the people's (social) welfare depends on the growth of non-state-owned economy. Therefore, the local government will release policies that benefit the continuous development of the private economy. Therefore, this will result in the different features of institutional developments between Jiangsu, Zhejiang, Guangdong and other areas[①].

(3) Equivalent average income level under the "class" and the reform of the start and implementation cost.

It was revealed that, until 1976, the income levels among various sectors of China were relatively consistent.

First, with the exception of regional gap, farmers had similar income levels. Income is related to the number of labor members in the family, that is, the more labor household, the higher the total household income. However, on average, the income level of each labor force is roughly the same, depending on hours worked.

Second, the relationship between each farmer and the land is the same. The land is owned by the public and each labor force is a part of the group. While the area of land is larger based on a larger workforce, on average, the area of the land owned by each labor force (including the degree of barrenness) is similar.

Third, the income level of urban workers is also even distributed, unless they

---

① Deng Hongtu, "The Evolution of China's Institutional Change in the Transitional Period: An Interpretation of the Evolution of Private Economy," Social Sciences in China, No. 5, 2004. There are many materials to support this proposition, see "China Statistical Yearbook" (1983, p. 226; 1984, p. 205; 1985, p. 319); "National Provinces, Autonomous Regions and Municipalities History-Compilation of Data Compiled (1949 – 1989.), 1990, p. 50.

belong to different ownership enterprises. The benefits of collectively-owned enterprises and enterprises owned by the public are different. For instance, for industries such as the steel and coal workers have a higher level of welfare than the average worker. This is due to more dangerous conditions and issues of safety.

Fourth, there is a disparity in income levels between the cadres and the masses. However, the difference in income levels is not drastic. Still, the difference in income levels can be readjusted through the "eight wage system". For instance, if a worker has a technical certificate of grade eight of fitters, then his income level may be much higher than the average cadre. With a certain degree of administrative power, the cadres may have a "potential source (avenue)" to increase their income. However, most of these "special ways (sources)" have been blocked by the political movements initiated by Chairman Mao Zedong. Therefore, the cadre's privileged status had always been suppressed, especially those of the middle and lower ranks of the cadres. The cadres had been judged and observed under the "sharp eyes" of the "masses". In rural areas, cadres of counties and commune had to visit the production team regularly and participate in manual labor. Although they physical stood out from the rest of the population, these differences were "strategically smoothed"①, due to Mao Zedong ideology and political requirements. In cities, government and business leaders also had to go to the workshop to participate in labor and learn from the workers. The ruling party established a policy which held that the status of workers and their labor power in the context of "political correct" and "ideological height"② .

Prior to the reform and opening-up policy, China's social and income differences were "institutionally flattened" by various policies, ideologies and even continuous political movements. And thus other powers openly challenged the form a power that is political and economic elements in Deng Xiaoping's reform and nor "strategy" (cause). There was a lack of class conflict due to the differences in the reality. People of all walks of life have a greater "intersection" about Mao Zedong's Thought

---

① Until his later years, to January 1976, Chairman Mao Zedong repeatedly showed his objection to the party to take the capitalist way of power, which also showed his objection to the aristocracy of workers and the privilege. He explicitly stated that the eight-wage systemis no different than was in the traditional society. These radicalistic ideas have a significant impact on the ruling party's cadre line. Therefore, we have reason to say that, until 1979, both in the party and out of the party, there is not a realistic form of decisive forces in the political and economic interests of the group to prevent Deng Xiaoping's implementation of his reform and opening up the political line. See also "Important Instructions of Chairman Mao (1)", Central Party Literature Press, 1998.

② The discussion of ideology is found in Mcfarquhar and J. K. Fairbank's book The Cambridge History of China: Revolutions within the Chinese Revolution (1966 – 1982)", China Social Sciences Press, 1992, pp. 87 – 112.

and socialist belief. So the start-up costs and implementation costs of the reforms were greatly reduced during the decade from 1979 to 1989①.

During this period, the land was collectively owned in the countryside regions of China. In contrast, the cities were owned by the state. Therefore, at the early stage of the open and reform period, the government developed policies on land in order to strengthen the reform and attract more foreign capital. Investors and construction units only needed to pay the country and the collective a very low rent to obtain the land. Advancements in investment and construction allowed many firms from foreign executives to significantly reduce the cost of land use. As a result, executives enjoyed a "policy bonus" from the reform and opening up policy. This increased the expected return on investment objectively, making the reform and opening up a predictable and cumulative self-reinforcing process.

(4) Opening and introduction in early 1970s.

During 1966 to 1969, all foreign trade relations stalled. After the tensions between China and the Soviet Union in the early 1960s, Mao Zedong had considered expanding economic and trade exchanges with the capitalist countries and introducing advanced equipment technology. He even suggested that the Japanese could come to Chinese to set up factories and mining, which was an opportunity to learn technological innovation and advancements. However, this was not possible due to the continued tension in the international situation and the expansion of the domestic class struggle (Zheng Qian, Zhang Hua, 2003)② .

In July 1971, the US President of the National Security Affairs Assistant Kissinger secretly visited China, in order to clear the obstacles for President Nixon to visit China. In October of this year, China resumed its legal seat at the United

① Harry Hardin wrote profoundly that "in the late 1980s, the reality seems to be contradictory, and the chaos of the Cultural Revolution is an important condition for the later reforms of Mao Zedong……Once this movement is over, it helps to form the economic and political liberation of the leadership……In short, if there is no Cultural Revolution, reform of post Mao Zedong period cannot go so far or so fast." However, Harding summed up from the experience. In fact, he should also be aware that the "Cultural Revolution" ideology, the impact of political power (resulting in a flat power structure) and the "diplomatic results" in late "Cultural Revolution" period made the future of China's reform and opening up costs And implementation costs "unexpectedly small". This made China's reform and opening up in the first decade (1979 – 1989) saw an absolute victory. Harding's essay is recorded in Macfarquhar and J. K. Fairbank's book "The Cambridge History of China: Revolutions within the Chinese Revolution (1966 – 1982)", China Social Sciences Press, 1992, pp. 211 – 219.

② Wuli, "Economic History of the People's Republic of China" (Volume 1), China Economic Publishing House, 1999, p. 709. Here quoted from Zheng Qian and Zhang Hua, "Mao Zedong era of China: 1949 – 1976" (Volume 3), the Communist Party of China History Publishing House, 2003, p. 289.

Nations with the support and assistance of friendly countries such as Africa. In 1972, President Nixon visited China. China and the United States signed the Sino-US Joint Communiqué in Shanghai, which marked the beginning of normal relations between the two countries. The normalization of Sino-US relations had also directly promoted the improvement of Sino-Japanese relations. Sino-Japanese relations achieved normalization of bilateral relations in September 1972. With these events as an opportunity, China established diplomatic relations with most developed countries or developing countries in Europe, the Americas and the South Pacific in the 1970s (Zheng Qian, Zhang Hua, 2003). This had created favorable conditions for China to expand foreign economic exchanges and the reform and opening up since 1979. From January 1972 onwards, with the support of Mao Zedong, Zhou Enlai decided to introduce complete sets of chemical fiber, fertilizer technology equipment from the western developed countries according to domestic needs. In January 1973, the State Council regarded that the capitalist countries were in a recession in the economic cycle, and the introduction of the equipment was beneficial to our country. Then they decided to introduce $4.3 billion of complete sets of equipment over the next five years. This included big projects such as 13 sets of large chemical fertilizer, 4 sets of large fiber, 3 sets of petrochemical factory, 10 alkyl benzene factory, 43 integrated coal mining units, 3 large power stations, Wuhan Iron and Steel 1700mm rolling mill, steam turbine, industrial steam turbine 3C factory and so on. This is the second large-scale introduction of the 156 projects introduced since the 1950s.① By the introduction of these equipment, together with the domestic through self-reliance production and equipment transformation, a total of 26 projects were built, with a total investment of about 21.4 billion yuan. By 1982, all of these projects were put into production (Zheng Qian, Zhang Hua, Vol. 3, 2003, pp. 289 – 292). It can be said that the China's diplomacy and the introduction of technology from the early 1970s to the middle of the 20th century, caused the following consequences of the 80s reform and opening up:

First, the introduction of fertilizer production lines and the scale of production improved the conditions of agricultural production. This created a "historical premise" for the 1984 food harvest (Cong Shuhai, 1999). As a result, farmers and urban residents had more favorable views towards reform and opening up (See Table 1 – 2).

---

① On the basis of these program, the introduction quota was added to 5.14 billion dollars.

Table 1 - 2 **Determined factors of grain production from 1973 to 1992: fertilizer or contract responsibility system**

Explanatory variables	Correlation coefficient	Standard deviation	T-statistic	Prob.
Constant term	14 045. 46	22 360. 69	0. 6281	0. 5427
Agricultural labor force	0. 0319	0. 2657	0. 1202	0. 9065
Grain sown area	-0. 1873	0. 2277	-0. 8227	0. 4281
Effective irrigated area	0. 8249	0. 3237	2. 5483	0. 0271
Fertilizer use	12. 7573	3. 9701	3. 2134	0. 0083
Total power of agricultural machinery	-0. 9611	0. 5771	-1. 6654	0. 1240
Disaster area	0. 0282	0. 0629	0. 4474	0. 6632
Virtual variable	1 055. 24	1 574. 27	0. 6703	0. 5165
Goodness of fit	0. 977400		D-W statistic	2. 053881
Adjusted goodness of fit	0. 963019		F-statistic	67. 96217

Note: Table 1 - 2 conclusions based on: "China Compendium of Statistics: 1949 - 2004", China Statistics Press, pp. 44 - 45, calculated using Eviews 5. 1. Variables that are not important should be removed to make the conclusion more precise, but even if it is not done, it is enough to explain the problem. In particular, this table shows the impact of grain-sown area, agricultural labor force, disaster area to grain production from 1973 to 1992 is margin. In fact, in the past 20 years, the agricultural labor force had always been surplus, so the marginal output of the labor force is almost zero. There was no growth in the area of food, and no major disasters had occurred, all of which were negligible. However, this table shows that irrigated area, especially fertilizer production increasing year by year, had a very important impact on grain production. Of course, Table 1 - 2 does not show the significant impact of technological progress on food production. Therefore, the impact of fertilizer on grain production may be somewhat high, but this is enough to explain that the fertilizer and other factors were on the key position of agricultural production. We took the virtual amount as 1 in 1959, 1960, 1961, and 1979, and in 1980, and the rest of the year as zero to express the impact of these policy changes or institutional changes on food production. The results showed that the impact of policy factors on grain yield is far from the effect of factors such as chemical fertilization and irrigated area. This conclusion is similar to that of Huang Zongzhi (2000). However, it is important to note that the core of these structures had been embedded in the general political and economic system of society as a political superstructure and ideology. For example, as seen in the multi-party cooperative system, there are the basic political principles of democratic consultation, the people's congress system, and the constitutional basis of the basic political order. We, thus, argue that these aspects are part of the basic elements of the country that consist of the "structural or supportive force" of a state government. At the same time, this concept has influenced the daily lives of the Chinese population, including their beliefs and values.

Second, the diplomatic success of the early 1970s provided important "historical conditions" for the subsequent reform and opening up. It reduced the cost and the "conversion cost" during making political and economic contract with developed and developing countries which was necessary to improve the international relationship. Since China welcomed the visit of US President Nixon in 1972, they would undoubtedly allow for the development of capitalism to enter into China's economic structure and ownership beginning in the 1980s.

3. Historical premise and logical starting point: summary statement

People in the discussion of traditional planned economic system might pay more attention to the specific structure of the system, but focus less on "system spirit" behind these specific political and economic structures. These "system spirit" are actually "born" and "embodied" by Chinese-style constitutionalism (as noted below). System change or historical evolution is very complex, and the key reason for determining the path or direction of change is, of course, structural; but it is important to note that the core of these structures had been embedded in the general political and economic system of society as a political superstructure and ideology. For example, the multi-party cooperative system, the basic political principles of democratic consultation, the people's congress system, the constitutional basis of the basic political order, and so on. These things work as the basic elements of the country to be the "structural or supportive force" of a state government. At the same time these things also work as the concepts that members of the whole society agree and the concept "infiltrated" to their daily life and determines their choice of dimensions and scope. Although the structure and ideology would change more or less with the passage of time, in a certain period of time, this change is potential, is step-by-step; before the decisive change took place, the original system structure and ideology were still the basic guarantee of social stability. The traditional political structure and belief system still play a role even after the change takes place and affects the "trajectory" and "process" of change.

A large number of facts show that the powerful political authority of the ruling party ensured its political mobilization. Relying on the political system and ideology established before 1977, the ruling party succeeded in establishing good expectations on reform for the social members of all levels of society in China. At the same time, the basic conditions for grain production are becoming more and more perfect by using the public necessary goods (such as collectively owned agricultural machinery, agricultural technology with spillover and shared by commune members, excellent varieties and public roads) for the farmland water conservancy facilities and agricultural production and management activities accumulated by the low labor force before the reform and opening up. Moreover, the fertilizer production line introduce from abroad in the early 1970s to the early 80s had been put into use. Therefore, the grain yield harvest had become a natural result that all these factors were together and were bound to produce.

It happened at this time that the people's commune disintegrated, rural implementation of the contract responsibility system as the core of the reform. This made decentralized management and food production and harvesting become a high correlation between the two historic events. This undoubtedly increases the attractiveness of decentralized reform ideas (such as contracting, etc.). However, as Huang Zongzhi has confirmed, the historic role of co-production contract responsibility system is to make the rural labor force have the opportunity to choose freely. The "urbanization" of the transfer of labor from rural to urban areas has been expanding and spreading along with the process of industrialization. Although this kind of organizational innovation may not be the real "main cause" of the food harvest in 1984, the commune team in the rural people's communes did not disappear with the disintegration of the communes. On the contrary, it became a positive factor in China's economic growth in the mid-1980s and mid-1990s. It promoted the industrialization and small urbanization of rural areas, absorbing a large number of rural surplus labors. In this way, before 1977, the social enterprises, (the ruling party's) political mobilization ability, the early 70s, the mid-term "opened" and the introducing policies, as well as the impact of the political movement on the interests of many factors "prompted" the economic system reform which started in early 80s. These factors were cumulative, so its release was gradually "launched". They made farmers and urban residents in the early stages of reform and opening up quickly enjoyed the "reform bonus" arising from the "historical heritage". So that members of the social strata had "good expectations" at the beginning of the reform. This common belief greatly reduced the "implementation costs" of the reform policy. On this basis, China's privatization began its progress (see Figure 1 - 8).

On the basis of self-reliance, China had established an independent industrial system with a well-equipped and well-developed infrastructure. In other words, till the mid-1970s, the basic framework necessary for China's modernization process had been basically completed. In 1949, China's agricultural output accounted for 70% of the total output value. In 1982, China's industrial output accounted for 80% of the total output value. This historical premise constitutes a solid foundation for China to adhere to reform and opening up and achieve rapid growth.

Emphasizing the decisive impact of the reform on the path of reform, does this mean that the reform is not important? It is not the case. There is evidence that the Soviet reforms were also beginning with local reforms (for example, the reforms of 1985 - 1989). The Soviet Union had also opted for outside reform, but in the Soviet, this reform had caused a recession, but led to sustained economic growth in China (Murphy, et al., 1992)[①]. Obviously, by the analysis logic of the use of reform

① Quoted from Yao Li, Zhang Jun, "Political Economy", Shanghai University of Finance and Economics Press, 2006, pp. 93 - 101.

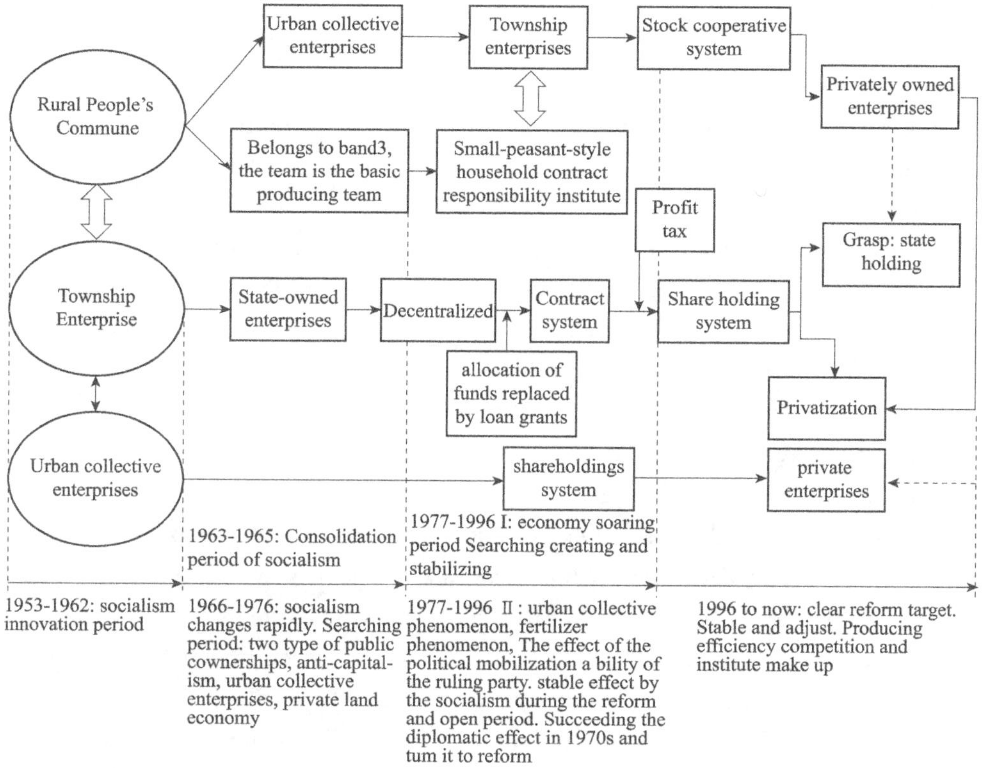

Figure 1 – 8 History of reform and opening-up policy: whether it is historical heritage or happened suddenly

Note: The time delineated in this diagram is only general and far from accurate, to illustrate the evolution of reform and opening up process. At the same time, it also explains the "decisive and historical role" of historical heritage to reform and opening up and its "evolutionary trajectory" and the exploration and system innovation on which the latter is based.

out of the government system, incremental reform, and double track transition cannot really explain the problem. We must analyze the ideal expectation brought to the public by the community enterprises, the people's commune system, and the ruling party's ability to mobilize behind the reform as well as the ideal ideology of the future reform of the traditional socialist ideology or belief structure from the end of 1970s to the mid and late 1980s. The combined effects of these factors determine both the economic performance of reform. But also reform began to win the moral and substantive success through the regional differences and difference in the system and out the system. Since 1969, the commune team began to develop with the "five small" industry. In 1972 the chemical industry production line began to be introduced.

In 1982 to 1983 the formation of large-scale production alleviated China's fertilizer shortage greatly. The results of the decision on the co-production, the responsibility system in the early reform of the successful wells have been "system consolidation". The success of the social enterprise and the success of the "five small" enterprises, to a certain degree, we shall thank to the urban-rural dualistic pattern and the planned economy itself under the planned economy. This has led to the beginning of the community to avoid the mandatory planning of the economy and in the supply and demand "shortage" in the case of "filling" the "shortage" of the legitimate reasons to develop. It not only increased the income of farmers, but also expanded the employment of rural areas. This alleviates the urban-rural conflict due to the differences in the three generated a considerable extent. On the contrary this makes the city feel the pressure. In the rural reform demonstration and induction, this pressure once became the external driving force of urban reform. From a historical point of view, the traditional Chinese planned economic system and the people's commune system have a duality for reform. On the one hand, it is the object of being reformed. On the other hand, under the start of the corresponding reform, the collective ownership of the "average land", the "relatively equal" social class, the "blossom" community enterprise, and the "mass production" of the fertilizer production line. The strong political mobilization of the ruling party, which is convinced of the funky feelings of the masses and the "ideological preferences" of the "legitimacy" of the "socialist system" of the socialist system, have, to a considerable extent, reduced the start of the reform. It weakened (potential) interest groups may bring resistance to the reform, threats and injuries, but also led to a series of late "system reform effect" That is, the rise of non-state-owned economy and private economy. Although these "reform consequences" are those of the strong tradition of the socialist followers are unexpected, the dual system or the binary or pluralistic pattern of the system is actually the natural product of the system changes that are under the expectation of the track and economic liberalization. In the history of the "dual structure" and "two-track operation" has been produced and continue to develop, in 1956 Mao Zedong's "on the Ten Major Relationships", in "political report" of the eighth national congress of the CCP, in 1969, in the large-scale development of the community enterprises, the self-remaining land economy along with the collective ownership, and in the existing historical status corresponding to the state ownership and collective ownership, the "dual structure" and "dual running" had been developing constantly, once the reforms are initiated or that, once the economic controls are relaxed, they will determine the "transition path" of system change in China in terms of system productivity competition and complement each other①.

1.2.2 System complementarity and productivity competition

1. Assumption, basic theory and "hypothesis"

Since the reform and opening up, the state-owned economy and the non-state economy are both competing (alternative) and complementary. The so-called competition, firstly, is manifested in the original monopoly by the state-owned enterprises in the market, and now allows township enterprises, private enterprises and foreign-funded enterprises to get in. This will reduce the monopoly profits of state-owned enterprises. The so-called complementary relationship, manifested in the state-owned enterprises and non-state-owned enterprises in the industrial structure in the front, back to the "production chain", their products occupy different but mutual market②. State-owned economy and non-state economy in the production, business activities constitute interdependence (see Figure 1 - 8). We define this as "complementary process". In addition, there are industries (industry) complementary. For example, many resource-based private enterprises for large state-owned enterprises to provide coal, nonferrous metals and other raw materials③. The development of the primary industry (such as state-owned mines) and the secondary industry (large-scale machinery processing enterprises) is always accompanied by the

---

① Amartya Sen believes that the development of literacy and basic health care measures help to promote the growth of market-based international companies and Mao Zedong's own wishes are different. (Although Marxist theorists may be interested in this dialectical contradiction) But these structural achievements before the reform were clearly a direct and valuable investment in China's economic boom after the reform (Chinese version, 2006). I would like to point out that Mori may underestimate the important impact of China's infrastructure before the reform, the independent industrial system on the subsequent reform and opening up, though he was quite objective and keenly aware of the internal logic of the social, economic and cultural (educational) structure before and after the teaching reform.

② For example, some township enterprises provide spare parts for large state-owned enterprises. Zhejiang's universal joint factory provides automotive universal joint assembly for many large car companies.

③ For example, Mengzi Mining and Metallurgy Co., Ltd., a company in Honghe, Yunnan, is a private enterprise with assets of one billion yuan. It produces and smelt aluminum ingots, zinc ingots, indium ingots and copper ingots directly to domestic state-owned (processing) enterprises. I had went to the mine for a six-day research in June, 2006.

development of the tertiary industry (such as services and services, such as various industries)①.

In addition, the relationship between non-state-owned economies and state-owned is competitive yet complementary. All the reform or evolution process of mutual penetration, mutual conditions, so that the reform of state-owned enterprises and the evolution of non-state economy presents a "complex form".

In the transition period of the system, participants or organizations in order to adapt to or solve external shocks and internal crises, competing to select or test a variety of organizational (governance) structure, in order to seek an efficient allocation of resources to replace the relatively low efficiency of the old (governance) structure. The "organization" can be defined as a "group of contractual arrangements". A contract structure is not the result of a random selection of participants, but rather the interaction of the participants in each of the strategies driven by their respective goals. Let us suppose:

(1) There are two domains in an economic (social) body: one is the state-owned economic domain, with G_s; the other is the non-state economic domain, represented by D_s, G_s and D_s are expressed in terms of time, such as the "system characteristics" of G_S^t at time t, state-owned economic domain (or state-owned enterprises), and G_s^t is expressed, at time t, the "system characteristics" in the non-state economic domain (or collective economy or private economy is faced with). The so-called "System characteristics" can be "portrayed" in a society related to state-owned economy (enterprise), collective economy (enterprise) or private economy (enterprise) related policies (or systems). These policies or systems determine the form of ownership and contractual structure of state-owned or non-SOEs.

In any society, government's policy or policy combinations (system) will directly or indirectly influence the economic entities' (or enterprises) way of exchange, transaction and profit-seeking. It makes the production of economic entities, operating results or closes or deviates from the "Pareto standard". For example, from 1979 to the present, the reform policy of state-owned (business) enterprises is a continuous and gradual process: first decentralization none other. Then there is price double track. The next is contract responsibility. (The factory director

① For example, large porphyry copper mine-Dexing copper mine, has a daily production of 100,000 tons of copper concentrate and its associated there are many private enterprises, such as copper metal products factory, cement plants, labor service companies, construction companies, etc. We had a 10-day study in August 2002 at the mine. The mine is ranked first in Asia, third in the world.

undertake the competent department of the corresponding product quality and quantity, and the staff and the factory contractor corresponding production and quality) and joint-stock system. In order to make the corresponding incentives for state-owned enterprises, the government has also implemented policies such as dial-up loans and government tax at the macroeconomic level. The implementation of each reform program will induce state-owned (state-owned) enterprises to adjust their internal governance structure, change their trading in order to maximize the use of these policies may be released from the system effects. In fact, the reform of the double track system not only makes the internal governance structure and behavior of the state-owned enterprises have a substantial change, but also to collective enterprises, private enterprises trading methods, internal governance structure has undergone substantial changes. State-owned enterprises, collective or private enterprises always want to get more unplanned sales from the government in order to get more profits through "profit balance". Many non-state enterprises cannot get unplanned sales of commodities from the government, and then it is likely through the internal transactions with the state-owned enterprises and illegal access to these goods unplanned right to operate. In the "market track" outside the "planning track", the ownership of "unplanned sales amount" means that there is a profit can produce excess monopoly concessions. It will induce the right to use the amount of state-owned enterprises and the right to use the amount of non-state-owned enterprises to carry out various trading activities. "Market economy" will "grow" inside of the planned economy because of the induction of these various policies. Therefore, for the purpose of economic analysis, we need to define the "social exchange domain" and see it as "system characteristics" to determine the economic transactions of the main way to describe the "economic volume." (see Figure 1 -9) .

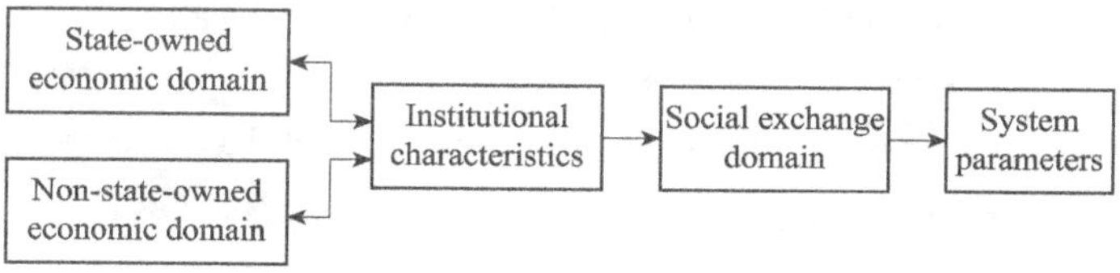

Figure 1 -9 Logical and "mapping" relationship among serval concepts

The economic quantities shown in Figure 1 - 9 will be used in the following analysis: use "system characteristics" to describe the "state-owned economic domain" and "private economic domain". They mainly refer to the policy system or combination associated with the state-owned economy and the private economy, and this system or combination will determine the way the economic entity deals. Each kind of transaction method contains some kind of resource allocation efficiency. Therefore, we use the "system parameters" to represent the "social exchange domain" of the "system characteristics", this variable will vary depending on the specific analysis logic and the analysis object. But in any case, they can be measured economic variables, such as transaction costs and resource allocation efficiency and so on.

(2) In the state-owned economic domain, there is a state-owned enterprise, represented by G_T; in the non-state economic zone, there is a non-state enterprise (such as collective enterprise or private enterprise), represented by D_T. In order to make these two concepts easy to analyze, we also assume that C_T^t and D_T^t, respectively, in time t, state-owned enterprises and non-state enterprises (such as collective enterprises or private enterprises) selected organizational or governance structure.

In the 1950s and 1960s and even the whole of the 1970s, the whole tendency policy of the state economy was that it could become the dominant force and control force of the economy and society to ensure the ruling foundation of the ruling party, to bring social benefits to the city workers, to provide social insurance, to maintain and increase employment opportunities. In this case, state-owned enterprises will focus more on production (i. e. gross product value) objectives and social objectives under the constraints, guidance or constraints of the system or policy and then is benefit target. This will of course affect the way the company produces, operates and contracts. After the reform and opening up, although after decentralization reform, contract reform, price reform and shareholding reform, we still find that state-owned enterprises have become more than ever stressed the importance of profit targets. But objectively the state-owned enterprises are still given the corresponding social responsibility or public responsibility. It can be understood that state-owned enterprises have pure economic profit targets, and, more importantly, have additional public responsibility for social welfare goals.

In the history of socialist construction in China, by 1957, the simple private economy had disappeared in the statistical data, after the rural cooperative and cooperative movement as well as the primary society, senior society and rural people commune, as well as the city of national industry and commerce, handicraft industry

Socialist transformation[①]. This situation did not begin to change until 1979. Since the beginning of this year, the national and local statistical yearbook began to individual economy, joint economy, and private economy into the statistical range. China since 1949, from the formal point of view, system changes seem to have occurred twice "reversed." One is the 1953 – 1957 carried out and basically completed the socialist transformation. And the other is the reform of ownership in 1979. But we have to hasten that the two seemingly different reversals actually have a logical inner consistency. Because the conditions of the two social transformations are not exactly the same, the behavior motive and value orientation of the private economic subject are not exactly the same as the result of the definition or prediction of neoclassical economics. They show a strong dependence on politics. In the last time, the guiding ideology and policy base of the ruling party began to shift from the new democracy marked by the "common program" to the Soviet Union. It makes the new democratic economic system no longer a relatively stable economic system. To gradually eliminate the private ownership as the main content of the socialist transformation were put on the agenda, since then, China entered into a period of dramatic changes in the economic system without any stop[②]. By 1957, the vast majority of the private economy was transformed into a state-owned capitalist economy in the form of public-private partnerships, and its profit motives and profit-seeking activities were strictly limited. The reforms that began in 1979, while the non-state economy, such as the collective economy, the individual economy and the private economy, were encouraged in policy, the intervention from administrative power was still relatively large. Thus, the private economy of the 1950s, despite its pursuit of profit, showed a strong "dependence" to the state and the socialist ideology. And after 1979, the private economy, the individual economy is clearly showing their "dependence" to the executive power or grass-roots government. It is reasonable to say that these two "dependencies" have utter difference. It would, to a considerable extent, distort the profitability of the private economy, so that the former in the pursuit of profit targets will be more to take care of the community's public (welfare) goals at the same time

① The transformation of private enterprises can be found in "Economic Profiles of the People's Republic of China (1953 – 1957) (comprehensive volume)" edited by the Chinese Academy of Social Sciences and the Central Archive, China Price Press, 2000, pp. 1119 – 1151.

② Wu Li: "Foreword", recorded in "Economic Profiles of the People's Republic of China (1953 – 1957) (comprehensive volume)" edited by the Chinese Academy of Social Sciences and the Central Archive, China Price Press, 2000, pp. 1 – 20.

and the latter will be more in the pursuit of their own interests while paying attention to and meet the specific interests of the public owner of the individual interest. Even so, in the analysis, for the sake of simplicity, we can still assume that private enterprises have only a simple profit motive and profit targets. However, discussions about state motives or preferences of state-owned (private) and private enterprises will be extremely useful in subsequent analyzes. They can derive and expand the rich political and economic connotations from the logical conclusions derived from our simple assumptions in an objective and practical way.

In addition, we also have the third hypothesis, which is:

(3) Supposing that there exists an average profit rate in the whole economic society, if an enterprise fails to reach this profit rate, it indicates that this enterprise would be replaced by another newly-rising enterprise of the same kind which possesses an advantage on organizing structure (or managerial structure) and production rate. Of certainty, we constantly hold that two enterprises exist in the whole economic society (only and at the same time). One is state-owned enterprises and another is private enterprises.

State the economic meanings of Figure1 – 10 with the above three hypotheses. "Series D" represents the evolutionary path ①→② of non-state-owned enterprises. On this path, D_s represents the System Characteristics of the economic environment where non-state-owned enterprises set their feet on. During non-state-owned enterprises' evolution along path ①, the System Field (System Characteristics) that it is in has not changed. However, the organizing form (or managerial structure) of non-state-owned enterprises has undergone transformation, turning into D_T^0 (the upper right sign is 0, showing that the non-state-owned enterprise is now at phase 0) to D_T^1 (the upper right sign is one, showing that the non-state-owned enterprise is now at phase 1). Due to technological concussion (for example, a technological innovation leads to changes in cost structures that intensify the competition) and market concussion (for example, a gap appears in the supply and demand of market and it causes a price fluctuation), non-state-owned enterprises find it necessary to coordinate resources more efficiently out of their need of survival and profit. If adjusting adaption is not carried out, enterprise organizations would lack competitiveness. The result of market selection is enterprise organizations change from $D_T^0 \rightarrow D_T^1$ ("→" represents "transformation", similarly hereinafter), which means a kind of managerial structure became another kind. However, although enterprise organizations make their own adjusting adaption under the effect of "system characteristics" of the given economic environment, system characteristics of economic environment, as "system parameters (such as D_s^0)"① in "social exchange field", would "insert into" the internal (managerial) structure of non-state-owned economic organizations. This kind of "system parameter" (such as D_s^0) is actually varied sorts of policies about civil operation launched by the government. Consequently, as an exogenous variable, it may promote or as well thwart enterprise organization to evolve towards the managerial structure which could bring a goal of resource allocation efficiency. The evolution process can also be described as, in the very beginning, system field D_s inserted into a non-state-owned economic organization D_T^0. Under the concussion from the market of technology, the non-state-owned economic organization transforms into D_T^1. At this point, D_s^0 is further inserted into the internal managerial structure of the newly-selected non-state-owned economy D_t^1 in the manner of "isomorphism"②, formulating or thwarting or promoting the "system constraints" of the evolution of non-state-owned economic organization. At this time, if D_s^0 is not capable of providing effective and lasting incentives for non-state-owned economic organization D_t^1, or internal members of the non-state-owned economic organization discover an available "system parameter" which is more effective, such as D_s^1, economy entities or internal members of enterprise organizations would put corresponding pressure onto policy makers (the government) after trials, comparisons and repeated contests with the government (policy makers) so that the latter can create a kind of system parameter that is compatible with new economic environment with having all kinds of advantages and disadvantages weighed, till the system expectation of this kind of "system parameter" is able to promote the approximation of economy entity's selective behavior towards the Pareto efficiency standard "system characteristic" D_s^1, which can totally replace the relatively poor D_s^0. The result is that a new kind of factor allocation and coordination system isomorphic to D_s^1 and D_T^1 shows up around D_t^1.

Evolutionary logic that mentioned above is also applicable for the changes of state-owned economic organizations. On ⑧ – ⑨ evolutionary paths in Figure 1 – 10,

---

① The author even deems system parameters as measurable economic magnitude like transaction cost thereupon. It is the predictable results of (economic) transaction entities' changes of behavior and management approaches caused by policies. However, it always exerts its influences on optional behaviors and managerial approaches of economic entities in the form of Prediction but not an actual result.

② Isomorphism mentioned here can be comprehended as the behavior approach and managerial approach that the system characteristic, which is embodied by policies, economy entities according to its original expectation.

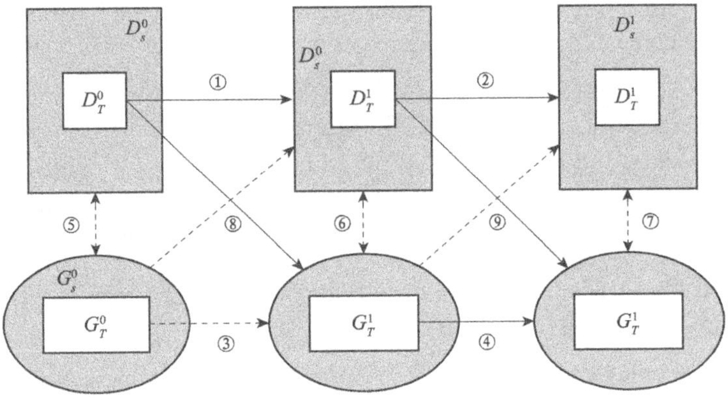

Figure 1 – 10 Mutual infiltration and institational complementarity in the reform of state-owned enterprises and the evolution of non-state-owned economy

as the system parameters corresponding to state-owned economy environment or policy systems, it represents the social exchange field where state-owned economy finds it position. It is expressed as G_s^0, and it is inserted with state-owned enterprises G_T^0. G_T^0 implies the organization form or internal managerial structure which fits the social exchange field or system characteristics. Just as non-state-owned enterprises, under a situation of being subject to external concussion, such as technological and market ones, state-owned enterprises would choose new organization forms or internal managerial structure to adapt to the system characteristic changes of economic environment. Therefore, state-owned economic organizations turn from G_T^0 to G_T^1. Finally, with the purpose of pursuing higher efficiency targets, state-owned economic organizations would make further efforts in adding to pressure on decision makers to have them select the system parameter with stronger incentive function, substituting G_s^0 with G_s^1.

It is necessary to further consider the possibilities of mutual influence and infiltration of system parameters of non-state-owned economy and state-owned economy (referred to the mutual influential and infiltrating paths of different system parameters shown in ⑤, ⑥ and ⑦ in Figure 1 – 10). This kind of mutual influence and infiltration between different system characteristics would differentiate the system changing path of the whole society from the evolutionary path of the monotonous state-owned economy or non-state-owned economy. Furthermore, as is illustrated in Figure 1 – 10, during phase 0, system characteristics or system parameters in non-state-owned economy environment would induce substantial impacts towards system parameters of state-owned economy environment in the succeeding phase (referred to path ⑧ in Figure 1 - 10). Similarly, during phase 0, system characteristics or system parameters in state-owned economy environment would induce substantial impacts towards system parameters of non-state-owned economy environment in the succeeding phase (referred to path ⑨ in Figure 1 - 10). The two kinds of system parameters are reciprocal causations and mutual infiltrations to each other, together composing or forming the system characteristics of the entire economic environment, which is the duality or the dual rail nature (system) of the system. In the transitioning society, between non state-own economy and state-owned economy are institutional complementarity and the competitiveness of system.

Aoki Masahiko and others have discussed more about the insertion and mutual interpenetration of individual system parameters and organizations, and they have not studied the possibilities of mutual infiltration of institutional system with different characteristics (1997, 1998, 1998b, 2000, 2001, 2001, Chinese Edition).

Based on the above discussion, we can present the following theorems:

Proposition E_1: The dual-track system is the historical premise of institutional complementarity and mutual competition. Due to the existence of institutional complementarity and competitiveness, system parameter of another institutional system would insert in the structure of the original institutional system and influence the evolution of the economic organizations of the original institutional system.

Proposition E_2: The degree of social openness and marketization forms a logical causal relationship with whether a system of the same society is embedded into and how deep embedded it is into another system. What is more, the mutual insertion of the system and system convergence depend on the degree of social openness and marketization. The two make two-way interaction, being a basis of one another.

Proposition E_3: The degree or extent of the insertion of a system into another system will greatly determine the path of organizational evolution of the embedded system. With different insertion degree, scope and approach, the evolution path would also be different. If a system infiltrate through another system with an incorrect prediction, the organization evolution path would not only exist with diversification but also tortuosity.

System complementarity and the production rate competition among systems would definitely lead to a relative change on factors (resources) price at last, which paves the way for the fortune distribution effect and price effect. The effects would obviously change the expected utility (function) structure and expected profit of economy entities (such as state-owned enterprises and non-state-owned enterprises), which would also change approaches of transaction and contracting of economy entities (such as state-owned enterprises and non-state-owned enterprises) , and it further influences the game relationship between economy entities and the government, which would cause changes in government policy preferences. As a consequence, we have the following inference:

Inference I: If an embedded system causes the change of resources and organizational resources so as to influence the relative price, which brings forward the price effect and the wealth distribution effect, economic entities will re-adjust their expectations and contracting mode, which will make the government's policy preferences change, and eventually lead to substantial deflections of the system changing path. The path of system change is the result of the game between the economic subjects and the government. It must meet the government's tax standard and the profit seeking standard of enterprises.

It is necessary to pay attention that, as Aoki Masahiko (2001) points out, under the condition of system complementarity, the balanced system arrangement may not be the optimal distribution pattern of social capital (such as institutions and organizations) that are embedded in each other. The game rules and structure of enterprises, interest groups and the government, and political skills and preferences of participants seeking innovative rent (internal members or third party), and so on, will jointly determine the nature of equilibrium system arrangements. Therefore, the synchronic correlation structure of holistic system arrangement[①] could be multiple and diversified. Although some system arrangement has shown certain convergence under the influence of market globalization and ICTs, we can still observe a significant diversification of system. In addition, system complementarity may also lead to system inertia or ratcheting of the system. The reason lies in that the change of some individual system would be restricted by old systems inserted inside itself, and thus it produces obstacles of revolutionary systems, which is explained thoroughly in Figure 1 -10.

2. Theoretical model: logical demonstration towards hypothesis

During the system change over the last 30 years, dual track system and price dual rail have objectively molded the power structure of the reform, which brought about

---

① The so-called synchronic correlation structure of holistic institutional arrangement can be simply comprehended as a distribution form that all system correlate with and influence each other in some time section.

substantial changes in the relationship between plan and market via the mutual infiltration and inlaying of state-owned economic region and non-state-owned economic region. Thus, it is important to show how plan and market were influenced by the historical conditions of the dual rail system. It is, therefore, important to as: would the market scope increase would it be the one of plan? This is reasonable to ask since state-owned enterprises and non-state-owned enterprises have shown a convergent governance structure.

To emphasis and clarify the analytical logic, it is important to consider the scenario that state-owned enterprises and non-state-owned enterprises produce homogeneous products. Thus we can further assume that:

· The price is on dual rails, which represents that there are two types of production materials (investment factors, including labor force) and product price. One is the market adjusted price while another is the nation planned price. State-owned enterprises examine and calculate according to the planned price within the scope of nation planned quota. As for products and investment factors outside the nation plan, it would be examined and calculated in accordance with the market price. When it comes to products and investment factors of non-state-owned enterprises, it shall totally be examined and calculated according to the market adjusted price.

· The labor and capital amount of the whole society is constant. If the labor force of state-owned enterprises is x_1, the labor investment of non-state-owned enterprises is $1-x_1$; if the capital amount that state-owned enterprises use is k_1, the capital investment of non-state-owned enterprises is $1-k_1$.

We decompose the competition between state-owned enterprises and non-state-owned enterprises into two stages. First, the two carry out the Stackelberg competition on output volume or market share. Second, given the output volume proportion determined in the first stage, two enterprises of different types would start the Bernard competition on price.

(1) The Stackelberg output volume of state-owned enterprises and non-state-owned enterprises is decisive to the market sharing.

Apparently, if state-owned enterprises and non-state-owned enterprises produce homogeneous products, the two would be in the midst of a competitive substitution relation. Taking the reality of two-tier price system, state-owned enterprises not only need to accomplish the nation planned quota (q_1) and calculate sales income according to the price p_0 set by the nation, but also need to sell the proportion y_1-q_1

that exceeding the planned quota according to the market-adjusted price p_1. In this situation, y_1 is the total amount that state-owned enterprises produce. The labor wage (w_1) and (investment) factor price k_1 of state-owned enterprises are given. All products of non-state-owned enterprises depend on the industry and the market. Its product price is the same of the ones outside plans of state-owned enterprises, both being p_1. The labor wage and factor payment price it provides are all decided by the market, respectively being w_2 and k_2. To make the issue briefer, it is assumed that under the conditions of the dual system or dual rail system, in face of the market rail, state-owned enterprises and non-state-owned enterprises have the same linear demand function and it can be expressed as:

$$p_i(Q) = \max[M - dQ], M, d > 0 \tag{1}$$

The total product provided to the market can be expressed as $Q \equiv y_1 + y_2 - q_1$. Supposing that state-owned enterprises are leaders while non-state-owned enterprises are followers, in stackelberg model, the strategy of two enterprises is the problem of choosing their output volume. Under the condition that the leaders have accomplished the nation quota, they resell surplus goods to the market. Given this output volume, the leaders would organize production according to market margin in order to realize a maximization of expected profits.

The state-owned enterprises' strategic space is simply given by $S_1 = \mathbf{R}_+$. Strategies and output volumes are corresponding to each other strictly, which is $y_1 = s_1 (q_1, y_1)$, $s_1 \in S_1$. On the other hand, the strategic space of non-state-owned enterprises' is:

$$S_2 = \{s_2 : \mathbf{R}_+ \to \mathbf{R}_+, y_2 = s_2(q_1)\}, \quad s_1 \in S_1$$

Given the strategic space and the payoff function π_i: $S_1 \times S_2 \to \mathbf{R}$. We can confirm that the profit every enterprise obtaining is as the following:

$$\pi_2(s_1, s_2) = y_2 \cdot [M - d(y_1 + y_2 - q_1) - w_2 \cdot (1 - x_1) - k_2 \cdot (1 - z_1)] \tag{2}$$

$$\pi_2(s_1, s_2) = (y_1 - q_1) \cdot (y_1 + y_2 - q_1) + q_1 \cdot p_0 - w_1 \cdot x_1 - k_1 \cdot z_1 \tag{3}$$

Solve the optimized condition in equation (2) (first-order condition) and it can be calculated as:

$$y_2 = \frac{M + dq_1 - dy_1}{2d} \tag{4}$$

Solve the optimized condition in equation (3) (first-order condition) and it can be calculated as:

$$y_1 = \frac{M + 2dq_1 - dy_2}{2d} \tag{5}$$

Solve the equation composed by equation (4) and (5), it can calculated that:

$$y_2 = \frac{M}{3d} \tag{6}$$

$$y_1 = \frac{M + 3dq_1}{3d} \tag{7}$$

According to equation (7), we can take the derivative of the product quantity that state-owned enterprises could freely sell on market apart from accomplishing the state planned quota:

$$y_1 - q_1 = \frac{M + 3dq_1}{3d} - q_1 = \frac{M}{3d} \tag{8}$$

It can be calculated that:

$$y_1 - q_1 = y_2 \tag{9}$$

As for a transition economy with both state-owned enterprises and private enterprises, there is planned administration deployment for resources and market deployment. A part of product price is up to plans while the other is up to the market. equations (6), (7) and (9) indicate that, given the historical premise of dual rail system, state-owned enterprises, as leaders, have an advantage on output volume ($y_1 > y_2$). However, once the rated capacity q_1 that planned rail requires state-owned enterprises to provide is left out, we find that state-owned enterprises and non-state-owned enterprises provide the same output volume on the market rail (seen in equation (9)), with both being $\frac{M}{3d}$ (seen in equation (8)). It suggests that if the resource scope that planned rail could adjust is getting smaller and smaller, and the rated capacity that the nation provides for state-owned enterprises is getting smaller, or the planning attribute of state-owned enterprises production is getting weaker, it indicates that q_1 in equation (7), (8) and (10) would become increasingly small while the market scope is becoming bigger and bigger. The result is that, as for no matter state-owned enterprises or non-state-owned enterprises, they would share the market outside planned quota in half. As a result, speaking in general, which means considering planned quota of planned rail and market rail outside the planned rail both, it is the Stackelberg competition that stands between state-owned enterprises and non-state-owned enterprises. State-owned enterprises take advantages on the aspect of input volume. However, if the market rail's deployment function towards resources is the only thing to consider, it seems to be the Cournot competition that stands between state-owned enterprises and non-state-owned enterprises, in which they share the market (space) beyond the planned rail. Obviously, with the transition in economy, the nation is setting an increasingly small planned quota towards state-owned enterprises, and the market space that private enterprises and state-owned enterprises share would be larger and larger. If $q_1 = 0$, state-owned economy and non-state-owned economy would cover the whole market in the form of sharing in half. Thus, the following statement can be inferred:

Theorem 1: Given the corresponding production technology, if the market need structures that state-owned and the non-state-owned economy face outside planned economy are equal, they will share the market outside planned quota. If the planned quota is equal to 0, the smaller the planned quota that state-owned and non-state-owned enterprises share is, the larger the components of marketization and non-state economy would be.

(2) Variant Bernard price competition

1. General discuss on price competitions under conditions of plan restriction and market restriction.

Next, we calculate the partial derivatives of π_1 sub x_1 and k_1; π_2 sub X_2, $(1 - x_2)$, k_2 and $(1 - K_2)$:

$$\frac{\partial \pi_1}{\partial x_1} = - w_1 \tag{10}$$

$$\frac{\partial \pi_1}{\partial k_1} = - z_1 \tag{11}$$

$$\frac{\partial \pi_2}{\partial x_1} = w_2 \tag{12}$$

$$\frac{\partial \pi_2}{\partial (1 - x_1)} = - w_2 \tag{13}$$

$$\frac{\partial \pi_2}{\partial k_1} = z_2 \tag{14}$$

$$\frac{\partial \pi_2}{\partial (1 - k_1)} = - z_2 \tag{15}$$

$1 - x_1$ in equation (13) and $1 - k_1$ in equation (15) are respectively the labor and capital investment of non-state-owned enterprises. This means that the labor and capital amount in the whole society is presumed as 1. Apparently, presumption like this is just for the convenience of discussing the issue and it does not influence our logic of analyzing problems.

To illustrate the economic meaning of equation (10) – (15), it is necessary to point out the followings. First, in the first 12 years of transition, such as 1979 ~ 1991, the economic environment of China is relatively tight, which implies that raw materials (such as steel material, cement and so on) have not got rid of shortages. Therefore, state-owned and non-state-owned enterprises share a strained relationship on the use of raw materials. Namely, state-owned enterprises use more while non-state-owned enterprises use less. Second, during the last decade or so, the potential supply of labor force has been infinite. What is more, after the disintegration of people's commune, the surplus labor in rural areas achieved unprecedented (on the career-choosing aspect) freedom. However, whether the wish of the surplus labor force finding its career in non-agricultural fields could come true depends on the following two basic conditions. First, whether the household registration system and the labor system of state-owned enterprises could make timely changes or reforms. Second, whether state-owned and non-state-owned enterprises could employ more labor force.

As apparent as it is, with only a simple inspection on China's changing history on systems it would be able to tell that compared with state-owned enterprises, collective enterprise, private and foreign-funded enterprises have a better flexibility in the labor system, which become the primary choice of migrant workers. When it comes to state-owned enterprises, the salary and labor system are rigid, which makes it tough to make flexible adjustment according to actual operating situations. Consequently, it makes sense to consider that:

$$|w_1| > |w_2| \qquad (16)$$

At the same time, from the early phase of transition to 1990, the supply of production materials is still tight, state-owned enterprises can purchase raw materials with the planned prices offered by the nation while non-state-owned enterprises can only obtain raw material they need via black markets outside the plans or some transactions with foreign enterprises. As a result, it is reasonable to consider that:

$$|z_2| > |z_1| \qquad (17)$$

According to equation (16) and (17), combined with equation (12) - (15), the following judgment can be inferred:

Judgment 1: Given a constant amount of available labor and capital, state-owned firms tend to replace labor force with capital, while non-state-owned firms tend to substitute labor for capital.

Considering there is a huge surplus labor force in rural China and because the household registration system and the labor system of state-owned enterprises are rigid and thus difficult to adjust, it can inferred that: $1 - x_1 \gg x_1$, which means $x_1 \ll 1/2$. As result, the factor market, especially the labor force market, would first be activated under the non-state-owned enterprises' decision of profit-seeking motives, and thus labor force prices under dual restriction are formed. The first restriction is the demand restriction under the infinite supply of labor force, which is a pure market restriction. The second restriction is the one of plans or systems. That is to say, it is hard for state-owned enterprises to adjust the amount of labor force and the remuneration level according to profit conditions. The two restrictions formulate two equilibriums with one being the market equilibrium of labor force salary, w_2 and another one being the "system (compulsory) equilibrium", w_1 of labor force salary under planned restrictions. Remuneration rate differences under this kind of dual restriction produce structural pressure on state-owned enterprises' supply and demand conditions of labor force decided by plans. Finally, this kind of structural pressure would urge the government to loosen its control towards the labor force market, and thus a unified labor force market is produced.

As for the production material market, this kind of change tendency exists as well. On one hand, state-owned enterprises enjoy the preferential policy of planned rail, receiving production material supplies in prices lower than the market ones. On the other hand, under the condition that the supply of production materials is relatively tight, non-state-owned enterprises can only purchase production materials with high price formed by the supply and demand structure which is in shortages. Therefore, two kinds of production material prices are bound to be produced by the dual restriction. One of them is the production material price under planned restriction, z_1; another one is the production material price under the restriction of market and the gap between supply and demand, z_2, $z_2 > z_1$. The difference of capital interest rate ($k_2 - k_1 > 0$) under this kind of dual restriction would produce a structural pressure on the supply and demand of production materials. Finally, this kind of structural pressure would urge non-state-owned enterprises to substitute capital with labor force to proceed production on one hand, and intensify their efforts on rent-seeking, obtaining production materials that they need with prices lower than the market ones but higher than the planned ones as far as possible, whose consequence would force decision makers to take measures eventually to realize the union of planned rail and market rail. In consequence, we have the following judgments:

Judgment 2: Under the condition that the labor and capital of the whole society remain unchanged, if the impact of technological change on the labor market is not within the scope of consideration and given that $w_1 > w_2$, the structural differences in labor force prices brought by the market-plan dual mechanism would result in a labor force market based on the unison of the whole society.

Judgment 3: Under the condition that the labor and capital of the whole society remain unchanged, if the impact of technological change on the labor market is not within the scope of consideration and given that $z_2 > z_1$, the structural differences in production material prices brought by the market-plan dual mechanism would result in a production material market based on the unison of the whole society.

2. Bertrand competition and privatization①

It is known from equation (6) and (7) that the consequence of the Stackelberg competition is that state-owned and non-state-owned enterprises share the market. Although state-owned enterprises also have a specific need q_1, plan rail, apart from this. This indicates that during the practical production and operating process, the market capacities owned respectively by state-owned and non-state-owned enterprises shall meet with the following condition:

$$y_2 = y_1 - q_1 \leqslant \frac{M}{3d} \equiv \bar{V} \tag{18}$$

Given the respective market capacities, the two enterprises are bound to conduct a price competition. And according to a hypothesis of equation (1), setting $i = 1, 2$ (1 stands for state-owned enterprises and 2 for non-state-owned enterprises) for every enterprise, it can be expressed as follows:

$$p_i \leqslant M \tag{19}$$

Then, the strategic space of state-owned enterprises and non-state-owned enterprises can be defined by Cartesian product $[0, \bar{k}] \times G_i$.

$$G_i \equiv \{g_i : [0, \bar{V}] \times [0, \bar{V}] \rightarrow [0, M], p_i = g_i(V_1, V_2)\}$$

V_1 and V_2 in the above equation are respectively the largest market capacities that state-owned and non-state-owned enterprises can get. c_1 and c_2 are corresponding to the two dimensions, representing the cost that state-owned enterprises and non-state-owned enterprises pay to open up V_1 and V_2 markets, which illustrates that state-owned

---

① About the Bertrand competition model setting and economic explanation, the author refers to Fernando Vega-Redondo: Economics and the Theory of Games. jointly published by Century Publishing Group and Shanghai People's Publishing House, 2006, pp. 156 – 160. Coincidentally, this model can well illustrate the price competition between state-owned enterprises and private enterprises in this part of the study, which will lead to further privatization. But according to the logic of the research, we don't agree with Redondo in writing $\left[\frac{M - p_1}{d} - \right]$ as $\left[\frac{M - p_i}{d} - \right]$ in equation (21) in this research. We believe that in the case of p_i, the potential demand (or maximum capacity) of the market is determined by the lowest price.

enterprises and non-state-owned enterprises both set prices depending on market capacity. Hence, we have the following discussion:

(i) If two enterprises carry out strategic actions directed against the output of the other party, making $p_i < p_j$ and $i \neq j$, it can be expressed as the following:

$$\pi_i(s) = \min\left[\frac{M - p_i}{d}, V_i\right]p_i - w_i \cdot x_i - k_i \cdot z_i - c_i V_i \tag{20}$$

$$\pi_j(s) = \min\left\{\max\left[\frac{M - p_i}{d} - V_i, 0\right], k_j\right\}p_j - w_j \cdot (1 - x_i) - k_j \cdot (1 - z_j) - c_j V_j \tag{21}$$

(ii) If two enterprises carry out strategic actions directed against the output of the other party, making $p_i = p_j$ and $i \neq j$, it can be expressed as the following:

$$\pi_i(s) = \min\left\{\frac{1}{2}\frac{M - p_i}{d} + \max\left[\frac{1}{2}\frac{M - p_j}{d} - V_j, 0\right], V_i\right\}p_i - w_i \cdot x_i - k_i \cdot z_i - c_i V_i \tag{22}$$

$$\pi_j(s) = \min\left\{\frac{1}{2}\frac{M - p_j}{d} + \max\left[\frac{1}{2}\frac{M - p_i}{d} - V_i, 0\right], V_j\right\}p_j - w_j \cdot (1 - x_i) - k_j \cdot (1 - z_i) - c_j V_j \tag{23}$$

The economic meaning of equation (20) and (21) is that when state-owned and non-state-owned enterprises proceed a price competition, if some enterprise i (which can a state-owned enterprise or a non-state-owned enterprise) puts forward the lowest price unilaterally, this would turn enterprise i into the one getting all needs of market capacity, which means $\min\left[\frac{M - p_i}{d}, V_i\right]$. Therefore, if $V_i > \frac{M - p_i}{d}$, which indicates that enterprise i would own all markets under the situation that the given price is p_i and there is no restriction until the market capacity equals $\frac{2M}{3d}$. This stems from:

$$\lim_{\substack{p_1 < p_j \\ t \to \infty}} V_j = 0$$

That is to say, if enterprise i adopts a low price strategy while enterprise j makes no adjustment on price, under the circumstances that $p_i < p_j$ and $i \neq j$, enterprise j may gradually lose the whole market capacity.

On the other hand, if $V_i < \frac{M - p_i}{d}$, which means that under conditions of the price being p_i, the actual market need can reach the level of $\frac{M - p_i}{d}$ with the largest capacity of enterprise i being V_i ($\leqslant \frac{2M}{3d}$). Therefore, enterprise i can merely fulfill a need reaching $\frac{2M}{3d}$. The remaining demand surplus $\left(\frac{M - p_i}{d} - V_i\right)$ of the market (or the remaining space of the market) shall be provided (or satisfied) by enterprise j.

Equation (22) and (23) state that if a state-owned and a non-state-owned enterprise adopt the same price, which means $p_i = p_j = p$, the two enterprises would share the market, with the scale of $\frac{1}{2}\frac{M - p}{d}$ respectively. However, if some enterprise, such as enterprise i, can not meet with the market needs that it gets by competing with another enterprise, j, or that it obtains according to theories, it means that, as for enterprise i, $\frac{1}{2}\frac{M - p}{d} > V_i$. That is to say, enterprise i still faces a failure in satisfying $(\frac{1}{2}\frac{M - p}{d} - V_i)$ of market capacity. The capacity that i fails to satisfy would turn to enterprise j to guarantee. This is the economic thought that equation (23) expresses. Correspondingly, if enterprise j can not fulfill $\frac{1}{2}\frac{M - p}{d}$ of market capacity according to theories, just as the same, the remnant would be taken up by enterprise i, which is the economic meaning that equation (22) expresses①.

Now, let's go back to the real world. In the transition condition, we found that, even if in the production of homogeneous products, such as electronic industry, textile industry, garment industry and even some of the heavy chemical industry, non-state-owned enterprises has a comparative advantage on the cost ratio compared with state-owned enterprises. First, they do not undertake the social responsibility like state-owned enterprises do, and they do not have to provide labor and health insurance for their employees. Their working conditions and wage quota are flexible and changeable. Unlike state-owned enterprises, non-state-owned enterprises do not have strong features of planning or rigidity, so the cost of unit production is much lower than that of state-owned enterprises. In addition, in the early stages of transition, due to the long-term implementation of the planned economy, China's various products, whether light industrial products, or heavy chemical products are in. Therefore, the market is concerned with the quantity of products more than the quality of products, and the whole market is still in an initial stage. Because producers are in a negotiating position with comparative advantage, non-state enterprises entering various industries

① The relevant proof process is omitted.

tend to realize their primitive accumulation by means of quantity expansion. They always produce and imitate similar products offered by state-owned enterprises with relatively low investment factors, so as to make z_2 approach z_1 as much as possible. That is to say, non-state-owned enterprises can use more primitive technology and their relatively poor quality investment factors to produce, and thus it leads to two consequences:

First, in the transition period, non-state-owned enterprises' unfair competition against state-owned enterprises leads to a price advantage of the former. Although state-owned enterprises enjoy the government quota in the purchase of raw materials, but the relative price advantage elements produced by this quota is offset by the brand imitation of non-state-owned enterprises.

Second, due to the relative price advantage non-state-owned enterprises obtain a production scale expansion to achieve rapid capital accumulation in a relatively short period of time, which actually prepares historical conditions in the next stage for non-state-owned enterprises in the technological innovation and brand aspect.

Given the above two consequences, the advantage of state-owned enterprises in the price of production materials will gradually become insignificant. Therefore, objectively this decision will induce decision makers to give up the "double track system" of price of production and carry out an abolition of the "plan track", making state-owned and non-state-owned enterprises achieve production materials they needed through the market rather than the plan amount or administrative power.

By equation (20):

$$\frac{\partial \pi_i}{\partial V_i} = c_i \tag{24}$$

$$\frac{\partial \pi_j}{\partial V_j} = c_j \tag{25}$$

equation (24) and (25) represent c_i and c_j are respectively the market opening cost that the enterprises have to pay for achieving the market share they ought to share theoretically. In the early period of the transition, because many non-state-owned enterprises seize the history opportunity like a seller market by making use of the imperfect market system and the national economy which is in shortage. Therefore, they are not only dominant in input prices, but also in the market transaction cost. The two present a causal logic, and with what Judgment 1 pointed out, non-state-owned enterprises do not pay attention to technological innovation in the regulatory period, and what they are more willing to do is to make use of their comparative advantage to substitute capital with more labor force. When all these factors take effect, the rapid development of private economy would become an inevitable logical result of the historical evolution.

1.2.3 Brief description of historical material and case study

1. Case study about agriculture and countryside

In 1984, with an abundant grain harvest in agriculture, the government abolished the state monopoly for the purchase and marketing of grain system and implemented the contract acquisition system. According to the contract, the government set a certain amount and purchased it at the price planned. The rest of the grain, whose price fluctuates caused by the supply and demand situation, would subject to market fluctuation. The double-track pricing system, the co-existence of stated fixed price and the market price, emerged. In the agricultural economy, there are two price, one is played by the rule of traditional planne economic system, while the other is played by the rule of market. The farmer faced two types of trading markets which were complementary (system).

However, the implementation of the double-track pricing system did not reach its expected result. The reason is that the market price is lower than the stated fixed price after the grain harvest in 1984. The rule that lower prices for grain negatively affected the peasants ability to efficient work and produce. As a result, the negative growth of the grain came into effect in 1985. In order to protect farmers interest, government implemented policies including prividing agricultural inputs, such as chemical fertilizer, in a planned price and charged a reserve fee.

Once published, the double-track pricing system would continue. This trading system① extended to the industry. The price of the product of the stated-owned enterprise was ruled by the double-track pricing system, which means that enterprises were able to sell the rest products to the market once achieve the quota set by the state. To a certain extent, enterprises' enthusiasm for production was motivated. It showed the evolutionary path that the rural "institutional innovation" penetrate into the urban industrial sector, (urban) industrial trading market and rural economic trading market constitute a "complementary system" and the institutional character of rural

---

① That is, double-track pricing system.

economic trading market influence the state-owned economy by "system penetration". This system penetration is the economic implication that path ⑤, ⑥, ⑦ as illustrated in Figure 1 – 10.

In fact, the decline of the grain production did not mean the stagnation of rural economy in 1985. At that time, the rural economic grew in a high speed because the comparative advantage of different field worked. With the contract system, farmers, whose percentage of non-agricultural income among overall income increased greatly①, had more options. Agricultural labor force diffused into individual operation, partnership operation and collective management. In the late 1980s, what made a stronger relationship between farmers and the land were the facts that the term of farmland contract extended to more than 15 years and that the contract could be transferred between farmers. Notably, the predecessor of township enterprise which rose in the vast rural area in China in the early and middle 1980s was the commune and brigade run enterprise which had produced in the late 1960s and early 1970s. With the help of marketed oriented economic reform, the commune and brigade run enterprise transformed to the more vibrant township enterprise. This process is the path ① and ② in the Figure 1 – 10. Path ① and ② are also the process of "diachronic diffusion"② . To paraphrase the analysis of Aoki Masahiko, this process can be defined as "diachronic linked games of system transformation"③ .

After the rural reform measures were taken, owing to the increase of free time and concurrent business of farmers, they had more options. The price of labor power increased. Therefore, farmer's input of marginal benefit changed. The reason was that the price of the marginal benefit changed under the stimulation of system innovation. On one hand, the increase of diversified economy raised farmer's

---

① Lin Yifu (2000) used to prove that exit right is a necessary condition for keeping the cooperative work effectively. In fact, "exit right" allowed farmers to diversify: on the one hand, it increased farmers' income; on the other hand, it led farmers to be the "specialist" in various field. In fact, in 1980s, there were numerous transportation specialists, weaving specialists and trading specialists. Later, many successful township enterprisers came from these specialists (Cong Shuhai, et al. , 1999). Once again, it proves that enterprisers are inseparable from the system. What the contract responsibility system brought to Chinese are not only the grain harvest, more importantly, but also the growth engine of institutional innovation. Many institutional transformation happened later could find the historic and logic starting point from the contract responsibility system.

② So-called "diachronic process" is the process of organization evolution and system transformation which has considers the time dimension. For instance, in time $t_0 \rightarrow t_1$, how did the organization evolve and how did the system transform.

③ See also Aoki Masahiko: "Comparative Institutional Analysis", Shanghai Far East Publishers, 2001, pp. 248 – 278.

income; on the other hand, it increased government's revenue. The reform, which was benefitted for farmers, workers in the city and government, got into a process of the increasing of marginal benefit. The reform became more and more irreversible. Under this historical condition, the success of the rural economic reform and the rise of township enterprise were easy to diffuse into the city. As mentioned above, "rural reform" led to the "urban reform".

In 1992, took Deng Xiaoping's south tour speech as an opportunity, rural economic reform further deepened. In 1984, the term of use right of land was 15 years. In 1993, it was further extended to 30 years. The circulation of the land contract was encouraged by policy. "Land subcontracting" provided "system platform" for conditional transfer of the land property right. It made the system character of rural economy changed. It penetrated inside the former rural economic organization, making the rural collective economic organization divide to new organization①, such as stock cooperative system, leading enterprises plus peasant households system and etc. The industry developed rapidly because numerous state-owned enterprises and state-holding enterprises transferred there and Taiwanese businesspeople regarded there as venture base. Everything would be unthinkable if there was no practical land transfer system.

The historical material above strongly proves "proposition E_1" and proves "proposition E_2" and "proposition E_3" to a certain extent.

2. Case study of agricultural industrialization

The agricultural industrialization, which started in the middle 1980s and flourished in the middle and late 1990s, can provide proof for the economic implication in Figure 1 – 10 and the hypothesis above.

Moreover, agricultural industrialization is a necessary stage in the development of rural economy in China. At present, China's population is 1.3 billion, but 70% of the population live in the countryside. The average area per person of land occupied is 0.24 hectare in the Chinese countryside. According to the current agricultural productivity rates, the agricultural population is roughly 100 million. However, in fact, 350 million people are engaged in agricultural production, which indicates that the entire population of agricultural surplus labor consists of 250 million. After China

---

① According to our investigation, Saifeiya Company in Ningcheng Town, Nei Monggol and textile factories in the villages around Baoding, Hebei Province, have all profited from the "subcontracting system".

joined the WTO, Chinese farmers faced direct pressure from the international market. For instance, China's agricultural products were higher than the average price in the international market (e. g. wheat, corn and cotton). Therefore, China could not compete with the cheaper international market prices.

In the next section, we look at the agricultural industrialization of Nanjie village and Sanwang village to illustrate the role of 'path dependency' in China's organization evolution and system transformation. In particular, we will examine how the circulation of the land property right and market breadth influenced the form of organization and the choice of contract structure. We are that both of these developments were critical to the historical developments of Chinese society.

(1) Case study of Nanjie village①.

Nanjie village, whose population is around 3 000, locates in 100 kilometer south of Zhengzhou, Henan province. In the early 1980s, like other villages, it distributed farmlands to household and carried out the household contract responsibility system. Afterwards, at the request of farmers, village committee of Nanjie village organized farmers to put the land distributed under the collective, purchase agricultural machinery, engage in production and operation together. Even though villagers in Nanjie village reestablish the position of collective economy, the collective economy was not as before simply. While they made the arrangement of agricultural production, villagers established village enterprises by fund raising and loan. Led by the village chief Wang Hongbin, they established 26 village enterprises which were producing instant noodle, packaging material, paint, etc. The property right of these village enterprises belongs to all villagers in Nanjie village. In terms of income distribution, Nanjie village distributed the income evenly according to the number of family members. And village provided standard apartment to every family. For the 20 years, this village whose output grew at 2 000 times hired 11 thousand migrant workers. Agriculture made up a small percentage of production in Nanjie village. Only 70 labors worked for agriculture, while there were only 67 hectare farmlands for traditional agriculture. Moreover, Nanjie village made considerable profit while it worked with Japanese enterprises for paper and paper products producing and worked with German enterprises for bear producing. Wang Hongbin claimed that they had emphasized working for collective economy and have taught villagers the thoughts of

---

① Both this case and the next case come from "Bungei Shunju" from Japan, April 2003, It's also recorded in Reference News, April 6th, 2003.

Mao Zedong all this time.

Although the development path of Nanjie village is not typical in the context of China's economic transformation, the system arrangements are worthy of discussion. "Path dependency" was prominent in the process of organization evolution in Nanjie village. From the point of view of "trading participant" with market awareness, thoughts of Mao Zedong were no longer adapted to the time. However, it became the link connecting the history in Nanjie village: they inherited the collective ownership system which formed under the context of planned economy, they embedded the structure of this ownership system into enterprises which competed in the market, and they made group members positive in production by teaching them the ideology of Mao Zedong's thoughts, avoiding the opportunism which was proofed by many economists repeatedly and the trouble of "tragedy of the commons" caused by the deficiency of individual quantification of property rights. So far, Nanjie village succeeds. In this case, collective economy, communal property rights and thoughts of Mao Zedong constituted the "system character" in the economic environment in Nanjie village. It is showed as G_s^0 in Figure 1 – 11. It continued all along, even though the internal organization of Nanjie village had been different from the organization which formed in the context of traditional collective economy (suppose that it is showed as G_t^0). It transferred to G^1 which fitted with the environment of market economy. We show the process of organization evolution in Nanjie village in Figure 1 – 11.

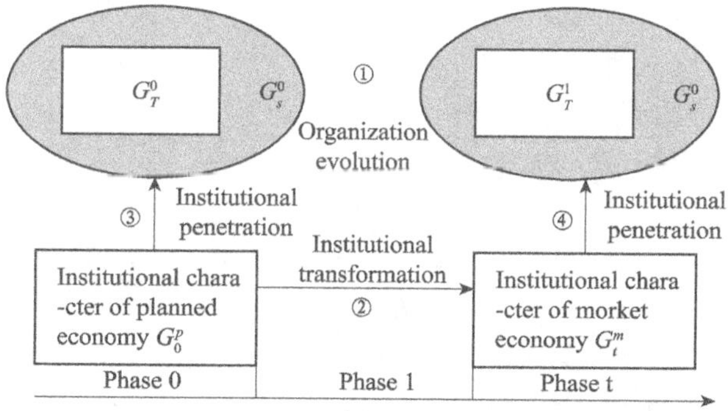

Figure 1 – 11 Nanjie village: organization evolution in time or history

As shown in Figure 1 – 11, the left part represents the organization form of Nanjie village (showed as G_t^0) in the context of planned economy (the institutional character is G_0^P). It is represented as "institutional character" (G_S^0) of collective ownership system. The right part represents the organization form of Nanjie village (showed as G_t^1) in the context of market economy (the institutional character is G_t^m). It is also wrapped in "institutional character" (G_S^0) of collective ownership system. Figure 1 – 11 expresses the crucial influence of the path dependency to the process of organization evolution. For instance, Nanjie village inherited the ideology of Mao Zedong, which lead to the "collective ownership system". Currently, the new organization form merged with institutional character G_t^m of market economy peculiarly. The experience of Nanjie village is not typical, but is significant in China's history. For instance, Figure 1 – 10 and Figure 1 – 11, implicit the diversity of China's institutional transformation. Figure 1 – 11 also shows the process of enterprise organization transformation: this organization developed from the collective economic organization and the traditional planned economy and transformed into a stock cooperative system with individual quantification of property rights.

(2) Case study of Sanwang village.

Nanjie village is located in the Zhongyuan District, Zhengzhou City, Henan province. In 1999, after negotiation with local governments, farmers and cultivation companies signed a contract allowing farmers to sell the use of the land. This situation allowed the farmer to still own the use right of the land (as the owner of the property rights of the land), but the use right of the land had to join the cultivation company as the stockholder. Payments for such use of land consist of two aspects: one was the land-use fee in which the company paid with products produced. For instance, the company paid 500-kilogram wheat for every use of the land. During the spring festival, the company paid farmers with meat, oil, fruits, etc., and allowed peasant shareholders to participate in annual bonus of course, peasants still hove "rations".

To ensure efficient production, the company hired about 400 farmers who were mostly local females whose annual salary was 3 500 RMB. Local male farmers were able to work outside or hold part-time jobs. As a result, these farmers' income increased 3-fold after the use right of the land joined the cultivation company. After becoming the stockholder of the cultivation company, farmers earned a relatively higher income and living standard. In addition to farmers, the local government and cultivation companies also benefited from this land use arrangement.

According to Figure 1 – 12, given the "institutional character" of the market economy, the form of the rural land collective ownership system changed from $G_s^0 \rightarrow G_s^1$. Originally, the use right of the land was family based. Now, the right to use the land has become a standardized enterprise. Even though the property of right to use the land is the same, the use pattern of the use right of the land has changed radically. It is neither "enterprise plus peasant household", nor stock cooperative system absolutely. It is now considered a "land-stock cooperative system" . The reason is that the female farmers were staff in the company whild they were also the "land-stock" holder. Therefore, the organization of the form has changed significantly.

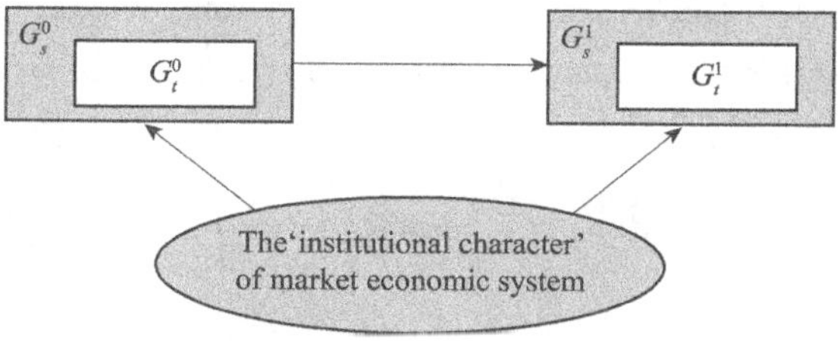

Figure 1 – 12 Sanwang village: land system transformation and organizational evolution

1. 2. 4 Organization momentum of economic growth

1. Deduction of hypothesis (proposition) E_1, hypothesis (proposition) E_2, hypothesis (proposition) E_3: organization evolution is more important than technical progress

This section discusses the basic structure of economic growth in China's transition. The key hypothesis of this section consists of the following: 'the historic and logic starting point' not only constituted the reason for economic reform, but also was decisive of the origins of the reform and path arrangement of economic organizational development. In particular, different economic organization evolutions were interactive and interpenetrative. Therefore, to understand the economic transition, we must first explain the complementarity of the system. In the next section, we described how our hypothesis (as stated above) can be tested using relevant data.

Deduction II: The main factor behind China's economic growth over a 20-year cycle is related to the "institutional transformation" in the context of economic reform. To a certain extent, the "institutional transformation" can be understood as "organization form evolution". According to observation, in the transition, the main content of institutional transformation is the change of ownership system. This refers to the percentage of public economy decreases constantly among the total economy while the percentage of non-public economy increases constantly. Furthermore, the relative ratio of state-owned economic organization operates on a downward trend, while the relative ratio of non-state-owned economic organization is constantly trending upward. However, instead of technical progress, institutional transformation is the underlying factor of China's exponential economic growth. In the transition, the key element of economic growth is economic institutional transformation. Overall, it could be argued that China's institutional transformation and organization evolution are more important than technical progress.

2. Organization momentum of economic growth: empirical evidence

Many studies have shown the process by which China's economy developed (which also include a discussion on its district economic growth). For instance, Xiao Geng (1997) used economic data of non-state sectors in district and province to show that the growth of non-state sector not only promotes the industrial growth, but also allowed for a more competitive environment for state-owned enterprises. At the same time, he also showed that the distribution of proportion of non-state-owned economy among total industrial production predicts the economic growth in different districts. The analysis of Liu Deqiang and Naoki Murakami shows that after considering the scale efficiency of production, compared to state-owned enterprise, township enterprise and village enterprise are relatively more efficient in the economy. For example, the machine tool industry and the clothing industry show how the non-state-owned economy (private enterprise) predominated in industrial structureadjustment in terms of human capital and industrial development. Furthermore, Yao Yang (1998) and Zhang Qi (2001) conducted empirical research about the internal and external effect of state-own enterprise and non-state-own enterprise (including collective enterprise, private enterprise, three-type joint enterprise and three-type joint enterprise of Hong Kong, Macau and Taiwan) and efficiency of industrial technology. The results revealed that the technical efficiency of private enterprise is higher than the technical efficiency of state-own enterprises. This created a "spillover effect" of township enterprise and three-type joint enterprises. In addition, this also created a prominent while the "spillover effect" of enterprise of Hong Kong, Macau and Taiwan, which is negatively associated. Thus, it is important to stress the powerful role of private enterprise on economic growth in China. However, the reason for the negative "spillover effect" is due to the industrial structure of enterprise of Hong Kong, Macau and Taiwan. In addition, Lin Yifu and Yao Yang (2003) found that the economic efficiency of township enterprise and the rural industry made a significant economic contribution to China. Overall, the literature shows that the technical progress should not be the key element of economic growth. Technology works in the context of corresponding system. For example, in the clothing industry, why the total factor productivity of village enterprise is higher than township enterprise's? Why the total factor productivity of township enterprise is higher than state-own enterprise's? Why the TPF[①] of associated enterprises and joint enterprise is higher than all other enterprise's (Liu Deqiang, Naoki Murakami, Chinese edition, 2000). The machine tool industry is the same. Normally, the technology in state-own enterprise is dominative absolutely. However, state-own enterprise which is dominative in technology is not dominative in efficiency (Liu Deqiang, Naoki Murakami, 2000).

Similarly, China's economic growth cannot be explained by growth in human capital. Given the same level of technology, the assertion that the human capital in Midwest is worse than in east is credible but needs to be further explained. The system element and organization element should be considered in the contribution of economic growth of human capital. It means that human capital is a variable that should be explained by system and organization.

In order to test the effect of different economic organization in economic growth, we estimate a production function which takes organization evolution as explanatory variable. The explained variable is the speed of GDP growth. There are two types of explanatory variables: firstly, represent the distribution of different economic distribution by the percentage of fixed investment of state-own and non-state-own economy in total investment. It implies the "evolution trend" of different economic organization and contribution of different economic organization to the local economic growth. The reason why can take the cross-section data to represent organization's evolution trend is that the benchmark of the discussion is the actual condition of Chinese economy before the reform. It constitutes "the historic and logic starting point". Comparing the distribution of economic organization in different district to before the reform, we can get the evolution trend of economic organization and its theoretical and economic significance to economic growth. Secondly, by taking the location of different economic organization as dummy variable, analyze how the

① TFP is total factor productivity.

structure of ownership or property right structure in different district, the types of economic organizations in different district and their detailed proportion affect the economic growth in that district. We "evaluate" different province, city and autonomous region as below:

(1) Take the western province as benchmark, the evaluation is 0, including: Tibet, Yunnan, Gansu, Qinghai, Shaanxi, Sichuan, Guizhou, Xinjiang, Chongqing and Ningxia.

(2) Inland region, the evaluation is 1, including: Jiangxi, Anhui, Hunan, Hubei, Henan, Heilongjiang, Inner Mongolia and Jilin.

(3) Eastern region, the evaluation is 2, including: Shanghai, Jiangsu, Zhejiang, Shandong, Beijing, Tianjin, Liaoning and Hebei.

(4) Special economic zone, the evaluation is 3, including: Guangdong, Fujian, Hainan and Guangxi.

Considering that the private economy in Guangxi and Hainan is not prosperous enough, in order to show their difference with Guangdong and Fujian, the evaluation of Guangxi and Hainan minus 0.5.

Currently, even though both Liaoning and Hebei belong to eastern region, but the private economy in the former is not prosperous and the state-own enterprise is prominent in the latter's total economy. In order to show their difference with other eastern cities, their evaluation minus 0.5, therefore, their evaluation is 1.5.

"Integrate" these evaluations to explain the variables of economic growth in different regions and express with "region element". In data processing, they get into the function as dummy variable.

Therefore, this is the rationale of our approach: organization types in different regions constitute the precondition of economic growth, and also constitute "the historic and logic starting point" of organization evolution in that region. Different logic starting point makes different evolution path of organization in these region, therefore, shows different economic performance. As the discussion in the front half in this section, the reason why Wenzhou people chose an economic system of small commodities production and management is the strained relation between and land caused by the scarcity of land, the convention and tradition of business and the unique dialect. The private economy developed fast here, and the "two-thirds of whole" economic pattern formed (two-thirds is private economy, one-third is state-own economy and collective economy). Economic performance must be explained by the dynamic efficiency of economic organization evolution, rather than technological transformation and human capital. Without the corresponding economic organization, human capital is not easy to play a role. Constrained by the limitation of collecting data, we regard the fixed investment of different economic organization in different district as "dynamic efficiency of economic organization evolution". It means that for a district, if its fixed investment of private economy is large and growing fast, we assert that dynamic efficiency of the private economy is high. Furthermore, the dynamic efficiency will promote the efficiency of resource allocation in this region.

We have collected data on fixed investment and growth of speed among 31 provinces, cities and autonomous regions in 2000. There are 248 samples[1]. In detailed analysis, we regard the percentage of fixed investment of collective economy, shareholding economy, enterprise of Hong Kong, Macau and Taiwan, foreign-funded enterprise, individual economy, state-own economy and associated enterprises among (these regions) total fixed investment and the dummy variable as explanatory variable. We do a regression of the growth rate of the gross domestic product (GDP) in different. We have found a series of valuable conclusions as are shown in Table 1-3.

Table 1-3 What decides the growth rate of economy?

Model	Unstandardized coefficients	Std. Error	Standardized coefficients	t	Sig.
	B		Beta		
Constant	93.819	5.680		16.517	0.000
Collective percentage	21.492	6.189	1.372	3.473	0.002
Share holding percentage	16.340	6.301	1.087	2.593	0.016
Hong Kong, Macau percentage	21.737	9.260	0.654	2.347	0.028
Foreign-funded percentage	14.394	7.345	0.462	1.960	0.062
Other percentage	11.218	8.096	0.511	1.386	0.179
State-owned percentage	15.292	5.790	1.684	2.641	0.015
Regional influence	0.341	0.223	0.278	1.533	0.139

Note: Explained variable, the GDP growth rate in 2000 in different regions (compared to last year).

The results from Table 1-3 are consistent with our expectation as all explanatory variables passed the T tests. For instance, the coefficient of "the percentage of collective economy", "the percentage of share-holding economy" and "the percentage of state-owned economy" are in the confidence interval of 99%; the coefficient of "the percentage of economy of Hong Kong, Macau" is in the confidence interval of 95%; the coefficient of the percentage of foreign-funded

① These data come form "China Ststistical Yearbook (2001)", China Statistics Press, 2001.

enterprise economy is in the confidence interval of 90%; the coefficient of the percentage of other economy is in the confidence interval of 80%. Compared to other variables, the impact of regional influence to economic growth is lowest. Compared to the impact in the middle of 1980s, even though the regional influence still works, its impact decreases. The flowing of human capital and technology become easy with the development of marketization. Many enterprises transferred from coastal areas to the inland region because of the pressure of industrial upgrading in coastal areas. However, regional influence should not be overlooked. Regions with high marketing degree, such as Shanghai and Guangdong, are still attracting numerous enterprises with their relaxed environment and advanced business awareness. Another reason about the low impact of regional influence is technical. It is relative with the dummy variables the author chose.

In order to understand the influence of technology, non-state economy, per capita farmland area and the percentage of rural population among private enterprise to economic growth rate, we collect more data of regions in 2001 (including 31 provinces, cities and autonomous regions). We take the growth rate of gross domestic product in the region as explained variable and take the four index mentioned above as explanatory variable. We do a regression and get the conclusion showed in Table 1 - 4. However, we should explain that we use the data of economic growth rate in 2000 to replace the data in 2001 because of the technical reason of data collection. It will not impact the reason of regression.

Furthermore, we conceptualize the per capita farmland area as a part of "the historic and logic starting point" of organization evolution of different province because the per capita farmland area represents the "relationship between people and land". According to the practical empirical observation, farmers in provinces whose per capita farmland area are lower than the national average, such as Zhejiang and Jiangsu, are easier to try innovative economic organization, under the conditional of scarcity of land, as to optimize the allocation of resource. Unfortunately, we fail to find the data about per capita farmland area in province, city or district before and after 1978. Therefore, we only are able to use the data in 2001. It will decrease the useful information of explanatory variable of "the historic and logic starting point". The distortion of the data quality will affect the result of regression greatly. Nevertheless, the impact of per capita farmland area to the economic growth rate is higher than the impact of (regional) technical volume (or trading volume). The latter is higher than the impact of the population of rural workers.

Table 1 - 4　Technology, non-state-owned enterprise, labor force and farmland

Variables	Unstandardized coefficients	Std. Error	Standardized coefficients	t	Sig.
	B		Beta		
(Constant)	105. 530	0. 849		124. 343	0. 000
Per capita farmland area	7. 027E-02	0. 020	0. 630	3. 596	0. 001
Labor force in private enterprise	1. 102E-03	0. 001	0. 191	1. 310	0. 202
Percentage of non-state-owned enterprise	5. 581	1. 739	0. 642	3. 209	0. 004
Technical volume	1. 313E-02	0. 004	0. 470	3. 550	0. 002

Note: Explained variable, economic growth rate (in 2000).

From Table 1 - 4, we find that the impact of economic organization to the economic growth rate is higher than the impact of technical volume to the gross domestic product. It can be explained by reason that technology can't influence the economic growth isolated. It becomes an inductive element through intermediary of organization and human capital.

In short, in this section, we explored the "evolutionary game track" of non-state-owned enterprise in detail by using methods like analysis of economic history. Specifically, this section proofs that there is a significant "historic and logic starting point" in both state-owned enterprise reform and non-state economic organization evolution. This original resource made the state-own enterprise reform show a serious of features, such as government-led, progressive, complicated, systemic and natural evolutionary.

This section discusses the non-state-owned economic evolution with a large portion. The development of non-state economy has unique historic significance in the overall economic reform. It made the reform go ahead step by step in the process of economic growth. It made China's economic reform goes beyond the categories of explanation of "Washington Consensus". By introducing Aoki Masahiko's theories, such as "system complementarity", "system penetration" and "relating game", we discussed organization choice and contract arrangement of township enterprise and private enterprise. Furthermore, we exploded the "historic logic" of organization evolution.

Moreover, we further constituted a basic pattern of organization evolution. This (already) expansive evolutional logic coincides with the theoretical model of contract choice and efficiency substitution in the other essay (Deng Hongtu, 2003). The former is the logical continuation of the latter. With the analysis, we aim to proof one conclusion: "system momentum", which exploded by organization evolution or system transformation, caused the continued economic growth in this 20 year. Other elements, such as technological choice and human capital, only can be explained accurately and completely under the frame of system analysis.

References

1. Alan Liu. Wenzhou Model and China's Modernization. Asian Survey, 1992 (8).

2. Aoki Masahiko. Comparative Institutional Analysis. Shanghai Far East Publishers, 2001.

3. Aoki Masahiko. Comparative Institutional Analysis: Causes and Some Preliminary Conclusions. Comparative Economic & Social Systems, 1997 (2).

4. Aoki Masahiko. Country Type as a Stable Game Result. Comparison, 2003 (5).

5. Aoki Masahiko. Information and Governance Structure of Silicon Valley Model. Comparative Economic & Social Systems, 2000 (1).

6. Aoki Masahiko. Institutional Changes Evolve along Equilibrium, Institutional, Contract and Organization-A Perspective from New Institutional Economics. Economic Science Press, 2003.

7. Aoki Masahiko. The Role of Government in Economic Development. Reform, 1997 (5).

8. Aoki Masahiko. Why the Diversity System Continues to Evolve. Comparative Economic & Social Systems, 2001 (6).

9. CaiKejiao. An Analysis of Wenzhou Humanistic Spirit. Journal of Zhejiang Normal University (Social Sciences Edition), 1999 (2).

10. Chang, Wang. The nature of the Township Village Enterprise. Journal of Compatative Economics, 1994 (19): 434 – 452.

11. Che, Qian. Insecure Property Rights and Government Ownership of Firms. Quarterly Journal of Economics, 1998.

12. Chen Jianbo. Institutional Change and Rural Informal System-Property Formation and Control of Chinese Township Enterprises. Economic Research Journal, 2000 (1).

13. Chen Jianbo. Non-private Property Rights and the Rapid Growth of Township Enterprises. Discover, 1995 (12).

14. Chen Jianbo. People's Commune System of Property Rights. Economic Research Journal, 1994 (7).

15. Chen Jianbo. Resource Allocation Efficiency of Township Industrial Enterprises, recorded in Lin Qingsong, Du Ying: Industrial Reform and Efficiency in China-A Comparative Study of State-owned Enterprises and Non-state-owned Enterprises. Yunnan People's Publishing House, 1997.

16. China Statistical Yearbook (2001). China Statistics Press, 2001.

17. China Statistical Yearbook (2002). China Statistics Press, 2002.

18. Cited from New Palegrave Economics Dictionary (Volume IV), Economic Science Press, 1992, pp. 44 -49.

19. Cong Shuhai, Zhang Bai. History of New China's Economic Development. Shanghai University of Finance and Economics Press, 1999.

20. Dai Yuanchen. Transitional Economy and Economic Transition. Reform, 1998 (6).

21. Deng Hongtu et al. Analysis of Contract Selection under Constraint Conditions and Continuity Condition of Contract Selection. Management World, 2002 (12).

22. Deng Hongtu. Economic Explanation for Organization, Organizational Evolution and Institutional Change. Nankai Economic Studies, 2003 (1).

23. Deng Hongtu. Relative Rational Research. Research of Institutional Economics, 2003 (1).

24. Deng Hongtu. The Logic of Organizational Evolution (Discussion Paper). Nankai University, 2003.

25. Deng Hongtu. The Official-merchant in History: An Economic Analysis. China Economic Quarterly, Volume 2, No. 3.

26. Deng Zhenglai. The Construction of Common-law Constitutional State: A Further Study of Hayek's Legal Theory. China Social Sciences Review, 2002 (1).

27. Dong Fureng, Zhao Renwei. Investigation on Rural Commodity Economy in Wenzhou and the Exploration of China's Rural Modernization. Economic Research Journal, 1986 (6).

28. Douglass. North. Structure and Change in Economic History. The Commercial Press, 1992: 46 -59.

29. Douglass North. Theoretical Outline of Institutional Change, recorded in Economics and China's Economic Reform. Shanghai People's Publishing House, 1995.

30. Douglass North. Transaction Costs, Institutional and Economic History, recorded in New Institutional Economics. Shanghai University of Finance and Economics

Press, 1998.

31. Edward J. Lopehz, Carlos D. Ramirez. Is Political Ideology Endogenous? Evidence from Business Cycle, 2000, papers. ssrn. com/sol3/papers. cfm? abstract_id = 257524.

32. Fan Gang. Chinese Culture, Rational System and Economic Development. Twenty-First Century, 1994 (2).

33. Fan Gang. Discussion on the Macroscopic Significance of Enterprise Reform. Tianjin Social Sciences, 1994 (1).

34. Fan Gang. On the Reform Process. Reform, Openness and Growth. Shanghai Joint Publishing, 1991.

35. Fan Gang. Political Economics Analysis of Gradual Reform. Shanghai Far East Publishers, 1996: 64 – 90.

36. Fan Gang. Two Reform Costs and Two Reform Methods. Economic Research Journal, 1993 (1).

37. FeiXiaotong. Trip to Wenzhou. Outlook Weekly, 1986 (20 – 22).

38. Feng Qu. On the Reform of Township Enterprises from the Fund-raising Mechanism: A Case of Institutional Change Dynamics. Reform, 2000 (5).

39. Feng Qu. The Progressive Track of China's Rural Industry Development. China Rural Survey, 2000 (5).

40. Feng Qu, Zhang Tao. Authority, Authoritative Organizations and Efficiency: Comment on the Path of Economic Transition. World Economic Papers, No. 5, 2002.

41. Hayek. The Constitution of Liberty. Joint Publishing, 1997.

42. Hu Wuhuan. The Inevitability and Progressive Significance of the Policy of Stressing Agriculture and Restraining Commerce, Agricultural History of China, No. 2, 1997.

43. Huang Shao'an. Hypothesis of Subject Change in Institutional Change and Its Explanation to China's Institutional Change-Commentary on Yang Ruilong's "Intermediate Diffusion Hypothesis" and "Three-stage Theory". Economic Research Journal, 1999 (1).

44. Huang Shao'an. Quaternary Main Body and Joint Innovation of China's Railway System-Analyze the Relaxation of China's Railway Regulation by Taking the Creation and Development of Sanmao Railway Company in Guangdong Province as an Example, A Case Study of Institutional Change in China (episode II). China Financial & Economic Publishing House, 1999.

45. Jin Xiangrong. A progressive Conversed Reform Path with Doexistence of a

Variety of Institutional Changes. Journal of Zhejiang University (Humanities &Social Sciences), 2000 (4).

46. Latan V. W. Theory of Induced Institutional Change. Property Rights and Institutional Change-A Collection of Translation of Property-right Economics and New Institutional School. Shanghai Joint Publishing, 1994: 327 –370.

47. Li Daokui. Fuzzy Property Right Theory in Transitional Economy. Economic Research Journal, 1995 (4).

48. Lin Yifu, Cai Pan, Li Zhou. China Miracle: Development Strategy and Economic Reform. Shanghai Joint Publishing, 1994: 20 –60.

49. Lin Yifu: On the Economic Theory of Institutional Change: Induced Institutional Change and Compulsory Institutional Change. Property Rights and Institutional Change: a Collection of Translation of Property-right Economics and New Institutional School. Shanghai Joint Publishing, 1994.

50. Lin Yifu, Liu Peilin. Viability and state-owned enterprise reform. Working Paper of China Center for Economic Research at Peking University, No. L2001005.

51. Lin Yifu, Yao Yang. China's Rural Industrialization in the Miracle of East Asia, Reflections on the Miracle of East Asia. China Renmin University Press, 2003.

52. Lin Yifu. On the Economic Theory of Institutional Change: Induced Institutional Change and Compulsory Institutional Change, written by North et al: Property Rights and Institutional Change. Shanghai Joint Publishing, Shanghai People's Publishing House, 1991.

53. Lin Yifu. Rural Movement and Domestic Demand Stimulation. China Center for Economic Research Series Briefing, 1999 (26).

54. Lin Yifu. Self-generating Ability and Deep-seated Problems of Reform, Comparative Economic & Social Systems, 2002 (2).

55. Lin Yifu. Some Opinions on Current Rural Policy, China Center for Economic Research Series Briefing, 2003 (29).

56. Lin Yifu. Viability, Policy Burden, Responsibility Attribution and Budget Soft Constraints. Comparative Economic & Social Systems, 2000 (4).

57. Liu Deqiang, Naoki Murakami et al. China's Industrial Reform: Past Achievements and Future Prospects. Shanghai Joint Publishing, Shanghai People's Publishing House, 2000.

58. Lu Changchong. Corporate Governance Structure and Relationship Theory between Three New and Old Committees. Economic Research Journal, 1994.

59. Mises. Human Action: A Treatise on Economics. San Francisco: Fox

&Wilkes, 1996: 23 -29.

60. National Bureau of Statistics. Statistics of China's Industrial Economy. China Statistics Press, 1987.

61. Nelson. The Source of Economic Growth. China Economic Publishing House, 2001.

62. Oi, J. Fiscal Reform and the Economic Foundations of Local State Corporatism in China. World Politics, vol. 45, No. 1.

63. Pan Wei. Farmer and Market. The Commercial Press, 2003.

64. Philip Kiefer, Ma M. Shirley. Formal and Informal System in Economic Development, Institutional, Contract and Organization-A Perspective of the Solution to the New Institutional Economics. Economic Science Press, 2003.

65. Ping Xinqiao, Jiang Guorong. Game Theory Analysis of "Triangular Debt" . Economic Research Journal, 1994 (1).

66. Qian Yingyi. Government and the Rule of Law. Comparison, 2003 (5).

67. Qin Hui. Looking at the Township from the Crossroads-Investigation Report on the Transformation of Township Enterprises in Tsinghua University. Reform, 1997 (6), 1998 (1).

68. Roger Franz. X-Efficiency: Theory, Evidence and Applications. Shanghai Translation Publishing House, 1993.

69. Sasaki Masahiro. Economic Analysis of China at Present Stage-Observation and Evaluation from Japan. Jilin People's Publishing House.

70. SchultzT. W. The System and Continuous Improvement of Economic Value of Man, recorded in North et al: Property Rights and Institutional Change. Shanghai Joint Publishing, Shanghai People's Publishing House, 1991: 251 -263.

71. Shi Jinchuan, Zhu Kangdui. Research on Wenzhou Model: Retrospect and Prospect. Zhejiang Social Sciences, 2002 (3).

72. Shi Lei. Analysis of an Enterprise Community Organization: HuaxiVillage. Academia Bimestris, 2000 (3).

73. State Administration of Taxation. Tax Year Book of China, China Tax Publishing House, 2000.

74. Statistics Bureau of Jiangsu Province. Statistical Yearbook of Jiangsu (1983), China Statistics Press, 1984.

75. Statistics Bureau of Shandong Province. Statistical Yearbook of Shandong (1983), China Statistics Press, 1984.

76. Stigler. The Division of Labor is Limited by the Extent of the Market. Selection

ofStegler'sPapers. The Commercial Press, 1999.

77. Sun Zao, Lu Zhengwei. From Government to Enterprise: A Summary of the Research Literature of Chinese Private Enterprises. Economic Research Journal, 2003 (4).

78. The situation of China's rural areas seen by Japanese journalists, Reference News, April 6, 2003, edition eight. Also contained in Japan art spring and autumn, April 2003 issued.

79. Tang Yinbi. Historical Research (Volume 1). Shanghai People's Publishing House 1997.

80. Wang Xiaoyi. Family System and Rural Industry Development. Chinese Social Sciences Quarterly, 1996 (16).

81. Wei Sen. Economic Analysis of Practice-New Development of Evolutionary Game Theory, recorded in Transitions and Growth. Shanghai Far East Publishers, 2002.

82. Wei Sen. Nature of Custom and Probe into Source of Growing Mechanism, recorded in Transitions and Growth. Shanghai Far East Publishers, 2002.

83. Xiao Geng. Property Right and China's Economic Reform. China Social Sciences Press, 1997.

84. Yang Ruilong. The Three-stage Theory of Institutional Change in China. Economic Research Journal, 1998 (1).

85. Yao Yang. The Influence of Non-state-owned Economic Components on China's Industrial Technology Efficiency. Economic Research Journal, 1998 (12).

86. Yao Yang, Zhang Qi. Analysis on Technical Efficiency of Chinese Industrial Enterprises. Economic Research Journal, 2001 (10).

87. Zhang Chunlin. On the Debt of State-owned Enterprises. Reform, 1996 (1).

88. Zhang Chunlin. Some Theoretical and Policy Issues on the Adjustment of State-owned Economy. Economic Research Journal, 1999 (8).

89. Zhang Jun, Feng Qu. An Analysis Framework for the Reform of Collective Ownership of Township Enterprises. Economic Research Journal, 2000 (8).

90. Zhang Weiying. Decision-making Right, Residual Claim Right and Performance: a Theoretical Analysis of the Reform of State-owned Enterprises in China. Chinese Social Sciences Quarterly (Hong Kong), Fall 1995.

91. Zhang Weiying. Regional Competition and Privatization. China Center for Economic Research Series Briefing, 1999 (20).

92. Zhao Wei. Wenzhou Strength. News of Economics, November 26, 1999.

93. Zhao Wei. Where Shall "Wenzhou model" Go? News of Economics, April 7, 2000.

94. Zhou Qiren. "Return of Control Right" and "Entrepreneur-controlled Enterprise" -A Case Study of Entrepreneur Human Capital Property in Public Ownership Economy. Economic Research Journal, 1997 (5).

95. Zhou Qiren. Companies in the Market: a Special Contract for Human Capital and Non-human capital. Economic Research Journal, 1996 (6).

96. Zhou Qiren. Countryside Rural Reform: Changes in the Relationship between State and Land Ownership-A Review of the History of Economic Institutional Change. Chinese Social Sciences Quarterly (Hong Kong), 1995 (6).

97. Zhou Qiren. The Nature of Public Ownership Enterprises. Economic Research Journal, 2002 (11).

98. Zhou Ye'an. Local Government Competition and Economic Growth. Journal of Renmin University of China, 2003 (1).

99. Zhou Ye'an. The Evolutionary Explanation of Institutional Change in China. Economic Research Journal, 2000 (5).

100. Zhou Ye'an. Theoretical Reflection on Institutional Change in China-A View of Evolutionary Theory. Internal discussion manuscript of Unirule Institute of Economics, 1998 (14).

101. Zhu Kangdui. Small Farm Culture and Wenzhou Rural Family Economy. Zhejiang Social Sciences, 1997 (5).

102. Zhu Kangdui. The Evolution of Industrial Organization in the Period of Economic Transition: A Preliminary Study on Wenzhou Regional Economy. China Rural Survey, 1999 (3).

Chapter 2

Dynamic Process of Private Economy Institution Innovations

This chapter consists of two parts, which discusses a dynamic analysis of private economic system innovation from different perspectives.

First, a model within the framework of endogenous economic growth is built in this chapter to study what is the optimal technological progress rate that the government should choose when promoting the development of private economy by establishing a patent system. This section focuses on the various factors that the government should consider when implementing patent protection and its implications for our country. Studies have challenged the degree to which technological progress of the private economy is actually faster.

Second, this chapter also constructs an endogenous economic growth model to analyze the effect of asymmetry of quality information on the growth of knowledge and the development of private economy. The conclusion of the model shows that the asymmetry of quality information will not only lead to the shrinking of the private economy product market finally, but also reduce the pricing of knowledge products, which will reduce the investment of R&D, thus hindering the knowledge growth of a country. As the growth rate of knowledge determines the long-term economic growth rate of a country, the asymmetry of quality information to the knowledge innovation will have a far-reaching negative impact on the private economy of a country. However, because the information asymmetry will reduce the level of social welfare of a country, so the community will give birth to some system arrangements to solve the problem of information asymmetry, thus to promote the development of private economy.

2.1 The matching of the development of private economy and the speed of technological progress

2.1.1 Introduction

The theory of modern economic growth is based on the Harrod (1939) and Domar (1946) model. In the Harrod-Domar model, the savings rate, the capital-output ratio and the population growth rate are independent of the exogenous variables of the economic system, and it is difficult to achieve and maintain an economic growth that both the labor and capital production factors are fully utilized. The balance of the Harrod-Domar is a kind of "balance on the blade". The most critical assumption of the Harrod-Domar model is the production function of the fixed technical coefficient. Solow (1956) and Swan (1956) amended this hypothesis to replace the neoclassical production function, which could be fully replaced between the elements of production, to establish the neoclassical growth theory. Because the main feature of the neoclassical production function is the diminishing marginal returns of the input factor, long-term sustained economic growth can only be achieved by exogenous technological progress.

Since the mid-1980s, and beginning with the studies by Romer (1986) and Lucas (1988), the issue of long-term economic growth has now become a focus of attention for economists. At this stage, the theory of economic growth is devoted to the study of how the sustained growth of a country's economy is endogenously determined by the economic system, that is, whether the endogenous growth theoryor new economic growth theory①. Is a faster technological progress better? In addition, does a faster technical progress mean it is better? It may be tempting to say "yes", but according to the concept of endogenous economic growth, the answer is "no". The argument is that rational people will choose the best path of technological progress, thus, fast technological progress is not necessarily ideal.

It is important to note that endogenous growth theory often leaves the government

① For an overview of Endogenous Growth Theory, see Pan Shiyuan and Shi Jinchuan (2002).

aside when studying the optimal technological path①. If the government can choose (or influence) the rate of technological progress through certain policies, it is not meaningful to ask if the progress of technology faster the better. This is mainly because in the economic reality, governments always regard the pursuit of rapid technological advances (high economic growth rates) as the most important goal. The role of the governments of developing countries in promoting technological progress is far greater than that of developed countries, therefore, the study of the optimal technological progress rate is more practical for developing countries. For example, since China's accession to the WTO, under the pressure of developed countries, the protection of intellectual property rights is increasing, but few people study the impact of intellectual property protection on China's technological progress and the level of people's welfare, as well as factors to be considered by China in the implementation of intellectual property protection.

According to Schumpter (1942), it has been widely believed that in order to stimulate innovation, it should give the innovator a certain amount of monopoly power. The patent system is a common system arrangement that gives the innovator monopoly power. Therefore, if the government wants to increase the rate of technological progress, then the protection of the patent system needs to be strengthened. Meanwhile, because the patent system that gives innovators market monopoly power will distort the allocation of social resources, enhancing the protection of the patent system will lead to a reduction in social welfare. As a result, high technological progress rates may not maximize the level of social welfare. The purpose of this study is to build a model that captures the endogenous economic growth of China. This consists of investigated the rate at which optimal technological progress occurred, which consists of identifying the role that the government placed in maximizing the social welfare as representing patent protection.

The study found a high rate of technological progress, which does not necessarily maximize social welfare. Therefore, the goal pursued by governments is not necessarily appropriate. Furthermore, we also will study the various factors that the government should consider when implementing the patent system, and analyze the enlightenment of the model conclusion on this basis. Next, we will then discuss the

---

① Some economists have studied the role of government in economic growth. For example, Barro (1990) studied the optimal tax rate and optimal economic growth rate that the government should choose in order to maximize social welfare. But his model is a simple AK model, and long-term economic growth does not take advantage of endogenous technological advances.

conclusion of this study.

2.1.2 Optimal technological progress rate

In a closed economy with a total population of L, everyone has no flexibility to provide 1 unit of labor to earn income and maximize utility:

$$U = \int_0^{\infty} \ln C(t) \cdot e^{-pt} dt \tag{1}$$

Where $C(t)$ represents the total consumption of consumers during the period t, and p represents the time discount rate. Equivalent consumption growth rate can be obtained by equation (1):

$$\dot{C}/C = r - \rho \tag{2}$$

Where, r represents the interest rate. Equation (2) shows that the lower the time discount rate, the higher the growth rate of consumption; on the contrary, the lower the growth rate of consumption. Low time discount rate means that the higher the substitutability of future consumption on the current consumption, the more profitable postponed consumption. Therefore, consumers will reduce the current consumption and increase the future consumption, thereby increasing the consumption growth rate.

Along with the research ideas of Dixit & Stigliz (1977) and Romer (1990), it is assumed that the production function of the i-th final product manufacturer is:

$$Y_i = L_i^{1-\alpha} \int_0^A (X_{ij})^{\alpha} dj \tag{3}$$

Where Y_i represents the output of the i-th manufacturer; L_i represents the labor input; X_{ij} denotes the input amount of the j-th intermediate product of the i-th manufacturer; A represents the number of intermediate products, that is, the technical knowledge level of a country, $0 < \alpha < 1$. This production function shows the diminishing marginal returns of labor inputs L_i and intermediate products inputs X_{ij}, but for all the input factors, the scale of income isunchanged.

After the invention of intermediate products, manufacturers are given a patent. As with the general endogenous growth model, this study assumes that the length of the patent is indefinite for the convenience of analysis and without loss of generality①. However, unlike general endogenous growth model, this study also describes different definitions of patent widths of vendor patent scholars from the

① Pan Shiyuan (2005) studies have shown that infinite patent length is not optimal. Assuming that the length of the patent is limited, it will not change the main conclusions of this study.

perspective of patent width. This study defines thepatent width as a difference between the characteristics of other non-infringing products and the characteristics of the patented product, along with the idea of Klemperer (1990)①. In this definition, it can be argued that the width of the patent is larger when the greater the difference between the quality of the imitated product and the patented product and when there is no infringement; on the other hand, the smaller the quality level of the imitated product and the patented product. In fact, the definition of patent width in this study is consistent with Gilbert & Shaplro (1990) who define the patent width as the ability of companies to raise the price of patented products. Obviously, the greater the imbalance between the quality of the imitated product and the patented product, the smaller the potential threat to the patented product, so the vendor can raise the price of the patented product; otherwise, the manufacturer can only make a lower price for the patented product. In this study, the government can influence the level of social welfare by selecting the patent width to influence the incentives for innovation. In other words, in this study, we argue that the government needs to balance the positive and negative effects of strengthening patent protection on the economy, thus selecting the optimal rate of technological progress.

Assuming that the manufacturer invented the cost of an intermediate product with a quality level of 1 is the final product Y in unit η; imitated product does not need to bear the R&D costs, but the quality level of the product is $0 \leqslant q \leqslant 1$. The marginal production costs of patented product and imitated product are 1 unit of final product Y②. Accordingly, $0 \leqslant \frac{1}{q} - 1 \leqslant \infty$ can be used to represent the patent width. That is, when the patent width is infinite, the quality level of the imitated product is $q = 0$; when the patent width is 0, the quality level of the imitated product is the same as that of the patented product, that is, $q = 1$.

From equation (3), when the price of the j-th intermediate product is p_j, the demand for the i-th intermediate product manufacturer for j-th intermediate products is:

$$X_{ij} = L_i \cdot (\alpha/p_j)^{1/(1-\alpha)} \tag{4}$$

The total market demand for the i-th intermediate product is given by equation (4):

① For definitions and measurements of different patent widths, see Denicolò (1996).

② Of course, in reality, even if the patent width is infinite, imitation vendors may also imitate the quality of products higher than 0. However, this does not change the conclusions of this study.

$$X_j = \sum_i X_{ij} = L \cdot (\alpha/p_j)^{1/(1-\alpha)} \quad (5)$$

Since the marginal cost of producing intermediate products is 1 unit of the final product, it is known from equation (5) that if there is no imitated product, then the monopoly price of the intermediate product is:

$$p_j = p = 1/\alpha \quad (6)$$

If there is imitated product, then for the sake of analysis, it is assumed that the intermediate products produced by the invention vendor and the intermediate products produced by the imitators are completely replaced. Accordingly, along with the research findings of Grossman & Helpman (1991), it is assumed that invention vendors and imitators have a Betrand price competition in the market. Because 1 unit imitated product is only equivalent to q unit invention vendor produced by the intermediate products, so if the quality level of imitated product is $q \geqslant \alpha$, then the invention vendor will price the j-thintermediate product as:

$$p_j = \frac{1}{q} \quad (7)$$

Accordingly, if the quality level of imitated product is $q < \alpha$, then the invention vendor will price the j-thintermediate product as:

$$p_j = \frac{1}{\alpha} \quad (8)$$

From equation (7), when the quality level of imitated product is $q > \alpha$, if the invention vendorprice its intermediate product as $\frac{1}{q} - \delta \cdot \frac{1}{q}$. If δ is any small positive real number, then imitated manufacturer can only produce its own intermediate products priced as $1 - \delta$, and at this time, imitated manufacturer has to withdraw from the market because it is impossible to obtain positive profits. Therefore, as long as the intermediate product is priced at $1/q$, invention vendor can have a permanent monopoly power. That is, when the patent width is not infinite, imitated product has a certain level of quality, in order to obtain monopoly profits, invent vendor will expose the imitated product out of the market by depressing the price. Correspondingly, it can be seen from equation (8) that when the patent width reaches a certain level, the quality level of imitated product is low, even if invent vendor sets the monopoly price to $1/\alpha$, Imitated manufacturer still cannot get a positive profit, and therefore has to withdraw from the market.

When the quality level of imitated product is $q < \alpha$, the change in the quality level of imitated product does not affect the pricing of patented product, and thus does not affect the entire economy. In other words, when the patent width is greater than $\frac{1}{\alpha} - 1$, the patent width of the change will not have an impact on the economy. Therefore, we only analyze the optimal patent width problem when the imitated product quality level is $q \geqslant \alpha$. When the price of the j-th intermediate product is $p_j = 1/q$, the total market demand of the j-th intermediate product is obtained from equation (5):

$$X_j = \sum_i X_{ij} = L \cdot (\alpha q)^{1/(1-\alpha)} \tag{9}$$

As the length of the patent is infinite, the present value of monopoly profits of the manufacturer is:

$$V = \int_t^{\infty} (1/q - 1) L(\alpha q)^{1/(1-\alpha)} e^{-\bar{r}(v,t)(v-t)} dv \tag{10}$$

In which, $\bar{r}(v,t) = \int_t^v r(u) du/(v-t)$ represents the average interest rate between time t and v. Assuming that the R & D market entry is completely free, each manufacturer can obtain the invention of the new intermediate product by paying the fixed cost η. Thus, the present value of the monopoly profit of the invention vendor should be equal to the fixed cost, that is:

From equation (5), we can see that the equilibrium interest rate satisfies:

$$\eta = \int_t^{\infty} (1/q - 1) L(\alpha q)^{1/(1-\alpha)} e^{-\bar{r}(v,t)(v-t)} dv \tag{11}$$

$$r = (L/\eta)(1/q - 1)(\alpha q)^{1/(1-\alpha)} \tag{12}$$

In order to study the problem of the optimal technological progress rate, it is necessary to analyze the relationship between the rate of technological progress and the level of social welfare. This depends on whether there is a transition in economic growth.

Proposition 1: Transitional dynamics does not exist in economic growth, the economy reached equilibrium at the outset, and the equilibrium rate of technological progress is $g = r - \rho$.

In fact, this model can eventually be transformed into an AK model. Thus, similar to the AK model, there is no transitional dynamics in economic growth, that is, the total (per capita) consumption, total (per capita) production and technical knowledge are growing at a balanced rate at the beginning①. As the transition dynamics does not exist ineconomic growth, therefore, on the basis of proposition 1,

① For a detailed analysis of the dynamics of the AK model, see Barro and Sala-i-Martin (1995).

the welfare level of the whole society can be calculated. So, there is proposition 2.

Proposition 2: The overall level of social welfare is:

$$W = \frac{\ln[\eta(\phi - g)A(0)]}{\rho} + \frac{g}{\rho^2} \tag{13}$$

In which, $\phi = \frac{L}{\eta}(\alpha)^{\frac{\alpha}{1-\alpha}}(q^{\frac{\alpha}{1-\alpha}} - \alpha q^{\frac{1}{1-\alpha}})$.

Due to patent the width will affect the rate of technological progress, therefore, Proposition 1 and Proposition 2 shows that the overall level of social welfare is related to the rate of technological progress. Equation (2) and (12), a wider patent width will promote innovation, thereby increasing the rate of technological progress. This will increase the value of g/ρ^2, thereby raising the level of social welfare. At the same time, by the expression equation of φ, the wider patent width will cause greater distortions on the market to reduce consumption, that is, to reduce $\eta(\varphi - g)A(0)$, thereby reducing the level of social welfare. Therefore, the government in pursuit of social welfare maximization can choose the optimal rate of technological progress.

Proposition 3: The optimal technological progress rate that maximizes social welfare is $g^* = (L/\eta)\alpha^{\frac{\alpha}{1-\alpha}}[(q^*)^{\frac{\alpha}{1-\alpha}} - (q^*)^{\frac{1}{1-\alpha}}] - \rho$, in which, $\alpha < q^* < 1$ is the solution of the equation $(L/\eta)\alpha^{\frac{\alpha}{1-\alpha}}q^{\frac{\alpha}{1-\alpha}}(q - \alpha) = \rho$.

2.1.3 Influencing factors of optimal technological progress rate and its enlightenment to China

Proposition 3 shows that the optimal technological progress rate is related to the total population of a country, the cost of producing intermediate products, and the patent width. Since q^* is the solution of the equation $(L/\eta)\alpha^{\frac{\alpha}{1-\alpha}}q^{\frac{\alpha}{1-\alpha}}(q - \alpha) = \rho$, therefore, $dq^*/d\eta > 0$. At the same time, the optimal technological progress rate is $g^* = (L/\eta)\alpha^{\frac{\alpha}{1-\alpha}}[(q^*)^{\frac{\alpha}{1-\alpha}} - (q^*)^{\frac{\alpha}{1-\alpha}}] - \rho$, therefore, $dg^*/d\eta < 0$. This suggests that the higher the cost of inventions, a country should maintain a relatively low rate of technological progress. The higher the invention cost is, the weaker the effect of strengthening patent protection on social welfare. Therefore, in order to maximize social welfare, the government should properly decrease the patent protection to reduce the degree of market distortions, which were caused by patent system; on the other hand, the government should also decrease the patent protection and thus reduce the patented product pricing. This will allow more end-product manufacturers can enjoy the benefits brought about by technological progress. Accordingly, if the invention costs are high, then in order to pursue the maximization of social welfare, a country should hold a relatively low rate of technological progress.

Since q^* is the solution of the equation $(L/\eta)\alpha^{\frac{\alpha}{1-\alpha}}q^{\frac{\alpha}{1-\alpha}}(q-\alpha) = \rho$, therefore, $dq^*/dL < 0$. At the same time, the optimal technological progress rate is $g^* = (L/\eta)\alpha^{\frac{\alpha}{1-\alpha}}[(q^*)^{\frac{\alpha}{1-\alpha}} - (q^*)^{\frac{1}{1-\alpha}}] - \rho$, therefore, $dg^*/dL > 0$. Thus, this suggests that the larger the total population, a country should maintain a relatively high rate of technological progress. In this study, we found that the invention cost has nothing to do with the total population; when people invent an intermediate product, the per capita cost is reduced as the population size expands, that is, the population has a scale effect. In other words, the expansion of population size is equivalent to the decline in inventive costs. Therefore, when the population size is expanded, a country should properly strengthen patent protection and improve the rate of technological progress.

China is a developing country with a large population, but relatively limited in its aterial capital and human capital respectively. In particular, invention and innovation are economic activities that require materials and human capital as important investments. Compared with other more developed countries, the cost of invention and innovation in China is relatively high. As a result, we argue that the Chinese government should reduce the protection costs of patents. On the one hand, this would reduce the degree of market distortions as caused by granting invention vendor the patent rights. On the other hand, this would also allow the reduction of cost for patented products, which would provide more incentives for customers. Therefore, we argue that due to the huge population size of China should gradually strengthen the protection of patents which would allow its people to enjoy the welfare improvement brought on by inventions. In other words, China's policy should consist of the following: China at this stage should be appropriate to reduce the protection of patents, then, with the rapid economic development, the protection of patents can be continuously strengthened. Since China's accession to the WTO, under the pressure of developed countries, intellectual property protection is increasingly strengthened, which may be able to promote China's invention①. However, we must be soberly

① If considering that lots of innovation nationally is obtained based on the digestion and absorption of foreign technology, so the cost at introduction of technology might be increased via the enhancement of implementation of property right protection, thus it will go against the technology innovation.

aware that, from the stage of economic development in our country, overly stringent intellectual property protectionmay make our people can not fully enjoy the benefits of technology, thereby reducing the welfare level of our people. Therefore, China should correctly handle the positive and negative effects of patent protection within the framework of the WTO "A greement on Trade-Related Aspects of Intellectual Property Rights" (TRIPs Agreement).

2.1.4 Conclusions

Overall, it is clear that governments regard the pursuit of rapid technological advances as the most important goal. However, does this mean that faster technological progress is better? Within the framework of endogenous growth theory, this study builds a model to study what the optimal technological progress rate that the government should choose when is choosing the degree of patent protection to maximize social welfare. The conclusion shows that the answer to the question that whether the faster the technological progress the better is negative. There is no doubt that the increase in technological progress will increase the level of social welfare in the event of other conditions unchanged. It is clear that the government needs to increase the rate of technological progress by strengthening the protection of the patent system. Because market monopoly power of innovators granted by the patent system will distort the allocation of social resources, the strengthening of the protection of the patent system will lead to the reduction of social welfare. Therefore, the high technological progress rate does not maximize the level of social welfare.

This study also shows that: (1) while the cost of new technology is continuously increasing, one country has maintained a relatively low rate of technological progress. When invention costs run high, it is weak to strengthen the patent protection to improve the social welfare function. Therefore, the government should reduce the patent protection in order to reduce the extent of market distortions resulting from the patent system, which should improve the level of social welfare. Additionally, when invention costs are high, the government should appropriately reduce the patent protection. This makes potentially imitated manufacturers a threat to the inventor, forcing the inventor to reduce the pricing of patented products. This results in more end-product manufacturers and consumers enjoying the benefits of technological progress and improving the level of social welfare. (2) In this study, since the cost of invention is not related to the total population. Thus, when people invent an intermediate product, the cost per capita is reduced as the population size expands. In other words, the expansion of population size is equivalent to a decline in inventive costs. Therefore, when a country's population is large, officials should properly strengthen patent protections and improve the technological progress rate.

This study is more applicable to developing countries because the role their governments play in promoting technological progress is far greater than that of developed countries. For example, since China's accession to the WTO, and due to pressure from developed countries, the protection of intellectual property rights is increasing. However, few people have studied the impact of intellectual property protection on China's technological progress and people's welfare, as well as factors to be considered in the implementation of intellectual property protection in China. This study shows that due to China's accession into the WTO, and the subsequent pressure placed by developed countries, there has been a shift towards increasing the protection of intellectual property rights, which in turn, encourages and promotes technological innovation in China. However, we must be cautious of being too harsh with intellectual property protection. From the stage of economic development in our country, strict intellectual property protection may make our people fail to enjoy the benefits of technology, thereby reducing the welfare of our people. Of course, due to the large population size and rapid economic development, China should gradually strengthen the protection of patents and enjoy the welfare improvement brought about by inventions.

2.2 Information asymmetry, adverse selection and private economic development

2.2.1 Introduction

Although the theory of economic growth has been around for a long time it remains an important topic in the study of economics. Harold (1939) and Dorma (1946) establish the basis of modern economic growth theory, as it marks the application of mathematical methodology to economic growth theory. However, the assumption of the fixed coefficient production function leads to the fact that their models can only be balanced on the edge of the blade, which is not very consistent with the economic reality.

Solo (1956) and Swan (1956) amended this hypothesis and replaced it with a neoclassical production function that could be fully replaced between the elements of production. Each independently established a model of economic growth, which is often referred to as the Solo-Swan model and is the second revolution of economic growth theory. However, because of the diminishing marginal returns of production factors, economic growth requires exogenous technological advances in the long run.

Perhaps due to limitations in the theory of economic growth and the lack of corresponding empirical research, the study of economic growth theory remained silent for almost 20 years. That is until the pioneering study of Romer (1986) and Lucas (1988), which revived economic growth theory and caused a boom in research①. This marked the difference of technical assumptions between birth of the theory of endogenous economic growth and the exogenous neo-classical economic growth theory. In the theory of endogenous economic growth, technological progress is born in a country's economic system, with a national research and development investment and other contributing factors.

For over the two decades that economic growth theory laid dormant, information economics made significant progress. Akerlof (1970) first pointed out that due to asymmetric information quality on the market, consumers have to average quality pricing. This results in high quality products being expelled from the market by low quality products, resulting in market atrophy and the loss of social welfare. Since then, Spencer (1973), Rothschild and Stiglitz (1976), Stiglitz and Weiss (1981) have studied the labor and insurance markets and information asymmetry in financial markets. Spencer (2002) and Stiglitz (2002) reviewed the development of information economics.

The development of information economics has also attracted the attention of researchers of economic growth theory. Due to the existence of asymmetric information, it is necessary for individuals to spend a lot of money in order to accurately understand an enterprise, which hinders the effective allocation of capital. Therefore, when the financial intermediaries collect information about enterprises, the financial intermediaries have economies of scale and can reduce the cost of information, resulting in efficient allocation of capital and economic growth

---

① For defailed information on Endogenous Growth Theory, see Pan Shiyi and Shi Jinchuan (2002).

(Greenwood & Jovanovic, 1990; King & Levine, 1993)[1].

The information asymmetry between the owner and the manager will lead to the problem of corporate governance as outlined by the principal-agent theory. Because the information has the nature of a public product, the financial intermediary has economies of scale in collecting information about the company. This information allows the owner of the company to supervise the company manager and improve corporate governance, thereby increasing the enthusiasm of money holders to buy the company's stock or bonds. This ultimately promotes capital accumulation and economic growth (Bencivenga & Smith, 1993).

When the investment of high-return projects in the economy is inseparable and huge, it is very important to mobilize the capital of the whole society in the process of economic growth. In order to better mobilize the capital of the whole society, we need to reduce the cost of mobilizing social idle capital. On the other hand, we need to reduce the information asymmetry, so that the savers can be assured to hand over the right to use capital. Sirri & Tufano (1995) show that banks are economically viable in raising social idle capital in order to reduce the cost of raising money. In addition, the credibility of banks and others will often make savers pay capital to it. Accordingly, Acemoglu & Zilibotti (1997) argue that financial arrangements conducive to capital mobilization, such as financial intermediaries, promote economic growth.

However, the asymmetry of the final product quality information on the intermediate product market and the impact of economic development have not yet attracted the attention of growth theory scholars. The World Bank (1998) noted that in developing countries, the final product quality information asymmetry is one of the more serious problems hindering economic development, as it leads to adverse selection and low quality final consumer goods will drive higher quality consumer goods out of the market. This is because low-quality final consumer goods, compared to high-quality consumer goods, contain high levels of technology (knowledge). This result in the final selection of consumer goods market expelling high-tech and high-quality consumer goods from the market, reducing the price of knowledge and investment in R&D. In the theory of economic growth, R&D investment is an important source of knowledge and economic growth. Accordingly, the impact of

---

① Levin (2004) excellently summarizes the theory and empirical literatures related to the relationship between the finance and economic growth.

information asymmetry on knowledge may have a far-reaching impact on the economy (as compared to information asymmetry) leading to the shrinking of the final product market. Therefore, this study constructs an endogenous economic growth model to analyze the effects of asymmetric quality information on knowledge growth and private economy development. The model's conclusions show that: the asymmetry of quality information will not only lead to the shrinking of the final private economic products market, but also reduce the pricing of knowledge products, which in turn, reduces the investment of R&D. This ultimately hinders the growth of knowledge in a country, as this knowledge determines the long-term economic growth of a country. Therefore, the asymmetry of quality information on knowledge innovation will have a far-reaching negative impact on a country's private economy. At the same time, because the information asymmetry will reduce the level of social welfare of a country, the community will give birth to system arrangements to solve the problem of information asymmetry, so as to promote a country's private economic development.

First, the impact of information asymmetry on the market of knowledge products is analyzed. Second, the knowledge growth and the development of a private economy is examined, and the influence of information asymmetry on the growth of knowledge and the development of private economy is analyzed. Thirdl, the endogenous problems of the system, and the impact of these solutions to the asymmetric information on economic development will be studied. Finally, a brief policy recommendation is put forward.

2.2.2 Information asymmetry and private economy development

The final consumer product quality market with information asymmetry may have different levels of quality of final consumer goods. Consumers cannot know exactly the level of quality of every specific consumer product in the market. However, consumers can know the quality of the product they buy after spending. According to this, assuming that the total population of a country's population is L, each person has no flexibility to provide 1 unit of labor to obtain income, thus maximizing utility:

$$U = \int_0^{\infty} \left[\frac{(C_1(t) + qC_w(t))^{1-\varepsilon} - 1}{1-\varepsilon}\right] e^{-\rho t} dt \qquad (1)$$

Among them, $C_1(t)$ and $C_W(t)$ represent the consumer's consumption of low-quality and high-quality consumer goods at time t, q indicates the high-quality level of consumer goods, and ε and ρ represent the reciprocal of cross-time alternative cost and time discount rates respectively. In the following section of the study, the time tt is omitted in the equation in order to avoid confusion.

The final consumer product needs to be put into the intermediate product, assuming that the intermediate product manufacturers can provide both high and low quality intermediate products, and accordingly, along the research approach of Romer (1990) and Grossman & Helpman (1991), assuming that the production function of the jth final consumer goods firm is:

$$Y_{wj} = L_{wj}^{1-\alpha}\int_0^{A_w}[X_{wj}(i)]^{\alpha}di \tag{2}$$

Or

$$Y_{1j} = L_{1j}^{1-\alpha}\int_0^{A_1}[X_{1j}(i)]^{\alpha}di \tag{3}$$

Among them, $0 < \alpha < 1$, L_{wj} represents the amount of labor input when the j-th final consumer product maker produces high quality consumer goods, X_{wj} (i) represents the amount of high quality intermediate product invested when the j-th final consumer goods manufacturer produces high quality consumer goods, and the quality level of high quality final consumer goods is $q > 1$. Accordingly, L_{1j}represents the amount of labor input when the j-th final consumer goods manufacturer produces low quality raw materials, X_{lj} (i) represents the amount of low quality intermediate product when the j-th final consumer product manufacturer produces low quality consumer goods, the quality level of the low quality final consumer product is 1, A_w and A_1 represent the number of high quality intermediate products and low quality intermediate products, respectively①. Since the expansion in the number of intermediate products means that new knowledge is generated, A_W and A_1 represent the total amount of high-quality and low-quality knowledge of a country, respectively.

Assuming the invention costs of high quality intermediate products is $q\eta_w$, the unit low-quality final product is Y_1, the invention cost of a low quality intermediate product is η_1, unit final product is Y_1, $q\eta_w > \eta_l$, but $\eta_w < \eta_l$. This suggests that the absolute cost of inventing high quality intermediate products is higher than the cost of

① Mistakes in one part of the production process may greatly reduce the quality of the product. In addition, the price of high quality intermediate products is often higher than the price of low quality intermediate products. Therefore, in the production of consumer goods, manufacturers should either put all into high-quality intermediate products, or put all into low-quality intermediate products.

inventing low quality intermediate products, but the cost per unit mass is lower[①]. If the cost per unit mass of invented high quality intermediate products is higher than the cost per unit mass cost of inventing low quality intermediate products, then through the consumer preferences and manufacturers of production technology we see that the invention cost of high-quality intermediate product is high. Thus, inventing high-quality intermediate products fail to promote economic development, thereby improving the level of social welfare and society will not give birth to some system arrangements to eliminate information asymmetry. However, in reality, we can see many arrangements have been made to eliminate information asymmetry. This research assumes that $\eta_w < \eta_1$, once the new product $X_w(i)$ or $X_1(i)$) is produced, the intermediate product manufacturers will always hold a monopoly over market power, and assume that the marginal cost of producing one unit of high-quality intermediate product is $q>1$ unit low-quality final consumer goods Y_1, while the marginal cost of producing a unit of low quality intermediate products is one unit low-quality final consumer goods Y_1.

Due to the existence of asymmetric quality information, consumers cannot know exactly the quality level of each specific final consumer product in the market. As a result, consumers price the expected average quality of the products in the market to purchase final consumer goods (including high quality final consumer goods and low quality final consumer goods). Because of the quality information asymmetry in final product market, consumers engage in single pricing in accordance with the average quality of high-quality, final consumer goods and low-quality final consumer goods. This leads to final consumer goods manufacturers knowing the quality of the intermediate products, and they are willing to pay the price of low-quality intermediate products in order to purchase high-quality intermediate products, thus lowering the price of high-quality knowledge. At this point, the cost of inventing high-quality intermediate products and the marginal cost of producing high-quality intermediate products is higher than the cost of inventing low-quality intermediate products and the marginal cost of producing low-quality intermediate products. This results in high-quality intermediate products being expelled from the market. In other words, the information asymmetry of the final consumer product quality ultimately

① In general, from the history of scientific and technological progress, mankind is always producing the low-quality intermediate products, prior to high-quality intermediate products. Thus, even if the low quality intermediate product is patented, the high quality intermediate product can be protected by the patent system on the basis of product quality improvement (Aghion & Howitt, 1998).

leads to the failure of high-quality intermediate products in market competition, and rational manufacturers will not invent and produce high quality intermediate product at the beginning of the economy (that is, at time 0)①.

Lemma 1: If there is an asymmetry in the final consumer goods market then when the market reaches equilibrium, only low-quality intermediates are sold②.

Since intermediate products are the input factor for the production of final consumer goods, when the market reaches equilibrium only low-quality final products are sold.

Lemma 2: If the final consumer goods market has asymmetric quality information, low quality final consumer goods will expel high-quality final consumer goods out of the market. In other words, when the market reaches equilibrium, only low-quality consumer goods are sold in the market.

The studies above show that the asymmetry of quality information led to high-quality final consumer goods being expelled from the market, eventually shrinking the market, and resulting in social welfare losses. However, this will also reduce the price of knowledge, R & D and reduces the balanced economic growth rate, indirectly resulting in social welfare losses. The first effect of the asymmetry of quality information on social welfare is emphasized by Akorov et al., yet they have not noticed the second effect of information asymmetry on social welfare, because they are not aware of the interaction between the final consumer goods market and the intermediate product market, which is what this research emphasizes.

When there is asymmetry of quality information, because high-quality intermediate products will be defeated by market competition, rational manufacturers (in the beginning of the economy) will not invent and produce high-quality

---

① Although the quality information of intermediate products market is completely symmetrical, when the market of final consumer goods have quality information asymmetry, the final consumer goods manufacturers do single pricing for high quality of intermediate products and low quality products. This is exactly similar to the intermediate product market which also has the quality of asymmetric information. Of course, if the time of the game between consumers and manufacturers is unlimited and the time discount rate is low, then when the market reaches equilibrium, the final consumer goods manufacturers will faithfully disclose the product quality information, so as to reach a cooperation between the Nash equilibrium. At this point, there will be no product quality information asymmetry. Since this study examines the impact of asymmetry of quality information on economic growth and social welfare, it is assumed that the discount rate is high and the Nash equilibrium with cooperation is excluded. In addition, even if some of the old product quality information asymmetry problems are resolved, the new product quality information asymmetry problem remains; therefore, it can be considered that the quality information asymmetry problem always exists.

② Interested readers can contact the task group to obtain the proof of lemma and proposition.

intermediate products. So, at time 0 only low quality intermediate products and low quality final products are sold in the market. At this point, if the purchase price of the low quality intermediate product X_1 (i) is P_1 (i), then the j-th final consumer product manufacturer will pursue profit maximization:

$$\max_{X_{1j}} \int_0^{A_1} [L_{1j}^{1-\alpha} X_{1j}(i)^{\alpha} - P_1(i) X_{1j}(i) - L_{1j} \cdot w] di \qquad (4)$$

Where w is the wage level, and the demand for low-quality intermediate products is determined by the first-order conditions that maximize the profit:

$$X_{1j}(i) = L_{1j}(\alpha/P_1(i))^{1/(1-\alpha)} \qquad (5)$$

Therefore, the market demand for the i-th intermediate product is:

$$X(i) = (\alpha/P_1(i))^{1/(1-\alpha)} \sum_j L_{1j} = L(\alpha/P_1(i))^{1/(1-\alpha)} \qquad (6)$$

Since the marginal cost of producing 1 unit of the i-th low-quality intermediate product is one unit Y_1, the manufacturer of intermediate production will maximize its profit by selecting the production of the i-th low-quality intermediate product:

$$(P_1(i) - 1) L(\alpha/P_1(i))^{1/(1-\alpha)} \qquad (7)$$

The monopoly price of the i-th intermediate product can be obtained from (7):

$$P_1(i) = P_1 = 1/\alpha \qquad (8)$$

Substituting (8) into (6) yields the market demand for the i-th intermediate product:

$$X_1(i) = X_1 = L\alpha^{2/(1-\alpha)} \qquad (9)$$

Since the intermediate product is completely symmetrical in this study, the monopoly profits of any low quality intermediate product invented at time tt are:

$$\pi = \int_t^{\infty} (P_1(i) - 1) X_1(i) e^{-\bar{r}(s,t)(s-t)} ds = L\left(\frac{1-\alpha}{\alpha}\right)\alpha^{2/(1-\alpha)} \int_1^{\infty} e^{-\bar{r}(s,t)(s-t)} ds \qquad (10)$$

Of which, $\bar{r}(s,t) = \int_t^s (u) du/(s-t)$ represents the average interest rate between t and s. Equation (10) shows that only when the price P_1 of the intermediate product exceeds the cost of production 1, the firm can make up for the cost of inventing, that is η_1, the new intermediate product by obtaining monopoly profits.

If the manufacturers in the invention market of new products, where manufacturers can freely enter and exit and invent low-quality products, the cost should be equal to it can get monopoly profits, namely:

$$\pi_1 = L\left(\frac{1-\alpha}{\alpha}\right)\alpha^{2(1-\alpha)} \int_1^{\infty} e^{-\bar{r}(s,t)(s-t)} ds = \eta_1 \qquad (11)$$

Equation (11) shows that for any time t, the invention of the monopoly profits should be equal to the cost of inventions η_1, so a balanced interest rate can be obtained:

$$r_1 = (L/\eta_1)\left(\frac{1-\alpha}{\alpha}\right)\alpha^{2(1-\alpha)} \tag{12}$$

When the economy reaches equilibrium, there is only low-quality products in the market-the final consumer goods are sold, (1) will change into:

$$U_1 = \int_0^{\infty}\left[\frac{(C(t))^{1-\varepsilon}-1}{1-\varepsilon}\right]e^{-\rho t}dt \tag{13}$$

The optimum consumption growth rate can be obtained by (13):

$$g_c = \frac{1}{\varepsilon}(r_1 - \rho) \tag{14}$$

Substituting (12), we can obtain:

$$g_1 = g_c = \frac{1}{\varepsilon}\left[(L/\eta_1)\left(\frac{\alpha}{1-\alpha}\right)\alpha^{2/(1-\alpha)} - \rho\right] \tag{15}$$

According to equation (15), the social welfare level can be obtained when the asymmetry of the quality information exists in the field.

Proposition 1: When there is an asymmetry of quality information, the level of social welfare is:

$$U_1 = 1/(1-\varepsilon)\{[\eta_1(\varphi_1 - g_1)A_1(0)]^{1-\varepsilon}/(\rho-(1-\varepsilon)g_1) - 1/\rho\} \tag{16}$$

Where $\varphi_1 = (L/\eta_1)(\alpha)^{2\alpha/(1-\alpha)}(1-\alpha^2)$, $A_1(0)$ represents the number of low quality intermediate products at time 0.

2.2.3 Symmetric information and the development of private economy

Based on the research above, it is necessary to study steady state economic growth rates and social welfare under symmetric quality information. Therefore, we can compare to the situation of asymmetric information in order to understand its influence on the knowledge products market and economic development.

Lemma 3: If there is no asymmetry of quality information, only high quality finished consumable products could be sold in the market it is balanced.

When there is no asymmetry of quality information, consumers would buy products of varying qulity at different prices. As a result, only the high quality intermediate consumable and high quality finished consumable products could be sold in the market at the beginning (when the time is 0) because of the relatively low cost and high profit of inventing high quality intermediate consumables①.

When there was no asymmetry of quality information, for the convenience of analysis, we regard high quality finished consumables as basic numeraire in the economy②. Similar to the analysis above, we can know that the price of high quality intermediate consumable is:

$$P_w(i) = P_w = 1/\alpha \tag{17}$$

Equation (17) indicates that when there was no asymmetry of quality information, the price of high quality intermediate consumable is q/α unit Y_1. Equation (8) indicates that when there was asymmetry of quality information, the price of low quality (high quality) intermediate consumable is $1/\alpha$ unit Y_1. It indicates that asymmetry of quality information could cause a decrease in the price of knowledge products③.

Equation (17) indicates that the market demand of high quality intermediate consumable is:

$$X_w(i) = X_w = L\alpha^{2/(1-\alpha)} \tag{18}$$

Equation (18) indicates that the market demand of high quality intermediate consumable is $q \cdot L\alpha^{2/(1-\alpha)}$ unit Y_1. Equation (9) indicates that the market demand of low quality intermediate consumable is $L\alpha^{2/(1-\alpha)}$ unit Y_1. It indicates that asymmetry of quality information could cause shrinkage of intermediate consumable market and finished consumable market.

Being the same as the calculation above, the market equilibrium rate is:

$$r_w = (L/\eta_w)\left(\frac{1-\alpha}{\alpha}\right)\alpha^{2/(1-\alpha)} \tag{19}$$

---

① Certainly, in real life, when the information is symmetric, due to the different preferences and budgets of consumers, low quality intermediate consumables could be sold in the market. However, this would not change the conclusions of this research.

② Knew form the formula of consumer's utility, when the information is symmetric, one unit of high-quality finished products Yw equals to q units of low-quality finished products Y_1. Therefore, we can use low-quality products as numeraire. It should be noted that thelow-quality finished products will not exist when the information is symmetric. Therefore, if we consider low-quality finished products as numeraire with price 1, then this price is the shadow price.

③ Certainly, it is possible that the finished consumable manufacturer buy the high quality intermediate consumable to produce high quality finished consumable and adulterate as producing low quality finished consumable. In the meanwhile, compared to the situation of no asymmetry of quality information, the number of high quality intermediate consumable bought by the finished consumable manufacturer decrease, then the profit of producing high quality intermediate consumable decrease. Finally, the asymmetry of quality information could cause the decrease of the price of knowledge products.

It will be seen form this that the growth rate of market equilibrium is:

$$g_w = g_c = \frac{1}{\varepsilon}\left[(L/\eta_w)\left(\frac{1-a}{\alpha}\right)\alpha^{2/(1-\alpha)} - \rho\right] \quad (20)$$

Equation (15) and (20) indicate that when comparing the situations where (1) the cost of per unit inventing of high quality intermediate consumables is lower than the one of low quality intermediate consumables, which means $\eta_w < \eta_l$, to (2) the situation of asymmetry of quality information of finished consumable, the growth rate of market equilibrium with symmetric of quality information will be higher. This means $g_w > g_1$. In other words, asymmetry of quality information could cause a decrease in the price of knowledge products, reducing the input of R&D and dampening economic development.

Based on the analysis above, we can determine social welfare in the condition of symmetry of quality information.

Proposition 2: When there was no asymmetry of quality information, social welfare is:

$$U_w = \frac{1}{1-\varepsilon}\left\{\frac{[(\eta_L + L\alpha^{2/1-\alpha})\eta_w(\varphi_w - g_w)A_1(0)/(\eta_w + L\alpha^{2/1-\alpha})]^{1-\varepsilon}}{\rho - (1-\omega)g_w} - \frac{1}{\rho}\right\} \quad (21)$$

Among it, $\varphi_w = (L/\eta_w)(\alpha)^{2\alpha/(1-\alpha)}(1-\alpha^2)$.

Comparing propositions 1 and proposition 2, we can determine that there is asymmetry of quality information, which influences society welfare in two ways. On one hand, it could influence the market capacity, impacting societial welfare, while on the other hand, influencing the growth rate and price of knowledge, having an impact on long term economic growth rate andsocietial welfare. Asymmetry of quality information could result in the shrinkage of the market, thereby reducing the welfare of society. It is to say that when the quality information is symmetric, market capacity is larger and society welfare is higher. In the meanwhile, when the quality information is complete, under the condition of symmetry of quality information, the long term economic growth rate would be higher, which is beneficial for the improvement of societial welfare. Thus, there is the proposition 3.

Proposition 3: $U_w > U_1$

With simple calculation, we get that:

$$\frac{1}{1-\varepsilon}\left\{\frac{[\eta_w(\varphi_w - g_w)A_1(0)]^{1-\varepsilon}}{\rho-(1-\varepsilon)g_w} - \frac{1}{\rho}\right\} > \frac{1}{1-\varepsilon}\left\{\frac{[\eta_1(\varphi_1 - g_1)A_1(0)]^{1-\varepsilon}}{\rho-(1-\varepsilon)g_1} - \frac{1}{\rho}\right\}$$

It indicates that when quality information is completely symmetric, the cost of inventing high quality intermediate consumable would be relatively lower, and the growth rate of knowledge and societial welfare would be higher. In the meanwhile, $\frac{1}{1-\varepsilon}\left\{\frac{[\eta_w(\varphi_w - g_w)A_1(0)]^{1-\varepsilon}}{\rho-(1-\varepsilon)g_w} - \frac{[\eta_1(\varphi_1 - g_1)A_1(0)]^{1-\varepsilon}}{\rho-(1-\varepsilon)g_1}\right\}$, it demonstrates the second effect of whether the information is symmetric to society welfare. $(\eta_L + L\alpha^{2/1-\alpha})/(\eta_w + L\alpha^{2/1-\alpha}) > 1$ indicates that when quality information is completely symmetrical, the cost of inventing high quality intermediate consumable would be relatively lower, enlargling market capacity therefore improving the welfare of society. At this point, $\frac{1}{1-\varepsilon}\frac{[\eta_w(\varphi_w - g_w)A_1(0)]^{1-\varepsilon}}{\rho-(1-\varepsilon)g_w}\left[\left(\frac{\eta_L + L\alpha^{2/1-\alpha}}{\eta_w + L\alpha^{2/1-\alpha}}\right)^{1-\omega} - 1\right]$. It demonstrates the first effect of whether the information is symmetric to societial welfare. The first effect of whether the information is symmetric to society welfare is what Akerlof and others emphasized, but they did not notice the second affect of the assymmetry of information to society welfare.

2.2.4 Internal institution and development of private economy: the exploration of product certification system

The asymmetry of quality information would make the low quality consumable push the high quality consumable out of the market. Thus, in order to survive in the market, high quality consumable manufacturers should differentiate themselves from the low quality ones by sending signals. These signals include: investing large funds for advertisement and taking part in the product certification. This likely solves the problems caused by asymmetry of quality information. At the same time, because the asymmetry of quality information would decrease economic growth and societial welfare, the government needs to establish a system to solve the problems caused by asymmetry of quality information. Establishing and implementing such a system would be costly. Neverthless, the government needs to impose a one-time tax on the manufacturer (or personal income). At the same time, because it is beneficial for all of society to establish and implement such a system, the manufacturer (individual) must be willing to pay the tax. Thus, the government should have the political will and ability to establish and implement this system in order to maximum societal benefits.

Product certification is an important system for many countries to implement in order to solve the problem caused by asymmetry of quality information. This is an expressd warranty for the product quality to society and consumer by the certification mark and prevents enterprises from adulteration[1]. The Product Certification System derived from England, in 1901, by the Engineering Standard Committee, which established the steel rail's dimensional standard and the architectural section steel's dimensional standard. Then, in 1903, it initiated the first "kitemark" which was composed of letter B and S to ensure that the steel rail comformed to dimensional standards. From the 1920s, developed countries adopted the Product Certification System consecutively. During the 1950s, this system was popular among all industrialized developed nations[2]. Later, from the 1970s, developing countries adopted the Product Certification System consecutively. Like most of developing countries, the Product Certification System started late in China. In 1978, after joined the International Standard Organization (ISO), China introduced the idea of quality certification. In May 1991, the State Council published the regulations of the People's Republic of China on the administration of product certification. It signified that product certification started to step into the legal track.

Why was the Product Certification System, which was introduced by the developed world at the start of the 20th cenytury, adopted so rapidly? Why was the product certification started to step into legal track in China in 1991? To answer these questions we must look at the factors that influenced the establishment and implementation of the Product Certification System. For the convenience of this analysis, we assume that a country established and implemented the Product Certification to solve all problems caused by asymmetry of quality information[3]. Preciesly, as seen in equation (21) and (16), the profit of the establishment and implementation of the Product Certification System is:

$$R = f \cdot A_1(0) \qquad (22)$$

Among it, the constant f is relative to ε.

We can determine from the formula of production of finished consumable, the production of finished consumables expanded as the number of intermediate consumables increased. Equation 2 demonstrates that the type and number of high

---

① In fact, for manufacturers, the Product Certification System is able to send signal. The Quality Certification System includes Product Certification System and Quality System Certification. Quality System Certification derived from Product Certification System in 1970s. Therefore, this study does not discuss the internal issue of Quality Certification System. Please refer to Luan Jun (1996) for defailed introduction of Quality Certification System and Quality System Certification.

② Please refer to Jiang Hongzhang (1995) for detail.

③ Assuming that the Production Certification System could only solve partial problems caused by assymmetry of the quality of information, this would not affect the main conclusion of this study.

quality consumable is's linear function of $A_1(0)$. Consequently, the production of high quality finished consumables account for the monotonic increasing function of $A_1(0)$. Obviously, an increase in production of high quality consumables requires more manpower and material resources are needed in the investment of Product Certification①. As a result, the implementation cost of Product Certification System increases as $A_1(0)$ increases②. Thereafter, we assume the cost of establishing and implementing the Product Certification System is:

$$\Omega = F + \varphi \cdot A_1(0) \tag{23}$$

Among it, F represents the cost of establishing a Product Certification System, which is a fixed cost; $\varphi \cdot A_1(0)$ represents the cost of implementating the Product Certification System, which is a mutable cost③.

We can determine from equation (22) and (23), only when $A_1(0)$ satisfies equation (24), that a country would establish and implement the product certification system:

$$A_1(O) > \frac{F}{f - \varphi} \tag{24}$$

We can estimate from equation (24) that when the production, type and number of high quality finished consumables reaches a certain size, the profit of establishing and implementing the Product Certification System would be higher than the cost. This is an ideal time for a country to implement the Product Certification System. On the contrary however, a country should not establish the Product Certification System after establishment.

After the industrial revolution in the 1850s, the world economy developed

---

① The Production Certification System which was recommended by ISO to every country is: type tests, quality system assess of supplier and supervision after certification—quality system review and market sampling inspection.

② In reality, we can understand the relationship between the cost of establishing and implementing the Product Certification System and the production of high quality finished consumables from two more angles. The larger the production of high quality finished consumable, the more manufacturers it means. In the meanwhile, there are more manufacturers to apply for the Product Certification (some products are compelled to apply for the Product Certification), so that the cost of implementation the Product Certification System will increase. In addition, people prefer diversity, so it can be considered that the larger the production of a high quality consumable, the higher the number of high quality consumables. In the meanwhile, there are more products that are needed to be applied for Product Certification, so that the cost of implementation the Product Certification System will increase.

③ No matter how many samples are checked, all procedures of sampling inspection need to be finished in accordance with the regulation. Thus, there are scale effect in sampling inspection. It means it is more rational to assume the mutable cost as $\varphi \cdot [A_l(0)]^{\beta}$, $0 < \beta < 1$. However, this will not change the conclusion of this study.

rapidly. The number of consumable products expanded significantly. It became harder and harder for consumers to understand these products. The problem of asymmetry of information became more and more serious. Compared to developing counties, the production and number of high quality finished consumables was larger in the West, which also meant that the damage of asymmetry of information was larger as well. Therefore, to a certain extent, equation (24) explains why the Product Certification System derived from developed countries was initially used in the beginning of 20th century and rapidly grew in popularity.

Before the reformation, China played catch up, prioritizing heavy industr. This improved the standard of living and the number of comsumables was small and allocated according through a coordinated and planned assignment strategy. Thus, the influence of asymmetry of quality information was almost non-existent at the time. After the reformation, China gave up on this catching-up strategy, and the socialist market economic system was established and developed. In the process of economic development, the problem of asymmetry of quality information emerged gradually as the number of consumables increase rapidly. For instance, in the 1980s, the made-in-Wenzhou and counterfeit leather shoes caused damage to the consumer. Therefore, to a certain extent, equation (24) explains why the Product Certification System started to step into legal track in China until 1991.

In fact, there are three main ways to solve the problem caused by asymmetry of quality information: government establish and implementation of a corresponding system; enterprise send signal; the conbination of establishment and the implementation of a corresponding system by government and sending signal by enterprise. As for the manufacturers, they can send a signal to public to demonstrate that their product meets certain criteria by passing production certification. As for the government, the Product Certification System is an important system to utilize in order to solve the problem caused by asymmetry of quality information. Thus, the Product Certification System discussed in this section is the third one. To solve the problem caused by asymmetry of quality information, governments can develop laws and regulations so that enterprises do not make public information inaccurate or they would be punished severely. Enterprise can solve the problem caused by asymmetry of quality information by establishing a brand. With the development of the economy, there are many famous brands now in China. Therefore, we will research the other two solutions for the problem caused by asymmetry of quality information further.

2.2.5 Conclusions

There are many studies that examine the relationship between finance and economic growth with the assumption of asymmetric information. However, there is almost no documented research on the influence of asymmetry of finished consumables quality information to the intermediate market and economic growth. Under the frame of internal economic growth theory, this study establishes a model to analyze the relationship between asymmetry of quality information and economic growth. The conclusion of the model is: the asymmetry of quality information would not only lead to the shrinkage of the finished consumable market, but also lower the price of knowledge and products while hampering the growth of knowledge as well as economic development. The knowledge growth decides the long term economic growth rate, so the obstacle of knowledge creation caused by the asymmetry of quality information has a deeply negative influence on the economy. In the meanwhile, because information asymmetry would lower the economic growth rate and societal welfare, there would be some system arrangement, such as Product Certification System, to solve the problem of information asymmetry and promote economic development.

In China, in the finished consumable market, the asymmetry of quality information is prevalent. Therefore, in order to increase the price of knowledge product, government should legislate corresponding law and implement strictly, reduce the asymmetry of quality information and promote the long term economic growth. On 13 October, 2004, in the sampling inspection of cement, industrial and commercial administration in Fujian province found that the qualified rate was only 67.5% of 120 samples from 69 distributors. Some national inspection-free products, such as "Xinan" and "Xingyan", were problematic in quality. And these two brands got their title of the National Inspection-free Product in 2003. According to the regulation, the term of validity is three years①. This event demonstrates that even though our country has established the Product Certification System, the implementation of this system has been problematic. Thus, in order to solve the problem of information asymmetry, government need to strengthen the implementation of Product Certification System.

① For defailed information, please refer to Sun Chen (2004).

References

1. Acemoglu, D. , Zilibotti, F. Was Prometheus Unbound by Chance? Risk, Diversification and Growth. Journal of Political Economy, 105: 709 – 751.

2. Aghion, Philippe, Howitt, Peter. Endogenous Growth Theory. Cambridge, MA: MIT Press, 1998.

3. Akerlof, George. The Market for Lemons: Quality Uncertainty and the Market Mechanism. Quarterly Journal of Economics, 1970 (84): 488 – 500.

4. Barro, Robert J. Government Spending in a Simple Models of Endogenous Growth. Journal of Political Economy, 1990 (98).

5. Barro, Robert J. , Xavier Sala-i-Martin. Economic Growth. McGraw-Hill, 1995.

6. Bencivenga, V. R. , Smith, B. D. Some Consequences of Credit Rationing in an Endogenous Growth Model. Journal of Economic Dynamics and Control, 1993 (17): 97 – 122.

7. Denicolò, Vincenzo. Patent Races and Optimal Patent Breadth and Length. Journal of Industrial Economic, 1996 (44).

8. Dixit, Avinash. , Joseph E. Stiglitz. Monopolistic Competition and Optimum Product Diversity. American Economic Review, 1977 (67).

9. DomerEvsey D. Capital Expansion, Rate of Growth, and Employment. Econometrica, 1946 (14): 137 – 147.

10. Gilbert Richard and Carl Shapiro. Optimal Patent Length and Breadth. RAND Journal of Economics, 1990 (21).

11. Greenwood, J. , Jovanovic, B. Financial Development, Growth, and the Distribution of Income. Journal of Political Economy, 1990 (98): 1076 – 1107.

12. Grossman, Gene M. , Elhanan Helpman. Innovation and Growth in the Global Economy. MIT Press, 1991.

13. Harrod Roy F. An Essay in Dynamic Theory. Economic Journal, 1939 (49): 14 – 33.

14. Jiang Hongzhang. New IS09000 Quality Management and Quality Assurance Series International Standard Application Guide. National Defense Industry Press, 1995.

15. King, R. G. , Levine, R. Finance, Entrepreneurship and Growth: Theory and Evidence. Journal of Monetary Economics, 1993 (32): 513 – 542. Klemperer, Paul. How Broad Should the Scope of Patent Protection be. RAND Journal of Economics,

1990 (21).

16. Levine, Ross. Finance and Growth: Theory, Evidence, and Mechanisms, in Aghion, Philipe and Durlauf, Steven eds: Handbook of Economic Growt. Amsterdam: North Holland, 2004.

17. Luan Jun. Quality Management Course. Shanghai Jiaotong University Press, 1996.

18. Lucas, Robert E. Jr. On the Mechanism of Economic Development. Journal of Monetary Economics, 1988 (22): 3-22.

19. Pan Shiyuan, Shi Jinchuan. Endogenous Economic Growth Theory: A Literature Review. China Economic Quarterly, 2002 (3).

20. Pan Shiyuan. Optimal Patent System. Economic Research Journal, 2005 (12).

21. Romer, Paul M. Increasing Return and Long-Run Growth. Journal of Political Economy, 1986 (94): 1002-1037.

22. Romer, Paul M. Endogenous Technological Change. Journal of Political Economy, 1990 (98).

23. Rothchild, Michael, Stiglitz, Joseph. Equilibrium in Competitive Insurance Market: An Essay on the Economics of Imperfect Information. Quarterly Journal of Economics, 1976 (90): 629-649.

24. Schumpeter, Joseph A. Capitalism, Socialism and Democracy. Harper, 1942.

25. Sirri, E. R. , Tufano, P. The Economics of Pooling, In D. B. Crane, et al. , Boston eds: The Global Financial System: A Functional Approach. MA: Harvard Business School Press, 1995.

26. Solow, Robert M. A Contribution to the Theory of Economic Growth. Quarterly Journal of Economics, 1956 (70): 65-94.

27. Spence, Michael. Job Market Signaling. Quarterly Journal of Economics, 1973 (87): 355-374.

28. Stiglitz, Joseph, Weiss, A. Credit Rationing in Markets with Imperfect Information. American Economic Review, 1981 (71): 393-409.

29. Stiglitz, Joseph. Information and the Change in the Paradigm in Economics. American Economic Review, 2002 (92): 460-501.

30. Sun Chen. Jurisprudence and Economics Rise in Revolt-national Inspection-free System is Precarious. China Business Journal, October 24, 2004.

31. Swan, Trevor W. Economic Growth and Capital Accumulation. Economic Record, 1956 (32): 334-361.

32. World Bank. Knowledge and Development. China Financial & Economic Publishing House, 1999.

Part Ⅱ

Development Barrier and Institution Innovation of Private Enterprise

Chapter 3

Entrepreneurial Behavior and Entrepreneur Environment of Private Enterprise

Professor Bygrave, the entrepreneurship research director of Babson College, once pointed out that the enterprising spirit is the most important strategic superiority in America. Since China's reform and opening up, the rise of private economy has been considered as a significant impetus for China's economy to achieve sustained and rapid growth. Appreciating folk strength and encouraging entrepreneurial behavior is of great strategic significance for China, especially in the 21st century. What's more, promoting the development of private enterprises, which are creative and possess a persistently enterprising spirit, has already become a common understanding. However, the current academia has been short of a real breakthrough in entrepreneurial behavior of private enterprises. The failure to deeply understand the type, pattern and characteristics of entrepreneurial behavior made it hard to discern the pertinent policies to construct a promoting environment for entrepreneurship and growth. This chapter aims at giving a better understanding of the characteristics of entrepreneurial behavior and identifying the inhibited factors in institutional environment which are not fit for business requirements, and ultimately cultivating the policy environment for startup and growth of private enterprises.

3.1 Characteristics of entrepreneurial activity in China

In recent years, the Global Entrepreneurship Monitor (GEM)[①] has begun to

---

① Global Entrepreneurship Monitor is the most comprehensive entrepreneurship investigation report around the world and is jointly produced by Babson College and London Business School. So far, 37 countries and regions have participated in it.

bring China, India and some other developing countries into their research perspective and applied the sampling survey method to investigate entrepreneurial activity. This proves that the entrepreneurial activity of developing country is a significant component of global entrepreneurial activity, among which the transition economy of China is of especially unique research value. This section will analyze the above problems on the basis of GEM framework and three foreign mainstream entrepreneurship research publications (JBV, ETP, JSBM), as well as two GEM reports (2002, 2003).

3.1.1 Some preliminary conclusions on entrepreneurial activity research from foreign scholars

This section adopts the GEM conceptual framework to sort out foreign studies on entrepreneurial activity in China.

GEM project provides a conceptual framework for entrepreneurship research which is presented in Figure 3 – 1. This model contains two sets of mutually independent and complementary mechanism. The first mechanism represents the relationship between existing enterprises and regional economic growth while the second emphasizes start-ups. As a matter of fact, the recently released 2003 GEM report has already improved the whole framework. For instance, in order to fully investigate the entrepreneurial activity, this framework analyzes the FEA index. Therefore, existing firms in the first mechanism still have the problems of seizing entrepreneurial opportunity, exploiting entrepreneurial capacity and promoting economic growth. Foreign mainstream entrepreneurship research publications have studied entrepreneurial activity of China in the following aspects.

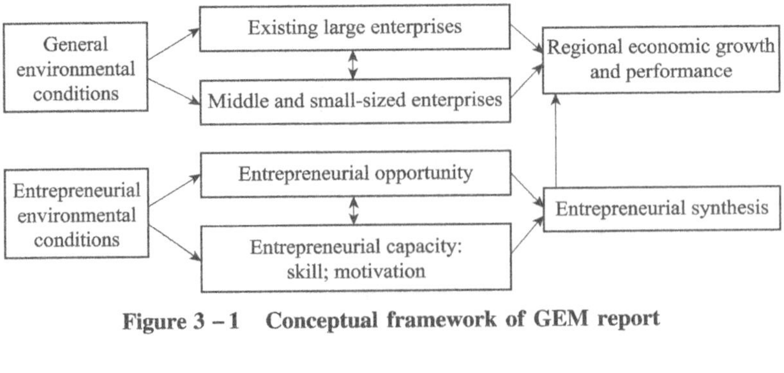

Figure 3 – 1 Conceptual framework of GEM report

1. Study on entrepreneurial environment conditions

Entrepreneurial environment conditions are influence factors of entrepreneurial opportunity and ability. Till now, GEM has exploits nine entrepreneurial environment conditions, which are financial support, government policy, government project, education and training, R&D transfer efficiency, business infrastructure, entry barriers, tangible infrastructure, cultural and social norms. Many scholars have analyzed how the evolution of social norms will influence entrepreneurial activity during the process of transition in China.

Ahlstrom and Bruton (2002) analyzed some institutional factors from the perspective of institutional economics. As a matter of fact, institutional factors have already been used to investigate entrepreneurial tendency (Busenitz, 1996), but were rarely used for entrepreneurial individuals and institutional interaction. These two researchers have demonstrated that under the circumstances of transitional economy, entrepreneurial enterprises will not only adapt to the environment, but also create a favorable institutional environment by altering certain conditions. Several studies have proved the evolution process of institution. On one hand, individual establishment of institution is not only rational and conscious, but also fragmentary and gradual (North, 1990; Powell, 1991). On the other hand, individuals can utilize informal institutional forces to reconstruct the system (Fligstein, 1997). Recent studies, regarding the entrepreneurial activity of China, have already made a breakthrough in considering institution as an available variable instead of simply an influence factor of individual entrepreneurial tendency.

Scott (1995a, 2002) once classified institution into three dimensions: regulatory, normative and cognitive. Among which, regulatory includes law, regulations and government policies at the national level; normative refers to powerful system and part which will instruct individual or organizational behavior; cognitive indicates circumscribed and incognizant variable which is not perceived by doers. During the period of transition, several gradually established norms have appeared; in the meantime, entrepreneurs have got to seek appropriate codes and standards to promote the legitimation of their entrepreneurial activity. In some regions in China, aligning with potent individual and organization will assist entrepreneurs in establishing unofficial norms (Schlevogt, 2001).

Relation is a core element in Chinese institution. People tend to do business with family members or trustable persons (Chen, 2001; Redding, 1990). However, most studies assume that relation is already existed and then focus on investigating its influences, instead of building relationships beforehand. In the study of utilizing and establishing relationships, Ahlstrom and Bruton have proposed and tested the following propositions:

Proposition 1: Successful entrepreneurs tend to locate their enterprises in regions where relationships are already built.

Proposition 2: Without prior contacts, successful entrepreneurs attempt to build trust relationships with potential customers and suppliers.

Proposition 3: If they fail to locate enterprises in related regions, successful entrepreneurs will build relationships by means of favoring and sending presents.

Proposition 4: Successful entrepreneurs often actively participated in charity activities in order to gain support of local government.

Both authors have verified that even without prior contacts, successful entrepreneurs will still be able to cultivate favorable relationships within a short period of time.

During the survey of 36 risk investors in 24 venture capital enterprises, Bruton and Ahlstrom (2003) found out that there are several differences in institutional environment between China and the West. This book has made comparisons in four parts: choosing promising enterprises, building relationships with invested companies and implementing supervision, increasing the value of invested companies, withdrawing.

Many successful risk investors discovered how to distinguish and utilize critical norms at various levels. For instance, in most cases, relationships will probably hinder due diligence because of failure to acquire useful information without established contacts. However, assume that investors do build some relationships or hire someone who has access to these relations, it should be beneficial to risk investors in seeking deals and supervising enterprises.

2. Study on entrepreneurial opportunity, ability and synthesis

Basic elements of entrepreneurial environment exert an important influence on entrepreneurial activity by creating entrepreneurial opportunity and enhancing entrepreneurial ability. With the combination of entrepreneurial opportunity and ability, entrepreneurial activity will come into being. We could see from the 2002 GEM China report that plenty entrepreneurial opportunities have been seen in our country within the last five years, especially now. Compared with other countries and regions participated in GEM, China has been holding the advantage. However, Chinese entrepreneurs have no vantage point of seizing or utilizing opportunities.

What's more, Chinese new ventures fall behind when it comes to information acquisition. As a result, the odds of establishing high-growth enterprises are relatively low when faced with numerous business opportunities.

Low and Busenitz (2001) studied the entrepreneurial cognitive pattern of Chinese small business owners and attempted to explain how they create, maintain and transform organizational forms. Based on the survey of 2 878 Chinese private enterprise owners, I found out that not only promises of entrepreneurs, achievement need and social environment will have influences on its start-up intention and expansion pattern, but also the entrepreneurs' cognition and comprehending of the environment (See Figure 3 - 2).

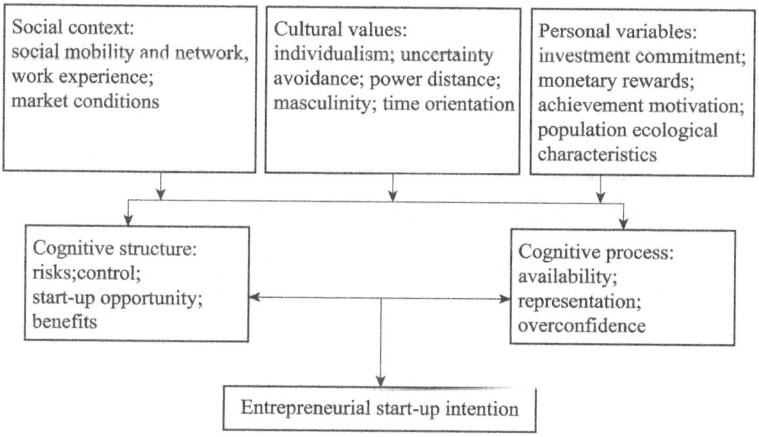

Figure 3 - 2 Analytical framework of entrepreneurial start-up intention (Busenitz Lau, 1996)

Their research verifies the prior assumption that social conditions and individual variables will have significant impacts on entrepreneurial start-up intention even in transition country as China. The transition period breeds plenty of growth opportunities, but entrepreneurial enterprises still face some limitations from traditional systems. This study also proves that the entrepreneurs' perceiving of market conditions and start-up intention are directly related with the means of achieving business growth.

By empirical comparison between small manufacturing enterprises and large traditional companies in Shanghai, Chow and Liu (2000) found out that middle and small-sized enterprises had less financial difficulties than we thought and more advantages in solving financial problems compared with traditional large companies. It also showed that the entrepreneurial ability of middle and small-sized enterprises is stronger than large ones.

There are many differences in economic conditions between transition countries and developed market economy countries. Because of underdeveloped and immature capital market, fixed asset investments of enterprises in developing countries depend more on bank credit. However, nationalized banks prefer state-owned firms which make most entrepreneurial firms hardly gain the support of nationalized banks. Chow and Fung (1996, 1997) found out that middle and small-sized entrepreneurial firms are more efficient than traditional state-owned enterprises. As a result, high management efficiency will make sure to generate large cash flows and satisfy the keen demand for long-term fixed asset financing. Besides which, these firms will also able to get loan funds from informal financing channels (Tam, 1986; Mckinnon, 1994).

Similar to other transition countries, capital market of China is also fragmentary. Non state-owned enterprises are pushed out of the nationalized bank financing system. However, traditional state-owned enterprises encountered more financing problems than middle and small-sized firms. We suspect that there are three possible explanations: (1) under the rapid growth of mixed ownership, middle and small-sized firms can generate enough cash flows to support fixed asset investment through market and management efficiency (2) state-owned enterprises which are in deep debt fall into an awkward position that they are losing the support of nationalized banks (3) middle and small-sized firms have access to large amounts of informal loan funds.

3. Entrepreneurship of existing large, middle and small-sized enterprises

As a matter of fact, domestic and overseas scholars have conducted many surveys of entrepreneurial activity in existing enterprises, such as internal entrepreneurship and identification of entrepreneurial enterprises within groups of middle and small-sized firms. This reveals that entrepreneurship of existing firms is also an important strength for economic growth. As previously noted, GEM project has begun to add studies about existing firms since 2003. But so far, existing researches have been focusing on developed market economy, especially internal entrepreneurship in transnational corporations. When it comes to the transition environment in China, we should consider the limitation of ownership condition.

Tan (2001) investigated the differences between administrators in state-owned enterprises and entrepreneurs in private enterprises when facing the same conditions. It turned out that there are distinct differences in the understanding of environmental features and strategy orientation. Compared with state-owned companies, entrepreneurial enterprises gain first-mover advantages through higher speed and more effective enforcement which in turn increases their odds of surviving. Therefore, we put forward two important hypotheses under the condition of China's transition economy:

Hypothesis 1: There is a huge difference in perceived regulation environment between administrators and entrepreneurs;

Hypothesis 2: There is a huge difference in motivation of innovation and risk taking between administrators and entrepreneurs.

As a matter of fact, the empirical research of these two types of people verified the above hypotheses (see Table 3 – 1). The administrators scored better than entrepreneurs in antagonism, dynamism and complicacy of environment; however, when it comes to innovation and risk taking, administrators fell behind.

Table 3 – 1 Differences between managers and entrepreneurs

Person	Manager			Entrepreneur			MANOVA	
Factor	N	Mean	SD	N	Mean	SD	F	Significance
Environment								
Antagonism	56	5.571	0.911	53	5.188	0.878	4.973	0.028
Dynamism	56	6.339	0.581	53	5.679	1.221	13.208	0.000
Complicacy	56	5.679	0.833	53	5.132	0.832	11.713	0.001
Strategy								
Risk taking	56	3.607	1.090	53	4.962	1.143	40.143	0.000
Innovation	56	3.786	1.155	53	4.622	1.078	15.243	0.000

Under the condition of China's transition economy, large amounts of regulations regarding competitive environment need to be improved. In the meantime, market environment has gone through dramatic evolvement and development. Various unsatisfied market niches are representations of entrepreneurial opportunities. There are two types of entrepreneurial activities: one is connecting different markets; the other is filling in the gaps of market. As a result, entrepreneurs are faced with a more turbulent environment when Chinese private entrepreneurs seek to create imbalance and act fast to fill in market niche (Tan, 1996). Small scale and simple structure make it more suitable for middle and small-sized entrepreneurial enterprises to tackle with the turbulent environment and adopt advanced action. Therefore, the volatility gives them a chance to break the status quo and destroy the rival's competitive edge (D'Aveni, 1994). These entrepreneurial enterprises will still be able to bell the cat and make fast decisions. even under the circumstances of incomplete information, Bird (1994).

Why do state-owned enterprises perceive a hostile environment even if many regulations are still in favor of them? Investigations find out that although the environment is unsatisfactory, many entrepreneurs believe it has been the best entrepreneurial environment since the founding of China, which is sharply contrasted with the answers from administrators. This suggests that even with the same objective conditions, different perception of the environment would bring different decisions.

Further analysis reveals that Chinese entrepreneurs adopt similar strategy orientation as western market economy (Bird, 1989), which is highly innovative motivation and high-risk tendency. As we found in previous investigations, entrepreneurs believe that the policy to support entrepreneurship will not change and therefore favorable environment will continue to exist. Because profits are directly correlated with them, hence entrepreneurial motivation of risk acceptance is sufficient. Besides which, the tolerance and adaptation of ambiguous and complex market environment make it possible for entrepreneurs to do better than administrators. That is to say, for entrepreneurs, success depends on complicacy, dynamism and antagonism of the market environment instead of consistency, stability and predictability.

4. Framework from environment, entrepreneurship to performance

The above are studies regarding each principal factor that has impact on the entrepreneurial activity in China. Several researches have turn their attention to an overall framework from environment, entrepreneurship to performance.

Based on the following framework (see Figure 3 – 3), Luo (1999) studied the entrepreneurial activity of township and village enterprises (TVEs) in China. He discovered some environmental features during the transition period, for instance, complicacy and dynamism have influence on perception towards uncertainty and potential which will in turn affect the entrepreneurs' strategy orientation. From data analysis, Luo found out that innovation, proactiveness and risk-taking are positively correlated with increasing dynamism of environment. When environment condition is complex or antagonistic, strategy are often drafted with great care.

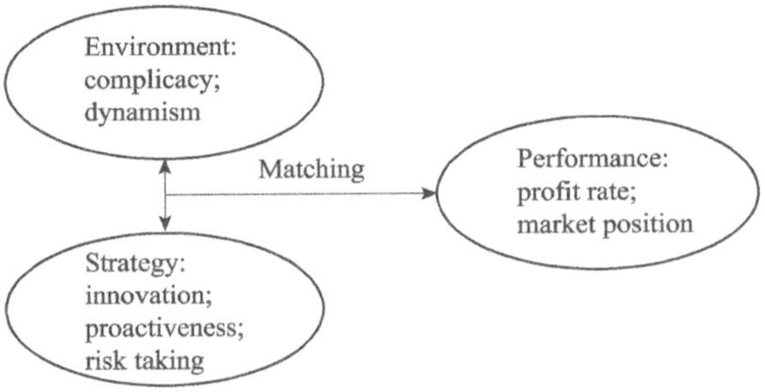

Figure 3 – 3 The conceptual model of environment, entrepreneurship and performance

Luo discovered that as the adaptation towards environment conditions, entrepreneurs in Chinese township and village enterprises adopted the role of a wary prospector instead of a pure prospector or defender. As a result, this strategic framework led to an outstanding performance in finance and market.

Unlike pure market economy, transition economy manifests a diversity of organizational forms instead of simple privately-owned business, which includes various economic forms such as state-owned enterprises, collectively owned enterprises, private enterprises and joint venture enterprises. The course of China's reform reveals that it has taken a method of shock therapy, which began with township and village enterprises and then led to decreasing ratio of state-owned business instead of purely privatization. In spite of their small scale, they are very efficient. They believed that township and village enterprises are effective carriers in saving transaction costs, adapting to institutional changes and opening up to various entrepreneurs Byrd (1992).

Due to the progressive features of China's reform and opening-up, entrepreneurs in township and village enterprises would benefit from both the planning and market departments (Nee, 1992). By becoming the major source of income in local government, township and village enterprises have gained a lot of help from it. In this way, a mutually dependent relationship has been developed between the two parties. As Nee (1992) pointed out that this institutional arrangement was an efficient way under the circumstances of incomplete market transition and weak structure.

In other transition economies, a lot of middle and small-sized firms in their initial stage find it very hard to obtain capital, technology, information, scarce resources and distribution channels. On the contrary, local governments in China are willing to help township and village enterprises to gain production factors, utilize infrastructures, arrange distribution channels and obtain government approval. Moreover, they would evaluate and disperse new venture's risks, even bear the cost of entrepreneurial failures. All the roles that the local governments are playing strengthen the innovative ability and adaptability of entrepreneurs in township and village enterprises.

The striking development of township and village enterprises is an important type of entrepreneurial activity. Many firms are dedicated to technological innovation while some others successfully adopt the advanced techniques at home and abroad. Under the unclearness of ownership, entrepreneurs of township and village enterprises manifest a characteristic of willing to take risks (Jefferson, Rawski and Zheng, 1992).

Due to the diversity of China's economy, organizations under the same cultural backgrounds are heterogeneous. Tan and Li (1996) found out that the reaction of northern township and village enterprises (such as Beijing and Tianjin) to external environment is a kind of hybrids between proactive and defensive model. As a hybrid strategy, analyzer-oriented strategy is good at opportunity exploitation and risk prevention (Hanbrik, 1983; Miles and Snow, 1978). This kind of strategy consists of two parts: one defending existing product markets while the other penetrating into new markets (Venkatraman and Prescott, 1990). Human ecologists believe that the survival and growth of organizations lie on environmental elements. Besides, the adjustment of strategy orientation is also an important factor (Miller and Friesen, 1983).

As a multidimensional structure, the market environment in China manifests features of invisibility, ambiguity, dynamism and accumulativeness (Boisot and Child, 1988). Under this circumstance, entrepreneurs obtain more competitive advantages which will further strengthen the adaptability and extensibility of township and village enterprises.

Empirical analysis results in Table 3 – 2 and Tabe 3 – 3 reveal that the reaction of entrepreneurs towards dynamic environment is highly innovative and proactive. However, in face of complexity, they tend to show unapparent features of risk taking which suggests that they are wary prospectors instead of pure prospectors. Due to the limitations of their own strength, entrepreneurs got to be more cautious of seeking product or market opportunities.

Table 3 – 2 Relationship between environment and strategy: results of multiple regression

Independent variable: environmental dimension	Dependent variable: strategic orientation			MANOVA results	
	innovation	proactiveness	risk taking	λ-value	F-value
Complicacy	0.26 *	0.29 **	0.17	0.83	2.33 **
Dynamism	0.44 ****	0.35 ***	0.39 ***	0.63	7.45 ***
R^2	0.22	0.19	0.29		
F	3.96	3.50	6.57		
p≤	0.01	0.05	0.001		
N	63	63	63		

Note: * represents $p < 0.10$; ** represents $p < 0.05$; *** represents $p < 0.01$; **** represents $P < 0.001$.

Multiple regression results in Table 3 – 2 show that the complicacy and dynamism of environmental dimension and innovation of strategic orientation are positively correlated. Similarly, the relationship between complicacy and dynamism of environment and proactiveness is also close. This reveals that when in face of a fleeting product or market opportunity, entrepreneurial township and village enterprises can only adopt the method of innovation and proactiveness in order to survive. The dynamism of environment is positively correlated with risk taking, whereas no significant correlation is existed between complicacy and risk taking.

Table 3 – 3 The relationship between strategy and performance: results of multiple regression

Independent variable: strategic orientation	Dependent variable: performance		MANOVA results	
	Profit rate	Market position	λ-value	F-value
Innovation	0. 38 ***	0. 37 ***	0. 72	5. 41 ****
Proactiveness	0. 34 **	0. 38 ***	0. 77	4. 38 ***
Risk taking	-0. 02	0. 08	0. 94	0. 90
R^2	0. 51	0. 60		
F	9. 66	12. 20		
p≤	0. 001	0. 001		
n	63	63		

Note: * represents p < 0. 10; * * represents p < 0. 05; * * * represents p < 0. 01; * * * * represents P < 0. 001.

We could see from Table 3 –3 that the correlation between innovation, proactiveness and profit rate, market position is significantly positive, whereas risk taking is not significant. This proves that innovation and proactivenss are important factors of entrepreneurial township and village enterprises in transition period.

3. 1. 2 Characteristics of entrepreneurial activity and entrepreneurial environment in China

From the studies of many foreign scholars, we could see that the entrepreneurial activity of China has an obvious characteristic of developing transition economy. For instance, the dynamism and complicacy of entrepreneurial environment is much higher than that of developed countries, especially dynamism, which will inevitably influence the behavior and results of entrepreneurial activity. Moreover, entrepreneurial activity in China also reveals some specific features such as treasuring relationships. In the following part, this book will further explain these features in three aspects.

1. Influence from transition economy

Due to the influence ofhighly-centralized planned economic system and traditional culture, China possesses a unique social and business background. As a matter of fact, private enterprises are facing a lot of restrictions, especially in acquiring essential entrepreneurial resources. Many entrepreneurial enterprises have to consider not only profit, market and other economic goals, but also political and other non-economic goals. China's enterprises are faced with two transition tasks: the first one is from planned economy to market economy; the second one is from traditional industrial economy to information, knowledge and service economy. Therefore, China's entrepreneurial activity has shown a different transitional characteristic from Eastern European and other socialist countries.

If we divide entrepreneurial activity into two categories: necessity entrepreneurship and opportunity entrepreneurship, we could see from the 2002 China GEM report that 60% of China's entrepreneurship belongs to necessity type while the other 40% are opportunity type. Necessity entrepreneurship is not only an important feature of China's reform and opening up, but also a significant force to maintain China's economic growth. But in the long run, opportunity entrepreneurship will play an important role in promoting the development of China's economy from "extensive" to "intensive".

Traditional analysis framework of environment-strategy-performance is mainly based on mature market economy countries, which means for unique transition country like China, the basic assumptions of management should be changed. For instance, environmental assumptions, finance, regulations and other institutional factors that have already been stereotyped in mature market economy countries, are still dynamic and changeful in China. For China, there are interactions between entrepreneurial activity and institutional factors. In a certain period of time, entrepreneurial activity has even become an important factor in institutional reform.

2. Influence from unique cultural values

China's unique cultural values also have a profound impact on entrepreneurial activity. For example, the Confucian culture has endowed the community with a strict hierarchical relationship which always put family members in priority. Therefore, many entrepreneurial activities have took place in local markets where trust is easy to build. Many scholars, who analyzed the unique element of "relationship", have consented to the fact that it is the most important feature of China. The relationship has been seen as a resource that can be traded when necessary, which is both an account receivable and an account payable (Tsang, 1998). However, the establishment of the relationship is very time-consuming. Due to the unusual importance of relational capital, the entrepreneurial ability of enterprises is sometimes in a secondary position.

Hamilton (1991) points out that family businesses are represented by a series of links that expand or contract as time and place change. As a matter of fact, firm boundaries are often vague because they cannot be defined entirely through property rights, ownership, and control power. On the contrary, they are defined by a network that associates people with social relationships. Chu Xiaoping (2003) believes that during the process of entrepreneurial growth of family business, various resources embedded in the relationship networkare continuing to be absorbed and integrated by enterprises, which results in the continuous evolvement of enterprise organization forms. Social network, on the one hand, acts as an intermediary to regulate the quantity, quality and approach of integrating financial and human capital; on the other hand, it is also a kind of social capital itself. During the process of integration of financial and human capital, social networks of business owners and their family members are also merged with a variety of social relations.

3. Entrepreneurial environment in China

From the 2002 GEM report, the integration of culture, economy, society, regulations and other entrepreneurial environment in transitional period embodies the unique conditions faced by China's entrepreneurial activities. In general, China's entrepreneurial environment ranked 23 in 37 GEM participating countries and regions, which is below average level. In accordance with entrepreneurial environment and entrepreneurial activity level, China belongs to the type of poor environment and high activity level among all GEM Asia participants. China has enough entrepreneurial opportunities and strong entrepreneurial motivation, but in the meantime, it lacks adequate entrepreneurial capacity. In other words, there is an urgent need to improve entrepreneurial capacity through entrepreneurship education.

Zhang Yuli (2003) conducted an empirical research on the relationship between entrepreneurs' characteristics and the external environment factors. Table 3 – 4 shows some preliminary conclusions.

Table 3 – 4 The relationship between environmental factors and entrepreneur traits

Entrepreneur traits	Cultural environment			Economic environment
	Respect for entrepreneur	Acceptance of income gap	Aware of entrepreneur	
Adventure	0.276 *	0.324 *	0.379 *	0.325 *
Competence and experience	0.378 *	0.300 *	0.455 *	0.284 *

Note: * represents $P < 0.05$ (two-tailed test).

Economic environment and cultural environment will influence entrepreneurial behavior through the impact on opportunity perception ability; individual adventurism will influence entrepreneurial behavior through the capacity of risk taking. What's more, the interaction between them has further strengthened the impact on entrepreneurship: favorable cultural and economic environment are conducive to the formation of entrepreneurial traits.

3.2 Entrepreneurial behavior of entrepreneurs

The previous section mainly discusses the process, influencing factors and environmental fit in of entrepreneurial behavior. Based on the above theories, this section attempts to verify theoretical assumptions and carry out some theoretical innovations through sample survey that crosses different regions and different level. In recent years, this research group has conducted three major entrepreneurship and growth survey. Firstly, from 2003 to 2004, we viewed MBA students and the general public as object of investigation, and conducted entrepreneurial behavior investigation in Beijing, Tianjin, Shenyang, Shenzhen and other seven cities; secondly, in 2004, we conducted a questionnaire and interview survey on top 100 private enterprises in Tianjin; thirdly, from 2004 to 2005, we carried out a comprehensive questionnaire survey on entrepreneurship and growth of small and medium-sized enterprises of science and technology in Tianjin, with the exception of exclusively foreign-owned enterprises and foreign holding enterprises, among which nearly 300 key enterprises had been interviewed. Based on the first survey, 3.2.2 shows the stage results of rational entrepreneurial decision-making and discrimination between opportunity-pulled entrepreneurship and poverty-driven entrepreneurship. In 3.2.3, it mainly discusses an empirical research of private enterprise on the relationship between entrepreneurial behavior and enterprise performance. The initial conclusion is that the entrepreneurial behavior will make for greater increase in enterprise performance only if joint efforts are created between entrepreneurial strategy of senior executive team and fostering internal business environment.

3.2.1 Empirical research

In order to understand the law of entrepreneurial behavior, we viewed MBA students and public groups as objects, conducted a random sample survey from October 2003 to April 2004 in Shenyang, Dalian, Beijing, Tianjin, Shijiazhuang, Nanjing, Shanghai, Changsha, Chengdu and Chongqing. Among them, Beijing,

Nanjing and Changsha only had the samples of MBA students, while Dalian, Chengdu and Chongqing only had public samples. During the survey, a total of 1 500 questionnaires were distributed, selected and sorted out. Those questionnaires with less than 80% key information were regarded as invalid (key information mainly included attitude towards entrepreneur, acceptance of income gap and expectations of economic environment) and the number of effective samples is 1 185 with an effective rate of 79%. Overall, the average age of the sample population is 35. Among which, there are 848 men and 337 women; the ratio of MBA students to the public is 0.85: 1. The systematic analysis of this report is based on 1 185 questionnaires.

This study refers to the public questionnaire of GEM (2002) to design a questionnaire for this report around the conceptual model, including seven aspects, namely, demographic characteristics, opportunity perception, entrepreneurial team, resource acquisition, cultural environment, economic environment, personal characteristics and so on.

Data collection was performed using random sampling method. The collection of MBA student sample was conducted in two ways: firstly, when teachers of Nankai University teach MBA courses in other places, they get the opportunity to adopt random sampling method in the classroom to fill out and collect questionnaires; secondly, they authorize local MBA professors to conduct the random sampling survey on their behalf by mail. In order to ensure effectiveness, we communicated with the teachers who participated in the distribution and collection of questionnaires in advance and asked them to ensure the randomness. The public samplewas randomly collected by way of road-side interview and used gifts to attract participants; some respondents were interviewed after the questionnaire was collected to ensure the validity of the information.

1. Composition and demographic characteristics of total sample

The number of total sample is 1 185, among which, there are 848 men and 337 women; besides, the ratio of MBA students to the public is 0.85: 1. The considerable number guarantees the credibility of the study. In addition to Tianjin (19.9%), Shanghai (15.1%) and Nanjing (10.7%), the gaps among the rest of the cities are small, which ensures the credibility. Table 3 – 5 shows the city distribution and MBA/public distribution of the total sample.

Table 3 – 5 City distribution and MBA/public distribution of total sample

City	Number	Ratio (%)
Beijing	79	6.6

Countinued

City	Number	Ratio (%)
Changsha	51	4.3
Chengdu	77	6.4
Dalian	54	4.5
Nanjing	128	10.7
Shanghai	181	15.1
Shenzhen	100	8.3
Shenyang	74	6.2
Shijiazhuang	113	9.4
Tianjin	239	19.9
Chongqing	89	7.4
Total	1 185	100
MBA	531	46.4
The public	627	53.6

The age of total sample is between 18 and 64 years old and fits a similar normal distribution. The ratio of 26-to-30-year-old sample is relatively high, while the ratio of the other age groups is relatively low; besides, the 26-year-old sample group has the highest ratio which is up to 8.8%, while 18-year-old and 64-year-old is the lowest with a ratio of less than 0.5%. The details are shown in Figure 3 - 4.

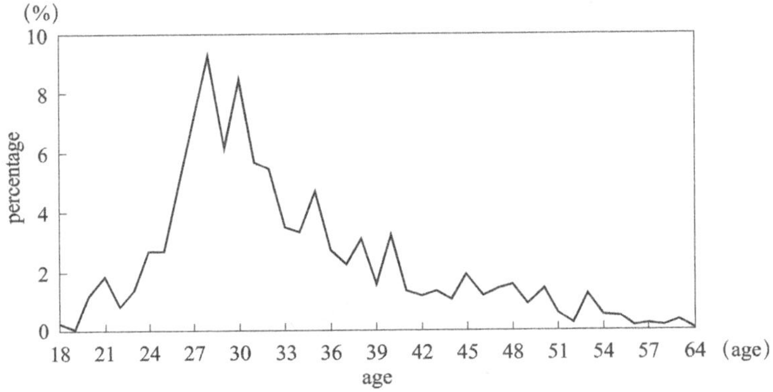

Figure 3 - 4 Age distribution of total sample

2. Demographic characteristics of overall entrepreneurship index and entrepreneurial motivation index

The overall entrepreneurial index is the ratio of entrepreneurial population to total sample, reflecting the overall level of entrepreneurship; the entrepreneurial motivation index is the ratio of people who are entrepreneurially motivated, reflecting the overall entrepreneurial motivation level. What's more, the gender distribution, residence distribution and age distribution of entrepreneurial index and entrepreneurial motivation index reflect the demographic characteristics (see Table 3 – 5 to Figure 3 – 7).

Table 3 – 6　　Gender distribution of overall entrepreneurship and entrepreneurial motivation index

(Unit: %)

Index	Male	Female	Total
Overall entrepreneurship index	15. 8	8. 4	24. 2
Entrepreneurial motivation index	33. 6	10. 8	44. 4

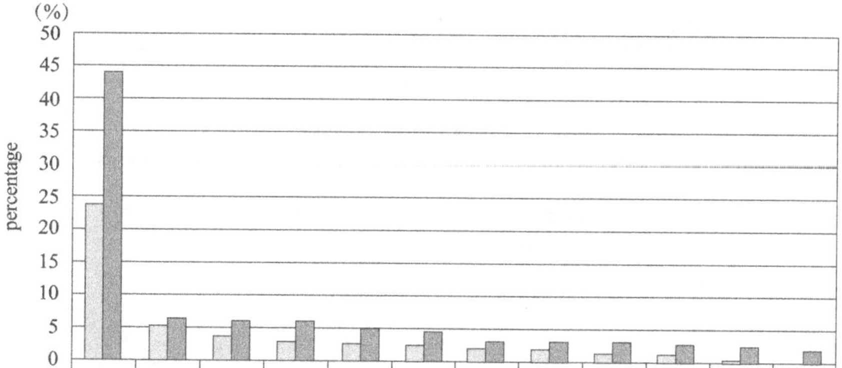

	total	Shang hai	Chong qing	Cheng du	Shijia zhuang	Nan jing	Shen yang	Shen zhen	Da lian	Tian jin	Bei jing	Chang sha
Overall entrepreneurship index%	24.2	5.22	3.60	3.00	2.73	2.39	2.10	1.93	1.38	1.30	0.53	0.10
Entrepreneurial motivation index%	44.4	6.17	6.12	5.99	4.75	4.57	3.14	3.13	3.13	2.85	2.57	1.99

□ Overall entrepreneurship index%　■ Entrepreneurial motivation index%

Figure 3 – 5　Residence distribution of entrepreneurial motivation index

Thus it can be seen that the overall entrepreneurship index and entrepreneurial motivation index is 24. 2% and 44. 4%; from gender distribution, men account for 15. 8% and 33. 6%, respectively, and women account for 8. 4% and 10. 8%, indicating that women's participation in social and economic activities has been greatly improved; from age distribution, the entrepreneurial population concentrate in age group from 27 to 35, while the entrepreneurial motive population concentrate in age group from 26 to 31; from residence distribution: 1) the level of entrepreneurship and entrepreneurial motivation are relatively higher in Shanghai, Chengdu and Chongqing; 2) the entrepreneurship level is low while the entrepreneurial motivation level is high in Tianjin and Beijing; 3) the level of entrepreneurship and entrepreneurial motivation are relatively lower in Changsha; 4) the level of entrepreneurship and entrepreneurial motivation are roughly the same in Nanjing,

Shenyang, Dalian, Shenzhen and Shijiazhuang.

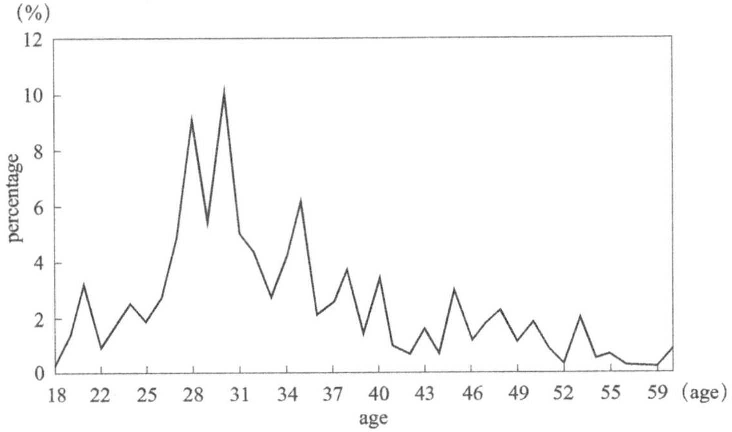

Figure 3 - 6 Age distribution of entrepreneurs

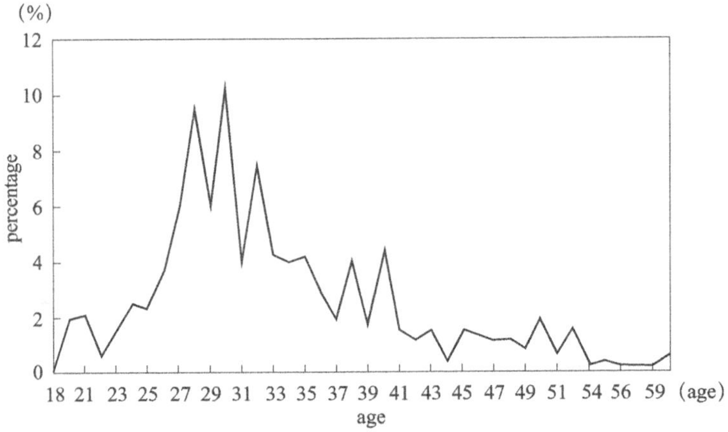

Figure 3 - 7 Age distribution of people with entrepreneurial motivation

3.2.2 Description of entrepreneurial behavior

1. Opportunity perception

Although some empirical studies have found positive correlations between opportunity perception and entrepreneurial motivation, entrepreneurial behavior, it does not come to a substantive conclusion that how decisions are made from opportunity perception to entrepreneurial behavior. Hills, Lumpkin and Singh (1997) believed that the perception of opportunity includes two logical stages: evaluation and analysis, which will ultimately lead to the occurrence of entrepreneurial behavior. Amit, Muller and Cockburn (1995) thought that the opportunity cost of entrepreneurial behavior is mainly determined by the entrepreneur's pre-entrepreneurial situation, which is expressed as vested interests (mainly including existing income level and education level). They found that the opportunity cost is the key factor in restricting venture decision-making after perceived business opportunity, which suggested that opportunity perception is a multi-stage decision-making process (Hills, Lumpkin and Singh, 1997). This report intends to draw some general rules of the decision-making process from opportunity perception to entrepreneurial behavior by describing the characteristics of the moment and doing inductive evaluation and analysis of the perceived opportunity.

The survey shows that more than 90% of entrepreneurs in the entrepreneurial population have chosen to start business from where they live. The ability to perceive opportunity is limited by the distance of space; in addition, the cost of obtaining information and finding new market opportunities, the barriers of entrepreneurial behavior and other factors will increase as the distance from residence increase.

The survey found that there are positive correlations between opportunity perception and entrepreneurial motivation, entrepreneurial motivation and entrepreneurial behavior with respective correlation coefficients of 0.316 ($p<0.05$) and 0.317 ($p<0.05$). There is negative correlations between opportunity cost and entrepreneurial motivation with a correlation coefficient of −0.341 ($p<0.05$), while no obvious correlation is existed between opportunity perception and entrepreneurial behavior. They also found that the entrepreneur's actual opportunity costs are lower: before entrepreneurship, annual business income of 50 000 yuan or less accounted for 42.4%, among which the group of 30 000 yuan or less accounted for 27.0%. Moreover, the group of more than 50 000 yuan accounted for 7.9%, of which 50 000 to 100 000 yuan accounted for 7.0%. On one hand, perceived entrepreneurial opportunities firstly promote entrepreneurial motivations and then lead to the occurrence of entrepreneurial behavior, which means entrepreneurial motivation is working as an intermediary; on the other hand, opportunity cost restricts the creation of entrepreneurial motivations and then prevents the occurrence of entrepreneurial behavior, that is, the more the entrepreneurial opportunity cost is, the less likely for entrepreneurs to abandon their current jobs. The combined effect of perceived opportunity and opportunity cost determines that the perceived entrepreneurship does not necessarily lead to entrepreneurial behavior. From the perception of opportunity to entrepreneurial behavior is a complex process in which entrepreneurs evaluate entrepreneurial opportunity by way of balancing the potential benefits and opportunity costs and make the decision of whether or not starting a business.

In summary, from the moment of opportunity perception, entrepreneurs tend to perceive the entrepreneurial opportunity around them and turn it into real realistic activities; from the process of perception to behavior, entrepreneurs are primarily engaged in making business decisions by comparing the potential benefits and opportunity costs (Zhang Yuli et al., 2003).

2. Comparison between opportunity and necessity entrepreneurship

The criteria for distinguishing opportunity and necessity entrepreneurship lie in the differences of entrepreneurial motivations. The motivation of the necessity type is that there is no better alternatives, which is why they have to participate in entrepreneurial activities to address the difficulties they face; and the motivation of the opportunity type lies in a strong desire of seizing existing opportunities. Investigations have found that there are clear differences between opportunity and necessity entrepreneurship in opportunity cost, team selection, industry choice, growth desire, innovativeness, financing channels, attitude towards social capital and other aspects.

(1) From the perspective of opportunity cost, the opportunity type is higher than that of necessity type: before entrepreneurship, the ratio of opportunity type's annual income above 50 000 yuan is 18.9%, while the other type is 5.7%; among which, the ratio of income that is above 100 000 yuan is 3.4% for opportunity type and zero for necessity type, indicating that the opportunity type is more adventurous.

(2) From the perspective of start-up team selection, the opportunity enterprenarship tends to become partnership while the necessity type prefers to start business on their own (see Table 3 - 7). The percentage of independent entrepreneurship and partnership is 48.3 and 51.7 in the opportunity type, while it is 51.4 and 48.6 in the necessity type.

Table 3 - 7 Comparison between opportunity and necessity entrepreneurship (Unit: %)

Type	Annual income level before start-up				
	Under 30 thousand yuan	Between 30 and 50 thousand yuan	Between 50 and 100 thousand yuan	Above 100 thousand yuan	Unanswered
Opportunity	42.2	33.6	15.5	3.4	5.3
Necessity	71.4	14.3	5.7	0	8.6

Type	Choice of start-up team		
	Alone	Partnership	Unanswered
Opportunity	48.3	51.7	0
Necessity	51.4	48.6	0

Continued

Type	Choice of industry				
	Primary industry	Secondary industry	Service industry	Emerging industry	Unanswered
Opportunity	2.6	13.8	54.3	18.1	11.6
Necessity	5.7	2.9	71.4	17.1	2.9

Type	Innovativeness		
	Complete innovation	Imitation	Unanswered
Opportunity	20.7	25.9	53.4
Necessity	14.3	42.9	42.8

Type	Attitude towards social capital			
	Very important	Averagely important	No difference	Unanswered
Opportunity	83.6	15.5	0.9	0
Necessity	80.0	11.4	2.9	5.9

Type	Number of planned increased employees in the following five years			
	1 ~ 74	75 ~ 124	Above 125	Unanswered
Opportunity	55.3	8.6	13.7	12.4
Necessity	65.9	6.6	5.2	22.3

Type	Choice of financing channels						
	Single financing channel					Mixed financing channel	Unanswered
	Equity fund	Financial institution	Venture investment	Other sources	Total		
Opportunity	31.0	7.8	3.4	7.8	50.0	46.0	4.0
Necessity	40.0	8.6	0	11.4	60.0	28.6	11.4

(3) From the perspective of industry choice, the necessity type prefers serviceindustry and primary industry, and the rates are respectively 74.1%, 5.7%, 54.3% and 2.6%; while the opportunity type tends to secondary industryand emerging industry, and the rates are respectively 13.8%, 18.1%, 2.9% and 17.1%.

(4) From the perspective of growth desire, the opportunity type is higher: whenit comes to the number of planned increased employees in the following five years, the percentage of over 75 employees is 22.3% inthe opportunity type, which is higher thanthat of the necessity type (11.8%); however, whenit comes to the low growth desire group, the necessity type has a percentage of 65.9 which is higher than 55.3 of the opportunity type.

(5) From the perspective of innovativeness, the opportunity type prefers complete innovation, and the rates are respectively 20.7% and 14.3%; while the other type tends to imitation, and the rates are respectively 42.9% and 25.9%.

(6) From the perspective of financing channels, the opportunity type prefers mixed financing channels, andthe rates are respectively 46.0% and 28.6%; while the necessity type tends to singlefinancing channels, and the rates are respectively 50.0% and 60.0%. Within the group of single financing channels, the necessity type prefers to equityfund and other sources (the rates are respectively 40.0%, 11.4%, 31.0% and

7.8%) while the opportunity type tends to venture investment (with a ratio of 3.4%).

From the perspective of attitude towards social capital, both types highlyvalue the rule of social capital played in the entrepreneurial process; while the ratio of people who believes that social capital has no impact on entrepreneurs in the necessity type is 2% higher than that of the opportunity type.

3. Start-up team

Entrepreneurs, as the main subject, play the role of decision maker in the process of entrepreneurship through the decision-making of a series of problems which will affect the success or failure of entrepreneurship (Hambrick, 1994). This book begins with the logical process of entrepreneurship, studies the decision-making elements before (start-up team selection and industry choice) and after (attitude towards social capital, innovativeness and growth desire) the founding of new enterprises, attempts to find the principles and methods of how to make entrepreneurial decisions, and then understand the general laws of entrepreneurship.

The choice of start-up team and industry are the main decision elements before the creation of new business. The survey found that the ratio of partnership venture was 60.5%, while the ratio of starting business alone was 39.5%, indicating that entrepreneurs preferred to partnership because of the advantages in dispersing the risk of entrepreneurial failure. The complementary skills among team members enhances the entrepreneurs' ability to cope with environmental uncertainty and thereby reduce the risk of failure for new enterprises. More importantly, the survey also found that stronger resource integration ability will ensure the acquisition of venture capital by way of acquiring capitals from various financing channels at the same time.

Entrepreneurial behavior are concentrated in service industry and emerging industry with a total ratio of 39.7%, . This is because of two aspects: on one hand, low entry and exit barriers and the characteristics of growth perioddetermine its higher long-term profitability; what's more, the new ventures are facing lower competitive risks compared with other industries. In contrast, the first and second industries, in mature or recession period, have lower profitability and higher entry and exit barriers, so the high risk has kept away many entrepreneurial enterprises.

After the establishment of new enterprises, thefocus of entrepreneurs or entrepreneurial teams has turn to making up for the disadvantages of the lack of resources and developing growth strategies and tactics to ensure that the new firms will smoothly go through the survival period. All of these are represented by the attitude towards social capital, innovativeness and growth desire. From the perspective of attitude towards social capital, entrepreneurs generally think that social capital is very important except for those in Chengdu, Dalian and Chongqing (see Table 3 - 8).

This is mainly because that through non-economic transactions within the social network nodes, new enterprises are able to get hold of a lot of external resources for external growth (the so-called external resources are things the entrepreneurs can dominate but do not have the ownership of, so the risk of entrepreneurial failure is largely reduced). In addition, the emphasis on social capital is relatively low in Chengdu, Dalian and Chongqing is probably because that these three cities don't have standardized entrepreneurial concepts and thus fail to recognize the role of social capital during the entrepreneurial process.

Table 3 - 8 City distribution of attitude towards social capital (Unit: %)

Attitude towards social capital	Very important	Averagely important	No difference	Unanswered
Chengdu	63.6	11.7	2.6	22
Dalian	46.3	9.3	1.9	42.5
Nanjing	28.2	0	0	71.8
Shanghai	27.6	1.7	0	70.7
Shenzhen	17.3	3.7	0	79
Shenyang	55.6	2.8	0	41.6
Shijiazhuang	37.3	6.8	0	55.9
Chongqing	65.2	18	2.2	14.6

From the perspective of innovativeness, the imitation type of entrepreneurial behavior accounted for 17.9% while the percentage of full innovation type is 8.8%. The reason is that, compared with imitative innovation, full innovation are faced with greater market risk and alternative risk: the former one is that once the market does not accept the new products or services, the entrepreneur's cumulative investment in innovation would go down the drain; the latter one is due to weaknesses such as resource scarcity, which makes it difficult for new firms to compete against improved alternatives and thus reduce the profitability of fully innovative products or services; besides, the interaction of market risk and alternative risk would further reduce the profitability of fully innovative products or services, which is why entrepreneurs tend to use imitative innovation products to avoid market and alternative risk and shorten the time from development to marketing.

In accordance with GEM (2002) method, this chapter divided growth desire into three categories: the normal growth desire is from 1 to 74 persons; the higher growth desire is from 75 to 124 persons; and the highest growth desire group is above 125 persons. The survey showed that the percentage of new enterprises with normal growth desire is the 18.4%; while the highest and higher group is 2.9% and 2.8%

respectively. Which indicates that only a small number of new enterprises have showed high growth aspirations while the majorities do not deliberately pursue high growth rate. This is mainly because, on the one hand, the entrepreneurial behavior is mainly concentrated in service and emerging industries where the demand for employees is relatively low; on the other hand, accompanied by the complexity of management and increasing risks, entrepreneurs find it difficult to manage the changes within and without the enterprises, leading to a rapid expansion of both development and failure risk of the new enterprises. As a result, avoidance of high growth indicates a way of risk-aversion.

To sum up, bearing the high risks of entrepreneurship to obtain high returns reflects the pioneering and adventurous spirit of the entrepreneurs. What's more, in order to control entrepreneurial risks, entrepreneurs prefer partnership venture, focus on service and emerging industries, value social capital, emphasize innovative imitation and do not deliberately pursuit high growth rate. Risk-aversion does not mean avoiding risk, and taking risk does not mean the pursuit of risk, these two thing are not contradictory, but mutually integrated and supportive. To a certain extent, entrepreneurship is the intertwined process between innovative spirit and rational judgment.

4. Resource acquisition

Entrepreneurship is the integration of resources and financial resources are the most important resources during early stage. This chapter divides financing method into two categories: a single financing method and a combination of multiple means. We found that the ratio of entrepreneurs using a single financing method is 6.2% lower than using mixed financing means, and the rates are respectively 26.0% and 32.2%. Besides, within the type of single method, the percentage of financing from entrepreneurs' social networks ranks the second place (19%). This is because: on the one hand, mixed financing method is conducive to ensuring the acquisition of venture capital and decentralize the financial risk of new enterprises; on the other hand, getting entrepreneurial funds through personal social networks will simplify financing procedures, shorten the time, and reduces some costs.

3.2.3 Relationship between exogenous factors and entrepreneurial behavior

1. General assessment

Table 3 – 9 shows the correlation between exogenous factors and opportunity perception, entrepreneurship motivation, entrepreneurial behavior. We can see that, 1) favorable cultural environment (including respect for entrepreneur, acceptance of income gap and aware of entrepreneur) can promote individual awareness of entrepreneurial opportunity: respect for and aware of entrepreneurs isconducive to the emergence of entrepreneurial motivation; respect for entrepreneur and acceptance of income gap is conducive to the generation of entrepreneurial behavior. Whereas, there are no direct correlations between acceptance of income gap and entrepreneurial motivation, aware of entrepreneur and entrepreneurial behavior; 2) individual risk-taking and experience is positively related to entrepreneurial motivation and entrepreneurial behavior, indicating that higher risk-taking and more necessary experience will tend to create entrepreneurial motivation and implement entrepreneurial behavior; 3) economic environment has an important impact on the overall level of entrepreneurship through the number of entrepreneurial opportunities: greater economic environment and more opportunities will make it easier to perceive entrepreneurial opportunity and promote entrepreneurship. What's more, there are obvious correlations between exogenous factors: in favorable cultural and economic environment, entrepreneurs tend to be more adventurous and have better belief in their competence and experience. The correlation coefficient between adventure and experience is 0.187 ($p < 0.05$), indicating that the higher the ability and experience is, the more risks they are willing to take.

Table 3-9 Correlation between exogenous factors and opportunity perception, entrepreneurship motivation, entrepreneurial behavior

Exogenous factors		Opportunity perception	Entrepreneurship motivation	Entrepreneurial behavior
Cultural environment	Respect for entrepreneur	0.462*	0.439*	0.431*
	Acceptance of income gap	0.084*	Not related	0.158*
	Aware of entrepreneur	0.008*	0.051*	Not related
Personal traits	Adventure	0.135*	0.064*	0.135*
	Competence and experience	0.294*	0.108*	0.294*
Economic environment		0.155*	0.074*	0.008*

Note: * represents $p < 0.05$ (two-tailed test).

Therefore, economic and cultural environment will affect entrepreneurial behavior by influencing the ability to perceive opportunity. Besides, individual risk-taking will also affect entrepreneurial behavior by influencing the entrepreneur's ability to take risks. From the microcosmic perspective, different choices of the same entrepreneurial opportunity is derived from the difference in individual risk-taking ability. Competence and experience will have an influence on entrepreneurial behavior by means of influencing the ability to perceive opportunity and increasing entrepreneurial confidence, which is represented by the ability and confidence in harness and avoidance of high uncertainty. Table 3 – 10 shows that favorable cultural and economic environment will promote the formation of entrepreneurial personal traits and then further strengthen the effects on entrepreneurship.

Table 3 – 10 Correlation between exogenous factors

Personal traits	Cultural environment			Economic environment
	Respect for entrepreneur	Acceptance of income gap	Aware of entrepreneur	
Adventure	0. 276 *	0. 324 *	0. 379 *	0. 325 *
Competence and experience	0. 378 *	0. 300 *	0. 455 *	0. 284 *

Note: * represents $p < 0.05$ (two-tailed test).

2. Mechanism of exogenous factors: the role of entrepreneurial opportunity cost perception①

Table 3 – 11 shows the distribution of cultural environment and entrepreneurial opportunity cost. From where the entrepreneur opportunity cost is more than 50 000 yuan, we could see that the respect for entrepreneurs, acceptance of income gap and awareness of entrepreneurs have the highest rate which are 6. 7%, 6. 7% and 6. 1% respectively. This indicates that, higher degree of social respect, more acceptance of income gap and more contact with entrepreneurs have made it more willing for the entrepreneurs to take on higher opportunity costs.

Table 3 – 11 Distribution of cultural environment and entrepreneurial opportunity cost

(Unit: %)

Attitude towards social capital	Annual income level before start-up			
	Under 30 thousand yuan	Between 30 and 50 thousand yuan	Between 50 and 100 thousand yuan	Above 100 thousand yuan
Respect	18. 2	11. 5	5. 9	0. 8
Neutrality	21. 6	10. 1	3. 4	0. 7
Disgust	22. 2	22. 2	0	0
Unanswered	38. 0	56. 2	90. 7	98. 5
Acceptance of income gap	Annual income level before start-up			
	Under 30 thousand yuan	Between 30 and 50 thousand yuan	Between 50 and 100 thousand yuan	Above 100 thousand yuan
Accept	17. 4	11. 0	5. 7	1. 0

① Entrepreneurial opportunity cost perception means the entrepreneur's attitude towards future entrepreneurial opportunity cost, which further represents the tendency to assume higher or lower entrepreneurial opportunity cost.

Continued

Reject	24. 1	12. 7	3. 8	0
Unanswered	58. 5	76. 3	90. 5	99. 0
Aware of entrepreneur	Annual income level before start-up			
	Under 30 thousand yuan	Between 30 and 50 thousand yuan	Between 50 and 100 thousand yuan	Above 100 thousand yuan
Aware	19. 5	11. 8	5. 6	0. 5
Not aware	12. 5	7. 1	1. 8	1. 8
Unanswered	68. 0	81. 1	92. 6	97. 7

Table 3 - 12 shows the correlation between economic environment and entrepreneurial opportunity cost. We could see that: 1) from where the opportunity cost is more than 50 000 yuan, better economic environment accounts for the most (10. 3%); 2) from where the opportunity cost is less than 50 000 yuan, worse economic environment accounts for the most (43. 9%). Which indicates that the better the economic environment is, the more willing for the entrepreneurs to take on higher opportunity cost.

Table 3 - 12 Distribution of economic environment and entrepreneurial opportunity cost

(Unit: %)

Economic environment	Annual income level before start-up			
	Under 30 thousand yuan	Between 30 and 50 thousand yuan	Between 50 and 100 thousand yuan	Above 100 thousand yuan
Better	18. 6	10. 5	9. 8	0. 5
Unchanged	16. 8	14. 4	3. 6	0. 6
Worse	34. 1	9. 8	3. 5	0. 3
Unanswered	30. 5	65. 3	83. 1	98. 6

From the view of personal traits, investigations have found positive correlation between opportunity cost and adventure with a correlation coefficient of 0. 133 ($p < 0.05$). There was a negative correlation between experience and opportunity cost with a correlation coefficient of - 0. 292 ($p < 0.05$), indicating that higher risks and weaker ability makes higher opportunity cost.

To sum up, the model of opportunity perception indicates that opportunity cost is the key factor in influencing entrepreneurial behavior. Exogenous factors (including cultural environment, economic environment and personal traits) will change the subjective attitude towards entrepreneurial opportunity cost and finally lead to different levels of entrepreneurship in different cultural and economic environment (see in Figure 3 -8).

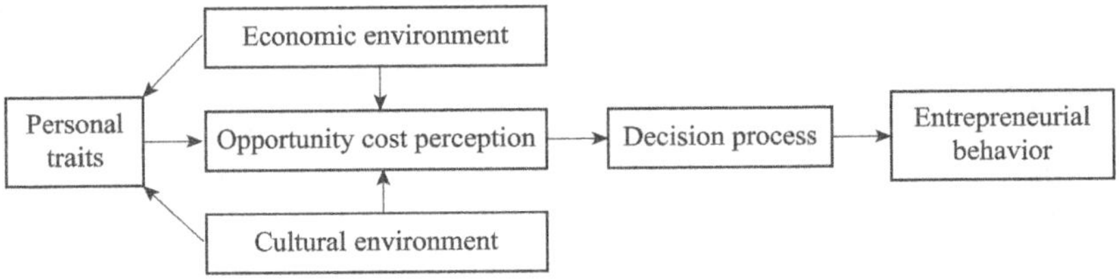

Figure 3 – 8 Integrated mechanism model of exogenous factors

3. 2. 4 Basic conclusions

1. Entrepreneurship is the intertwined process between innovative, adventurous spirit and rational decision making

The rationality of entrepreneurial behavior is represented by the scientific nature of entrepreneur's access to entrepreneurial resources and response to environmental uncertainty, such as preferring partnership venture, focusing on service and emerging industries, valuing social capital, emphasizing innovative imitation and so on to control and reduce entrepreneurial risks. What's more, the intertwined process between innovative, adventurous spirit and rational decision making will finally determine the growth of new enterprises. This process is represented by a series of innovative behaviors that will promote and maintain the growth and development of new enterprises. Eventually, the rational elements of this kind of behavior will be integrated into the institution, culture, strategy and other parts of the enterprises (see Figure 3 – 9).

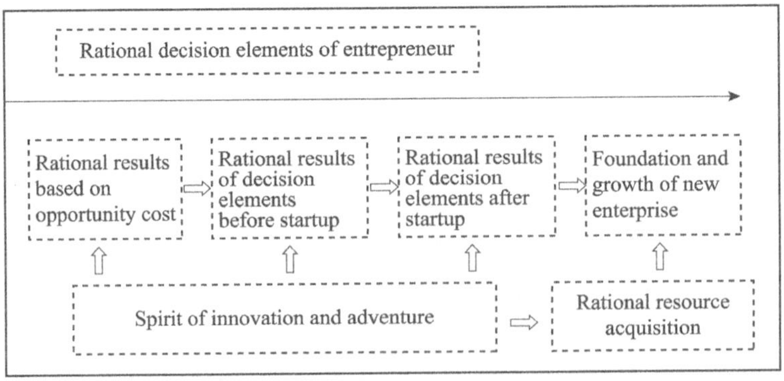

Figure 3 – 9 Intertwined model of entrepreneurial spirit and rational entrepreneurship

2. Comparison between opportunity and necessity entrepreneurship

Compared with the opportunity type, on the one hand, the necessity type is more reluctant to bear the risk of entrepreneurship; besides, the entrepreneurial purpose is to seek changes in the state of survival instead of the pursuit of self-realization. From the perspective of survey subjects, the MBA group is mainly concentrated in the opportunity type which is based on seizing opportunities, while the mass group is focused on necessity entrepreneurship which is based on getting out of poverty. In addition, the difference between opportunity and necessity entrepreneurship will influence the entrepreneurial process in terms of growth desire and choice of financing channels. On the other hand, by distinguishing the differences between opportunity and necessity entrepreneurship, it is helpful to identify policy recommendations for poverty-driven entrepreneurship, meet their unique policy needs and improve the level of necessity entrepreneurship, which is of great practical significance to address the problems facing vulnerable groups in China.

3. The fundamental difference between MBA and the public on the basis of entrepreneurial logic process

From the perspective of opportunity cost, the MBA group is higher than the public group: the entrepreneur opportunity cost of more than 50 000 yuan is 3.4% higher in the MBA group than the public, while the cost of less than 50 000 yuan is 28.9% higher in the public than the MBA group. From the perspective of decision-making elements before establishment, the MBA group is more preferred to partnership; after the establishment, the MBA group leans to imitative innovation, value of social capital and higher growth desire.

It can be seen that the difference in entrepreneur opportunity costs is the primary source of differences in entrepreneurial behavior between MBA and the public. Higher opportunity costs, on the one hand, make the MBA group show lower level of entrepreneurship and higher motivations where the entrepreneurship index and entrepreneurship motivation index is 4.7% and 3.0% higher than that of the public group; on the other hand, the decision results of preferring partnership venture, emphasizing innovative imitation, utilizing social capital and showing higher growth desire all combine to reduce entrepreneurial risks. Thus, the MBA community is in actual need of a favorable cultural and economic environment that will encourage it to take on higher opportunity costs and carry out entrepreneurial activity.

3.3 Entrepreneurial activity and enterprise performance

Based on the samples of 55 Chinese private enterprises in their growth period, this section has used the two-path and three-way contingency method to reconstruct the evaluation index of entrepreneurial activity, and has empirically studied its impact on the enterprises' performance. Similar to previous studies, we found that there was a significantly positive correlation between entrepreneurial activity (EA) and firm performance (EP). In the meantime, we've also reached some other meaningful conclusions based on the background of Chinese enterprises.

3.3.1 Introduction

In terms of entrepreneurship research, people try to figure out a basic proposition which is how entrepreneurial activity (EA) will affect enterprise performance (EP). At the macroeconomic level, after five years of continuous research, the GEM report found that the positive correlation between entrepreneurial activity at the national or regional level and economic growth of subsequent years has passed the statistical test. At the enterprise level, many scholars had focused on the relationship between entrepreneurial activity and enterprise performance, and had conducted a lot of theoretical and empirical surveys.

Previous studies have made some ambiguous and even self-contradictory discoveries. Some studies found that the enterprises who used entrepreneurial strategy have achieved better performance (such as, Wiklund, 1999; Zahra, 1991; Zahra and Covin, 1995). However, these studies are not final conclusions. For example, Smart and Conant (1994) did not find a significant correlation between entrepreneurial orientation and performance; Hart (1992) argued that in certain contexts, entrepreneurial strategy would lead to worse performance.

There are different explanations for these ambiguous conclusions. Firstly, contradictory conclusions may come from the lack of measuring tools for entrepreneurial activity; secondly, they may also come from different disturbing variables in theory. Therefore, we still need to further study these questions, such as will entrepreneurial orientation, corporate entrepreneurship assessment instrument (CEAI), or entrepreneurial management be able to reflect entrepreneurial activity at the enterprise level? How does entrepreneurial activity affect enterprise performance? Does this relationship be influenced by environmental perception?

In order to answer these questions, we have reconstructed the evaluation index system of entrepreneurial activity after evaluating the theoretical sources of three measurement tools, then evaluated independent effects of some variables through this system, and analyzed the effects of two-path and three-path interactions. The whole study was based on a sample of 55 private enterprises in their growth period and we attempted to make the following contributions. Firstly, we have done a detailed literature review and found that there are three main measuring tools that reflect entrepreneurial activity at the enterprise level with some deficiencies. Therefore, we used factor analysis to build our own measuring tools, which is EO and IEE (Internal Entrepreneurship Environment), and found that entrepreneurial orientation is not always a dependent dimension. In this chapter, entrepreneurial orientation is divided into two dimensions: innovation and proactiveness (EO_1), risk taking (EO_2). Secondly, based on three indicators that are commonly used to reflect financial performance and development of enterprises, we have constructed an operational enterprise performance indicator. Thirdly, based on empirical evidence from Chinese private enterprises, we have verified the relationship between entrepreneurial activity and enterprise performance.

This chapter follows the following logic. Above all, a literature review of the measuring tools for entrepreneurial activity at the enterprise level is presented. We propose a general theoretical model to explain the EA – EP relationship. In addition, we emphasize that we should pay more attention to the reality which is far more complex than general models. Therefore, we propose two kinds of contingency models (two-path and three-path interactions)①, and we think that they are superior to the general models. Finally, we present and discuss the implications for entrepreneurs and practitioners in the field of entrepreneurship.

3.3.2 Literature review and research hypothesis

1. Measuring tools of entrepreneurial activity on enterprise level

It can be seen from relevant literature that there have been three types of

---

① Wiklund J., Shepherd D., Entrepreneurial Orientation and Small Business Performance: a Configurational Approach. Journal of Business Venturing, 2005, 20: 82 – 83.

important measuring tools on the enterprise level, which is entrepreneurial orientation (Miller, 1983; Covin and Slevin, 1991; Lumpkin and Dess, 1996), evaluation tools (Kuratko et al., 1990, 2002) and entrepreneurial management (Brown et al., 1998, 2001). Because of different theoretical backgrounds, these three types of measuring tools have different contents and different perspectives.

(1) Entrepreneurial orientation.

Miller (1983) was the first one to move his focus from individuals to enterprises, that is, from the intrinsic characteristics of entrepreneurs to the entrepreneurial process itself, and the organizational factors that motivate or hinder entrepreneurial activity. Miller's contribution is that he has brought about a new and broad perspective, which is a positive signal for the enterprises. Based on contingency theory, we can strengthen enterprise's long-term competitive advantage by stimulating entrepreneurial activities as long as we try to find the right organizational factors.

Based on Miller's contribution, some scholars have done a lot of important research work. Covin and Slevin (1991) constructed a conceptual framework that uses the concept of entrepreneurial status to measure entrepreneurial orientation. According to Miller's definition, they argue that entrepreneurship can be defined as a set of strategic trends, including risk-taking tendencies, competitive tendencies, proactive behavior and innovation activities. They think that entrepreneurial behavior at the enterprise level is an important and effective predictor of enterprise performance, and they have also identified 44 research propositions which has become the basis of many follow-up empirical researches.

Lumpkin and Dess (1996) believe that entrepreneurial orientation is consists of five important dimensions, which is autonomy, voluntary innovation, risk taking, positive tendencies and proactiveness toward market opportunities. Besides, they have made a clear distinction between entrepreneurship and entrepreneurial orientation. New entry behavior is the creation of new business through existing enterprises or internal entrepreneurial activities. Therefore, they believe that the essential behavior of entrepreneurship is the new entry behavior. However, entrepreneurial orientation refers to the organization that lead to the process, practice and decision-making activities of new entry behavior.

We can see that the focus of entrepreneurial-oriented research is why entrepreneurial activity happen at this level, and its theoretical basis is the basic assumption that "attitudes affect behavior", which is based on theories such as psychology and organizational behavior. The features of innovation, proactiveness and risk taking will not only occur at individual level, but also at organizational level. The meaning of entrepreneurial-oriented research is that the entrepreneurial behavior at enterprise level can be affected by creating a certain organizational strategy, structure, institution and culture.

(2) Evaluation tools.

Using the sample of top 500 enterprises in the United States "Fortune", Kuratko (1990) adopted the method of quasi-experimental design and developed Intrapreneurial Assessment Instrument (IAI), which included three major dimensions (Management support for internal entrepreneurship, organizational structure, availability of remuneration and research) and 21 sub-dimensions. And then, through a group of senior management training projects, they ultimately found that the internal entrepreneurial environment perception of employees has been significantly improved by targeted training programs.

Later, based on two sets of large-scale comparative samples and management perception of middle managers, Hornsby et al. (2002) developed a comprehensive set of measuring tools called the company's entrepreneurial assessment tool (CEAI). CEAI includes five dimensions: management support, job freedom, reward, time availability, and organizational boundaries. The cumulative interpretation of these five factors is 43.3%, which suggests that the company should focus on the construction of its internal entrepreneurial environment. The basic assumption is that the company management activities can be effectively managed.

(3) Entrepreneurial management.

Similar to the study of Kuzatko, Brown's (2001) human study is directly influenced by Stevenson et al. (1983, 1985, and 1990) and is based on the development of a group of measuring tools called entrepreneurial management.

Stevenson (1983) defines entrepreneurial management as a set of management practices based on opportunity development that can help companies stay energized and ultimately contribute to value creation activities at the enterprise and society level. In his early works, Stevenson divided this kind of management behavior into two categories (promoter and trustee) and six dimensions, which is strategic orientation, opportunity commitment, resource commitment, resource control, management structure and reward philosophy (Stevenson, 1983; Stevenson and Gumpert, 1985). In the following studies, he made some changes by adding two more dimensions: entrepreneurial culture and growth orientation (Stevenson and Gumpert, 1985; Stevenson and Jarillo, 1986, 1990).

After two previous tests, Brown et al. (2001) obtained a large sample of more than 1 200 specimens based on a random sampling in different sizes, governance structures and industrial attributes. The results show that it is feasible to carry out the operational research based on Stevenson's theory, and to separate six dimensions: strategic orientation, resource orientation, management structure, reward philosophy, growth orientation and entrepreneurial culture.

They further validated that the six dimensions of entrepreneurial management only interacted with entrepreneurial orientation partly. Besides, these two operating tools were positively correlated, and reflected, measured different parts of entrepreneurial activity.

From the literature review above, the three types of measuring tools are based on two major basic disciplines: psychology and organizational behavior, management. Entrepreneurial orientation is trying to answer the question why entrepreneurial activity happens with its main contributors as Miller et al. (1983). Whereas, the entrepreneurial assessment tools and entrepreneurial management are trying to answer the questions how entrepreneurial activity occurs. Its main contributors are Stevenson et al. (1983, 1985, 1990). The above differences are shown in Table 3 – 13.

Table 3 – 13 Differences among three measuring tools

Measuring tools	Entrepreneurial orientation	Evaluation tools	Entrepreneurial management
Researchers	Miller (1983) Covin, Slevin (1991) Lumpkin, Dess (1996)	Kuratko et al. (1990) Hornsby et al. (2002)	Brown et al. (2001)
Disciplines	Psychology, sociology, organizational behavior, Miller et al. (1983)	Management, Stevenson et al. (1983, 1985, 1990)	—
Questions	Why: origin of entrepreneurship	How: management of entrepreneurial behavior	—

2. Empirical research on relationship between entrepreneurial activity and enterprise performance

On the basis of the above measuring tools, many scholars have conducted empirical researches on relationships between entrepreneurial activity and enterprise performance (see Table 3 – 14 for some empirical conclusions). And most of them adopted EO system while only a few empirical studies used CEAI or EM system. The following are some preliminary conclusions from their analysis:

(1) Generally speaking, entrepreneurial activity does have certain correlations

with enterprise performance and can be used as a predictor for it. This conclusion has been supported by many empirical studies from the Americas, Europe and Asia, but some studies have also yielded insignificant or opposite conclusions. Chinese scholars should also carry out more in-depth studies on the basis of actual situation in enterprises under transitional conditions.

(2) The complex relationship between entrepreneurial activity and enterprise performance is caused by the influence of third-party variables, and their effects will lead to different performance or even negative ones. In view of the influence of third party variables and the relationship between "entrepreneurial activity and enterprise performance", Coventry and Slavin (1991) proposed a complete conceptual framework, and subsequent empirical researches are conducted around these factors.

(3) The long-term impact of entrepreneurial activity on enterprise performance is better than short-term forecasting. From the view of longitudinal research approach used by Zahra (1995) and Wiklund (1999), long-term performance is better than short-term one in regression results, which is very similar to the conclusion of GEM. Therefore, the entrepreneurial strategy is a long-term strategy instead of short-term tactical behavior.

Table 3 - 14 Empirical research of relationship between entrepreneurial activity and performance

Author & Year	Method & Data	Effective samples	Statistical analysis	Contributions & Conclusions
Zahra, Covin (1995)	Based on research of Miller and Friessen (1982); primary and secondary data within 7 years	108 firms in various segmented markets	Regression analysis	The effectiveness of corporate entrepreneurship has increased, especially in antagonistic environment
Becherer, Maurer (1997)	Questionnaire survey; EO	Entrepreneurialenterprise, 147 valid questionnaires	Correlation analysis; Multiple regression analysis	Entrepreneurial orientation will directly influence corporate profit
Wiklund (1999)	Questionnaire survey; EO; Longitudinal study within 3 years	Swedish small enterprise, 132 valid questionnaires	Multiple regression analysis	EO is positively correlated with performance of small enterprise; available assets is of great importance to entrepreneurial activity and performance
Knight (2000)	Semi-structured interview; questionnaire survey; Based on Miller's EO study	American manufacturing small business owner	Structural equation model; Correlation analysis; Regression analysis	Entrepreneurial orientation will promote the implementation of market strategy and thus enhance performance

Continued

Author & Year	Method & Data	Effective samples	Statistical analysis	Contributions & Conclusions
Zahra (2000)	Questionnaire survey; Based on Miller's (1983) three dimensions	American international manufacturers, 98 valid questionnaires	Correlation analysis; Regression analysis	Entrepreneurial orientation is positively correlated with ROA and revenue growth rate;
Yusuf (2002)	Questionnaire survey; EO	Manufacturing and merchandising enterprise; 86 valid questionnaires	Multiple regression analysis	Performance is positively correlated with EO, competitive uncertainty and financing uncertainty
Brizek (2003)	Questionnaire survey; CEAI	522 valid questionnaires in catering industry	Stepwise regression; Correlation analysis	Work satisfaction is positively correlated with perceived entrepreneurial culture and CEAI
Eliasson, Davidsson (2003)	Telephone interview and questionnaire survey; EM	Swedish middle and small-sized private enterprise, 957 and 574 valid questionnaires	Hierarchical regression	EM will affect entrepreneurial activity; entrepreneurial activity will affect profit rate
Arbaug, Cox, Amp (2003)	Questionnaire survey; EO five indexes	1045 firms in 17 countries	Factor analysis; regression analysis	Entrepreneurial orientation has general meaning under international background and is positively correlated with some performance indexes
Jarna, Kaisu (2003)	Questionnaire survey; similar to CEAI	184 employees in Finnish small enterprise	Correlation analysis	Interior entrepreneurial environment is positively correlated with customer satisfaction and work satisfaction
Wiklund, Shepherd (2005)	Questionnaire survey; Based on Miller's (1983) three dimensions	413 valid questionnaires from Sweden	Stepwise regression (three interactive variables)	EO is positively correlated with performance; EO will overcome the limitations of environment and resources

3. Deficiencies of measuring tools

From the literature review above, we can see that the relationship between entrepreneurial activity and performance requires more research. Some studies have determined the organization of entrepreneurial activity by scoring of management perception, are prone to the following results.

One situation is that the organization's top management team has a high entrepreneurial orientation, but does not establish an effective internal entrepreneurial institution and a good entrepreneurial culture, therefore, the grassroots employees do not have high entrepreneurial orientations. As a result, good institutions and policies cannot be effectively implemented at the grassroots level, and it is also difficult for organizations to seize fleeting business opportunities.

Another situation is that lower-level employees have recognized the unmet needs of the market or the resources that are not being developed within the organization (Kirzner, 1997), but senior managers do not provide appropriate support and motivations, thus some employees may go out to start their own businesses.

CEAI is mainly based on the perception of middle managers, although including the support from some senior management, it does not fully reflect the entrepreneurial orientation of senior managers which is of great importance.

The above method is a general one, which assumes that each predictor variable (independent variable) has a separate, additional, and independent effect on the standard variable (dependent variable), but is not subject to other disturbing variables (Aiken and West, 1991).

In fact, enterprise-level entrepreneurial activity is influenced by both senior managers and the entrepreneurial spirit of all employees. Although these factors are in particular order, it is difficult to determine the real impact on performance by neglecting some effects.

4. Integrated entrepreneurial activity system on enterprise level

Hart (1992) examined the relationship between strategic decision-making patterns and enterprise performance. He found that only if high-level managers' decision-making patterns are matched with the behavior patterns of general organizational members will the enterprise achieve better performance. If the senior management team's strategic decision-making model is "total control" and the general organization members are "sheep", it can only bring low performance (role imbalance); if the senior management team is "strategic abdication", and the general members are "wild ducks", it will also lead to low performance. Only when high-level management teams are in the "sense of strategic direction", and the general organization members are "active players", will it be possible to bring high performance (role balance).

Hart's thought is in line with the theory of contingency which holds the view that the relationship between two variables is influenced by a third-party variable, thus scholars must consider interference effects of the third one (Arnlod, 1982). There are also many scholars calling for the use of contingency methods to verify complex relationships between independent variables and dependent variables (such as,

Ginsberg and Venkatraman, 1985; Hay and Morris, 1991; Robinson and McDougall, 2001).

Therefore, previous researches often view entrepreneurial-oriented perception of high-level management as the evaluation indicators of entrepreneurial activity, or look at the internal business environment based on the management of middle-level or grass-roots staff. We believe that these two methods are both somewhat deviated from the practice. If the organization wants to achieve high performance through entrepreneurial activities, it must be done in two ways: senior management entrepreneurial orientation (EO) and cultural and institutional aspects of the internal entrepreneurship environment (IEE) within the whole organization. Then we can get to the following conceptual research framework, as shown in Figure 3 – 10.

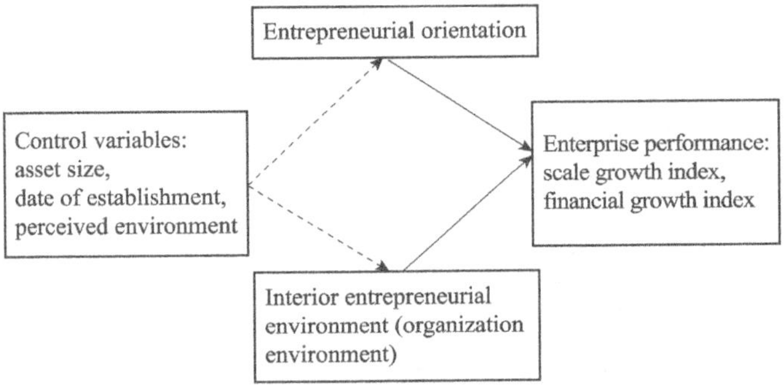

Figure 3 – 10 Conceptual model of relationship between entrepreneurial activity and performance

5. Research hypothesis

From the above literature review and conceptual research framework, we can get the following research hypotheses.

Miller (1983) and other studies have tried to transplant personal entrepreneurial-oriented results to entrepreneur's entrepreneurial research, the basic conclusion is that an entrepreneurial organization is firstly embodied as a senior management team with entrepreneurial spirit. From the above theoretical and empirical researches on EO, the entrepreneurial orientation perceived by senior management team has a significantly positive correlation with enterprise performance, so we get to hypothesis one.

Hypothesis 1: There is a significantly positive correlation between enterprise performance and entrepreneurial orientation perceived by senior management teams.

With the in-depth studies on entrepreneurial spirit of existing enterprises, especially large enterprises and even multinational enterprises, it is clear that the high-level management team's entrepreneurial orientation is hard to represent the entire organization. Besides, whether the general middle and lower employees are able to perceive the culture and environment that encourages entrepreneurship is one of the cruces to the effectiveness of entrepreneurial strategy. Thus, we get to hypothesis two.

Hypothesis 2: There is a significantly positive correlation between enterprise performance and internal entrepreneurial environment perceived by general staff.

According to the study of Hart (1992), Bartlett and Ghoshal (1997) found that only the entrepreneurial orientation of the senior management team or the entrepreneurial enthusiasm of the staff is not enough, it has to create a culture of entrepreneurial orientation throughout the whole organization. Only when entrepreneurial culture is perceived by the entire staff and they all work together will enterprise performance be continuous. The studies of Bartlett and others have shown that high, medium and low managers all play a different role in grasping opportunities, integrating resources and creating values in high-efficient organizations. In entrepreneurial activities, senior managers often play the role of developing a set of opportunity criteria and performance standards, and middle managers' role is to cultivate staff, evaluate and support their creativity, while the grass-roots managers create and seek new opportunities. Combined with the above analyses, we can get to hypothesis three.

Hypothesis 3: In terms of the predictive effects of general models on performance, a contingency model that integrates the interactions between entrepreneurial orientation and internal entrepreneurial environment is more effective in predicting enterprise performance.

Many studies have shown that the dynamics, complexity and antagonism of environment are important driving factors of entrepreneurial activity. They also consider the entrepreneurial team's perception towards environment (dynamic, complex, antagonistic) as an important factor. After investigating 63 township enterprises in China, Luo (1999) has discovered that environmental dynamics are significantly related to EO, but the correlation between complexity and risk-taking is not significant. Rumblekin and Days (2001) have found that, proactiveness is suitable for enterprises in early stage of industrial growth under turbulent environment, while competitive enthusiasm is more applied to mature enterprises under competitive environment. From Wei Kelunde's (1999) conclusion, we could see that available asset has a significant impact on the relationship between entrepreneurial activity and enterprise performance, where asset size is viewed as one of the disturbing variables. In the meanwhile, we should also consider the life-span of enterprise as a disturbing variable because some studies have shown that entrepreneurship will go through cyclical changes. For instance, Edith argued that in the enterprise's life cycle, the entrepreneurship would first be strong and then get weak. Therefore, we can get to the hypothesis four.

Hypothesis 4: The environmental changes perceived by enterprises, the scale of assets, and the life-span of enterprise have a significant disruption to the relationship between entrepreneurial activity (EO and IEE) and enterprise performance.

3.3.3 Research method

1. Data sample

Our sample includes 55 enterprises with total assets ranging from 8.6 million yuan to 450 million yuan. The average total assets is 343 million yuan and the standard deviation is 694 million yuan. The average number of employees in our sample is 629 person, with an average founding time of 7.4 years. In terms of industrial distribution, it includes real estate, steel, chemicals, food and pharmaceutical industry. These samples are limited to the top 100 private enterprises in Tianjin instead of being randomly selected.

The initial questionnaire was in English and was pretested by a group of EMBA students, and then was translated into Chinese by back-to-back procedures. The distribution of questionnaires is by mail and then collected by someone within the research group. All the respondents are department managers and above. All the data were collected in August 2004. The descriptive statistics of the overall sample are shown in Table 3 – 15.

Table 3 – 15 Descriptive statistics of total sample (2003)

Features	Sample size	Minimum	Maximum	Average	Standard deviation
Enterprise age (year)	55	2.5	20	7.40	4.00
Total assets (10 thousand yuan)	55	860	45 000	34 264.94	69 389.03
Staff (person)	55	15	4 300	629.33	769.22
Sales revenue (10 thousand yuan)	55	643	385 679	30 992.74	71 335.76

From the enterprises' characteristics of life-span, total assets, number of employees and sales revenue, these samples are not a homogeneous group of enterprises.

2. Variables and measurement

Based on a detailed literature review on entrepreneurship, we have sorted out a set of questions to describe entrepreneurial activity at the enterprise level. The questions are based on the following studies of some well-known scholars, including Miller (1983), Brown (2001), Hornsby (2002) and so on. The measurement system of entrepreneurial orientation and internal entrepreneurial environment, as well as the perceived dimensions of environmental changes have used a 5-level Likert scale and factor analysis. The following statistical analysis has used SSPS 11.5.

(1) Enterprise performance.

There was no consistent and uniform measurement system for the performance of entrepreneurial firms, and past researches tended to more available variable information (Cooper, 1995). Scholars believed that growth was the most important indicator when observing the enterprise performance (such as Brush and Vanderwerf, 1992; Chandler and Hanks, 1993; Fombrun and Wally, 1989; Tsai, MacMillian and Low, 1991; Wiklund and Shepherd, 2005) and also more accurate and available than any other accounting data.

Hoy et al. (1992) stressed that many scholars have reached a consensus that the growth of sales revenue is the best growth measurement indicator, which not only reflects the short-term changes, but also reflects the long-term changes in the enterprise; besides, it is easy to obtain. Other scholars such as Buckham (1996) believed that entrepreneurs see sales growth as the most common performance indicator. The creation of new jobs has attracted wide attention, thus the growth of the number of employees and assets are also considered as important aspects of performance. Therefore, when we use growth as an important indicator, sales revenue, number of employees and assets will all provide important and complementary performance information. As a result, this study uses several performance indicators to carry out hypothesis testing.

Because our sample contains different industries, the overall evaluation of the indicators is not appropriate and cannot be compared. They are enterprise in their growth period, thus the growth indicator is the most important. At the same time, growth indicator can also be compared among different industries. Therefore, we have chosen three growth indicators, two of them are scale growth indicators (assets growth, AG and employee growth, EG) and the other one is financial growth indicator, that is, sales growth rate SG. The calculation formulas are shown below:

$$\text{Total asset growth rate (AG)} = (\text{total asset}_{2003} - \text{total asset}_{2001}) / \text{total asset}_{2001}$$

$$\text{Employee growth rate (EG)} = (\text{employee}_{2003} - \text{employee}_{2001}) / \text{employee}_{2001}$$

$$\text{Sales revenue growth rate (SG)} = (\text{sale revenue}_{2003} - \text{sale revenue}_{2001}) / \text{sale revenue}_{2001}$$

Table 3 – 16 provides the average, standard deviation and Pearson correlation on three types of performance indicators for factor analysis.

Table 3 – 16 Average, standard deviation and correlation coefficient of 3 performance index

Performance index	Average	Standard deviation	AG	EG
Total asset growth rate (AG)	1.95	5.21	1	
Employee growth rate (EG)	0.61	0.77	0.524 **	1
Sales revenue growth rate (SG)	2.91	10.09	0.862 **	0.444 **

Note: ** represents $p < 0.01$, two-tailed test (Pearson correlation).

You can see these three types of growth indicators were significantly correlated from 0.444 to 0.862, but did not reach the level of mutual substitution. By using the Cronbach α coefficient to measure its reliability, the three indicators in our sample has a Cronbach α value of 0.660, which is in line with the 0.7 standard.

Then we used factor analysis to analyze these three types of performance indicators and found that they were classified as one type. The KMO value is 0.613, which is suitable for factor analysis. The cumulative explanatory value of the variables is 74.78%. So we get a comprehensive performance indicator EP with its factor load matrix (see Table 3 – 17).

Table 3 – 17 Factor load matrix of enterprise performance [a]

Performance index	Factor
	1
Total asset growth rate (AG)	0.939
Employee growth rate (EG)	0.726
Sales revenue growth rate (SG)	0.913

Note: Extraction method is principal component analysis; "a" means extracting a factor.

(2) Measurement of entrepreneurial activity.

Miller (1983) summarized the characteristics of entrepreneurial enterprises as below: entrepreneurial enterprises are committed to product or market innovation, and are engaged in adventurous cause and proactive actions which will always leave their components a fatal hit. Based on this, many scholars agree that entrepreneurial orientation is mainly embodied in three dimensions: innovation, proactiveness and risk taking. Thus, entrepreneurialism encompasses a tendency to continually update market offerings, adventurously bring out new and uncertain products, services, or markets and always capture market opportunities before competitors (e. g. Covin and Slevin, 1991; Knight, 1997; Miller, 1983; Wiklund, 1999; Zahra and Covin, 1995). We also agree with the above point of view.

Based on the scales used by Miller (1983), Hansby (2002), Brown (2001) and so on, this research has made an operational definition of entrepreneurial orientation and internal entrepreneurial environment. For EO and IEE, we have used 12 items which are all required. Among which, the two most extreme situations are on both ends while the other five ranks are in between. In order to avoid misleading judgments, we have adopted reverse judgment and putted the entrepreneurial and non-entrepreneurial status on both ends. The Cronbach α value for EO and IEE is 0.787, which suggests a satisfactory reliability. Table 3 – 18 shows the descriptive statistics of EO and IEE.

Table 3 – 18 Descriptive statistics of EO and IEE (Y1 – Y12)

Item	Sample size	Minimum	Maximum	Average	Standard deviation
Y1	55	2.00	5.00	4.055	0.731
Y2	55	1.00	5.00	2.855	0.891
Y3	55	1.00	5.00	3.564	0.856
Y4	55	2.00	5.00	3.636	0.930
Y5	55	2.00	5.00	4.164	0.714
Y6	55	2.00	5.00	3.982	0.733
Y7	55	2.00	5.00	3.255	0.700
Y8	55	3.00	5.00	4.182	0.641
Y9	55	2.00	5.00	3.709	0.712
Y10	55	3.00	5.00	4.291	0.685
Y11	55	2.00	5.00	3.891	0.629
Y12	55	3.00	5.00	4.091	0.646

Note: EO means entrepreneurial orientation; IEE represents interior entrepreneurial environment.

We did a factor analysis on items from Y1 to Y5, which made up the entrepreneurial orientation. We found that they were composed of two factors instead of a single dimension, namely proactiveness (EO1: Y1, Y4, Y5) and risk taking (EO2: Y2, Y3). This result is consistent with the conclusions of some other scholars. We found that in this report, innovation and proactiveness are classified as one dimension. The KMO value of Y1 to Y5 is 0.657, which is suitable for factor analysis, and the interpretation of the whole variables is 66.22%. Table 3 – 19 shows the factor load matrix of EO.

Table 3 - 19 **Factor load matrix of EO [a]**

Item	Factor	
	1	2
Y1	0. 667	0. 209
Y2	-0. 022	0. 912
Y3	0. 361	0. 766
Y4	0. 768	0. 055
Y5	0. 820	0. 091

Note: Extraction method is principal component analysis; rotation algorithm is variation maximum method; "a" means three-step iterative.

By conducting factor analysis on items from Y6 to Y12, we found that they could form a singly dimension, which is internal entrepreneurship environment (IEE) with a KMO value of 0. 804. The interpretation of the variables is 45. 98%. The factor load matrix is shown in Table 3 - 20.

Table 3 - 20 **Factor load matrix of IEE [a]**

ITEM	Factor
	1
Y6	0. 722
Y7	0. 494
Y8	0. 721
Y9	0. 841
Y10	0. 567
Y11	0. 574
Y12	0. 758

Note: Extraction method is principal component analysis; "a" means extracting a factor.

(3) Control variables.

Enterprises of different sizes and life-spans will show different organizational and environmental characteristics, which will in turn affect performance. Therefore, we regard age and total assets (here we use the data from the end of 2003) as control variables. Besides, some previous studies have also attached importance to these variables (e. g. Chandler and Hanks, 1994). Previous studies have also found that entrepreneurial activity and performance are interfered by environmental perception, which is consisted of three types: antagonism, complexity and dynamics (Zahra, 1993; Miller, 1988; Wiklund, 2005). Just as the dimensions of EO and IEE are constructed, the perception of environment is based on a large number of previous studies, uses a 5-level Likert scale and conducts factor analysis (due to space limitations, the results are omitted here).

3. Analysis

In order to verify the hypotheses, this report has used the method of hierarchical regression. Based on careful checking of the data, each step adds a higher level of interaction (two-path and three-path interactions, respectively), and the significance of the increased R^2 and F value are evaluated. In order to evaluate the interaction of the variables, it is common practice to first add independent arguments and then observe the effects on dependent variable (Cohen and Cohen, 1983). This arrangement allows us to evaluate the effect of independent variables on dependent variable under the influence of variable interaction. Table 3 – 21 shows the correlations of quantifiable variables.

Table 3 – 21 Correlation analysis of quantifiable variables

Variables	1	2	3	4	5	6	7	8
1. Enterprise age	1							
2. Total asset (2003)	0.087	1						
3. Environmental resistance	0.013	0.129	1					
4. Environmental complexity	-0.289*	-0.242	-0.303*	1				
5. Environmental dynamics	0.189	0.130	-0.215	0.135	1			
6. Enterprise performance	-0.194	0.188	0.070	-0.186	-0.187	1		
7. IEE	-0.045	0.330*	0.025	-0.095	0.265	0.187	1	
8. Innovative cognition and action	-0.087	0.187	-0.161	0.120	0.148	-0.212	0.565**	1
9. Risk – taking	-0.111	0.061	0.043	0.165	0.059	-0.043	0.258	0.247

Note: * represents $p < 0.05$, ** represents $p < 0.01$, two-tailed test (Pearson correlation).

We can see that the age of enterprise is negatively correlated with perceived environmental complexity ($p < 0.05$), which is in line with the characteristics of the growth firms. During the growth period, the entrepreneurial enterprise has a relatively clear understanding of its industry status and competitive information. We can also see that the antagonism of the environment is negatively correlated with complexity ($p < 0.05$), indicating that the three dimensions of environmental perception do not necessarily constitute a single indicator and, in some cases, are separate from each other. There is also an important finding that the total assets in 2003 were positively correlated with internal entrepreneurial environment ($p < 0.05$), which was consistent with the conclusions of some previous literatures. When the enterprise grows to a certain stage, we must strengthen the internal entrepreneurial environment and institution construction instead of relying on entrepreneurs or entrepreneurial teams alone. Another finding is that the internal entrepreneurial environment and innovation (EO_1) are positively correlated ($p<0.01$), which can be explained by the fact that the sample is directly from the top 100 private enterprises in Tianjin, thus they behave better in internal entrepreneurial environment and innovation but not in risk taking (EO_2).

3. 3. 4 Results and conclusions

In order to verify the hypotheses, we first add control variables, then independent variables, and then the two-way interaction, and finally the three-path interaction. The three control variables of total assets, firm age and environmental perception explain 6% of performance, but not statistically significant. On the basis of previous analysis, the next general model evaluates the independent effects of EO and IEE, and the total interpretation of performance is 20. 1% (adjusted R^2), which is the second column data in Table 3 – 21 ($p<0.05$). The interactions of two-way and three-path are respectively reflected in contingency model Ⅰ and Ⅱ. We can see that the adjusted R^2 was 0. 262 ($p<0.05$) and 0. 280 ($p<0.05$) with the explanations of 26. 2% and 28%, respectively. Table 3 – 22 shows the results of the above regression.

Table 3 – 22 Entrepreneurial activity and enterprise performance: general model & contingency model (sample size = 55)

Entrepreneurial activity (EA)	Enterprise performance (EP)			
	Control variable	General model	Contingency model Ⅰ	Contingency model Ⅱ
Enterprise age	–0. 220	–0. 181	–0. 100	–0. 091
Total asset (2003)	0. 165	0. 146	0. 087	0. 089
Environmental resistance	–0. 048	–0. 123	–0. 057	–0. 050
Environmental complexity	–0. 236	–0. 141	–0. 224	–0. 232
Environmental dynamics	–0. 130	–0. 219	–0. 154	–0. 142
Interior entrepreneurial environment (IEE)		0. 470 ***		
Innovative cognition and action (EO_1)		–0. 474 ***		
Risk – taking (EO_2)		–0. 041		
IEE × EO_1			–0. 080	
IEE × EO_2			–5. 255 *	
EO_1 × EO_2			4. 142 **	
IEE × EO_1 × EO_2				5. 559 ***
R^2	0. 150	0. 324	0. 418	0. 432
Adjusted R^2	0. 060	0. 201 **	0. 262 **	0. 280 ***
S. E.	0. 985	0. 908	0. 872	0. 862
F	1. 659	2. 636	2. 682	2. 836
Sig.	0. 163	0. 019	0. 011	0. 008

Note: In Contingency model Ⅱ, interaction effect of EO_1 and EO_2 is eliminated due to collinearity; * represents $p<0.10$, ** represents $p<0.05$, *** represents $p<0.01$.

Thus, hypothesis 1 is partly supported by the fact that the entrepreneurial orientation perceived by senior managers is broken down into two parts: EO_1 (innovation and proactiveness) and EO_2 (risk-taking). Among which, EO_1 is negatively correlated with enterprise performance, but not significant, while EO_2 is significantly positively correlated with enterprise performance. Hypothesis 2 is supported, and the internal entrepreneurial environment perceived by the whole organization has a significantly positive correlation with enterprise performance. At the same time, hypothesis 3 has also been supported. Taking into account the interaction of the contingency model has better improved the interpretation than general models.

From general model 1, it can be seen that internal entrepreneurial environment is positively related to performance, but innovation and proactivess are negatively correlated with performance, and this conclusion is similar to other experts who study Chinese issues. For example, Tan and Li (1996), Luo (1999) found that for private enterprises in northern China (Beijing and Tianjin), their response to external environment is a mixed type between proactiveness and defense. They are considered as "cautious advancers" because their attitude towards complex external environment is not always risky, and it is difficult for them to make a careful and detailed analysis before making decisions. This kind of strategy-environment architecture will lead to excellent financial and market performance.

When we assess the standard regression coefficients of control variables such as corporate age, firm size (total assets), and environmental perception, there are no clear conclusions. All control variables have some changes in different models and some effects on relationship between entrepreneurial activity and enterprise performance. However, it is not statistically significant, so hypothesis 4 is partially supported. Through the above analysis, we can get the following regression analysis results.

Based on 55 private enterprises in China and the analysis of contingency models, we find a significantly positive correlation between entrepreneurial activity and enterprise performance. This conclusion is of great importance for entrepreneurial management, that is, if we want long-term competitive advantage and extraordinary performance, we have to take care of two aspects: one is the senior management of entrepreneurial orientation; the other is the internal entrepreneurial environment and the institutional and cultural construction within the whole organization. But because our samples are manufacturing enterprises in traditional industries, there are more antagonism and competitiveness but less complexity and dynamics compared with high-tech enterprises. We will use the sample of high-tech enterprises for further verifications in follow-up studies.

There are some limitations should be noted. Frist, the sample size of this survey is not large; second, this report is also limited by some common problems, such as, there may be some cognitive bias problems due to the same answerer for questions of entrepreneurial-oriented, internal entrepreneurial environment and enterprise performance. The use of longitudinal research methods and engaging of more investigators may make up for some of the current shortcomings. Besides, structural equation models such as LISREL and longitudinal case studies are also within the future directions (Zahra et al., 1995; Wiklund, 1999).

References

1. Ahlstrom D., Bruton G. D. An Institutional Perspective on the Role of Culture in Shaping Strategic Actions by Technology-focused Entrepreneurial Firms in China. Entrepreneurship Theory and Practice, 2002, 26 (4): 53 –69.

2. Aiken A. W., West S. G. Multiple Regression: Testing and Interpreting Interactions. Sage: Newbury Parks, CA, 2001.

3. Brockhaus R. H. Risk-taking Propensity of Entrepreneurs. Academy of Management Journal, 1980 (23): 509 –520.

4. Bruno A. V., Tyebjee T. T. The Environment for Entrepreneurship. In C A. Kent, D. L. Sexton, K. H. Vesper (Eds.), Encyclopedia of Entrepreneurship, 1991: 288 –307, Englewood Cliffs, NJ. Prentice Hall.

5. Brush C. G., Vanderwerf P. A. A Comparison of Methods and Sources for Obtaining Estimates of New Venture Performance. Journal of Business Venturing, 1992, 7 (2): 157 –170.

6. Busenitz L. W. A Cross-cultural Cognitive Model of New Venture Creation. Entrepreneurship Theory and Practice. 1996, 20 (4): 25 –39.

7. Carland J. A., Carland J. W. An Empirical Investigation into the Distinctions between Male and Female Entrepreneurs and Managers. International Small Business Journal, 1991, 9 (3): 62 –72.

8. Chandler G. N., Hanks S. H. Measuring Performance of Emerging Business. Journal of Business Venturing, 1993 (8): 3 –40.

9. Chandler G. N., Lyon D. W. Methodological Issues in Entrepreneurship Research: the Past Decade. Entrepreneurship Theory and Practice, 2001, 25 (4):

101 – 113.

10. Chow C. K. W., Fung M. K. Y. Firm Dynamics and Industrialization in the Chinese Economy in Transition: Implications for Small Business Policy. Journal of Business Venturing, 1996, 11 (6): 489 – 505.

11. Chu Xiaoping. Social Relationship Capital and Chinese Familial Enterprise' s Entrepreneurship and Development. Nankai Business Review, 2003 (6): 8 – 12.

12. Covin J. G., Slevin D. P. A Conceptual Model of Entrepreneurship as Firm Behavior. Entrepreneurship theory and Practice, 1991 (16): 7 – 25.

13. Dana L. P. Small Business as a Supplement in the People's Republic of China (PRC). Journal of Small Business Management, 1999, 37 (7).

14. D'Aveni R. Hypercompetition. New York: Free Press, 1994.

15. DruckerP. F. Innovation and Entrepreneurship. Hainan Publishing House, 2000.

16. Drucker P. F. Our Entrepreneurial Economy. Harvard Business Review, 2010 (35): 614.

17. Fligstein N. Social Skill and Institutional Theory. American Behavioral Scientist, 1997 (40): 397 – 405.

18. Fombrun C. J., Wally S. Structuring Small Firms for Rapid Growth. Journal of Business Venturing, 1989, 4 (2): 107 – 122.

19. Gartner W. B. A Conceptual Framework for Describing the Phenomenon of New Venture Creation. Academy of Management Review, 1985, 10 (4): 696 – 706.

20. Hambrik D. C. Some Tests of the Effectiveness and Functional Attributes of Miles and Snow's Strategic Types. Academy of Management Journal, 1983 (26): 5 – 26.

21. Hambrick D. C. Top Management Groups: A Conceptual Integration and Reconsideration of the" Team" Label. In L. L. Cummings, B. M. Staw (Eds.): Research in Organizational Behavior, 1994: 171 – 214, Greenwich, CT: JAI Press.

22. Hamilton G. Business Networks and Economic Development in East and Southeast Asia. HongKong: Center for Asian Studies, 1991.

23. Hay D. A., Morris D. K. Industrial Economics and Organization: Theory and Evidence. Oxford University Press, 1991.

24. HuttM. A., Erin D. Strategic Entrepreneurs: Creating a New Type of Intellectual Pattern. Economic& Management Publishing House, 2002.

25. Jiang Yanfu, Gao Jian, Cheng Yuan, QiuQiong. Global Entrepreneurship Monitor China Report (2002). Tsinghua University Press, 2003.

26. Kirnzer I. Entrepreneurial Discovery and the Competitive Market Process: an Austrian Approach. Journal of Economic Literature, 1997 (35): 60 -85.

27. Kuratko D. F., Montagno R. V., Hornsby J. S. Developing an Intrapreneurial Assessment Instrument for an Effective Corporate Entrepreneurial Environment. Strategic Management Journal, 1990 (11): 49 -58.

28. Lumpkin G. T., Dess G. G. Clarifying the Entrepreneurial Orientation Construct and Linkingit to Performance. Academy of Management Review, 1996, 21 (1): 135 -172.

29. McKinnon R. I. Financial Growth and Macroeconomic Stability in China, 1978 - 1992: Implications for Russia and Other Transitional Economies. Journal of Comparative Economics, 1994, 18 (3): 438 -469.

30. North D. Institutions, Institutional Change and Economic Performance. Cambridge: Cambridge University Press, 1990.

31. Per Davidsson, Johan Wiklund. Values, Beliefs and Regional Variations in New Firm Formation Rates. Journal of Economic Psychology, 1997 (18): 179 -199.

32. Raphael Amit, Eitan Muller, Iain Cockburn. Opportunity Cost and Entrepreneurial Activity. Journal of Business Venturing, 1995 (10): 95 -106.

33. Robinson K. C., McDougall P. P. Entry Barriers and New Venture Performance: a Comparison of Universal and Contingency Approaches. Strategic Management Journal, 2001 (22): 659 -685.

34. Sexton D. L., Bowman N. B. The Entrepreneur: A Capable Executive and More. Journal of Business Venturing, 1985 (1): 129 -140.

35. Shane S., Venkataraman S. The Promise of Entrepreneurship as a Field of Research. Academy of Management Review, 2000, 25 (1): 217 -226.

36. Smart D. T., Conant J. S. Entrepreneurial Orientation, Distinctive Marketing Competencies and Organizational Performance. Journal of Applied Business Research, 1994, 10 (3): 28 -38.

37. Staley E., Morse R. Developing Entrepreneurship: Elements for a Program, In Kilby (Ed), Entrepreneurship and Economic Development, 1971: 357 -384, New York: Free Press.

38. Stevenson H. H. A Perspective on Entrepreneurship. Harvard Business School Working Paper, 1983 (9): 384 -131.

39. Stevenson H. H., Gumpert D. E. The Heart of Entrepreneurship. Harvard Business Review, 1985 (2): 85 -94.

40. Stevenson H. H., Jarillo-Mossi J. C. Preserving Entrepreneurship as

Companies Grow. Journal of Business Strategy, 1986, 7 (1): 10 -23.

41. Stevenson H. H. , Jarillo-Mossi J. C. A Paradigm of Entrepreneurship: Entrepreneurial Management. Strategic Management Journal, 1990 (11): 17 -27.

42. Tsang E. W. K. In Search of Legitimacy: the Private Entrepreneur in China. Entrepreneurship Theory and Practice. Entrepreneurship Theory & Practice, 1996 (21): 76 -80.

43. Venkatraman N. , Prescott J. E. Environment-Strategy Go Alignment: An Empirical Test of its Performance Implications. Strategic Management Journal, 1990 (11): 1 -23.

44. Waddell F. T. Factors Affecting Choice, Satisfaction, and Success in the Female Self-employed. Journal of Vocational Behavior, 1983 (23) 294 -304.

45. Wilklund J. , Davidsson Per, Delmar F. What Do They Think and Feel about Growth? An Expectancy Value Approach to Small Business Managers'Attitudes towards Growth. Entrepreneurship Theory and Practice, 2003, 27 (3): 247 -270.

46. Williamson O. E. Comparative Economic Organization: the Analysis of Discrete Structural Alternatives. Administrative Science Quarterly, 1991 (36): 269 -296.

47. Zahra S. A. Predictors and Financial Outcomes of Corporate Entrepreneurship: an Explorative Study. Journal of Business venturing, 1991 (6): 259 -285.

48. Zapalska A. M. , Edwards W. Chinese Entrepreneurship in a Culture and Economic Perspective. Journal of Small Business Management, 2001, 39 (3): 286 -292.

49. Zhang Yuli, XueHongzhi, Yang Jun. Rational Analysis of Entrepreneurial Activity. Research on Economics and Management, 2003 (5): 9 -13.

50. Zhang Yuli. Entrepreneurial Management: New Challenge of Management Work. Nankai Business Review, 2003 (6): 4 -7.

51. Zhang Yuli, Yang Jun. Empirical analysis of Entrepreneurial Activity. Business Management Journal, 2003 (20): 19 -26.

Chapter 4

Analysis on Financing Obstacles for Private Enterprises

China's private economy has achieved rapid development during 30 years of reform and opening up. However, the development of private economy in different regions is very different, as well as financing channels and financing environment. The questions worth exploring here are how to treat the financing problems of private enterprises? What are the differences in financing mechanism of private enterprises among different regions? Is there a difference in the level of financing convenience? In developed areas, the proportion of financial resources which private economy has gained from state-owned and other formal financial channels is very small. This leads to a question: why is it difficult for private economy to obtain funds needed for development from formal financial channels? Why has it developed so fast? The possible explanation is that although the financial resources gained from formal channels are limited, private finance has played a huge role in promoting private economy, which leads to the second question: whether the private economy has obtained enough financial support from private finance? If so, then how to regulate future development of private finance? If not, it means that the private economy could have developed faster, so how we should promote the reform of financial system in the future? In underdeveloped areas, what is the main factor that has restricted the development of private economy? How can we do to get rid of the backward status? And so on. Analyzing these questions will be helpful to understand the internal mechanism of private economy development and its finance supporting system, to reveal the constraints faced by private enterprises in different regions and different growth stages, and to give more specific and feasible solutions.

Overall, the financing channels of China's private enterprises are not smooth. But it is not enough to just leave the analysis at this level. Due to the differences of initial endowment and institutional rent level in each region, different game strategies have been adopted by relative stakeholders during the process of economic development. As a result, different development modes and evolution paths have took shape, as well as some specific financing models that are appropriate to that particular modes. This kind of financing model is something that matches the development model of private economy, but not necessarily the optimal one. For private enterprises in different modes of private economy development, the constraints are different; at the same time, for those in different growth stages, the demand for funds and the constraints are also different. Therefore, in study of financing problems of private enterprises, we should first explore the evolution mechanism of private economy, and then analyze specific modes of private enterprise financing mechanism and its constraints. What's more, according to the characteristics of various financing models and its constraints, we should combine it with the growth stage of private enterprises in order to fully understand the internal mechanism and bring about more targeted countermeasures.

4.1 Different endowments and financing choice for private economy in initial stage

The institutional rent level and its reduction rate are determined by endowment and its dynamic changes, which stipulates the development mode and evolution path of private economy in specific regions. The process itself also endorses the financing choice of private economy in initial stage. "History is always important. Its importance is not only that we can learn from the past, but also because the present and the future are connected with the past through the continuity of a social system. The choice of today and tomorrow is determined by yesterday. "① In study of financing problems of private enterprises in China, western corporate finance theory has some guiding significance, but at the same time we must consider the specific institutional state within specific period. During early stage of reform and opening up, the economic form mainly includes state-owned and collective economy. In order to guarantee capital supply for state-owned economy, our country allocated financial

① Douglas C. N., "Structure and Changes in Economic History (Chinese version)", Shanghai Joint Publishing, Shanghai People's Publishing House, 1994, pp. 225 - 226.

resources by plan and as a result, the state-owned finance was in monopoly position within the whole financial system. The development of financial system has seriously lagged behind, making private economy which stays outside the system difficult to obtain state-owned financial support.

4.1.1 Growth stage and financing choices

Enterprises in different stages of development have different financing capacity and demand for funds. For various reasons, it is difficult for enterprises in initial stage to obtain external funds. Plus the lag of financial system arrangements and monopoly position of state-owned finance during the process of marketization, it is more difficult for private enterprises to obtain external funds. Enterprises in different stages of life cycle, will have different growth characteristics, different financing capacity and different financing needs. The following are described separately.

1. Characteristics and financing choices of initial period

Private enterprisesare developing very slowly during the initial period where the life cycle curve is of small slope and also small change. Although the pace is not fast, there is a good phenomenon that the enterprises are growing. The early stage is characterized by great operational risk, high cost, low credibility, small scale and weak profitability. The control of the enterprise is mainly in the hands of the entrepreneur. During middle and late period of entrepreneurship, capital demand will increase while the sustainable management ability is still weak, the probability of bankruptcy or suspension is large, the information disclosure is not enough, the difficulty of value evaluation is larger, and the external financing capacity is weak. Start-up enterprises generally have the characteristics of originality, high growth and high risk. They need to avoid various risks (such as technical risk, market risk, financial risk and management risk) to gain development, while the potential return is high. Therefore, based on the high-risk and high-yield characteristics of start-ups, venture capital is more popular. The financing platform for start-up enterprise is mainly composed of entrepreneurs, venture capitalists and creditor investors, where financial leasing is also a common choice.

From the experiences of western developed countries, the majority of small and medium-sized enterprises have start their businesses mainly by endogenous financing, that is, self-financing and corporate retained earnings. Early financing targets of US small and medium-sized enterprises include: personal savings, friends and relatives. As shown in Table 4 – 1, small and medium-sized enterprises in the United States, Japan and the United Kingdom mostly rely on internal financing. Although Japan has the lowest proportion of internal financing, it is still close to 60%.

Table 4 – 1 Financing structures of enterprise entrepreneurship in some countries

Country	Period	Capital ratio (%)		External fund (%)	
		Internal financing	External financing	Direct financing	Indirect financing
U. S.	1958 – 1962	65. 1	34. 9	42. 9	57. 1
	1980 – 1984	73. 7	26. 3	65. 4	34. 6
Japan	1958 – 1962	24. 0	76. 0	73. 7	26. 3
	1980 – 1984	59. 1	40. 9	85. 5	14. 2
U. K.	1958 – 1962	62. 0	38. 0	44. 7	55. 3
	1980 – 1984	81. 1	18. 9	88. 3	11. 7

Source: Wang Yuzhen, "An Institutional Analysis of Capital Structure for State-owned Enterprises", 1999, China Economic Publishing House.

2. Characteristics and financing choices of growth period

If enterprises can survive early period of hardships and get some development, it will generally enter the high-speed growth stage. This stage is characterized by fast development, small fluctuations, enhanced strength, gradually standardized management and compliant governance. In this stage, the enterprise not only has strong vitality, but also strong strength, so the development will be fast. The research which the Mckinsey business management consulting firm once conducted in 1983 has shown that the sales of 70 member companies (all of which are high-speed, medium-sized enterprises) of the American Entrepreneurs Association have increased at least 15% in the past five years. In 1982, the sales of medium-sized enterprise in US grew by an average of 12% while the average rate of return on capital increased by 10%. Among which, the first batch of enterprises' annual growth rate of sales reached 43% and the average rate of return reached 14%. In terms of sales and return on capital, these enterprises have all gone beyond the 250 major companies listed in the "Happiness".

The life cycle curve of growth period is known as positive curve slope and large value. During this period, the enterprises need a lot of capital investment to maintain the rapid development trend, while self-financing and internal financing are not enough. In the meantime, the enterprises also have certain accumulations and material basis, which make it possible to go through other financing channels, such as debt financing, equity financing, venture capital and so on. Because the enterprises have the characteristics of good growth and high risk, they should be very consistent with the investment standards of venture capital. So many growth companies view venture capital as an important financing channel.

3. Characteristics and financing choices of mature period

After high-speed development, the enterprises will enter a mature period with the characteristics of lower development pace but more benefits, good corporate image, declined innovative spirit and rigid system. As the mature enterprises have good financial situations, large scale, stable development, nearly saturated market, widely-known product and high credit, thus the corporate financing channels are wide. At this point, the pace of development of private enterprises is slow. And from the view of corporate scale, the enterprises have already developed to a relatively high level. At this time, it is relatively easy for private enterprises to obtain bank loans and establish a close, win-win relationship with banks due to strong ability and high credibility. As a result, the access to stable banking support is the main financing mode for private sector during this period. At the same time, we should pay more attention to debt financing to promote equity financing and refinancing, so that these two financing modes will encourage and influence each other and a reasonable financing structure will be developed. Borrowing from banks and other financial institutions or issuing bonds in capital market will increase corporate debt and asset-liability ratio. Compared with equity financing, one of the most important features of debt financing is that it will ensure the control of shareholders. Because creditors have no right to participate in decision making, the way in which enterprises take debt financing will not decentralize shareholders' control over the company (corporate) as with issuance of stocks. In addition, debt interest expense can be paid before income tax, so the actual burden of capital cost is low; and the increase of the company's (corporate) debt is conducive to the role of financial leverage. No matter how much the company earns, it only needs to pay a fixed interest on the debt, and more income can be used to allocate among shareholders or stay in the company (business) for reinvestment, which will in turn increase the wealth of shareholders and companies. However, debt financing must pay interest on a regular basis and repay the principal in the end, which will also bring higher financial risk. At this time, the main financing methods include endogenous financing, debt financing, equity financing and so on.

4. Characteristics and financing choices of recession period

When enterprises go into the recession period, they will show up the following characteristics: increasingly serious "large enterprise disease"; backward technology and obsolete technical equipment; shrinking production and reduced efficiency; increased liability and deteriorated financial situation. In this period, the decline of product sales and profits will accelerate. The enterprises may even get loss because of lack of product competitiveness, aging equipment, backward technology and weak innovative awareness. As a result, a variety of enterprise diseases may emerge. At this time, the operational risk and financial risk are both very large.

The emergence of various unfavorable conditions made it very difficult for corporate financing. Creditors are often worried about the bankruptcy of enterprises and thus require them to repay the debt in advance; most of the funds accumulated in the early stages are used to repay the debt and to achieve a smooth transition of relevant expenses; corporate stocks will continue to decline due to the deterioration of operating conditions and the ability of direct financing is greatly frustrated. At this time, the enterprise should seek the chance of mergers through reorganization of assets and other strategic reorganization. However, if the debt is too large, it will constitute a substantial obstacle to the realization of these measures.

To sum up, the financing methods that enterprises should adopt at different stages are summarized in Table 4 - 2.

Table 4 - 2 Financing choices in different stages

Financing choice	Initial period	Growth period	Mature period	Recession period
Self-raising	√	√	√	√
Venture investment	√	√		
Growth enterprise market		√		
Main board market			√	
Indirect financing	√	√	√	

Source: sorted out by the author according to relevant information.

4.1.2 Different endowments and financing choice in initial stage of China's private economy: an empirical analysis

On the whole, the venture capital of China's private enterprises are mainly from their own accumulations while the funding channels of external sources are narrow. At the same time, due to different government power and marketization degree in different regions, the funding sources and financing structures in initial stage are also different. At the beginning of the reform and opening up, although our country has relaxed the restrictions on private economy, the impact of traditional planned economic system is still exist to a certain extent. The systematic difference between state-owned (financial) sector and private (economic) sector is still significant. Besides, market awareness and local government attitude towards private economy are also different. In this case, the way that private economy take to obtain start-up funds will be completely different. In areas where market degree is relatively high, government power is relatively small and institutional rent level is low, the entrepreneurial process of private enterprise is from scratch. In this process, individual entrepreneurship is basically in a spontaneous status: start-up enterprises are difficult to obtain external funds so they can only rely on themselves to raise and accumulate. Thus, the entrepreneurs carry out primitive accumulation through various commercial activities and, if necessary, conduct private lending to obtain funds. This type of capital accumulation is characterized by self-accumulation, small scale and slow development. Therefore, this private economic development mode in initial stage is relatively slow. But when it develop to a certain stage, its market advantages will fully show up and private lending will play an important role. With the development of marketization process and enhancement of their own financing capacity, it will be easier for private enterprises to obtain external funds and get more financial support. In areas where marketization level and government power are higher, the system rent is higher. At this time, the private enterprise (mainly the collective enterprise) will have some collective accumulation, and the government will use its own advantages to provide financial intermediation from state-owned financial channels. Because this mode has certain basis and access to a large scale of funds, it will have faster development in early stages of development. But with the increasing degree of economic marketization, the drawbacks will be exposed and the government power will inevitably decline. In areas with low degree of marketization and high government power, the system rent is usually high and the state-owned economy is more important. The development of private enterprises is limited by the environment and lack of external financial support, so it is difficult and slow to develop. In areas with low degree of marketization and government power, the system rent is higher. However, due to the slow development of industrialization in this region, the private economy and entrepreneurial financing are more out of the question.

1. Data source, variable definition and preliminary verification

According to relevant macroeconomic data, the regression analysis method is used to analyze the relationship between financing choice, endowment and the system rent factors in initial stages. On the whole, it can be seen that the early stage of reform and opening up is the initial stage for private enterprises. At this point, corporate financing method is single, banks are monopolized in financial system, and bank credit is the most important source of external funds. Therefore, according to the data of all financial institutions in all regions of China from 1999 to 2001, we can roughly estimate the status of bank credit funds obtained by private enterprises in initial stage, which will reflect the financing situations and influencing factors of the private enterprises. The data used in this section are inter-provincial data from 1999 to 2001① and contains a total of 29 provinces, autonomous regions and municipalities. Hainan and Chongqing are excluded due to data reasons. The data are derived from 2000 – 2002 "China Statistical Yearbook", "China Private Economy Yearbook", "China Population Statistical Yearbook", "China Business Yearbook", "China Industrial Administration Statistical Yearbook", "China Agriculture Yearbook", "New China Fifty-Five Years Statistical Data Collection" and so on. For individual data that cannot be obtained, we made some appropriate adjustments based on other indicators. For the definition of variables, we continued the method in previous regression analysis and made appropriate adjustments based on the availability of sample data as follows:

In order to measure the amount of loans obtained from formal financial institutions at initial stage, we exclude the amount of state-owned economy loans from all local financial institutions to measure the amount of money acquired by private economy. Because the loans from financial institutions mainly flow to state-owned economic sectors, we use the following method to estimate the share of loans in the private sector:

Total financial institution loans $F_i = \beta_0 + \beta_1 {}^*$ (total industrial output value) $+ \gamma_i$

From the stochastic error term γ_i in the above equation, we can get the balance of loans, $\beta_0 + \beta_i$, which are not related to the state-owned economy. In the following analysis, the estimate of $\beta_0 + \beta_i$ is used as an independent explanatory variable. We use this value to approximately represent the share of loans that flows to the private sector. For data reasons, we can only use this indicator for approximate analysis. Financial institution loans is an important source of corporate finance, and the amount of loans from this channel in our country is closely related to regional systems, endowments, ideologies and other factors. Thus, analyzing through this indicator is

① The reason of using data between 1999 and 2001 is that: In 1992, Deng Xiaoping's speech gave a better policy and market environment for the development of private economy, but the detailed data on individual and private economy before 1999 were not available. At the same time, the caliber changed after 1999 (the state-owned economy in and after 1999 include state-owned and state-controlled enterprises).

of important inspiration and will also explain some important phenomena in private enterprise financing. Other explanatory variables are defined as follows:

Influence of state-owned economy: we use two variables to measure the influence of state-owned economy. The first one is the scale of loans from all financial institutions expressed by per capita loans: the balance of loans from all financial institutions/total population; the second variable is the size of state-owned economy expressed by per capita state-ownedindustrial output value, that is, total industrial output value of enterprises owned by the whole people/total population of each region.

Power of local government: we use three variables to measure the power of local government. The first one is the proportion of households that did not use all-round contracts at the end of 1983, indicating the political power and leadership of local governments, that is: households that did not use all-round contract at the end of 1983/ total households in contract responsibility system; the second variable is per capita initialcommunity industrial output value, which shows the development of collective industry and the accumulation of physical capital and human capital by local government at the beginning of the reform. It can be expressed by per capita initialcommunity industrial output value, that is, total community industrial output value in 1979/total rural population in 1981; the third one is per capita collective investment in fixed assets: collective amount of total investment in fixed assets/total population (local fiscal expenditure indicator is not used here due to the limitations of data).

Marketization degree: we use four variables to measure the marketization degree. The first variable is the initial marketization level, which is expressed by per capita urban and rural market turnover in 1981: urban and rural market turnover/total population; the second variable is product marketization degree which can be expressed by urban and rural market turnover/total population, indicating that the higher the degree of product market, the more convenient the circulation of goods, and the more conducive for private economy to get raw materials and sell products; the third variable is urban population ratio which is calculated by town population/total population. This indicator can measure the level of urbanization: the higher the level of urbanization, the more active the market and the higher the degree of marketization; the fourth variable is financial deepening degree expressed by savings deposits of urban and rural residents/total population, which indicates that the higher the degree of financial deepening, the higher the degree of marketization.

Here, we use year dummy variables from 1983 – 1984 to eliminate the effects of some time-varying factors (such as ideology, inflation, etc.). Because some of the changes in macroeconomic policies have already been partially controlled by variables such as the scale of state-owned economic loans, the dummy variables here mainly represent changes in ideology throughout the country and other factors that may change over time. At the same time, some variables (such as the proportion of households that do not use all-round contract, etc.) do not change over time, which can partially eliminate some of the differences between regions. Here, we will not introduce all regional dummy variables and still divide 29 provinces into six regions① according to geographical environment and other characteristics, in order to eliminate the influences of natural conditions and national non-equilibrium policies on the development of local private economy. The descriptive statistics of each variable are shown in Table 4 –3.

Table 4 –3 Descriptive statistics of each variable

Variable	Average	Maximum	Minimum	Standard deviation
Proportion of private economy in total financing institution loans (γ_i^*)	38. 20	303. 4	– 150. 8	67. 69
Per capita financial institution loans (p_g)	0. 057	0. 274	0. 006	0. 056
Per capita state-owned industrial output value (p_h)	0. 072	0. 554	0. 0057	0. 102
Proportion of households that did not use all-round contract (p_j)	0. 067	0. 546	0. 0014	0. 114
Per capita initial community industrial output value (p_k)	0. 0067	0. 042	0. 0009	0. 009
Per capita collective investment in fixed assets (p_m)	0. 0026	0. 0168	0. 0003	0. 003
Initial marketization level (i_m)	0. 0025	0. 0054	0. 0007	0. 001
Financial deepening degree (p_n)	0. 0133	0. 058	0. 003	0. 01
Product marketization degree (q_q)	0. 0042	0. 01	0. 0013	0. 002
Urban population ratio (p_q)	0. 342	0. 699	0. 057	0. 16
Influence of state-owned economy (m_1)	1. 688	11. 75	0. 23	2. 18
Power of local government (m_2)	0. 058	0. 44	0. 002	0. 092
Marketization degree (m_3)	0. 11	0. 196	0. 039	0. 036
Institution rent level (r_t)	0. 305	2. 44	0. 0042	0. 49

Note: Because of the estimation method used in the text, the minimum value of the private economic share γ_i^* in all financial institutions is negative. The results of the estimates here are only representatives of the relative level of private economic shares in financial institution loans in each region. We should know that they are not absolute amount.

Source: Sorted out by the author.

① According to geographical location and natural environment, we divided 29 provinces into six regions: the northern region (including Heilongjiang, Jilin, Inner Mongolia, Shanxi, Anhui, Hebei, Henan); the southern region (including Hunan, Hubei, Jiangxi, Guangxi); the northwest region (including Shaanxi, Gansu, Ningxia, Qinghai, Xinjiang, Tibet); the southwest region (including Sichuan, Guizhou, Yunnan); in addition, we separately consider six coastal provinces (Liaoning, Shandong, Jiangsu, Zhejiang, Fujian and Guangdong) as a region, because they had been one step ahead in the reform and opening up; moreover, we view the three major cities of Beijing, Tianjin and Shanghai as a region, because they are smaller in geographical area and rural scale. Thus, there are six regional dummy variables.

In order to obtain some information on the relationship between the development of private economy and each variable, we first choose Zhejiang (mainly based on individual and private economy), Jiangsu (dominated by township collective economy) and Qinghai (less developed private economy) as examples. The comparison of relationships among all variables can be seen in Table 4 – 4. It can be seen from the table that in early stages of the reform and opening up, the balance of financial institutions' loans excluding the share of state-owned economy is highest in Jiangsu, and then in Zhejiang and Qinghai. Per capita state-owned industrial output value is lowest in Qinghai, and then in Zhejiang and Jiangsu. Zhejiang's per capita financial institution loan is lower than that in Jiangsu, and the power of local government, which is measured by the proportion of households that did not use all-round contract, is higher than that of Jiangsu. However, the per capita initial community industrial output value and the per capita collective investment in fixed assets are lower than those of Jiangsu. The influence of state-owned economy is highest in Jiangsu, and then in Zhejiang and Qinghai; while the power of local government and the marketization degree are both highest in Zhejiang, and then in Jiangsu and Qinghai. Although the power of local government is higher in Zhejiang, its institution rent level is lower than that of Jiangsu because of higher marketization degree. In Zhejiang, due to high marketization degree, the institution rent level is rapidly decreasing while private economy went through rapid development. Besides, local government also plays a coordinating function to get more financial institutions loans; In Jiangsu, although the institution rent level has rapidly reduced, because of higher power of local government, the overall institution rent level is still high. Private economy has gone along the evolution of collective economy mode and has achieved a large amount of bank loans. This also shows that the initial marketization level has a significant impact on the development of private economy. Although the institution rent level is low in Qinghai, because of low degree of marketization, the local government has not fully played their roles, the marketization process has been slow, the institution rent level has decreased very slowly and the private economy has been stagnant. All of which has made it difficult to acquire financial institutions loans.

Table 4 – 4 Comparisons of variables of Jiangsu, Zhejiang and Qinghai in 1983

Variables	Jiangsu	Zhejiang	Qinghai
Balance of financial institutions' loans excluding the share of state-owned economy (s_f)	12.61	11.91	2.95
Per capita financial institution loans (p_g)	0.037	0.028	0.027
Per capita state-owned industrial output value (p_h)	0.055	0.038	0.03

continued

Variables	Jiangsu	Zhejiang	Qinghai
Proportion of households that did not use all-round contract (p_j)	0.017	0.052	0.02
Per capita initialcommunity industrial output value (p_k)	0.014	0.008	0.0019
Per capita collective investment in fixed assets (p_m)	0.0035	0.0025	0.00038
Initial marketization level (i_m)	0.00318	0.00379	0.00065
Financial deepening degree (p_n)	0.005	0.0094	0.0093
Product marketization degree (q_q)	0.0041	0.0049	0.0015
Urban population ratio (p_q)	0.2	0.23	0.19
Influence of state-owned economy (m_1)	0.05	0.035	0.029
Power of local government (m_2)	0.027	0.047	0.017
Marketization degree (m_3)	0.088	0.104	0.054
Institution rent (r_t)	1.205	1.14	1.119

Source: sorted out by the author.

2. Models and regression results

In the following part, we use regression analysis method to conduct an empirical analysis on correlations between all variables, in order to further explore financing choices and institutional factors in the initial stage of private enterprises. The model used here is:

$$Y_{it} = C + \beta X_{it} + \delta_{it}$$

We use three models to verify specific financing factors in initial stage of private enterprises. The explanatory variables Y_{it} in each model represents the balance of loans obtained from financial institutions by province i in year t. In the first model, X_{it} represents institution rent level; in the second model, X_{it} represents the influence of state-owned economy, the power of local government and the marketization degree; in the third model, X_{it} represents specific variables, such as per capita state-owned industrial output value. Here, we use inter-provincial data from 1983 – 1985 to do general OLS regression analysis. The results are shown in Table 4 – 5.

Table 4 – 5 Regression results of each variable

Variables	Model Ⅰ	Model Ⅱ	Model Ⅲ
C	84.55 (0.25)	–17.27 (0.84)	–259.50*** (0.01)
Institution rent (r_t)	–134.01*** (0.00)		
Influence of state-owned economy (m_1)		–28.8*** (0.00)	
Power of local government (m_2)		–18.46 (0.86)	
Marketization degree (m_3)		621.54*** (0.01)	
Per capita financial institution loans (p_g)			2 511.55*** (0.00)
Per capita state – owned industrial output value (p_h)			–986.64*** (0.00)

continued

Variables	Model Ⅰ	Model Ⅱ	Model Ⅲ
Proportion of households that did not use all - round contract (p_j)			-52.37* (0.07)
Per capita initialcommunity industrial output value (p_k)			1 713.28 (0.15)
Per capita collective investment in fixed assets (p_m)			-1 486.16 (0.15)
Initial marketization level (i_m)			13 757.73 (0.32)
Financial deepening degree (p_n)			-2 466.48 (0.17)
Product marketization degree (q_q)			7 869.12*** (0.01)
Urban population ratio (p_q)			11.26 (0.61)
P_v1983 time dummy variable	61.84*** (0.00)	44.16*** (0.01)	1.59 (0.94)
P_w1984 time dummy variable	24.91* (0.07)	16.80 (0.23)	-10.41 (0.53)
r_1 area dummy variable	-130.83*** (0.01)	-79.44 (0.15)	136.47* (0.06)
r_2 area dummy variable	-48.47*** (0.00)	-29.64 (0.11)	15.07 (0.51)
r_3 area dummy variable	38.20** (0.04)	38.79** (0.04)	35.89** (0.03)
r_4 area dummy variable	33.96 (0.11)	28.98 (0.16)	14.92 (0.44)
r_5 area dummy variable	35.15** (0.04)	36.07** (0.04)	13.93 (0.36)
R^2	0.46	0.50	0.72

Note: 1) ***, **, * indicate significance at 1%, 5%, 10%, respectively; the significant level of corresponding variables are within the brackets; 2) The sample size is 87; 3) DW Value and F statistic are in accordance with the corresponding test, indicating no autocorrelation or multiple collinearity between variables.

In model Ⅰ, we use institution rent as the explanatory variable, and introduce both the time and area dummy variable to explore its influence on the loans obtained from financial institutions by private economy. In this model, the coefficient of institution rent is significantly negative, the time dummy variable P_v and P_w are significantly positive, the area dummy variable r_1 and r_2 were significantly negative while r_3, r_4, r_5 are positive (r_4 is not statistically significant). This indicates that the higher the level of institution rent, the more disadvantageous for private economy to obtain loans from the state-owned financial institutions; with the change of people's understanding, the share of loans that private economy has obtained from financial institutions will increase; and regional macroeconomic policies will be conducive for private economy to obtain loans. In early days of the reform and opening up, this situation is not difficult to understand. The higher the level of institution rent, the more constraints are against private economy through institutional arrangements and ideology. Besides, formal financial institutions mainly provide loans to state-owned economic sector, which makes it harder for private economy to obtain loans from them (mainly state-owned financial institutions).

In model II, we use the influence of state-owned economy, the power of local government and marketization degree as explanatory variables to further analyze the impact of these factors on financing choice of private economy in the initial stage. In this model, the coefficient of influence of state-owned economy is significantly negative; the coefficient of power of local government is negative, but not statistically significant; the degree of marketization is significantly positive. The time dummy variable P_v and P_w are both positive, while the latter is not statistically significant; the area dummy variable r_1 and r_2 were not significantly negative while r_3, r_4, r_5 are positive (r_4 is not statistically significant). This shows that the greater the impact of state-owned economy, the more difficult for private economy to obtain loans from financial institutions in the initial stage, which is not difficult to understand. Because in places where the influences of state-owned economy are great, most loans will be occupied by the state-owned economy which makes private economy ignored and excluded. The influence of the power of local government on loans from financial institutions is vague, probably related to the behavioral characteristics of local government: the more powerful the local government is, the more difficult will be for the private economy to obtain loans from financial institutions; when the local government power is large, it always encourages the development of collective economy and use their own advantages to help them get access to loans from state-owned financial institutions. Thus the greater the local government power, the more conducive for collective economy to obtain financial institutions loans. The higher the degree of marketization, the more favorable the regional institutional arrangement and ideology will be for the development of private economy, which makes it easier for the private economy to obtain loans from financial institutions.

In model III, we use specific indicators to analyze the impact of various institution rent factors on financing options of private economy in the initial stage. In this model, the coefficient of per capita financial institution loans is significantly positive, while per capita state-owned industrial output value is significantly negative, which further shows that the higher the proportion of state-owned economy, the more disadvantageous for private economy to obtain financial institutions loans; the more developed the state-owned financial market, the more financial resources, the more favorable for private economy to obtain loans. The coefficient of the proportion of households that did not use all-round contract is significantly negative; the coefficient of per capita initial community industrial output value is positive, but not statistically significant; the coefficient of per capita collective investment in fixed assets is not significantly negative. This shows that when the local governments have high enthusiasm to promote the development of collective economy, they will also be motivated to help it obtain loans; when the power of local government is strong, it will be harder for private economy to acquire loans, which may be correlated with specific political risks in early reform. The coefficient of initial marketization level is positive, but not statistically significant; the financial deepening degree is negative but also not statistically significant; the product marketization degree and the ratio of urban population are both positive while the latter one is not statistically significant. This shows that the initial marketization level does have certain impact on the development of private economy and access to financial institution resources. But in early stages of the reform and opening up, the marketization degree of the whole society is generally low and the private economy has been faced with a great deal of uncertainty, thus the market itself has little impact on loans. The higher the degree of financial deepening, the stronger the ability of individual capital accumulation. Relatively speaking, this means the demand for financial institutions loans is smaller. The higher the degree of product marketization, the more conducive to the development of private economy and the improvement of marketization degree in the whole region, and thus financial institutions will be more willing to provide credit support. The coefficients of all dummy variables are not described here in detail.

3. Research conclusions

Through the above analysis, we can draw some following conclusions:

First, the venture capital of private enterprise mainly come fromself-accumulation because of the narrow financing channels. During entrepreneurship, external funds mainly come from private lending and bank loans, while the latter has a very low proportion.

Second, Institutional factors will have an important impact on financing options of private enterprises in the initial stage. In different regions, the financing structures are different. The higher the level of institution rent, the more constraints private economy will be faced with. While most formal financial institutions will provide credit support for state-owned economic sector, which makes it difficult for private economy to obtain loans from them (mainly state-owned financial institutions).

Third, the influence of state-owned economy, the power of local government and marketization degree have different action mechanisms on financing choice of private enterprises. In places where the influences of state-owned economy are great, most loans will be occupied by state-owned economy which makes private economy ignored and excluded. The influence of the power of local government is vague, probably related to the behavioral characteristics of local government: the more powerful the local government is, the more difficult will be for the private economy to obtain loans from financial institutions; when the local government power is large, it always encourages the development of collective economy and use their own advantages to help them get access to loans from state-owned financial institutions. Thus the greater the local government power, the more conducive for collective economy to obtain financial institutions loans. The higher the degree of marketization, the more favorable the regional institutional arrangement and ideology will be for the development of private economy, which makes it easier for the private economy to obtain loans from financial institutions.

From the above analysis, we can summarize the relationship between financing choice of private economy and the level of government power and marketization in Figure 4 – 1.

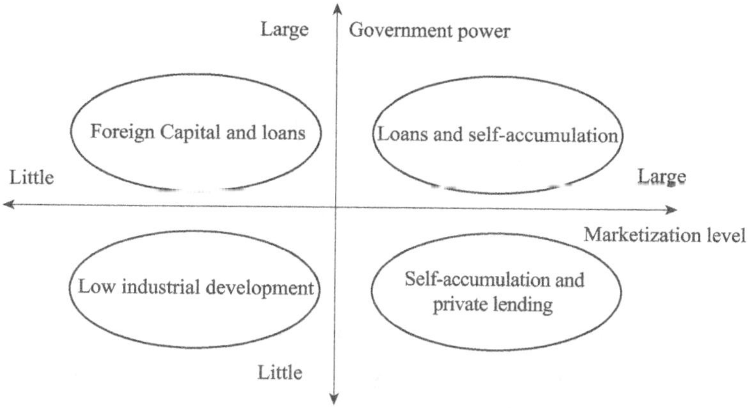

Figure 4 – 1 Government power, market level and financing choice in the initial stage

In the initial stage, different combinations of government power and marketization level will first determine whether or not private economy in this region can develop and the possible development model. If this region does not have the motivation to develop private economy, then financing problems will not matter. As can be seen from Figure 4 – 1, the initial stage of reform is characterized by large government power, low degree of marketization and high level of institution rent. At this time, the development of private economy is mainly driven by the government and has taken foreign or collective economic form, with the corresponding source of funds of foreign capital and state-owned financial institutions loans. In places where government power and marketization degree are both high, the development of private economy mainly adopts the form of collective economy with various sources of funds, including loans, foreign capital and self-accumulation. In the above areas, the government power is high, which means they can help private enterprises to obtain loans and institution rent through their own relationship with the state-owned financial institutions. In places where government power is small but marketization degree is high, the main body of private economic development is private economy, with the corresponding sources of funds of self-accumulation and private lending; this development model also contains the basis of private finance. In places where government power and marketization degree are both low, the private economy cannot develop, let alone financing problems.

4.2 Institutional rent changes and financing choice for private enterprise

China's private enterprises have been faced with a very special development environment from the outset. Due to the fact that the financing channels are single, the state-owned financial system is highly centralized, and the private enterprises have "system defects", thus, in the initial stage, private enterprises have huge difficulty to obtain external funds and have to rely on self-accumulation for development; but in the development process, self-accumulation is far from enough. What's more, in order to obtain financial support from the state-owned financial channels, the collective economy, as a kind of private economy with the form of compatibility, has gained rapid development under the financial incentive of the local government. The state-owned financial system monopolizes most of the financial resources and provide financial support mainly for state-owned economic sector; during the process of the development of private economy, acquiring the access to financial institution loans will be very critical; this is closely related to the credit links between the state-owned financial system and the state-owned economy. Financial rent caused by institutional arrangements are mainly divided among state-owned economic sectors, which makes it very difficult for private economy to obtain institutional rent. With the rapid development of private economy and the reduction of institution rent, the share of loans obtained by private enterprises has slowly increased and the credit funds on the development of private economy has far from played a catalytic role. In the context of increasing contributions of private economy to national economy, if the financial institution loans still flow mainly to the state-owned economic sector, the private economy will inevitably face the situation of shortage of external funds; after all, the total amount of this piece of cake is limited. Therefore, share of financial institution loans by private economy, institutional changes of state-owned enterprises financing system, and development of financial system marketization are all mutually linked aspects in the process of institutional changes in China. The formation and evolution of state-owned enterprise financing system has its historical inevitability. In order to analyze the relationship between private enterprises and banks, it is necessary to first describe the historical process of the state-owned enterprise financing system.

4.2.1 Institutional rent changes and private enterprise financing

1. Financial control and institutional rent

Although the reform of state-owned enterprise financing system did not fundamentally solve the problem of inefficient operation of state-owned enterprises, with the advancement of marketization, the overall institution rent scale has tended to decline. In the planned economy period, the leading form of state financing is: through low wages and price scissors, bringing over the income which is derived from urban and rural residents and can be used for long-term savings, and "secretly" making it for state-owned capital by way of profits in state-owned enterprises. These initial capitals have been used directly to start and operate state-owned enterprises. It is impossible to form a contractual relationship between the state and the individual residents because these income have never been assigned to them. Since all of the residents' future consumption income have been used for the accumulation of state-owned capital, the government should bear the corresponding future consumption expenses, such as pension, medical and so on. At this time, the whole economic system is highly centralized with the government playing the central role in financing system, while the whole society has a very low degree of marketization and a high level of institution rent. The price of various elements is distorted. Within the socially affordable range and in accordance with the needs of development strategy, our country has reached the highest level of institutional rents and shared them with the state-owned enterprises. The subsequent reform changed the pattern of national income distribution, but the state did not give up the administrative allocation of capital. The only thing that has changed is the government's identity of financing intermediary between capital owners and users. As the accumulated income finally be allocated to the hands of individual residents, the way in which our country raise money from the residents has changed from "secretly take" to "obviously borrow". Through banks and other institutions, our country has built a debt contract relation with individual residents by bearing clear debt service obligations. The real interest rate is very low or even negative, but after all, it still formed a certain constraint to the state-owned enterprises; thus, compared to free financial grants, this is still a big step forward. Borrowing from the residents, the state can absorb resident savings through banks or issue financial bonds. According to the World Bank estimates, from 1987 to 1995, the ratio of China's non-financial public sector debts to GDP is 10.8%. Among which, the ratio of loans from the banking system to GDP is 9.0% while the ratio of state-owned enterprises to GDP is 8.6%[1]. The state continues to act as a financing intermediary through tax credit, income financing and debt financing, although this role is gradually fading. At this time the institution rent level has been reduced, but still at a relatively high level, which can be roughly seen from rent scale in used funds. The so-called rent effect is shown in Figure 4-2: through the government control of finance, the state-owned financial institutions have transferred a large number of rents from the residents and the public sector has obtained a funding price which is much lower than the equilibrium market price so they have gained huge hidden subsides.

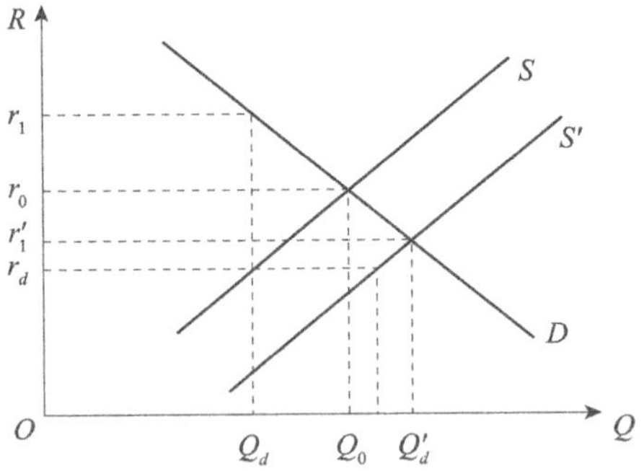

Figure 4-2 Interest rate control and financial rent

① World Bank. The Chinese Economy: Fighting Inflation, Deepening Reforms. Washington: the World Bank, 1996, p. 66. Quoted from Fan Gang. Financial Development and Enterprise Reform. Economic Science Press, 2000, p. 61.

In the market economy system, the equilibrium interest rate is r_0 and the supply of funds Q_0. But if the government controls interest rate, then the deposit rate will be r_d, the supply of funds will be Q_d, the loan interest rate will be r_1, and the balance of $r_1 - r_d$ will be the economic rent of the bank. At this time, the loan interest rate is higher than that without intervention, and the rent that the banks get from the residents and enterprises is $r_0 - r_d$ and $r_1 - r_0$, respectively. Under the financial control policy, the bank and the business sector share this financial rent due to the deposit and loan interest rates and the control of credit scale. In the case where the income of the resident sector continues to grow and there is not enough alternative financial assets to choose, and the residents are forced to hold much larger amount of savings than the equilibrium amount which leaves the state-owned banks more credit resources. When the bank's capital supply curve moves right to S', the equilibrium loan rate will fall to r'_1 and loan quantity expand to Q'_d, which will lead to a typical rent effect. From the perspective of state-owned enterprises, due to the government's policy of capital control, the bank's low-cost financing from the resident department is allocated to key state-owned enterprises in a low-cost way. The financial rent is divided between state-owned enterprises, $r_0 - r'_1$, and the banks, $r'_1 - r_d$, while it is difficult for private enterprises to obtain such rent.

Some scholars have estimated the size of rent in our country. According to the estimates of Hu Heli (1989)① and Wan Anpei (1995)②, inter-commodity spreads, interest margins and rate differences have accounted for the majority of rent scale in China since 1988. It can be roughly estimated that, since the reform of double-track system, the ratio of rent scale to national income is between 30% and 40%. With the accelerated reform of marketization, the ratio of rent scale to national income has gradually decreased while the absolute amount has increased. This is mainly due to the lag of institutional reform and the particularity of China's progressive reform. The characteristic of changes in the source of rent in China is that the rents in the commodity market are relatively shrinking, while the rents on the factor market are expanding. This is consistent with the process of market reform in China. During the reform process, the market mechanism has developed, but the sectors within the system, especially the monopolized industry, are not fundamentally touched.

---

① Hu Heli, Estimation of the Value of China's Rent in 1988, Comparative Economic & Social Systems, No. 5, 1989, pp. 20 - 26.

② Wan Anpei, A Dynamic Study of Rent Scale, Economic Research Journal, No. 2, 1995, pp. 75 - 80.

According to Hu Angang's (2001) [1]estimates of the rent of some monopolies in China, it can be found that from 1995 to September 1998, the rent in three monopoly industries (electricity, medical, transportation, post and telecommunications) reached 130 to 202 billion yuan / year. In addition, illegal incomes in part of the monopoly industry amounted to 53 billion yuan, accounting for 0.60% of the country's GDP.

In financial sector, the rent scale is huge. It is estimated that China's loan interest margin reached 198.3 billion in 1992 (Wan Anpei, 1995). According to another calculation of Hu Lian, the amount of China's total loan was 2200 billion yuan in 1992. Because the interest rate was too low and the demand for funds was so strong, private commissions were at least up to 10% (Hu Lian, 1994). According to "China Finance", at the beginning of 1993, the balance of bank loans was 260.812 billion. The difference between the bank interest rate and the market interest rate is roughly within 231.95 and 394.73 billion yuan. It was also estimated that from 1988 to 1995, China's loan interest margin was 1472.8 billion yuan with an average of 184.1 billion yuan per year. Such a large amount of financial rent was all swallowed by banks and state-owned enterprises, while the cash-strapped private enterprises had no access to bank credit.

In this situation, the soft budget constraint of enterprises (including banks) has not been fundamentally resolved and the state has still directly or indirectly played the role of financing intermediary. Under the circumstances of limited governance mechanism and serious insider control, the soft budget constraint will only be a transformation from one form to another.

Many problems of the state-owned enterprises are rooted in the financing system inherited from the planned economic system, which views the state as the sole intermediary, that is, the state provide financial support for the development of state-owned enterprises. It will leave the enterprises with free capital illusion. Coupled with the lack of supervision and hard constraints, the enterprises will inevitably behave inefficient when utilize funds. Many problems of the state-owned enterprises can largely be attributed to a single national financing system. Market reform, on the one hand, will lead to changes in financing methods of state-owned enterprises; on the other hand, will have great influence on the operation of state-owned enterprises and the change of banking system.

---

① Hu Angang, China: Challenge Corruption. Zhejiang People's Publishing House, 2001, pp. 118 - 126.

2. Institutional rent changes and financing mechanism of state-owned enterprise

The existence of institutional rent has caused state-owned banks and state-owned enterprises the illusion of free capital; soft budget constraints and the lack of governance mechanism have made the state-owned enterprises rely highly on bank funds and have high asset-liability ratio. According to the results of verification of 302,000 state-owned enterprises, the asset-liability ratio was 38.7% in 1980 and 69.3% in 1995. Of which, the total amount of assets was 7 472.1 billion yuan and the total amount of liabilities was 5 176.3 billion yuan, with an ownership interest of 2 295.9 billion yuan; if we take out the loss of assets, the actual asset-liability ratio would be as high as 76.1%. Among them, the number of enterprises with the asset-liability ratio of more than 100% is 51,000; among the enterprises with asset-liability ratio below 100%, there are 61,000 enterprises on the verge of insolvency. Corresponding to this, there also have been a large number of bad loans① within the financial assets of the state-owned banks. From the perspective of the world level, corporate debt ratio in the US and UK is generally between 35% and 45%, Germany is around 60% while Japan has decreased from 70% to 60%.

According to the data released by the People's Daily on May 9, 1996, the total assets of the state-owned enterprises in the national budget was 7.28 trillion yuan and the total liabilities was 5.17 trillion yuan with a debt ratio of as high as 71%. As can be seen from Table 4 – 6, the survey of the branch of Industrial and Commercial Bank of China in Hunan Province shows that the average debt ratio of all state-owned industrial enterprises was 68.21%.

Table 4 – 6 The liability situation in state-owned industrial enterprise (Unit: %)

Industry	Asset-liability ratio	Current liability	Industry	Asset-liability ratio	Current liability
Total	68.21	93.63	Metallurgy	62.32	92.88
Non-ferrous metal	70.63	95.75	Machinery	75.49	90.69
Automobile	75.06	91.42	Power	48.23	81.75
Coal	64.12	92.65	Petroleum	58.31	75.13
Chemistry	74.75	104.42	Petrochemical	56.12	70.48
Pharmaceuticals	76.49	95.10	Building material	68.11	92.00
Textile	81.58	166.69	Light	80.33	104.32

Source: Branch of Industrial and Commercial Bank of China in Hunan Province. Liu Bingwen, "Research on Financing issues of State-owned Enterprises", 2002, p48.

① Chi Fulin, State-owned Enterprise Reform and Debt, Foreign Languages Press, 1998, pp. 7 – 8.

Of course, with the deepening of the reform and the improvement of the market system, the rapid development of non-state economy and the decline of institutional rent have externally given state-owned enterprises a certain degree of competitive pressure and relatively strong hard constraints. The asset-liability ratio of the state-owned enterprises has improved on the book, but not fundamentally. Data shows that in 1996, the asset-liability ratio of national industrial and commercial enterprises is 65.25%, of which 65.5% are state-owned enterprises, both are lower than the previous year; therate of shareholders value maintaining and increasing is 119.6%, of which the state-owned enterprises is 118.8%. From the reform of the pilot situation, the level of various types of enterprises is slightly different. By the end of 1996, the asset-liability ratio of 100 pilot enterprises was 63.9%, decreased by 26% compared with last year; the ratio of state-holding enterprises was 67.1%, down by 5.8%. From different types of property rights organizations, the asset-liability ratio of the joint-stock company is the lowest (63.2%) with a decrease of 6.3%; the ratio of the wholly state-owned company is 63.3%, down by 2.6%; while the ratio of the limited liability company is the highest (71.4%), only fell by 0.72%①.

Although theactual interest rate is very low or even negative, it is still a burden for state-owned enterprise which have turned financing channels to the banks. However, the problem is that the operating mechanism of the state-owned enterprises has not changed correspondingly. Under the circumstances of market competition and the development of non-state economy, when the funds come with a price, the soft budget constraints still exist and operating efficiency is not improved, the situation of the state-owned enterprises will inevitably deteriorate and lead to the coexistence of high debt and low efficiency. In the state-owned independent accounting industrial enterprises, the ratio of loss to profit has remained below 10% during 1978 – 1988, but rapidly increased to 24% in 1989. In the next two economic cycles, this ratio never fell back below 50%. In the first four months of 1996, the loss of state-owned industrial enterprises exceeded the profit for the first time, resulting in a net loss. After May, although the situation improved month by month, there was no fundamental change. From January to August, 45.7% of the state-owned independent accounting industrial enterprises suffered a loss, and the net profit fell 79.7% compared with the same period last year②. The inefficiency of the state-owned

① Ru Xin, Lu Xueyi, Shan TianLun, Analysis and Forecast of Social Situation in China in 1998, Social Sciences Academic Press, 1998, pp. 24 – 25.

② Fan Gang, Financial Development and Enterprise Reform. Economic Science Press, 2000, p. 51.

enterprises is widespread. From 1988 to 2001, the amount of loss has been continuously increasing (see Table 4 – 7).

Table 4 – 7　　Deficits of state-owned enterprise

Year	1988	1990	1992	1995	1997	2000	2001
Deficit (100 million yuan)	80	349	369	581	607	704	686

Source: China Statistical Yearbook (1995 – 2002).

By comparing the return on investment and the borrowing rate of 5 000 industrial enterprises, some scholars believe that China's corporate profitability is poor, the average return on investment is less than half of one-year bank borrowing rate, and the financial leverage is negative (see Table 4 – 8).

Table 4 – 8　　Profitability and debt rate of 5000 industrial enterprises　　(Unit: %)

Year	Return on assets	Return on equity	Yearly savings rate	Return on investment based on return on assets	Return on investment based on return on equity	Lending rate
1994	3.2	9.1	10.98	10.5	12.3	12.0
1995	2.4	6.5	10.98	10.3	11.5	12.0
1996	1.4	3.7	9.22	9.0	9.1	10.0
1997	1.3	3.4	7.17	6.3	7.0	7.5

Source: Xiong Lianhua, "Status Analysis of Chinese Enterprise's Direct Investment", Financial Times, August 1, 1998.

Compared with the profitability of other types of enterprises, the efficiency of state-owned enterprises is lower than the average of all enterprises, as well as private enterprises and joint-equity enterprises (see Table 4 – 9).

Table 4 – 9　　Comparison of funds utilization efficiency of enterprises in China　　(unit: %)

Enterprise type	Profit rate on funds	Profit rate on capitals
State-owned enterprise	3.22	7.70
Collectively-owned enterprise	4.90	13.91
Private enterprise	6.21	14.80
Joint enterprise	5.43	13.91
Joint-equity enterprise	11.64	15.39
Foreign-funded enterprise	8.71	15.57
Hong Kong, Macao and Taiwan enterprise	5.57	12.70
Other enterprises	10.64	25.48
Total	4.22	9.96

Source: Lu Zhengfei, "Theoretical Analysis and Empirical Research on Moderate Corporate Debt", Economic Research Journal, No. 2, 1996, pp. 52 – 58.

Soft budget constraints and the lack of governance mechanism have, on the one hand, led to inefficient operation of state-owned enterprises; and on the other hand, resulted in insufficient bank capital and large numbers of bad loans. By the end of 2001, the capital adequacy ratio of four major state-owned commercial banks was only

4.4%, far below the international standard of 8%; the average asset profitability of the four banks is 0.105%, far below 1.56% of Citibank and 1.77% of HSBC; in 2001, the total amount of bad assets of all financial institutions in China was about 3 trillion yuan, accounting for 25% of the total loan balance; among which, the bad assets of wholly state-owned commercial banks was 1765 billion yuan, accounting for more than 60% of all bad assets and 18.4% of GDP①. Compared with other countries, the ratio of bad loans in China is particularly high (see Table 4-10). In recent years, with the stripping of bad assets and the strengthening of supervision, the operational condition has improved in state-owned banks. However, this situation is hard to be fundamentally changed unless we promote the establishment of effective corporate governance mechanism or the implementation of privatization reform.

Figure 4-10 Comparison of banks' bad assets in several countries and regions (Unit: %)

Project	China	Singapore	Hong Kong, China	the Philippines	India	Indonesia	Korea
Target ratio	20	2.0	2.1	3.4	17	9.2	18
Peak ratio	>25	>8	>8	10-15	>15	>40	>25

Source: Wang Jinbin, "Financial Control, Risk Elimination and Economic Growth", Economic Research Journal, No. 4, 2000, pp. 11-18.

In the transition period, the relationship between the state-owned enterprises and the banks is far from the credit relationship under market situations. The soft budget constraints to the banks have indirectly constituted the soft constraints to the state-owned enterprises. With the development of capital market, state-owned enterprises have become the main force in the securities market and obtained a great deal of financial resources through direct financing. However, China's securities market was established at the beginning to solve the financing problems of the state-owned enterprises and to raise huge amount of development funds through the approval system and other measures. During the change of financing system in state-owned enterprise, the government has always been the leading force. Of course, with the development of the market and the diversification of the main body, the overall state of the state-owned enterprises has been improved, but the fundamental problem remains unresolved. With the rapid development of market economy and openness, and the sustained and rapid development of the non-state economy, the state-owned enterprises are facing increasingly hardened budget constraints and increasingly fierce market competition environment. At this time, state-owned enterprises will not

① Chen Yun, A Study on Non-governmental Finance in China's Market Reform, South China Normal University, 2004.

survive unless they try to improve the governance mechanism within the framework or enhance operational efficiency by means of privatization reform. After years of efforts, the overall situation of the state-owned enterprises tends to improve. But we should also see that this is inseparable from the privatization of state-owned enterprises. Some of the state-owned enterprises have been privatized and most of the enterprises that have been left are monopoly industries. The only reason they survived is because of monopoly power instead of increased efficiency. Therefore, for state-owned enterprises, there are only two options: either improve operational efficiency or implement privatization reform.

3. Institutional rent changes and financing mechanism of private enterprise

From a historical point of view, the Chinese financial system, with banking industry as its main body, was highly concentrated from the beginning. With continuous development of the economy, although the financial system is gradually reformed and the institution rent tends to decline, the status of the country as property owners has not changed. From this perspective, China's top-down government-driven financial system reform is still to meet the government's preferences and utility, and to serve the financing needs of state-owned enterprises. Theoretically, a financial system is mainly designed to reduce financial transaction costs, but in China it is mainly for financing. The reform of the banking industry is closely related to the reform of state-owned enterprises. State-owned banks monopolize financial resources, and state-owned enterprises account for the vast majority of bank resources (see Table 4 – 11). State-owned banks are in absolute dominance of all bank assets and total loans. At the same time, with the reduction of institutional rents, non-state financial institutions have developed. The proportion of total bank assets and loans has slowly increased, but the absolute amount is still low.

Table 4 – 11 The proportion of assets and loans among all banks (unit: %)

Year	1993	1994	1995	1996	1997	1998.9
Proportion of assets in non-state-owned banks	13.32	14.99	16.18	16.47	16.36	15.33
Proportion of loans in non-state-owned banks	11.66	13.43	14.13	14.01	14.51	14.62

Note: Non-state-owned banks include urban credit cooperatives, urban cooperative banks and rural credit cooperatives. Bank statistics include the People's Bank of China, state-owned commercial banks, policy banks, other commercial banks, credit cooperatives, finance companies, financial trust and investment companies (including leasing company).

Source: The calculation is based on "Statistical Quarterly of the People's Bank of China", No. 4, 1998. Fan Gang, "Financial Development and Enterprise Reform", Economic Science Press, 2000.

Despite the great development of non-state economy after the reform and opening up, the financial resources, especially obtained from state-owned financial institutions, are still very limited. This shows that the resources of state-owned financial institutions mainly flow to the state-owned economic sector where state-owned enterprises are the main customers of bank loans, while the non-state-owned economic sector have no choice but to acquire development funds from other channels. High liabilities of state-owned enterprises coexist with low liabilities of private enterprises. Institutional rent is mainly divided between state-owned banks and state-owned enterprises, while it is difficult for private enterprises to obtain (see Table 4 – 12 to Table 4 – 14).

Table 4 – 12 The proportion of non-state-owned enterprise in total financial institution loans

(unit: %)

Year	1991	1992	1993	1994	1995	1996	1997
The proportion of loans to non-state-owned enterprises by all financing institutions	8.76	9.93	10.66	13.27	12.38	12.83	14.24
The proportion of loans to non-state-owned enterprises by state banks	7.16	7.5	7.51	9.05	7.98	8.1	8.85

Source: The data before 1996 is from "China Financial Yearbook (1997)"; the data in 1997 is from "China Statistical Yearbook (1998)"; the specific gravity coefficient is based on relevant data. Fan Gang: "Financial Development and Enterprise Reform", Economic Science Press, 2000.

Table 4 – 13 Changes of loan flow in financial institutions

Year	1952	1985	1990	1997	2002	2003
Total amount of loans in all financial institutions (100 million yuan)	108.0	5 905.6	17 680.7	74 914.1	131 293.9	158 996.2
Amount of loans to collective and private enterprises (100 million yuan)	0.5	321.3	1 017.3	5 422.5	7 871.1	9 123.2
Proportion of loans to collective and private enterprises (%)	0.46	5.44	5.75	7.24	6.0	5.74

Source: "China Compendium of Statistics", "China Statistical Yearbook (2003 – 2004)".

Table 4 – 14 The proportion of enterprise number and credit in state-owned enterprises (1996)

Number of state-owned-enterprise	Aggregate (ten thousand)	11.38
	Large-sized state-owned-enterprise (%)	5.97
	Middle-sized state-owned-enterprise (%)	13.18
	Small-sized state-owned-enterprise (%)	80.85
Credit	The proportion of credit of state-owned enterprises to total credit (%)	81.37
Asset	The proportion of assets of state-owned enterprises to total assets (%)	58.61

Source: "China Statistical Yearbook", "China Financial Yearbook (1997)". Fan Gang: "Financial Development and Enterprise Reform", Economic Science Press, 2000.

The reduction of institutional rent has created a relatively more relaxed financing environment for private enterprises and eased the financial difficulties. However, the operation and governance mechanism of state-owned enterprises and state-owned banks have not fundamentally changed, which makes it still difficult for private enterprises to obtain development funds from state-owned financial institutions in the context of fund shortage. Besides institutional constraints and ideology preferences of the state-owned banks, another reason why private enterprises have difficulty in acquiring loans is closely related with their own credit level. On the one hand, some fast-developed and large-scale private enterprises have no problem of loans; but it is worth noting that the vast majority of private enterprises are small and medium-sized enterprises, which have less standard governance, opaque information and low credit (see Table 4 – 15). For example, from the perspective of organizational form, although private enterprises are gradually improving, there are still a lot of private enterprises that do not have a modern enterprise system (see Table 4 – 16). Most private enterprises have adopted family-based governance system, which has certain advantages in early stage of development. But with the expansion of enterprise scale, it has to transfer into modern enterprise governance system. While in China, this process is relatively slow. In this case, the bank's access to information is difficult, and the loan costs are high. In the absence of competition, state-owned banks are more willing to lend money to small-risk state-owned enterprises instead of small and medium-sized private enterprises. Compared with the financing system in transition period, the governance mechanism of private enterprises is not the most fundamental. With the gradual establishment of market-oriented financing system, the governance problem of private enterprises will become more prominent. Because in the process of transition, the reason of financing difficulties in private enterprise is not only a problem of their own, but also the external environment constraints.

Table 4 – 15 Credit rating of small and medium-sized private enterprises in some provinces

Whether to participate in credit rating	Yes		Ratings Score					
Provinces	Sample size	ratio (%)	A sample size	ratio (%)	B sample size	ratio (%)	C sample size	ratio (%)
Fujian	113	51.13	76	67.26	31	27.43	6	5.31
Guangdong	61	51.69	30	49.18	29	47.54	2	3.28
Hunan	56	40.58	28	50	18	32.14	10	17.86
Jiangxi	118	76.13	96	81.36	21	17.8	1	0.85
Liaoning	24	35.82	13	54.17	11	45.83	0	0

continued

Whether to participate in credit rating	Yes		Ratings Score					
Provinces	Sample size	ratio (%)	A sample size	ratio (%)	B sample size	ratio (%)	C sample size	ratio (%)
Sichuan	39	72. 22	14	35. 9	18	46. 15	7	17. 95
Hubei	108	39. 85	46	42. 59	47	43. 52	15	13. 89

Note: A, AA level and above; B, A level and below, and BB level and above; C, B level and below.

Source: Sorted in accordance with the National Bureau of Statistics 2001 Enterprise Survey Corps data. Sample number is the number of enterprises with the primary and secondary sources of funds in corresponding options, while the ratio is the number of enterprises divided by total samples in the provinces.

Table 4 – 16 Evolution of organizational forms of private enterprises in China

Year	1991	1993	1995	1997	1999	2001
Single Ownership	56. 2	48. 4	46. 0	40. 3	34. 7	43. 1
Partnership	37. 6	23. 8	18. 1	13. 6	7. 0	8. 2
Limited Liability Company	6. 2	27. 8	35. 9	46. 1	58. 3	48. 7

Source: Li Lixia, "Research on Financing System of Small and Middle-Sized Enterprises in China", Science Press, 2005.

4. 2. 2 Institutional rent changes and financing choice of private enterprises: an empirical analysis

On the whole, with the reduction of institutional rent, private economy tends to obtain more loans from financial institutions, including state-owned banks. Private economy is developing rapidly while the increase in loans is slow. Thus, the bank loans have not played a sufficient role in promoting the development of private economy. In China's market-oriented reform, the size and reduction rate of institutional rent are different among regions, which will have a significant impact on the development of local private economy and its access to financial institutions loans. In the following part, we use inter-provincial data from 1999 to 2001① and adopt the method of empirical analysis to explore the impact of change of institutional rent, government power and marketization level on private economy financing.

① The reason of using data between 1999 and 2001 is that: In 1992, Deng Xiaoping's speech gave a better policy and market environment for the development of private economy, but the detailed data on individual and private economy before 1999 were not available. At the same time, the caliber changed after 1999 (the state-owned economy in and after 1999 include state-owned and state-controlled enterprises).

1. Data source and variable definition

The data contains 29 provinces, autonomous regions and municipalities. Hainan and Chongqing are excluded due to data reasons. The data are derived from 2000 – 2002 "China Statistical Yearbook", "China Private Economy Yearbook", "China Population Statistical Yearbook", "China Business Yearbook", "China Industrial Administration Statistical Yearbook", "China Agriculture Yearbook", "China Financial Yearbook", "New China Fifty-Five Years Statistical Data Collection" and so on. For individual data that cannot be obtained, we made some appropriate adjustments based on other indicators.

In the case where specific statistical data cannot be obtained, we remove the loans to local state-owned economic departments from all state-owned bank loans in to approximately represent the amount of loans obtained by private enterprises from state-owned financial institutions. And then, we divide this value by local private economic output value and use the quotient as an independent explanatory variable. The higher the quotient, the greater the contributions of local state-owned bank loans, and the easier for private economy to obtain state-owned bank loans. State-owned banks include Bank of China, Agricultural Bank of China, China Construction Bank, Industrial and Commercial Bank of China and China Agricultural Development Bank. We use the amount of loans from 1999 to 2001 in these five major banks to represent local state-owned financial institutions loans, and use industrial output value of state-owned and state-owned holding enterprises to measure state-owned economic sector loans. According to the relationship between gross domestic product (GDP) and the balance of all financial institutions in 1999 – 2001, we can see that the ratio between them is basically 1: 1. And here we assume that each unit of state-owned industrial output value also corresponds to a unit of state-owned bank loan. According to this, we can estimate the amount of state-owned bank loans occupied by the state-owned economic sector, and then use the total amount of state-owned bank loans minus the total industrial output value of state-owned and state-owned holding enterprises to measure the amount of state-owned bank loans obtained by private economy. For data reasons, we can only use this indicator for approximate analysis. Financial institution loans is an important source of corporate finance, and the amount of loans from this channel in our country is closely related to regional systems, endowments, ideologies and other factors. Thus, analyzing through this indicator is of important inspiration and will also explain some important phenomena in private enterprise financing. Other explanatory variables are defined in the previous chapter and will not be repeated here.

2. Preliminary verification

The results show that, from 1999 to 2001, the total amount of loans from five major state-owned banks in all 29 provinces was 18 114. 106 billion yuan, of which the amount of loans provided to the private economy was 6 494. 226 billion yuan, accounting for 35. 85% . This is in close proximity to the conclusion of Fan Gang (2000) that the proportion of all bank credit assets occupied by non-state-owned economy is about 30%. Therefore, we believe that the above estimates can basically reflect the real situation.

From the absolute number of loans provided by state-owned banks to private sector in Table 4 – 17, we can see that the eastern region is much higher than the central and western regions, while the western region is the lowest. In the meantime, the amount of loans in all three regions tends to increase, while the gap between them tend to expand. This may be related to the contraction strategy of state-owned banks, whose business is mainly concentrated in economically developed regions and cities; at the same time, the more developed the private economy is, the easier for them to get access to state-owned financial institutions loans. The comparison of share of state-owned bank loans on private economy output value shows that, during the period from 1999 to 2001, the western region is much higher than the central and eastern regions, while the central region is the lowest. The low value in 2000 was mainly related to state-owned commercial banks' dealing with bad loans (such as debt-to-equity) and structural adjustment policies. This shows that the less developed the private economy is, the more dependent they will be on state-owned bank loans; the more developed the private economy is, the easier it will be for them to get access to financial institutions loans; and for private economy in the middle stage, it will be urgent for them to get support from financial institutions loans. This may be because in developed areas, private enterprises have a high level of credit and state-owned financial institutions have a strong sense of marketization, thus they are willing to provide financial support for private economy. However, the growth rate of loans is much lower than that of private economy, and thus the unit share of loans in private economy output value is relatively low. In less developed areas, the self-accumulation ability of private economy is weak and the financial method is single, thus they can only rely on financial institutions to obtain funds. While in the middle stage, state-owned financial institutions are reluctant to provide financial support to immature private enterprises, and local governments cannot meet the funding demands of private enterprises. Therefore, they have to rely on their own. With the development of private economy and financial market, the financial support of the state-owned financial system to the private economy tends to increase.

Table 4 – 17 Regional comparison of share of state-owned bank loans on private economy output value

Region	Year 1999		Year 2000		Year 2001	
	Absolute amount	Relative value	Absolute amount	Relative value	Absolute amount	Relative value
East	11 044. 9	0. 293 4	9 763. 3	0. 251 0	12 259. 56	0. 273
Middle	7 816. 14	0. 336 5	5 645. 31	0. 218 9	6 283. 43	0. 234 7
West	4 262. 42	1. 442 2	3 705. 07	1. 096 7	4 162. 13	1. 185 4

Note: The east, middle and west region are divisions of 29 provinces, excluding Hainan and other provinces.
Source: Sorted by the author.

From the perspective of sub-sector, the state-owned bank loans mainly flow to the state-owned economic sector and private economic sector. Here, we first view the total state-owned bank loans as explained variables, and then view the output value of state-owned economy and the output value of private economy as explanatory variables, and finally test that to what extend do state-owned enterprises and private enterprises rely on state-owned bank loans. Table 4 – 18 shows that the coefficient of the output value of state-owned economy and private economy are both significantly positive, but with huge difference. This indicates that although the state-owned bank loans have certain role in promoting the development of the state-owned economy and private economy, the former is more dependent on state-owned bank loans. When we consider the unit share of state-owned bank loans in private economy as the explanatory variable, the coefficient of state-owned and private economic output value are both negative, but the latter is not statistically significant. This shows that the larger the scale of state-owned economy is, the less the unit share of state-owned bank loans in private economy will be; the more developed the private economy is, the less dependent it will be on state-owned bank loans.

Table 4 – 18 Regression results of state-owned bank loans with state-owned economic output value & private economic output value

Explanatory variable	Total amount of loans in state-owned banks	(Total amount of loans in state-owned banks) / (Output value of private economy)
C	404. 43 *** [0. 00]	1. 18 *** [0. 00]
Output value of state-owned economy	1. 101 *** [0. 00]	-0. 0003 * [0. 06]
Output value of private economy	0. 045 *** [0. 01]	-4. 61E-5 [0. 14]

continued

Explanatory variable	Total amount of loans in state-owned banks	(Total amount of loans in state-owned banks) / (Output value of private economy)
R^2	0.82	0.16

Note: 1) ***, **, * indicate significance at 1%, 5%, 10%, respectively; the significant level of corresponding variables are within the brackets; 2) The sample size is 87.

3. Models and regression results

In the following part, we use the amount of loans in unit private economic output value as explained variable, and consider the institutional rent and other variables (the definition of variables see corresponding part in Chapter 3 and Chapter 4; due to data reasons, some variables are slightly adjusted) as explanatory variables, to explore the influence factors of private economy's availability to state-owned financial institutions loan. The model we used here is:

$$Y_{it} = C + \beta X_{it} + \delta_{it}$$

First of all, we verified the relationship between the change rate of institutional rent and the amount of loans obtained from state-owned financial institutions by private economy. Table 4 – 19 shows that change rate of institutional rent is significantly negative, which means the faster the reduction rate is, the less the amount of loans depended on financial institutions will be.

Table 4 – 19 Regression results of loan share of financial institutions and change rate of institution rent

Explanatory variable	Coefficient
C	0.99 [0.24]
Change speed of institution rent [rr]	-4.00^{***} [0.00]
r_1 area dummy variable	-2.18^{***} [0.00]
r_2 area dummy variable	0.53^{**} [0.02]
r_3 area dummy variable	0.34 [0.20]
r_4 area dummy variable	0.66^{**} [0.03]
r_5 area dummy variable	0.41^{*} [0.10]
R^2	0.60

Note: 1) ***, **, * indicate significance at 1%, 5%, 10%, respectively; the significant level of corresponding variables are within the brackets; 2) The sample size is 87.

We believe that the above regression result does not mean that the faster the reduction rate is, the more reluctant it will be for state-owned banks to provide loans to private economy. However, this is probably because that the faster the reduction rate is, the faster the development of private economy will be. In this case, the financing channels for private economy are relatively wide. At this time, although the absolute amount of loans from financial institutions is relatively large, the amount of loans for unit private economic output value will be less due to the fact that the growth rate of private economy is larger than that of loans in financial institutions. This can also be seen from the negative correlation between the unit share of state-owned financial institution loans for private economy and the output value of private economy (the correlation coefficient is-0.35). The more developed the private economy is, the less amount of loans obtained from state-owned financial institutions by unit private economic output value will be. This may indicate that, on the one hand, the development of private economy is faster than that of state-owned financial institutions; on the other hand, it also shows that private economic development has other sources of funding support and state-owned financial institutions have failed to meet the funding demands of private enterprises.

We use three models to verify the specific impact on private enterprises to obtain loans from state-owned financial institutions. The explanatory variables Y_{it} in each model represents the share of financial institution loans on unit private economy output value in province i and year t. In the first model, X_{it} represents institutional rent; in the second model, X_{it} represents the influence of state-owned economy, the power of local government, and the marketization level; in the third model, X_{it} represents various specific variables, such as per capita state-owned industrial output value. In this case, we carried out a common OLS regression using inter-provincial data from 1999 to 2001. The results are shown in Table 4 – 20.

Table 4 – 20 Regression results of all variables

Variables	Model Ⅰ	Model Ⅱ	Model Ⅲ
C	−4.83*** [0.00]	−0.56 [0.46]	−1.02 [0.36]
Institution rent (r_t)	4.44*** [0.00]		
Influence of state-owned economy (m_1)		−0.51*** [0.00]	
Power of local government (m_2)		27.41*** [0.00]	
Marketization degree (m_3)		−3.49*** [0.00]	
Per capita financial institution loans (p_g)			0.10 [0.46]
Per capita state-owned industrial output value (p_{h1})			−1.30*** [0.00]
Proportion of households that did not use all-round contract (p_j)			9.84*** [0.00]
Per capita initialcommunity industrial output value (p_k)			150.07*** [0.00]
Per capita collective investment in fixed assets (p_m)			−8.59** [0.04]
Initial marketization level (i_m)			−336.4*** [0.00]

continued

Variables	Model Ⅰ	Model Ⅱ	Model Ⅲ
Financial deepening degree (p_n)			-1.09** [0.04]
Product marketization degree (q_q)			-0.004 [0.53]
Urban population ratio (p_q)			-2.42*** [0.00]
P_v1999 year dummy variable	-0.39** [0.04]	-0.15 [0.20]	0.19 [0.22]
P_w2000 year dummy variable	-0.13 [0.50]	-0.02 [0.41]	0.20 [0.18]
r_1 area dummy variable	3.99*** [0.00]	0.90*** [0.01]	2.54*** [0.00]
r_2 area dummy variable	0.69*** [0.00]	0.11 [0.35]	0.46* [0.10]
r_3 area dummy variable	-0.07 [0.65]	-0.10 [0.31]	0.48** [0.04]
r_4 area dummy variable	0.13 [0.34]	0.41*** [0.01]	0.74*** [0.00]
r_5 area dummy variable	0.39* [0.10]	0.36** [0.03]	0.55** [0.04]
R^2	0.65	0.88	0.82

Note: 1) ***, **, * indicate significance at 1%, 5%, 10%, respectively; the significant level of corresponding variables are within the brackets; 2) The sample size is 87; 3) DW Value and F statistic are in accordance with the corresponding test, indicating no autocorrelation or multiple collinearity between variables.

In model I, when institutional rent is used as an explanatory variable, its coefficient is significantly positive. This result is different from the previous conclusions. We believe that this may be related to the year of the data. At the beginning of the reform and opening up, the whole society is very exclusive of the private economy and the state-owned economy is more influential. By this constraint, financial institutions are reluctant to provide funds to the private economy; at the same time, the local government did not dare to actively help the private economy get access to financial resources. Therefore, the higher the institutional rent is, the less loans the financial institutions will be willing to provide to private sector. After years of reform and marketization development, on the one hand, the whole society's attitude towards the concept of private economy has changed. Although the state-owned economy still plays a leading role, its influence has weakened; On the other hand, the market orientation of financial institutions has been enhanced, and they are willing to lend money to qualified private enterprises. In areas where the institutional rent is low, the marketization level is high and the government power is small, thus the private economy develops rapidly and the financing ability gets stronger. This time, the marketization trend of financial institutions also gets stronger. But overall, the rate of increasing loans is slower than the rate of private economy development, thus the share of financial institutions loans on unity private economy output value is less. In addition, the higher the institutional rent is, the lower the marketization level and the larger the government power will be: on the one hand, private economy develops slowly and the financing method is single; on the other hand, local governments are more active to use their own advantages to help private economy get access to development funds, which leads to larger share of loans on unit private economy output value.

In model II, we use the influence of state-owned economy, the power of local government and marketization level as explanatory variables to further analyze the impact of these factors on financing of private economy. We found that, the coefficient of influence of state-owned economy and marketization level is significantly negative; while the coefficient of the power of local government is significantly positive. This shows that although China's market-oriented reforms have endeavored for many years, the institutional inertia of state-owned economy still exists. The state-owned economy mainly relies on state-owned bank loans, and the resources of state-owned financial institutions mainly flow to state-owned economic sectors. The greater the influence of state-owned economy, the closer the relationship between state-owned enterprises and state-owned banks, and the harder it will be for private economy to obtain loans from financial institutions. As time goes by, the influence of local government power on the loans obtained from financial institutions by private economy has changed. The local government power has a significantly positive effect on private enterprises. This is related to behavioral characteristics of the local governments: with the advancement of marketization, economic expectations tend to be stable and the local government's ideological concerns are eliminated. Thus, in order to develop private economy, especially collective economy, local government often use their own advantages to help private enterprises acquire state-owned finance institutional loans. Therefore, the larger the local government power is, the more conductive it will be for collective economy to obtain financial institution loans. This also means that the local private economy is still in a relatively low stage of development. The higher the degree of marketization, the more favorable regional institutional arrangement and ideology will be for the development of private economy. At this time, although the market-oriented operation of financial institutions gets intense and the absolute amount of loans increase, the share of state-owned financial institution loans on unit private economic output value is still low.

In model III, we use specific indicators to analyze the impact of various institutional rent factors on the financing of private enterprises. In this model, the coefficient of per capita financial institution loans is positive, but not statistically significant; the coefficient of per capita state-owned industrial output value is significantly negative, which further shows that the higher the proportion of state-owned economy, the more unfavorable it will be for private economy to get access to financial institutions loans; the more developed the state-owned financial market is, the more financial resources are, the more favorable it will be for private economy to obtain financial institutions loans. But the allocation of state-owned financial resources are often associated with the proportion of high state-owned economy, which is not conducive to financing of private economy. The coefficients of proportion of households that did not use all-round contract and per capita initialcommunity industrial output value are significantly positive, while the coefficient of per capita collective investment in fixed assets is significantly negative. This shows that the stronger the executive power is, the more motivated it will be for local government to help them get access to financial institutions loans; and the more enthusiastic the local government is to develop collective economy, the faster the development rate for private economy will be. This shows that the local government has two sides in the development of private economy. The coefficients of initial marketization level, financial deepening degree, and urban population ratio are significantly negative; while the product marketization degree is negative, but not statistically significant. This may suggest that the higher the level of initial marketization, the stronger the self-accumulation ability will be in the development of private economy; at the same time, the more sources of other funds, the faster the private economy will develop and the fewer contributions of state-owned financial institutions will make. The higher the degree of financial deepening, the stronger the ability of individual capital accumulation. Relatively speaking, the demand for financial institutions loans will be smaller. The higher the degree of product marketization, the more conducive it will be for the development of private economy and the improvement of marketization level in the whole region. In addition, financial institutions will be more willing to provide credit support. Since self-financing capacity of private economy also gets stronger, this kind of relationship will be vague. The higher the ratio of urbanization, the faster the development of private economy and other financial institutions. Since various financing tools are available and financing environment gets loose, the loans obtained from state-owned financial institutions by private economy will be relatively reduced. The coefficients of dummy variables are not described here in detail.

4. Research conclusions

Through the above analysis, we can draw some conclusions:

First, private enterprises obtaining financial institution loans is closely linked to and the financing system change of state-owned enterprise. The source of financing loans in state-owned enterprises tend to diversify and state-owned banks are gradually lending money to eligible private enterprises. During this process, the change of institutional rent is of great importance. The decline rate of institutional rent, on the one hand, has a crucial impact on the development rate of private economy and determines the financing choice of private enterprises. The faster the decline of institutional rent, the faster the development of private economy and the more financing choices there will be. In the case of rapid market development, the market orientation of the state-owned banks is stronger and the amount of loans to private economy will increase. Of course, the increase rate in the amount of loans is still lower than the development rate of private economy, thus the share of loans in unit private economic output value will be lower.

Second, institutional rent level has a significant impact on whether the private enterprises will get loans from financial institutions. The lower the institutional rent, the lower the share of loans in unit private economic output value will be. Specifically, the greater the influence of state-owned economy is, the more difficult it will be for private enterprises to obtain financial institutions loans; in the process of marketization, the greater the local government power is, the more willing for local government to help private economy get access to financial loans, which also indicates a relatively low development stage of the private economy; the higher the degree of marketization, the higher the market orientation of financial institutions will be, and the absolute amount of loans obtained by private economy will also increase. This also shows that the marketization process of state-owned financial institutions has lagged far behind that of private economy. In areas where the private economy is more developed, the dependence on loans from state-owned financial institutions will be smaller.

Third, in the process of marketization, the role of local government is very critical. In the case of low degree of marketization, in order to develop private economy, local government can help private enterprises obtain funds by cultivating the market system and using their own links with state-owned financial institutions. With the increase of marketization degree, local governments should reduce the degree of participation in the economy and focus on coordinating the healthy operation of market mechanisms.

Fourth, the expansion of private enterprise financing channels depends on the optimization of state-owned enterprise financing mechanism. The key to reforming state-owned enterprises and state-owned banks is to raise the hard constraints on their financing. With gradual improvement of market mechanism and development of non-state-owned economy, the increase of financing methods outside the system provides available financing choices for the state-owned enterprises; and the high capital utilization efficiency of private economy will also create external pressure for the state-owned enterprises and force them to improve their efficiency. The accumulation of private capital and the increase of financing channels have also formed certain competitive pressure on state-owned banks. Under these circumstances, developing private finance and encouraging private capital get into the financial industry, especially the banking industry, are conducive to solving private enterprise financing problems and improving the efficiency of capital use. In the meantime, this will also greatly promote the reform of state-owned banks and state-owned enterprise property rights. Changes in the financing system of state-owned enterprises and the establishment of market-oriented mechanism of state-owned banks will in turn greatly promote the development of private economy and the optimization of financing mechanism.

These conclusions are of great significance. In the developed areas of private economy, private enterprises have various financing channels and strong financing ability. The main function of the government is to shape the favorable development environment and guide the various financing mechanisms which is endogenously produced during the development process of private economy. In the less developed areas of private economy, due to the weak financing ability and single financing channels, the government must strive to cultivate the regional marketization level and broaden the financing channels of private enterprises so as to promote the rapid development of private economy.

4.3 Mode selection and governance of financial subject privatization

According to ownership structure, China has no shortage of private financial institutions. Urban credit cooperatives, urban commercial banks and rural credit cooperatives are all non-public enterprises and private financial institutions where individuals account for the vast majority of shares.

City credit cooperative is a kind of credit cooperative organizations. It is based on collective economy and individual industrial and commercial households and was established in 1980s. In the next 10 years, it had increased to more than 5 000. However, under the control of non-public economy, urban credit cooperatives did not develop as well as we would expect. On the contrary, they had some great risks at that time. In the mid-1990s, the government decided to reorganize city credit cooperatives and set up commercial banks. So far, there have been 108 commercial banks. In the formation of urban commercial banks, local governments generally invest 25% to 30%, and the remaining 75% to 70% are corporate shares, especially non-public enterprises and individual holdings. Therefore, according to ownership structure, "these city commercial banks are still dominated by private capital and belong to private banks"①.

In addition, China Minsheng Bank Corp in 1996 and Zhejiang Bank in 2004 are all typical private banks due to the fact that their ownership structure are owned 100% by private enterprises.

The history of rural credit cooperatives is more distant and can be traced back to Sino-foreign joint "China Huayang disaster relief meeting" and the credit cooperatives established by farmers in Zhejiang in the 1920s. Since then, in the Anti-Japanese War and the Liberation War, credit cooperatives led by Communist Party had gone through certain development; till 1947, there were more than 880 credit cooperatives in the whole liberated area. After the founding of new China, the development of credit cooperatives was considered as part of the entire cooperative movement, in which its fate were closely related to the choice of overall economic model and gone through twists and turns. It was not until august 1996 that the State Council promulgated "the Decision on the Reform of Rural Financial System" and established the goal of market-based cooperative financial system with the theme of "rebuilding cooperation system", which requires the rural credit cooperatives to be in accordance with the principle of cooperation: rural credit cooperatives and agricultural banks are completely "decoupled", and we should restore the nature of cooperative finance by viewing grassroots rural credit cooperatives as legal person; In 1997, the "Regulations on the Management of Rural Credit Cooperatives" defined credit cooperatives as "consisting of membership shares, running by democratic management and providing financial services for members"; In 1998, the State Council forwarded the Notice of the People's Bank of China on "the Opinions of

① Wu Xiaoling. China Business Times, January 24, 2003.

Reform and Rectification of Rural Credit Cooperatives". The principle of cooperation was interpreted as "voluntary shares, democratic management and mainly serving members"; In 2003, the restructuring work of rural credit cooperatives began to focus on the construction of property rights system and improvement of governance structure of rural cooperative banks and rural commercial banks, and eight pilot provinces gradually extended to the whole country①. In cooperation with the reform, the state has given financial subsidies, tax relief, floating interest rates, Central Bank refinancing and a series of preferential policies. The reform of rural credit cooperative has also achieved initial results: by the time of September 2006, rural credit cooperatives have set up 85 banking institutions throughout the country, including 12 rural commercial banks and 73 rural cooperative banks.

It is estimated that China's private capital has controlled 14.6% of the total assets in joint-stock commercial banks and no less than 7.4% of the premium income of insurance companies; private capital's proportion in shareholding and holding of the securities companies is more than 13 %; half of the 12 financial leasing companies in the country are controlled by private enterprises; in addition, three out of more than 40 trust and investment companies in China are private holding companies (Jinxin Trust, Jinxin Trust and Aijian trust); two out of more than 70 financial companies are private financing companies (Oriental Group Finance Company and Wanxiang Finance Company).

Therefore, the number of financial institutions controlled by private capital is high. However, if we judge from the three principles of whether it is in accordance with the principles of market economy, whether it is different from state-owned financial institutions in corporate governance mechanism, and whether its service objects are mainly private enterprises, there will be no private financial organizations in real sense.

4.3.1 Path selection of private financial market access

To guide private capital into the financial field is inevitable due to financial deepening. But for emerging market economy countries, under the condition of incomplete financial institution and financial system, the market access of private

① Thirty provinces have carried out the reform of rural credit cooperatives except for Tibet where there is no rural creditcooperatives.

finance is particularly cautious. China's current policy of financial privatization is not clear yet and has not developed a unified market access rule for private financial institutions; what's more, the policy environment needs to be improved and financial supervision needs to be strengthened. At present, we should take the following policy measures to promote the development of private finance:

First, we should gradually implement the privatization strategy of financial main body. In order to solve the financing obstacles of private economy and to guide the private capital to run in compliance with the regulations, the development of private finance is not only a necessary content of the establishment of financial infrastructure, but also an effective measure of improving financial macro-control. However, the technical complexity and high risks of financial industry have asked for a high entry threshold to avoid overcrowding of the financial industry.

In the mid-1980s, China had gone through a similar issue of low market access to urban credit cooperatives which led to the phenomenon of institution expansion and "excessive bank". In order to avoid vicious and disorderly competition caused by excessive open of private finance, we should first make clear provisions on the legal qualifications of investors, the scope of access to funds and the minimum amount of registered capital. For the establishment of rural private financial institutions, it can be differentiated according to regional differences, and should be lower than the city standard to fill the gaps in financial services. Relying on large-scale private enterprise groups or financial companies, this kind of set-up acquires relatively large initial investment which will increase social costs and lead to excessive financial institutions; but the new institutions do not have historical burden, have clear property rights, and are easy to design in the organization's equity structure and corporate governance structure. The privatization of existing financial institutions, including the establishment of small and medium-sized private banks on the basis of urban credit cooperatives and urban commercial banks; the introduction of private capital into existing commercial banks; the transformation of rural credit cooperatives and rural commercial banks in the same way; and the formation of new community banks by selling some branches of state-owned banks to private capital (Shi Jinchuan, 2003). The privatization reform of existing financial institutions through capital operation may leave some historical problems, and the assessment of property rights and assets of the original financial institutions will be relatively difficult. From the policy point of view, it is necessary not only to encourage the privatization reform of original financial institutions, but also to support the set-up of market-oriented private financial organizations. The experience of private finance development suggests that private investment should be encouraged and allowed in all financing areas where foreign investment are allowed to enter.

Second, we should run in accordance with the rules of the market, promote competition in the financial industry, and improve financial efficiency. For example, the development of private securities companies can use private enterprise funds, and this will help securities companies improve structure and promote standardized development. In addition, for the characteristics of high-risk in individual investment, we can establish a number of private industry investment funds which are under standardized operation and run by professional management so as to concentrate scattered funds to participate in social infrastructure and public utilities investment such as bridges, roads and others (Qian Xiaoan, 2003). On March 21, 2002, the People's Bank of China initially implemented the interest rate liberalization pilot in eight rural credit cooperatives in Zhejiang, Fujian, Jilin, Heilongjiang and Inner Mongolia which regulated that the floating range of the deposit rate is 30% while the floating range of the loan interest rate is 100%. The smooth operation of the pilots shows that the development of private financial institutions needs the rules of marketization, and the interest rate marketization also made private funds into the normal business of private financial institutions, played as the intermediary role in private financial institutions, standardized the activities of private finance, enhanced the strength of private financial institutions, and promoted the development of private economy and private finance.

4.3.2 Institutional guarantee of smooth operation in private finance

The ability of private finance to resist financial market risk is the main concern of the Central Bank on private financial industry. In order to ensure the stability of financial order, to enable private financial institutions to survive in the competitive environment of state-owned and foreign-funded financial institutions, the corresponding system and safeguard measures must be complete and advanced. These measures include deposit insurance system, final lender system, social credit system, corporate governance mechanism and so on.

1. Construction of a perfect deposit insurance system

Deposit insurance is an ex post facto remedy that protects the interests of depositors, stabilizes the financial system and financial institutions. After the outbreak of the economic crisis in 1929 – 1933, the Federal Deposit Insurance Corporation (FDIC) was formally established on January 1, 1934, in order to protect the interests of depositors and restore public confidence in the banking system. Since the 1960s, many countries have established a deposit insurance system that is suitable for their own national conditions.

The credit base of China's private finance and state-owned financial is different, it is not possible to rely on the state to provide the final credit guarantee for depositors. In order to enhance public confidence in private finance, we can legislate to establish an initial deposit insurance institution, which is managed by the People's Bank of China and not for the purpose of profit making, and clearly stipulate the purpose of deposit insurance (to protect the interests of depositors and maintain the confidence in rural private financial institutions), insurance principles, insured objects and insurance qualifications. The funding resource is consisted of government funding and deposits which are payed by other banks; in the early stage, we can set up a lower rate; when things are ripe, we should determine different insurance rates according to the bank's capital adequacy ratio, asset liquidity, risk assets ratio and other indicators, and periodically review the adjustments. And then we can expand the scope of insurance, set up nationwide deposit insurance institutions, and require gradual participation of the state owned banks so as to gradually weaken the rely of state-owned commercial banks on the credibility of the country, construct a fair market competition environment for small and medium-sized banks, and ensure funding sources of deposit insurance. In addition, in the insurance market, we can also set up a private deposit insurance company, require full participation of private banks which engage in the deposit business, and make sure the whole banking system is going to be more secure. When the financial institutions enter the bankruptcy liquidation procedures, the financial regulatory authorities should utilize their own power, authority and strong professional knowledge to arrange the drop-out of the financial institutions, transfer it to the deposit insurance institutions and leave the specific settlement work to them.

2. Establishment of a final lender system

The lender of last resort is an institutional arrangement in which the Central Bank offer financial assistance and implement rescue operations for problematic banks. When commercial banks go into a cash flow dilemma, the Central Bank loans is the only way to solve the problem of solvency. Of course, for banks who have disordered operation, liquidity problems and high risks, they need to be taken over, be suspended for rectification, and go bankruptcy and other mandatory measures, instead of the lender of last resort.

For private financial institutions, China needs to establish the final lender system, and the Central Bank acts as the lender of last resort. This will not only ensure that private banks have sufficient liquidity and maintain the stability of the financial system, but also be conducive to strengthening the central bank's supervision of private banks. The establishment of the final lender system can take a variety of forms. First, the Central Bank dependently acts as the lender of last resort and rescues the problematic private banks; second, the Central Bank and private banks mutually set up a fund to exercise the role of the lender of the last resort; third, large banks consortium acts as the lender of last resort and rescues the problematic private banks (Zhang Qingliang, 2005).

Of course, after the privatization of financial entities, saturated state may appear. Financial institutions, which are of poor management and accumulated risks, will be taken over, dissolved, revoked or even declared bankruptcy. Therefore, there should be clear boundaries between the withdrawal mechanism of financial institutions and the final lender system. If the banks go into the bankruptcy liquidation procedure, they will not be suitable for the final lender system. This will create a reverse demonstration effect that for banks of poor operation and high risks, they would be expelled.

3. Construction of a social credit evaluation system

It is also necessary to create a good credit environment so as to support the development of private finance. What's more, we should also build a social credit evaluation system to reduce the degree of information asymmetry between enterprises and financial institutions, financial institutions and regulatory authorities.

The credit system and the legal system are the basis for the benign development of the market economy. The establishment of a unified, open and effective credit rating system and evaluation system for enterprises and individuals is a basic condition for the healthy development of financial industry and an important guarantee for the healthy development of small and medium-sized private banks. During the transition period, China's social credit is generally missing: the financing difficulties of small and medium-sized enterprises and the shortage of bank credit coexist, indicating that the enterprises and banks are both in their own predicament. To solve this contradiction, it is necessary for the whole social system and economic system to improve at the same time. Through the construction of social credit evaluation system, small and medium-sized private banks can choose customers through the enterprise's credit records and collateral assets, thus greatly reduce the business risk. The establishment of private enterprise credit and guarantee system will also help private enterprises to break through the financing barriers and create a good credit environment for the development of private finance.

4. Implementation of prudential supervision measures

Due to the low transparency of private finance, the effectiveness of financial supervision is weak and it is easy to accumulate financial risks. Besides, financial risk is transitive, which means the poor operation of a single private financial institution will transmit risks to the entire financial system. Therefore, for the development of private finance, it is necessary to strengthen the supervision and make sure that the improvement of financial supervision and the development of private financial go on simultaneously (Fan Gang, 2002).

The implementation of prudential supervision measures include market access, exit, regulatory concept, comprehensive supervision and other aspects; in addition, corporate governance and the qualifications of directors and senior management staff should also be contained within the scope of supervision. Specifically speaking: in the aspect of market access to private financial institutions, we should formulate appropriate market access rules and effective market exit mechanism according to the characteristics of different types of financial institutions and the development reality of financial groups; in order to prevent moral hazard, we should establish appropriate protection system and gradually establish explicit security measures (such as the deposit insurance system) to avoid the fact that private financial institutions may pass the risks to the government (Qian Xiaoan, 2000); in order to deal with the relationship between regulation and innovation, we should encourage private financial institutions to carry out business innovation, develop new products and improve operational efficiency; we should constantly improve financial regulatory indicators and measures in accordance with the latest development in financial innovation, and fully utilize on-site supervision, off-site supervision and other means to strengthen the supervision on private finance so as to prevent private financial regulatory gaps and ensure sound operation of private finance.

5. Perfection of corporate governance for private financial institutions

There are many particularities in the corporate governance of financial institutions. The perfection of corporate governance is an important guarantee for scientific decision-making and an important measure to prevent financial risks.

First, the corporate governance of private finance should pay more attention to the interests of stakeholders, not just to the shareholders themselves (Li Wei'an, 2003). In the field of corporate governance, the debate of whether the company should maximize the interests of shareholders or should pay more attentions for the interests of stakeholders has a long history. The mainstream viewpoint is that the shareholders are the owners of the company and the company's control naturally belongs to the shareholders. This theoretical logic is often referred to as "shareholder supremacy." In this theory, the shareholder-based client model views the shareholders as the main body. The emerging "stakeholder theory" argues that the "ownership" is mutual and that the company should take care of the interests of the stakeholders as much as possible, since the shareholders are only part of the stakeholders. The main basis of the stakeholder theory is: (1) as with shareholders, creditors, employees, suppliers, customers and communities all bear the corresponding risks of the company, and should share the ownership of the company; (2) shareholders, especially dispersive and passive shareholders, are usually at a disadvantage in a large company, but other stakeholders, especially workers, may be in a dominant position to exercise all relevant rights and responsibilities. For the above reasons, this theory see the enterprise as a contract for stakeholders, and thus the company's goal is to maximize the company's value.

If the "shareholder supremacy" and "stakeholder theory" are still controversial in the field of corporate governance, we should firmly support the "stakeholder theory" when it comes to corporate governance in financial institutions. This is because the particularity of financial institutions. As an important pillar for the national economy, financial institutions' risk loss will seriously threaten all aspects of social and economic life. Thus, we should pay more attention to the interests of stakeholders in private financial organizations. In the banking industry, the Basel Committee requires corporate governance to address the following issues: (1) establishing clear bank objectives; (2) ensuring normal business operations on a daily basis; (3) taking full account of the interests of stakeholders; (4) ensuring the safe and sound operation of banks under the judicial and regulatory system; (5) ensuring the interests of depositors.

Second, the objectives of corporate governance of private finance should not only be the maximization of corporate value, but also the organization's security. Financial institutions are not only an important financing channel for industrial and commercial enterprises and an indispensable payment system for the whole society, but also provide credit and liquidity support under special market conditions. Therefore, financial organizations, as the key sectors of the national economy, are often included in government safety system and become the focus of government regulation and control objectives. From the perspective of business objectives, financial companies and general companies are different. The goal of the company is to achieve the maximization of the company's value (especially the shareholders' wealth). The financial industry, as an important part of the special industry of the national economy, should take into account the macroeconomic stability in addition to maximizing its own interests. Private financial institutions should pay attention to their own safety and stability because there is no government credit for guarantee.

Third, due to the limited role of external governance mechanism, the governance mechanism of private financial should focus on internal governance and selectively utilize external governance mechanism. The external governance mechanism of financial institutions has the following shortcomings: (1) inadequate market competition will weaken the product market competition mechanism as the basic role of external governance mechanism; (2) in the aspect of corporate governance, the creditor's rights are different from the stock rights. The absence of the creditor's supervision caused by special capital structure of the financial industry makes the external governance mechanism unable to play; (3) huge costs of mergers and acquisitions will also restrict the role of external regulatory mechanism. In view of the differences in the external governance mechanism and the differences in the degree of emphasis on the external governance mechanism, the prudent use of external governance mechanism is in line with the theoretical norms. In addition to the progressive characteristics of China's transition economy and market system construction, such considerations are in line with the reality (Li Wei'an, 2003).

At present, private financial institutions should improve corporate governance from the following aspects: (1) strengthening the functions of the board. This includes: to enhance the authority and independence of the board, especially to introduce a certain number of independent directors; to establish a director evaluation system and clarify the responsibilities of directors; to improve the internal organizational structure of the board and set up risk management committee, nomination committee, remuneration committee and audit committee; (2) improving the incentive mechanism, especially the establishment of senior management incentives; (3) emphasizing supervision and restraint. This includes two specific contents: one is to establish and improve the internal and external supervision system, and to ensure the fairness and objectivity of these supervisory bodies; the second is to promote information disclosure, especially the accounting statements, in order to accept a wide range of social supervision; (4) reforming the appointment and removal of senior management and assessment system, and gradually trying the market-oriented operation mechanism.

References

1. All-China Federation of Industry and Commerce. Almanac of China's Private Economy (1996). China Chamber of Commerce and Industry Publishing House, 1996.

2. All-China Federation of Industry and Commerce. Almanac of China's Private Economy (1997 – 1999). Sino-culture Press, 2000.

3. All-China Federation of Industry and Commerce. Almanac of China's Private Economy (2000 – 2001). China Chamber of Commerce and Industry Publishing House, 2003.

4. Anders Isaksson. The Importance of Informal Finance in Kenyan Manufacturing. United Nations Industrial Development Organization (UNIDO) Working Paper, 2002, No 5, www. unido. org/en/doc/5003.

5. Avery R. B. , Bostic R. W. , Samolyk K. A. The Role of Personal Wealth in Small Business Finance. Journal of Banking and Finance, 1998, 22 (3): 1019 – 1061.

6. Barbosa E. , Moraces C. Determinants of the Firm's Capital Structure: the Case of the Very Small Enterprises. Working Paper from Econpapers, 2003.

7. Brau J. C. Do Banks Price Owner-manager Agency Costs? An Examination of Small Business Borrowing. Journal of Small Business Management, 2002, 40 (4): 273 – 286.

8. Cai Fang. Logic and Successful Conditions for the Reform of Property Rights Regime of Township Enterprises. Economic Research Journal, 1995 (10): 35 – 40.

9. Cao Jinsheng. Bank Financing in the Development of Enterprises. Economic & Management Publishing House, 2002.

10. Chen Weihong. "Relationship Financing" and its Expansion in Private Enterprises. Management World, 2004 (10): 143 - 144.

11. Chen Xiaofeng, Lin Qiu. "Market Failure" during the Process of Credit Financing in China's Private Enterprises. Inquiry into Economic Issues, 2003 (8): 53 - 57.

12. Chen Xiaohong, GuoShengkun. Financing of Small and Medium Enterprises. Economic Science Press, 2002.

13. Chen Yan. Action Agenda of Private Bank in China. Economic& Management Publishing House, 2003.

14. Cheng Lei. Interpretation of Private Enterprise Financing Behavior and Comment on Private Enterprise Financing Practice in Wenzhou. Journal of Wenzhou University, 2002 (1): 31 - 35.

15. Cheng Lei. Empirical Research of Private Finance. Finance& Trade Economics, 2004 (2): 39 - 42.

16. Cheng Siwei. Reform and Development: Promoting China's Rural Finance. Economic Science Press, 2005.

17. China Society for Finance and Banking. Almanac of China's Finance and Banking (2000 ~ 2003).

18. Cole R. A., Walranen N. Banking Consolidation and the Availability of Credit to Small Business. Board of Governors of the Federal Reserve System Working Paper, 1998.

19. Cui Lijin, Li Jiang, Wu Liang. Survey and Thinking of Underground Financial Market in Zhejiang, Fujian and Guangdong. Reporter Observation, 2002 (3): 18 - 21.

20. Editorial Board of Almanac of China's Economy. Almanac of China's Economy, 2003.

21. Fang Jian, etc. Discussion on Bond Financing Mode in China's Small and Medium-sized Enterprises. China Soft Science, 2003 (10): 52 - 57.

22. Fan Gang. Financial Development and Enterprise Reform. Economic Science Press, 2005.

23. Fang Xiaoxia. Enterprise Financing in China: Institutional Changes and Behavioral Analysis. Peking University Press, 1999.

24. Feng Qu. On the Reform of Township Enterprises from the Perspective of Fund Raising Mechanism: A Case of Institutional Change Dynamics. Reform, 2000 (5): 58 - 64.

25. Grossman s. , Hart O. One-Share-One-Vote and the Market for Corporate Control. Journal of Financial Economics, 1988 (20): 175 - 202.

26. Guo Bin, Liu Manlu. Private Finance and Development of Small and Medium-sized Enterprises: An Empirical Analysis of Wenzhou. Economic Research Journal, 2002 (10): 40 - 46.

27. He Liping. To Overcome the Asymmetric Information Barriers between Financial Institutions and Small and Medium-sized Enterprises. Reform, 1999 (2): 14 - 16.

28. He Sijiang. Institutional Distortion and Financial Arrangement during the Process of Regional Economic Development: A Case of Wenzhou. Zhejiang Social Sciences, 2003 (3): 42 - 47.

29. Helwege J. , Liang N. Is There a Pecking Order? Evidence from a Panel of IPO Firms. Journal of Financial Economics, 1996 (40): 429 - 458.

30. Horworth C. A. Small Firms' Demand for Finance: A Research Note. International Small Business Journal, 2001, 19 (4): 78 - 86.

31. Hou Li. On the Financing of Private Enterprises in China from the Perspective of Changes in American Enterprise Financing Modes. Economic Theory and Business Management, 2002 (12): 52 - 54.

32. Hu Xiaoping. Financing of Small and Medium Enterprises. Economic & Management Publishing House, 2000.

33. Huang Jiaye, XieRuiqiao. The Development and Evolution of Taiwan's Private Finance. Finance& Trade Economics, 2003 (3): 91 - 94.

34. Jean C. Oi. Rural China Takes Off: Incentives for Industrialization. Berkeley: University of California Press, 1997: 191 - 204.

35. Jiang Xuzhao. Chinese Folk Finance Research. Shandong People's Publishing House, 1996.

36. Jin Xiangrong, Zhu Xiwei. The Origin and Evolution of Specialized Industrial Zone: A Historical and Theoretical Perspective. Economic Research Journal, 2002 (8): 74 - 82.

37. Jing Xuecheng, Shen Bingxi. The Marketization Process of China's Interest Rate. China Financial & Economic Publishing House, 2000.

38. Li Fuyou. Regional Differences in Endogenous Financing of Private Economy. Reform, 2006 (1): 100 - 105.

39. Li Wei'an, Cao Tingqiu. Ownership Structure, Governance Mechanism and Urban Bank Performance: Survey Evidence from Shandong and Henan. Economic

Research Journal, 2004 (12): 4-15.

40. Li Yang, Yang Siqun. Financing and Banking of Small and Medium-sized Enterprises. Shanghai University of Finance and Economics Press, 2001.

41. Lin Hanchuan, Guan Hongxi. Financial Status and Countermeasures of Small and Medium-sized Enterprises: Questionnaire Survey Report from Small and Medium-sized Enterprises in Hubei, Guangdong. The Journal of Quantitative & Technical Economics, 2002 (2): 107-110.

42. Lin Hanchuan. Research of Development Mechanism in China's Small and Medium-sized Enterprises. The Commercial Press, 2003.

43. Lin Yifu, Li Yongjun. The Development of Small and Medium-sized Financial Institutions and Financing of Small and Medium-sized Enterprises. Economic Research Journal, 2001 (1): 10-18.

44. Lin Yifu, Sun Xifang. Information, Informal Finance and SME Financing. Economic Research Journal, 2005 (7): 35-44.

45. Liu Hongmei, Wang Keqiang. Research of China's Corporate Finance Market. China Price Press, 2002.

46. Liu Jing, Zheng Zhenlong. Institutional Changes of Folk Finance. Finance and Economics, 1999 (7): 18-20.

47. Liu Wei. Property Rights of Contemporary Chinese Private Capital. Economic Science, 2000 (2): 5-14.

48. Liu Yong, Li Shan Tong. Foreign SME Financing and its Revelation. Financial Digest, 2001 (10): 12-13.

49. Luo Zhengying, etc. Credit Chain: the Association Strategy of SME Financing. Accounting Research, 2003 (7): 50-52.

50. Modigliani F., Miller M. Corporation Income Taxes and the Cost of Capital: A Correction. American Economic Review, 1963 (53): 433-443.

51. Myers S. C. Capital Structure. Journal of Economic Perspectives. 2001 (15): 81-102.

52. National Bureau of Statistics of the People's Republic of China. 2003 China Development Report. China Statistics Press, 2003.

53. Otsuka, Keijiro. Rural Industrialization in East Asia. Mimeo, Tokyo Metropolitan University, 1996.

54. Petersen M. A., Rajan R. G. Dose Distance Still Matter? The Information Revolution in Small Business Lending. Journal of Finance, 2002, 57 (6): 2379-2403.

55. Qian Xiaoan. Financial Privatization and Financial Infrastructure Construction. Journal of Financial Research, 2003 (2): 1 – 11.

56. Scherr F. C. , Hulburt H. M. The Debt Maturity Structure of Small Firms. Financial Management, 2001 (Spring): 85 – 111.

57. Shaw, Edward S. Financial Deepening in Economic Development. Oxford University Press, 1973.

58. Shi Jinchuan, etc. Development of Zhejiang Private Financial Industry. Zhejiang Social Sciences, 1998 (5): 23 – 28.

59. Shi Jinchuan et al. Research on the Development of Small and Medium-sized Financial Institutions and Enterprises: Taking Examples of Wenzhou and Taizhou. Zhejiang University Press, 2003.

60. Stiglitz J. , Weiss. Credit Rationing and Markets with Imperfect Information. American Economic Review, 1981 (71): 393 – 411.

61. Stiglitz, Joseph E. The Role of the State in Financial Market. The World Bank Economic Review, 1994 (8): 57 – 68.

62. Strahan, Philip E. , Weston, James P. Small Business Lending and the Changing Structure of the Banking Industry. Journal of Banking and Finance, 1998 (22): 821 – 845.

63. Sun Li. China's Private Financial Development and Financial System Changes. Shanghai Journal of Economics, 2000 (5): 62 – 65.

64. Tan Liwen. Financing Planning. Democracy and Construction Press, 2001.

65. TianGuoqiang. Frontier Development of Modern Economics and Finance. The Commercial Press, 2002.

66. Timothy Besley, Stephen Coate, Glenn Loury. The Economics of Rotating Savings and Credit Associations. American Economic Review, Sep, 1993, Vol. 83, No. 4: 792 – 810.

67. Tucker J. , Lean J. Small Firm Finance and Public Policy. Journal of Small Business and Enterprise Development. 2003, Vol. 10, No. 1: 42 – 54.

68. Wang Ning. Research on Enterprise Finance. Social SciencesAcademic Press, 2002.

69. Wang Tingting. Analysis of Finance Support for Private Enterprises. Finance and Insurance, 2002 (8): 14 – 16.

70. Wang Xiao, Zhang Jie. Bank Credit Rationing and SME Loans: A Theoretical Model of Internalized Collateral and Enterprise Size. Economic Research Journal, 2003 (7): 68 – 75.

71. Wang Xiaolu, Fan Gang. The Changing Trend and Influencing Factors of Regional Gap in China. Economic Research Journal, 2004 (1): 33 -44.

72. Wang Xiaolu, Fan Gang. The Trend and Influencing Factors of Income Gap in China. Economic Research Journal, 2005 (10): 24 -36.

73. Wang Xuanyu. The Impact of Information Disclosure Mechanism on Private Enterprise Financing Decisions. Economic Research Journal, 2002 (10): 31 -39.

74. Wei Shouhua, Liu Guanghai, Shao Dongtao. Indirect Financing Characteristics and Strategy of SME in Industrial Clusters. Finance and Trade Research, 2002 (9): 53 -60.

75. Yang Ruilong. The Institutional Change of "Central Diffusion" and Innovative Behavior of Local Government: Case Study of Self-financed Economic and Technological Development Zone in Jiangsu Kunshan, recorded in the second set of Case Study of China's Institutional Change. China Financial & Economic Publishing House, 2002.

76. Ying Zhanyu. The Financing Situation and Policy Analysis of China's Small and Medium-sized Enterprises. Finance& Trade Economics, 2004 (10): 33 -38.

77. Yu Guangyuan. From the Wenzhou Model to "a System of Multi-style" . Ta Kung Pao, 1992. 1. 28.

78. Yu Li, Jiang Chunhai. An Empirical Analysis of Absorbing Labor Employment in China's Township Enterprises. Management World, 2003 (3): 76 -82.

79. Yu Li, Jiang Chunhai. An Empirical Analysis of the Sources of Output of China's Township Enterprises. Industrial Economics Research, 2003 (5): 1 -12.

80. Yu Li, Wu Xueliang. Vertical Restrictions on Economic Logic and Antitrust Policy. China Industrial Economics, 2005 (8): 20 -26.

81. Zeng Deming, Gong Hong. Stakeholder Evaluation Method Based on Enterprise System and Enterprise Theory. Nankai Business Review, 2004 (1).

82. Zeng Deming, Zhou Rong. Research on the Relationship between Environmental Dynamics, Capital Structure and Enterprise Performance. Finance and Trade Research, 2004 (3): 67 -74.

83. Zhang Chenghui. Investigation Report on Financing Situations of Private Enterprises. Journal of Central South University of Technology, 2001 (3): 242 -250.

84. Zhang Gaiqing. China's Corporate Bond Market Development and Private Enterprise Financing. Commercial Research, 2003 (10): 127 -128.

85. Zhang Jianhua, Zhuo Kai. Informal Finance, Institutional Change and Economic Growth: A Literature Review. Reform, 2004 (3): 36 -41.

86. Zhang Jianjun, Yuan Zhonghong, Lin Ping. From Private Loan to Private

Finance: Industrial Organization and Trading Rules. Journal of Financial Research, 2002 (10): 101 - 109.

87. Zhang Jie. Structure and Change of China's Financial System. Shanxi Economic Publishing House, 1988.

88. Zhang Jie. Analysis of China's State-owned Financial System Changes. Economic Science Press, 1998.

89. Zhang Jie. Financial Arrangements for Growth outside the System in China. Economist, 1999 (2): 38 - 43.

90. Zhang Jie. Financial Dilemma and Financing Order of Private Economy. Economic Research Journal, 2000 (4): 3 - 10.

91. Zhang Jie. System, Gradual transition and China's Financial Reform. China Financial Publishing House, 2001.

92. Zhang Jie. Relational Loan and Bank Organizational Structure of Small and Medium-sized Enterprises. Economic Research Journal, 2002 (6): 32 - 37.

93. Zhang Jie, Wang Xiao. Financial Growth Cycle and Financing Structure Change of Small and Medium-sized Enterprises. The Journal of World Economy, 2002 (9): 63 - 70.

94. Zhong Tianli, Mi Yuexu, Wang Lichun. Information Asymmetry and SME Financing Market Failure. Accounting Research, 2003 (8): 42 - 44.

95. Zhu Delin, Hu Haiou. China's Gray-black Finance. Lixin Accounting Publishing House, 1997.

96. ZuoBaiyun. Research on Private Finance. Financial Theory & Practice, 2001 (5): 21 - 22.

Chapter 5

Governance Issues in the Growth of Private Enterprises

At present, family governance has a relatively dominant position in the study of governance structure and governance mechanism of private enterprises. Researchers not onlyaffirm the superiority of family governance in entrepreneurship and early development stages ofprivate enterprise, but also explore the obstruction it will create when it grows to a certain size. This kind of family-owned private enterprise is mainly based on individual households. In the transition process from the planned economy to the market economy, this new type of business originated in the gaps of the original national enterprises and collective enterprises. Most studies believe that: because family business usually has the characteristics of poor product knowledge, flexible market operation and relative lack of operational capacity, thus the evolution of the relationship between business owners and professional managers is indeed worthy of attention. Family governance is able to facilitate internal management and accelerate decision-making; therefore, it is the preferred mode of business during start-up period. But the family governance model is difficult to grow with the development of enterprises. When the enterprise reaches a certain scale and seeks further development, the limitations and deficiencies of the family governance model become the "bottleneck". At this time, they will need a transform into modern corporate governance model.

However, this study found that the overall judgment on the governance of private enterprises is not comprehensive. This study argues that the research on the key issues of corporate governance in the development of private enterprises should be based on the following understandings.

First of all, characteristics of different groups of private enterprises are increasingly obvious. Private enterprise, as the micro-subject of private economy, has an imperfect governance model. Small and medium-sized private enterprises, which are low-tech and self-generated, and private technology enterprises, which are based on higher technical resources and technology entrepreneurship, have shown their distinctive features in the enterprise growth and governance issues.

Second, the development of private enterprises began to encounter deeper issues of governance structure and governance mechanism. Governance structure, as a set of institutional arrangements and mutual check-and-balance relationships among various subjects of rights, and governance mechanism, as a series of rules and the sum of the mechanism which ensure the healthy operation of enterprises, have shown a new phenomenon worthy of attention. New phenomena have arisen in the intergenerational transmission of control rights, in the process of introduction of professional managers, and in the venture capital governance of control configuration venture capital investors and entrepreneurial managers.

This requires us to consider the new group and level hierarchical characteristics of private enterprises, to focus on the change of ownership and control rights and the internal governance elements that influence the development of the enterprise, to explore the barriers to private enterprise governance, to analyze the microeconomic mechanism of the development of private economy under the new situation, to find the root of the development of private economy through institutional innovation, and to put forward effective policy recommendations.

5.1 Governance "inflection point" in the growth of private enterprises: institutional obstacles and property rights concern

Institutional innovation is the micro-institutional basis which supports the development of China's private economy. In order to analyze the transformation of institutional innovation reference system of China's private enterprise under the dual background of economic globalization and transition of state-owned economy, and explore the evolution of private enterprise development modeunder the multi-interactive framework of relationship among state-owned enterprise reform, foreign enterprise participation and private economic evolution, we should use the corporate governance concept which is different from the general corporate governance and conduct in-depth study on governance structure and governance mechanism.

5. 1. 1 Macro-background of private enterprise governance

After more than 20 years of reform and opening up, private economy has become an important force in China's economic development. As the basis of private economy, private enterprises originated from limitations but showed strong vitality. After more than 20 years of tenacious development, it has occupied a significant proportion of the entire GDP. According to recent statistics, the number of China's private enterprises is more than 30 million, the annual output value is about 5 trillion yuan, and the annual growth rate of various economic indicators is more than 20%.

However, the sustainable development of private enterprises have faced with severe challenges under the improvement of external development environment. The entry of international competitors in the WTO framework has challenged private enterprises that have grown up in relatively closed environments. Relying solely on flexible operating mechanism will not able to meet the demands of the international competitive environment. The upgrading of enterprise institution has become a key to sustainable growth of private enterprises. In this regard, a large number of private enterprises which had already came out of the original accumulation stage, reached the "inflection point" of "personal property rights concern". Private enterprise governance, with the innovation of property right system as its core, is becoming the bottleneck which restricts the development of private enterprises.

At present, the overall governance state of private enterprises in China is shown as below: (1) Entrepreneurship-based family property structure still dominates. The average proportion of corporate capital owned by enterprise owners is as high as 76.7%; here is a lack of contractual relationship among the shareholders of the enterprise and there are hidden dangers of property rights disputes; (2) Among ownership, cooperation and limited liability, the proportion of limited liability companies grows the fastest: from 58.4% in 1999 to 68.0% in 2001; (3) The unification of family governance and family management has led to corporate socialization and low degree of publicity. The special principles of choice of operators has formed the barriers to entry of social human resources. Currently, 96% of the business owners are director or manager; only 30% of the executives and the main technical staff hold shares with a total share of only 9%; (4) Compared with listed companies, general private enterprises are short of a mandatory supervision mechanism from government securities regulatory authorities, corporate control market and a number of shareholders. They protect the non-standardized market secrets through low degree of information disclosure. (5) A considerable part of the limited liability company is a strategic choice which the company's board of directors does not have a core position in the governance structure.

The change of constraint conditions changes the game payoff of the private enterprise, which requires that the driving mode of enterprise value should change from individual entrepreneurship to team production, and the external expansion mode should change from single capital to joint property right. These governance barriers have become the key to limiting the growth of private enterprises, which directly affects the internal and external integration of enterprise property rights: not only makes it difficult for enterprise to form a team incentive mechanism to meet the conditions of property rights compatibility, but also leads to the financing obstacles to the growth of enterprises. Therefore, to achieve a flexible mechanism and a standardized institution is the pursuit and urgent goal of private enterprise governance.

The governance barriers of private enterprises have a distinct historical background. Since the 16th National Congress of the Communist Party of China, a series of ideas have been realized in the aspects of value theory, people's livelihood and private property protection, so that the theoretical basis of the definition of private enterprise property has been markedly shifted, and the initial state of private enterprises and the operating environment have been changed substantially. With the characteristics of growth and innovation, the technical characteristics of the private enterprises determine the important position of human capital in capital structure. The coordination between human capital and monetary capital is the key to improving the governance mechanism. In other words, the key to breaking the bottleneck of private enterprise is not only property rights adjustment in monetary capital sense, but also reconstruction of governance structure after the introduction of human capital property rights.

The evolution of the economic system is the result of the interaction between government, enterprises and markets. It is necessary to study the interactive mode of game between various economic forms and explore the evolution mechanism of private enterprise system. The development model of private economy has once become a hotspot in economic research. But now it seems that the spontaneous expansion of Wenzhou mode, which is mainly developed by private businessmen, or the mode of southern Jiangsu developed by collective enterprises, or the fast development of the Pearl River Delta mode by means of foreign investment, or Zhongguancun mode features private technology enterprises, are all faced with increasingly prominent regional limitations during the expansion. We believe that China's private economic development mode is neither forced by the government alone, nor is it a simple folk spontaneous evolution, but a comprehensive mode consists of government policy, state-owned enterprises transition and private enterprises profit-seeking. In the context of state-owned enterprise reform, participation of foreign-funded enterprises and evolution of private economy, private enterprise system must change from "institution vacancy" to "institutional innovation" under the background of the diversity of interaction beyond geographical mode.

After joining the WTO, the dual role of state-owned enterprises in the development and complementarity of private enterprises and the intensification of competition from foreign-funded enterprises have made the "productivity competition" among private enterprises, foreign-funded enterprises and state-owned enterprises unprecedented; the development of private enterprise is faced with a serious "institutional bottleneck". Only through the innovation of governance structure and property rights system, would it be possible to enhance the competitiveness of private enterprises and achieve a successful convergence to international market.

5.1.2 Institutional obstacles and property rights concern

Many problems of private enterprise governance can be generalized by two keywords of "property right" and "family system". In terms of property rights, the problem of private enterprises in China is complicated: the overall property rights of the private sector is clear, but there is also a problem of property rights definition among internal core members, and a situation where the ownership is clear but is short of property rights benefits. The study found that the entrepreneur-based family structure is still dominant. The average proportion of capital owned by enterprise owners is up to 76.7%. The fuzzy property rights of township enterprises have led to rapid growth during early period, but now it has become an obstacle in the new period. The study of governance obstacles from the perspective of institutional barriers and property rights concern is the most important basis for the design of incentive system under the new background. The property rights of private enterprise is the basis of corporate governance and the hotspot in current research. At present, researchers have studied this topic in different types of private enterprises.

1. Property rights of township and village enterprises

The fuzziness of property rights of private enterprises are reflected in the initial property rights, value-added assets, "anchored" property rights and other aspects. Li Daokui (1995) argues that the fuzzy property rights theory of township enterprises explains the reasons of efficient operation under the conditions of imperfect market and incomplete legal system. Weitzman (1995) explains the growth of township enterprises from the perspective of "cooperation", which is formed by fuzzy property rights structure, and believes that the high efficiency of collective township enterprises are based on the cooperative culture; Tian Guoqiang points out the reason why the collective ownership of property rights is optimal, which is due to the middle state of the degree of economy freedom and market imperfection; Shi Lei (2000) analyzes the organizational form of Huaxi Village in Jiangsu, and reveals the path dependence of organizational evolution and the complexity of organizational form; Some scholars have studied the further development of southern Jiangsu mode from the perspective of property rights reform (Fan Conglai, 1995, 2001).

2. Property rights of private enterprises

In general, the property rights of private enterprises is relatively clear; nevertheless, it has attracted the attention of theorists. The overall property rights of the private sector is clear, but there is a definition problem among internal core members; thus, the situation is clear but it is short of property rights benefits; Mao Sanyuan claims that the property right structure of private enterprise is the reason why its life cycle is so short; Liu Wei emphasizes the importance of property rights definition to the development of private capital in China; some scholars have made an international comparison of family control (Su Qilin et al, 2003); Wang Lianjuan et al. (2000, 2001) studies the institutional change of family business from the perspective of property rights; some other scholars focus on the relationship between institutional lock-up and institutional innovation of family business, and others study the regional private enterprise property right system.

3. Familization of private enterprises

Since the late 1990s, family business has become a hotspot in the research of China's private economy. Some scholars believe that the family business should gradually move towards modern enterprise system; some believe that the existence of family business has its rationality; some study the change of family business system from the perspective of property rights; some study family business from pan-familism and its integration with social capital; some have studied the relationship between trust and governance cost structure in the established cultural system environment through the coordination game model, and pointed out that the trust and loyalty factors have led to the plight of recruiting managers in family enterprises; some have focused on family businesses in rural China.

5. 1. 3 Analysis framework of obstacles in private enterprise governance

This study breaks through the limitations of existing enterprise theory, explores the optimal design of ownership arrangement and governance mechanism from the perspective of institutional innovation, and puts forward some policy suggestions on the improvement of private economy (see Figure 5 – 1).

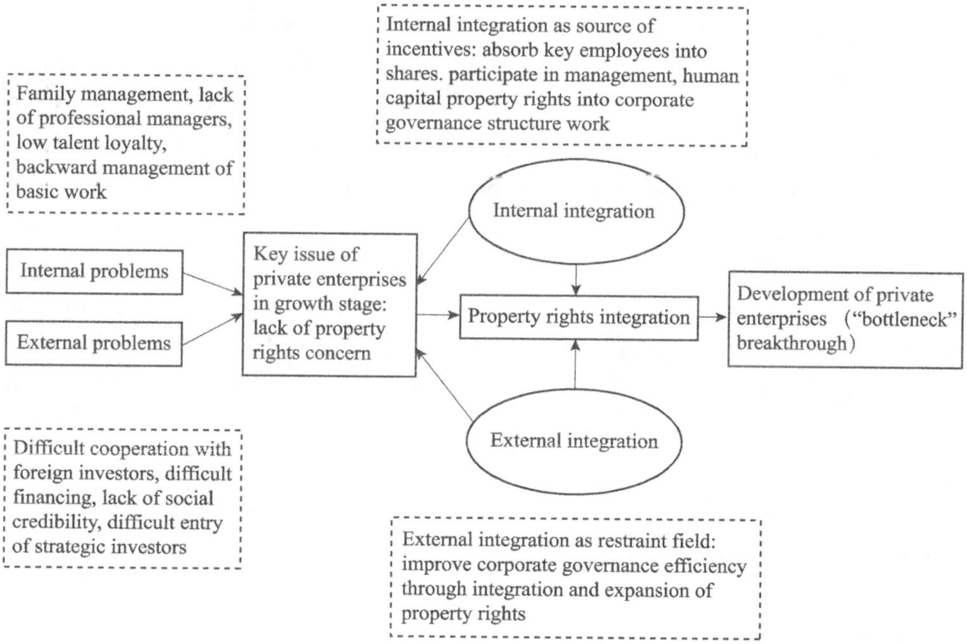

Figure 5 – 1 Analysis framework of obstacles in private enterprise governance

In terms of the characteristics of family system of private enterprises, current researches are concentrated mainly on trust mechanism, organization form, information network and other aspects, which have attracted a lot of attentions. However, the governance of private enterprise has shown obvious regional complexity, type heterogeneity and stage dissimilarity. The main problem faced by the governance of private enterprise is not the supervision of professional operators under the general meaning of principal-agent chain, but its internal scientific decision-making barriers, and the internal and external integration difficulties during the process of property rights expansion. The perfection of external management system of private enterprises must be based on the need of internal governance mechanism; and the improvement of internal management behavior should also depend on its internal governance mechanism. The key to understanding the current problem of private enterprise governance is through systematic theoretical demonstration, typical case analysis and effective empirical analysis on the growth and transformation of human capital and monetary capital in different types of private enterprises. We believe that we should face up to the characteristics of private enterprise governance, which is different from mainstream corporate governance, effectively identify the barriers to internal and external governance through systematic theoretical exploration and extensive empirical analysis, and put forward the idea of solving the problem.

A large number of private enterprises, which have gone through continuous rapid development, began to encounter the business owners' "inflection point" of "personal asset concern", and thus are faced with increasingly prominent internal governance barriers. The problem of private enterprise development is characterized by: the confusion of property rights, the erosion of shareholders' rights and interests, the loss of internal management, the change of business direction, and the sharp decline or even disintegration of enterprise efficiency. Private enterprises urgently need to seek further development opportunities through institutional innovation. In face of the entry of international competitors after joining the WTO, private enterprises, which grew up in a relatively closed market environment, have encountered new competitive challenges and great contrast of institutional environment. How to move from the original advantage to adapt to the modern market competition will be the key to overcoming the governance barriers in private enterprises.

5.1.4 Private enterprise governance: from governance structure to governance mechanism

At present, the research of corporate governance in private enterprises is mainly aimed at the family characteristics of private enterprises and concentrated on trust mechanism, organizational form and so on. From the perspective of corporate governance, Wu Jinglian (2001) points out that private enterprises also have "a dominance"; Cai Jiming et al (2000) divide private enterprise governance mode into two categories: one is market-oriented type, the other is network-oriented type. And they emphasize that there is no governance problem in family business; only larger private enterprises and collective enterprises have governance problems; Chen Ling points out that in order to achieve large-scale, family business may use interpersonal relationships to change to strategic network organization; some scholars generalize and summarize the governance mode from the perspective of corporate governance system, such as the family governance mode research; Cao Yuanzheng (2000) points out that to further develop the private economy, we must improve its governance structure; some scholars study the issue of private enterprise governance from the perspective of different ownership enterprises; some scholars study the governance structure arrangement during the process of transformation of township enterprises; in terms of the relationship between human capital and monetary capital in corporate governance, some scholars point out that we should not excessively emphasize any part and the interests of both sides must be included in the scope of corporate governance; some scholars study the governance issues of technology enterprises and small and medium-sized enterprises.

On the whole, the current researches on corporate governance at home and abroad are mainly based on property right system and corporate governance structure in micro level, and have not paid much attention to governance mechanism; this will easily lead to the return of "nationalization of private enterprise" system.

The key to the corporate governance of private enterprises in China is not to establish the formal system or structure, but to form a governance mechanism which has a direct effect on governance behavior in the enterprise. For private enterprises, the governance mechanism includes decision-making mechanism, incentive mechanism and restraint mechanism.

1. Decision-making mechanism

At present, in the internal decision-making mechanism of private enterprises, investor decision-making (mainly includes boss decision-making and family decision-making) occupies a dominant position, senior management decision-making accounts for a certain proportion while the proportion of board of directors is the minimum.

This reflects that the decision-making mechanism of private enterprises has yet to be optimized. Of course, this may be related to the relatively small size of the national private sector.

In general, most private enterprises have not yet established a scientific decision-making mechanism; most family businesses adopt the paternalistic management mode and everything is the decided by one person, which is lack of effective internal and external supervision, feedback and constraints. If the business operator is impetuous and make wrong decisions, it is easy to cause bad consequences and bring about a lot of decision risks. Decision-making, which is based on personal experience and subjective discretionary, is a common problem in private enterprises.

The basic reform direction of the decision-making mechanism of private enterprises is from family governance to the board governance, including: realize the rationalization of investment decision-making and decision-making process, promote and supervise the system construction and organization construction of various operation links within the enterprise, make these links routinized, transparent and rationalized, and promote the institutionalization and rationalization of the internal control mechanism. In major decision-making management process, we should emphasize the template decision-making process and regular management mechanism. Board decision-making mainly includes three major elements: development strategy, property rights adjustment (such as employee holdings, etc.) and risk control.

Corporate governance requires specialized skills that are best implemented by the committee. There may be a number of committees, including the audit committee, the remuneration committee, the nomination committee, the development strategy committee, the investment and financing committee and the corporate governance committee. The members of these committees shall consist mainly of external directors and independent directors. In this process, we should improve the scientificity of strategic decision-making and investment decision-making.

In private enterprises, the decision-making advisory committee composed of external experts may be established, which can be part of the board of directors (such as, the board of advisers).

From the experience of foreign countries, the introduction of the independent director system in the United States was mainly used to assist the company to make strategic decisions; that is, independent directors (the main source is active or retired enterprises, certified public accountants and lawyers) can help CEOs make strategic decisions. Therefore, we believe that private enterprises (including non-listed corporate private enterprises) should also pay attention to the introduction of independent directors, and its main purpose may not be monitoring function, but to participate in strategic management.

In particular, it should be noted that non-family members should have a certain proportion in the board of directors, including some of the executives.

In addition, the optimization of decision-making mechanism is also correlated with the opening of property rights and the introduction of talents. The introduction of social capital and the change of property rights structure can improve the enterprise decision-making system. And through the introduction of talents, we can make up for the lack of decision-making ability and optimize the decision-making mechanism. At the same time, private enterprises may also have the risk of loss of control (see Figure 5 -2).

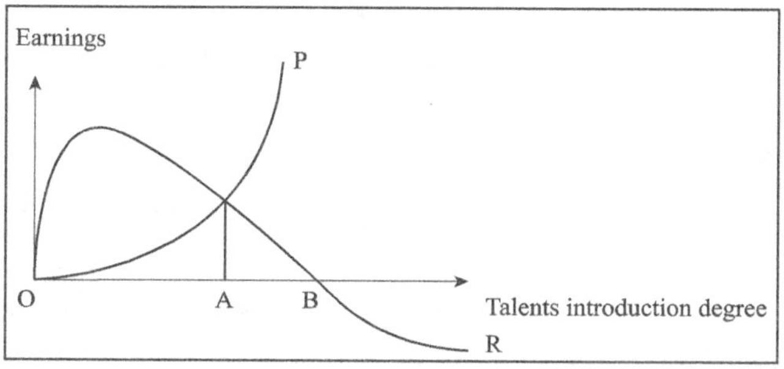

Figure 5 -2 Relationship between optimization of decision-making mechanism and talents introduction

In Figure 5 - 2, the curve P represents the increase in the cost of private enterprise governance, while the curve R represents the introduction of talents caused by changes in corporate earnings. It can be seen from the figure that in the early stage of introduction of talents, the income will increase; while with the deepen of the talents introduction degree, the risk factors begin to highlight, the talents begin to abuse their power to seek personal gain and the earnings decline. The main reason is that most private enterprises introduce talents when their own capacity do not adapt to the development, therefore, the ability to control talents is weak and the restraint mechanism is incomplete.

It can be seen from the figure that there is a degree in introducing talents, A is the best point, and after point B, the introduction will only bring in negative income.

The best point of talents introduction is coordinated with the control ability of private entrepreneurs. In practice, the choice of different private enterprises will be different. In particular, if we consider subsidiaries, the relationship between the introduction of talents and the optimization of decision-making mechanism will be more complex. We do not do too much discussions here.

2. Incentive and constraint mechanism

For private enterprises, the incentive mechanism is particularly important. This chapter argues that the overall growth of private enterprises is inseparable from its high-intensity incentive mechanism. However, with the conversion of economic background and the adjustment of competitors, the incentive mechanism of private enterprises should also be changed and the basic direction is to strengthen long-term incentives. As the incentive mechanism involves a wide range, this chapter focuses on private equity incentive. In fact, compared with state-owned enterprises, private enterprises have better conditions to implement equity incentive; because there are many obstacles in the implementation of equity incentive for state-owned enterprises, such as easy to be accused of loss of state assets. Private enterprises should seize the opportunity to build their own institutional advantages.

Good corporate governance mechanism not only has a good incentive mechanism, but also needs a complete set of constraints mechanism. Constraint mechanism involves a wide range, this chapter here mainly analyzes the constraints of private enterprise insider control. Insider control is used to refer to the situation in which managers controlled the enterprises during the transition period of state-owned enterprises reform. This book refers specifically to the situation that the professional manager overheads the business owner in private enterprises.

Most private enterprises introduce talents when their own capacity do not adapt to the development. However, if the talent's quality is better than the owner, then there will be low-quality owners controlling high-quality managers. Once the control is not good, it is possible to lose the enterprise resources and go into insider control. With the development of the enterprise scale, the gap between the owner and the manager will become increasingly larger, that is, the owner is more difficult to control the manager and the risk of losing the enterprise is also growing.

According to the individual capacity of private business owners and the degree of openness of corporate property rights (especially the degree of openness to operational control), this chapter builds four combinations, as shown in Figure 5 – 3. In the upper left quadrant, the ability of business owners is strong and the enterprise property rights is closed, so the owners themselves control the enterprises. In the upper right quadrant, the ability of business owners is strong and the enterprise property rights is open, so the business owners and professional managers control the enterprise together. In the lower left quadrant, the ability of business owners is weak, but the enterprise property rights is closed, so the owners themselves control the enterprises and its main purpose is to guard against risks (such private enterprises are usually in the development of stagnant platform). In the lower right quadrant, the ability of business owners is weak, but the enterprise property rights is open, this is prone to insider control phenomenon (see Figure 5 -3).

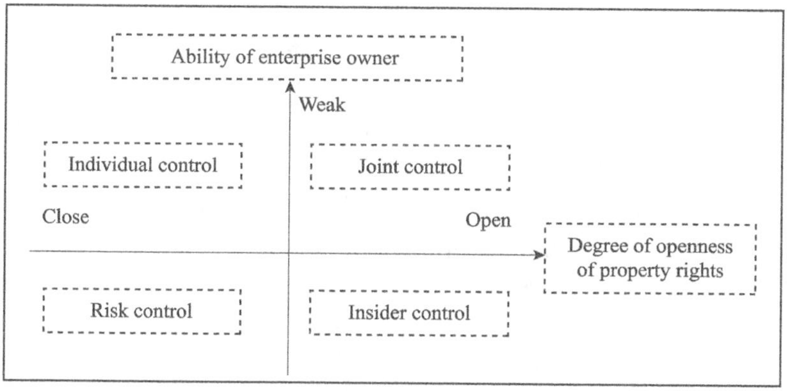

Figure 5 -3 Combinations of property rights ability in private enterprises

As can be seen from Figure 5 -4, with the rise of corporate value, the trust between private business owners and professional managers is likely to decline. When the scale of enterprise is small, such as the growth period, the two sides can often maintain a high degree of trust. On the contrary, once the enterprise reaches a certain size, there is prone to crisis of confidence and to insider control issue (see Figure 5 -4).

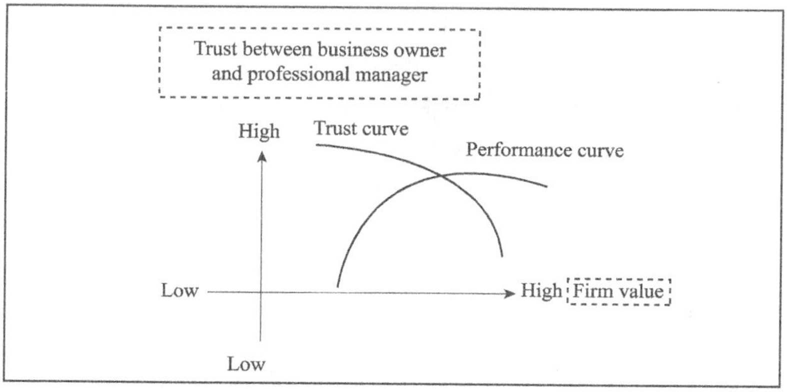

Figure 5 -4 Trust and insider control in private enterprises

In order to prevent insider control, private enterprises can try the following strategy portfolio:

(1) Before the adoption of separation of powers or the introduction of professional managers, private enterprises should first improve the internal control system (including financial audit system).

(2) Private enterprises should conduct standardized operations before hiring managers. For example, once the manager's demand is not satisfied or conflict with the interests of the owners, the manager will use the irregularities of the enterprises to blackmail the owner.

(3) Owners should try to improve the substitutability of operating positions to reduce the bargain ability of the managers. The purpose is to reduce the owner's dependence on the operator. In other words, companies cannot rely too much on a single manager and should form a manager's team. Once there is an unusual situation, you can have a second echelon. But it should be noted that it will also reduce the enthusiasm of managers, and the trust between the manager and the owner is difficult to form. Therefore, the owner of private enterprises should master the degree of incentive and restraint.

5.2 Principal-agent relationship and control transfer in family business

Modern family business is a very common form of organization in the global context. China's family business is an important part of China's private economy. A large number of private enterprises are generated in the form of family business or quasi-family business. Mainstream academia believe that only through institutionalized change will the family business ensure sustainable development; However, in reality, China's family business has begun to experience the transfer of wealth and power between two generations. The succession of blood inheritance and the succession of professional managers is increasingly concerned by academics and industry. This chapter tries to provide a useful reference for the inheritance model of the management of family business in our country through the comparative analysis of the internal driving factors and the management conditions.

5.2.1 Effectiveness of family governance model: internal control and growth

Family business is prevalent in the whole world. Scholars have analyzed the governance mode of family business from the perspective of property rights theory, enterprise organization theory, enterprise life cycle and other different angles. The effectiveness of family management mode for enterprise development is shown in four aspects:

First, the integration of two rights effectively reduce the cost of principal-agent. The separation of ownership and control yields an agency relationship. But the agency relationship does not naturally produce agency problems. When the agent's goal is exactly the same as the principal, the agency problem will not arise. In the family business, the integration makes the owner's personal interests consistent with business goals, thus the common ownership of the owners and their family members have complete residual claims and they can protect the family organization from opportunistic violations.

Second, the cohesion of the enterprise is strong. Family members consider the enterprise assets as family property and the business as part of family business; thus, there exists a consciousness that the enterprise is the extension and simulation of the family. Under the influence of this concept, family members, which are based on kinship and marriage, can integrate the ethics and emotions within the family into the enterprise, and thus it is easier to form a strong cohesion.

Third, the stability of the enterprise is high. In family business, family members control both the ownership and the management, making the business management controlled by family's ethical norms. It is precisely because of the constraints of family ethics that make family business maintain a high stability.

Fourth, business decisions is quickly. As the operation and management of the family business is under the constraints of family ethics, therefore, the highest authority in the family will become the highest leaders of the enterprise. He can make decisions on his own, and this will save decision-making time and ensure the rapid decision-making process. At the same time, because the family members are consistent with each other in the interests, ideas and understandings, and they have absolute obey to family ethical norms, therefore, the decision of leaders are easy to be understood by other family members and can quickly be implemented in the enterprise. This will greatly avoid the time delay phenomenon and, to some extent, ensure that the decision-making process is rapid.

5.2.2 Internal transmission of operational control in family business

The internal transmission of operational control in family business refers to intergenerational transmission within the family. The entrepreneur's absolute or relative control of the family business is based on ownership or entrepreneurial talent. In fact, the transmission of control power is the transmission of property, prestige and social status. This process begins with the heirs' entry into the family business and end up with the total exit of the old leader, with its purpose of protecting the continuation of family business.

Internationally speaking, Johnson & Johnson, Ford, Wal-Mart, Procter & Gamble, Motorola, IBM, Hewlett-Packard and Disney are all successful examples of family business control transmission; the maturity period of China's family business began in the 1990s. During this period, some family business leaders began to pass their leadership to the second generation. For example, Lu Weiding (Lu Guanqiu's son) became the president of Vientiane Group, Xu Yongan (Xu Wenrong's son) served as chairman of Hengdian Group.

The reason why these family businesses retain the family control of the enterprise, lies in that this mode of family governance is effective on the enterprise's internal control and growth. Li Wei'an (2001) points out that the family governance mode refers to the integration of ownership and management rights, the main control power is allocated within family members. In this mode of governance, the ownership of the enterprise is mainly controlled by the family members composed of blood, kinship and marriage. The main management rights are controlled by the family members. The enterprise decision-making procedure is carried out according to the family procedure[①]. Thus, the internal transmission of operational control in family business is considered as an optimized approach which will continue this kind of governance mode.

---

① Li Wei'an, Corporate Governance, Nankai University Press, 2001, pp. 197 - 198.

1. Driving factors

(1) Property rights characteristics and incentive compatibility.

The integration of ownership and control is one of the salient features of family business in terms of property rights. The separation of these two powers in modern enterprises has led to the generation of principal-agent relationship and agency costs. In the family governance mode, there is no principal-agent chain, which effectively guarantees the basic consistency between the operator and the owner's goal. At the same time, the operator will receive double incentives and restraints from family interests and family affection. For the first generation of entrepreneurs, their business behavior is often for better lives, as well as for their future generations. For the second generation of operators, to carry forward the cause of their fathers, to preserve or increase the value of family members' assets and to maintain the family affection, is the main mechanism of incentive and restrain. Thus, compared with non-family-member successors, the moral hazard and individualistic tendency of family-member successors is less likely to occur, which will reduce the cost of governance and regulation.

(2) Emotional foundation and trust relationship.

Family is a group consists of blood relations. The internal transmission of control can guarantee the continuation of integration of family and business. The succession mode of "father-to-son" can be traced back to the emergence of human family. Lansberg believes that for parents, the best way to keep their hopes and dreams is to pass on the causes they have established to their descendants from generation to generation, which is human nature. The degree of trust and understanding among family members is much higher than that of non-family members; therefore, they only bear a lower psychological contract costs. The mechanism of family action will form affinity and family network, so as to build a unique trust relationship among family members and construct relatively low communication costs, which is a strong guarantee for competitive advantage. Family business is more able to resist impact, especially in early stage of entrepreneurship or under poor external environment. The succession mode of "father-to-son" stems from the basic concept that traditional Chinese society focus on family ethics. As Mr. Fei Xiaotong said, China's society is self-centered, blood-linked and concentric circles, that is, "differential pattern." At the same time, family business is entrepreneurs' long years of hard work and testimony, and most entrepreneurs have a deep feeling of their family business;

therefore, the ownership and control power of family business is usually controlled by a family and passed on from generation to generation within the family. Mao Lixiang, chairman of Fang Tai, did not shy away from selecting his son as the successor, and he believed that deliberately choose other person may be hypocritical.

(3) Management style and inheritance of decision making.

Family business is operated and managed under the constraints of family ethics, therefore, the leader can dictatorially command the cause and ensure the rapid decision-making process. Under these circumstances, family business entrepreneurs are willing to continue their own management style and management policies, respect for the authority of the elders. It can be said that this is the transplantation of family culture in the management of enterprise. The internal transmission of control makes it more likely for family members to form a consistency in interests, concept and understanding of the problems. Thus, the decisions that the successor made is easier for family members to understand and can be implemented quickly in the enterprise.

(4) Perfect manager market and lack of social credit system.

The cultivation and selection of professional manager market is not achieved by an enterprise or an enterprise group; it is gradually formed and perfected under the action of a mature market mechanism. Experts pointed out that China has not yet established a professional manager market; family businesses or other forms of enterprises cannot find professional managers in the market. The external transmission of control will face subjective induced moral hazard and adverse selection issues. Family business itself cannot rely on their own power to implement effective incentives and control on managers.

Drucker proposed that, for family business to survive and maintain effective operation, there has to be at least one non-family member within senior managers. But this book argues that this approach should be based on the establishment of a relatively perfect social credit system and the manager market as a prerequisite. The process of authorizing a professional manager is actually a process of sharing confidential information and confidential resources with someone. In spite of the reasons of cultural traditions and the characteristics of social transition, Chinese family business owners are more likely to become centralized monopolies of corporate secret and information. However, in the absence of social credit system, we cannot use mature reputation mechanism to stimulate, supervise and effectively evaluate the manager class.

Therefore, the problem of no restriction on the betrayal of managers made that the family business owners cannot appoint and authorize professional managers, even if they have strong management experience and professional competence. Lifan Group once put an "outsider" manager in an important position, who leaked out the enterprise's core technology and caused irreparable damages.

2. Key factors

The transmission of family business leadership to the second or third generation may lead to division, dissolution and bankruptcy. Sometimes, when the second generation of candidates do not get the support of family members, it will lead to a split crisis. In the transition process of family power, internal contradictions among family members will consume the energies of the enterprise and put its daily business in trouble. So, what factors will affect the success of this process?

(1) Definition of primitive property subject.

The definition of the original property rights of the family business is mainly manifested in two aspects. First, the definition between family members are unclear. At the beginning, enterprises are in urgent need of funds and manpower and the absorption of family members into the enterprise is the common practice. Second, the relationship between family business and external property is unclear. In order to obtain the support of various national or local government policy, family enterprises often linked to state-owned or collective units, that is, "red cap" enterprises.

In the early stage of development, the unclearness of property rights between family members have certain inevitability and rationality. The inevitability shows that this kind of arrangement is deeply influenced by the concept of family in cultural traditions. Unlike individualism, advocated by the Western countries, our country's cultural tradition attaches great importance to the concept of family: family property should be owned by the whole family and there is no need to make a division between individuals. Rationality is manifested that: it can effectively utilize family members' inexpensive human capital, low supervision costs and low financing costs to complete early capital accumulation. However, when the enterprises develop to a certain size, the shortcomings of unclear property rights will be fully exposed. Although family is regarded as the most stable and cohesive structure in the social structure, the kinship among family members can be impacted by economic interests, and the loyalty among family members can also be eroded by the interests of assets. The unclearness of original property subject is bound to affect the object selection of control transmission. In most cases, the control of entrepreneurial family business is based on ownership. Therefore, we believe that the unclearness of internal property rights will form a hidden dilemma of intergenerational transmission disputes. The requirement to define property rights between individual members is also insurmountable among siblings.

Wearing "red cap" can bring certain benefits for family business, such as preferential policies, secured loans, good reputation and reduced risks. However, it also makes the enterprise's property rights fuzzy and leads to a number of legal disputes. As a result, the enterprises get into a "property lawsuit" trap. When it comes to selecting the successor, it is inevitable that there will be a dispute between the government-delegated candidate and the transmission within family.

(2) Entrepreneurs' willingness to withdraw.

An important factor in the failure of intergenerational transmission is that entrepreneurs are reluctant to give up the control power and do not consciously cultivate successors, says Prof. Joachim Schwass from IMD Business School in Switzerland. In many Chinese family businesses, the selection of successor is the founder's personal decision; as to when they abdicate, there is no rules to follow. Most entrepreneurs are deeply influenced by traditional Chinese culture, hope to maintain the authority and control intensity of the enterprise, and feel a great sense of loss about abdication. This kind of behavior often have two bad consequences. First, "reign behind a curtain", that is, intervening the development strategy and business behavior of the successor; second, psychologically and actually avoid inheritance problems. In the event of an accident, enterprises will fall in intricate internal contradictions and operational difficulties. On the contrary, if the leaders plan to train the successor and timely exit the control role, the family business will continue prosperity.

(3) Successor's ability and inheritance motive.

Family mechanism takes the method of "designated successor" to solve the problem of family succession. But this method may lead to dislocation of power transmission, that is, the designated person is not suitable for the role. In the transmission between the first generation and the second generation, the relationship between two generations is often very tense and the contradictories mainly focused on whether the heir is willing to become the heir of the family business, and whether the heir has professional knowledge and management experience to ensure the existence of the enterprise.

Entrepreneurial talent cannot be replaced by knowledge from the books. Some successors lack the ability and vision of their parents, but are anxious for blind expansion, which will finally shake the foundation. When the successor lacks enough authority and courage, the family business will be prone to split and factional struggle. Zhang Mingtian, the founder of Hong Kong Overseas Trust Bank, suddenly died in 1982. After that, the huge commercial kingdom fell apart in the following three years. The overseas trust banks were also on the brink of bankruptcy and had to be taken over by the government of Hong Kong SAR.

(4) Choice of intergenerational delivery timing.

The intergenerational transmission of control will cause a great deal of shocks not only within the family, but also to non-family members in the enterprise; therefore, choosing the right time to achieve the full conversion of power is extremely important. Usually, when the enterprise has a certain scale and the management conditions are fine, the internal relations will be in a relatively stable state and will provide a better transmission environment. In addition, before the handover phase, the entrepreneur needs to do a succession plan, so that the successor and the existing leadership team will have a harmonious relationship. At the same time, the successor should grasp the timing of exit, and coordinate the relationship between the new management and the old management to ensure the balance of power and unity of the atmosphere.

3. Implementation

The internal transmission of control powerinevitably have to face the selection and training of heirs; coordinate contradictory relationships; develop and implement transmission plan.

(1) Selection and cultivation of internal successor.

The selection and cultivation of internal successor is a very critical part. The founder definitely hope that the future generations will inherit his mantle and carry it forward. In family businesses, the success or failure of the enterprise depends largely on the judgment, selection and cultivation of successors. When the control power is transferred to the next generation, the shortage of sufficient authority and courage will make the family business prone to internal division and factional struggle. Therefore, the selection and cultivation of family business successors is a crucial issue.

(2) Coordination mechanism of internal inheritance contradiction.

In order to smoothly carry out the transmission process, it is necessary to establish a sound transfer system (coordination mechanism). The system must create a united, open atmosphere and environment. Every member of the family business is encouraged to express their views and participate in the successor's decision. Together we discuss each other's needs and expectations, so that the power transfer is achieved in mutual communication.

Family meeting is a more concise and persuasive way to solve the problem of succession. Family meeting (may invite some non-family stakeholders to participate in) is hold by family business owners. After fully negotiations, they would determine a preliminary program; or directly form a formal program in the family representative meeting; or directly hold family meetings and the family business owner submit the succession plan. Dennis Jeff has listed ten indicators for a family meeting to address a range of family business issues. One of them is the "guidelines for succession and accession". It can be seen that the family meeting is indeed a better way to solve the problem of family business succession.

Carlo and Ward highlighted the role of "Family Agreement" in supporting family equity. Family agreements can reduce friction and conflict on the condition that they are based on unanimous consent; all family members know their content; they are consistently implemented; family members can modify them according to current situations. The family agreement forms a policy of accomplishing family tasks, which makes the family change from personal credit to institutionalized credit. The family agreement should include relevant matters on the transmission of ownership and control power①.

5.2.3 External transmission of operational control in family business

The intergenerational transmission mode of control power is a relatively effective inheritance model which will ensure the stability of the family business and internal controllability. But this model may also put family business in crisis during full transmission phase, including: (1) internal friction crisis. In the transfer of family power, the employed management group cannot be "neutral", they will inevitably receive the threats or interests of family members, or take the opportunity to misappropriate corporate property as "insiders"; (2) split crisis. When successors compete fiercely for the wealth and power of a family business, it is common for a family member to lead his followers to live in a separate house; (3) loss of control crisis. This kind of crisis is most likely to occur in stock company. When the family

① Randall Carroll, John Ward, Strategic Planning for the Family Business, CITIC Press Group, 2002, pp. 88.

members have different views, it is easy for non-family members of the third party to seize the right of management.

The debate on the inheritance of family business management and the succession of professional managers is a hot topic in academia and industry. There are mainly two ways for the transmission of control power: one is internal succession, that is, to develop their own son to inherit; the second is external search, that is, to look for professional managers from outside the enterprise. From the perspective of capacity, external search is better than internal succession, because the chance of selecting a good professional manager is much higher and close relatives are prone to contraction phenomenon. From the point of view of loyalty and trust, managers as "outsiders" are likely to infringe the owner's rights and interests and lead to the failure of management. Will Chinese family businesses be able to introduce professional managers to achieve the professionalization of management control?

1. Limitations of internal delivery

(1) Emergence of agency risk.

In the early stage of family business, the ownership and control right are highly integrated. In this case, the entrepreneur is not only the owner and but also the operator of the enterprise, and the profit or loss is shared or undertaken by the entrepreneur himself; therefore, there is no agency problem at the beginning. However, when the control power is transmitted to the second generation or third generation, core family groups will be more and more, and family property will be constantly subdivided due to the divergent distribution of family members. Due to the closeness of internal kinship and the endowment difference of management ability, the control power can only be concentrated in the hands of few family members who have a close relationship with the leader and have the operation capacity. At this time, the separation of ownership and control will emerge. For family members who do not have the control right, they actually transfer the control of the enterprise to some family members through a written or invisible proxy contract. Because of the inconsistency of family members who have the control of family business and who do not have the control of family business, the former sometimes violates the interests of the latter for their own interests. In this way, the risk of principal-agent in modern enterprises appears in the family business.

(2) Inheritance and continuity of family culture.

The intergenerational inheritance of the family business is the inevitable result of the natural law, of course, this does not rule out some unexpected events. No matter what the circumstances will be, the management of the family business is undoubtedly a challenge. Lanceberg argues that the transition of leadership in a family business sometimes involves only changes in managerial group, sometimes involves fundamental changes in the structure and culture of the company. Gaelsick further sums up the change process into two words: inheritance and continuity. Inheritance reflects a change in the state, but this change is a "double-edged sword": on the one hand, it will bring new things to the enterprises and avoid rigid management; on the other hand, the power transmission is also very destructive. To minimize the destruction, it requires the enterprises to maintain a certain part of the original group within the new generation. It can be seen in the intergenerational transmission of family business that, to ensure the continuity of management, we must pay attention to dealing with the balance between inheritance and continuous. To some extent, the business culture of the first generation is the reflection of the founder's personality. It will inevitably lead to the change of corporate culture because the personality cannot be inherited. In China, this kind of cultural conflict is particularly prominent: the cultural level of the first generation is generally low, but they dare to endure hardship and are good at business, so their entrepreneurship is formed in the business; while the second generation of successors are mostly highly educated, many of them are foreign doctors and MBA elites. They have a more in-depth understanding of industry technology, development situation and management models. They are basically no entrepreneurial experience. This difference of growth process will inevitably lead to divergences of culture and system between the two generations.

It can be said that with the emergence of the second generation of entrepreneurs, the family business will be integrated into the components of system management. However, the "inheritance" and "continuity" is very important during the change of corporate culture and system. Whether the external environment or the internal environment cannot digest too much culture and institutional changes. Bruno and others believe that the power transmission process is like a relay race, where there will be a run-up process, that is, a power transmission period. Mao Lixiang, chairman of Fang Tai Group, believes that this period is up to 5 years, and some others say even to 10 years. We believe that the length of this term is determined by when we will find the convergence of culture and system within the two generations. Of course, in order to do this successfully, these two generations should have a common goal and keep good communications.

(3) Closeness of "inbreeding" and talents selection system.

Family business is an economic organization which views blood ties as the basic link, views family interests as the primary goal, views actual control power as the basic means, views kinship as the first principle, and views enterprise as the organization form. The principle of selecting senior management staff is kinship first and ability second. Under the constraints of this principle, family business will naturally form a "dual structure" which consists of a "hard core" (include united family members) and a "periphery" (include outsiders that lack of identity and possess centrifugal force). Generally speaking, family business open their management positions to outsiders according to the principle of "the confidentiality degree of management". Under normal circumstances, they tend to open production technology sector and routine management sector which have relatively lower degree of confidentiality, while financial and sales sector are usually held within their own hands. The double standard of talent selection in family business has seriously restricted the inflow of external talents. In the case of family members in the "dual structure", under the constraints of this criterion, the selection scope of senior managers presents a divergent model of limited areas with kinship constraints. In this divergent mode, when the family business grows up, the owners will assign the management rightsto many children, such as father as the chairman, son as general manager, daughter as the chief financial officer; this kind of interpersonal relationship will have some cohesive force toward certain group of people while the others will be repelled. Its closeness has made it exclusive for the introduction of human resources. For those who have entrepreneurial talent is far away from the trust circle and is difficult to be appointed; even if the appointment do happens, it is still easy to generate internal and external psychological separation.

2. Dilemma of implementing principal-agent mechanism in Chinese family business

The manager market is a special human capital market, in a certain sense, it is a hiring market for "professional" entrepreneur[1]. The integration of family business and social human capital is achieved through the establishment of a principal-agent mechanism. However, the factors that hinder the effective operation of this mechanism

---

① Li Xinchun, Manager's Market Failure and Family Business Governance, Management World, No. 4, 2003.

are multiple: the strength of the owners' "centralized complex", the confidentiality of the internal information, the trust between the owners and the professional managers, the development of the professional managers' market, etc. These directly or indirectly affect the efficiency of the principal-agent mechanism, thus setting the barriers to the transfer of operational control outside the family.

(1) Internal system and cultural constraints in family business.

When family business integrate the human resources of managers, they will encounter a crucial problem: business owners must re-allocate corporate control, that is, transfer part of the control power to professional managers. Reading and Fukuyama have conducted an in-depth study of this problem. Reading believes that, for overseas Chinese enterprises, there are obvious difficulties in the transfer of power to professional managers and the separation of control and ownership. This is why Chinese family business cannot escape the family control mode. Fukuyama believes that Chinese family business is usually vigorous and has impressive profits, but when they want to institutionalize the company and do not rely on the family's financial resources, they will encounter great difficulties. Business owners are mostly reluctant to introduce professional managers, because it needs to cross the family contact circle, and their trust toward the outsiders is very low. At present, the motivation of breaking through the closeness of human capital is increasing. However, the risk of information sharing and "centralized complex" have become the main obstacles for integrating professional managers.

First, entrepreneurial authority and centralized complex. "Entrepreneurial authority" prevents the establishment and operation of principal-agent mechanism. The principal-agent relationship can be considered as a set of contracts between the client and the agent in the event of uncertainty and information asymmetry. The establishment of a contractual relationship necessarily entails a prerequisite that the two parties are equal in their status, which is in sharp conflict with "entrepreneurial authority"① . At the same time, the personal loyalty and trust of family members toward the entrepreneur is absolute, thus preventing the development of rational and professional management system. "It is difficult to push Chinese family business to implement the so-called 'management revolution', that is, the transfer of power to professional managers and the separation of control and ownership②.

---

① Guo Qiang, Personal Power and Decline of Enterprise, Management World, No. 3, 2001, p. 163.

② Lei Ding, The Management Thought of Overseas Chinese Entrepreneurs: Cultural Background and Style, SDX Joint Publishing (Shanghai) Co. Ltd., 1993, p. 240.

The existence of "position view" makes it difficult for family members to let out the management "power." According to the framework and management structure of modern enterprise system, the management of family business is changed from family to professional, the management personnel is changed from family members to experts, the supervision of the enterprise is changed from law-abiding to the market. It is a painful and difficult process to realize the manager's revolution. The so-called difficulty is because it is the re-allocation of corporate management power: to give up some of the power and leave it for professionals to manage. The so-called pain is because the victory over kinship is much harder than to overcome the general interpersonal relationships, and overcome oneself is harder than the victory over family.

Second, paying attention to the cultural roots of blood inheritance. Lensberg believes that the best way to keep their parents' hopes and dreams is to pass on the creatures that they are engaged in to their descendants from generation to generation, that is human nature. In China, "family" and "pan-family" will be the main form of integration within the family business in a very long time, therefore, it has set obstacles for external transmission of family business management control. But we also note that the continuation of China's familial management is not confined to "inheritance". China's cultural traditions have changed fundamentally today. The advancement of birth control system and the infiltration of Western culture have made traditional family culture which are built on blood relations gradually replaced by some new networks of relations. In some developed central cities, families, communities and other concepts are gradually fading, even the links between relatives are weakening (Li Xinchun, 1998). The influence of these changes on the intergenerational heritage of the family business will be manifested as the gradually expansive scope of internal training from son to relatives, friends, classmates and fellows.

Third, the constraints of information system. Information is the basic unit of the era of knowledge economy and an important component of modern productive forces. The important features of information are normality and dispersion. Normality refers to the degree of clarity and specificity of the information at the time of transaction; dispersion is the degree to which the relevant information that can be reached in the transaction is grasped by the public. In a relatively centralized economic system, the transaction-related information is usually in the hands of a few people, and the flow of information is often subject to strict system constraints; while decentralized economic society will help the information scattered in every corner of the market economy. Anyone can freely use this information to participate in market transactions. Generally speaking, the degree of normality and dispersion is proportional. Members of family business mainly come from the family and are linked by blood relationship. Disputes outside the family are usually settled according to the principle of egoism through the contract; however, disputes within the family is usually settled according to the principle of altruism in a more efficient way of obedience or tacit understanding. In such an enterprise, the information is centralized and not standardized, the exchange of information is greatly restricted, and the diffusion of information can only be achieved by face-to-face actual contact. The information is focused on the hands of entrepreneurs, and rely on his or hers personal charm to establish a hierarchical structure: it is difficult to integrate with the principal-agent mechanism which are based on standard contract.

(2) Environmental constraints of external manager market.

First, the development of manager market. The development stage of China's market economy has made China's talents market, especially the manager market be in a state of just getting started. We can see from research data that more than half of people believe that China's current manager market needs to be improved and the family business owners are immature①. Although this set of data reflects the subjective understanding of the current situation of the manager market in China, it can explain the stage of manager market and the necessity for improvement to some extent.

From the development trend point of view, there will be more and more family business owners realize that enterprise, after all, is not a family; and the modern society which is full of commercial competition is not the traditional family society. Therefore, paying attention to the quality, technology and education level of the talents, recruiting talents from the whole community, combining family, loyalty and talents together, will gradually become the most important means for the integration of human capital. However, this may be a relatively long process in China. From actual situation, a considerable number of family businesses have been hit during the reform, in which the Yellow River Group in Lanzhou is a typical. Due to the lack of effective institutional resources, those enterprises which have failed the reform returned to strengthen the family system and thus formed a path dependence. At present, most business owners are still not optimistic about the management of professional managers.

---

① Zhang Houyi, et al., China's Private Enterprise Development Report (2001), Social Sciences Academic Press, 2001, p. 72.

China has not yet formed a class of professional managers, the reason is: the vast majority of enterprises in China have not yet achieved the separation among ownership, corporate property and operation right, which is the necessary conditions for the generation of professional managers. Professional manager market includes social market and internal market; professional managers are employed in the market. The professional role of the professional manager is absent, and the overall level of professional managers' quality is not high. Among which there is a reason that directly restricts the emergence of professional manager class in China, which is the credit problems. The supervision, security and incentive mechanism are not perfect, thus the credit of professional managers cannot be guaranteed.

The imperfection of the manager market has created at least two kinds of difficulties for family business to find external agents: first, the lack of market channels. In most cases, the recommendation of friends and family members makes it difficult to ensure the suitability of agents; second, the lack of a competitive unified market, managers can evade market supervision.

China is currently facing a real situation that there is not sufficient business ethics, business rules and business orders between enterprises and customers. The lack of contract between enterprises and employees and the lack of rigidity of the whole social credit relationship make the credit chain very fragile. So to a certain extent, family management has become a kind of self-defense.

Second, the lack of manager restraint mechanism. Another reason for the failure of formation of the professional managerial hierarchy is that the market-oriented manager constraint mechanism is imperfect, thus leading to a crisis of trust in the agent. On the basis of egoism, western enterprises have constructed an effective preventive system, which creates a behavioral pattern that only through altruism will achieve egoism. Therefore, the business goals and individual goals can be met under the premise of mutual agreement. The non-institutional management characteristics are obvious in early stage of Chinese family business. We can find that almost all successful enterprises are strongly dependent on excellent entrepreneurial qualities and abilities, instead of system advantages[①]. Thus, family business in China has been aware of the self-interest of others, while the distrust towards outsides has been strengthened.

---

① Liu Xiaoxuan, China's Classical Business Model: Entrepreneurial Business, Management World, No. 6, 1999, p. 35.

In the transitional period of market economy, the social moral restraint is weak and the personal information cannot be obtained. The objective function of the manager and the owner is usually not the same: inconsistent interest and asymmetric information will inevitably lead to the increase of supervision costs. At this stage in China, this cost of supervision will be particularly expensive. Because the client (owner) and the agent (manager) have no kinship to maintain and no professional ability to match. The lack of restraints and the increase of agent costs means that the principal-agent system has lost its implementation basis.

Third, the relationship between family business owners and professional managers. At present, the attention of the theoretical community is focused on regulating the pursuit of both sides, and they believe that the problem of information asymmetry is actually impossible to solve. The focus of domestic theoretical community is mainly on two aspects: one is to require professional managers to improve their professional ethics; the other is to motivate professional managers to keep in line with their bosses through the design of incentive mechanisms. Foreign theoretical community have further considered how to reduce the conflicts between professional managers and business owners through the design of enterprise capital structure[①]. In competition and internationalization, the more common model is to share the control power between the family and managers[②]. Stock option incentive mechanism is widely recognized in academia, but I believe that when managers have to withdraw from the family business, the risk and loss will be greater. The absence of reputation mechanism also increases the manager's "moral hazard". This also means that the cost of agency will increase and the barriers for the establishment of elimination mechanism will be created.

3. Implementation of external transmission of operational control

(1) Non-family-member managers' access into the family business.

According to the definition of family business and family governance model, family members have the absolute or relative control power within family enterprise. Even so, there will still be a large number of non-family members in family business. Non-family managers mainly rely on internal promotion, social recruitment

---

① Yu Bin, Cornerstone of Principal-agent Mechanism in Private Enterprises: Constraint Based on Supervision, Economist, No. 2, 2003, p. 68.

② Li Xinchun, Manager's Market Failure and Family Business Governance, Management World, No. 4, 2003.

and friends' recommendation. However, for different types of non-family members, the selection criteria is different.

Entrepreneurs have different criteria for managers and other types of staff because managers play an important role in the development of family business. The indirect reason is that the managers' trust crisis that we have discussed earlier will exist for a long time. The solution to this problem needs to be based on the improvement of the manager's market and the establishment of market-oriented manager selection, incentive and restraint mechanisms.

(2) Internal incentives and constraints of professional manager.

The development of professional manager market in our country is still immature, thus the incentives and constraints of professional managers will be relatively weak. Under existing external conditions, the role of internal incentive and restraint mechanism is particularly important.

5.2.4 Family business inheritance: an analysis based on corporate control theory

1. Corporate control issues in the development of family business

When the private enterprises develop to a certain size, they may encounter management bottlenecks, which means relying on the entrepreneurial spirit of the founder alone cannot effectively manage the enterprise. Family businesses need to establish a series of standardized decision-making, human resources and financial systems. However, entrepreneurship and general management are two different management activities, a successful entrepreneur is probably not a good manager. Many private enterprises want to introduce professional managers from outside the family to solve the problem of management bottleneck. However, in the introduction of professional managers, family businesses have encountered a lot of problems. On the one hand, after the introduction of professional managers, the entrepreneur will have to authorize, but the authorization is likely to lead to professional managers' opportunistic behavior. For example, to transfer corporate assets, to steal the core technology and information, "collective rebellion", excessive consumption and other behaviors. On the other hand, these acts of professional manager have led to a high agency costs. As a result, many family business who introduced professional managers were finally caught in the trap of "empowerment-loss-retake control".

For professional managers, if you want to play a role in the management of family business, you should be fully authorized by the founder. However, professional managers often complain that he cannot get the trusts of the founder and other family members, and cannot make decisions on even daily stuff. Finally, they have to resign.

The dilemma that often occurs in the process of introducing a professional manager in a family business can be attributed to the high agency costs caused by the opportunistic behaviors that professional managers may have, and the value of the family's control over the firm (the management of family members can give the family a sense of honor). The cost of agency is determined by whether the laws and regulations are perfect, whether the manager's market is mature, whether the organizational structure within the enterprise is perfect. With the development of the manager's market and the continuous improvement of the legal system, the agency costs between the family business and the professional managers are decreasing. Ownership control can give the founder and other members of the family some private benefits. The family may attach a great deal of importance to the control of the enterprise. They see the business as part of family property and do not want outsiders to control the business. However, employing professional managers inevitably needs to empower outsiders, which can lead to the loss of private benefits.

Therefore, although the family hopes to get help from external forces to improve the management level; but the agency problem between the family and professional managers and the consumption problem of family's private benefits have hindered the decision to hire professional managers. At present, "inherited his father's" is still the main mode of family business succession.

Li Xinchun (2000) and Chu Xiaoping, Li Huaizu (2003) attributed this dilemma to the lack of trust in Chinese society. They believe that Chinese society is a low-trust society. As the lack of trust, it is difficult for family business to absorb external management resources, thus restricting the growth of family business. Studies of Eastern European countries and Viet Nam (McMillan, Woodruff, 2000; Johnson, McMillan, Woodruff, 2002) have suggested that in countries where the legal system is imperfect, the law is weak in the protection of transactions and property rights, and the execution of contracts depends mainly on relational contracts and social networks. Relational contracts are self-enforcing, and social networks are often closed. Therefore, the information of the breach can be spread out quickly in the network, and the penalty mechanism can be implemented by expelling the breaching party from the network. Family businesses in China and Southeast Asia mainly use social network (formed of race, kinship or marriage) to replace legal system in the protection of trade and property rights. Therefore, the root cause of the dilemma in the family business succession is not the lack of trust, but the imperfection of the legal system.

Burkart, Panonzi and Shaleifer (2003) have provided a family business succession model which is similar to this chapter. One of the key issues faced by family businesses is that entrepreneurs must choose between hiring career managers and letting their successors to manage their business; in the meantime, they should also decide on the number of shares sold in the securities market. In different legal environments, the founders have different options: (1) when the legal protection of property rights is very good, the founder should sell out the ownership and make it decentralized holding company running by professional managers; (2) when the legal protection of property rights is ordinary, the founder should hire a professional manager, but at the same time retain the status of major shareholders to supervise the professional managers; (3) when the law is weak, the founder should continue to retain the family nature of the enterprise and manage the business by himself or other family members, even if the talent of these two is far less than that of professional managers. However, Burkart et al. did not consider the private benefits of the control power.

Graceman and Hart (1986), Hart and Moore (1990), Hart (1995) divided ownership into residual usufruct and control power. Aghion and Tirole (1997), Baker, Gibburn and Murphy (1999) further subdivided the control power into "nominal control right" and "actual control right" or "formal authority" and "real authority". In family holding companies, the formal authority and the real authority is unified. In a public listed company, shareholders delegate control power to the manager, the shareholders only maintain partial control power and have final voting rights only for some important matters such as election of directors, modification of the articles of association, bankruptcy and reorganization; in other words, shareholders only enjoy nominal control right. Therefore, what is commonly referred to as the "separation of powers", which is the separation of ownership and control, is simply a non-standard statement. The exact argument should be the separation of ownership and actual control right (Hansmann, 1996). The distribution of control power is multidimensional, for example, the manager has the right of advice and enforcement, while the owner has decision-making control and supervision power (Fama & Jensen, 1983).

In family business, the founder hires professional managers to operate the enterprise and authorizes (partial) actual control right to them, but retains the nominal control right. At any time, the founder can recover the actual control right from the hands of professional managers. In this way, the professional manager and the founder share the enterprise's (actual) control right. Li Xinchun (2003) also argues that because of the imperfection of the manager's market, the split of actual control right between the family and professional managers is a kind of institutional arrangement which can circumvent the agency costs.

This book considers the question of whether the family business transfers the actual control right to the professional manager while retaining residual claim. The model assumes that business managers can be sought from within the family members and on the manager's market. The benefits of promotion within the family business are familiar family members, information symmetry, and consistent benefits, so the agency costs between managers and the family are very low. However, the family does not always have the right person. If we look for managers from the outside, the business will have to pay a relatively high salary, the professional managers may have opportunistic behaviors, and the family must also give up partial actual control right. However, if the professional managers can bring great improvements in management, then the introduction of professional managers will be worthwhile. Family businesses need to weigh between the introduction of professional managers and the promotion of family members.

Under certain conditions, the promotion of successors from within the family may be better than finding the right person from the manager's market. However, when the size of the enterprise is growing, the cost of agency between the family and the external manager will be reduced, the introduction of external professional managers will become more attractive.

2. Model framework

Here we use a simple model to describe the decision on the choice of successor. Consider such a family business: when the enterprise reaches a certain size, the number of decisions that the founder needs to make is getting higher and higher. In addition, a successful entrepreneurial entrepreneur is probably not a good manager. Therefore, in order to achieve long-term development, many private enterprises want to introduce professional managers from outside the family to solve the problem of management bottleneck, and to establish standardized decision-making, human resources, financial and other systems.

If a family business wants to increase the level of management by introducing professional managers, it is necessary to strike a balance between improving corporate performance, losing private benefits and triggering agency costs. As long as the benefits of introducing professional managers is greater than possible losses, the family business will introduce professional managers.

The distribution of control power is multidimensional, for example, the manager has the right of advice and enforcement, while the owner has decision-making control and supervision power. To simplify the analysis, this study assumes that the control power is one-dimensional. Assume that the transmission of control power to professional manager is i, $0 \leq i \leq 1$. $i = 0$ or 1 respectively represent that the family or professional managers have complete control right of the enterprise. This report further assumes that if the family business chooses a professional manager, the control power transmitted to them must be greater than the lower bound i: this is because if a professional manager is to be introduced, he or she must be given a certain amount of power in terms of personnel, finance, investment and so on. The improvements on management of introducing professional managers is the function of the transmission of control power $R(i)$ ($R'(i) > 0$, $R''(i) < 0$). In other words, the more the transmission, the more likely for professional managers to play their management skills and the greater the improvement of management. However, this increase in management growth is getting smaller and smaller.

In addition, the transmission of control power to the manager also means that the founder and the family will lose partial private benefits $B(i)$. $B'(i) \geq 0$, $B''(i) > 0$, $B'''(i) < 0$, $B'(0) = 0$, $B'(1) = 0$. Its economic significance is that the marginal loss of private benefits from control transmission will increase from zero and then decrease to zero. When the amount of transmission is small, the marginal private benefits that the family has lost is less; when the amount of transmission increases to a certain extent, the marginal benefits reaches the maximum; then, the marginal benefits begins to decrease, until the control power is completely transferred to the manager. At this time, the founder's marginal costs of transmission is zero. The intuitive meaning is: when the transfer of control is less, the founder will not feel that the authorization has brought so much loss. When the transfer of control reaches a critical value, further transfer of control will make the founder feel that he will lose the control of the enterprise. Although the founder has the nominal control right of the enterprise, once the professional managers have the enterprise personnel appointment and removal rights, investment and financing decision-making power, it will bring great shock to the enterprise and cause immeasurable losses by removing the professional managers and recovering the control power. At this time, the marginal cost of transfer reaches the maximum.

Similarly, if the manager has a great deal of control power, it will be possible for him or her to take opportunistic behaviors. Assuming that the agent cost between the founder and the manager is $A(i)$, $A'(i) \geqslant 0$, $A''(i) > 0$, $A'''(i) < 0$, $A'(0) = 0$, $A'(1) = 0$. The explanation here is similar to the marginal loss of private gains from the transfer of control: the marginal agency costs increase from zero and then decrease to zero.

Thus, the total cost of transfer control to the founders is $C(i) = B(i) + A(i)$, $C'(i) \geqslant 0$, $C''(i) > 0$, $C'''(i) < 0$, $C'(0) = 0$, $C'(1) = 0$.

Of course, in addition to hiring professional managers from outside, the founders can also choose to cultivate their relatives. The benefit of doing so is that the agency costs between the founders and relatives are much lower than that between the founders and professional managers. As the control power is still in the hands of the family, the loss of private benefits is relatively low. However, the family does not necessarily have a competent manager. Therefore, compared with hiring professional managers from the outside, choosing relatives as the manager will lose part of the efficiency. Assuming the benefits, the marginal loss of private income and the marginal agency costs of choosing relatives to be managers are $r(i)$, $b(i)$, $a(i)$, $r(i) < R(i)$, $b(i) < B(i)$, $a(i) < A(i)$; for $0 \leqslant i \leqslant 1$, $c(i) = b(i) + a(i)$.

3. Cost-benefit analysis of introducing professional manager

(1) Static framework.

The founder chooses between "reliable" and "capable". If the founder hires professional managers, the optimal amount of transmission will be the solution of the following equation:

$$C'(i) = B'(i) + A'(i) = R'(i)$$

The solution is i^* and the net income of the transmission is:

$$\Pi^* = \int_0^{i^*} R'(i) - [B'(i) + A'(i)] \mathrm{d}i$$

If the founder chooses a relative, the optimal amount of transmission will be the solution of the following equation:

$$c'(i) = b'(i) + a'(i) = r'(i)$$

The solution is i^{**} and the net income of the transmission is:

$$\Pi^{**} = \int_0^{i*} r'(i) - [b'(i) + a'(i)]di$$

If $\Pi^* > \Pi^{**}$, the founder will introduce professional managers. If $\Pi^* < \Pi^{**}$, the founder will choose relatives to manage the business. This report will further analyze how the control power is transferred to the hands of professional managers.

As shown in Figure 5 – 5, the RR curve is the expected benefit after the introduction of professional managers. Assuming that when the family business begins to transfer the control power to the manager, the benefits of improved management are significant; as the control power is gradually transferred to the manager, the increase in revenue is diminishing. The CC curve represents the costs for family business to give up the control power, which includes the loss of private benefits and the expected costs incurred by the manager engaging in activities that will do harm to the interests of the owner. According to the hypothesis, the CC curve is an inverted U, when the control right begins to transfer, because most of the control power is still in the family, the losses of control transfer is very small; when the transfer of control is getting more and more, the private loss of the family and the agency costs between the manager and the owner will be greater. When the transfer of control reaches a certain proportion, because the family has lost the absolute or relative control of the enterprise, further transmission will bring to the maximum loss and then to a downward trend.

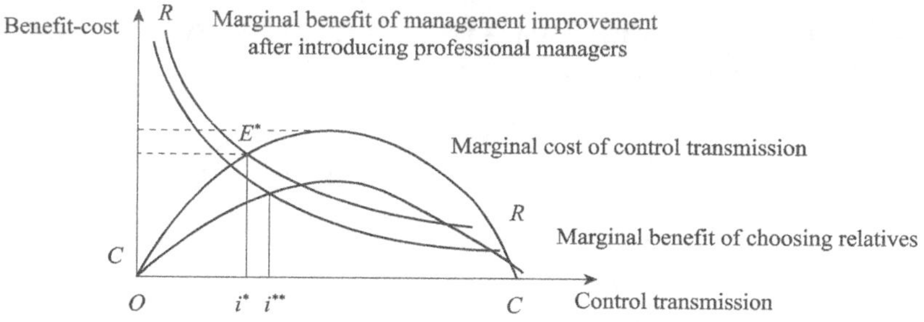

Figure 5 – 5 Cost-benefit analysis of control transmission in family business: partial transmission

A. Partial transmission. When the agency costs between the family business and professional managers are large while the expected benefits of management improvement are small, the optimal transmission point of the founder is at point E, and the amount of transfer is i^*.

B. No feasible transmission. When the family business' evaluation of private income is very high or the agency costs between the family and professional managers are very high, the costs of control transfer will be relatively higher compared to the improvement of management efficiency. The transfer of control will be relatively lower in equilibrium as point i_1 shown in Figure 5 – 6. However, if the transfer of control is not completely divisible, for example, the amount of control power that the family business will transfer should be larger than i; while on the right side of point i_1, the cost of control transfer is greater than the benefits of management improvements, thus the transfer of control is not feasible. At this time, the family business will not introduce professional managers. In reality, although the family hopes to improve management level with the help of some "external brain", the agency problem between family and professional managers, and the family's consumption of private benefits brought by control power will all affect the decision-making of hiring professional managers. This has led to the fact that "father-to-son" is still the main mode of family business succession.

C. Complete transmission. Figure 5 – 7 shows that when the efficiency of management is much higher than the cost of control transfer, that is, the RR curve is higher than the CC curve, the transfer of control is feasible at any time. At this point, the enterprise reaches a larger scale and the organization becomes a huge enterprise, relying solely on the founder's adventurous spirit is not enough. Only through the introduction of professional managers and the establishment of sound management rules will the enterprises survive the rapid growth stage and move into a stable period.

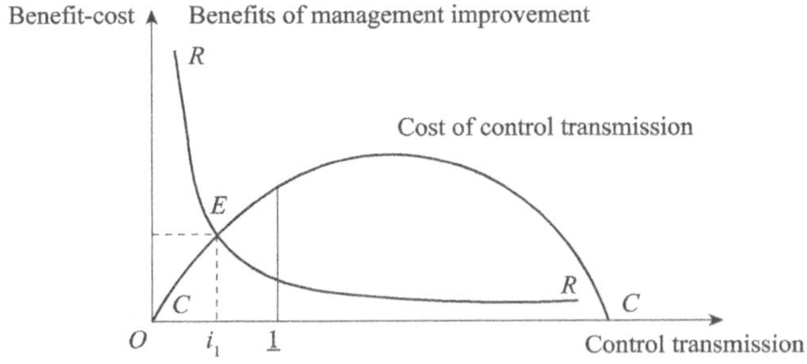

Figure 5 – 6 Cost-benefit analysis of control transmission in family business: no transmission

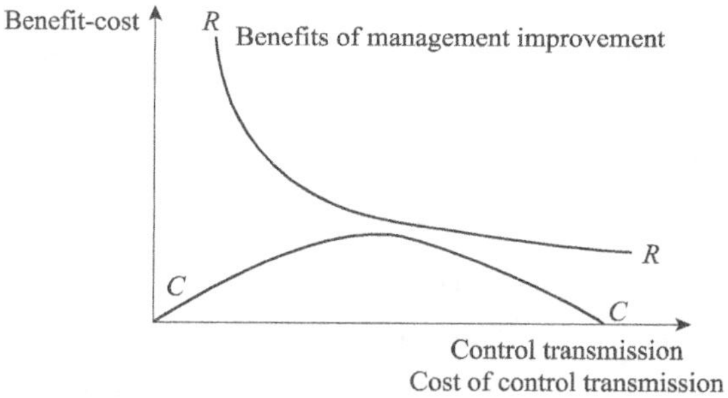

Figure 5 -7 Cost-benefit analysis of control transmission in family business: transmission is not feasible

In the early development stage, the enterprise relies on the entrepreneurial spirit of the founder and the ownership of the enterprise is unified with (nominal) control right. When the enterprise develops to a certain stage, it will need standardized regulations. At this time, the professional managers should be introduced and the founders and professional managers will share the control power. When the enterprise reaches a considerable scale and the legal protection of property rights is very perfect, the benefits of the introduction of professional managers will be greater than the loss. The control power will be transferred to the hands of professional managers and the ownership and management will be separated.

(2) Dynamic perspective.

When the scale of enterprises is getting bigger, the agency costs of introducing professional managers will get smaller than the management improvement brought by the introduction of professional managers. When the legal system is getting more perfect, the opportunist behavior of professional managers will receive restrict limitations. When the manager's market becomes more standardized, the opportunistic behavior will have a serious impact on their reputation. Therefore, professional managers will be self-restraint of their behavior to a certain extent. The above changes are conducive to the introduction of managers by family business. This is shown in the figure that the decrease in the marginal cost curve brought by the transfer of control, and the increase in the marginal yield curve RR brought by the improvement of management after the introduction of professional managers.

4. Conclusions

When the family business develops to a certain scale, it may encounter management bottlenecks: relying solely on the founder's entrepreneurial spirit cannot effectively manage the business. Therefore, the founder decides to authorize the control power to family members or professional managers. Choosing a career manager will lead to improved management efficiency, but it can also lead to higher agency costs; the family will lose some private benefits by giving up partial control power. Since the family does not have the appropriate operator, therefore, choosing family members will not produce agency costs, but the improvement of management will be limited. Thus, the founder has to weigh between family members and professional managers. Under certain conditions, it is effective to transfer the control power to professional managers; however, since the control power is not completely separable, the transfer of control is not feasible. With the expansion of the scale of the enterprise, the perfection of the legal system environment and the maturity of the manager's market, the benefits of introducing professional managers is getting bigger and bigger and the agency problem is gradually solved, thus the family business will tend to transfer the control power to professional managers.

Therefore, the root cause of the dilemma in Chinese family enterprises is not the lack of trust, but the imperfect legal system. In order to make full use of the advantages of the modern enterprise system, we should strengthen the protection of private property rights and increase the costs for professional managers to steal the core technology of the enterprise. The family enterprise should also improve the audit and control mechanism to avoid opportunistic behavior; at the same time, we should establish an effective incentive mechanism, including equity incentive, pay system and promotion system, to ensure that the interests of professional managers and family business are united.

References

1. Aghion P. , Tirole J. Formal and Real Authority in Organizations. Quarterly Journal of Economics, 1997, 105 (1): 1-29.

2. Baker G. , Gibbons R. , Murphy K. J. Informal Authority in Organizations. Journal of Law Economics & Organization, 1999, 15 (1): 56-73.

3. CaiJiming etc. International Comparison of Corporate Governance Structure: Governance Structure and Enterprise Innovation of Private Enterprises in China. Nankai Economic Studies, 2000 (2).

4. Cao Yuanzheng. Development of Private Economy and Improvement of Governance Structure. Macroeconomics, 2000 (6).

5. Chao Shang. On the Intergenerational Transmission of Family Business Power. Nankai Business Review, 2002 (5).

6. Chen Jiagui, Huang Qunhui. Comparison and Improvement of Governance Structure among Different Ownership Enterprises. China Industrial Economics, 2001 (8).

7. Chen Ling. Information Characteristics, Transaction Costs and Family Organizations. Economic Research Journal, 1998 (7).

8. Chu Xiaoping. Family Business Research: a Topic of Modern Significance. Social Sciences in China, 2000 (5).

9. Chu Xiaoping. Career Managers and Family Business Growth. Management World, 2002 (4).

10. Chu Xiaoping, Li Huaizu. An Analysis of Family Business Transformation. Economic Theory and Business Management, 2002 (10).

11. Chu Xiaoping, Li Huaizu. Trust and Growth of Family Business. Management World, 2003 (6).

12. Dai Yuanchen. Problems of Family System in the Development of Private Enterprise. South China Journal of Economics, 2001 (11).

13. Fan Conglai. The Development of Southern Jiangsu Model and Reform of Property Rights of Township Enterprises. Management World, 1995 (4).

14. Fan Conglai etc. Research on Reform Model and Ownership Structure of Property Rights Regime of Township Enterprises. Economic Research Journal, 2001 (1).

15. Gan Dean. Research on Family Business in China. China Social Sciences Press, 2002.

16. Gelshik C. The Proliferation of Family Business. The Economic Daily Press, 1998.

17. Grossman S., Hart O. The Costs and Benefits of Ownership: A Theory of Vertical and Lateral Ownership. Journal of Political Economy, 1986, 94 (4): 691 - 719.

18. GuoQiang. Personal Power and Decline of Enterprise. Management World, 2001 (3).

19. Hansmann H. The Ownership of Enterprise. Cambridge: the Belknap Press, 1996.

20. Hart O. Firms, Contracts and Financial Structure. Oxford University Press, 1995.

21. Hart O., Moore J. Property Rights and the Nature of the Firm. Journal of Political Economy, 1990, 98 (6): 1119 –1158.

22. Jin Chengnan. Re-examine Korean Economic Development Model. The Journal of World Economy, 1999 (6).

23. Johnson Simon, McMillan John, Christopher Woodruff. Courts and Relational Contracts. Journal of Law Economics & Organization, 2002, 18 (1): 221 –277.

24. Li Daokui. Fuzzy Property Rights Theory in Transition Economy. Economic Research Journal, 1995 (4).

25. Li Ji, Li Lin. Survival and Development of Small and Medium-sized Enterprises: Competition, Governance Mechanism and Incomplete Advantages. Reform, 2001 (5).

26. Li Wei'an, Wu Lidong. Corporate Governance of Corporate Groups: Starting Point, Governance Boundary and Subsidiary Governance. Nankai Business Review, 1999 (4).

27. Li Wei'an. Corporate Governance. Nankai University Press, 2001.

28. LiXinchun. China's Family Regime and Enterprise Organization. Chinese Social Science Quarterly (Hong Kong), fall 1998.

29. Li Xinchun. Management Revolution of Family Businesses. Academic Research, 2001 (5).

30. LiXinchun. Trust, Loyalty and Familyist Dilemma. Management World, 2002 (6).

31. LiXinchun. Manager's Market Failure and Family Business Governance. Management World, 2003 (4).

32. LiYa. Corporate Governance of Private Enterprises. China Fangzheng Press, 2003.

33. Liang Tongying, Lu Zhenghua, Huang Jianhuan. Financing Arrangement and Governance Structure Improvement in the Transformation of Township Enterprises: a Case Study of Vinda Company. Management World, 2001 (6).

34. LvFeishi, Wu Desheng. Research on Governance Costs in Corporate Governance Change. Jianghan Forum, 2006 (12).

35. Mao Yunshi. Family Business: Formation, Transition and Change. Academic Research, 2001 (5).

36. McMillan John, Christopher Woodruff. Private Order under Dysfunctional Public Order. Michigan Law Review, 2000, 98 (8): 2421 –2458.

37. Pan Bisheng. Problems of Family Management in Township Enterprises. China

Rural Survey, 1998 (1).

38. Redding S. B. Management Thought of Overseas Chinese Entrepreneurs: Cultural Background and Style. Shanghai Joint Publishing, 1993.

39. SuQilin, Wan Junyi, OuXiaoming. International Comparison of Family Control and Family Business Governance. Foreign Economics & Management, 2003 (5).

40. Tang Qingquan. The Challenges and Countermeasures of Family Enterprises' Successful Operation. Management World, 2002 (9).

41. Tirole J. Corporate Governance. Econometrica, 2001, 69 (1): 1 -35.

42. Wang Xiaoyi. Private Enterprises and Family Economy in Rural China. Shanxi Economic Publishing House, 1996.

43. Wang Zheng. Agency Costs, Family System and China's Private Enterprises. Economy and Management, 2002 (9).

44. Weitzman, Xu Chenggang. China's Township Enterprises as Cooperatives with Vague Property Rights. Economic Translation, 1995 (1).

45. Wu Desheng. An Analysis Framework for Corporate Ownership and Control Arrangements: from Corporate Governance to Enterprise Governance. In the Proceedings of the 3rd International Symposium on Corporate Governance, Nankai University Press.

46. WuJinglian. Private Enterprises Also Have a "Dominant" . Beijing Youth Daily, June 25, 2001.

47. XieShujiang. Some Problems in the Governance Structure of Private Enterprise in China. Tianjin Social Sciences, 2001 (2).

48. Xu Jingyong. Retrospect and Prospect of Property Rights Regime Reform of Private Enterprises in Wenzhou. Economy and Management, 2000 (6).

49. Yan Ruosen. The Composition of Corporate Governance Cost and the Optimization of Corporate Governance Efficiency. Accounting Research, 2005 (1).

50. Yang Hao. Nature Definition and Property Right Analysis of Private Enterprises. Shanghai Journal of Economics, 2001 (3).

51. Yang Jiguo. Human Capital Property Rights: A Proposition that Challenges Corporate Governance Theory. Economic Sciences, 2002 (1).

52. Yao Xiantao, Wang Lianjuan. Chinese Family Business. Enterprise Management Publishing House, 2002.

53. Ying Huanhong. "Family System" and Institutional Innovation of Private Enterprises. Zhejiang Academy of Social Sciences, 2001 (5).

54. Ying Huanhong. Research on Property Right System of Private Enterprises in Zhejiang province. China Soft Science, 2001 (12).

55. Yu Lizhi. Institutional Lockout and Innovation of Private Family Enterprises in Zhejiang province. Zhejiang Social Sciences, 2002 (7).

56. Zhang Kezhong. Reflections on Institutional Obstacles to China's Family-oriented Private Enterprises during Transition Period. Modernization of Management, 2000 (6).

57. Zhou Qingjie. Corporate Governance Efficiency: An Analysis Based on Institutional Economics. Finance & Economics, 2003 (3).

Chapter 6

Institutional Environment in International Development Process of Private Enterprises

This chapter mainly studies the bottleneck of various systems encountered in the process of international development of private enterprises. First of all, according to the classic paradigm "structure-conduct-performance" in industrial organizational theory, this book analyzes the relationship between private enterprises export behavior and its performance. Secondly, from the perspective of international division of labor and value chain, this book analyzes the typical market "separation" problem in the export of private enterprises. Finally, taking Zhejiang province as an example, this book studies the institutional obstacles and supply problems in the development of private enterprises' export, and draws some enlightening conclusions and puts forward relevant policy suggestions.

6. 1 Characteristics of export behavior of private enterprises

In the past 20 years, the development of private enterprises has been an important supporting force in China's sustained and rapid economic growth. The growth performance of private enterprises has a profound impact on China's economic development prospects. With the advent of the era of economic globalization, the international division of labor and international market competition has been further deepened. The impact of foreign trade on a country's economic growth has become increasingly significant[①]. Studying the export behavior and performance of Chinese private enterprises will become an important aspect of China's economic growth research. This paper follows the classical paradigm SCP in industrial organizational theory, analyzes the current situation of Chinese private enterprises' export behavior, puts forward some problems and gives corresponding policy suggestions.

6. 1. 1 Present situation of export behavior of private enterprises in China

After 20 years of reform and opening up, a large number of private enterprises have moved from the start-up stage into the mature stage. While actively maintaining and opening up the domestic market, more and more private enterprises have been participating in the international market competition by way of providing export sources for foreign trade sector or through foreign trade agents and other indirect ways or through self-export and other direct ways. Figure 6 – 1 shows the share of collective and private enterprises in China's total exports from 1994 to 2002 and the amount of exports in collective and private enterprises in China from 2000 to 2002.

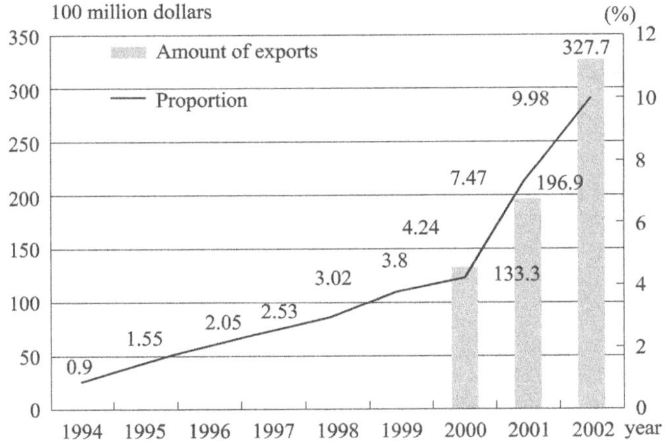

Figure 6 – 1 The share of collective and private enterprises in China's total exports from 1994 to 2002 and the amount of exports in collective and private enterprises in China from 2000 to 2002

Source: Sorted out from China Customs Statistical Yearbook in relevant years.

---

① Lin Yifu and Li Yongjun (2003) proved that exports have always been one of the major contributions to China's rapid economic growth. If foreign trade exports increase by 10%, China's national economy will increase by 1%.

As can be seen from Figure 6 - 1, on a nationwide scale, the share of private enterprises in China's foreign trade has steadily increased. Taking into account the restructuring problem in a large number of township enterprises and foreign joint ventures, as well as some local foreign trade companies, the actual operating performance of collective and private enterprises should be higher than the statistics from the customs. It is worth noting that in more developed areas of the market economy, private enterprises have shown a more important position in foreign trade. Taking the example of Zhejiang province, where foreign trade and private economy are more developed, the current export business entity has been divided into the pattern of state-owned, foreign and private enterprises. Diversified and balanced development of the business entity has become the main reason for the rapid growth of foreign trade export and national economy in Zhejiang, which can be seen in Figure 6 - 2.

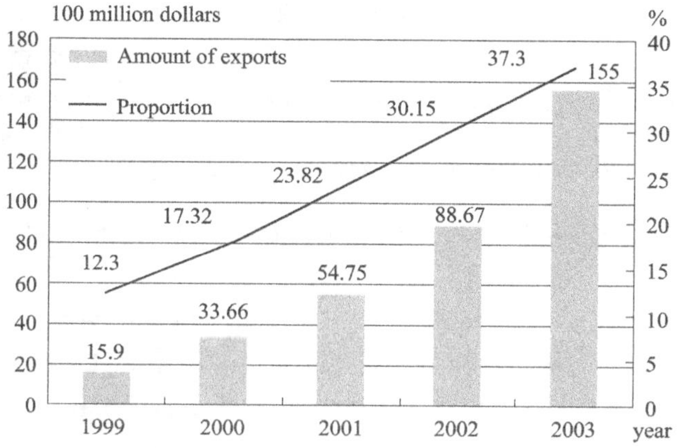

Figure 6 - 2 Exports of collective and private enterprises in Zhejiang province from 1999 to 2003

Note: the data of 2003 is based on the data from January to August in 2003.

Source: Sorted out from Foreign Trade and Economic Cooperation Department in Zhejiang province: "Zhejiang Province Foreign Trade Statistics" in relevant years.

6.1.2 Problems and analysis of the export of private enterprises in China

Most private enterprises in China are typically traditional enterprises which have relied on the natural accumulation of private capital to form and evolve. Thus, it is difficult for management system and governance structure to provide an effective micro-institutional basis for enterprise innovation and fierce market competition. We should face up to the existing problems in the high-speed growth of private enterprises export.

In 1776, Smith compared the price under monopoly and the price under free competition, and emphasized the importance of market structure. Cournot (1838) proposed the theory of the first seller oligopoly. Since the 1950s, the classical paradigm "Mason-Bain" in the theory of industrial organization, that is, the SPC paradigm, emphasized the influence of market structure on the behavior of market players, and the main behavior's impact on market performance. As an important aspect of the market structure, product differentiation has received considerable attentions in theory and application. In particular, the theory of industrial organization divides product differentiation into horizontal differentiation and vertical differentiation, and analyzes the market equilibrium and social welfare. Based on the theory of industrial organization, we conclude the problems of private enterprises into two aspects. At the same time, combined with the reality of the export of private enterprises in China, we consider market concentration as an important analysis point.

1. Horizontal differentiation of product

(1) Imitation of competition and vicious price competition are quite common, the enterprise lack market forces.

Most of our private enterprises are close to the atomic type and the horizontal differentiation is not significant. From the perspective of a single enterprise, the scale of private enterprises in China is generally small① and the production of similar products is huge, so the behavior of one enterprise will have no significant impact on other manufacturers. Enterprises do not distinguish between limited horizontal differentiation and other companies. The lack of ability to transform this limited horizontal differentiation into "market forces", that is, the lack of ability to influence and control market prices, has led to the downward of price competition with other firms. Because the horizontal differentiation of product is not normally compensated, this has led to imitative competition (Jin Xiangrong, 2003). The imitative competition will further intensify horizontal homogenization and downward vicious price competition.

① Taking Zhejiang for example, at the end of 2001, the registered capital of the province's private enterprises is only 804 300 yuan / household and the market structure is characterized by "small and scattered" form.

(2) Coexistence of horizontal differentiation and horizontal homogeneity.

Private enterprises, which product similar products, usually gather in a specific geographical area and form external economies of scale and economy of scope on the basis of ultra-fine specialized division of labor; besides, they breakthrough "production possibility frontier" of horizontal differentiation and form a higher level of horizontal differentiation which is based on enterprise clusters. In larger enterprise clusters in Zhejiang province, there are plentiful product varieties, specifications and colors. Obviously, for the whole enterprise cluster, the higher the level of horizontal differentiation, the more important role it will play for external economies of scale and the formation of learning economy. But at the same time, due to the fact that a large number of similar private enterprises find it difficult to form a "price collusion", a single enterprise cannot rely on enterprise clusters to obtain market power which is brought about by the external economy. For example, many industrial products in Zhejiang province have occupied a large share of the national and international markets. But the price competition strategy is widely adopted among enterprises, so that the price is reduced to the level of production costs (Jin Xiangrong, 2003). Table 6 - 1 shows the distribution of main private enterprise clusters in Zhejiang province. As can be seen from Table 6 - 1 that, on enterprise cluster level, private economy in Zhejiang province has occupied a large market share in domestic market. These products are not only sold in domestic market, but also have certain competitiveness in international market. At the same time, the number of similar enterprises in the cluster is huge, thus the transfer of market power from cluster level to enterprise level is still a problem to be solved.

Table 6 - 1 Distribution of private enterprises in Zhejiang province

Major product	Region	Number of enterprise	Output value (100 million yuan)	National production proportion (%)
Tie	Shengzhou	1 200	80	80
Low-voltage apparatus	Leqing	3 800 *	155	66
Hardware tools	Yongkang	6 500	190	25
Lighter	Wenzhou	260	20	94
Pen-making	Wenzhou	151	16	33
Leather	Haining	5 688	120.88	25 *
Plastic products	Taizhou	10 081 *	121 *	14.3 *
Lock-making	Wenzhou	400	50	65
Shoe-making	Wenzhou	6 000 *	300	20
Glasses	Wenzhou	500 *	45	80
Wood industry	Jiashan	248 *	41.6 *	41.3
Children's garments	Huzhou	6 600	25	15

continued

Major product	Region	Number of enterprise	Output value (100 million yuan)	National production proportion (%)
Clothing	Ningbo, Wenzhou	3 300	333.6	15

Note: * for data in 2000, the rest are in 2001.

Source: Jin Xiangrong et al., Research of Specialized Industrial Area during the Process of Industrialization in Zhejiang province, working papers, 2002.

2. Vertical differentiation of product

(1) Lack of incentives.

Most of our private enterprises developed from the original "classical enterprise", which have the general characteristics of extensive, endogenous and expansive in the market competition, and focus on the production and sale of low-quality products for a long time. For example, private enterprises in Zhejiang province still cannot get out of the low-end line. They lack the "learning-by-doing" experience in high-quality product market and the trial cost is quite large. Besides, because the industrial organization of private economy is small and scattered, the development of high-end product has become a "luxury" consumption to a certain extent. The above two aspects have led to the huge costs of upward vertical differentiation in private enterprises. At the same time, due to the imperfection of market and institution environment, and the prevalent imitation competition, the upward product innovation income is difficult to be effectively protected and innovation income is likely to be dispersed in a short time. As a result, China's private enterprises lack the incentive of upward vertical differentiation.

(2) Entry barriers.

Production of high-quality products have some requirements for enterprise in equipment, capital, technology, management, scale and other aspects, which is unattainable for original private enterprises. As already mentioned, even if entry barriers can be exceeded, after cost-benefit analysis, the private enterprises which demand maximized profits still lack incentives for upward vertical differentiation. In fact, even if most private enterprises are willing to carry out upward vertical differentiation, they will still find it difficult to go beyond entry barriers. In addition, the current foreign trade "separation" has strengthened this kind of entry barriers from another aspect, and made it difficult for private enterprises to grasp market demand, and made it less possible for them to sense product innovation, technology innovation, and institution innovation invoked by market opportunities, and finally led to the fact that these enterprises have become the workshop for low-quality products.

As a result, China's private enterprises generally adopted the strategy of vertical differentiation for low-quality products. The problem is that the way to maximize the differentiation by reducing product quality will be narrower and narrower. Table 6 – 2 shows the price movement index of export products in some of the private enterprises in China. Based on the export price index in 1995, the international market prices of many export products are declining. A more detailed survey shows that among 25 export products from 1995 to 1998, the price of ten products increased, and the price of one product remained the same while the price of the other 14 products decreased. By 2002, 17 of them decreased. Moreover, low-quality products have the characteristics of low income elasticity, thus, the market share is gradually shrinking.

Table 6 – 2 Price movement index of major export products (1995 = 1)

Product name	1998	2002	Product name	1998	2002
Sewing machine	1.26	0.71	Canned pork	0.95	0.77
Leather shoes	1.04	0.90	Canned mushroom	0.86	0.80
Plastic products	—	0.91	Carpet	0.89	0.40
Lock	—	0.92	Thermos	1.08	0.91
Umbrella	1.10	0.81	Clock	0.71	0.65

Source: China Statistical Yearbook in relevant years.

It is noteworthy that the process of product differentiation of private enterprises in China is not optimistic. In recent years, relying on private enterprises and its strong comparative cost advantage, the export trade developed rapidly. However, from the perspective of SPC framework, private export enterprises generally use vicious price competition. This also partially explains why China's private enterprises have suffered frequent anti-dumping issues in international market.

3. Market concentration

Low concentration of market structure has led to the lack of market power in private export enterprises in China. Market concentration is an important aspect of the market structure. There is a positive relationship between market concentration and market performance or profitability. China's private economy is led by core-free atom-oriented enterprises, and has "small and scattered" industrial organization. In the case of Zhejiang province, where private economy and foreign trade are relatively developed, according to the basic unit survey database in 2001, the number of industrial independent accounting units is 154 789, among which the number of above a designated scale units (including all state-owned enterprises and non-state-owned industrial enterprises which have annual product sales income more than 5 million yuan) is 18 626, on accounting for 12%. This is a good description of Zhejiang private enterprises' "small and scattered" market structure. Through careful finishing, we give the amount of exports in four major private export enterprises and its share in total exports in Zhejiang province from 1999 to 2002. As a weak evidence, we can see this indicator as the market concentration index CR4 of private enterprises in Zhejiang province. It is generally believed that when CR4 is greater than 80%, it belongs to high-concentrated market structure; when CR4 is less than 20%, it belongs to low-concentrated market structure. As can be seen from Figure 6 – 3, the export of private enterprises in Zhejiang province belongs to a typical low-concentrated market structure. Although the total exports increased rapidly, the low-concentrated market structure has not been improved. In fact, the export situation of private enterprises in Zhejiang province can also reflect the export realities in China.

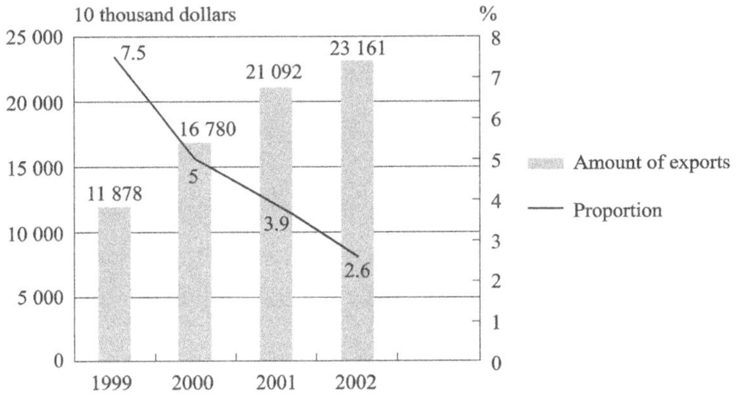

Figure 6 – 3 The amount of exports in four major private export enterprises and its share in total exports in Zhejiang province from 1999 to 2002

Source: Sorted out from Foreign Trade and Economic Cooperation Department in Zhejiang province: "Zhejiang Province Foreign Trade Statistics" in relevant years.

Low market concentration of industrial organization structure led to imitation competition, crowded phenomenon in the use of resources and the lack of power and capacity to change from family traditions to modern management; thus, it is difficult to obtain scale economy advantages in wholesale and distribution. So far, China's private economy has not yet formed a large-scale core or leading enterprise to internalize other "small and scattered" enterprises; due to the similar size of many small businesses, a certain degree of "price collusion" is difficult to form. The low concentration of similar market has led to Bertrand competition: the lack of market power, the sharp decline of market profits, and even vicious price competitions. These enterprises suffer from export losses and foreign anti-dumping litigation.

6. 1. 3 Conclusions and policy recommendations

Through the aforementioned analysis of market structure and market behavior, we have shown that the export performance of private enterprises in China needs to be further improved, and the key issue is to promote the process of product differentiation and realize the market power based on the enterprise level.

Product differentiation is closely related to and intertwined with the process of industrialization, marketization and modernization. The price competition behavior of private enterprises export is a typical kind of market failure. The government should improve and optimize the environment, policies and conditions of enterprise product differentiation to promote the process of differentiation in private enterprises.

For enterprises, the focus is on the implementation of product differentiation strategy, the improvement of market concentration and the access to business market power. First, the formation of enterprise alliances. In this regard, low-voltage electrical appliances in Wenzhou and Yueqing is a successful case. In the production of low-voltage electrical appliances, Chint, Delixi, Samsung and other leading enterprises have formed a number of business alliances or brand clubs through holding, equity and production license, which greatly improved the level of differentiation. The production of low-voltage electrical appliances have formed a high degree of market concentration and market power in Liushi. Second, correctly deal with the relationship between self-export and export agent; there are two meanings: first, correctly deal with the relationship between self-export and professional foreign trade agency; second, correctly deal with the relationship between self-export and common agent. In the short term, private enterprises cannot completely achieve self-export; but in the long run, the "separation" caused by professional foreign trade companies will create more and more obstacles for private enterprises. Leading enterprises, which are based on the integration of resources, will be conducive for small and scattered enterprises to obtain market power. Low-voltage electrical appliances in Liushi have built their own marketing system based on brand and achieved economies of scale.

For the government, the focus is to promote the process of enterprise product differentiation, to help integrate the loose industrial organization, and to support enterprises to obtain market power. First, to promote the reform of the Chamber of Commerce, to strengthen the intermediary organizations of industry norms and services, to reorganize the Chamber of Commerce and Industry Association, to cultivate the agency function of the Chamber of Commerce, to amend the "Anti-Unfair Competition Law" and "Anti-monopoly Law", and to give "monopoly" right to the Chamber of Commerce, associations and other organizations in export trade and other aspects. Second, the construction of regional product innovation system is conducive to promoting the process of product differentiation. The government should support large enterprises to establish their own technology development institutions; strengthen the support of R & D; increase the investment in government research. Third, to encourage and develop all kinds of higher education, especially vocational and technical education. The implementation of product differentiation strategy is highly relied on the support of talents. Higher education, especially vocational and technical education which is closely related to actual industry, can quickly and effectively reduce the entry barriers in the production of high-quality products. Fourth, to combine the construction and development of various industrial parks with the promotion of product differentiation. The construction of industrial park should pay attention to the protection of cooperation system. The government should focus on the design and guide of system, mechanism and policy, support and encourage the implementation of product differentiation strategy. For example, to encourage the establishment of enterprise alliance and attract similar famous enterprises at home and abroad. To consider the brand, market power (rather than market share), economic density, technological innovation and internationalization as measuring indicators for the construction of industrial park.

6.2 Institutional obstacles and institutional supply in the export development of private enterprises in Zhejiang province

The comparative benefits obtained through international division of labor and trade are not only depended the optimization of export commodity structure on technical level, but also on system innovation on organizational level. In the competitive situation of trade integration, expanding the export of private manufacturing enterprises is an inevitable choice for China to establish an open foreign economic and trade system. Based on the fertile soil of private economic development, the foreign trade of Zhejiang, especially the development of export trade, is unique in the whole country. The export of private production enterprises has built a new growth point in export and a source of sustained growth in export trade. However, there are some institutional obstacles in the process of export development of private enterprises, such as high entry barriers, lagging export tax rebates and difficult export quotas. There is a need to achieve institutional supply and innovation in government, enterprises and intermediate organizations.

6. 2. 1 Relaxation of foreign trade control and export of private manufacturing enterprises

The transition from a non-market economy to a modern market economy is the formation of regulations and rules. Studying how the competitive management system in the field of foreign trade is formed is of great theoretical and practical significance to analyzing the changes of foreign trade organization system and the reshaping microscopic subjects. Foreign trade control refers in general to the government's direct intervention in foreign trade activities, including various fields from macro to micro; it narrowly refers to the government-led foreign trade management system. Both the mercantilist policy of the capitalist countries and the national monopoly system of the traditional socialist countries, are within the scope of foreign trade control. The relaxation of foreign trade regulation generally refers to the process of trade liberalization. In the narrow sense, it is the process of decentralization of foreign trade, that is, from government-led to enterprise-oriented.

Before the reform and opening up, China's foreign trade system was based on mandatory planning, foreign trade ownership, leadership and management rights were all concentrated in the central government. The main form of the Chinese government's control over foreign trade is to restrict access and to limit the number of imports and exports. For those who engaged in government-encouraged economic activities are given the priority, and the government used domestic policy to encourage preferred trade activities; priority enterprises can achieve more protection.

The continuous advancement of China's economic system reform has increasingly solved the external constraints of relaxation of trade control, and the conditions for effective competition have gradually matured. The dilemma between the liberalization of foreign trade and the maintenance of business order is gradually being lifted. The principle of easing foreign trade regulation is: first, to reduce the entry barriers for foreign trade industry, so that the market share of state-owned foreign trade enterprises will decline and the entry of other business enterprises will become easier, thus, a competitive market structure will be formed; second, the elimination of supply bottlenecks and the gradual abolition of quotas, permits and other administrative interventions; third, to promote the privatization of foreign trade system. There are two main ways of privatization: one is the institutional innovation of property rights system of public-owned enterprises; the second is to allow the entry of private enterprises and to build foreign trade micro-foundations which is in line with market economy.

In the transition from the domestic market to the international market, the production and marketing organization of private production enterprises mainly depends on the transaction cost. The cost of any commodity can be divided into two parts: one is the production cost of the commodity itself; the other is a series of transaction costs for exchange activities. The transaction costs are: (1) the cost of research activities, that is, mutual search, and research on product quality and manufacturer credibility; (2) negotiation costs, that is, management costs during the bargaining process; (3) contract execution fees. In the past, manufacturing enterprises usually transferred the risk of export trade to foreign trade companies: the transaction costs of indirect export through foreign trade companies were the lowest, but the degree of control and profits were also the lowest. With the changes of market environment and the promotion of open economy, enterprises are increasingly absorbing export sales activities into their own organizational systems. With the increasing accumulation of cross-border operation experiences, as well as the establishment of private enterprise business reputation, the advantages and importance of choosing self-export mode are increasingly apparent.

The traditional subjects involved in international economic competition are state-owned professional foreign trade companies, which are the only way for production enterprises to enter the international market. The reform of foreign trade management system is the breakthrough for the reform of foreign trade system. The main body of foreign trade management evolved along the trajectory of national-local-enterprise, professional foreign trade companies have changed from original administrative appendages to intermediary service organizations, and the business model have gradually changed from acquisition system to agency system. Efficient trading system is eliminating various entry barriers in the competition process and can greatly improve the efficiency of China's foreign trade operations. The gradual decline of licenses, quotas and other foreign trade tools have exacerbated the fight for policy resources. From national monopoly business model to multi-level, multi-form foreign trade business, there has been a new pattern in which foreign trade enterprises, foreign-invested enterprises and production enterprises compete with each other. With the weakening of the traditional public ownership and the promotion of the non-public ownership, the institutional innovation in the field of foreign trade will become an effective form in the development of foreign trade operation subjects. This is outstandingly represented as the decentralization of foreign trade rights, as well as the continuous decline of the threshold for import and export.

There are important links between the changes of access conditions for foreign trade export market and the development of private enterprises in Zhejiang. In 1988 the state decided to give the production enterprises the right to import and export. However, due to policy constraints, private enterprises can only conduct foreign trade business through false collective, fake joint venture and other "wearing a hat" ways. On January 1, 1999, the pilot approach of giving private enterprises foreign trade import rights is promulgated and implemented, private enterprises began to obtain foreign trade rights. Private production enterprises whose registered capital is more than 5 million yuan, private scientific research institutes whose registered capital is more than 2 million yuan, and high-tech enterprises, and mechanical and electrical products manufacturing enterprises, are all in line with the declaration conditions; at the same time, to abolish original assessment criteria such as sales revenue and export supply. On July 10, 2001, the former Ministry of Foreign Trade and Economic Cooperation reduced the access restrictions on foreign trade in non-public sector and promulgated "relevant provisions on the management of import and export business qualification", unified the management of import and export business qualifications on all types of enterprises (foreign-invested enterprises, commercial materials, supply and marketing cooperatives enterprises, small trade enterprises, except for enterprises in special economic zones and Pudong New Area), and changed the import and export business qualification system into registration and approval system. In 2003, the Ministry of Commerce further relaxed the right to operate foreign trade, promulgated and implemented "the Notice on Adjusting the Standards and Approval Procedures for Import and Export Business", unified the management of import and export business qualification of domestic enterprises; for private enterprises whose registered capital is more than 500 000 yuan, they are in line with the declare conditions for import and export right.

The liberalization of foreign trade right is beneficial to more direct and more extensive participation in China's foreign trade activities for private enterprises, which will greatly promote the development of private enterprises. With the liberalization of foreign trade business right and the continuous relaxation of market access, the exports of private enterprises in Zhejiang province have developed rapidly. From 1999 to 2000, the number of enterprises in Zhejiang province who have been approved the right to operate foreign trade is about 2 500, which is two times the cumulative number of the first 20 years; among which, collective and private enterprises accounted for 4/5. By the end of October 2003, there were 9 573 production enterprises with import and export right, accounting for 81.3% of the total number of foreign trade enterprises within the province, of which 80% were private production enterprises (see Table 6 – 3). In October 2002, the monthly export volume of production enterprises exceeded that of professional foreign trade companies for the first time (see Table 6 – 4).

Table 6 – 3 Approval of foreign trade right in Zhejiang province

Type of enterprise	Cumulative number (until the end of October 2003)	New batch from January to October in 2003
Total	11 773	3 519
Distribution company	2 156	813
Foreign trade corporation	1 948	809
Commercial supply company	79	4
Manufacturing enterprise	9 573	2 702
Others	41	1

Source: statistics from Foreign Trade and Economic Office in Zhejiang.

Table 6 – 4 Comparison of the export of three types of companies in Zhejiang province

(unit: 100 Million douars)

Time	Specialized foreign trade enterprise	Self-production enterprise	Foreign-invested enterprise
March, 2002	7.58	5.80	7.10
October, 2002	9.10	9.17	8.08
April, 2003	10.96	12.02	10.42

Source: statistics from Foreign Trade and Economic Office in Zhejiang.

6.2.2 Institutional obstacles in the export of private enterprises

When private enterprises are entitled the access to import and export rights, they will enjoy same treatment as state-owned, collective self-employed import and export production enterprises; the bias of ownership and the inequality of foreign trade policy are gradually eliminated. However, from the perspective of creating a fair environment, there are still some institutional obstacles in the market environment, such as market access restriction, legal environment, export agency, intermediary organization, tax rebate system and national treatment.

1. Restrictions on market access

(1) The standards for private enterprises to obtain foreign trade circulation qualifications is higher than that of general state-owned enterprises.

The industry monopoly of foreign trade professional company still exists, which mainly allows the access for state-owned capital. The entry of foreign capital has begun to pilot. For example, Sino-foreign joint ventures foreign trade companies have been established in Shanghai Pudong, but the establishment of private professional foreign trade enterprises are still strictly limited. This kind of restrictions on market access is unfair to the development of private enterprises and does not conform to the unified rules of international trade.

(2) Private enterprises have not yet fully liberalized in the field of foreign investment and engineering contract.

The legitimate channels of "going out" for private enterprises are not smooth, thus restricting the initiatives for private economy to participate in foreign economic activities and restricting private enterprises to promote export trade through overseas investment. The approval of overseas investment projects in private enterprise has the characteristics of "many departments, complex procedures, low efficiency and long period".

(3) Entry barriers to domestic market.

Due to historical restrictions, there are still many restrictions on the development of private enterprises, including entry barriers to administrative access control, entry barriers to ownership discrimination, entry barriers to local protection, and entry barriers to administrative monopoly. The scope of industry which private enterprises are able to enter is relatively narrow, mainly concentrated in low-tech labor-intensive traditional industries, such as textiles, clothing, manufacturing, processing, catering, etc. However, oil, natural gas, mineral exploration, basic industries and other 30 industries have certain access restrictions on private enterprises. The entry barriers of the domestic market has led to the fact that the export products of private production enterprises can only concentrated in general trade and the market risk is huge. Taking Zhejiang as an example, private industrial enterprises are mainly concentrated in textile industry, clothing and other fiber products manufacturing, general machinery manufacturing, electrical machinery and equipment manufacturing, metal products industry and other manufacturing industries. In 2002, the total output value of these five industries respectively accounted for 21.6%, 8.1%, 7.7%, 7.3% and 6.1% of the total industrial output value. Under the impact of industrial structure, the export growth of private enterprises in Zhejiang province mainly come from general trade.

(4) Entry costs for export trade.

The entry costs for private enterprises to carry out import trade are: first, the cost of information. The information sources of private enterprises are relatively original and the comprehensive services provided by government departments is very limited, therefore, the export or overseas investments of private enterprises has certain blindness, which will increase the risk of foreign trade. From the perspective of information consultation and auxiliary system, the establishment and operation of the relevant government departments are mainly for state-owned enterprises, private enterprises will find it difficult to effectively obtain overseas economic information, business consulting and other services. Second, the cost of booths. The supply and distribution mechanism of the Canton Fair booth has made it impossible for private enterprises to participate in through formal channels. Some private enterprises have to buy stalls from state-owned enterprises through private transactions, which greatly increased the operating costs and risks. Third, the cost of bidding. The current tender and quota allocation system led to a serious shortage of supply of quotas for private enterprises. Private enterprises can only buy required quota indicator through underground transactions, which will significantly increase export costs. Fourth, financing costs. The difficulty in financing leads to high capital cost. Fifth, non-productive costs.

2. Legal environment

A good legal environment is the basis for the healthy development of enterprises. However, the effective coverage of existing laws on private enterprises is not enough and the legal protection of private enterprises is still insufficient. For example, the multilateral investment security system is a measure established by the government to protect the economic interests of enterprises' foreign investment. It is usually composed of government, insurance companies, mutual funds and specific enterprises. At present, the multilateral investment protection agreement led by China's government has covered few private enterprises and the overseas investment of private enterprises is difficult to get effective protection from government policies. Compared with foreign-funded enterprises, private enterprises lack the corresponding policy protection. In China, foreign-funded enterprises enjoy preferential policies that go beyond national treatment, while private enterprises are subject to non-national policy discriminations, the contrasts between them are clearly manifested in industry access and tax incentives. Therefore, private enterprises have greater difficulties in the process of moving to the international market.

In addition, the protection of intellectual property rights in private enterprises is not enough. Although some new products have applied for the design of the patent, but according to China's law, the process from application to formal approval, and to finally obtain a patent certificate, will generally take a year. Coupled with the weak awareness of intellectual property protection in domestic enterprises, these enterprises have suffered serious losses.

3. Export agency system

The foreign trade agency system of state-owned foreign trade companies has played a positive role in improving the overall efficiency and international competitiveness of the economy and promoting the development of import and export business. However, with the changes of foreign trade enterprises and private enterprises in organizational structure, production and business scope, activity function and other aspects, coupled with the adjustment of domestic policy, the drawbacks of foreign trade agency system have been increasingly obvious.

On July 10, 2001, the former Ministry of Foreign Trade and Economic Cooperation further reduced the access restrictions on foreign trade in non-public sector and promulgated "relevant provisions on the management of import and export business qualification", unified the management of import and export business qualifications on all types of enterprises (foreign-invested enterprises, commercial materials, supply and marketing cooperatives enterprises, small trade enterprises, except for enterprises in special economic zones and Pudong New Area), and changed the import and export business qualification system into registration and approval system. But for enterprises who apply for foreign trade circulation right and import and export right, the registered capital should not be less than three to five million yuan. As the development time is short and the production scale is small, the number of enterprises which can meet the application conditions is less. For those who don't have import and export right, it is necessary to invite state-owned foreign trade companies to carry out agents for them. However, the procedures are complicated, the time is long, the cost is high and the information is blocked; these have greatly inhibited the initiatives of small and medium-sized private enterprises to participate in foreign trade. At the same time, foreign trade companies have controlled the sources of intermediate products and the sales channels of final products. Therefore, small and medium-sized private enterprises are difficult to directly contact with foreign enterprises and cannot directly enter the international market; and the phenomenon of market "separation" emerged. These enterprises will eventually degenerate into the production workshop for state-owned foreign trade companies.

4. Intermediary organization service

Since more than 20 years of reform and opening up, China has established a number of foreign trade intermediary organizations, such as International Chamber of Commerce and the Import and Export Trade Associations and its member institutions; but the Import and Export Trade Associations are mainly divided from the industry authorities, it is not suitable to the intense international market competition. There is an urgent need to improve the service mode, enrich the service content, improve the organizational system, and establish an effective coordination and supervision mechanism. At present, China's foreign trade intermediary organizations have some main problems: First, as the coordinating intermediaries, export associations are over-reliant on administrative coordination measures and have taken on too much government functions. Second, the functions of the import and export chambers of commerce are unknown: lack of unified and standardized coordination system; enterprise self-discipline, industry self-discipline and other economic and legal coordination are weak; coordination scope is narrow, especially for non-quota management of commodities, coordination is not enough; the awareness of active service and quality service is not strong; the ability to provide full-service for government and enterprises is not enough, the timeliness and effectiveness of the service is poor. Members of the Chamber of Commerce are still dominated by state-owned foreign trade companies, foreign-funded enterprises and private manufacturing enterprises which account for more than 70% of China's foreign trade exports are excluded from the Chamber of Commerce. This seriously affected the functions of the

Chamber of Commerce. Third, the division of export associations is unreasonable and has not yet established a systematic, efficient coordination and service mechanism. In general, the existing foreign trade intermediary organizations mainly view state-owned foreign trade companies as the object of service, thus providing some institutional barriers for the development of private enterprises export. The existing industry associations still bear a large number of government functions, while the concern of development of private enterprises is not enough.

5. Financial support

Private enterprises in Zhejiang province are highly developed and the private capital is abundant. However, because the difficulty for small and medium-sized private enterprises to obtain loans, and the difficulty for banks to supervise private enterprise and protect creditor's right, the prospective borrowers of four major state-owned banks and some large commercial banks are mainly state-owned enterprises and large and medium-sized enterprises; In addition, due to the lack of small non-state-owned financial institutions and private financing channels, the issue of "financing difficulty" is quite prominent in small and medium-sized private enterprises. On the one hand, the banks are reluctant to loan; on the other hand, private enterprises which are urgent for funds cannot get loans. According to the nature of ownership, the output structure and financing structure is extremely asymmetric in Zhejiang province.

The financial system structure and related policy discrimination have limited the financing channels of private enterprises and the scale of foreign capital. The use of international capital markets and the development of Sino-foreign joint ventures are important means and ways for private enterprises to enhance their scale and strength, introduce advanced technology, improve management level and improve comprehensive competitiveness of the market. However, most of our private enterprises have started up, expanded and operated through self-financing or informal financing channels for a long time. The ratio of domestic bank loans and capital market financing is very low; the number of foreign capital which involved in private enterprises is quite small; and the amount of financing through international capital market, such as overseas listing and issuing bonds, is few, let alone credit businesses. The sample survey, which was conducted by State Economic and Trade Commission and the International Finance Corporation in 1999 on private enterprises in Beijing, Wenzhou and other cities, shows that only 3 to 4 private enterprises have been listed in domestic stock market and no companies have ever obtained capital from foreign capital markets. And 15% of companies plan to finance through the stock market, 23% of companies want to establish joint ventures with foreign companies, and 11% of them expressed the willingness to borrow money from foreign banks.

6. Export tax rebate system

From 1999 to 2002, the average annual growth rate of China's export tax rebate amount is 36.3%, while the actual growth rate of central government revenue over the same period is only 18.2%. According to the statistics of the State Council Development Research Center, by the end of 2002, the state's fiscal arrears of export tax rebate has reached 247.7 billion yuan; it is expected that by the end of 2003, the state's fiscal arrears of export tax rebate will exceed 340 billion yuan.

Private enterprises have to face up with double pressure caused by tax arrears, that is, cash flow dilemma and capital costs increase. In addition, the export tax rebate indicators are not sufficient, the export tax rebate rate is not stable, and the export tax rebate is seriously lagging behind in Zhejiang province. When tax department audit tax rebates, they always give priority to state-owned enterprises and foreign-funded enterprises, while private enterprises rank at the bottom. The lagging period of export tax rebate for private enterprises is up to a year and a half, which not only takes up a lot of money, but also increases operating costs. In the case of insufficient export credit, the lag of export tax rebate has led to cash flow difficulties; the incentives for small and medium-sized private enterprises to export are not sufficient; some companies have already compressed production and export scale to avoid increasing financial pressure. On October 13, 2003, the State Council issued a "decision on the reform of current export tax rebate mechanism": from January 1, 2004, China's average export tax rebate rate will be reduced by 3%. According to the investigation of Ministry of Commerce, if the export tax rebate rate decreases by 1%, the general trade export costs will increase by about 1% and the export growth rate will decline by 4.9%. But compared with the high amount of tax arrears, many private enterprises would rather take a small amount of export tax rebates to speed up the issuance of tax rebates to ease the financial pressure.

7. Unequal competitive environment

In the competition with the state-owned foreign trade companies, due to the unequal system, private enterprises are often subjected to low national treatment.

(1) It is more difficult for private enterprises to obtain quota for export commodities.

The export quota management in China is only for partial export commodities and is divided into active quota management and passive quota management. For those who have access to active quota management, they must be foreign trade enterprises, production enterprises or "foreign-funded" enterprises. Passive quota is mainly textile quota, its distribution principle is: the utilization of the first half of export quota, the price level, the contribution to textile exports and the implementation of textile quota requirements. Only enterprises who have textile operation right and export performance are eligible for application. In the face of strong state-owned enterprises and foreign-funded enterprises, private enterprises are mostly small and, generally lack of more than three years of export business performance, therefore, they cannot get quota commodity management rights. At the same time, to obtain the right to operate quota goods, they must also join the relevant import and export Chamber of Commerce.

(2) It is more difficult for private enterprises to obtain stalls in Canton Fair.

The annual turnover of the Canton Fair accounts for 1/3 of China's annual general trade exports, thus, it is an important way for professional foreign trade companies and production enterprises to expand overseas markets. Although the booth has been increasing in recent years, the total supply is still seriously inadequate. The allocation mode of the Canton Fair booth is planned distribution, resulting in inequality between private enterprises and state-owned enterprises, foreign companies, and limitations of the export channels of private enterprises. Among them, guarantee booths are used for high value-added enterprises (the annual export value is more than 50 million dollars); maintenance booths are used for foreign trade backbone enterprises with economies of scale and operating profitability (the annual export amount is more than 40 million dollars, while remote and poor provinces have to reach 15 million dollars); the first two types of booths are designated to large enterprises by the Ministry of Foreign Trade; exhibition booth is not suitable for distribution and is allocated by six chambers of commerce; allocation booths is assigned to the booth of the exhibitors by the trading group according to the current method, mainly for foreign trade companies and foreign-funded enterprises. In the 90th Canton Fair in 2001, the number of private enterprises among all exhibitors was less than 1% (except for Guangdong province).

6.2.3 Institutional supply in the export development of private enterprises

With the deepening of regional economic integration and China's formal accession into the WTO, the development of private economy is facing new market environment and development opportunities. At the same time, the development of private economy in Zhejiang province has begun to enter the critical stage of "second takeoff". In the process of developing an open economy and accelerating the export of private enterprises, Zhejiang should implement system supply and innovation from the aspects of enterprises, governments and intermediate organizations.

1. Enterprise level: to establish the basic status of private enterprises in the development of market economy and locating the focus of foreign trade activities on private production enterprises or groups.

(1) Establishment of a new type of foreign trade agency system.

Under the market economy conditions, production enterprises should consider comparative advantage and economic performance as criteria. On the one hand, production enterprises have strong advantages in production, technology, scientific research and other aspects; on the other hand, foreign trade companies have obvious advantages in customer, talents, information and other aspects; therefore, the combinations of industry and trade, skill and trade, technology and trade, will be an invincible path for various export enterprises in China to achieve complementary advantages, enhance overall competitiveness and be successful in international competitions. Production enterprises have the right to import and export, this does not mean that the export of every self-produced products and the import of raw materials and equipment should be operated on their own. In fact, the enterprises can choose proprietary trading or foreign trade companies under the premise of cost accounting. In this way, it will form a long-term economic relationship in the division of labor between industry and trade.

(2) Implement of brand competition strategy.

Core competence is the organic combination of core technology, enterprise management level, organizational learning ability and marketing strategy. In the face of brand-oriented international non-price competition, manufacturers should gradually cultivate core competitiveness, continuously improve the brand's reputation and market share, actively adopt international standards and international quality certification system, and enhance competitiveness; enterprises who has a certain scale, should carry out exclusive agent, conduct good after-sales service work, and expand export through the international chain network.

(3) Promotion of the "going out" international business strategy.

Private enterprises can use local advantages to organize production, carry out foreign materials processing and promote exports. Private production enterprise is based on marketing its own products. Through the formation of enterprise groups and the establishment of subordinate import and export companies, private production enterprises can make single products into a series of exports and promote the transformation to commodity business; some large self-employed enterprises should gradually set up subsidiaries or branches abroad, engage in direct foreign investment, and practice China's international strategy in the process of constantly seeking dynamic comparative advantages and competitive advantages.

2. Government level: to achieve innovation of foreign trade management system and establish foreign trade and economic promotion system which is in line with WTO rules.

In accordance with the principle of "norm, unity, efficiency, service, transparency", we should establish an efficient government management system, which is in line with the requirements of the WTO, to provide convenient and thoughtful service for private enterprises to participate in international competitions.

(1) Reform of foreign trade administration system.

In the macro-management system of foreign trade and economic cooperation in Zhejiang province, responsible institutions at all levels should regulate in accordance with the requirements of open market economy, weaken administrative intervention on micro-economy, strengthen indirect macro-management, strengthen the guidance of foreign trade and economic planning, policy guidance, administrative services and supervision, change the government priority from approval and management of specific matters to planning and policies of foreign economic and trade development, so as to create a better institutional environment. The relevant policies, such as the quota for import and export commodities, should be standardized and published in the form of government announcements. In order to jointly create a better environment for the development of private enterprise, the government should strengthen the sense of service, strengthen the coordination and cooperation with customs, immigration inspection and quarantine, taxation and other departments, and implement unified and transparent policies and administrative rules.

(2) Establishment of foreign trade and economic promotion system.

Specifically, first, to use tax rates, exchange rates, interest rates and other economic means to adjust foreign trade and economic activities, so that unnecessary administrative power will gradually withdraw from the market; to improve the export tax rebate mechanism to achieve full and timely tax rebates; to ensure that private enterprises and other enterprises are treated equally without discrimination. Second, to establish and improve the export credit system, to adjust the use of foreign trade development fund, to establish a synchronous growth mechanism for export growth and credit scale, and to provide necessary financial support for small and medium-sized private production enterprises to expand exports; to expand the scale and field of export credit insurance and to provide a comprehensive policy of investment and trade insurance business for private enterprises; to establish export enterprises financing guarantee fund to solve the problem of insufficient financing. Third, to provide quality service and policy support for enterprises in Zhejiang province in terms of foreign exchange management and foreign affairs management. Fourth, to take some financial support measures. Such as the implementation of export subsidies to optimize export structure and expand export scale; the foreign trade and financial sector should give some subsidies for enterprises to participate in overseas exhibition booths; to encourage brand competition.

(3) Achievement of both inside and outside development strategy.

In terms of external opening up, it should improve the degree of regional economic openness; in terms of internal opening, it should view private capital and private enterprises as the main body and carrier, actively promote the integration process of Yangtze River Delta and achieve active regional development strategy. Among them, the internal opening-up policy of strengthening the integrated linkage of the Yangtze River Delta is an important component in the formation of a high-level, multi-field and all-round policy system in Zhejiang private economy.

3. Intermediate organization level: to establish industry associations and chambers of commerce organizations, and to improve foreign trade intermediary service system.

With the breakout of the national foreign trade monopoly system, the relationship between the government and the enterprise has changed: the government will indirectly manage enterprises through economic means and legal means, which objectively requires the establishment of an intermediate link between macro-management and micro-business to provide coordination services and prevent the order of foreign trade from getting out of control. Since the industry associations and intermediary organizations cannot provide coordination and services needed for the development of private economy, thus a new "bottom-up" intermediary organization, that is, civilian chamber of commerce, has come into being and taken on the functions of industry associations and intermediary organizations in Zhejiang province. The civilian chamber of commerce, which is characterized by civil autonomy, service and specialization, represents the overall interests of the industry and maximizes the overall interests of the whole industry or group by coordinating the relationships between concerned parties. Since the establishment of the first batch of civilian chamber of commerce in 1988, it has been 15 years. These gradually improved civil society organizations, are key factors which promote the prosperity and development of private economy and the rapid growth of private enterprises in Zhejiang province. Therefore, we should learn from the experience of Zhejiang, promote the reform of chambers of commerce and associations, modify the Anti-Unfair Competition Law and the Anti-monopoly Law, and give certain "monopoly" immunity to the chambers of commerce, associations and other organizations in export trade. In the meantime, we should focus on the cultivation of the following functions:

At present, the world's foreign trade promotion intermediaries and their activities include: (1) associations, the main activities are advisory and consultants, small seminars, trade promotion and communications; (2) Chamber of Commerce, which is working as a cooperative and coordinating body for the import and export of similar commodities, the activities are coordination, supervision and arbitration; (3) trade fairs; (4) trade delegations, business tours and project missions; (5) professional firms, consulting services companies. Intermediary organizations are working as bridges and links between the government and enterprises, enterprises and enterprises. They provide coordination services, design programs, protocol strategies, assess credit and promote negotiations, and they implement self-management and self-restraint within member companies in the organization. In the future, we should further promote the reform of import and export chambers of commerce, develop the information service function of research and consulting institutions, and provide the following services for private export enterprises: product and market exploitation, including information service trade, foreign market and opportunity analysis, market information intelligence preparation, export promotion project design; export management support, including marketing management, transportation and packaging management, export service management, the provision of support staff in foreign trade fair, organization of vendors delegation; other services, such as small and medium-sized private enterprise support projects, professional skills training services and quality standards control services.

In the future, trade associations should change their functions as soon as possible: from an administrative role that focuses on management and control, to an economic community with the functions of coordination, negotiation and industry constraints. To fully play the role of industry associations and strengthen the pre-filing counseling work; to improve the industrial damage warning mechanism and to play its service function to the industry and enterprises; to strengthen the external contact and exchange, and gradually establish contact system with relevant national institutions; to strengthen the contact with relevant agencies in WTO, and actively participate in dispute settlement. And strive to make the industry association a true self-disciplined organization, to play its role in protecting domestic industry and supporting domestic enterprises to enhance international competitiveness.

4. Construction of foreign trade and economic information service system to provide platform for the innovation of foreign economic and trade system.

(1) To start online projects for export enterprises, to support and guide private export enterprises to carry out international e-commerce, to promote enterprises to take the road of information.

To help enterprises to develop international market and expand online transactions. To speed up the construction of large-scale e-commerce trading platform between domestic and foreign enterprises to help enterprises to establish a relatively reliable and stable trade supply and demand chain, and enhance the ability of enterprises to obtain business information. To jointly solve the problems in the e-commerce process such as electronic payment, foreign exchange settlement, tax and other issues and to build a good e-commerce environment with the help of customs, banks, foreign exchange administrations, tax and other department. To improve the logistics environment in e-commerce, establish a foreign trade transport network, simplify the transaction process and reduce transaction costs.

(2) To improve the e-government system of government departments such as foreign trade and economic cooperation.

To establish and improve the network systems and automation systems, establish an efficient and convenient communication feedback mechanism between government and enterprises, improve policy transparency, management efficiency and service levels, strengthen the construction of important databases, provide timely and accurate policies and regulations, business information, market conditions and other comprehensive information services for import and export enterprises.

References

1. Jin Rongxiang etc. Joining WTO and Zhejiang's Economic System Innovation. Zhejiang University Press, 2001.

2. Jin Rongxiang etc. Research on Zhejiang Specialized Industrial Area during the Process of Industrialization. Working paper, 2002.

3. Jin Rongxiang. Problems and Countermeasures in the Process of Product Differentiation in Zhejiang Province. Wenzhou Forum, 2003 (4).

4. Liang Neng. International Business. Shanghai People's Publishing House, 1999.

5. Lin Yifu, Li Yongjun. Export and China's Economic Growth: Demand-oriented Analysis. China Economic Quarterly, 2003 (3): 779 – 794.

6. Stigler G. J. Industrial Organization and Government Regulation. Shanghai Joint Publishing, 1989.

7. Sun Zao, Lu Zhengwei. From Government to Enterprise: A Literature Review of Chinese Private Enterprises. Economic Research Journal, 2003 (4): 79 – 87.

8. Yang Shengming. The Frontier of China's Foreign Trade Theory. Social Sciences Academic Press, 1999.

Part Ⅲ

Evaluation and Countermeasure of Private Economy and Enterprise Development

Chapter 7

Evaluation on the Governance of Private Listed Companies

Chinese private economy has experienced a rapid development since China's entry into the WTO, and the quantity and quality of private enterprises have also achieved great breakthroughs with the institutional form evolving from single ownership or corporation to joint-stock form. In 1992, Huayuan industrial co. , LTD in Shenzhen initiated by Huayuan electronic technology co. , LTD went listed in Shenzhen Stock Exchange as the first private listed company, marking the Chinese private companies (PCs) entering into a new era of cooperate governance. The number of private listed company (PLC) in Shenzhen and Shanghai Stock Exchanges has reach 197 until the end of 2006.

There is a significant phenomenon in the group of the increasing number of PLCs, which is their performance and ROI have been decreasing since going public. According to Table 7 - 1, the performance of PLCs fluctuates to some degree and exhibits a decreasing trend overall from fore-and-aft look. The ROEWA and the EPSWA drop from 0. 3956 Yuan and 13. 44% in 1993 to 0. 0674 Yuan and -0. 8051% in 2004 respectively, marking a great decrease. Crosswise comparing, the ROEWA of PLCs outnumbered that of the total public companies before 2000, but the situation reversed after 2001 and the EPSWA experienced similar change. Xie & Xie (2003) demonstrated that the overall performance of PLCs was lower than that of Non-PLCs and not higher than the state-owned listed companies (SOLCs) under the current market conditions. Zhang & Zhang (2003) argued that PLCs had advantages in operation situation, profit, capital structure and market evaluation but of varying quality and faced greater risk (see Table 7 - 1).

Table 7 – 1 Overall performance (average) of PLCs and comparison with total Listed companies

Year	ROEWA (Yuan)		EPSWA (%)	
	Total	Private	Total	Private
1993	0.33	0.3956	13.55	13.44
1994	0.32	0.4720	14.06	14.96
1995	0.25	0.3862	10.8	14.15
1996	0.23	0.2938	9.59	11.31
1997	0.2726	0.2828	11	11.37
1998	0.1993	0.2349	7.97	9.69
1999	0.2069	0.2417	8.31	10.42
2000	0.1754	0.2170	6.95	8.71
2001	0.1369	0.0420	5.56	1.76
2002	0.1481	0.096	5.82	3.22
2003	0.1953	0.128	7.37	4.63
2004	0.1421	0.0674	4.59	-0.8051
2005	0.1434	0.0683	4.23	-0.7702

Notes: data sources include PLCs Dataset of Nankai University, Xie & Xie (2003), Xie & Lu (2004) and annual reports of relevant Listed companies.

The direct factor of corporate performance is market competition. PLCs come from family companies or privatized medium and small SOEs, which generally running in competitive industries. Compared to the government reliant non PLCs with advantages in resource capturing, this might jeopardize the improvement of their performance. Nonetheless, PLCs have stronger entrepreneurship since they have solved the problems of unclear property right and owner's absence existing in SOEs, which will offset the negative impact of the external environment. Therefore, it is necessary to shift the study view to the organizational factors affecting the performance of PLCs. Xie & Xie (2003) used to propose that the agent problem between big and small stock holders derived from equity division influenced the improvement of corporate performance but did not explore further into the mechanisms. Xie & Wu (2003) examined the relationship between governance structure and performance using the sample of 276 PLCs in Shenzhen and Shanghai, concluded the negative correlation between the positions of controlling shareholders in the border of directors and corporate value. These studies suggest that the corporate governance (CG) of PLCs has turning into an organizational factor not to be neglected, which is a problem need to be solved in the growing process of PCs.

It is considered that the PCs have found their ecological niche (Hannan & Freeman, 1998) after going public, which is a process of delaminating uncertainty from external environment. The problem of adaption to the change of environment through the adjustment of internal organizational factors has become a vital factor, in which CG plays a key role and the trouble here will decrease the adaptive capability of the organization. Tang (2002) indicated that the nepotism out of the absence of mechanism to trust in external people existing in PCs will increase the opportunity cost of employment, weakening the organizational adjustment capability, where the sound governance institution is the base of trust in outsiders. Chu (2002) analyzed the organizational closeness of PCs from the perspective of information capture and demonstrated that the owner would not authorize the non-family manager access to the whole information which weakened the organizational efficiency. However, there was another situation that the non-family manager might set up another company as a competitor once he has the access, which resulted in the serious principle agent problem between family and non-family members. Recent studies suggest that the principle agent problem existed inside the family of PLCs. For instance, Wang & Gu (2004) studied 94 PLCs empirically and found that at the beginning of PLCs development, the contractual governance played a positive role and the altruism resulted in the agent problem among family members which affected the organizational efficiency. Wang & Zhou (2006) examined the negative impact of altruism on corporate performance in PLCs.

The theoretical and empirical analysis around PLCs suggest that the CG of PLCs is a complex topic to be explored thoroughly. The complexness lies in the multiple-agent problem derived from the multiple stake holders' network and the absence of clear and comprehensive knowledge of the internal mechanism behind the scene right now. Consequently, it is important to evaluate the CG mechanism of PLCs, discover and conclude the specific law as the logical starter to treat the essential nature of their governance appropriately.

7.1 Analytical framework of corporate governance for private listed companies

The listing of Shenhuayuan (000014) in 1992 marked the birth of the first PLC in China. The PC Xiwang Group went listed after transforming into joint-stock enterprises (Xinxiwang, 000876), marking a substantial breakthrough for PCs' entry into stock market and the increasing of the numbers, while the listing of PCs is still restricted by quota management. Since 2000, the way of listing changed from examination and authorization to approval system, prompting the market oriented reform of stock issuing system, offering sound institutional environment for PCs' listing and the PLCs entered a fast track of growing.

7.1.1 Basic characteristics of private companies

1. Existence of multiple ways of listing

There are three ways for PCs to go listed, namely Initial Public Offering (IPO), Reverse Merger (RM) and Management Buyout (MBO). Before 1997, IPO nominated as the major way for the listing of PCs when the stock market was oriented to solve the financing problem for SOEs and the entry barrier was high for PCs with only 4.24% of PLCs in the total listed companies. PCs generally are faced with financing constraints and have great eagerness for the direct financing of stock market. RM got adopted as a new method to go public by some PCs to overcome the barrier of IPO. PCs have started to do this since 1994 and the number has grown gradually since 1997. With the strategic adjustment of state-owned economy and the implementation of invigorating large enterprises while relaxing control over small ones strategy, some medium and small SOEs launched privatization reform through MBO and PCs started to go public by the same way after 1999, while the ratio remained low due to the absence of relevant law and regulation and the detailed way of implementation remains to be discussed further.

Table 7-2 describes the development path of PLCs from 1992 to 2002. During this decade, the number of PLCs grew with a high annual rate of 83.3%. Among these 197 PLCs, 71 of them went public by IPO, accounting for 36%, 6 by MBO with 3% and 120 by RM with 61%.

Table 7-2 Development of the PLCs 1992-2002

Year	IPO	RM	MBO	Total	Number of listed companies	Number of PCs	Ratio of PCs
1992	1	0	0	1	53	1	1.89
1993	2	0	0	2	183	3	1.64
1994	4	2	0	6	291	9	3.09
1995	0	0	0	0	323	9	2.79
1996	10	4	0	14	530	23	4.24
1997	9	12	0	21	745	44	5.91
1998	5	22	0	27	851	71	8.34
1999	9	22	2	33	949	104	10.96

continued

Year	IPO	RM	MBO	Total	No. of Listed Companies	No. of PCs	Ratio of Pcs
2000	18	23	2	43	1 088	146	13. 42
2001	12	10	1	23	1 160	169	14. 57
2002	2	25	1	28	1 224	197	16. 09

Source: Zhang & Zhang (2004).

2. Characteristics of the pan-family control

The color of family firm is dense in Chinese PCs and family share accounts for a big part after going public generally (See Figure 7 – 1). For instance, Tiantong Holdings was the first to go public controlled by the status of natural person, where Guangtong Pan and his son Jianqing Pan held the 21. 48% shares totally turning into the biggest shareholder and became the actual controller of the company through reformation.

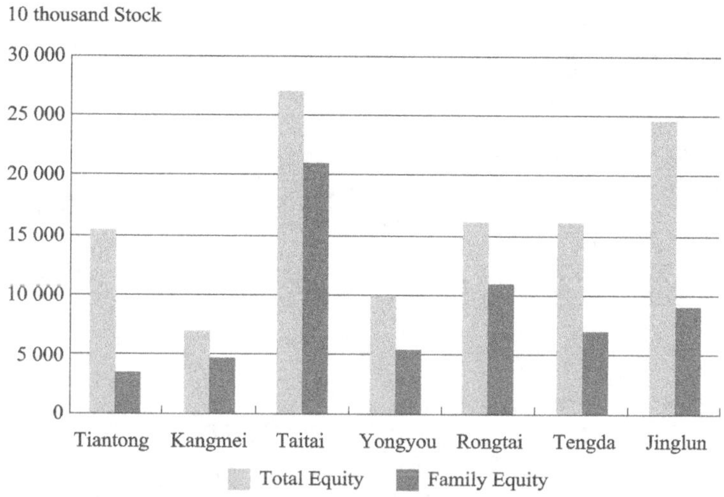

Figure 7 – 1 Ratios of the family held shares in total shares for several PLCs

The PLCs exhibit the characteristic of family control in this situation. Family shareholders perform their decision-making right more actively, hence the president or manager of PLCs are usually the direct delegate of the majority shareholder or himself, unifying the interest of manager and shareholders. In the meanwhile, PLCs can solve the problem of owner's absence in SOEs and minimize the moral hazard of managers, achieving the rigid constraint of budget. According to relevant statistics, the average LEV of PLCs is 23%, far below that of state-holding listed companies which is 40%, implying that the invest risk of PLCs is lower. Therefore, the agency cost emphasized by the mainstream principle agent problem is pretty low. Meanwhile, the majority positions in boards of directors, supervisors and managers are held by family shareholders or related family members, endowing the family control entity of PLCs dual characteristic of capital and personnel unification (see Table 7 –3).

In the meantime, to strengthen the control power, PLCs may exclude the entry of non-family members in to the core management level. For example, the board of directors are all family members after the retirement of two former directors in a PLC named Zhejiang Glass listed in Hong Kong GEM. What's more, the phenomenon of chain directors is very normal in PLCs, which means the executives of directors and supervisors hold the position of executives in the related companies. Based on this, PLCs and their related companies consist of the company group with its extent and density growing.

Table 7 –3 Family control situation of certain PLCs

Name	Family member	Position	Shareholding ratio (%)	Way of holding
Guangdong Rongtai	Yang	Chairman of the Board	37.5	Indirect
	Piao Suojuan (wife)	—		
	Li Linkai (son in law)	Vice Chairman of the Board, General Manager	27.81	
	Yang Hejing (daughter)	Supervisor	1.88	
	Huang Mian (son in law)	ViceGeneral Manager		
Jiankangyuan	Zhu Baoguo	Chairman of the Board	47.54	Indirect
	Liu Guangxia (wife)	ViceChairman of the Board	4.90	
	Liu Miao (mother)	Shenzhen Sales Deputy Manager	19.19	
	Zhu Baoan (younger brother)	Director	2.33	
Tiantong Holdings	Pan Guangtong	Chairman of the Board	11.03	Direct
	Pan Jianqing (son)	Vice Chairman of the Board and General Manager	10.45	
	Pan Meijuan (daughter)	Shenzhen Sales Deputy Manager	1.35	
	Pan Jianzhong (son)	Purchasing Department of Raw Materials Procurement Deputy Manager	1.20	
	Du Haili (daughter in law)	General Manager Office Vice Director	0.89	
Chuanhua Holdings	Xu Guanju	Chairman of the Board	24.58	Direct
	Xu Guanju	Director	14.71	
	Xu Chuanhua (father)	—	13.75	

Data source: Zhang Jianwei, "Political Structure, Guanxi Network and Governance Reconstructing of Stock Market" and other relevant materials.

3. Generally adoption of group governance structure

Some of the PLCs in China transit from the way that manager holds the major share or MBO during the process of the SOE privatization, and others from IPO or RM of PCs. The capital constraint faced by the owners of either kind of PLCs is very different from that of the agent of state-owned capitals supported by administrative resources and they are faced with more uncertainties of operational environment. Therefore, under the orientation of overcoming resource reliance and contracting environment, PCs have stronger motivation to go public and the group structure is a vital method in this process, which refers to that investors construct the control status through multiple layers of holding and cross holding.

Group structure can generate leverage effect on resource control, which means the lawful control right can be obtained by the ownership formed by minority shareholdings rather than majority holdings and to control massive wealth. As the example in Berle & Means (1932), the Swolingen Brothers control eight first grade rail firms of 2 billion dollars value through the control of investment of less than 20 million dollars. Fuguang Huang & Yinfeng Qi (2001) proved that the higher level of group control, the leverage effect stronger. Hence, it is a key method for PCs to break through the resource reliance employing the leverage effect of group structure and it is good to reduce invest risk and manage the uncertainties of the environment through the group control form of cross holding and multiple-layer holding. Therefore, family group control is common in PLCs, such as the Delong Group. The Tangs' Four Brothers constructed a complex group governance structure through purchase of stock of Xinjiangtunhe, Xianghuoju, Hejintouzi and STzhongyan between 1996 and 2001, embedding their governance structures into the group network based on family control.

Group control has been criticized a lot since 1990 due to the inefficiency of resource allocation (Scrfstein & Stein, 2000). Especially in the Asian family firms group, Shleifer & Vishny (1997) indicated that dominant family controls multiple public companies through family firms on top of the group directly or indirectly and executive management behavior, shifting the agency problem from between owners and managers to dominant family shareholders and medium and small shareholders, especially when dominant shareholders hold minority shares, they will adopt management encroachment to pursue family goal and private interest. While Morck & Yeung (2004a, 2004b) suggest further that the agency problem of dominant family shareholders in group structure is more severe than normal manager agency problem in general corporate governance, since managers in the latter are constrained by capital and production markets where hostile takeover, shareholder's lawsuit and accountability will force their demission, while in family group structure, when the direct or indirect share of family exceeds 50% , there will be conspiracy between the dominant shareholders and managers usually due to the existence of family contract and powerful control from family shareholders. However, medium and small shareholders are not able to dismiss the dominant shareholders and managers when they betray their own interest, invalidating the governance mechanism of the above companies.

Family group control will intrigue the generation of tunneling (Johnson & La Porta, 2002), referring to that under the authorization of dominant family, asset transfer in favor of family interest will happen among the internal companies, transferring company asset with cash flow directed to social shareholders to member companies with cash flow directed to dominant family shareholders. The root of tunneling derives from two sources of individual and organizational ones. On the one hand, the inheritor of dominant family prefer to employ his own wealth and influence to gain competitive advantage through the embezzlement of the interest of external small shareholders and political rent-seeking since entrepreneurship and endowment are not able to be inherited (Morck & Yeung, 2003).

On the other hand, group structure has effect on the interest structure of dominant family. For example, Johnson & La Porta (2000) suggested that the bigger bias of control from cash flow right, the more motivation dominant family has to pursue private benefit.

7. 1. 2 Agency relationships in private licted companies

1. Triple-ring model in the agency relations of family companies

From a more broad view, either kind of PLC is a pan-family enterprise (Li, 2005). The triple-ring model of family companies' governance constructed by Tagiurihe & Davis (1982) offers a referential framework to analyze the agency problem in PLCs. In Figure 7 – 2, the above ring indicates owners, the below left one family members and below right managers. F indicates pure family members, O pure owners, M pure managers, FO family owners, FM family managers, OM external owners and managers, FOM family owners and managers.

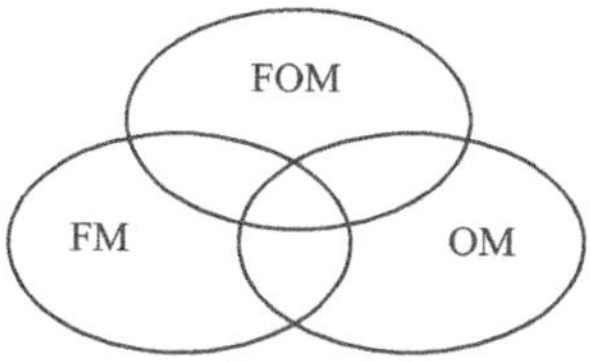

Figure 7 – 2 Triple-ring model of the family companies' governance

Source: Tagiuri, R. & J. Davis, 1982, "Bivalent attributes of the family firms", working paper, Harvard Business School, Cambridge, MA.

The following agency relations in family companies can be summarized based on the triple-ring model: (1) The agency relation between FO, FOM and FM; (2) The agency relation between dominant FO, FOM and other FOM, FM; (3) The agency relation between FO, FOM, FM and M; (4) The agency relation between FO, FOM and O, OM; (5) The agency relation between O, OM and FOM, FM; (6) The agency relation between O and M; (7) The agency relation between FOM, FM and M.

2. Complex agency relationship in Chinese PLCs

The agency problem in Chinese PLCs lies between dominant shareholders and medium and small ones (the forth type) and among family members (the first and second types). Shao & Tian (2005) analyzed a sample of 114 PLCs empirically and found that cases with agency problem between dominant shareholders and medium and small shareholders account for 31.3% of the total problems, those between owners and managers (the fifth type) 7.83%, while the cases with high centralization of ownership, control right and management 57%. The authors concluded that most PLCs did not meet the requirements of modern company institutions which are the most agency cost-saving and efficient governance mode based on the mainstream principle-agent model. Going back to the triple-ring model, we can find this kind of analysis overlooked the internal agency problem among family members. Shultze et al. (2001) concluded that there is agency problem among internal family members due to altruism and the self-control problem of the owners through an empirical study of 1 376 family companies.

It is in favor of foster loyalty of each other and making commitment to the long-term goal of the company, reducing agency cost to bring the altruism from family to

PLCs for family members. Altruism will encourage each family member hired by the family company playing as the actual owner of the company and entitles them with faith to possess the residual claimant right of the family asset, which helps employ the internal human resources, private savings and external social capital of family members. Thanks to altruism, principle and agent have perfect dual altruism and regard the interest of each other as his own as stewardship theory suggests that family agent will act as owners wholeheartedly. However, Schultz et al. (2000, 2002, 2003a) argued that after the initial period of company, especially when it went public, altruism would turn into reverse altruism, i. e. the agency problems of family agent free-riding, self-control and so on. In the meanwhile, they would result in complicated agency problems mixed with the control of owners and managers, which would offset the saving of altruism.

Therefore, there are more complex agency relations in Chinese PLCs. How these complex agency relations will affect the governance structure of the public companies? What characteristics and rules will be exhibited in the governance structure? These are all challenging topics to confront studying PLCs.

7.1.3 Governance structure, ultimate controller's behavior and enterprise performance: theoretical framework

The analysis of the question of how to influence the behavior of the ultimate controller and how to influence the governance structure of the listed companies after the formation of group control in private listed companies will more correctly grasp the internal mechanism of the group control. As the starting point of the question, the utility function of the subject determines the behavior choice.

1. Revenue structure, revenue cost and UC behavior

The revenue structure of UC in listed companies includes two parts: one is control right revenue and the other is benefits of cash flow. Control right revenue refers to the total value the UC possesses through the execution of the control right on the public company, including self-transaction, the employment of opportunities from the company, the revenue from insider trading, excessive reward, perquisite consumption and so on (Grossman & Hart, 1988), which are defined by Dyck and Zingales (2001) that the revenue is only entitled to the UC and not shared by the medium and small shareholders. Benefits of cash flow refers to the dividend income through holding the stock of the company. Plenty of studies argued that when control right revenue consisted the majority of the UC's revenue, his behavior would exhibit strong encroachment effect and supervision effect would stand out otherwise. The studies of La Porta (1998) proved that the benefits of cash flow of the dominant shareholders helped increase the value of company and medium and small shareholders could thumb a lift from the effort of supervision (supervision effect), while they would be encouraged to choose tunneling behavior when the control right revenue grew, jeopardizing the value of the listed company (encroachment effect). Therefore, it is possible to distinguish whether the behavior of the UC possesses supervision or encroachment effect through comparing his revenue from control right and cash flow.

For the UC of the PLC, the behavior choice is the result of maximizing his own utility. The nature of the major shareholder of private ownership determines that he neither pursue pure control right revenue nor cash flow one, but rather their combination. Therefore, the utility function is $u\ (R_x,\ R_y)$, R_x and R_y are control right and benefits of cash flow respectively①, and there is due to the constraint of resource, referring to that the increasing of revenue from control right will decrease that from cash flow.

The UC is faced with the following problem:

$$\begin{aligned} & \max u(R_x, R_y) \\ s.t.\quad & c_1 R_x + C_2 R_y \leqslant I \\ & R_x > 0 \\ & R_y > 0 \end{aligned}$$

Hereby I is the resource invested by the UC of the PLC, $C_1R_x + C_2R_y \leqslant I$ indicates the resource constraint he confronts with. There is certain cost when obtaining revenue either he has control right or management right (Burkart, Gromb & Panunzi, 1997) and C_1、C_2 are the effort (cost) he has to make to obtain one unit of control right or benefits of cash flow respectively. In this way, it reaches the optimized utility equilibrium point on the point of tangency of utility and constraint curves.

Figure 7 – 3 describes that how to get the equilibrium revenue for the UC. To analyze the endogeneity of his behavior objectively, we assume that the preferences for both revenue are the same, i. e. the utility curves are symmetry around OB where

---

① Due to the scarcity of the listed company shell, the ultimate controller of PLCs generally has a strong incentive to keep the shell, who pursues that the upper limitation of control right revenue is to keep benefits of cash flow above zero. The ultimate controller will turn losses through earnings management when there is loss report. Therefore, it is assumed that $R_y > 0$ and obviously, $R_x > 0$.

OB curve is the track where two kinds of revenue equal. Given to the assumed conditions, the left side of OB is encroachment effect dominant part and the right side is supervision effect dominant part. AB is the resource constraint curve. When the UC put all the resource into the attainment of controller right revenue, he will get I/C_1 unit of revenue, while I/C_2 unit when into benefits of cash flow. When the equilibrium point is E_1, i. e. the behavior of the UC corresponding to the encroachment effect part, $I/C_1 > I/C_2$, i. e. $C_2 > C_1$, which means that benefit-cost is the main factor of his behavior choice. In the case that external pressure forced him to choose E_2, the equilibrium would not be stable since the utility level would be decreased despite of the positive effect. As long as $C_1 < C_2$, the UC would pursue more control right revenue to achieve the maximum of his utility, which would generate stronger encroachment effect.

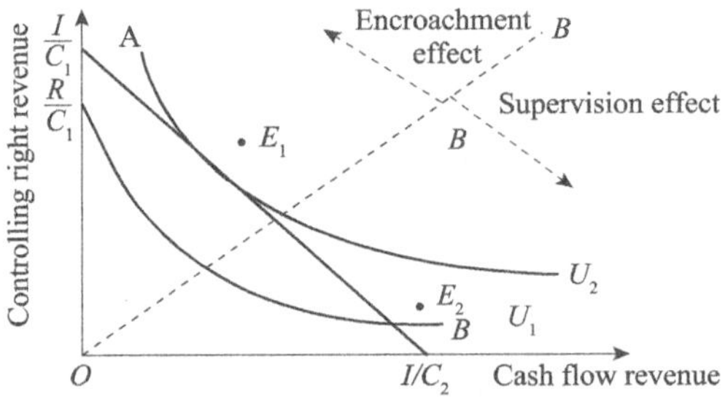

Figure 7 - 3 Revenue equilibrium model

The impact on benefit-cost comes from the intensity of external supervision and market competition factor (Nickell, 1996) as well as the internal organizational aspect of the UCs in PLCs, including group control, governance structure and so on. The impact of group control and governance structure on benefit-cost will be emphasized in the following part, which will relate them through benefit-cost analysis.

2. Impact of group control on the UC's behavior

In the group control structure, the control right revenue from one unit of resource input outweighs that of the benefits of cash flow due to the bias between control right and cash flow right (La Porta, 1999)①, i. e. $C_1 < C_2$ and the input to produce one unit of control right revenue is less than that of benefits of cash flow, hence $I/C_1 >$

① According to the computing method proposed by La Porta (1999), control right is CON = min ($\alpha_1, \alpha_2, \cdots, \alpha_n$), $\alpha_1, \alpha_2, \cdots, \alpha_n$ are the share ratio of each company on the control chain. Benefits of cash flow is CASH = $\Pi\alpha_i$ ($i = 1, 2, \cdots, n$) and i is the control layer. Under the condition of group control, CON > CASH with the growing of control layers is called the bias between control right and cash flow right.

I/C_2. At this moment, the revenue structure curve of the UC in the PLC runs as AB in Figure 7 – 3. Under the given resource constraint, the UC's utility reaches the max level of U_2 at the point of E_1, when E_1 lies on the left of OB, indicating that his behavior implies strong encroachment effect. In the case that the UC choose the behavior with positive externality, as at E_2, the utility level U_1 ($U_1 < U_2$), he would not achieve the maximization of the utility. Therefore, E_1 is the rational choice. It is thus evident that, in the group control structure, with the increasing of the bias between control right and cash flow right, the cost of control right revenue runs lower, the motivation for the UC to choose encroachment behavior is stronger and will jeopardize the performance of the company. In other words, with the decreasing of the cost C_1 for control right revenue in Figure 7 – 3, the equilibrium point E_1 runs further from OB and the encroachment effect of the UC is stronger.

3. Comprehensive impact of governance structure and group control on the behavior of the UC

Well governance structure can restrain the behavior of the UC. The factors of equity structure and board structure will be introduced on the base of group control in this part and the impact of governance structure in PLCs on the UC's behavior in the condition of group control will be discussed.

From the perspective of the public company only, according to the theory of check-and-balance ownership structure, it is not easy to generate check and balance power for centralized equity structure and the cost for the controlling shareholders to introduce projects in favor of increasing control right revenue but inefficient for the company will be reduced, increasing the private revenue of control right. With the existence of multiple majority shareholders, the check and balance between them will increase the cost for the control right revenue and force them to adopt the behavior of supervision effect (Gomes & Novaes, 2005). Plenty of empirical studies indicate that the more average of the distribution of major shareholders, the stronger of the check and balance power generated (Laeven & Levine, 2004; Maury & Pajuste, 2005). Yet the endogeneity of equity structure implies that whether the equity distribution is centralized or decentralized depends on the goal of the utility maximization of the controlling shareholders. Generally speaking, equity structure is the choice of controlling shareholders between the revenue from stock market liquidity generated by equity decentralization and that from the effective supervision on managers generated by equity centralization, which is the tradeoff between risks taking and controlling.

Existing empirical studies on relation between equity structure and CP overlooked the factor of group control generally. As shown in Figure 7 – 4, from the perspective of equity check and balance, for Beijing Yongyou, which is the biggest shareholder of the listed company Yongyou Software, the other several major shareholders are able to exert powerful constraining force on him. However, these shareholders are the persons acting in concert with Beijing Yongyou, which are all subject to the same UC Jingwen Wang, excluding the existence of check and balance power.

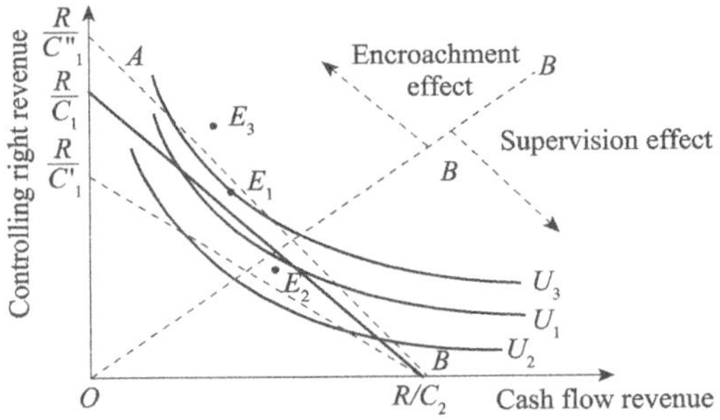

Figure 7 – 4 Movement of the equilibrium revenue

The UC choose the following equity structure for the sake of controlling the listed company effectively and spreading risks autonomously, where there are several major shareholders called the internal shareholder group subject to one UC and other major ones not related to him called the external shareholder group.

Under the condition of group control, the UC will take the action of positive effect when the power of the external shareholder group is strong, as Nickell, Nicolistas & Dryden (1997) proposed that the external shareholder group performed better than the internal one to make sure of realization of the value maximization goal, when the equilibrium point of the UC moves from E_1 to E_2 and the utility level drops from U_1 to U_2. Nevertheless, when the internal group accounts for the major ratio or the major shareholders are subject to the same UC, the factor of equity check and balance which will increase the cost will be no longer in existence and reduce the cost of benefits of control instead, which will reinforce the encroachment behavior. The UC will move his equilibrium point of behavior from E_1 to E_3 to reach a higher utility level of U_3 when the cost of benefits of control drops from C_1 to C''_1.

Hence, in the group control structure, the cost to gain controlling revenue will drop when the internal group accounts for the major ratio and the CP will be jeopardized since the encroachment effect of the UC's behavior will be reinforced. In Figure 7 – 4, with the increasing of the ratio of internal shareholder, the cost to gain controlling revenue drops from C_1 to C_2, the equilibrium point from E_1 to E_3 and the encroachment effect of the UC's behavior is reinforced.

The factor of board of directors is introduced in the remaining part to analyze how group structure affects the behavior of the UC in the listed company under the mutual effect of equity structure and the board structure. The board of directors as the endogenous mechanism to solve the internal contract problem can improve the quality of company decision with its effect on supervising the long-term operation strategy and employment, accessing and motivating the top managers etc. (Fama & Jensen, 1983; Hermalin & Weisbach, 2001). The reform of corporate governance in China has been prompted around the constructing of the board institution. In 2002, China Securities Regulatory Commission and State Economic and Trade Commission issued *The Governance Standards of China's listed Companies* jointly due to the frequent happening of major shareholder's tunneling incident and proposed the requirement of enhancing the independence of the board. With the high independence level of the board, the external directors account for a high ratio and can represent the interest of other shareholders, when any selfish behavior is exposed to risks and increase the cost to gain controlling revenue in this case.

In Figure 7-4, the cost of benefits of control increases from C_1 to C'_1 and the equilibrium point of the UC's behavior moves from E_1 to E_2, where E_2 indicates that the UC's benefits of cash flow outweighs the benefits of control whose behavior exhibits strong supervision effect, while his utility drops from U_1 to U_2, making the equilibrium at E_2 unstable. The UC will reinforce his control on the board to reduce the cost to gain benefits of control and increase his utility level. La porta (1998) used to argue that the major approach to reinforce the controlling right is to get hold of certain ratio of positions on the board and the position of president etc., when the equilibrium point of the UC is E_3 rather than E_2. With the growing number of the external directors, the cost to gain benefits of control drops from C_1 to C''_1 and equilibrium point from E_1 to E_3, when the encroachment effect of the UC's behavior is reinforced.

Under the condition of group control, the UC will reinforce his control on the board to reduce the cost to gain benefits of control. Therefore, the higher of the external director's ratio, the stronger the encroachment effect of the UC's behavior which will deteriorate the company's performance.

7.2 Evaluation of equity structure and shareholders' behavior of private listed companies

Equity structure is the basis of effective CG and has important influence on the operation of other governance mechanisms and the company's performance. With the separation of ownership and corporate control in the company's development, two kinds of principle-agent problems emerge. One is the two rights separation problem, which means the agent problem between the owner and the manager. In particular, under the condition of highly dispersed equity structure, the opportunism behavior is severe when it is hard for each shareholder to supervise the managers and to act jointly, leaving the manager level gets hold of the actual controlling right of the company. Under this circumstance, the agent cost goes high and the CP is deteriorated. Then the goal of CG is to make sure that the managers as the agent will act for the sake of shareholders' interest, make decision for the sake of maximizing company's value, maximize shareholders' value and reduce the owner-manager agent cost. The other is caused by the diversification and the asymmetry of shareholders structure, i. e. the agent problem between major and minor shareholders. In particular, under the condition of highly centralized equity structure and the existence of controlling shareholders, on the one hand, the controlling shareholders need to take the major cost of the managerial decision that deteriorates company's value (Demsetz & Lehn, 1985) which motivates and entitles them to supervise managers and take all or part of the related cost, while the benefits are shared by all the shareholders. Other shareholders can free ride and this is called helping hand of the controlling shareholders. On the other hand, due to the existence of private controlling benefits, the controlling shareholders have motivation to intervene to make the company take actions in favor of themselves but against other non-controlling shareholders' interest using their controlling power, i. e. tunneling behavior which deteriorates the overall value of the company. When the motivation of controlling shareholders to grab benefits using their controlling position grows and results in the behavior of encroaching resource and deteriorating value of the company, the total benefits will be enjoyed by the controlling shareholders exclusively while the cost shared by all, making other shareholders' benefits deteriorated and this is called grabbing hand of the controlling shareholders. The choice of controlling shareholders' behavior depends on the cost-benefit relation under the condition of particular CG mechanism and external supervision environment. Therefore, dispersed equity structure results in high owner-manager agent cost and moderate centralized one is in favor of shareholders' effective supervision on agents and reduce the agent cost. In the meanwhile, the high centralization of equity results in another kind of transaction cost called tunneling effect yet. Therefore, effective CG mechanism needs to take the situation that agent cost varies with the distribution of equity into account to minimize the overall agent cost.

The implicit assumption in the above perspective of analysis is only the equity structure on the first level exerts influences on CG and CP and overlooks the ultimate controlling problem and its impact. With the existence of UCSs, it is hard to examine the impact by considering the first level structure only. Generally, shareholders' cash flow and controlling benefits are symmetry without ultimate controlling or with the existence of only one equity structure. Even not, the bias is generally little. In the case of ultimate control, most UCSs take the approach of cross-shareholding or tower-shareholding to control the company, which results in the bias between cash flow and control rights. Under the condition of the asymmetry, the cost for UCSs to encroach company's benefits is lower and acquired benefits higher, making their motivation stronger. The behaviors of UCSs exert important effect on CG and CC.

7.2.1 Effect of equity structure on enterprise performance: literate review

Scholars argued from various perspectives around different problems brought by ES. Proper ES should accord with the specific institution environment, which helps minimize the overall agent cost. The studies on relations between ES and CP are summarized in Table 7 -4.

Table 7 -4 Studies on ES and CP

Scholars	Conclusion
Berle & Means (1932); Jensen & Meckling (1976); Grossman & Hart (1988)	Highly decentralized ownership structure will reduce corporate performance
Shleifer & Vishny (1997); Holderness & Sheehan (1988); Xu et al. (1997); Sun (1999); Zhang (2000); Shi (2000); Xu & Chen (2003)	Moderate concentration of equity is conducive to the improvement of corporate value

continued

Scholars	Conclusion
Baraclay & Holderness (1989); Wolfenzon and Daniel (1998) LaPortaet al. (1999); Johsonet al. (2000); Harrisand Raviv (1988); Claessenset al. (2000); Ye et al. (2002); Su et al. (2003); Xu et al. (2005)	The higher the deviation from controlling shareholder's rights and cash flow rights, the less favorable the improvement of the value of the company
Li et al. (2004, 2006); Xu & Wu (2005)	The higher the shareholder behavior index, the more help the company to improve the value
Winton (1993); Bennedsen and Wolfenzon (2000); Edwardsand Weichenrieder (1999); Volpin (2001)	The existence of a competitive structure of multiple major shareholders helps to enhance the value of the company
Stulz (1998); Morck, Shleifer, and Vishny (1988); McConnelland Servaes (1990)	There is a non-linear relationship between management holding and corporate performance

7.2.2 Empirical analysis on relationship between equity structure and enterprise performance in private listed companies

1. Data source and variable definition

The sample in this part is 235 PLCs including 85 on Shenzhen and 150 on Shanghai stock exchanges. The data is collected from the information in corporate annual reports, excluding ST and small and medium board companies on Shenzhen stock exchange.

Based on the above theoretical analysis, we construct the following ES and CP variables to examine the relation between ES and CP:

Cash flow right (xjllq). Following the method of La Porta (1999), with the existence of multilayer controlling shareholding, the cash flow right of the UCSs $CASH = \Pi\alpha_i$ $(i = 1, 2, \cdots, n)$. In the case of multiple holding, the cash flow right of the UCSs is the sum of the cash flow right on each controlling chain.

Degree of deviation (pld). In the case of multiple controlling, a listed company may be controlled by another one and the shareholding ratio of the latter company may be subject to certain UC directly or indirectly. Ultimate control right is the control right of the UC on listed companies in this circumstance. Following the method of La Porta (1999), the ultimate controlling right of pyramid shareholding structure $CON = \min(\alpha_1, \alpha_2, \cdots, \alpha_n)$, $\alpha_1, \alpha_2, \cdots, \alpha_n$ is the ratio of each listed companies' shareholding on the controlling chain. In the case of multiple holding, the ultimate control right ratio equals to the sum of vote right of each control chain. The deviation between ultimate control and cash flow rights is measured by ultimate control right/cash flow right.

Herfindahl index (hindex). It is the square sum of the shareholding ratios of the top five controlling shareholders. This index measures the Matthew effect of the shareholding ratio, i. e. the gap between different shareholders' holding ratios stands out with the amplification of squared gap between the larger and smaller ratios. It is generally recognized that Herfindahl index is an ideal indicator since it measures the level of equity concentration and the evenness of distribution on the one hand, and avoids the problem of dimension by converting the shareholding ratio to the non-dimensional index. It is introduced following Demsetz and Lehn. The gap among the top five shareholders is larger with the closeness of H index to 1. Dongzhi Yu (2001) calculated H index of the top five shareholders and take 0. 3 as the dividing line. The shareholding ratios of the top five controlling shareholders are not even when the index is bigger than 0. 3.

Number of the internal shareholders (nbgdrs). It is measured by the number of persons acting in concert.

Ratio of loan guarantee (dkdbbl). It is measured by the external guarantee value/net assets.

Frequency of general meeting (extraordinary general meeting included) (gddhcs). It is measured by equity held by the attended shareholders/total equity of the company.

In addition, we introduce the following two indicators to measure the CP level.

Tobin-Q. Most foreign scholars take Tobin-Q to measure the corporate value proposed by economist Tobin, which equals to the ratio of market value and replacement value of the corporate assets. The market value equals to the share price multiplied by the total shares. There are two types of shares namely tradable and non-tradable ones in the equity of Chinese listed companies. It will overestimate the market value of non-tradable shares measuring with the product. Therefore, the product is multiplied by 0. 8 to measure the market value of non-tradable shares to get the modified Tobin-Q.

Return on assets (ROA). ROE is the commonly used method to measure the performance, but easily manipulated. One classic example is that many companies manipulate their information to meet the 10% standard of the ROE in recent 3 years set by China Securities Regulatory Commission (Sun, Huang, 1999). Compared to

ROE, ROA is not as easily manipulated and shrink the management space of corporate surplus. Hence, we introduce ROA calculated by net benefits/total assets (see Table 7 -5) .

Table 7 -5 Variable names and definitions

Variable name	Code	Definition
Tobin-Q	Tobin-Q	(Equity market value + debt market value) / total assets book value
Return on assets	ROA	Net profit / total assets
Cash flow right	Xjllqg 1	CASH = $\Pi\alpha_i$ ($i = 1$, 2, …, n)
Degree of deviation	Pldg 2	Cash flow right / ultimate control right
Herfindahl index	Hindexg 3	Squared sum of the shares of the top five shareholders of the company
Number of the internal shareholders	Nbgdrsg 4	Number of the ultimate controlling shareholders with unanimous actions
Ratio of loan guarantee	Dkdbblg 5	Loan guarantee amount / net assets
Frequency of general meeting	Gddhcsg 6	Frequency of the annual general meeting
Attendance ratio of annual general meeting	Gddhrsblg 7	Attendance at the meeting shareholders / total share capital

2. Descriptive analysis

Based on the sample company data, the preliminary statistical analysis of each variable is conducted and the governance situation and performance distribution can be observed.

(1) Cash flow right.

Figure 7 -5, Table 7 -6 and Table7 -7 show the distribution of PLCs' cash flow rights and descriptive statistics. The results show that the minimum value of sample companies' cash flow right is 0. 01, maximum is 0. 66, average is 0. 19 and standard deviation is 0. 12, which means a small disparity among companies. 57. 02% of the values drop between 0 and 0. 2, 91. 49% between 0 and 0. 4, exhibiting a low level. With the increasing cash flow right, the number of the sample companies drops.

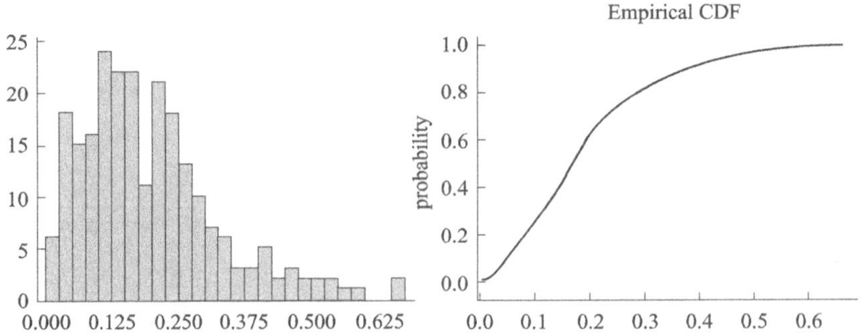

Figure 7 -5 Column figure and empirical cumulative distribution function figure

Table 7 - 6 **Descriptive statistics**

Mean	Min	Max	Median	Standard deviation	Skewness	Kurtosis
0. 19	0. 01	0. 66	0. 16	0. 12	1. 08	4. 2

Table 7 - 7 **Distribution of the cash flow right**

Value	Count	Percent	Cumulative count	Cumulative percent
[0, 0. 2)	134	57. 02	134	57. 02
[0. 2, 0. 4)	81	34. 47	215	91. 49
[0. 4, 0. 6)	18	7. 66	233	99. 15
[0. 6, 0. 8)	2	0. 85	235	100. 00
Total	235	100. 00	235	100. 00

(2) Number of the internal shareholders.

The number distribution of the internal shareholders and descriptive statistics are shown in Figure 7 - 6, Table 7 - 8 and Table 7 - 9. The results show that the minimum value of sample companies' internal shareholders is 0, maximum is 6, average is 1. 69 and standard deviation is 1. 21, which means a big disparity among companies. 64. 68% of the values are 1, 84. 68% between 1 and 2, exhibiting the serous internal shareholders situation.

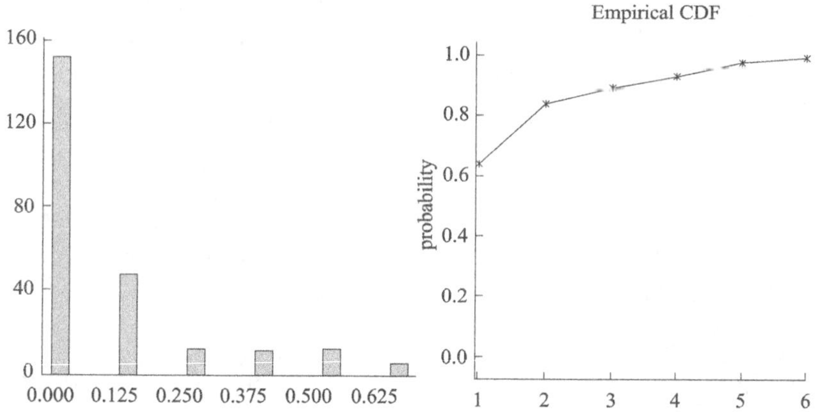

Figure 7 - 6 Column figure and empirical cumulative distribution function figure

Table 7 - 8 **Descriptive statistics of the number of the internal shareholders**

Mean	Min	Max	Median	Standard deviation	Skewness	Kurtosis
1. 69	1	6	1	1. 21	1. 96	6. 04

Table 7 - 9 **Distribution of number of the internal shareholders**

Value	Count	Percent	Cumulative count	Cumulative percent
1	152	64. 68	152	64. 68
2	47	20. 00	199	84. 68
3	11	4. 68	210	89. 36
4	10	4. 26	220	93. 62
5	11	4. 68	231	98. 30
6	4	1. 70	235	100. 00
Total	235	100. 00	235	100. 00

(3) Deviation.

The descriptive statistics and distribution of the deviation between control right and cash flow right are shown in Figure 7 - 7, Table 7 - 10 and Table 7 - 11. The results show that the minimum deviation of sample companies is 0, maximum is 0. 61, average is 0. 15 and standard deviation is 0. 12, which means a small disparity among companies. 72. 34% of the values fall below 0. 2, 95. 32% below 0. 4. Despite of the low deviation level of some companies, plenty of them have serious deviation between control right and cash flow right and this situation is more serious for PLCs. With the increasing deviation, the number of the sample companies increases.

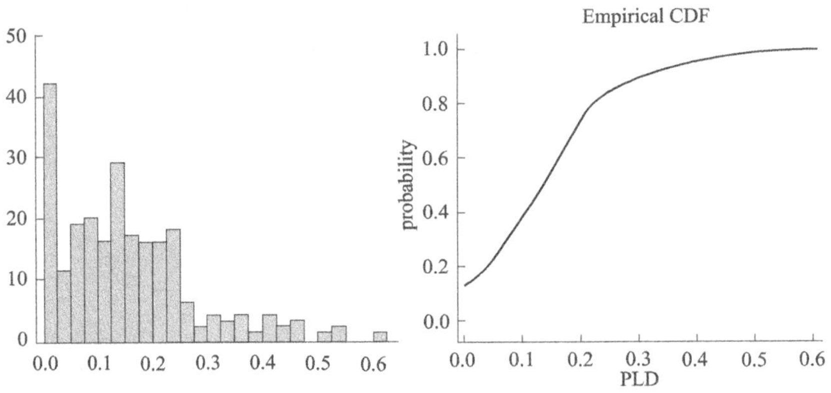

Figure 7 - 7 Column figure and empirical cumulative distribution function figure

Table 7 - 10 **Descriptive statistics of the deviation**

Mean	Min	Max	Median	Standard deviation	Skewness	Kurtosis
0. 15	0	0. 61	0. 14	0. 12	1. 05	4. 2

Table 7 – 11 **Distribution of the deviation**

Value	Count	Percent	Cumulative count	Cumulative percent
[0, 0.2)	170	72.34	170	72.34
[0.2, 0.4)	54	22.98	224	95.32
[0.4, 0.6)	10	4.26	234	99.57
[0.6, 0.8)	1	0.43	235	100.00
Total	235	100.00	235	100.00

(4) Loan guarantee ratio.

The descriptive statistics and distribution of the loan guarantee ratio are shown in Figure 7 –8, Table 7 – 12 and Table 7 – 13. The results show that the minimum loan guarantee ratio of sample companies is 0, maximum is 16.11, average is 0.3 and standard deviation is 1.18, which means a big disparity among companies. 99.15% of the values fall between 0 and 5. Sample companies have different degrees of security behavior.

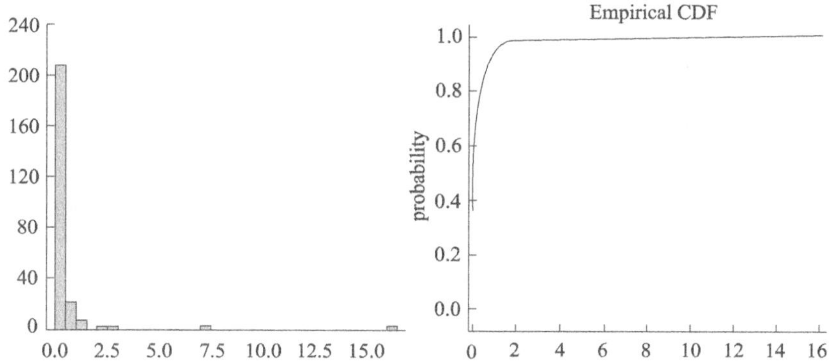

Figure 7 –8 Column figure and empirical cumulative distribution function figure

Table 7 – 12 **Descriptive statistics of the low guarantee ratio**

Mean	Min	Max	Median	Standard deviation	Skewness	Kurtosis
0.3	0	16.11	0.06	1.18	11.14	142.18

Table 7 – 13 **Distribution of the low guarantee ratio**

Value	Count	Percent	Cumulative count	Cumulative percent
[0, 5)	233	99.15	233	99.15
[5, 10)	1	0.43	234	99.57
[15, 20)	1	0.43	235	100.00
Total	235	100.00	235	100.00

(5) Frequency of general meeting.

The descriptive statistics and distribution of the frequency of general meeting are shown in Figure 7 – 9, Table 7 – 14 and Table 7 – 15. The results show that the frequency of general meeting of sample companies is 1, maximum is 8, average is 2.27 and standard deviation is 1.08, which means a big disparity among companies. 27.23% of the sample companies call the general meeting once, 60.85% once to twice, 88.51% once to three times and more than 10% four to eight times. Despite that the growing frequency of meeting increases the coordination cost among shareholders, it shows that the role of medium and small shareholders taking part in CG is more important and there is no absolute controlling shareholders alone have the say situation in the company, which has positive effect on CP.

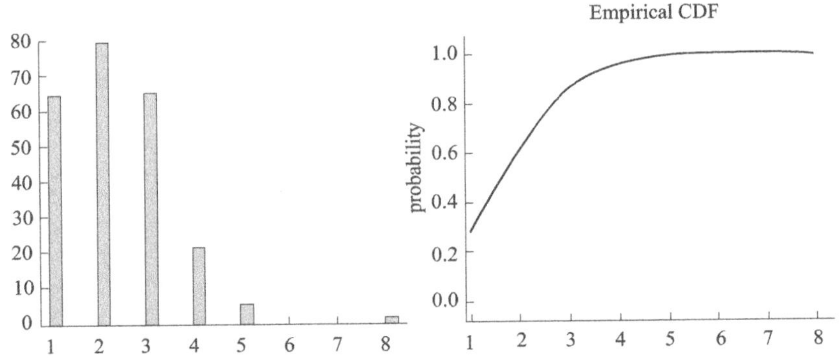

Figure 7 – 9 Column figure and empirical cumulative distribution function figure

Table 7 – 14 Descriptive statistics of the frequency of general meeting

Mean	Min	Max	Median	Standard deviation	Skewness	Kurtosis
2.27	1	8	2	1.09	0.96	5.3

Table 7 – 15 Distribution of the frequency of annual general meeting

Value	Count	Percent	Cumulative count	Cumulative percent
1	64	27.23	64	27.23
2	79	33.62	143	60.85
3	65	27.66	208	88.51
4	21	8.94	229	97.45
5	5	2.13	234	99.57
8	1	0.43	235	100.00
Total	235	100.00	235	100.00

(6) Attendance ratio of Annual General Meeting

The descriptive statistics and distribution of the attendance ratio of annual general meeting are shown in Figure 7 – 10, Table 7 – 16 and Table 7 – 17. The results show that the attendance ratio of annual general meeting of sample companies is 0. 1, maximum is 0. 8, average is 0. 55 and standard deviation is 0. 14, which means a small disparity among companies. 72. 34% of the values fall between 0. 2 and 0. 4, 44. 26% between 0. 4 and 0. 6 and 40% 0. 6 and 0. 8. The attendance ratios of the sample companies are generally low, which may be related to the only one big share problem and imperfection of governance mechanism for medium and small shareholders. In this situation, the controlling shareholders are able to manipulate the general meeting and tend to encroach the benefits of medium and small shareholders.

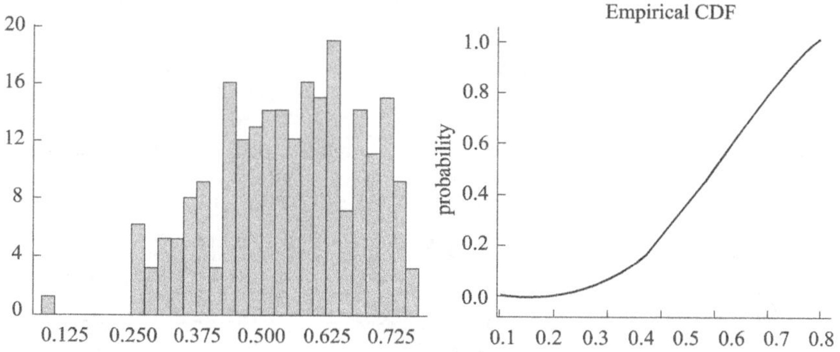

Figure 7 – 10 Column figure and empirical cumulative distribution function figure

Table 7 – 16 Descriptive statistics of the attendance ratio of annual general meeting

Mean	Min	Max	Median	Standard deviation	Skewness	Kurtosis
0. 55	0. 1	0. 8	0. 57	0. 14	-0. 36	2. 5

Table 7 – 17 Distribution of the attendance ratio of annual general meeting

Value	Count	Percent	Cumulative count	Cumulative percent
[0, 0. 2)	1	0. 43	1	0. 43
[0. 2, 0. 4)	36	15. 32	37	15. 74
[0. 4, 0. 6)	104	44. 26	141	60. 00
[0. 6, 0. 8)	94	40. 00	235	100. 00
Total	235	100. 00	235	100. 00

(7) Herfindahl index

The descriptive statistics and distribution of the Herfindahl index are shown in Figure 7 – 11, Table 7 – 18 and Table 7 – 19. The results show that the Herfindahl index of sample companies is 0. 01, maximum is 0. 46, average is 0. 15 and standard deviation is 0. 09, which means a small disparity among companies. 32. 77% of the values fall between 0 and 0. 1, 48. 83% between 0. 1 and 0. 2 and 14. 89% 0. 2 and

0. 3. The Herfindahl indexes are generally high and the equity is concentrated relatively.

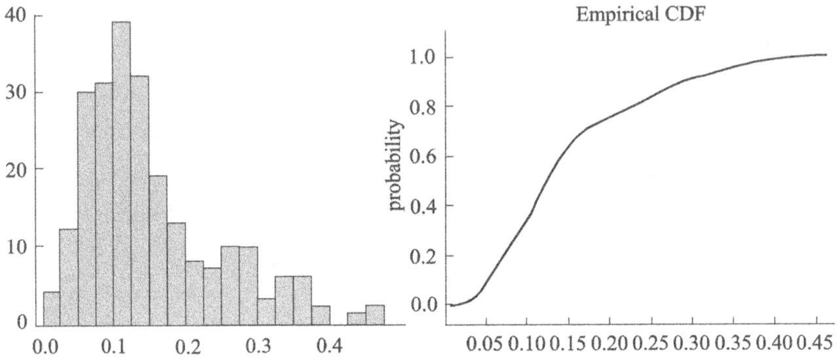

Figure 7 - 11 Column figure and empirical cumulative distribution function figure

Table 7 - 18 Descriptive statistics of the Herfindahl index

Mean	Min	Max	Median	Standard deviation	Skewness	Kurtosis	JB statistics
0. 15	0. 01	0. 46	0. 13	0. 09	1. 12	3. 79	55. 52

Table 7 - 19 Distribution of the Herfindahl index

Value	Count	Percent	Cumulative count	Cumulative percent
[0, 0. 1)	77	32. 77	77	32. 77
[0. 1, 0. 2)	103	43. 83	180	76. 60
[0. 2, 0. 3)	35	14. 89	215	91. 49
[0. 3, 0. 4)	17	7. 23	232	98. 72
[0. 4, 0. 5)	3	1. 28	235	100. 00
Total	235	100. 00	235	100. 00

Finally, we summarize the descriptive statistics on equity structure and shareholder behavior in Table 7 - 20.

Table 7 - 20 Descriptive statistics on equity structure and shareholder behavior indicators

Variable Name	Mean	Min	Max	Median	Standard deviation	Skewness	Kurtosis	JB statistics
Xjllq	0. 19	0. 01	0. 66	0. 16	0. 12	1. 08	4. 2	45. 69
nbgdrs	1. 69	1	6	1	1. 21	1. 96	6. 04	240. 68
Pld	0. 15	0	0. 61	0. 14	0. 12	1. 05	4. 2	62. 69
Dkdbbl	0. 3	0	16. 11	0. 06	1. 18	11. 14	142. 18	194 536
Gddhcs	2. 27	1	8	2	1. 09	0. 96	5. 3	88. 4
gddhrsbl	0. 55	0. 1	0. 8	0. 57	0. 14	- 0. 36	2. 5	7. 4
hindex	0. 15	0. 01	0. 46	0. 13	0. 09	1. 12	3. 79	55. 52

3. Regression analysis

Regressions on the relations between the indicators of ES and shareholders' behaviors and CP are run to explore the relation between the indicator of ES and CP based on the variable data of sample companies. In the regression analysis, we introduce 13 control variables $Indus_i$ (I = 1, 2, 3, 4) classified by industry①. Meanwhile, to control for the effect of company scale on its performance, we take the natural logarithm of total assets LnA as a control. To control for the effect of regional environment, we introduce regional dummies AR1 and AR2②. The regression model is as followings:

$$\text{Tobin} - \text{Q}(\text{ROA}) = C + \rho X + \alpha_i \sum_{i=1}^{13} Indus_i + \pi \text{Ln}A + \Phi AR_1 + \Phi_2 AR_2 + \bar{o}$$

Whereby X are variables of ES and shareholders' behavior and each of them is analyzed in the remaining part. It is to examine the relation between the indicator of ES and CP and lay foundation for the following rating. Therefore, we explore the coefficients of corresponding ES variables and dummies are not discussed here.

(1) Cash flow right and CP.

The regression results of cash flow right on CP are shown in Table 7 – 21. The coefficients are positive significantly when Tobin-Q and ROA is included as the explanatory variable. The relation between cash flow right and CP is positive and the higher the cash flow right level, the better the CP. This suggests that the increasing of ultimate control shareholders' cash flow right level helps improving CP.

Table 7 – 21 Regression results of cash flow right on CP

Regression results	Tobin-Q		ROA	
	Coefficient	Prob.	Coefficient	Prob.
C	6.73	0.00	-0.18	0.06
Cash flow right	0.0014	0.02	0.0004	0.11
R-squared	0.28		0.03	

(2) Deviation and CP.

The regression results of deviation on CP are shown in Table 7 – 22. The coefficients are negative significantly when Tobin-Q and ROA are included as the

① The classification bases on those of CSRC and Shenzhen Stock Exchange and is adjusted slightly, which contains 14 industries finally. To avoid the multicollinearity problem, we introduce 13 industry dummies.

② The nation is divided into the eastern, middle and western parts and two dummies are included in the regression.

explanatory variable respectively. The relation between deviation and CP is negative and the higher the deviation level, the worse the CP. This suggests that the increasing level of deviation between cash flow and control rights level helps improving CP.

Table 7 – 22　　　　　Regression results of deviation on CP

Regression results	Tobin-Q		ROA	
	Coefficient	Prob.	Coefficient	Prob.
C	-6.74	0.00	0.18	0.07
Deviation	-0.37	0.01	-0.01	0.13
R-squared	0.28		0.025	

(3) Herfindahl index and CP.

Based on the previous theoretical analysis, moderate equity concentration helps reduce the agent cost of managers and improves CP in the situation of dispersed equity. While the holding ratio of the biggest shareholder is as high as the level of controlling position, moderate dispersion of the equity helps reducing the agent cost between major and minor shareholders. Therefore, the relation between Herfindahl Index and CP should be nonlinear. For this point, we introduce the control of the holding ratio of the biggest shareholder to examine the effect of equity concentration on CP excluding its impact when analyzing the relation between Herfindahl index and CP. The regression result of Herfindahl index on CP is shown in Table 7 – 23. The coefficient is negative significantly when Tobin-Q is included as explanatory variables and not significant when ROA is the control. Generally speaking, the relation between Herfindahl index and CP is negative and the higher the Herfindahl index, the worse the CP. This suggests that the concentration of equity in Chinese PLCs goes against improving CP. This situation may be related to the common existence of the single-large shareholder in the ES of Chinese companies. Due to the high holding ratio of the biggest shareholder, the ES is regarded as equity concentrated, which means competitive ES helps reducing the encroaching motivation of controlling shareholders and improving CP.

Table 7 – 23　　　　Regression results of Herfindahl index on CP

Regression results	Tobin-Q		ROA	
	Coefficient	Prob.	Coefficient	Prob.
C	6.82	0.00	-0.18	0.07
Hindex	-0.78	0.04	-0.02	0.18
R-squared	0.28		0.02	

(4) Number of the internal shareholders and CP.

The coefficients of number of the internal shareholders are not significant in the regressions. Considering the possible nonlinear relation between them, we introduce the squared term of the number of the internal shareholders, and the holding ratio of the biggest shareholder as the control. The results are shown in Table 7 – 24. The relation between number of the internal shareholders and CP is reverse U type when Tobin-Q and ROA is included as the explanatory variable respectively. It is significant only for Tobin-Q while not for ROA. Overall, the relation between number of the internal shareholders and CP is reverse U type. With the increasing number of the internal shareholders, CP increases and drops hereafter. This suggests that in Chinese PLCs, when the controlling shareholders control some other shareholders by various ways to maintain their control power, the positive effect is stronger. Yet when the controlling shareholders control many other shareholders and even the company completely, the motivation to encroach company's benefits grows and goes against improving CP.

Table 7 – 24 Regression results of the number of internal shareholders on CP

Regression results	Tobin-Q		ROA	
	Coefficient	Prob.	Coefficient	Prob.
C	6. 70	0. 00	–0. 18	0. 07
Number of the internal shareholders	0. 22	0. 03	0. 004	0. 19
Squared number of the internal shareholders	–0. 32	0. 05	–0. 0004	0. 22
R-squared	0. 30		0. 03	

(5) Loan guarantee and CP.

The regression results of loan guarantee on CP is shown in Table 7 – 25. The coefficients are negative significantly when Tobin-Q and ROA are included as the explanatory variable respectively. The relation between loan guarantee and CP is negative and the higher the loan guarantee level, the worse the CP. This suggests that in Chinese PLCs, when the loan guarantee grows, the encroachment of company benefits for the controlling shareholders increases and goes against improving CP.

Table 7 – 25 Regression results of loan guarantee ratio on CP

Regression results	Tobin-Q		ROA	
	Coefficient	Prob.	Coefficient	Prob.
C	6. 73	0. 00	–0. 18	0. 05
Loan guarantee ratio	–0. 0007	0. 00	–0. 0002	0. 00
R-squared	0. 31		0. 14	

(6) Frequency of general meeting and CP.

The regression results of frequency of general meeting on CP are shown in Table 7 - 26. The coefficients are negative and positive when Tobin-Q and ROA are included as explanatory variables respectively and only significant in the first model. Overall, the relation between frequency of general meeting and CP is negative. Moderate frequency of general meeting helps improving CP, while oversized frequency implies the imperfection of CG mechanism and goes against improving CP.

Table 7 - 26 Regression results of frequency of general meeting on CP

Regression results	Tobin-Q		ROA	
	Coefficient	Prob.	Coefficient	Prob.
C	6. 84	0. 00	-0. 17	0. 08
Frequency of general meeting	-0. 02	0. 08	0. 001	0. 28
R-squared	0. 28		0. 02	

(7) Attendance ratio of annual general meeting and CP

The regression results of attendance ratio of annual general meeting on CP is shown in Table 7 - 27. The coefficients are positive and negative when Tobin-Q and ROA are included as explanatory variables respectively and only significant in the first model. Overall, the relation between frequency of general meeting and CP is negative. The relation between attendance ratio of annual general meeting and CP is positive and the higher the attendance ratio of annual general meeting, the better the attendance of shareholders, which helps improving CP.

Table 7 - 27 Regression results of attendance ratio of annual general meeting on CP

Regression results	Tobin-Q		ROA	
	Coefficient	Prob.	Coefficient	Prob.
C	6. 83	0. 00	-0. 18	0. 07
Attendance ratio of annual general meeting	0. 0005	0. 09	-0. 0003	0. 28
R-squared	0. 28		0. 027	

7. 2. 3 Rating system for indicators of equity structure and shareholders' behavior in private listed companies

1. Principle statement on rating for indicators of ES and shareholders' behavior

Based on the relations between the rating indicators and CP derived from the above empirical models, we can confirm the final rating basis and specific principle for governance indicators of ES and shareholders' behavior as followings specifically. Cash flow right of the ultimate controlling shareholder in positive relation with CP. Empirical evidences from various nations suggest that cash flow right is a sound indicator for the positive incentive effect of the biggest shareholder. We assign values on cash flow right of the ultimate controlling shareholder with a distance of 5% between groups. Number of the internal shareholders in reverse U shape with CP. We assign the highest value with one internal shareholder since the peak value is smaller than 1 and the value is lower with the increasing number of the internal shareholders. The maximum value is 6 with the assigned value of 1, 5 with 2, 4 with 4, 3 with 6, 2 with 8 and 1 with 10. Deviation between voting and cash flow rights of the biggest shareholders in negative relation with CP. We assign values on deviation with a distance of 5% between groups.

Ratio of the guarantee value in net assets in negative relation with CP. Four values higher than 100% are listed as outliers. The sample is divided into 10 groups with a distance of 10% between groups, among which 90% is the first group and values are assigned from high to low accordingly. Frequency of general meeting in negative relation with CP. One general meeting gets the highest value and increasing number reduces the value accordingly.

Attendance ratio of annual general meeting in positive relation with CP. 0.095 188 is the outlier and the distance between groups is 0.792 4 − 0.258 3/10 = 0.053 41. Herfindahl index in negative relation with CP. The values are assigned with a distance of 5% between groups. The detailed cases are as Table 7 − 28 and Table 7 − 29.

Table 7 − 28 Rating principle and indicators of ES and shareholders' behavior

Indicator Name	Relation with Performance	Evaluation Criteria
Cash flow right	Positive	The higher the better
Degree of deviation	Negative	The lower the better
Herfindahl index	Negative	The lower the better
Number of the internal shareholders	Inverse U	First rise and then down, 1best, the more the worse
Ratio of loan guarantee	Negative	The lower the better
Frequency of general meeting	Negative	1 best, the more the worse
Attendance ratio of annual general meeting	Positive	The higher the better

Table 7 – 29 Rating principle on indicators of ES and shareholders' behavior

Score	Cash flow right (%)	Number of the internal shareholders	Degree of deviation (%)	Ratio of loan guarantee%	Frequency of general meeting	Attendance Ratio of A. G meeting	Herfindahl index (%)
Group Gap	5	1	5	10	1	0. 053	5
1	0 – 5	6	45	90	10	0. 053 – 0. 311	45
2	5 – 10	5	40 – 45	80 – 90	9	0. 311 – 0. 364	40 – 45
3	10 – 15		35 – 40	70 – 80	8	0. 364 – 0. 417	35 – 40
4	15 – 20	4	30 – 35	60 – 70	7	0. 417 – 0. 470	30 – 35
5	20 – 25		25 – 30	50 – 60	6	0. 470 – 0. 523	25 – 30
6	25 – 30	3	20 – 25	40 – 50	5	0. 523 – 0. 576	20 – 25
7	30 – 35		15 – 20	30 – 40	4	0. 576 – 0. 629	15 – 20
8	35 – 40	2	10 – 15	20 – 30	3	0. 629 – 0. 682	10 – 15
9	40 – 45		5 – 10	10 – 20	2	0. 682 – 0. 753	5 – 10
10	45	1	0 – 5	0 – 10	1	≥0. 735	0 – 5

2. Descriptive statistics for scores of governance evaluation indicators of ES and shareholders' behavior

For scores of governance evaluation indicators of ES and shareholders' behavior, we take two approaches of column figure and table. It is worth mentioning that the horizontal axis represents the score and vertical represmts number of companies with the corresponding score, while the descriptive statistics for the evaluation indicators' scores are summarized in the table.

(1) Cash flow right of the UCSs (XJLLQFS).

The descriptive statistics of the UCSs evaluation indicator score are shown in Figure 7 – 12. The average score is 4. 24, medium is 4. 00 and standard deviation is 2. 40, which means a big disparity among companies. Overall, the UCSs evaluation indicator scores are relatively low and most of them are below 5. In the sample, the cash flow right level is generally low in PLCs, which may be related to the common existence of cross and tower holding structure.

(2) Number of the internal shareholders (NBGDRSFS).

The descriptive statistics of number of the internal shareholders evaluation indicator score are shown in Figure 7 – 13. The average score is 8. 62, medium is 10. 00 and standard deviation is 2. 39, which means a big disparity among companies. Overall, number of the internal shareholders evaluation indicator scores are relatively high and most of them are above 7. 5. In the sample, number of the internal shareholders is generally small which may be related to the common existence of the single-large shareholder in Chinese PCs. Due to the high holding ratio of the controlling shareholder, there is no need to look for more internal shareholders' support to control the company.

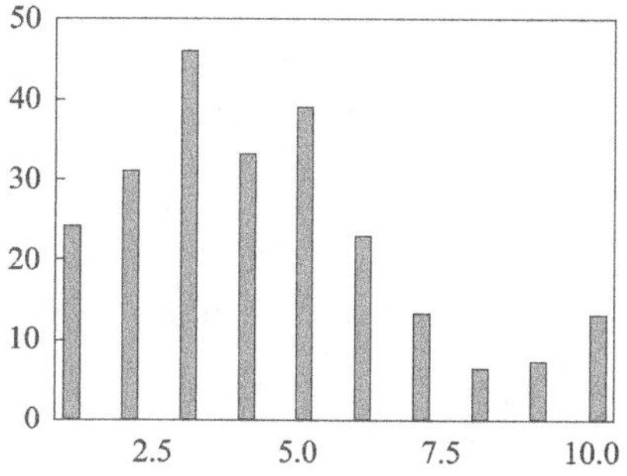

Figure 7 – 12 Column figure of cash flow right of the UCSs indicator score

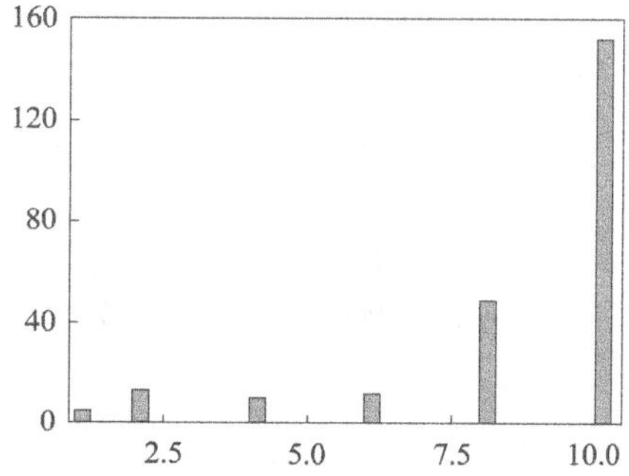

Figure 7 – 13 Column figure of number of the internal shareholders indicator score

(3) Deviation between voting and cash flow rights of the UCSs (PLFDFS).

The descriptive statistics of deviation between voting and cash flow rights of the UCSs evaluation indicator score are shown in Figure 7 – 14. The average score is 7.56, medium is 8.00 and standard deviation is 2.21, which means a big disparity among companies. Overall, evaluation indicator scores of the deviation are relatively high and most of them are above 5. In the sample, the deviation level is not very high in most of the PLCs.

(4) Ratio of the guarantee value (DKDBBLFS).

The descriptive statistics of the ratio of the guarantee value evaluation indicator score are shown in Figure 7 – 15. The average score is 8.43, medium is 10.00 and standard deviation is 2.50, which means a big disparity among companies. Overall, evaluation indicator scores of the ratio are relatively high and most of them are above

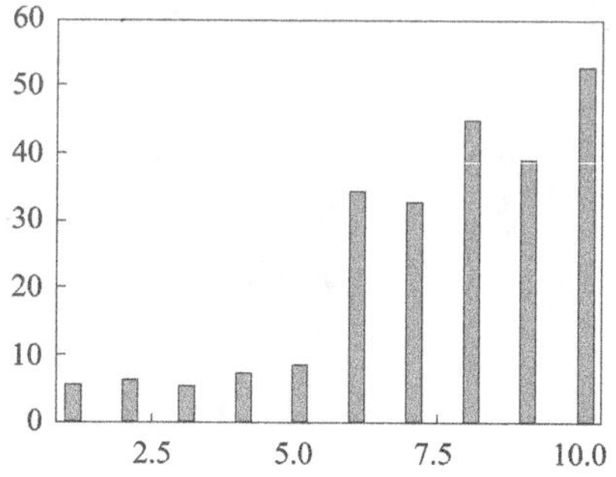

Figure 7 – 14 Column figure of the deviation between voting and cash flow rights of the UCSs indicator score

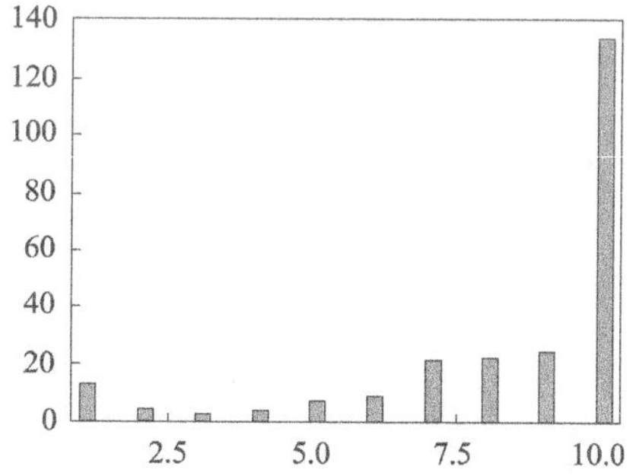

Figure 7 – 15 Column figure of ratio of the guarantee value indicator score

8. In the sample, the deviation level is low in most of the PLCs.

(5) Frequency of general meeting (GDDHFS).

The descriptive statistics of the frequency of general meeting evaluation indicator score are shown in Figure 7 – 16. The average score is 8.73, medium is 9.00 and standard deviation is 1.09, which means a small disparity among companies. Overall, evaluation indicator scores of the frequency of general meeting are relatively high and most of them are above 7.5. In the sample, the frequency is moderate in most of the PLCs.

(6) Attendance ratio of annual general meeting (GDDHCXLFS).

The descriptive statistics of the attendance ratio of annual of general meeting evaluation indicator score are shown in Figure 7 – 17. The average score is 6.07, medium is 6.00 and standard deviation is 2.56, which means a big disparity among companies. Overall, evaluation indicator scores of the attendance ratio follow the normal distribution.

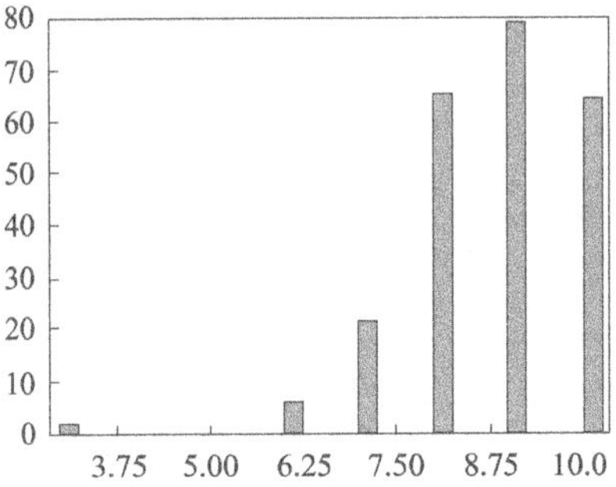

Figure 7 – 16 Column figure of the frequency of general meeting indicator score

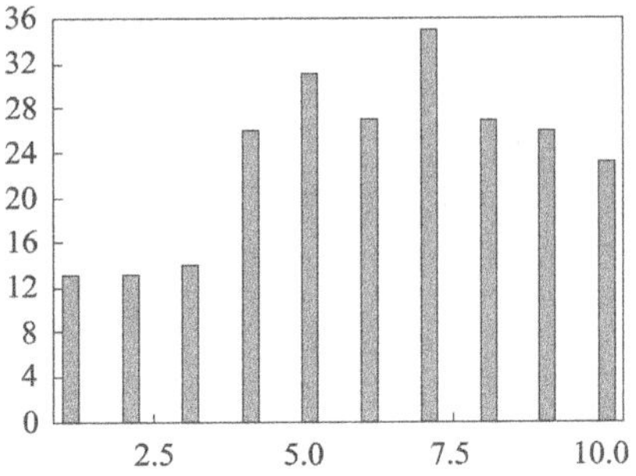

Figure 7 – 17 Column figure of the attendance ratio of annual general meeting indicator score

(7) Herfindahl index (HINDEXFS).

The descriptive statistics of the Herfindahl index evaluation indicator score are shown in Figure 7 – 18. The average score is 7.49, medium is 8.00 and standard deviation is 1.86, which means a small disparity among companies. Overall, evaluation indicator scores of the Herfindahl index are low.

(8) Total score of governance evaluation indicators of ES and shareholders' behavior for PLCs.

The descriptive statistics of the total score of governance evaluation indicators of ES and shareholders' behavior for PLCs are shown in Figure 7 – 19. The average score is 51.23, medium is 51.00 and standard deviation is 5.51, which means a big

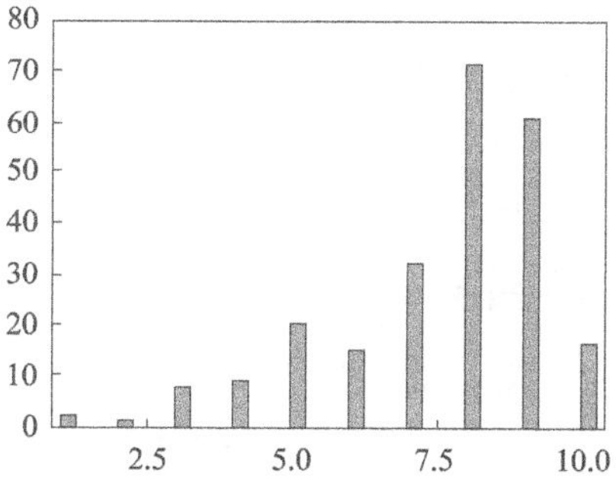

Figure 7 – 18 Column figure of the Herfindahl index indicator score

disparity among companies. Overall, the total scores follow the normal distribution, which indicates the reasonability of the evaluation method. The total scores are generally high and those of the most sample companies are higher than 45.

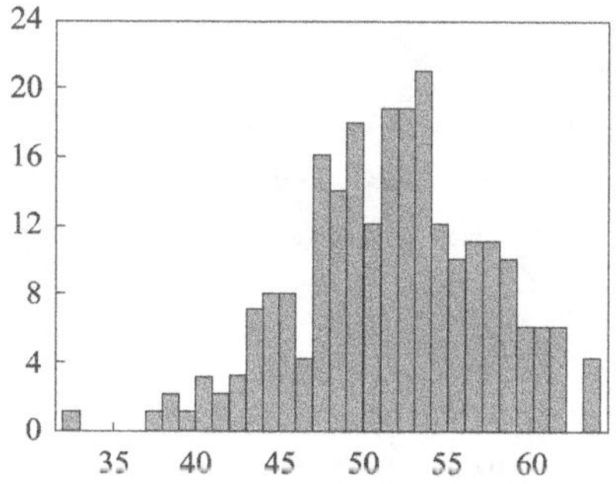

Figure 7 – 19 Column figure of the total score of governance evaluation indicators of ES and shareholders' behavior (arithmetic sum)

(9) Summary descriptive statistics of the indicator score of ES and shareholders' behavior.

Table 7 – 30 Summary descriptive statistics of the indicator score of ES and shareholders' behavior

Variable	Mean	Median	Standard deviation	Skewness	Kurtosis	JB statistics
Xjllqfs	4.24	4.00	2.40	0.71	2.93	20.02
Nbgdrsfs	8.62	10.00	2.39	–1.87	5.52	199.71
Pldfs	7.56	8.00	2.21	–1.03	3.74	47.07
Dkdbblfs	8.43	10.00	2.50	–1.80	5.37	181.51
Gddhfs	8.73	9.00	1.09	–0.96	5.30	88.40
Gddhcxlfs	6.07	6.00	2.56	–0.25	2.16	9.36
Hindexfs	7.49	8.00	1.86	–1.10	3.84	54.73
Gdxwzf	51.23	51.00	5.51	–0.26	3.07	2.69

Most scores of the remaining indicators are high with means higher than 6 except for the cash flow right scores based on the column Figures and descriptive Tables of the indicator score of ES and shareholders' behavior for the PLCS. Overall, the PLCs performs well in the indicator score of ES and shareholders' behavior.

3. Regional and industrial disparities of the total score of governance evaluation indicators of ES and shareholders' behavior

With the total score of governance evaluation indicators of ES and shareholders' behavior for PLCs as research objects, the regional disparity and industrial characteristics are analyzed in in the renaming part. The horizontal axis represents the score and vertical axis represents the number of companies.

(1) Regional disparity of the total score of governance evaluation indicators of ES and shareholders' behavior.

We adopt the classification index to represent the regional disparity with 1 indicating the eastern, 0 the central and -1 the western[①]. We present the regional disparity of the total score of governance evaluation indicators of ES and shareholders' behavior in Table 7 - 31 with the descriptive statistics and in Figure 7 - 20 using columns.

Table 7 - 31 Regional disparity of the evaluation score of ES and shareholders' behavior

Variable	Mean	Median	Max	Min	Standard deviation	Skewness	Kurtosis	JB statistics
Eastern (135)	51.57	52.00	63.00	32.00	5.74	-0.42	3.32	4.60
Central (47)	50.50	50.00	63.00	40.00	5.38	0.13	2.41	0.82
Western (53)	51.00	52.00	63.00	39.00	5.03	-0.17	2.98	0.27

Notes: numbers in brackets of the first row indicates the number of the PLCs in the region.

The above table implies that the regional difference is not very large and the mean scores are very close with 51.75 for the eastern, 50.50 for the middle and 51.00 for the western. The score of the eastern is slightly higher than the western and the middle and the number of companies in the eastern is significantly higher than the remaining area in the meantime. The maximum values are the same for the three regions, with the minimum value 32.00 for the eastern, 40.00 for the middle and 39.00 for the

① The eastern area includes Liaoning, Hebei, Tianjin, Beijing, Shandong, Jiangsu, Shanghai, Zhejiang, Fujian, Guangdong and Hainan. The middle area includes Heilongjiang, Jilin, Shanxi, Henan, Anhui, Hubei, Hunan and Jiangxi. The western includes Shaanxi, Gansu, Ningxia, Qinghai, Xinjiang, Sichuan, Chongqing, Yunnan, Guizhou, Tibet, Inner Mongolia and Guangxi.

western. The standard deviation of the scores for the western, middle and eastern companies is 5. 74, 5. 38 and 5. 03 respectively. The standard deviation of the eastern is relatively large and the changes in means and deviations are similar for all the regions.

Figure 7 – 20 presents the column figures of the scores of governance evaluation indicators of ES and shareholders' behavior for the eastern, middle and western. The figures indicate that scores of the eastern companies follow the right skewed normal distribution and most scores are high. Scores of the middle companies follow the left skewed normal distribution and most scores are low. Scores of the western companies follow the normal distribution.

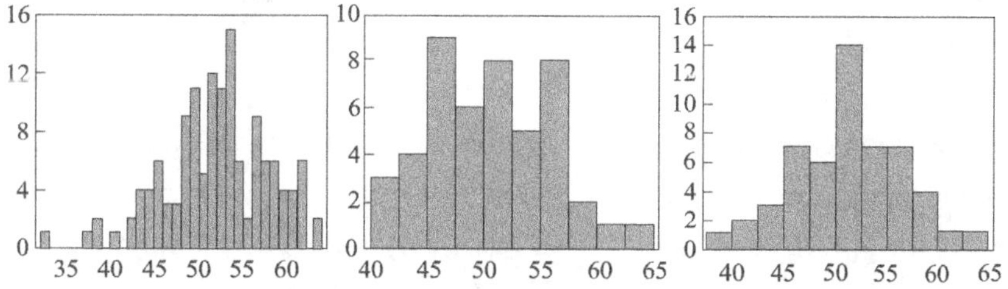

(a) Eastern (b) Central (c) Western

Figure 7 – 20 Column figures of scores of the regional disparities of ES and shareholders' behavior

(2) Industrial disparity of the total score of governance evaluation indicators of ES and shareholders' behavior.

We classify the PLCs into different industries according to the CSRS industrial classification standard[1] and employ classification index to present the industrial disparity, with the characters corresponding to the numbers. We present the industrial disparity of the total score of governance evaluation indicators of ES and shareholders' behavior in Table 7 – 32 with the descriptive statistics.

① CSRC industry classification standards are released by China Securities Regulatory Commission and are non-mandatory, whose basic classification units are the listed companies listed on the stock exchanges in the PRC, which are applicable to all relevant units and departments in the securities industry for the statistics, analysis and other related work of classified information of listed companies. The structure and codes are as followings: A, Agriculture, forestry, animal husbandry and fishery; B, Mining; C, Manufacturing; D, Electricity, gas and water production and supply; E, Construction; F, Transportation and warehousing; G, IT; H, Wholesale and retail trade; I, Finance and insurance; J, Real estate; K, Social service; L, Communication and cultural industries; M, Miscellaneous. During assignment, we assign A to 1, B to 2, and so on.

Table 7 - 32 **Industrial disparity of the evaluation score of ES and shareholders' behavior**

Variable	Mean	Median	Max	Min	Standard deviation	Skewness	Kurtosis	JB statistics
1 (7)	51. 29	53. 00	61. 00	41. 00	7. 32	-0. 19	1. 82	0. 45
3 (143)	51. 00	51. 00	63. 00	32. 00	5. 58	-0. 26	3. 33	2. 26
5 (6)	53. 83	54. 50	61. 00	47. 00	5. 15	-0. 05	1. 86	0. 33
7 (16)	52. 81	52. 50	60. 00	44. 00	5. 04	0. 05	1. 90	0. 81
8 (12)	51. 33	52. 00	59. 00	40. 00	5. 18	-0. 54	3. 15	0. 60
10 (14)	49. 57	51. 00	56. 00	38. 00	5. 40	-0. 99	3. 02	2. 28
11 (6)	55. 00	56. 00	63. 00	47. 00	6. 07	-0. 14	1. 73	0. 42
13 (22)	50. 91	51. 50	58. 00	42. 00	4. 80	-0. 24	1. 91	1. 29
Others① (9)	50. 89	51. 00	60. 00	43. 00	5. 97	0. 11	1. 74	0. 62

Notes: numbers in brackets of the first row indicates the number of the PCs in the region.

Table 7 - 32 implies scores of the companies in social service and construction industries are higher than the others with the means are 55. 00 and 53. 83 respectively. Companies in real estate industry get the lowest score with a mean of 49. 57. The median of companies in social service industry is largest with the value of 56. 00 and those of the other are smaller. The standard deviation of companies in agriculture industry is largest with the value of 7. 32 and smallest for general companies with the value of 4. 80. In the meantime, most of the PLCs concentrate in manufacture industry with the number of 143, accounting for 58% of the sample. Figure 7 - 20 presents the distributional figures of the scores of governance evaluation indicators of ES and shareholders' behavior in different manufacture companies. The figure indicates that scores of the manufacture companies follow the right skewed normal distribution and the scores are high and moderate.

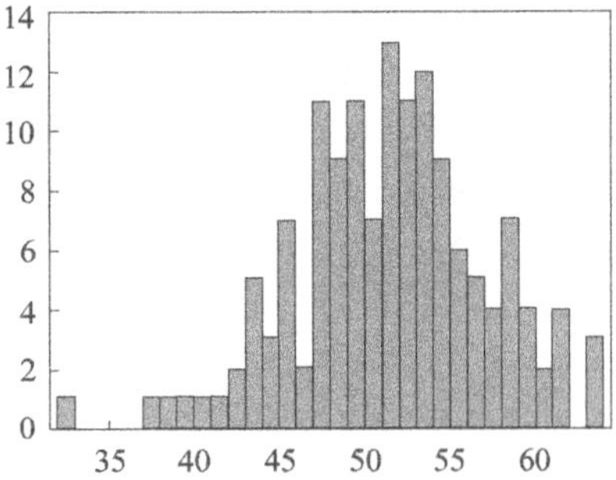

Figure 7 - 21 Indicator scores of ES and shareholders' behavior for companies in manufacture samples

① The others include the following industries: B, Mining; D, Electricity, gas and water production and supply; F, Transportation and warehousing; I, Finance and insurance; L, Communication and cultural industries. They were merged due to that the numbers of the listed companies belonging to these industries are small and the industry has a monopoly attribute.

7.3 Structure and operation of the board of directors in private listed companies

7.3.1 Structure, behavior, compensation of the board of directors and enterprise performance in private listed companies

In this section, the empirical work is divided into two parts to improve the credibility and convincingness of the results. The first part examines the governance indicators of the board listed in the above section employing the PLCs related data from CCER public database from 2002 to 2005 and the second one focuses on the missing indicators in CCER database based on the manually collected PLCs related database of 2005 by our group.

1. Empirical study employing CCER data

(1) Variable selection.

A. CP. In this part, EPS, NAVPS and ROA of the selected companies are employed to proxy the CP.

B. Governance situation of the board. According to the previous theoretical and empirical analysis, the governance situation is measured from the perspective of structure, behavior and compensation of the board. To be specific, ratio of the independent directors in the board is to measure its independency, annual frequency of meetings called by the board is to measure its behavior and total compensation of the top 3 directors to measure the salary level.

C. Controls. We control the possible disturbances to exclude their impact on the relation between the governance situation of the board and CP and to explore it more precisely, including the features of the company and its governance. To be specific, we control share ratio held by shareholders attending the annual shareholder meeting, scale of the board of directors, number of the independent directors, scale of the board of supervisors, meeting annual frequency called by the board of supervisors, debt equity ratio and scale of the company etc.

The Table 7 – 33 below shows all variables, abbreviation and implication used in this section.

Table 7 - 33　　Variables, abbreviations and implications list

Variable type	Abbreviation	Implication
Explained variables	EPS	Earnings per share
	NAPS	Net asset per share
	ROA	Return of asset
Explanatory variables	Independence	Independence of the board of directors
	SQ_indepd	Squared independence of the board of directors
	Times_dsh	Annual frequency of meeting called by board of the directors
	SQ_times_ds	Squared annual frequency of meeting called by board of the directors
	Lnpay_ds	Logarithm of the sum of the top three directors' remuneration
Controls	Attendence	Proportion of the shares represented by the shareholders at the annual general meeting
	Size_dsh	Scale of board of the directors
	Number_indp	Number of independent directors
	Size_jsh	Size of the board of supervisors
	Times_js	Annual frequency of meeting called by board of the supervisors
	LEV	Debt asset ratio
	LnTA	Natural logarithm of scale of the company

(2) Data sources.

The basic databases include the CCER PLCs database and the general corporate finance database. Samples with missing variables in this study are excluded and the outliers are corrected according to Juchao Info Web, which leaves a sample of 858 companies from 2002 to 2005, with 126 for 2002, 186 for 2003, 245 for 2004 and 301 for 2005. In this case, the data is an unbalanced panel which helps avoid the unobservable heterogeneity bias common in cross sectional analysis and expand the sample volume to improve the credibility of the results.

(3) Empirical strategies and regression models.

Panel data features with both cross section and time dimensions, making the choice of appropriate models far more complicated than that of the cross section case. If the observable variables control the correlated features of the individuals, no unobservable features will exist. In this case, non-observable effect will be excluded and pooled OLS regression can get the exact estimation. If not, the unobservable effect may be correlated to any explanatory variable and the regression estimation will be affected by the unobservable heterogeneity. Even if the unobservable effect is not correlated to any observable variable, the unobservable effect will result in inefficient estimates and invalid standard error. In this case, it is necessary to choose fixed or random effect model to estimate based on the feature of the data itself.

Hausman and Taylor (1981) argued that fixed effect framework offered a general and unbiased approach to control the effect of missing variables. In the following regression analysis, we choose the appropriate regression model using Durbin-Wu-Hausman approach from fixed and random effect models.

On the above assumption and variables' definition, the adopted regression models are as followings.

$$EPS = b_0 + b_1 * Independence + b_2 * Attendence + b_3 * Size\_dsh + b_4 * Number\_indp + b_5 * Size\_jsh + b_6 * Time\_js + b_7 * LEV + b_8 * LnTA + e \quad (14)$$

$$EPS = b_0 + b_1 * Independence + b_2 * SQ\_indepd + b_3 * Attendence + b_4 * Size\_dsh + b_5 * Number\_indp + b_6 * Size\_jsh + b_7 * Time\_js + b_8 * LEV + b_9 * LnTA + e \quad (15)$$

$$NAPS = b_0 + b_1 * Independence + b_2 * Attendence + b_3 * Size\_dsh + b_4 * Number\_jndp + b_5 * Size\_jsh + b_6 * Time\_js + b_7 * LEV + b_8 * LnTA + e \quad (16)$$

$$NAPS = b_0 + b_1 * Independence + b_2 * SQ\_indepd + b_3 * Attendence + b_4 * Size\_dsh + b_5 * Number\_indp + b_6 * Size\_jsh + b_7 * Time\_js + b_8 * LEV + b_9 * LnTA + e \quad (17)$$

$$ROA = b_0 + b_1 * Independence + b_2 * Attendence + b_3 * Size\_dsh + b_4 * Number\_indp + b_5 * Size\_jsh + b_6 * Time\_js + b_7 * LEV + b_8 * LnTA + e \quad (18)$$

$$ROA = b_0 + b_1 * Independence + b_2 * SQ\_indepd + b_3 * Attendence + b_4 * Size\_dsh + b_5 * Number\_indp + b_6 * Size\_jsh + b_7 * Time\_js + b_8 * LEV + b_9 * LnTA + e \quad (19)$$

$$EPS = b_0 + b_1 * Times\_ds + b_2 * Attendence + b_3 * Size\_dsh + b_4 * Numfjer\_indp + b_5 * Size\_jsh + b_6 * Time\_js + b_7 * LEV + b_8 * LnTA + e \quad (20)$$

$$EPS = b_0 + b_1 * Times\_ds + b_2 * SQ\_times\_ds + b_3 * Attendence + b_4 * Size\_dsh + b_5 * Number\_indp + b_6 * Size\_jsh + b_7 * Time\_js + b_8 * LEV + b_9 * LnTA + e \quad (21)$$

$$NAPS = b_0 + b_1 * Times\_ds + b_2 * Attendence + b_3 * Size\_dsh + b_4 * Number\_indp + b_5 * Size\_jsh + b_6 * Time\_js + b_7 * LEV + b_8 * LnTA + e \quad (22)$$

$$NAPS = b_0 + b_1 * Times\_ds + b_2 * SQ\_times\_ds + b_3 * Attendenre + b_4 * Size\_dsh + b_5 * Number\_indp + b_6 * Size\_jsh + b_7 * Time\_js + b_8 * LEV + b_9 * LnTA + e \quad (23)$$

$$ROA = b_0 + b_1 * Times\_ds + b_2 * Ailendence + b_3 * Size\_dsh + b_4 * Number\_indp + b_5 * Size\_jsh + b_6 * Time\_js + b_7 * LEV + b_8 * LnTA + e \quad (24)$$

$$ROA = b_0 + b_1 * Times\_ds + b_2 * SQ\_times\_ds + b_3 * Attendence + b_4 * Size\_dsh + b_5 * Nuniber\_indp + b_6 * Size\_jsh + b_7 * Time\_js + b_8 * LEV + b_9 * LnTA + e \quad (25)$$

$$EPS = b_0 + b_1 * Lnpay\_ds + b_2 * Attendence + b_3 * Size\_dsh + b_4 * Number\_indp$$

$$+ b_5 * Size\_jsh + b_6 * Time\_js + b_7 * LEV + b_8 * LnTA + e \quad (26)$$

$$NAPS = b_0 + b_1 * Lnpay\_ds + b_2 * Attendence + b_3 * Size\_dsh + b_4 * Number\_indp$$
$$+ b_5 * Size\_jsh + b_6 * Time\_js + b_7 * LEV + b_8 * LnTA + e \quad (27)$$

$$ROA = b_0 + b_1 * Lnpay\_ds + b_2 * Attendance + b_3 * Size\_dsh + b_4 * Number\_indp$$
$$+ b_5 * Size\_jsh + b_6 * Time\_js + b_7 * LEV + b_8 * LnTA + e \quad (28)$$

Model (1) – (6) are used to examine the relation between board independency and CP. Model (7) – (12) are used to examine the relation between frequency of meetings called by the board of directors and CP. Model (13) – (15) are used to examine the relation between total compensation of the top three directors and CP.

(4) Empirical results and analysis.

A. Descriptive statistics and correlation analysis.

Table 7 – 34 presents the four-year average descriptive statistics of the variables employed from 2002 to 2005 and Table 7 – 35 present the descriptive statistics year by year. Table 7 – 34 indicates that the average EPS during the four years is negative with –0. 0275 yuan and the revenue situation is not ideal in these years. Among these observations, the highest EPS is 1. 3637 yuan, lowest – 14. 0837 yuan and the standard deviation is 0. 7852, which means a large disparity in the sample. Table 7 – 35 suggests that the average EPS is positive with 0. 0449 and 0. 0665 in 2002 and 2003 respectively, but negative with –0. 1086 and –0. 05 in 2004 and 2005 respectively.

Based on the statistical results in Table 7 – 34 and Table 7 – 35, the four-year average NAVPS is 2. 2981 yuan/share, highest 9. 2828 yuan/share, lowest –12. 4813 and the standard deviation is 1. 8162, which means a big disparity. The NAVPS in 2002 is 2. 3573 yuan/share, increases to 2. 5252 yuan/share in 2003, decreases to 2. 175 3 yuan/share in 2004 and increases to 2. 2329 yuan/share in the following year. The four-year average ROA is –0. 0229 with the value of each year is –0. 0046, –0. 0124, –0. 0359 and –0. 0266 respectively.

Table 7 – 34 Descriptive statistics of the average from 2002 to 2005

Variable	N	Minimum	Maximum	Mean	Std. deviation
EPS	858	– 14. 084	1. 364	–0. 028	0. 785
NAPS	858	– 12. 481	—	2. 298	1. 816
ROA	858	– 1. 787	0. 511	–0. 023	0. 185
Independence	858	0. 125	1. 000	0. 525	0. 206
Times_ ds	858	1. 000	29. 000	8. 259	3. 569
Lnpay_ ds	858	10. 073	16. 754	12. 598	0. 905
Attendence_ gd	858	0. 220	1. 000	0. 555	0. 171
Size_ dsh	858	1. 000	16. 000	6. 020	1. 647
Number_ indp	858	1. 000	6. 000	2. 970	0. 799
Size_ jsh	858	1. 000	9. 000	3. 680	1. 159

continued

Variable	N	Minimum	Maximum	Mean	Std. deviation
Times_js	858	1.000	11.000	3.625	1.705
LEV	858	0.068	23.799	0.715	1.445
LnTA	858	16.884	23.187	20.754	0.927

Table 7 – 35 Descriptive statistics of the average from 2002 to 2005

Year	Varaible	N	Minimum	Maximum	Mean	Std. deviation
2002	EPS	126	–1.474	0.702	0.045	0.326
	NAPS	126	–1.385	6.022	2.357	1.414
	ROA	126	–0.999	0.152	–0.005	0.121
	Independence	126	0.125	1.000	0.372	0.205
	Times_ds	126	1.000	16.000	6.550	2.875
	Lnpay_ds	126	10.386	16.754	12.191	0.872
	Attendence_gd	126	0.220	1.000	0.552	0.140
	Size_dsh	126	2.000	13.000	6.840	1.874
	Number_indp	126	1.000	4.000	2.300	0.707
	Size_jsh	126	2.000	8.000	3.920	1.217
	Times_js	126	2.000	8.000	3.480	1.424
	LEV	126	0.112	10.375	0.602	0.906
	LnTA	126	17.553	22.759	20.616	0.892
2003	EPS	186	–3.303	0.971	0.067	0.479
	NAPS	186	–2.739	9.283	2.525	1.726
	ROA	186	–1.431	0.219	–0.012	0.172
	Independence	186	0.200	1.000	0.515	0.125
	Times_ds	186	2.000	23.000	9.300	3.336
	Lnpay_ds	186	10.166	15.384	12.419	0.834
	Attendence_gd	186	0.220	1.000	0.542	0.143
	Size_dsh	186	3.000	12.000	6.150	1.461
	Number_indp	186	1.000	6.000	3.070	0.706
	Size_jsh	186	2.000	7.000	3.820	1.080
	Times_js	186	2.000	9.000	4.130	1.681
	LEV	186	0.099	23.799	0.720	1.760
	LnTA	186	16.884	23.041	20.757	0.918
2004	EPS	245	–14.084	1.364	–0.109	1.173
	NAPS	245	–9.856	7.966	2.175	1.852
	ROA	245	–1.787	0.510	–0.036	0.242
	Independence	245	0.333	1.000	0.552	0.137
	Times_ds	245	3.000	27.000	8.540	3.739
	Lnpay_ds	245	10.073	16.077	12.646	0.900
	Attendence_gd	245	0.235	1.000	0.545	0.167
	Size_dsh	245	3.000	16.000	5.960	1.606
	Number_indp	245	2.000	6.000	3.160	0.698
	Size_jsh	245	1.000	9.000	3.750	1.124
	Times_js	245	1.000	11.000	3.600	1.786
	LEV	245	0.068	19.867	0.789	1.795
	LnTA	245	17.061	23.154	20.758	0.939

continued

Year	Varaible	N	Minimum	Maximum	Mean	Std. Deviation
2005	EPS	301	-5.010	1.045	-0.050	0.665
	NAPS	301	-12.481	8.021	2.233	1.979
	ROA	301	-1.542	0.144	-0.027	0.159
	Independence	301	0.333	1.000	0.573	0.258
	Times_ds	301	3.000	29.000	8.100	3.566
	Lnpay_ds	301	10.290	15.490	12.840	0.888
	Attendence_gd	301	0.271	1.000	0.573	0.200
	Size_dsh	301	1.000	10.000	5.650	1.562
	Number_indp	301	1.000	6.000	3.030	0.828
	Size_jsh	301	1.000	7.000	3.450	1.175
	Times_js	301	1.000	11.000	3.330	1.671
	LEV	301	0.070	14.474	0.698	1.046
	LnTA	301	17.122	23.187	20.805	0.936

The four-year average frequency of meeting called by the board of directors is 8.2587, highest is 29, lowest is 1. The average frequency in 2002 is low with 6.54776, while that of 2003 to 2005 is high with 9.3011, 8.5388 and 8.1030 respectively. The frequency in 2002 is lower with 16 and is high in three other years with 23, 27 and 29 respectively.

The four-year average frequency of meeting called by the board of supervisors is 3.6247. The average frequency in 2003 is high with 4.1312, while that of the other years is lower than 4 with 3.4841, 3.6041 and 3.3256 respectively in 2002, 2004 and 2005. The four-year average ratio of independent directors is 52.50%. The average ration is 37.21%, increases to 51.49% rapidly and is 55.23% and 57.30% in 2004 and 2005 respectively.

The share ratio held by shareholders attending the annual shareholder meeting is 55.53% on average and doesn't changes much from 2002 to 2005. The average ratio in 2003 is the lowest with 54.10%, highest in 2005 with 57.30% and 55.24% and 54.51% in 2002 and 2004 respectively. The biggest value in these four years is 100% and the lowest 22%.

The average scale of the board of directors is 6.02 from 2002 to 2005 and shows a decreasing trend. The value in 2002 is the biggest and decreases to 5.65 in 2005, the scale is 6.15 and 5.96 in 2003 and 2004 respectively. Similarly, the scale of the board of supervisors is 3.68 in these four years and shows a decreasing trend as well. The average scale in 2002 is 3.92 and decreases to 3.45 in 2005. The average frequency of meeting called by the board of supervisors is 3.627 4 and shows an increasing first and decreasing after trend. The average frequency in 2002 is 3.48 and 4.13 in 2003, then the ratio decreases in the following two years with 3.6 and 3.33.

The correlation analysis results are present in Table 7-36 and frequency of meeting

Table 7 – 36 **Correlation results among variables**

	(1)	(2)	(3)	(4)	(5)	(6)	(7)
Eps(1)	1	0. 652 (**)	0. 933 (**)	0. 018	0. 076 (*)	0. 236 (**)	0. 303 (**)
Naps (2)	0. 560 (**)	1	0. 499 (**)	0. 024	0. 127 (**)	0. 309 (**)	0. 280 (**)
Roa (3)	0. 734 (**)	0. 528 (**)	1	0. 007	0. 088 (**)	0. 164 (**)	0. 324 (**)
Independence (4)	-0. 051	0. 040	-0. 018	1	0. 079 (*)	0. 095 (**)	0. 068 (*)
Timesjds (5)	0. 187 (**)	0. 144 (**)	0. 080 (*)	0. 132 (**)	1	-0. 065	-129 (**)
Lnpay_ds (6)	0. 119 (**)	0. 278 (**)	0. 096 (**)	0. 104 (**)	-0. 047	1	0. 072 (*)
Attendence (7)	0. 193 (**)	0. 300 (**)	0. 198 (**)	0. 034	-102 (**)	0. 073 (*)	1
Size_dsh (8)	0. 070 (*)	0. 017	0. 047	-563 (**)	-0. 065	0. 022	0. 007
Number_indp (9)	0. 014	0. 064	0. 079 (*)	0. 398 (**)	0. 069 (*)	0. 190 (**)	0. 089 (**)
Sizejsh (10)	0. 006	-0. 015	-0. 022	-187 (**)	-0. 062	-0. 070 (*)	-0. 038
Times_js (11)	-0. 012	-0. 062	0. 028	0. 032	0. 311 (**)	-107 (**)	-0. 035
LEV (12)	-0. 216 (**)	-0. 378 (**)	-0. 616 (**)	-0. 041	0. 000	-0. 068 (*)	-125 (**)
LnTA (13)	0. 237 (**)	0. 481 (**)	0. 389 (**)	0. 030	0. 025	0. 417 (**)	-0. 027

	(8)	(9)	(10)	(11)	(12)	(13)	
Eps(1)	0. 007	0. 083 (*)	0. 000	-0. 055	-0. 400 (**)	0. 361 (**)	
Naps (2)	-0. 008	0. 068 (*)	-0. 034	-0. 086 (*)	-0. 563 (**)	0. 495 (**)	
Roa (3)	0. 001	0. 052	0. 005	-0. (M7	-0. 486 (**)	0. 203 (**)	
Independence (4)	-0. 525 (**)	0. 571 (**)	-0. 170 (**)	-0. 034	0. 033	0. 049	
Timesjds (5)	-0. 125 (**)	0. 075 (*)	-0. 044	0. 327 (**)	0. 149 (**)	0. 024	
Lnpay_ds (6)	0. 039	0. 180 (**)	-0. 059	-106 (**)	-0. 079 (*)	0. 407 (**)	
Attendence (7)	0. 026	0. 082 (*)	-0. 037	-0. 029	-0. 316 (**)	-0. 031	
Size_dsh (8)	1	0. 263 (**)	0. 322 (**)	0. 049	0. 005	0. 074 (*)	
Number_indp (9)	0. 285 (**)	1	0. 103 (**)	0. 089 (**)	0. 025	0. 180 (**)	
Sizejsh (10)	0. 309 (**)	0. 108 (**)	1	0. 064	o. mi	0. 105 (**)	
Times_js (11)	0. 089 (**)	0. 112 (**)	0. 054	1	0. 066	-0. 0Q3	
LEV (12)	0. 012	-0. 060	0. 078 (*)	-0. 039	1	0. 020	
LnTA (13)	0. 068 (*)	0. 189 (**)	0. 076 (*)	-0. 001	-0. 364 (**)	1	

Note: the Pearson correlation is showed on the left down corner and the Spearman correlation is showed on the right up corner. * indicates the 95% significant level (two-tailed) and ** 99% significant level (two-tailed).

called by the board of directors is positively correlated with EPS, NAVPS and ROA with a significant level of 5% or 10% and Pearson correlation coefficient is 0.187, 0.144 and 0.080 respectively, which means that the increasing of frequency of meeting called by the board of directors may positively correlated with CP. Total compensation of the top 3 directors is positively correlated with CP as well and the significant level is 5%. The correlation coefficient is 0.119, 0.278 and 0.096 respectively. The board independency is not significantly correlated with CP.

The correlation between the controls and the explained variable indicates that EPS is positively correlated with the share ratio held by shareholders attending the annual shareholder meeting, scale of the board of directors and total asset and negatively correlated with assets debt ratio. NAVPS and ROA are not correlated with scale of the board of directors significantly and the relations of other controls with EPS are the same as among themselves.

B. Regression results and analysis.

We regress the above equations respectively using fixed and random effect model, whose results are present in Table 7 –37 and the first column of each equation shows the fixed effect results and second random effect results. The appropriate approach is chosen using Hausman test.

According to the regression equation (1) and (2), Table 7 –37 presents the linear and non-linear regression results between frequency of meeting called by the board of directors and EPS. The Hausman test results direct to the choice of fixed effect method i. e. model (A) and (C). In model (C), the coefficients of board meeting frequency and its squared term are significant on the level of 1%, which means that the relation between board meeting frequency and EPS is non-linear. Take one more step, according to the results, with other conditions constant, EPS is the highest when board meeting frequency is 7.37.

Table 7 –37 Results of the regression between board meeting frequency and EPS

MODEL	EPS			
	A	B	C	D
Variable	Fixed effect	Radom effect	Fixed effect	Radom effect
Times_ds	-0.0329 ***	-0.0406 ***	0.0762 ***	0.0797 ***
	0.0118	0.0079	0.0289 ***	0.0230
SQ_times_ds	—	—	-0.0052 ***	-0.0054 ***
	—	—	0.0013	0.0010
Attendence	0.6118	0.7960 ***	0.7765 *	0.8386 ***
	0.4083	0.1653	0.4037	0.1620

continued

MODEL	EPS			
	A	B	C	D
Variable	Fixed effect	Radom effect	Fixed effect	Radom effect
Size_ dsh	0. 0535 *	0. 0291 *	0. 0643 **	0. 0406 **
	0. 0288	0. 0177	0. 0284	0. 0174
Number_ indp	-0. 0281	-0. 0209	-0. 0235	-0. 0322
	0. 0505	0. 0344	0. 0497	0. 0339
Size_ jsh	0. 0924 *	-0. 0012	0. 0877 *	-0. 0067
	0. 0521	0. 0256	0. 0513	0. 0251
Times_ js	0. 0318	0. 0262	0. 0226	0. 0140
	0. 0223	0. 0160	0. 0221	0. 0159
LEV	0. 0336	-0. 0549 ***	0. 0392	-0. 0531 ***
	0. 0348	0. 0200	0. 0343	0. 0196
LnTA	0. 6163	0. 2016	0. 6050	0. 1949
	0. 1244	0. 0353	0. 1225	0. 0344
Constant	-13. 6055 ***	-4. 4906 ***	-13. 9755 ***	-4. 9072 ***
	2. 6267	0. 7459	2. 5863	0. 7327
R-sq	0. 1043	0. 2283	0. 1345	0. 2715
F_u_i	1. 77 (0. 0000)	—	1. 78 (0. 0000)	—
F	7. 09 (0. 0000)	—	8. 39 (0. 0000)	—
Wald chi^2	—	127. 19 (0. 0000)	—	163. 11
Hausman	23. 37 (0. 0029)		22. 81 (0. 0066)	

Note: *** indicates the 99% significant level, ** 95% significant level and * 90% significant level. The value in brackets under the coefficient is the standard error. F test and Hausman test results are present in the Table, t test is adopted in fixed effect model and z test in random effect model.

According to the regression equation (3) and (4), Table 7 -38 presents the linear and non-linear regression results between annual frequency of the board of directors and NAVPS. The Hausman test results direct to the choice of fixed effect method i. e. model (E) and (G). In model (E), annual frequency of the board of directors is significantly correlated with NAVPS. However, in model (G), the coefficients of board meeting frequency and its squared term are not significant, which means that board meeting frequency may negatively correlated with NAVPS.

Table 7 -38 Results of the regression between board meeting frequency and NAVPS

MODEL	NAPS			
	E	F	G	H
Variable	Fixed effect	Radom effect	Fixed effect	Radom effect
Times_ ds	-0. 0404 *	-0. 0435 ***	0. 0454	0. 0400
	0. 0145	0. 0128	0. 0361	0. 0339
SQ_ times_ ds	—	—	-0. 0041	-0. 0038
	—	—	0. 0016	0. 0014

continued

MODEL	NAPS			
	A	B	C	D
Variable	Fixed effect	Radom effect	Fixed effect	Radom effect
Attendence	1. 9250 ***	2. 8918 ***	2. 0545 ***	2. 9404 ***
	0. 5040	0. 3252	0. 5035	0. 3250
Size_ dsh	0. 0386	0. 0238	0. 0471	0. 0326
	0. 0355	0. 0297	0. 0355	0. 0298
Number_ indp	-0. 0501	-0. 0472	-0. 0465	-0. 0505
	0. 0623	0. 0545	0. 0620	0. 0543
Size_ jsh	0. 1905 ***	0. 0689	0. 1868 ***	0. 0662
	0. 0644	0. 0484	0. 0640	0. 0483
Times_ js	0. 0722 ***	0. 0406	0. 0649 **	0. 0328
	0. 0276	0. 0250	0. 0276	0. 0250
LEV	-0. 0187	-0. 1031 ***	-0. 0143	-0. 0990 ***
	0. 0430	0. 0333	0. 0428	0. 0332
LnTA	0. 9749 ***	0. 8666 ***	0. 9660 ***	0. 8618 ***
	0. 1536	0. 0795	0. 1528	0. 0794
Constant	-19. 7039 ***	-17. 2530 ***	-19. 9949 ***	-17. 5682 ***
	3. 2425	1. 6796	3. 2255	1. 6814
R-sq	0. 2035	0. 3635	0. 2144	0. 3623
F_ u_ i	6. 60 (0. 0000)	—	6. 67 (0. 0000)	—
F	15. 56 (0. 0000)	—	14. 74 (0. 0000)	—
Wald chi^2	—	312. 18 (0. 0000)	—	320. 43 (0. 0000)
Hausman	47. 57 (0. 0000)		47. 33 (0. 0000)	

Note: *** indicates the 99% significant level, ** 95% significant level and * 90% significant level. The value in brackets under the coefficient is the standard error. F test and Hausman test results are present in the Table, t test is adopted in fixed effect model and z test in random effect model.

According to the regression equation (5) and (6), Table 7 - 39 presents the linear and non-linear regression results between annual frequency of the board of directors and ROA. The Hausman test results direct to the choice of fixed effect method i. e. model (I) and (K). In model (K), the coefficients of board meeting frequency and its squared term are significant on the level of 10% and 5% respectively, which means that the relation between board meeting frequency and EPS is non-linear. Take one more step, according to the results, with other conditions constant, ROA is the highest when board meeting frequency is 8. 83.

Table 7 - 39 Results of the regression between board meeting frequency and ROA

MODEL	ROA			
	I	J	K	L
Variable	Fixed effect	Radom effect	Fixed effect	Radom effect
Times_ ds	-0. 0026	-0. 0039 ***	0. 0106 *	0. 0093 **
	0. 0024	0. 0015	0. 0060	0. 0045

continued

MODEL	ROA			
	I	J	K	L
Variable	Fixed effect	Radom effect	Fixed effect	Radom effect
SQ_times_ds	—	—	-0.0006 **	-0.0006 ***
	—	—	0.0003	0.0002
Attendence	0.1819 **	0.1486 ***	0.2018 **	0.1528 ***
	0.0835	0.0300	0.0835	0.0298
Size_dsh	0.0105 *	0.0044	0.0118 **	0.0056 *
	0.0059	0.0033	0.0059	0.0033
Number_indp	-0.0078	-0.0034	-0.0073	-0.0047
	0.0103	0.0065	0.0103	0.0065
Size_jsh	0.0211 **	0.0002	0.0205 *	-0.0004
	0.0107	0.0046	0.0106	0.0046
Times_js	0.0038	0.0040	0.0027	0.0028
	0.0046	0.0030	0.0046	0.0030
LEV	-0.0412 ***	-0.0655 ***	-0.0405 ***	-0.0654 ***
	0.0071	0.0037	0.0071	0.0037
LnTA	0.1604 ***	0.0440 ***	0.1590 ***	0.0433 ***
	0.0255	0.0061	0.0253	0.0061
Constant	-3.5334 ***	-0.9718 ***	-3.5782 ***	-1.0188 ***
	0.5373	0.1300	0.5350	0.1301
R-sq	0.3266	0.5198	0.3345	0.5286
F_u_i	1.36 (0.0000)	—	1.36 (0.0008)	—
F	29.52 (0.0000)	—	27.15 (0.0000)	—
Wald chi^2	—	611.65 (0.0000)	—	628.24 (0.0000)
Hausman	33.40 (0.0000)		33.40 (0.0001)	

Note: *** indicates the 99% significant level, ** 95% significant level and * 90% significant level. The value in brackets under the coefficient is the standard error. F test and Hausman test results are present in the Table, t test is adopted in fixed effect model and z test in random effect model.

According to the regression equation (7) and (8), Table 7-40 presents the linear and non-linear regression results between board independency and EPS. The Hausman test results direct to the choice of fixed effect method i. e. model (M) and (O). In the two models, the regression results are both not significant, which means that the relation between board independency and EPS is not significant in the sample we studied.

Table 7-40 Results of the regression between board independency and EPS

MODEL	EPS			
	M	N	O	P
Variable	Fixed effect	Random effect	Fixed effect	Random effect
independence	-0.0116	-0.2023	-0.6405	-0.2786
	0.3774	0.2126	1.0901	0.6376
SQ_indepd	—	—	0.2870	0.0270
	—	—	0.4667	0.2126

continued

MODEL	EPS			
	I	J	K	L
Variable	Fixed effect	Random effect	Fixed effect	Random effect
Attendence	0.6884 *	0.9134 ***	0.7049 *	0.9118 ***
	0.4144	0.1681	0.4155	0.1686
Size_ dsh	0.0615	0.0205	0.0429	0.0171
	0.0386	0.0260	0.0491	0.0370
Number_ indp	-0.0518	-0.0074	0.0068	0.0000
	0.0724	0.0475	0.1196	0.0756
Size_ jsh	0.0891 *	0.0059	0.0859	0.0058
	0.0526	0.0263	0.0529	0.0263
Times_ js	0.0086	-0.0005	0.0091	-0.0005
	0.0209	0.0155	0.0210	0.0155
LEV	0.0309	-0.0563 ***	0.0310	-0.0564 ***
	0.0352	0.0204	0.0352	0.0204
LnTA	0.6037 ***	0.1981 ***	0.6046 ***	0.1980 ***
	0.1258	0.0365	0.1258	0.0365
Constant	-13.5318 ***	-4.6303 ***	-13.3704 ***	-4.5961 ***
	2.6859	0.7905	2.7004	0.8327
R-sq	0.0900	0.1756	0.0907	0.1758
F_u_i	1.81 (0.0000)	—	1.81 (0.0000)	—
F	6.02 (0.0000)	—	5.39 (0.0000)	—
Wald chi^2	—	97.69 (0.0000)	—	97.61 (0.0000)
Hausman	20.93 (0.0000)		21.49 (0.0107)	

Note: *** indicates the 99% significant level, ** 95% significant level and * 90% significant level. The value in brackets under the coefficient is the standard error. F test and Hausman test results are present in the Table, t test is adopted in fixed effect model and z test in random effect model.

According to the regression equation (9) and (10), Table 7 - 41 presents the linear and non-linear regression results between board independency and NAVPS. The Hausman test results direct to the choice of fixed effect method i. e. model (Q) and (S). In the two models, the regression results are both not significant, which means that the relation between board independency and NAVPS is not significant in the sample we studied.

Table 7 - 41 Results of the regression between board independency and NAVPS

MODEL	NAPS			
	Q	R	S	T
Variable	Fixed effect	Random effect	Fixed effect	Random effect
Independence	0.2360	0.4165	-0.8159	0.2814
	0.4657	0.3549	1.3447	1.0120
SQ_ indepd	—	—	0.4801	0.0518
	—	—	0.5757	0.3630

continued

MODEL	NAPS			
	I	J	K	L
Variable	Fixed effect	Random effect	Fixed effect	Random effect
Attendence	2. 0565 ***	3. 0190 ***	2. 0840 ***	3. 0167 ***
	0. 5113	0. 3253	0. 5125	0. 3260
Size_ dsh	0. 0655	0. 0675 *	0. 0342	0. 0624
	0. 0476	0. 0410	0. 0606	0. 0543
Number_ indp	-0. 1139	-0. 1334 *	-0. 0160	-0. 1204
	0. 0893	0. 0742	0. 1476	0. 1179
Size_ jsh	0. 1878 ***	0. 0741	0. 1825 ***	0. 0735
	0. 0649	0. 0487	0. 0652	0. 0488
Times_ js	0. 0444 *	0. 0121	0. 0452 *	0. 0122
	0. 0258	0. 0236	0. 0259	0. 0236
LEV	-0. 0200	-0. 1026 ***	-0. 0199	-0. 1028 ***
	0. 0435	0. 0336	0. 0435	0. 0336
LnTA	0. 9662 ***	0. 8682 ***	0. 9675 ***	0. 8681 ***
	0. 1552	0. 0802	0. 1552	0. 0802
Constant	-19. 9131 ***	-17. 8611 ***	-19. 6432 ***	-17. 8086 ***
	3. 3144	1. 7255	3. 3312	1. 7628
R-sq	0. 1913	0. 3566	0. 1925	0. 3562
F_u_i	6. 60 (0. 0000)	—	6. 59 (0. 0000)	—
F	0. 1913 (0. 0000)	—	12. 87 (0. 0000)	—
Wald chi^2	—	298. 35 (0. 0000)	—	298. 17 (0. 0000)
Hausman	42. 88 (0. 0000)		45. 52 (0. 0000)	

Note: *** indicates the 99% significant level, ** 95% significant level and * 90% significant level. The value in brackets under the coefficient is the standard error. F test and Hausman test results are present in the Table, t test is adopted in fixed effect model and z test in random effect model.

According to the regression equation (11) and (12), Table 7 -42 presents the linear and non-linear regression results between board independency and ROA. The Hausman test results direct to the choice of fixed effect method i. e. model (U) and (W). In the two models, the regression results are both not significant, which means that the relation between independency of the board of directors and ROA is not significant in the sample we studied.

Table 7 -42 Results of the regression between board independency and ROA

MODEL	ROA			
	U	V	W	X
Variable	Fixed effect	Random effect	Fixed effect	Random effect
Independence	0. 2360	0. 4165	-0. 8159	0. 2814
	0. 4657	0. 3549	1. 3447	1. 0120
SQ_ indepd	—	—	0. 4801	0. 0518
	—	—	0. 5757	0. 3630

continued

MODEL	ROA			
	I	J	K	L
Variable	Fixed effect	Random effect	Fixed effect	Random effect
Attendence	2. 0565 **	3. 0190 ***	2. 0840 **	3. 0167 ***
	0. 5113	0. 3253	0. 5125	0. 3260
Size_dsh	0. 0655	0. 0675	0. 0342	0. 0624
	0. 0476	0. 0410	0. 0606	0. 0543
Number_indp	-0. 1139	-0. 1334	-0. 0160	-0. 1204
	0. 0893	0. 0742	0. 1476	0. 1179
Size_jsh	0. 1878 *	0. 0741	0. 1825 **	0. 0735
	0. 0649	0. 0487	0. 0652	0. 0488
Times_js	0. 0444	0. 0121	0. 0452	0. 0122
	0. 0258	0. 0236	0. 0259	0. 0236
LEV	-0. 0200 ***	-0. 1026 ***	-0. 0199 ***	-0. 1028 ***
	0. 0435	0. 0336	0. 0435	0. 0336
LnTA	0. 9662 ***	0. 8682 ***	0. 9675 ***	0. 8681 ***
	0. 1552	0. 0802	0. 1552	0. 0802
Constant	-19. 9131 ***	-17. 8611 ***	-19. 6432 ***	-17. 8086 ***
	3. 3144	1. 7255	3. 3312	1. 7628
R-sq	0. 3251	0. 5166	0. 3254	0. 5154
F_u_i	1. 37 (0. 0000)	—	1. 36 (0. 0007)	—
F	29. 33 (0. 0000)	—	26. 04 (0. 0000)	—
Wald chi^2	—	603. 54 (0. 0000)	—	604. 08 (0. 0000)
Hausman	35. 01 (0. 0000)		35. 47 (0. 0000)	

Note: *** indicates the 99% significant level, ** 95% significant level and * 90% significant level. The value in brackets under the coefficient is the standard error. F test and Hausman test results are present in the Table, t test is adopted in fixed effect model and z test in random effect model.

According to the regression equation (13), (14) and (15), Table 7 - 43 presents regression results between total compensation of the top three directors and CP. The Hausman test results direct to the choice of fixed effect method i. e. model (Y), (AA) and (AC). In these three models, the relations are all positively significant. To be specific, the significant level of the coefficient of compensation and EPS is 5%, that of compensation and NAVPS 10 and that of compensation and ROA 5%, which means that the increasing of total compensation of the top three directors and improvement of CP are highly correlated. This may resulted from the high motivation inspired by increasing compensation for the directors.

Table 7 – 43 Results of the regression between compensation of the top three directors and CP

MODEL	EPS		NAPS		ROA	
	Y	Z	AA	AB	AC	AD
Variable	Fixed effect	Random effect	Fixed effect	Random effect	Fixed effect	Random effect
Lnpay_ ds	0. 1311 **	-0. 0113	0. 1365 *	0. 0029	0. 0266 **	-0. 0102
	0. 0625	0. 0354	0. 0773	0. 0620	0. 0127	0. 0063
Attendence	0. 6354	0. 9152 ***	1. 9643 ***	3. 0129 ***	0. 1768 **	0. 1643 ***
	0. 4095	0. 1693	0. 5062	0. 3256	0. 0832	0. 0301
Size_ dsh	0. 0574 **	0. 0384 **	0. 0443	0. 0345	0. 0101 *	0. 0052
	0. 0288	0. 0180	0. 0356	0. 0298	0. 0059	0. 0033
Number_ indp	-0. 0286	-0. 0364	-0. 0554	-0. 0746	-0. 0047	-0. 0034
	0. 0512	0. 0354	0. 0633	0. 0555	0. 0104	0. 0066
Size_ jsh	0. 0746	0. 0063	0. 1715 ***	0. 0716	0. 0179 *	0. 0001
	0. 0528	0. 0265	0. 0652	0. 0491	0. 0107	0. 0047
Times_ js	0. 0016	-0. 0004	0. 0364	0. 0110	0. 0006	0. 0010
	0. 0211	0. 0156	0. 0261	0. 0238	0. 0043	0. 0029
LEV	0. 0383	-0. 0546 ***	-0. 0144	-0. 1054 ***	-0. 0399 ***	-0. 0647 ***
	0. 0351	0. 0206	0. 0434	0. 0339	0. 0071	0. 0038
LnTA	0. 6425 ***	0. 2064 ***	0. 9998 ***	0. 8597 ***	0. 1672 ***	0. 0486 ***
	0. 1261	0. 0397	0. 1559	0. 0840	0. 0256	0. 0068
Constant	-12. 6310 ***	-4. 7916 ***	-18. 6779 ***	-17. 4567 ***	-3. 3430 ***	-0. 9740 ***
	2. 6715	0. 7818	3. 3019	1. 7080	0. 5428	0. 1333
R-sq	0. 0981	0. 1698	0. 1961	0. 3558	0. 3310	0. 5092
F_u_i	1. 85 (0. 0000)	—	6. 59 (0. 0000)	—	1. 39 (0. 0003)	—
F	6. 62 (0. 0000)	—	14. 85 (0. 0000)	—	30. 13 (0. 0000)	—
Wald chi^2	—	96. 48 (0. 0000)	—	296. 82 (0. 0000)	—	598. 45 (0. 0000)
Hausman	25. 49 (0. 0013)		53. 07 (0. 0013)		33. 54 (0. 0000)	

Note: *** indicates the 99% significant level, ** 95% significant level and * 90% significant level. The value in brackets under the coefficient is the standard error. F test and Hausman test results are present in the Table, t test is adopted in fixed effect model and z test in random effect model.

2. Empirical analysis using manually collected data

(1) Data, variables and regression equation.

According to the manual collection of the public disclosed information, we acquire the information on employment in the biggest shareholder's company of the directors, total compensation of the independent directors and attendance ratio of the independent directors. In this part, the relations between these three indicators and CP are analyzed empirically.

Limited by number of words and to avoid repetition, the basic statistics of the employed variables will not be analyzed in this part and the regression equations are present here.

$$EPS = a_0 + a_1 * Ratio\_gdrz + a_2 * Times\_dsh + a_3 * Size\_dsh + a_4 * Diverge + a_5 * Shl + a_6 * Sh2 + a_7 * LEV + a_8 * LnTA + e \quad (28)$$

$$NAPS = a_0 + a_1 * Ratio\_gdrz + a_2 * Times\_dsh + a_3 * Size\_dsh + a_4 * Diverge + a_5 * Shl + a_6 * Sh2 + a_7 * LEV + a_8 * LnTA + e \quad (29)$$

$$ROA = a_0 + a_1 * Ratio\_garz + a_2 * Times\_dsh + a_3 * Size\_dsh + a_4 * Diverge + a_5 * Shl + a_6 * Sh2 + a_7 * LEV + a_8 * LnTA + e \quad (30)$$

$$EPS = a_0 + a_1 * Lnpay\_indp + a_2 * Times\_dsh + a_3 * Size\_dsh + a_4 * Diverge + a_5 * Shl + a_6 * Sh2 + a_7 * LEV + a_8 * LnTA + e \quad (31)$$

$$NAPS = a_0 + a_1 * Lnpay\_indp + a_2 * Times\_dsh + a_3 * Size\_dsh + a_4 * Diverge + a_5 * Shl + a_6 * Sh2 + a_7 * LEV + a_8 * LuTA + e \quad (32)$$

$$ROA = a_0 + a_1 * Lnpay\_indp + a_2 * Times\_dsh + a_3 * Size\_dsh + a_4 * Diverge + a_5 * Shl + a_6 * Sh2 + a_7 * LEV + a_8 * LnTA + e \quad (33)$$

$$EPS = a_0 + a_1 * Ratio\_attend\_indp + a_2 * Times\_dsh + a_3 * Size\_dsh + a_4 * Diverge + a_5 * Shl + a_6 * Sh2 + a_7 * LEV + a_8 * LnTA + e \quad (34)$$

$$MAPS = a_0 + a_1 * Ratio\_attend\_indp + a_2 * Times\_dsh + a_3 * Size\_dsh + a_4 * Diverge + a_5 * Shl + a_6 * Sh2 + a_7 * LEV + a_8 * LnTA + e \quad (35)$$

$$ROA = a_0 + a_1 * Ratio\_attend\_indp + a_2 * Times\_dsh + a_3 * Size\_dsh + a_4 * Diverge + a_5 * Shl + a_6 * Sh2 + a_7 * LEV + a_8 * LnTA + e \quad (36)$$

Equation (16) to (18) are used to analyze the relation between ratio of the employment in major shareholders' companies of the directors and CP, regression results are present in model (BA) to (BC). Equation (19) to (21) are used to analyze the relation between total compensation of the independent directors and CP. Equation (22) to (24) are used to analyze the relation between attendance ratio of the independent directors and CP.

Table 7 - 44 present the names, abbreviations and implications of the variables used in this part.

Table 7 – 44 **Variables, abbreviations and implications list**

Variable type	Abbreviation	Implication
Explained variables	EPS	Earnings per share
	NAPS	Net asset per share
	ROA	Return of asset
Explanatory variables	Ratio_ gdrz	Ratio of the employment in major shareholders' companies of the directors
	Lnpay_ indp	Compensation of the independent directors
	Ratio_ attend_ indp	Attendance ratio of the independent directors
Controls	Times_ dsh	Annual frequency of meeting called by board of the directors
	Size_ dsh	Scale of board of the directors
	Diverge	Difference between voting and cash flow rights of the controlling shareholders
	Sh1	Ratio of share held by the largest shareholder
	Sh2	Ratio of share held by the second largest shareholder
	LEV	Debt asset ratio
	LnTA	Natural logarithm of scale of the company

(2) Regression results and analysis.

According to the regression results between ratio of the employment in major shareholders' companies of the directors and CP present in Table 7 – 45, significant test of the regression on model BA fails and the coefficient in the other two models is positive and negative respectively with failure of the significant tests neither. This means that in our sample, in board of the directors, the employment in major shareholders' companies of the directors doesn't affect CP negatively as predicted by the theoretical analysis above. The reason may be that the sample scale is too small. Additionally, the indicators of ratio of the employment in major shareholders' companies of the directors and CP are of the same year, regarding the lagging feature of the governance effect, more negative effects may be discovered using the CP indicator of 2006.

Table 7 – 45 Regression results between ratio of the employment in major shareholders' companies of the directors' compensation of the independent directors and FP

Independent Variable	EPS	NAPS	ROA	EPS	NAPS
Model	BA	BB	BC	BD	BE
Ratio_ gdrz	4. 1639	4. 4868	-0. 0035	—	—
	3. 5415	3. 6327	0. 0331	—	—
Lnpay_ indp	—	—	—	0. 6251	0. 4967
	—	—	—	0. 8819	0. 9052
Times_ dsh	0. 0675	0. 0704	-0. 0037 ***	0. 0551	0. 0608
	0. 1216	0. 1247	0. 0011	0. 1236	0. 1268

continued

Independent Variable	EPS	NAPS	ROA	EPS	NAPS
Size_dsh	0. 3267	0. 3636 *	0. 0015	0. 2663	0. 3139
	0. 2130	0. 2185	0. 0020	0. 2263	0. 2323
Diverge	0. 5034	0. 5115	0. 0234	0. 3114	0. 3791
	3. 9380	4. 0394	0. 0368	4. 0413	4. 1481
Sh1	3. 2237	4. 5046	-0. 0229	3. 7384	4. 9323
	4. 9857	5. 1141	0. 0465	5. 0867	5. 2211
Sh2	-1. 2551	-0. 8913	-0. 0624	-1. 9769	-1. 6287
	5. 9468	6. 1000	0. 0555	6. 0082	6. 1670
LEV	-6. 9987 **	-10. 1807 ***	-0. 1067 ***	-6. 8620 **	-10. 1163 **
	2. 5936	2. 6604	0. 0242	2. 6767	2. 7475
LnTA	0. 3021	0. 8828	0. 0165	0. 2803	0. 8795
	0. 5217	0. 5351	0. 0049	0. 5508	0. 5654

Note: *** indicates the 99% significant level, ** 95% significant level and * 90% significant level. The value in brackets under the coefficient is the standard error.

According to the regression results between compensation of the independent directors and firm performance present in Table 7 -45 and Table 7 -46, significant test of the regression fails similarly with that of the above regression and all the independent variables' coefficients are not significant. According to the regression results between compensation of the independent directors and firm performance present Table 7 -46, attendance ratio of the independent directors is positively correlated with firm performance significantly. The significant level with EPS is 5% and those with NAVPS and ROA are both 1%, which accords with the theoretical analysis. High attendance ratio of the independent directors in the board of the directors meeting is the important guarantee to perform the duty and vital ways to participate in the corporate decisions for the independent directors.

Table 7 -46 Regression between compensation, attendance of the independent directors and FP

Independent Variable	ROA	EPS	NAPS	ROA
Model	BF	BG	BH	BI
Lnpay_indp	-0. 0057	—	—	—
	0. 0082	—	—	—
Ratio_attend_indp	—	22. 1471 **	25. 6582 ***	0. 0163 ***
	—	8. 7109	8. 9028	0. 0049
Times_dsh	-0. 0036 ***	0. 0817	0. 0877	0. 0192
	0. 0011	0. 1203	0. 1229	0. 0822 ***
Size_dsh	0. 0018	0. 3357	0. 3747 *	-0. 0036
	0. 0021	0. 2107	0. 2153	0. 0011
Diverge	0. 0254	0. 6093	0. 6191	0. 0015
	0. 0374	3. 8915	3. 9772	0. 0020

continued

Independent Variable	ROA	EPS	NAPS	ROA
Sh1	-0.0266	3.7758	5.1376	0.0232
	0.0471	4.9336	5.0423	0.0367
Sh2	-0.0622	-1.2641	-0.8466	-0.0226
	0.0556	5.8591	5.9882	0.0466
LEV	-0.1145 **	-6.1540 **	-9.2165 ***	-0.0612
	0.0248	2.5741	2.6308	0.0553
LnTA	0.0185 **	0.2094	0.7717	-0.1063 ***
	0.0051	0.5174	0.5288	0.0243
Constant	-0.2850 **	-28.4731 **	-40.4598 ***	-0.2740 **
	0.1025	13.1787	13.4691	0.1244
R^2	0.1689	0.0705	0.1132	0.1593
F	5.61 (0.0000)	2.13 (0.0338)	3.59 (0.0006)	5.33 (0.0000)

Note: *** indicates the 99% significant level, ** 95% significant level and * 90% significant level. The value in brackets under the coefficient is the standard error.

(3) Study results and evaluation indicators of governance of the board of directors.

According to the theoretical analysis, literature review and empirical analysis using the two samples, we evaluate the governance situation of board of the directors in PLCs from the following perspectives: structure of board of the directors, motivation of board of the directors and behaviors of board of the directors.

To be specific, structure of board of the directors includes two indicators of ratio of the independent directors and ratio of the employment in major shareholders' companies of the directors, motivation of board of the directors includes two indicators of total compensation of the top three directors and that of the independent directors and behaviors of board of the directors includes two indicators as well, which are annual frequency of board of the directors meeting and attendance ratio of the independent directors.

7.3.2 Indicators for governance situation of the board of directors in private listed companies

1. Summary statistics of evaluation indicators for governance situation of the board of directors

We present descriptive statistical analysis of the basic situation of evaluation indicators for governance situation of board of the directors in Chinese PLCs in 2005.

(1) Structure of the board of directors.

A. Ratio of the non-executive directors in board of the directors

Histogram and empirical cumulative distribution functions figure of ratio of non-executive directors in board of the directors are present in Figure 7 – 22 and detailed frequency distribution table is not present constrained by the space. Ratio of the non-executive directors falls between 30% and 60% in most PLCs. To be specific, the ratio falls below 30% in 20% of the PLCs, the ratio falls below 44.4% in 52.77% of the PLCs and the ratio falls above 60% in 9.79% of the PLCs.

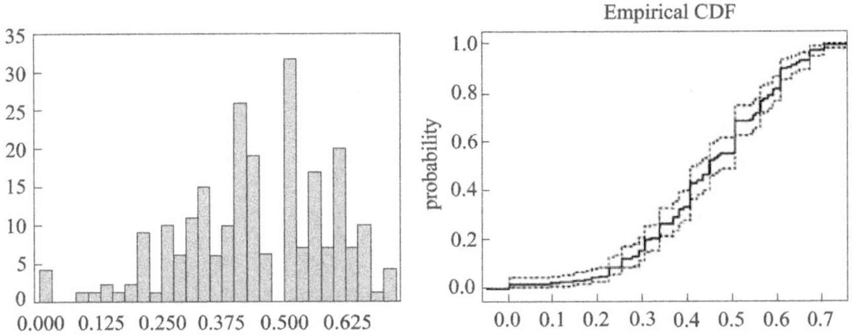

Table 7 – 22 Histogram and empirical CDF figure of ratio of non-executive directors in the board

Table 7 – 47 presents descriptive statistics summary of ratio of non-executive directors in board of the directors. The average value is 44%, biggest 79% and the standard deviation is 0.15, which means a big disparity among companies. The skewness is –0.49 indicating right skewed distribution of the data.

Table 7 – 47 Descriptive statistics of ratio of non-executive directors in the board

Variable	Mean	Median	Max	Min	Standard deviation	Skewness	Kurtosis
Numeric value	0.44	0.44	0.79	0.00	0.15	–0.49	3.04

B. Employment in major shareholders' companies of the directors

This indicator reflects control of the biggest shareholder on board of the directors and degree of due diligence of the directors. Histogram and empirical cumulative distribution functions figure of employment in major shareholders' companies of the directors are present in Figure 7 – 23. Average ratio of employment in major shareholders' companies of the directors is 27%, biggest 87.5%, which means most directors take other positions in shareholders' companies. The skewness is 0.87 indicating left skewed distribution of the data.

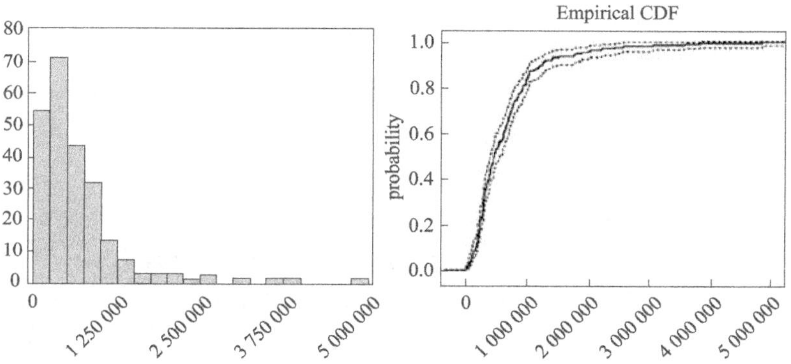

Figure 7 – 23 Histogram and empirical CDF figure of ratio of employment in major shareholders' companies of the directors

Table 7 – 48 Descriptive statistics of ratio of employment in major shareholders' companies of the directors

Variable	Mean	Median	Max	Min	Standard deviation	Skewness	Kurtosis
Numeric value	0. 27	0. 23	0. 875	0. 00	0. 16	0. 87	3. 96

(2) Motivation for the board of directors.

A. Total compensation of the top three directors

Distribution of the total compensation of the top three directors is present in Figure 7 – 24, the basic summary statistics are listed in Table 7 – 49. The average compensation is 646. 2 thousand yuan, highest 4. 816 million and lowest 453. 5 thousand yuan. The highest is more than 10 times of the lowest and the standard deviation is 63. 11, which means a big disparity among different companies. However, the distribution figure in Figure 7 – 24 shows that most values are under 1 million and only a few of them are higher than the average. The skewness is 2. 97, which indicates a left skewed distribution of the sample data.

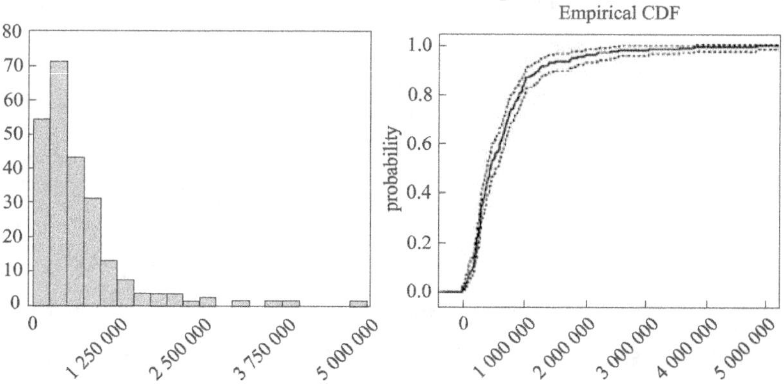

Figure 7 – 24 Histogram and empirical CDF figure of total compensation of the top three directors

Table 7 - 49 **Descriptive statistics of total compensation of the top three directors**

Variable	Mean	Median	Max	Min	Standard deviation	Skewness	Kurtosis
Numeric value	64.62	45.35	481.6	0	63.11	2.97	15.38

Note: the units are all 10 thousand.

B. Total compensation of the independent directors

Histogram and empirical cumulative distribution functions figure of total compensation of the independent directors are present in Figure 7 -25 and the basic descriptive statistics are listed in Table 7 -50. The average compensation is 117.4 thousand yuan, highest 280 and the standard deviation is 5.34, which means a big disparity among different companies. The skewness is 0.32, which indicates a left skewed distribution of the sample data. The compensation in most companies falls between 70 to 160 thousand yuan. Compared to the top three directors, compensation of the independent directors is far lower and the disparity among individuals is much smaller.

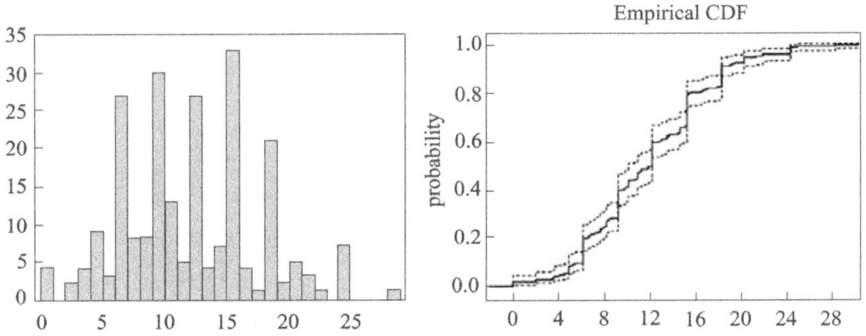

Figure 7 -25 Histogram and empirical CDF figure of total compensation of the independent directors

Table 7 -50 Descriptive statistics of total compensation of the independent directors

Variable	Mean	Median	Max	Min	Standard deviation	Skewness	Kurtosis
Numeric value	11.74	12	28	0	5.34	0.32	2.79

(3) Behaviors of the board of directors.

A. Frequency of Board of the Directors Meeting

Histogram and empirical cumulative distribution functions figure of total compensation of frequency of board of the directors are present in Figure 7 -26 and the basic descriptive statistics are listed in Table 7 -51. The average frequency of meeting is 8.01, median 7 and highest 26, which is much higher than that of the regular meetings. On the one hand, major adjustment of the management strategy may emerge and decisions needed to be made by board of the directors meeting increases. On the other, board of the directors may not reach a consensus on some issues internally and have to communicate and coordinate repeatedly. The smallest frequency of board of the directors is 2, standard deviation 3.54 and skewness is 2.04, which indicates a left skewed distribution of the sample data.

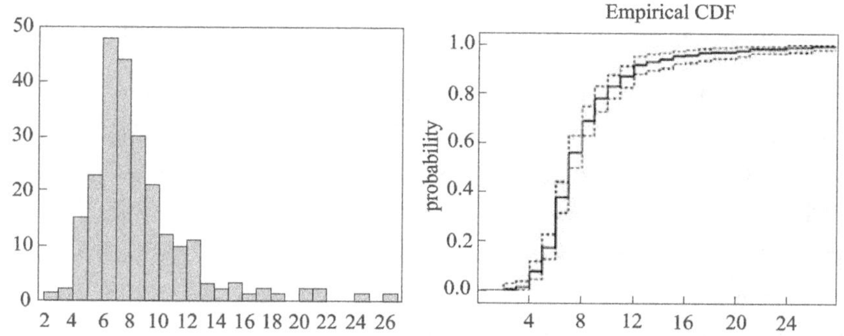

Figure 7 – 26 Histogram and empirical CDF figure of frequency of the board meeting

Table 7 – 51 Descriptive statistics of frequency of the board meeting

Variable	Mean	Median	Max	Min	Standard Deviation	Skewness	Kurtosis
Numeric value	11.74	12	28	0	5.34	0.32	2.79

B. Attendance ratio of the independent directors

Histogram and empirical cumulative distribution functions figure of attendance ratio of the independent directors are present in Figure 7 – 27 and the basic descriptive statistics are listed in Table 7 – 52. The average ratio is 98%, which means most independent directors take part in all the board of the directors meetings. The smallest ratio is 60% in companies of 2005 and the standard deviation is 0.05, which means that the disparity among the companies is small and Figure 7 – 27 shows this feature as well. The skewness is −3.87, which indicates a right skewed distribution of the sample data.

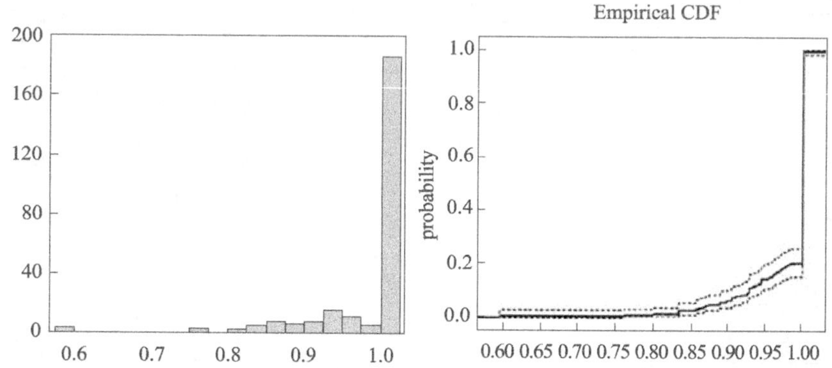

Figure 7 – 27 Histogram and empirical CDF figure of attendance ratio of the independent directors

Table 7 - 52 Descriptive statistics of attendance ratio of the independent directors

Variable	Mean	Median	Max	Min	Standard deviation	Skewness	Kurtosis
Numeric value	0. 98	1. 00	1. 00	0. 6	0. 05	-3. 87	23. 57

2. Rating principles on indicators of governance of the board of directors

(1) Independence of the board of directors.

A. Ratio of non-executive directors. The higher the ratio of non-executive directors, the better the governance situation. The rating takes 7% as group gap.

B. Employment of directors and supervisors in the biggest shareholder's companies. The lower the employment ratio, the better the governance situation. It takes 0. 09 as group gap and is rated from the largest to the smallest.

(2) Motivation of the board of directors.

A. Total compensation of the top three directors. The higher the compensation, the better the governance situation. The rating takes 0. 48 million as group gap.

B. Total compensation of the independent directors. The higher the compensation, the better the governance situation. It takes 24 thousand as group gap.

(3) Behaviors of the board of directors.

A. Frequency of board of the directors meeting. The optimal frequency is 8 or 9 times. The lager the distance from the optimal frequency, the worse the governance situation. The rating takes 2 times as group gap.

B. Attendance ratio of the independent directors. The higher the ratio, the better the governance situation. It takes 0. 02 thousand as group gap.

Detailed rating rules of each indicator are present in Table 7 - 53.

Table 7 - 53 Rating principles of indicators on construction and operation of the board of directors

Rating	fzxdsfs	gcontrolfs	Dsbcfs (10 thousand)	dldsbcfs	dshcsfs	dldschfs	dshgmfs
Group gap	7	0. 09	48	2. 4	2	0. 02	1
1	0 - 7	0. 81 -	0 - 48	0 - 2. 4	0 - 2	-0. 82	5 - 6
2	7 - 14	0. 72 - 0. 81	48 - 96	2. 4 - 4. 8	2 - 4	0. 82 - 0. 84	6 - 7
3	14 - 11	0. 63 - 0. 72	96 - 144	4. 8 - 7. 2	4 - 6	0. 84 - 0. 86	7 - 8
4	21 - 28	0. 54 - 0. 63	144 - 192	7. 2 - 9. 6	6 - 8	0. 86 - 0. 88	8 - 9
5	28 - 35	0. 45 - 0. 54	192 - 240	9. 6 - 12. 0	8 - 10	0. 88 - 0. 90	9 - 10
6	35 - 42	0. 36 - 0. 45	240 - 288	12. 0 - 14. 4	10 - 12	0. 90 - 0. 92	10 - 11
7	42 - 49	0. 27 - 0. 36	288 - 336	14. 4 - 16. 8	12 - 14	0. 92 - 0. 94	11 - 12
8	49 - 56	0. 18 - 0. 27	336 - 384	16. 8 - 19. 2	14 - 16	0. 94 - 0. 96	12 - 13
9	56 - 53	0. 09 - 0. 18	384 - 432	19. 2 - 21. 6	16 - 18	0. 96 - 0. 98	13 - 14
10	63 - 70	0. 00 - 0. 09	≥432	≥21. 6	≥18	0. 98 - 1. 00	≥15

3. Descriptive statistics of rating results of the governance of the board of directors

Bar Chart and table are used to present the rating descriptive statistics. In the following Bar Chart, horizontal axis indicates the score and vertical axis indicates the number of corresponding companies.

(1) Scores of structure status of the board of directors.

A. Scores of ratio of non-executive directors.

Figure 7 – 28 is distribution Figure of scores of ratio of non-executive directors in board of the directors and Table 7 – 54 presents the descriptive statistics of each sub indicator and overall indicator on construction and operation of board of the directors. The average score of ratio of non-executive directors is 6. 82, median is 7, skewness is – 0. 45 and the distribution follows a right-skewed trend, which is shown in Figure 7 – 28 straightforwardly. The distribution of rating results in Table 7 – 55 shows that companies scored lower than 5 take up 26. 82% and those higher than 7 take up 44. 68%. The number of companies scored 8 is the largest with 51 and take up 21. 70%, those scored 6 follow with 42 and take up 17. 87% of the total sample.

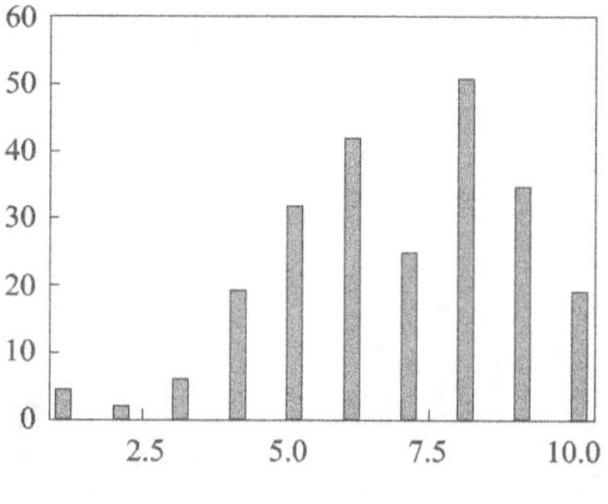

Figure 7 – 28 Scores of ratio of non-executive directors

Table 7 – 54 Descriptive statistics of scores on construction and operation of the board of directors

Variable	Mean	Median	Standard error	Skewness	Kurtosis
Fzxdsfs	6. 82	7. 00	2. 05	– 0. 45	2. 75
Gdcontrolfs	7. 55	8. 00	1. 82	– 0. 78	3. 67
Dsbcfs	1. 86	1. 00	1. 41	3. 00	14. 59
Dldsbcfs	5. 41	5. 00	2. 30	0. 27	2. 26
Dshcsfs	4. 11	4. 00	1. 67	1. 48	5. 67
Dldschfs	9. 25	10. 00	1. 87	– 2. 82	10. 48
Dshzf	39. 86	40. 00	5. 80	– 0. 14	4. 03

Table 7 –55 **Distribution of scores of ratio of non-executive directors**

Value	Count	Percent	Cumulative count	Cumulative percent
1	4	1. 70	4	1. 70
2	2	0. 85	6	2. 55
3	6	2. 55	12	5. 11
4	19	8. 09	31	13. 19
5	32	13. 62	63	26. 81
6	42	17. 87	105	44. 68
7	25	10. 64	130	55. 32
8	51	21. 70	181	77. 02
9	35	14. 89	216	91. 91
10	19	8. 09	235	100. 00

B. Scores of employment of directors in the biggest shareholder's companies

Figure 7 – 29 is histogram of scores of employment of directors in the biggest shareholder's companies and combined with Table 7 – 54, it is present that the average score is 7. 55, median is 8, standard deviation is 1. 82 and skewness is –0. 78 and the distribution follows a right-skewed trend. The distribution of rating results in Table 7 – 56 shows that companies scored lower than 5 take up 11. 49% and the number scored 10 is 39 and takes up 16. 60%. 22. 13% of the companies score 9, 21. 28% score 8 and the number of companies with these two scores is the largest.

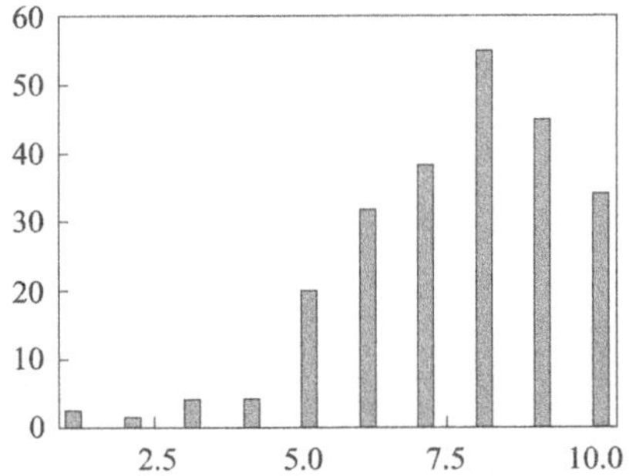

Figure 7 – 29 Scores of employment of directors in the biggest shareholder's companies

Table 7 –56 **Distribution of scores of employment of directors in the biggest shareholder's companies**

Value	Count	Percent	Cumulative count	Cumulative percent
1	1	0. 43	1	0. 43
2	2	0. 85	3	1. 28
3	4	1. 70	7	2. 98
4	1	0. 43	8	3. 40
5	19	8. 09	27	11. 49

continued

Value	Count	Percent	Cumulative count	Cumulative percent
6	27	11. 49	54	22. 98
7	40	17. 02	94	40. 00
8	50	21. 28	144	61. 28
9	52	22. 13	196	83. 40
10	39	16. 60	235	100. 00
Total	235	100. 00	235	100. 00

(2) Scores of motivation of board of the directors.

A. Scores of total compensation of the top three directors

Figure 7 –30 is distribution fgure of scores of total compensation of the top three directors and combined with Table 7 –54, it is present that the average score is 1. 86, standard deviation is 1. 14 and skewness is 3 and the distribution follows a left-skewed trend. The distribution of rating results in Table 7 – 57 shows that 52. 77% of the companies only score 1 and not up to 20% score over 2, which means that motivation effect of the compensation of directors in Chinese PLCs is weak and it is hard to play a motivation and constraint role.

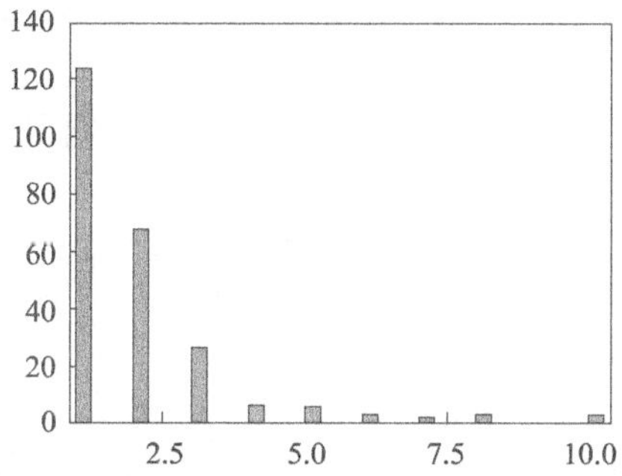

Figure 7 –30 Scores of total compensation of the top three directors

Table 7 –57 Distribution of scores of total compensation of the top three directors

Value	Count	Percent	Cumulative count	Cumulative percent
1	124	52. 77	124	52. 77
2	68	28. 94	192	81. 70
3	26	11. 06	218	92. 77
4	5	2. 13	223	94. 89
5	5	2. 13	228	97. 02
6	2	0. 85	230	97. 87
7	1	0. 43	231	98. 30
8	2	0. 85	233	99. 15
9	2	0. 85	235	100. 00

B. Scores of total compensation of the independent directors

Figure 7 – 31 is histogram of scores of total compensation of the independent directors and combined with Table 7 –54, it is present that the average score is 5. 41, median 5, standard deviation 230 and skewness 0. 27 and the distribution follows a left-skewed trend. The distribution of rating results in Table 7 – 58 shows that companies scored lower than 3 take up 22. 13% and the number scored 8 or higher takes up 20%. 18. 3% of the companies with the largest number 43 score 5, 17. 87% scored 4 follows and the number of companies is 42.

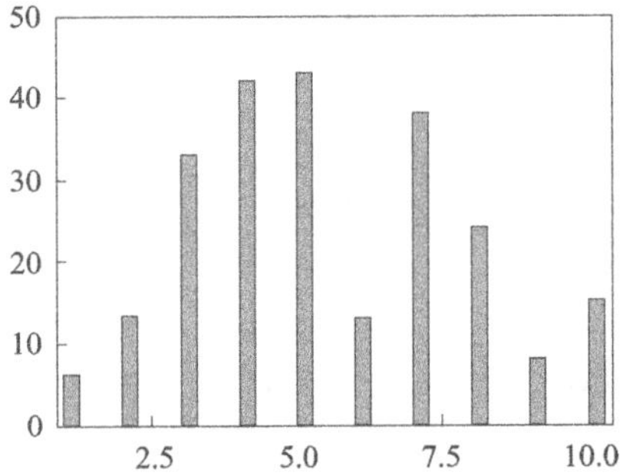

Figure 7 –31　Scores of total compensation of the independent directors

Table 7 –58　Distribution of scores of total compensation of the independent directors

Value	Count	Percent	Cumulative count	Cumulative percent
1	6	2. 55	6	2. 55
2	13	5. 53	19	8. 09
3	33	14. 04	52	22. 13
4	42	17. 87	94	40. 00
5	43	18. 30	137	58. 30
6	13	5. 53	150	63. 83
7	38	16. 17	188	80. 00
8	24	10. 21	212	90. 21
9	8	3. 40	220	93. 62
10	15	6. 38	235	100. 00

(3) Scores of behavior of the board of directors.

A. Scores of frequency of board of the directors meeting

Figure 7 –32 is distribution figure of scores of total compensation of the top three directors and combined with Table 7 –54, it is present that the average score is 4. 11, median is 4, standard deviation is 1. 67 and skewness is 1. 48 and the distribution follows a left-skewed trend. The distribution of rating results in Table 7 – 59 shows that 15. 32% of the companies score lower than 6 and 45. 33% score over 8. Those scored higher than 8 and 9 take up to 24. 68% and 23. 83% respectively with the largest number 58 and 56.

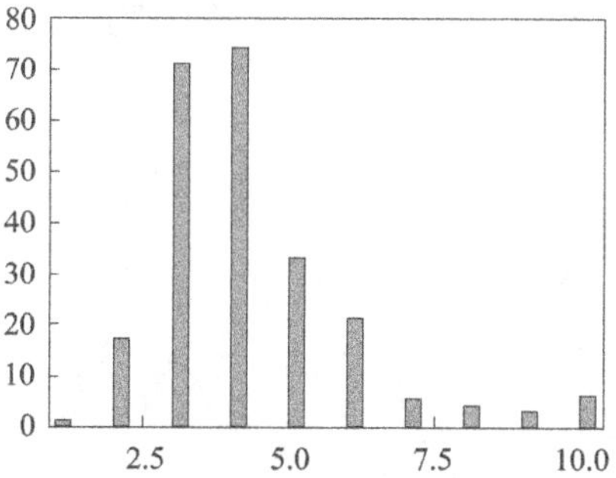

Figure 7 – 32　Histogram of scores of frequency of the board meeting

Table 7 – 58　　Distribution of scores of frequency of the board meeting

Value	Count	Percent	Cumulative count	Cumulative percent
1	7	2. 98	7	2. 98
2	2	0. 85	9	3. 83
3	1	0. 43	10	4. 16
4	4	1. 70	14	5. 96
5	4	1. 70	18	7. 66
6	18	7. 66	36	15. 32
7	34	14. 47	70	29. 79
8	58	24. 68	128	54. 47
9	56	23. 83	184	78. 30
10	51	21. 70	235	100. 00

B. Scores of attendance ratio of the independent directors

Figure 7 – 33 is histogram of scores of attendance ratio of the independent directors and the detailed distribution status is present in Table 7 – 60. It is present that the average score is very concentrated. 189 companies score 10 and take up 80. 43%. Only 8. 51% of the companies score under 7. This means that most independent directors take active parts in board of the directors meetings and lay solid foundation for their sound performance of duty and obligation in PLCs.

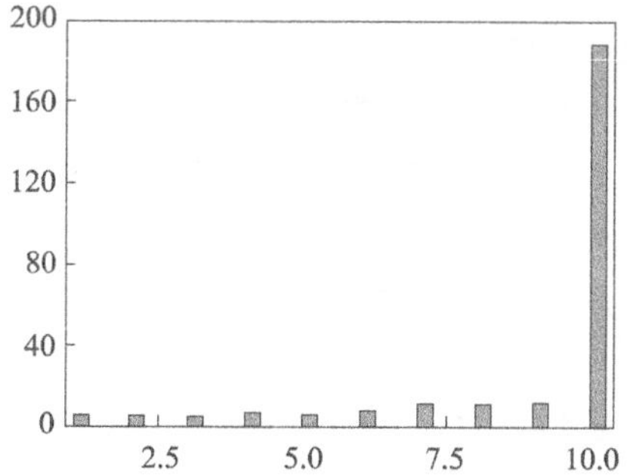

Figure 7 – 33　Scores of attendance ratio of the independent directors

Table 7 - 60 **Distribution of scores of attendance ratio of the independent directors**

Value	Count	Percent	Cumulative count	Cumulative percent
1	3	1.28	3	1.28
2	3	1.28	6	2.55
3	2	0.85	8	3.40
4	4	1.70	12	5.11
5	3	1.28	15	6.38
6	5	2.13	20	8.51
7	9	3.83	29	12.34
8	8	3.40	37	15.74
9	9	3.83	46	19.57
10	189	80.43	235	100.00

(4) Total scores of construction and running of the board of directors.

Figure 7 - 34 is distribution figure of total scores of construction and running of board of the directors and combined with Table 7 - 54, it is present that the average score is 39.86, median is 40, standard deviation is 5.80 and skewness is -0.14 and the distribution follows a right-skewed trend. Total scores fall between 36 and 48.

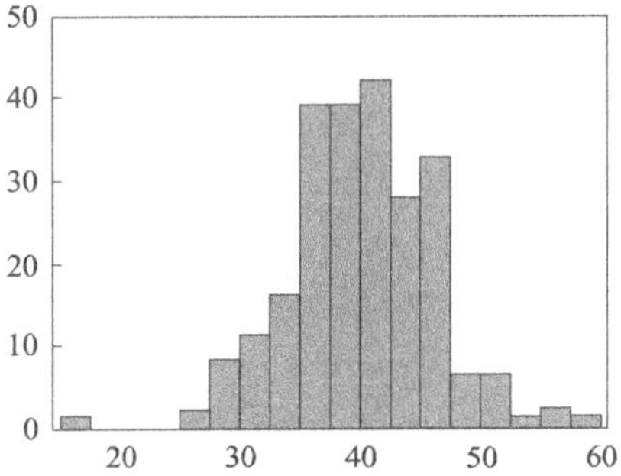

Figure 7 - 34 Total scores of construction and running of the board of directors

4. Regional and industrial differences of the evaluation results of the board of directors governance

(1) Regional differences of the evaluation results of the board of directors governance.

We divide all the provinces into three regions according to their locations, namely the eastern, the central and the western[①]. Then the differences of the board of directors' governance situation are compared. Table 7 - 61 present descriptive statistics of board of the directors' governance scores, from which we can see there are 135 PLCs in the eastern, 53 in the western and 47 in the central. The scores in the western

① As specified before.

are the highest with 40. 26, those in the central are lower with 39. 15 and those in the eastern are the lowest with 39. 94. However, the company with the best governance locates in the eastern and the best in the central only gets a score of 51.

Table 7 – 61 Regional difference of construction and running of the board of directors

Area	Observations	Mean	Median	Max	Min	Standard Deviation	Skewness	Kurtosis
Eastern	135	39. 94	40. 00	58. 00	26. 00	5. 82	0. 09	3. 30
Central	47	39. 15	39. 00	51. 00	16. 00	6. 16	- 1. 07	5. 67
Western	53	40. 26	40. 00	56. 00	29. 00	5. 46	0. 36	3. 18

As for the deviation of board of the directors' governance inside different regions, the standard deviation of the central is the largest with 6. 16, the eastern follows with 5. 82 and the western is the smallest. As for the normality of the distribution, the skewness of the eastern and the western is 0. 09 and 0. 36 respectively following the left-skewed distribution, but the central's skewness is – 1. 07 following the right-skewed distribution (see Figure 7 – 35 to Figure 7 – 37).

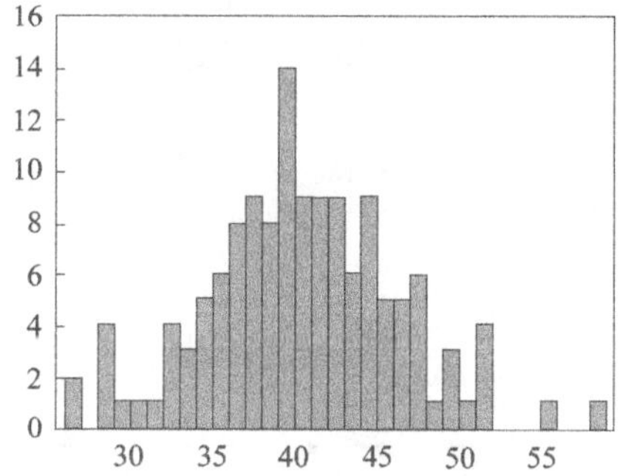

Figure 7 – 35 Distribution of the board of directors' governance in the Eastern

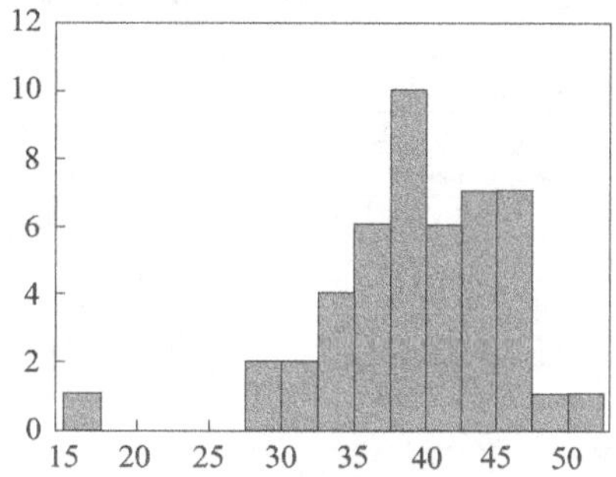

Figure 7 – 36 Distribution of the board of directors' governance in the Central

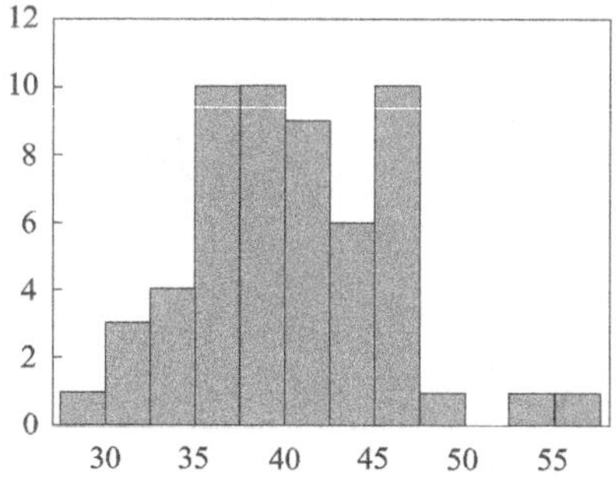

Figure 7 – 37 Distribution of the board of directors' governance in the Western

(2) Industrial difference of the evaluation results of the board of directors governance.

The industries of all the PLCs are divided according to the CSRC① industry classification standard. The classification index indicates industrial difference and letters correspond to numbers.

Table 7 – 62 present the basic statistics of board of the directors governance scores from different industries. Industries of B (extractive industry), D (production and supply of electricity, gas and water), F (transportation and storage industry), I (finance and insurance) and L (communication and cultural industry) get the highest average score of 44.44. In the PLCs of 2005, the governance of construction companies is the best with the score of 41.17, real estate industry follows with 40.50, the worst is social service industry with 37.50 and the second worst is wholesales and trade industry with 38.92. Figure 7 – 38 presents the histogram of manufacture companies' board of the directors' governance, which follows the normal distribution basically.

Table 7 – 62 Industrial difference of scores of construction and running of the board of directors

Industry	Observations	Mean	Median	Max	Min	Standard deviation	Skewness
Agriculture (7)	38.57	39.00	44.00	31.00	4.21	-0.44	2.55
Manufacture (143)	39.83	40.00	55.00	16.00	5.61	-0.62	4.80
Construction (6)	41.17	40.5	48.00	38.00	3.71	1.09	3.02
IT (16)	39.25	38.00	49.00	30.00	6.14	0.32	1.98
Wholesales and Trade (12)	38.92	38.00	47.00	32.00	5.66	0.14	1.46
Real estate (14)	40.50	40.50	51.00	28.00	5.80	-0.30	2.99
Social service (6)	37.50	37.50	41.00	34.00	2.74	0.00	1.64
Comprehensive (22)	39.36	39.00	51.00	26.00	6.09	0.11	2.95
Others (9)	44.44	46.00	58.00	32.00	9.84	-0.09	1.66

Note: 1) Others include industries of B, D, F, I and L. They are merged into one classification since number of the companies is small and they are of monopoly nature. 2) Numbers in the brackets are the numbers of PLCs in the corresponding industry.

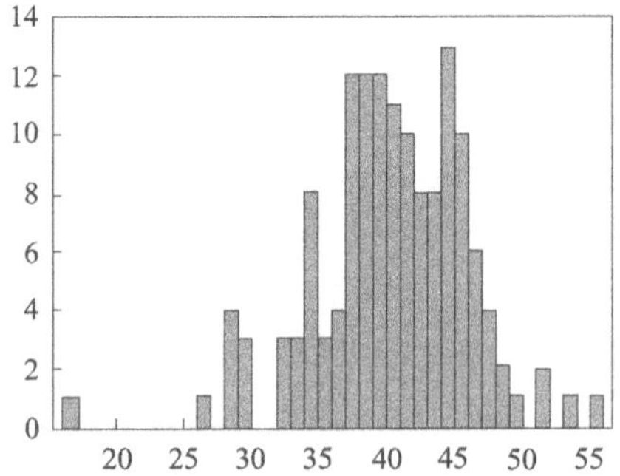

Figure 7 – 38 Histogram of the board of directors' governance in manufacture PLCs

① As illustrated before.

7.4 Governance Evaluation of the board of supervisors in private listed companies

7.4.1 Study on governance evaluation of the board of supervisors

Compared to the other parts in CG evaluation, there are only three evaluation systems involved with evaluation of governance of board of the supervisors①, namely Nankai University CG Evaluation System, Chinese Taiwan Fu Jen Catholic University CG and Evaluation System and CG Rating System for Public Companies developed by Pengyuan Company and Shenzhen Securities Information Company. Among them, Nankai University CG Evaluation System take governance of board of the supervisors as an individual system to evaluate. From the indicator systems published in 2003 and 2005 respectively, we can tell the system gets more scientific but the data are harder to acquire in practical uses, which makes it not practical without conducting the survey. Optimized evaluation system gets the advantage of data access but some extra subjective indicators are included. The comparison between the two systems is present in Table 7 -63 and Table 7 -64.

Table 7 -63 Indicators of evaluation of $CCGI^{NK}$ system of board supervisors published in 2003

Main factor level	Sub factor level	Notes
Supervisor's ability to ensure performance	The non-worker represents the candidate for the nomination of the supervisor	Reflect the independence and enthusiasm of the supervisory board members themselves
	Professional degree of the supervisory board	
	Working hours in the company of the external supervisor guaranteed	
	Compensation level of the external supervisor	

① The reasons are from multiple ways. First, there is no board of the supervisors in mainstream Britain and American companies with monistic governance mode. Therefore, although some well-known companies including Standard & Poor's, Deminor and Calyon Securities launched their own CG evaluation system, they don't come down to the governance evaluation of board of the supervisors. Second, Chinese CG model follows the binary mode which are generally adopted by Japanese and Germany companies. However, the Japanese and Germany stock markets are not mature and their management levels play dominant role in CG structure, which makes the evaluation of them less referable.

continued

Main factor level	Sub factor level	Notes
Operation effectiveness of board of the supervisors	Structural and scale effectiveness of board of the supervisors	Reflect the efficiency and effectiveness of the supervisory board in the course of operation
	Convening of the provisional shareholders meeting in the past three years	
	Effectiveness of the meetings of board of the supervisors	
	Effectiveness of the supervisory authority exercising the supervisory authority	
	Completeness of the supervisory record of board of the supervisors	

Source: Nankai University CCGI Study Center.

Table 7 – 64 Indicators of evaluation of $CCGI^{NK}$ system of board supervisors published in 2005

Main factor level	Sub factor level	Notes
Operation status of the board of supervisors	Frequency of meetings of board of the supervisors	Assess the actual situation of the board of supervisors to perform their functions and play a supervisory role
	Independent opinions status issued by board of the supervisors	
Structure and scale of board of the supervisors	Number of the supervisors on board	Assess board of the supervisors to perform the functions of the supervisory staff and the board of supervisors on behalf of the staff and the interests of shareholders
	Supervisors set up for the staff	
	Supervisors set up for the small and medium-sized shareholders	
Competence of the supervisors	Professional background of chairman of board of the supervisors	Assess effects of the supervisors' academic qualifications, professional background and the status of ownership on their competencies
	Educational background of chairman of board of the supervisors	
	Age of chairman of board of the supervisors	
	Shares held by chairman of board of the supervisors	
	Whether chairman of board of the supervisors changed ever	
	Professional background of other supervisors	
	Educational background of other supervisors	
	Age of other supervisors	
	Shares held by other supervisors	

Source: Nankai University CG Study Center.

Different from $CCGI^{NK}$ System, Chinese Taiwan Fu Jen Catholic University CG and Evaluation System and CG Rating System for Public Companies developed by Pengyuan Company and Shenzhen Securities Information Company don't take board of the supervisors as an individual sub-system to evaluate and combine it with the evaluation of board of the directors. Chinese Taiwan Fu Jen Catholic University CG and Evaluation System and CG Rating System mainly involves with component of board of the supervisors and focus on its professionalism and independency. To be specific, the indicators include maximum number of members of the board of directors as supervisors, the number of supervisors and other shareholders as supervisors' ratio (Ye, Li & Ke, 2002). These two systems lack systematisms compared to the Nankai system.

7.4.2 Choice of indicators for evaluation of the board of supervisors

Based on experience of the current evaluation systems, this book demonstrates that the design of indicators for evaluation of board of the supervisors should take full consideration of the features and functions of the supervisory institution. Scientificity is the top priority and access to data is the guarantee to ensure its performance. Scientific and appropriate evaluate system can be designed only when these two dimensions are combined both. In the meanwhile, it is necessary to grasp its generality, but also to examine its own particularity when evaluating the governance of board of the supervisors in PLCs. For example, on the basis of constructing the supervisory index of the board of supervisors, Li & Wang (2005) analyzed the influence of the guarantee ability of the board of supervisors and the effectiveness of the board of supervisors on the financial early warning coefficient and argued that the nature of ownership of large shareholders has a significant impact on the performance of the board of supervisors, and private listed companies are significantly better than state-owned listed companies. They argued that possible reasons may be that most of the PLCs in the early days of the company can be in accordance with the requirements of the law, combined with their own characteristics, the establishment of a standardized system of supervisors, non-employee representatives on behalf of supervisors nomination, external supervisors in the company's working hours to ensure the level of external supervisors And so on are more competitive than SOEs. In fact, the difference might result from their behavioral difference. For example, in Hebei Dawu Agriculture and Animal Husbandry Group (non-listed companies), Sun Dawu designed "private enterprise constitutional monarchy system", through which the family supervise the operation of enterprises and would certainly have an important impact on the behavior of board of the supervisors. Based on this, we believe that the board of supervisors exercises the power of supervision and be responsible for the shareholders general meeting as the company's internal full-time supervision agencies and representatives of the identity of the investors. Its basic functions are to supervise the board of directors and general manager of the company, to monitor all the company's business activities and financial situation. In the supervision process, it should require the board of directors and managers to correct violations of the articles of association of ultra vires at any time. Based on the conclusion and enlightenment of the existing research, according to the structure and behavior characteristics of the board of supervisors which may be brought by private listed companies, based on the internationally accepted principles and standards of corporate governance, combined with the special historical stage of Chinese listed companies. Considering the consistency of the "Corporate Law of Listed Companies in China", "Company Law" and "Securities Law", the consistency of the logical connotation of "independence", "initiative", "supervisory function" and on the basis of the indicators design that Nankai University has constructed in the evaluation index system of the board of supervisors of private listed companies, we construct our own system specifically including the following four indicators.

1. Proportion of employee supervisors

From the source of the members of the board of supervisors of listed companies in China, Article 118 of the Company Law of the People's Republic of China stipulates: "The board of supervisors shall include the representatives of the shareholders and of the employees in the appropriate proportion, and the proportion of the employee representatives shall not be less than 1 / 3, the specific proportion is set by the articles of association". In other words, at present, the supervisors of listed companies in China include both shareholder supervisors and employee supervisors, and some listed companies also introduce independent supervisors. Shareholders' supervisors, as representatives of shareholders, often lead to the board of supervisors weakening the supervision of the board of directors and managers. While the independent supervisors are conducive to making judgments independent on those of the other members of the board of supervisors, the independent supervisors are subject to factors such as the time of work in the company and the access to information. What's more, the internal information they obtain is inadequate, and at this stage does not yet have its full play of the conditions (such as the developed manager market, if the introduction of the corresponding supporting mechanism is needed). On the contrary, employee supervisors are the internal staff of enterprises, in the process of supervision and decision-making they have sufficient information advantage. When board of the directors and managers commit irregularities, taking into account the corresponding consequences, they often give full play to their supervisory functions. At the same time, the full participation of employee supervisors to corporate oversight decision can not only enhance the sense of responsibility of the staff master, but also bring about the scientific and democratization of decision-making and bring about the strengthening of supervision[①]. To this end, the increase in the proportion of employee supervisors will be conducive to the board of supervisors.

2. Employment of members of the board of supervisors in the biggest shareholder's companies

The typical characteristic of modern company is the separation of ownership and control, which results in the corporate governance framework under the dual principal-agent problem in practice. One is the agent problem between shareholder and manager in the form of operator's moral hazard and opportunistic behavior, that is, operators under the cover of corporate interests pursue his maximization of personal interests. The second is the agent problem between the major shareholders and the small and medium shareholders, that is, the controlling shareholders through the pyramid ownership structure encroach the interests of minority shareholders. In practice, the main contradiction in the governance of listed companies in China is very different from Anglo-American. In the Anglo-American countries, the main problem of corporate governance lies in the issue of separation of ownership and management rights under the condition of the decentralization of shares. Therefore, the main supervisory objects are the selfish behaviors of executive directors and managers. And this is not the main contradiction in China at present, the main contradiction exists between the major shareholders and small and medium shareholders (Li, 2004). The controlling shareholders of the company control the board of directors, managers and the board of supervisors to engage in the abuse of the interests of the minority

---

① For example, in the German board of supervisors, the board of supervisors consists of 12, 16, or 20 persons, depending on the number of workers. Of which half are representatives of employers; the other half is the labor representatives. Labor representatives are elected by laborers, management staff and trade unions. At the same time, the chairman of the board of supervisors is elected by the representatives of the party, the vice chairman elected by the labor representatives. The chairman of the board of supervisors has the final voting power if the number of votes is the same. This co-decision system created an opposing and coordinated institution for German employers and workers.

shareholders (Li, 2004). This agent problem in PLCs is more prominent. Qiu et al. (2005) argued that controlling shareholders implemented close control on the management of listed companies in the use of assets, personnel and other means. This make the second type of agency problem through unfair related party transactions, illegal guarantees and other means against other investment has been very serious in Chinese PLCs. To this end, to strengthen the supervision and checks and balances of the largest shareholder, safeguarding the interests of small and medium shareholders has become an important issue in the theoretical and practical circles.

From the shareholding ratio view, in the case that the largest shareholder has the absolute advantage, because of its advantage of controlling the company and driving force of abuse of the company's independent personality, he often manipulates the general meeting, elects to his own "trusted directors, supervisors and general manager" as representative of interests in the enterprise in pursuit of his own interest based on the controlling status and having more control of the company in his own hands. To this end, as the main supervisory body of listed companies, more major shareholders acting the members of board of the supervisors will not help the implement of supervision and cannot avoid encroachment of major shareholders on small and medium ones. In this regard, Li et al. (2006) pointed out that "a dominant" system is not conducive to governance of board of the supervisors and union governance of a few major shareholders is more conducive to the improvement of governance performance of the board of supervisors. To this end, listed companies have to optimize the ownership structure as a breakthrough to fundamentally improve the performance of the board of supervisors and construct the monopoly competitive structure where the major shareholders check and balance in order to strengthen the competition for the company's control. In fact, it is eventually designed to achieve effective supervision by constructing members' structure in board of the supervisors. Based on this, we use the proportion of the total number of supervisors employed by the largest shareholder's companies to reflect the largest shareholder's control on board of the supervisors.

3. Average shares held by the supervisors

The members of board of the supervisors of the enterprise have nature of the manager which determines that they are not always loyal to the client in pursuit of maximizing their own utility. At the same time, they may be bought by the inefficient agent and conspired with the agent to encroach on the principles' interest (Tirole,

1986). In the principal-agent relationship between the owner and the supervisor[①], if the owner is able to fully grasp the relevant information of the supervisory action, the owner may impose rewards and punishments on the supervisors in accordance with the observed action. However, information is asymmetric in reality and the owner cannot fully observe the behavior of supervisors, making it necessary to achieve incentive compatibility for the supervisors. Mirrlees (1974, 1976), Holmstrom (1979) modeled the agent's incentive mechanism using the "parametric approach to the distribution function", whose expression is as followings[②]:

$$\max_{a,\, s(x)} \int v(\pi - s(x)) f(x, \pi, \alpha)\, dx \tag{1}$$

$$\text{s. t. } (IR) \int u(s(x)) f(x, \pi, a)\, dx - c(a) \geqslant \bar{u} \tag{2}$$

$$(IC) \int u(s(x)) f(x, \pi, a)\, dx - c(a) \geqslant \int u(s(x)) f(x, \pi, a')\, dx - c(a') \tag{3}$$

Among which, $a \in A$ is the action of the client (for example, work hard or not), π is the output (such as profit), $f(x, \pi, a)$ is the distribution density function, $s(x)$ is the proxy return function $v(\pi - s(x))$ and $u(s(x))$ is the utility function of the principal and the agent respectively; who wants the agent; $\bar{u}$is the agent's preserved utility, $c(a)$ and $c(a')$ is the utility loss respectively, for the agent takes action a and a' (such as the input time). The above formula shows that the maximization of the utility of the client, in addition to the agent's participation constraint (IR)[③], must also be faced with an incentive compatibility constraint (IC), which means that it must be given some incentive to make the goal of the agent consistent with that of the principle. According to this, it can be seen that in order to make the supervisors' behaviors do not deviate from the owner too far, it is necessary to give some incentives when giving responsibility to board of the supervisors, which is one of the important prerequisites to achieve the effect of supervision. Only then can we achieve the goal of effective supervision. The traditional incentive mainly includes the basic salary plus annual bonus, whose assessment criteria is usually the company's previous year's performance, which in a sense has certain incentive effect. However, this type of incentive effect, may makes the stakeholders only cares about the economic benefits of the current year and

---

① Some scholars argue that it should be trust relationship between them.

② This model is referred to Zhang (2005, pp. 241) and the assumptions are referred to pp. 239 - 241.

③ The expected utility of the agent in accepting the contract cannot be less than the maximum expected utility available when the contract is not accepted.

contributes to its short-term behavior, while stock options can make up for the shortness of the annual salary system (Chance, Kumar & Todd, 2000; Core & Goay, 1999). To this end, to allow supervisors to hold a moderate share of the company not only help create a good incentive mechanism for the effective supervision of supervisors, but also is conducive to the supervisors to recognize that "effective supervision" is not only in line with the interests of the company also in line with their own interests, The fiduciary duty. Based on the above analysis, we use the "average number of shares held by supervisors" to reflect the enthusiasm of the members of the board of supervisors.

4. Frequency of the board of supervisors meeting

As we all know, the convening of the board of supervisors is an indispensable process for the exercise of the board of supervisors. The meeting of the board of supervisors is the place where the supervisors fulfill their obligations and supervise the full exchange of information. The regular meetings of the board of supervisors will facilitate the exchange of supervisory information between the external supervisors and the internal supervisors and resolve the problems in time. Wang (2006) also demonstrated that the efficiency of governance of the board of supervisors (the main measure of frequency of meetings of the board of supervisors) has an important influence on the performance of supervisors through the gray relational analysis of the efficiency of the board of supervisors. Therefore, the quality of the meetings of the board of supervisors plays a key role in the efficiency of the board of supervisors. In terms of the process and form of operation of the board of supervisors, we use frequency of meetings held by the board of supervisors to measure the effectiveness of the meetings of the board of supervisors. Based on this, we got the evaluation index system of the board of supervisors as shown in Table 7 – 65.

Table 7 – 65 Evaluation indicators system for governance of the board of supervisors

Target level	Main factor level	Notes
Indicators system for governance of the board of supervisors in Chinese private listed companies	Proportion of employee supervisors	Reflects the democratization of supervision and decision-making
	Employment of the members of the board of supervisors in the largest shareholder's companies	Reflects the control of the board of supervisors by the major shareholders
	Average holdings of supervisors	Examine the enthusiasm of the members of the board of supervisors
	Frequency of Board of the Supervisors Meeting	Examine the efficiency of the board of supervisors

7.4.3 Formation and analysis of governance index of the board of supervisors

1. Descriptive statistics of the indicators

Before proceeding with the specific evaluation, we will first analyze the proportion of the employee supervisors of the sample companies, the performance of the members of the board of supervisors in the largest shareholder units, the average number of shares held by supervisors and the number of meetings of the board of supervisors.

(1) Proportion of employee supervisors.

Of the 235 private listed companies, 210 listed companies do not have employee supervisors, which not only do not comply with the relevant provisions of our company law, but also is not conducive to the democratization of the board of supervisors and scientific. Article 118 of the Company Law of the People's Republic of China stipulates: "The board of supervisors shall include the representatives of the shareholders and the proportion of the employees in the appropriate proportion, and the proportion of the employee representatives shall not be less than one third, and the specific proportion shall be stipulated in the articles of association." While only 10.21% of the companies in the sample company met this requirement. In the company to meet the requirements, 5.96% of the companies are just to meet the requirements as in Table 7-66. In addition, the distribution of employee supervisors in the sample companies is shown in Figure 7-39.

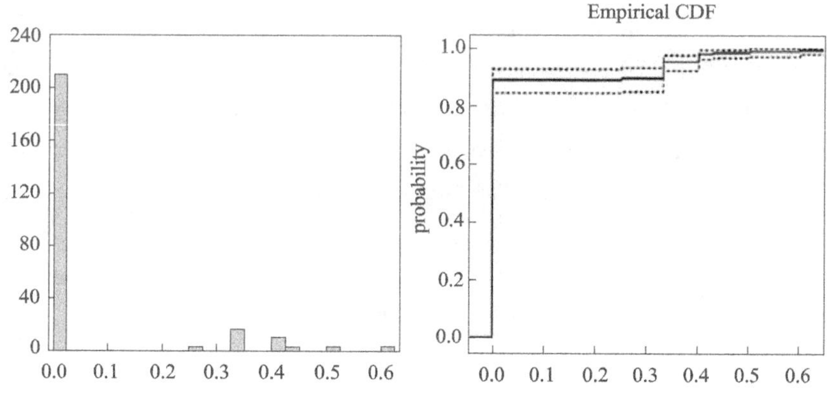

Figure 7-39 Histogram and empirical cumulative distribution function figure of employee supervisor proportional distribution

Table 7 – 66 **Distribution of employee supervisor**

Value	Count	Percent	Cumulative count	Cumulative percent
0. 000000	210	89. 36	210	89. 36
0. 250000	1	0. 43	211	89. 79
0. 333333	14	5. 96	225	95. 74
0. 400000	7	2. 98	232	98. 72
0. 428571	1	0. 43	233	99. 15
0. 500000	1	0. 43	234	99. 57
0. 600000	1	0. 43	235	100. 00
Total	235	100. 00	235	100. 00

Further, we also counted the other indicators of the proportion of employee supervisors in the sample companies. The maximum value is 0. 6, the mean is 0. 04, the standard deviation is 0. 12, the skewness is 2. 76, and the kurtosis is 9. 19, see Table 7 – 67.

Table 7 – 67 **Descriptive statistics of proportion of employee supervisors**

Mean	Median	Max	Min	Standard deviation	Skewness	Kurtosis
0. 04	0. 00	0. 60	0. 00	0. 12	2. 76	9. 19

(2) Employment of the members of the board of supervisors in the largest shareholder's companies.

The sample shows that only 1. 7% of the private listed companies in China are currently not working in the largest shareholder's companies. In the private listed companies with members of the board of supervisors working in the largest shareholder's companies, the highest rate of service was 87. 5%, with an average of 27%. Also, the standard deviation of the sample is relatively small, only 0. 16, as in Table 7 – 68. So much from the largest shareholder's companies of the proportion of supervisors is not conducive to the prevention of major shareholders of the invasion of small and medium-sized shareholders of the supervision, which is the second type of agent problem and the situation is more prominent. In addition, the histogram and the empirical cumulative distribution of the membership of the board of supervisors in the largest shareholder's companies are shown in Figure 7 – 40.

Table 7 – 68 **Employment members of the board of supervisors in the largest shareholder's companies**

Mean	Median	Max	Min	Standard deviation	Skewness	Kurtosis
0. 27	0. 23	0. 875	0. 00	0. 16	0. 87	3. 96

(3) Average dings of supervisors.

In the sample company, the maximum holdings of supervisors were 4 726 033

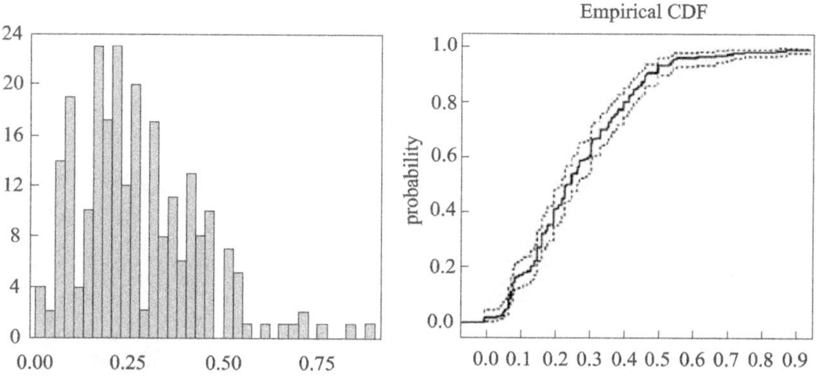

Figure 7 – 40 Histogram and empirical cumulative distribution function figure of employment of the members of the board of supervisors in the largest shareholder's companies

shares, with an average of 78 066. 59 shares, and the differences among the different companies in the sample were significant. In fact, in 235 private listed companies, accounting for 62. 55% (i. e. 147) of the company, the average holdings of supervisors is 0 as shown in Table 7 – 69. To this end, although the equity incentive measures for board of the directors in PLCs have been improved than before, the overall implementation effect is not good. The histogram and empirical cumulative distribution of the average holdings of supervisors are shown in Figure 7 – 41.

Table 7 – 69 Descriptive statistics of average holdings of supervisors

Mean	Median	Max	Min	Standard deviation	Skewness	Kurtosis
78 066. 59	0. 00	4 726 033	0. 00	41 925 507	7. 84	76. 30

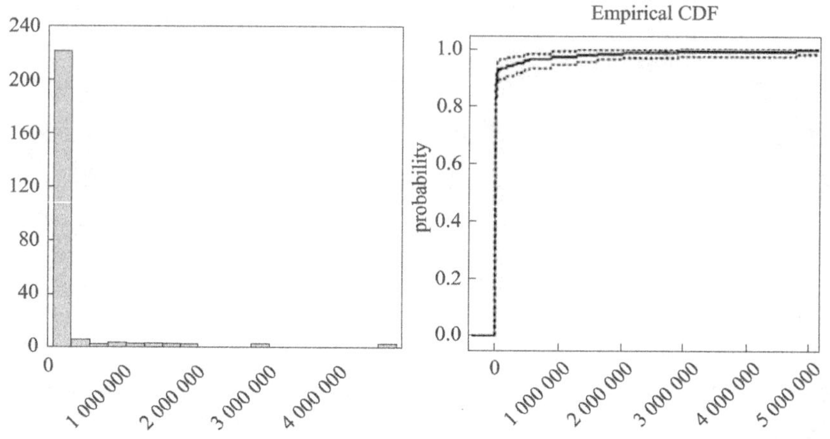

Figure 7 – 41 Histogram and empirical cumulative distribution function figure of average holdings of supervisors

(4) Frequency of the board of supervisors meeting.

Among the 235 private listed companies, the frequency of board of the supervisors meeting is 3 times (including 3 times) in 155 companies, which account for 65.96% of the total sample. Of these, 15.74% of the companies only convened the meeting once, 30.64% only held twice. 91.06% of the companies held under 5 times (including 5 times) as in Table 7 – 70. At the same time, the histogram and empirical cumulative distribution of frequency of board of the supervisors meeting are shown in Figure 7 – 42.

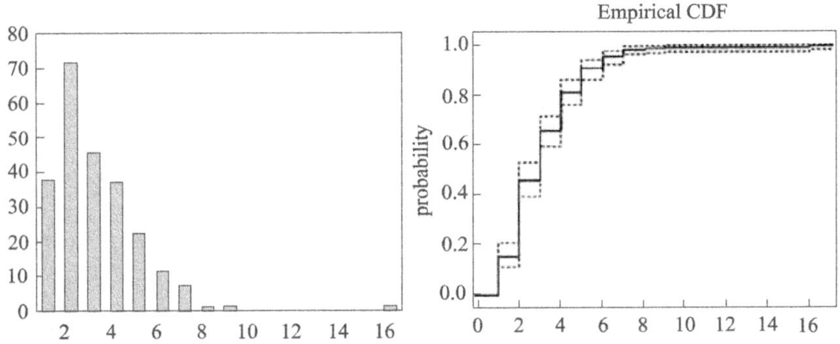

Figure 7 – 42 Histogram and empirical cumulative distribution function figure of the meeting frequency of board of supervisors

Table 7 – 70 Distribution of the meeting frequency of board of supervisors

Value	Count	Percent	Cumulative count	Cumulative percent
1	37	15.74	37	15.74
2	72	30.64	109	46.38
3	46	19.57	155	65.96
4	37	15.74	192	81.70
5	22	9.36	214	91.06
6	11	4.68	225	95.74
7	7	2.98	232	98.72
8	1	0.43	233	99.15
9	1	0.43	234	99.57
10	1	0.43	235	100.00
Total	235	100.00	235	100.00

Further statistics on the number of other supervisors of the number of board of supervisors, it can be seen that the average value of the meetings of the board of supervisors is 3.09 times, the maximum is 16 times and the standard deviation is 1.83. It can be seen that the annual frequency of most companies is low and is not conducive to communication between members of the board of supervisors. Other statistics are shown in Table 7 - 71.

Table 7 - 71 Descriptive statistics of the board of supervisors meeting frequency

Mean	Median	Max	Min	Standard deviation	Skewness	Kurtosis
3.09	3.00	16.00	1.00	1.83	2.04	12.68

2. Rules and principles of indicators of governance of the board of supervisors

In order to reduce the subjective judgment as far as possible, we first judge the relationship between the indicators and the performance indicators, count the maximum and minimum statistics of the indicators, and determine the group gap using 10 points-scale to rate. Finally, the total score of governance of board of the supervisors is the sum score of each indicator.

First, the relationship between the board of supervisors' governance evaluation indicators and performance. According to the above analysis, we can get the possible relationship between the above indicators and supervisory performance. In this way, theoretically speaking, it is different from the performance of the enterprise because the corporate performance is the result of the common effect of corporate governance and management under certain environmental conditions. The reflections in reality are the relevant indicators in the accounting report, such as earnings per share and profit per share. While supervisory performance emphasizes the efficiency and effectiveness of the supervisory function of the board of supervisors and other possible impacts. From the practice of internal supervision system arrangement, supervisory performance includes two aspects: direct supervisory performance that manifests supervisory function and indirect supervisory performance derived from supervision process. Direct supervisory performance refers to the duties such as checking the company's financial affairs, supervising the day-to-day business activities of the board of directors and the manager, maintaining the legitimate rights and interests of the shareholders, and ensuring the scientific and legal nature of the company's decision-making. To this end, we defined the company's financial supervision level, the quality of information disclosure, the level of board of the directors' governance and management governance as the direct supervision performance. The derived supervisory performance mainly emphasizes the externalities caused by the supervision process. In practice, the most likely externalities of supervision are the impact on the stakeholders. Based on this, the five variables of "financial supervision level", "board governance index", "manager governance index", "information disclosure index" and "stakeholder governance index" are used as the standard to measure supervisory performance and derive the possible effect of each evaluation indicator on for the supervisory performance as shown in Table 7 – 72.

Table 7 – 72 Relationship between governance indicators of the board of supervisors and performance

Varible	Stakeholder governance	Level of financial supervision	Board governance	Managerial governance	Information disclosur equality
Proportion of employee supervisors	↗	↗	↗	↗	↗
Employment of board of the supervisors in the largest shareholder's companies	↘	↘	↘	↘	↘
Average holdings of supervisors	↗	↗	↗	↗	↗
Frequency of board of the supervisors meeting	↗	↗	↗	↗	↗

Note: ↗ indicates positive effect and ↘ indicates negative effect.

Second, the group gap to determine and rating principle. First, proportion of employee supervisors (zgjsbl). The proportion of supervisors should be positively related to supervisory performance. According to this, we determine the classification principle, which takes 10% as the group gap and rates from the small to large; second, employment of members of board of the supervisors in the largest shareholder's companies (control). Because it will have a negative impact on supervisory performance. According to this, we determine the classification principle, which takes 0.09 as the group gap and rates from the large to small; third, the average number of shares held by supervisors (jspcg). Consider the effect of the average holding of supervisors on supervisory performance. The classification principle takes 4 000 as the group gap and rates from the small to large; Fourth, the frequency of board of the supervisors meeting (jshcs). As stated in the previous judgment, the frequency of board of the supervisors meeting has a positive impact on the supervisory performance. According to this, we determine the classification principle, which takes 1 as the group gap and rates from the small to large; the rating principles of the above indicators are further shown in Table 7 – 73.

Table 7 – 73 Principles on governance indexes of the board of supervisors

Score	zgjsbl	gdcontrol	jspcg	jshcs
Group gap	0.1	0.09	4 000	1
1	0 – 0.1	0.81 –	0 – 4 000	1

continued

Score	zgjsbl	gdcontrol	jspcg	jshcs
2	0. 1 – 0. 2	0. 72 – 0. 81	4 000 – 8 000	2
3	0. 2 – 0. 3	0. 63 – 0. 72	8 000 – 12 000	3
4	0. 3 – 0. 4	0. 54 – 0. 63	12 000 – 16 000	4
5	0. 4 – 0. 5	0. 45 – 0. 54	16 000 – 20 000	5
6	0. 5 – 0. 6	0. 36 – 0. 45	20 000 – 24 000	6
7	0. 6 – 0. 7	0. 27 – 0. 36	24 000 – 28 000	7
8	0. 7 – 0. 8	0. 18 – 0. 27	28 000 – 32 000	8
9	0. 8 – 0. 9	0. 09 – 0. 18	32 000 – 36 000	9
10	0. 9 – 1. 0	0. 00 – 0. 09	36 000	16

Finally, the board of supervisors' governance index. After the evaluation of each indicator, the sum of each score will be the supervisory board governance index, that is, the board of supervisors governance index = zgjsbl + control + jspcg + jshcs. In other words, the highest score of governance of the board of supervisors is 40 points.

3. An empirical analysis of governance indexes of the board of supervisors in PLCs

In accordance with the above criteria, we have evaluated the governance of the board of supervisors of private listed companies and derived the score of each indicator and the board of supervisors' governance index.

(1) Descriptive statistics of scores of the evaluation indicators on board of the supervisors governance index.

A. Descriptive statistics of the proportion of employee supervisors. In the sample company, generally speaking, the score of proportion of employee supervisors in the board of supervisors is lower. Among them, companies scoring 1 point accounts for 89. 36% of the sample, 14 companies get 4 points accounting for 5. 96%, the highest score of the company is only 7 points, and there is only one listed company. Table 7 – 74 presents the rest situation.

Table 7 – 74 Distribution of evaluation scores for proportion of employee supervisors

Value	Count	Percent	Cumulative count	Cumulative percent
1	210	89. 36	210	89. 36
3	1	0. 43	211	89. 79
4	14	5. 96	225	95. 74
5	8	3. 40	233	99. 15
6	1	0. 43	234	99. 57
7	1	0. 43	235	100. 00
Total	235	100. 00	235	100. 00

B. Descriptive statistics of employment of members of board of the supervisors in the largest shareholder's companies. In general, 34 companies (14.47%) achieve the highest score of 10 points. Companies scoring 8 points account for 23.40% with the largest numbers, followed by companies scoring 9 points accounting for 19.15%. See Table 7 -75 for other related scores.

Table 7 -75 Scores for employment of the board of supervisors in the largest shareholder's companies

Value	Count	Percent	Cumulative count	Cumulative percent
1	2	0.85	2	0.85
2	1	0.43	3	1.28
3	4	1.70	7	2.98
4	4	1.70	11	4.68
5	20	8.51	31	13.19
6	32	13.62	63	26.81
7	38	16.17	101	42.98
8	55	23.40	156	66.38
9	45	19.15	201	85.53
10	34	14.47	235	100.00
Total	235	100.00	235	100.00

C. Descriptive statistics of the average holdings of supervisors. In terms of the average holdings of supervisors in PLCs, the highest score is 10 points and there are 18 listed companies to achieve this level. At the same time, companies scoring 1 point account for 79.15% of the sample. Combined with the aforementioned analysis, of the 186 listed companies, the vast majority of them (specifically 147) do not implement the supervisors' shareholding institution. And 84.68% of the companies only score below 2 points (including 2 points), which is not conducive to the improvement of the enthusiasm of supervisors. Other details see Table 7 -76.

Table 7 -76 Distribution of evaluation scores for average holdings of supervisors

Value	Count	Percent	Cumulative count	Cumulative percent
1	186	79.15	186	79.15
2	13	5.53	199	84.68
3	8	3.40	207	88.09
4	1	0.43	208	88.51
5	5	2.13	213	90.64
6	4	1.70	217	92.34
10	18	7.66	235	100.00
Total	235	100.00	235	100.00

D. Descriptive statistics of frequency of board of the supervisors meeting. In terms of frequency of board of the supervisors meeting, 65.96% of the company scores are 3 points or below (see Table 7 – 77). There were only one company scoring the 8 points, 9 points and 10 points respectively in the sample, and 37 of the companies score 4, 22 of the companies score 5 and 11 score 7. It can be seen that in 2005, the scores are not satisfactory.

Table 7 – 77 Evaluation scores for frequency of the board of supervisors meeting

Value	Count	Percent	Cumulative count	Cumulative percent
1	37	15.74	37	15.74
2	72	30.64	109	46.38
3	46	19.57	155	65.96
4	37	15.74	192	81.70
5	22	9.36	214	91.06
6	11	4.68	225	95.74
7	7	2.98	232	98.72
8	1	0.43	233	99.15
9	1	0.43	234	99.57
10	1	0.43	235	100.00
Total	235	100.00	235	100.00

Further statistics on the other indicators above are summarized in Table 7 – 78. Table 7 – 78 shows that the average proportion of employee supervisors is 1.37 and the standard deviation is 1.11. The mean value of employment of the board of supervisors in the biggest shareholder's companies is 7.55 and the standard deviation is 1.82; the average score of the supervisors' average holdings is 2, the standard deviation is 2.5; the standard deviation of frequency of board of the supervisors meeting is 3.06, the standard deviation is 1.69. In comparison, situation on employment of the board of supervisors in the biggest shareholder's companies is better than the other three aspects and scores on proportion of employee supervisors perform worst.

Table 7 – 78 Descriptive statistics of evaluation indicators of the board of supervisors' governance

Variable	Mean	Median	Standard deviation	Skewness	Kurtosis
Zgjsblfs	1.37	1.00	1.11	2.87	10.10
Controlfs	7.55	8.00	1.82	-0.78	3.67
Jspcgsfs	2.00	1.00	2.50	2.60	8.34
Jshcsfs	3.06	3.00	1.69	1.03	4.13

(2) Descriptive statistical analysis of governance indexes of private listed board of supervisors.

A. Overall situation of board of the supervisors in PLCs. Through the descriptive statistics on the governance index of the private board of supervisors, we have obtained the statistical results of Table 7 – 79 and the distribution of the governance index of the board of supervisors in Figure 7 – 43. On the whole, the level of governance of the board of supervisors of private listed companies shows a trend of normal distribution. The maximum value of governance index of private board of supervisors is 26 points, the minimum value is 4 points, of which companies scoring 10 points or below accounts for 13. 19%, 20 points or below for 94. 47%, only one listed company gets 10 points. On this basis, the further use of statistical methods finds the average value of 13. 98 points and the standard deviation of 3. 43. The above statistics show that the current level of private listed companies' supervisory board governance level is generally not high and how to strengthen the board of supervisors' governance has become a key issue for firm performance in PLCs.

Table 7 –79 Evaluation scores for employee of board of the supervisors in the largest shareholder's companies

Value	Count	Percent	Cumulative count	Cumulative percent
4	1	0. 43	1	0. 43
7	1	0. 43	2	0. 85
8	9	3. 83	11	4. 68
9	3	1. 28	14	5. 96
10	17	7. 23	31	13. 19
11	22	9. 36	53	22. 55
12	28	11. 91	81	34. 47
13	34	14. 47	115	48. 94
14	34	14. 47	149	63. 40
15	21	8. 94	170	72. 34
16	18	7. 66	188	80. 00
17	11	4. 68	199	84. 68
18	7	2. 98	206	87. 66
19	10	4. 16	216	91. 91
20	6	2. 55	222	94. 47
21	9	3. 83	231	98. 30
22	2	0. 85	233	99. 15
24	1	0. 43	234	99. 57
26	1	0. 43	235	100. 00
Total	235	100. 00	235	100. 00

B. Regional differences in governance of board of supervisors in private listed companies. In order to analyze the regional differences in the governance of the board of supervisors, we first divided the listed companies into the eastern, central and western regions. There were 135 listed companies in the east, 53 in the west and 47

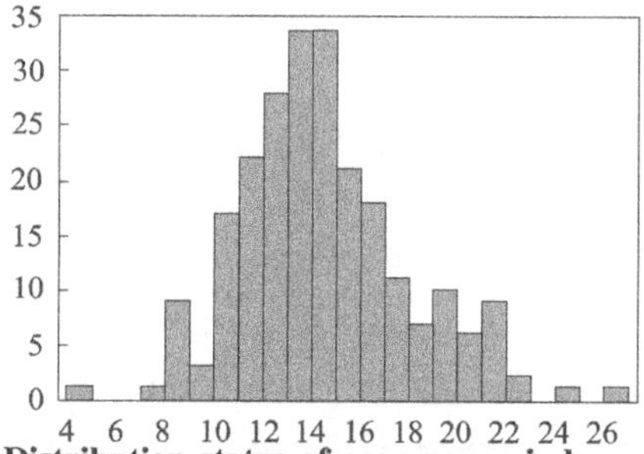

Figure 7 – 43 Distribution status of governance indexes of the board of supervisors in private listed companies

listed companies in the central as in Table 7 – 80. Further, according to the location of the listed company after the division of the board of supervisors governance indicators were descriptive statistics, see Table 7 – 81. Statistics find that the central region compared to the west and east, the overall level of governance of the board of supervisors is lower, and the best in the west, followed by the east.

Table 7 – 80 Regional division of PLCs sample

Region	Number of provincial district	Number of companies	Names of provincial district
Eastern	8 provinces and 3 cities	135	Liaoning, Hebei, Tianjin, Beijing, Shandong, Jiangsu, Shanghai, Zhejiang, Fujian, Guandong, Hainan
Central	8 provinces	47	Heilongjiang, Jilin, Shanxi, Henan, Anhui, Hubei, Hunan, Jiangxi
Western	6 provinces, 1 city and 5 autonomous regions	53	Shaanxi, Gansu, Ningxia, Qinghai, Xinjiang, Sichuan, Chongqing, Yunnan, Guizhou, Tibet, Inner Mongolia, Guangxi

Table 7 – 81 Regional differences in governance of board of supervisors in private listed companies

Region	Mean	Median	Max	Min	Standard deviation	Skewness	Kurtosis
Eastern	13. 81	13. 00	24. 00	7. 00	3. 58	0. 57	2. 85
Central	13. 70	14. 00	21. 00	4. 00	3. 16	-0. 08	3. 94
Western	14. 66	14. 00	26. 00	8. 00	3. 22	0. 98	4. 80

C. Industrial differences in governance of board of supervisors in private listed companies. According to the CSRC industry classification standard on the listed private companies for industry division, the industrial differences of the indexes are analyzed and the results are present in Table 7 – 82. Table 7 – 82 shows that the governance index of the board of supervisors of private listed companies shows a certain difference in different industries. Among them, the construction industry and the real estate industry compared to other industries in terms of the overall level of governance of the board of supervisors is better (especially the social services, information technology industry). The possible reason is that the construction industry and the real estate industry have developed rapidly in recent years, and the improvement of the supervisory level of the board of supervisors has been promoted by the shareholders, employees, the media and the government. This indicates that it is helpful to promote the participation of other stakeholders (employees) in the governance of the board of supervisors and enhance the governance level of the board of supervisors.

Table 7 – 82 Industrial differences in governance of the board of supervisors in private listed companies

Industry	Mean	Median	Max	Min	Standard Deviation	Skewness	Kurtosis
Agriculture (7)	13.71	14.00	17.00	10.00	2.14	-0.26	2.89
Manufacture (143)	14.04	14.00	26.00	4.00	3.47	0.50	3.73
Construction (6)	16.33	17.00	21.00	11.00	4.89	-0.12	1.17
IT (16)	12.19	12.50	17.00	7.00	2.83	0.13	2.29
Wholesales and Trade (12)	14.75	14.50	19.00	11.00	2.49	0.44	2.40
Real estate (14)	14.64	13.50	22.00	10.00	3.84	0.59	2.28
Social service (6)	11.33	12.00	13.00	8.00	1.97	-0.85	2.29
Comprehensive (22)	14.05	14.50	21.00	8.00	3.58	0.38	2.64
Others (9)	14.23	14.00	21.00	10.00	3.08	0.92	3.69

Notes: 1) Others include industries of B, D, F, I and L. They are merged into one classification since number of the companies is small and they are of monopoly nature. 2) Numbers in the brackets are the numbers of PLCs in the corresponding industry.

7.5 Evaluation on managerial governance of private listed companies

7.5.1 Review of managerial governance and evaluation

In recent decades, the research on managerial governance at home and abroad has focused on the empirical analysis of the effect of reward incentive and restraint mechanism. Murphy (1985) suggests that managerial pay is significantly associated with firm performance, and Adobe (1990) further argues that the previous level of compensation is associated with current operational performance sensitivity. Bruck &

Buck (1996) and Mcknight & Tomkins (1999) have shown that stock options have a significant effect on corporate performance. Li & Zhang (2003) constructs the managerial evaluation indicator system and the index system, and evaluates the governance of listed companies in China from the three dimensions of appointment and removal, enforcement guarantee and incentive and restraint. Li et al. (2003, 2004) finds that the level of remuneration, salary incentive and managerial shareholding of managers in Chinese listed companies are significantly positively correlated with earnings per share. Xue & Wu (2004, 2005) analyzes the composition of incentive mechanism of managers in listed companies and analyzes the relationship between them.

Private listed companies' development are accompanied by the reform and transformation of China's economy and they are the constantly growing strength playing an increasingly important role. Most people believe that the low income, irrational remuneration structure, single form and absence of market-oriented long-term incentive of state-owned enterprises is the reason of insufficient incentive for state-owned listed companies' managers. Then as an emerging force, whether managers of private listed company have overcome such problems, and is there any distinction with those of the state-owned listed companies? Li & Zhang (2005) finds that when the largest shareholder is private, the managerial evaluation index of listed companies is high and the executives' problems are outstanding. Reasonable and effective managerial incentive and restraint mechanisms can improve financial security, reduce corporate governance risk and governance costs. Tian & Cheng (2006) uses the data of the replacement of managers of private listed companies from 1998 to 2002, and proves that the possibility of replacement of managers in private listed companies is negatively correlated with performance, and insider succession is better than that of outsiders to improve performance.

In general, the study of managerial behavior in listed companies in China mainly focuses on the empirical research on managerial salary, shareholding ratio and corporate performance, and draws a lot of meaningful conclusions. However, the common problem is that the number of samples is small and there is no robustness check on the econometric results. What's more, the private listed companies manager behavior research does not sum up the particularity of private listed companies managerial behavior, because in the final analysis of private listed companies manager management, rules must be the general principles of corporate governance and be combined with the particularity. Samples in existing researches are the total listed companies and there are no literatures on the evaluation indexes of private listed companies in China at present. This part tries to establish the management evaluation index of private listed companies from both theoretical and practical aspects.

7.5.2 Theoretical and empirical study on evaluation index of managerial governance

According to the previous theoretical research review, the management evaluation of private listed companies firstly needs to focus on the incentive mechanism for managers to effectively encourage the manager to have the will, motivation and actively achieve the realization of their own interests to maximize the interests of shareholders. Taking into account of data collection difficulty and availability, we chose two indicators on the incentive for managers disclosed in the listed company's annual report: total compensation of the top three executives (not including directors and supervisors) and shareholding ratio of the manager. In terms of the appointment and removal institution and the security of implementation, this study does not involve because the data collection is difficult. In terms of constraints for the management governance, we select the indicator on independence of the board to study the relationship between independence of board of the directors and incentive of manager. In order to examine the relationship between managerial governance and the control characteristics of private shareholder groups in private listed companies, we have examined the empirical relationship between the proportion of internal shareholders representing the group control index and managerial remuneration.

1. Variables selection and data sources

Our total sample is private listed companies listed from 2002 to December 2005. However, because of the data discontinuity (mainly refers to that the indicators are changed in the process of selection) and robustness of the econometric results, the sample is divided into two subsets. The first subset is private listed companies listed from December 2002 to December 31, 2004 and the total number is 318. After screening, we excluded those key regulatory companies marked with " * ST", 30 companies listed in Shenzhen small and medium board in 2004 and Delong Group companies managed by Huarong Asset Management Company. In addition, we also excluded several sample companies whose information disclosure is not complete and the final remaining 224 sample companies are the research object. The second subset is the private listed companies in 2005 and with the same screening, the final remaining 235 companies are used for the study. The data mainly comes from the comprehensive utilization of the database of private listed companies of Nankai University Corporate Governance Research Center, the Senuofen database of PKU, Guotai'an Database and the annual report of listed companies published by China Securities Regulatory Commission website.

Part of the company's performance indicators are earnings per share (EPS) and we use manager's shareholding ratio and total compensation of the top three executive to represent the manager's incentive indicators. First of all, we have to verify the relationship between manager's incentive indicators and corporate performance. Control variables include region and industry dummy variables, logarithmic main business income to control the size of assets and debt assets ratio to control the company's financial leverage. Variable symbols, variable meaning are present in Table 7 – 83.

Table 7 – 83 List of variable symbols and meanings

Category	Symbol	Meaning
Dependent variable	EPS	Earnings per share (net profit)
Independent variables	SR	Shareholding ratio of the general manager
Controls	MR	Total compensation of the top three executive (not including directors and supervisors) (10 thousand Yuan)
	Sfdum	Region dummies
	Hydum	Industry dummies
	Lnzy	Logarithmic main business income
	LEV	Debt assets ratio

Note: 1) 1 is for the eastern, 0 for the central and – 1 for the western; 2) 3 is for the manufacture industry, 2 for the comprehensive, – 1 for the real estate, – 2 for the others and – 3 for wholesales. Other industries include culture, electricity etc.

2. Empirical analysis methods and regression models

We use different empirical methods for the regression of the two sample subsets to explore the robustness of the empirical results. For the sample of private listed companies from 2002 to 2004, we use the unbalanced panel data model. For the sample of private listed companies in 2005, we used the cross-sectional data model. The variables set is the same and the results show that the symbols of the variable coefficients in two models are the same, which indicates that the econometric results of our models are relatively robust since they are not affected by the time period.

The unbalanced panel data from 2002 to 2004 are analyzed using econometric method for unbalanced panel data, Hsiao (2001) pointed out that the panel data contains the observed values of N individuals in T time periods and compared to cross-sectional data whose T = 1 or time-series data whose N = 1, the degree of freedom is naturally much higher, so it is more likely to avoid problems caused by multiple collinearity and low degree of freedom and can more accurately estimate the parameters of interest. Moreover, by comparing the differences between individuals and the dynamic characteristics of this difference, the researcher can establish a much more complex behavior hypothesis than the cross-sectional data or time series data model. One of the challenges of the panel data model is how to capture the effects of non-observed heteroscedasticity in the model, thus making appropriate inferences about the effects of the variables we are interested in. In general, the solution is to put into the error term, and the relationship between the decomposition of the error term and the explanatory variable is divided into fixed effect model and random effect model. In econometric sense, the estimator of the model is consistent and effective as long as the model is set correctly and. The drawback is that the estimator is inconsistent when there is a correlation between the stochastic influence and the explanatory variables considered into the model and the advantage of the fixed effect model is that it allows to explain the fundamental differences between the variables, but also allows to consider the correlation between the explanatory variables of the model and the error terms, but the disadvantage is caused by the typical accompanying parameter problem, that is, The unknown parameter increases with the increase of N and T. In this section, we examine the relationship between managerial incentive indicators and corporate performance indicators, and it is certain that managerial incentives are only part of the performance of the firm and that there are many other indicators that affect firm performance, from corporate governance The influence of the shareholders' checks and balances, the governance of the board of directors and the supervisory situation of the board of supervisors. These factors are classified into the residual items in the model. However, there is a relationship between the governance of the board of directors and the governance of the board of supervisors, There is a correlation between the explanatory variables, in which we should choose the fixed effect model, but considering the accompanying parameter problem and that T is relatively small, we can set the time fixed effect model. In econometrics, we still have to use Hausman test to determine whether the model is a random effect or a fixed effect model, the model is set as follows:

$$EPS_{it} = \alpha_1 + \beta_1 MS_{it} + \beta_2 Control_{it}(hydum_{it}, sfdum_{it}, lnzy_{it}, Lev_{it}) + e_{it} \quad (1)$$

$$EPS_{it} = \alpha_1 + \beta_1 SR_{it} + \beta_2 Control_{it}(hydum_{it}, sfdum_{it}, lnzy_{it}, Lev_{it}) + e_{it} \qquad (2)$$

Taking into account the particularity of managerial governance, we present the results of pooled regression estimation in panel data regression. This is mainly based on the little variability of the managerial sample data of the private listed companies. We assume that the three-year samples are from the same population. The F-statistic is used to select from pooled estimation model and fixed effect model. The pooled estimation model is set as follows:

$$EPS = \alpha + \beta_1 MS + \beta_2 Control(hydum, sfdum, lnzy, Lev) + e \qquad (3)$$

For the 2005 cross-sectional data of private listed companies, we use the least squares (OLS) regression model. Because it is cross-section data, it is not necessary to consider the autocorrelation factors. In the model we also use industry, region, asset size, debt assets ratio and other control variables as controls, but the White test found that it still cannot eliminate the impact of heteroscedasticity. In order to eliminate the influence of heteroscedasticity on the consistency of estimators, the classical method developed by Newey – West in 1987 is used to deal with the heteroscedasticity in the model. Considering the large sample size (235), it is basically considered that using this method, we can get the covariance estimation of covariance matrix under the existence of heteroscedasticity of the model. Therefore, the estimated coefficients and statistics have high accuracy. The model is set as follows:

$$EPS_i = \alpha + \beta_1 MS_i + \beta_2 Control_i(hydum_i, sfdum_i, lnzy_i, Lev_i) + \varepsilon_i \qquad (4)$$

$$EPS_i = \alpha + \beta_1 SR_i + \beta_2 Control_i(hydum_i, sfdum_i, lnzy_i, Lev_i) + \varepsilon_i \qquad (5)$$

3. Empirical results and analysis of managerial incentive model

As the data collection is sufficient, the descriptive statistics of the samples of private listed companies will provide us with some intuitive understanding. Table 7 – 84 lists the descriptive statistical analysis results for each of the years from 2002 to 2005. It is clear that since we excluded the ST companies in the sample, the earnings per share of the private listed companies in the four years are positive on average every year. In 2004, the earnings of private listed companies fell to a low level, starting from 2005, the highest among them in four years Of the earnings per share of 1.95 yuan, the lowest for – 14.08 yuan, the standard deviation of the largest 1.73, indicating that private listed companies there is a big difference between the sample companies.

Table 7 - 84 Descriptive statistical results on manager variables

Year	Earnings Per Share (EPS)			
	Mean	Standard deviation	Min	Max
2002	0. 13	0. 39	-3. 09	0. 92
2003	0. 13	0. 53	-3. 56	1. 35
2004	0. 02	1. 73	-14. 08	1. 95
2005	0. 10	0. 38	-2. 22	0. 86
Year	Total compensation of the Top Three Executives (MS)			
	Mean	Standard deviation	Min	Max
2002	15. 33	17. 68	1. 16	157
2003	18. 39	17. 32	1. 40	163
2004	20. 25	19. 8	2. 20	170. 67
2005	39. 78	43. 92	3. 75	345
Year	Ratio of Shares Held by the General Manager (MS)			
	Mean	Standard deviation	Min	Max
2002	0. 0043	0. 0244	0	0. 2270
2003	0. 0071	0. 0334	0	0. 2915
2004	0. 0075	0. 0330	0	0. 2915
2005	0. 0065	0. 0309	0	0. 2523

From views of the two incentives for the manager which are the pay and equity, total compensation of the top three executives began to rise from the beginning of 2002, the average rose from 150 000 yuan in 2002 to 40 million in 2005. The maximum and the minimum values are more than doubled, but it is worth noting that the standard deviation of the sum of the compensation continued to rise, indicating that the remittance of the sample manager of the company is increasing and the rise of proportion of general manager shares from 2002 to 2005 is small. There is no significant variation observed from the sample data.

The correlation between the performance of the private listed companies and the manager's main incentive variables is shown in Table 7 - 85. This table is calculated using the sample of private listed companies in 2005.

Table 7 - 85 Coefficient of explanatory variables on corporate performance and manager

Variable	EPS	MS	SR
EPS	1	0. 091	0. 027
MS	0. 091	1	0. 037
SR	0. 027	0. 037	1

From Table 7 - 85, we can see that the relation between compensation and shareholding is positive, indicating that the manager's salary incentive and shareholding incentives are related to the performance of private listed companies positively. Seeing from the correlation coefficients, these two types of incentives can effectively mobilize the enthusiasm of managers of listed companies. The pay directly inspires managers and shareholding gives the agent manager certain amount of corporate residual claims, making the goals of client shareholders and managers consistent, leading to a higher level of managerial effort and improved performance. But it must be noted here that our correlation coefficient does not pass the significance test and must using empirical econometric analysis to further verify the conclusions drawn through descriptive statistics.

Results of the two empirical models of managerial incentive and corporate performance of private listed companies are shown in Table 7 -86. The results of the fixed effect model of the unbalanced panel data from 2002 to 2004 are on the left and the results of the regression analysis in 2005 are on the right.

Table 7 -86 Regression results on empirical model on corporate performance and manager Level explanatory variables

Varaible	EPS		EPS	
Mcthod	Unbalanced Panel Data Model		OLS	
Sample	PLCs from 2 002 to 2 004		PLCs in 2 005	
Model	(3)	(1)	(4)	(5)
Variable	Pooled Model		Time Fixed Effect	OLS
MS	0. 004455 ***	0. 006759 ***	0. 001434 ***	—
	(0. 001664)	(0. 001983)	(0. 000422)	—
SR	—	—	—	0. 279060
	—	—	—	(1. 018166)
Sfdum	0. 039649	0. 045733	—	—
	(0. 044870)	(0. 045213)	—	—
Hydum	-0. 000416	0. 015939	—	—
	(0. 016387)	(0. 018944)	—	—
Lnzy	—	—	—	—
	—	—	—	—
LEV	—	—	—	—
	—	—	—	—
Constant	—	-0. 108841 *	—	0. 095054 ***
	—	(0. 060416)	—	(1. 018166)
R-squared	0. 022	0. 036	0. 003	0. 001

Note: *** indicates significance level of 1%, ** indicates 5% and * indicates 10%; the values in the parentheses of the equation coefficients are the standard error. R-squared is reported, but it is not meaningful in the panel model. The Hausman and F statistic tests results in the panel model indicate that the fixed effect model is used. Since the Newey-West method is used in the OLS regression model to obtain the heteroscedasticity consistent estimate of the model, the control variables can be discarded in the OLS model.

The empirical results of the panel model and the OLS model show that there is a significant positive correlation between the total compensation of the top three executives and the performance of the company. In this sense, we can think that the result that total compensation of the top three executives has positive motivation on the company performance is robust. In the least squares regression model, it is found that although the proportion of the general manager's shareholding is positively related to the firm's performance, but the estimation didn't pass the significance test. In the preceding literature review, the results show that the executive compensation has a positive effect on the firm's performance. In the literature review, we pointed out that Han et al. (2006) argued that there was non-linear relationship between management holding and corporate performance in 78 private listed companies in Shenzhen Stock Exchange in 2004, and benefit convergence effect and trench benefit alternated. We use the 2005 sample data to continue to validate and try to establish a non-linear model of earnings per share and shareholding of general managers. Heteroscedasticity is still handled using Newey – West's classic approach developed in 1987 and the results of the fitting model are shown in Table 7 – 87.

Table 7 – 87 Regression results of non-linear model on corporate performance and general manager's shareholding ratio

Vairiable	EPS
Method	OLS (non-linear model)
Sample	PLCs in 2005
Variable	—
Vairiable	EPS
SR	15.84006 ***
	(0.000422)
SR^2 (squared term)	188.0139 ***
	(66.07023)
SR^3 (quadric term)	507.8523 ***
	(189.9252)
Constant	0.086477 ***
	(0.026419)
R-squared	0.028

Note: *** indicates significance level of 1%, ** indicates 5% and * indicates 10%; the values in the parentheses of the equation coefficients are the standard error. R-squared is reported.

From the analysis results in Table 7 – 87, we can see that the non-linear model of corporate performance and the proportion of the total holdings of private listed companies is fitted well, whose R-squared has been significantly improved from 0.001 in (5) to 0.028 in the nonlinear model and the estimators of the manager's shareholding ratio in the nonlinear model are all significant at the level of 1%. Therefore, there is a nonlinear relationship between the managers of the private listed companies and the performance of the listed companies. The final model is written as:

$$EPS_i = 0.086\,477 + 15.840\,06SR_i - 188.013\,9SR_i^2 + 507.852\,3SR_i^3 \quad (6)$$

The first-order derivative of the above model indicates that when SR = 5.06%, the company's performance reaches its maximum; when SR = 19.62%, the company's performance reaches its minimum. When 0 < SR < 5.06%, the general manager's shareholding is positively related to the performance of the firm. The performance of the company increases with the increase of the proportion of the general manager. When 5.06% < SR < 19.62%, the firm's performance and manager's shares are related negatively, which means with the increasing of management of the shareholding ratio, the management of the company's control increases, the original external binding on the manager is gets weaker, so the manager at this time acts in the broader range of the pursuit of personal interests, thereby enhancing agency costs and reduce corporate performance and value; when 19.62% < SR < 1, the company's managerial interests and shareholders' interests are closely linked, the manager works harder to improve corporate performance and value under the incentive of large shareholding ratio. We use Eviews 5.0 to get the numerical fit of model (6) as Figure 7-44, it can be clearly seen from the figure that the model reaches the maximum at 0.0506 and reaches the minimum value at 0.1962. Taking into account the fact that in 2005, the highest proportion of shareholding of the general manager was 25.23% disclosed in private listed companies annual report, the SR maximum value is set to 0.26 in Figure 7-44.

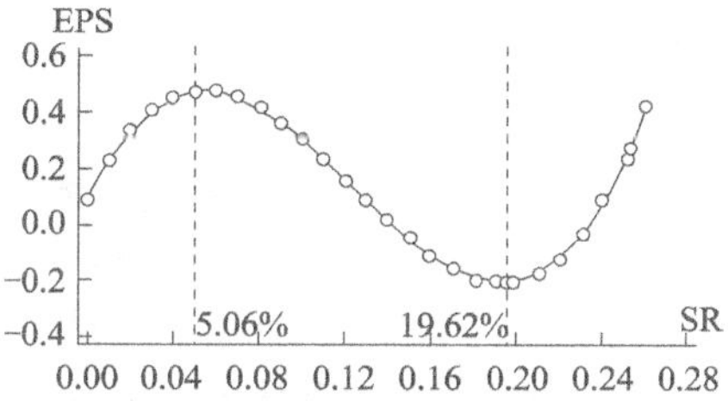

Figure 7-44 Numerical simulation results of non-linear model (6) on corporate performance and general manager's shareholding ratio

Note: Seeing from the non-linear model of the third-order polynomial function numerical simulation image, the company's performance EPS reached the maximum and minimum at 5.06% and 19.62% respectively, which are marked with two vertical lines, indicating that there is a nonlinear relationship between the company's equity motivation and the manager.

From the empirical results above of the managerial salary and equity incentive in private listed companies, the result is different from the state-owned listed companies since the private listed company's largest shareholder has a private ownership nature①. In addition, corporate governance research literature (Li, 2004) suggests that the

① When drawing samples, we tend to go back to the ultimate controller of the private listed companies remuneration and equity incentive effect on the manager is relatively small since the absolute proportion of state-owned shares and legal person shares cannot flow in the state-owned listed companies. In PLCs, the remuneration and equity incentives can effectively motivate managers due to the relatively clear property rights. Our robust empirical results also show that the clarity of property rights can improve the management level of the manager.

4. Empirical results and analysis of manager's compensation, board independence and group control

In the previous section, we confirmed the incentive effect is more significant in private listed companies with clear property rights. We are going to discuss another question that on the level of governance mechanism of managers, whether we can combine the current characteristics of private listed companies to find the characteristics of private listed companies' management. We just look for preliminary evidence in this part and explore the relationship among managers in private listed companies, independence of the board and group control.

Li (2004) proposed that checks and balances on "insider control" is the main line through the management of managerial governance indicators of listed companies. This is mainly based on the fact that managers who occupy the majority of the board of directors or appointed by a few people sent by the major shareholders are of the ultimate control and conduct the self-evaluation, making the general meeting of shareholders and board of the directors in name only. Combined with private listed companies literature Wu et al. propose that family control and group control are more serious in PLCs, then what is the relationship between the manager and the ultimate control of the private listed company in controlling the internal shareholder group, whether the board of private listed companies can play the supervisory and binding role of the managers of the private listed companies, and we will discuss the above problems in the econometric analysis.

Due to the limited managerial index of private listed companies, we have selected the explanatory variables of the top three executive compensation (MS) of the private listed companies as the explanatory variables of the model. Considering that the executive compensation is closely related to the performance of the firm, EPS is controlled and then we come to explore the impact of degree of independence and control group on executive compensation, where we use the external shareholders ratio to measure independence of the board (Independence of DB). Internal shareholders ratio (Nbgdbl) is used to measure the level of group control and the specific meaning is that the shareholder is a major one when his holding ratio is more than 5% and this indicator is defined as the ratio of major shareholders and all major shareholders belonging to the same ultimate controller. The final model is set as followings.

$$MS = \alpha + \beta_1 \text{Independence} + \beta_2 \text{Control(EPS)} + \varepsilon \quad (7)$$

$$MS = \alpha + \beta_1 \text{nbgdrs} + \beta_2 \text{Control(EPS)} + \varepsilon \quad (8)$$

The descriptive statistics of the independence of the board and the proportion of internal shareholders can be seen from Table 7 – 88, the proportion of internal shareholders of private listed companies has declined in recent years, from 23% in 2003 to 17% in 2005, and the maximum value from 89% to 60%, but we also found that private listed companies in the independence of board of the directors fell faster with 30% drop in 2005. It is still in doubt whether group control phenomenon in private listed companies is in the mitigation or intensification, which is a question worthy of further study, naturally there is information disclosure problem in the annual report as well.

Table 7 – 88 Independence of the board of directors and ratio of internal shareholders

Year	Ratio of internal sharehold (Nbgdbl)				Independence of board of the directors (Independence)			
	Mean	Standard deviation	Min	Max	Mean	Standard deviation	Min	Max
2002	0. 19	0. 13	0. 11	0. 89	0. 77	0. 14	0. 43	1
2003	0. 23	0. 19	0. 17	0. 86	0. 78	0. 14	0. 45	1
2004	0. 20	0. 14	0. 13	0. 87	0. 79	0. 13	0. 45	1
2005	0. 17	0. 12	0. 10	0. 60	0. 43	0. 14	0	0. 7

Logically, if the managers of private listed companies directly belong to or subordinate to the control group①, then with the increase in the proportion of internal shareholders, control groups can more effectively control the entire listed companies and get access to benefits. Managers share the benefit of group control as executives and get their compensation increased. At the same time, since the independence of the board of directors is a balancing effect on the control of the internal shareholder group (Wu, 2006), with the increase in the independence of the board of directors, the supervision and restraint of the internal shareholder group will be strengthened and the manager's pay will be checked and balanced. Therefore, the independence of the board of directors should be negatively related with the compensation. The econometric results are given in Table 7 – 89.

From Table 7 – 89, we can see that obvious positive correlation exits between managerial remuneration and the proportion of internal shareholders in private listed

① At present, we cannot find the relationship between the company manager and internal shareholders from the private listed companies ' annual report and a lot of information is not disclosed.

companies in the two-period econometric models, indicating that the econometric results are relatively robust, so we think that executives of private listed companies is correlated to the internal control group somehow and they are closely linked. The game model of the private listed companies control right by Zhang (2006) shows that the internal shareholder control group strengthen the control of listed companies through a variety of ways, resulting in that the manager has to accept a distorted contract, or collude with the control group to encroach to get the additional income, which is justified by our econometric model. As for the ways in which the internal control group and the managers of private listed companies obtain the benefits, we need to study further in the follow-up work; but our econometric results also find that the managerial compensation and the independence of the board do not correlated negatively as we think. The two models show that the estimated coefficient of independence of the board are not significant, so the relationship between independence of board of the directors and the manager is worth continuing to study and research.

Table 7 – 89 Regression on managerial remuneration and control and board independence

Variable	MS		MS	
Method	Unbalanced Panel Model		OLS	
Sample	PLCs between 2002 and 2004		PLCs in 2005	
Model	(7)	(8)	(7)	(8)
Variable	Time fixed effects	Time fixed effects	—	
EPS	3.389 099 ***	3.524 897 ***	9.831 429	9.227 715
	(0.903 075)	(0.923 436)	(8.999 758)	(8.575 025)
Independence of DB	−5.689 713	—	10.186 67	—
	(5.838 037)	—	(18.227 01)	—
Nbgdbl	2.660 507 ***	—	42.017 44 *	
	(0.685 943)	—	(23.390 70)	
Constant	22.628 50 ***	14.187 95 ***	34.521 18 ***	31.814 15 ***
	(4.620 822)	(1.358 789)	(9.154 422)	(4.596 726)
R-squared	0.022	0.062	0.010	0.022

Note: *** indicates significance level of 1%, ** indicates 5% and * indicates 10%; the values in the parentheses of the equation coefficients are the standard error. R-squared is reported, but it is not meaningful in the panel model. The Hausman and F statistic tests results in the panel model indicate that the fixed effect model is used. Since the Newey-West method is used in the OLS regression model to obtain the heteroscedasticity consistent estimate of the model, the control variables can be discarded in the OLS model.

This part is only a preliminary study of characteristics of management of private listed companies, we find that managers and ubiquitous control group in private listed companies are correlated to some degree. But it is worth noting that in our panel data model, the compensation of managers in PLCs is significantly related to the company's performance indicators, which fully demonstrates that private listed companies are still closely tied to managerial pay and performance. As for the governance characteristics of private listed companies, we believe that with the expansion of private listed companies and the disclosure of information norms, we will have a deeper discovery in the follow-up study.

7.5.3 Evaluation and status quo of managerial governance

Based on our previous review of private corporate governance literature and theoretical and empirical research conclusions in this section, we have selected two variables to measure the management of private listed companies' manager: general manager shareholding ratio (SR) and sum compensation of the top three senior managers of listed companies (MS). According to the empirical research in front of this part, sum compensation of the top three senior managers is positively related to the performance of the company, and share ratio held by the general manager is nonlinear with the firm's performance. In this part, we will be in accordance with the above two indicators of private listed companies in 2005 to evaluate the management in PLCs. First of all, we study the descriptive statistics of the two indicators for private listed companies' manager in 2005.

1. Descriptive statistics of managerial governance evaluation variables

We selected 235 private listed companies on Shenzhen and Shanghai stock markets as the sample, including 85 on Shenzhen market and 150 on Shanghai market. In the selection process, we removed the ST companies and those of SME sector on Shenzhen market (see Figure 7-45, Table 7-90).

(1) Descriptive statistics of general manager's shareholding ratio (SR).

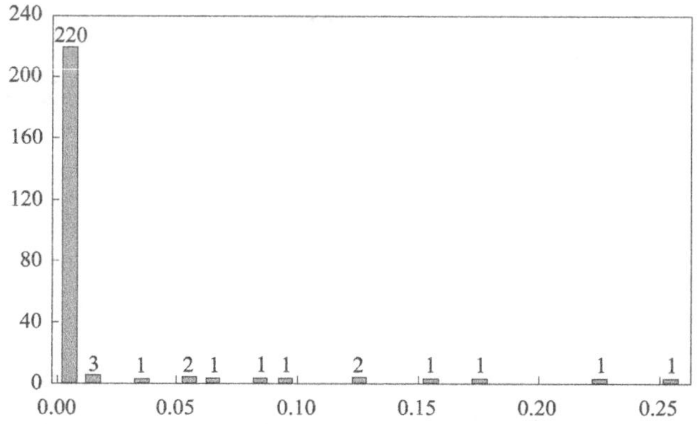

Figure 7-45 Histogram of general manager's shareholding ratio

Table 7 - 90 **Descriptive statistics of general manager's shareholding ratio**

Mean	Median	Max	Min	Standard deviation
0. 0065	0. 00	0. 2523	0. 00	0. 0309

From descriptive statistics of general manager shareholding ratio, we can see that private listed companies with the general manager holding shares in the sample are still the minority. There are 180 private listed companies where the general manager does not hold any share and 220 companies' managers holding less than 2. 5%. Taking into account the empirical results we find in the previous study that when shareholding ratio of general manager falls between 0 to 5. 06%, the equity can effectively stimulate the private listed company managers, so we should encourage appropriate holdings of private listed companies' manager. Those who really make a significant contribution to the development of the companies get the appropriate company equity, reflecting their value.

(2) Descriptive statistics of total compensation the top three executives' compensation (SR)

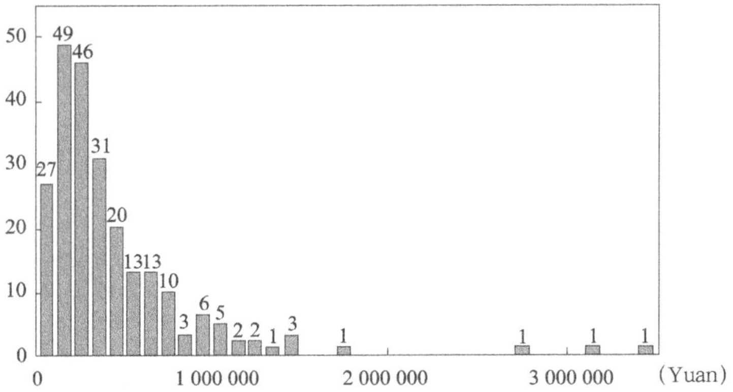

Figure 7 - 46 Histogram of total compensation of the top three executives

Note: In previous econometric model, the unit of the sum of top three executive compensation of private listed companies is ten thousand yuan, while the unit in this figure is yuan; from the perspective of econometric model, this will not change the robustness of the measurement results. It is equivalent to multiplying the estimated coefficient by 10 000.

Table 7 - 91 Descriptive statistics of total compensation of the top three executives

Mean	Median	Max	Min	Standard deviation
414 950	289 200	3 452 600	4 300	438 800

From descriptive statistics of total compensation of the top three executives in private listed companies, we can see that the average value of total compensation of the top three executives is high at 0. 41 million, with the compensation of managers in 183 private listed company under 0. 50 million. Combined with the empirical results of our previous model, the compensation can effectively motivate the manager, and is positively correlated to the company performance. Therefore, from this point of view, we believe that compensation incentive for the manager is more fully in companies with clear property rights. But from the histogram we also find that the compensation distribution is right skewed, and the standard deviation is large, indicating that the company in the compensation incentive differences are large.

2. Principle explanation for managerial governance evaluation index rating

(1) General manager's shareholding ratio (SR): Due to the non-linear relationship between the shareholding ratio of the general manager and the firm's performance, we use two different principles to rate.

Principle 1: in accordance with Figure 7 – 45, taking into account the 224 companies holding the proportion of 5. 06% or less, only a small number of enterprises, the proportion of general manager of more than 5. 06% stake, the results published in Table 7 –92; Principle 2: because the numerical difference among other enterprises is large, the group gap is the power of 10 and according to the order from small to large. For example, 10^{-6} is given for 4.

(2) Total compensation of the top three executives (MS): since the empirical model shows that the sum of executive compensation is positively correlated to firm performance, the following rating principle is used: the absolute value of 10 000 is the group gap and according to the order from small to large. Results are present in Table 7 –93.

Table 7 –92 Scores for special shareholding ratios

Stock Code	Company's Name	Holding Ratio	Score
600570	G Hengsheng	0. 057314402	10
600527	G Gaoxian	0. 057340549	10
600537	G Haitong	0. 064272590	8
600352	G Longsheng	0. 089220212	7
600330	G Tiantong	0. 098262105	6
600594	G Yibai	0. 122388060	4
600499	G Yuekeda	0. 128206811	3
600405	G Dongliyuan	0. 159161606	2
600446	G Jinzheng	0. 175660070	1
600355	G Jinglun	0. 227060053	2
600521	G Huahai	0. 252281252	3

Table 7 - 93 Principle explanation for managerial governance evaluation index rating

(Unit: 10 thousand Yuan)

Indicator	SR	MS
Group gap	10^{-1}	1
Score	—	—
10	$(3-5)\times 10^{-2}$	≥90
9	$(1-2)\times 10^{-2}$	80 - 90
8	10^{-3}	70 - 80
7	10^{-4}	60 - 70
6	$(6-9)\times 10^{-5}$	50 - 60
5	$(1-5)\times 10^{-5}$	40 - 50
4	10^{-6}	30 - 40
3	—	20 - 30
2	—	10 - 20
1	0	0 - 10

3. Descriptive statistics for managerial governance evaluation index rating

This part gives the descriptive statistics of the scores of managerial governance evaluation index rating for private listed companies. It should be noted that in the histogram, x axis represents the score, y axis represents the corresponding score of the number of private listed companies.

(1) SR governance index score histogram situation.

We can see that private listed companies are particularly deficient in the equity incentive of the manager, and the scores are low (see Figure 7 - 47). Of which 181 companies get a minimum score of 1, accounting for 77% of the sample. This shows once again the private listed companies in the manager of the equity incentive this one has a larger room for improvement. Because equity incentive is a long-term incentive means, it is necessary to attach importance to the equity incentive this one, to reflect the long-term efforts of managers and corporate performance and the dynamic relationship between the value of enterprises in the smooth development of the enterprise managers also bring huge remuneration, Because private listed companies can consider appropriate to increase the proportion of managerial shares to encourage their long-term business behavior.

(2) MS governance index score histogram situation.

Figure 4 - 48 shows that executive pay score distribution than the equity incentive score has been greatly improved in the private listed companies, indicating that private listed companies pay more attention to the manager of the explicit incentive.

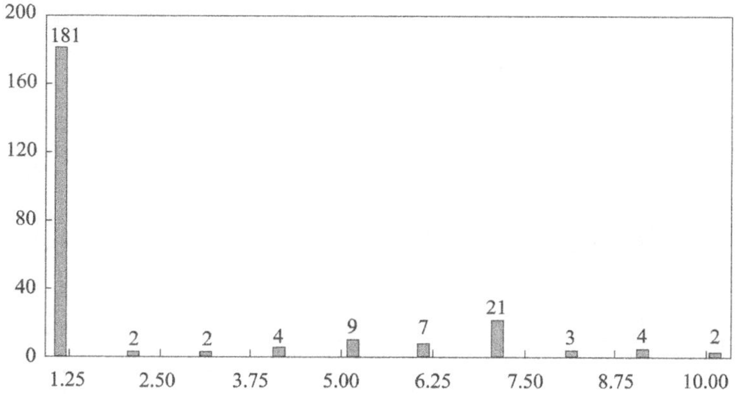

Figure 7 – 47　SR governance index score histogram

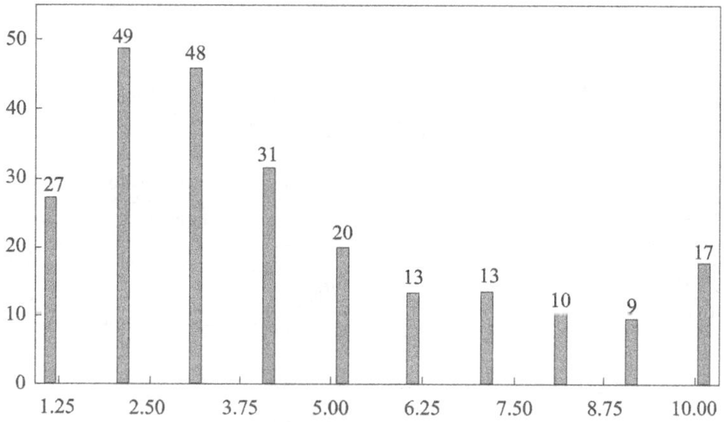

Figure 7 – 48　MS governance index score histogram

(3) Managerial governance index overall score histogram.

In Figure 7 – 49, we can see that the overall score distribution of managerial governance indicators is more balanced, but still follows the right skewed distribution, there is still a lot of room for improvement.

(4) Managerial governance indicators score descriptive statistical summaries.

Table 7 – 94 shows the summary of descriptive statistics of managerial indicators of private listed companies. It can be seen from the figure that the average score of the managerial evaluation index is low, which indicates that there is a big difference between the managerial governance and the corporate governance of the private listed companies. There is an urgent need to further improve the governance of the managers of the private listed companies. Management level governance indicators and the performance of the total score of the regression model results, the management of governance indicators for each additional 0. 1 points, the company's performance increased 0. 0013428 yuan (see Table 7 – 95) .

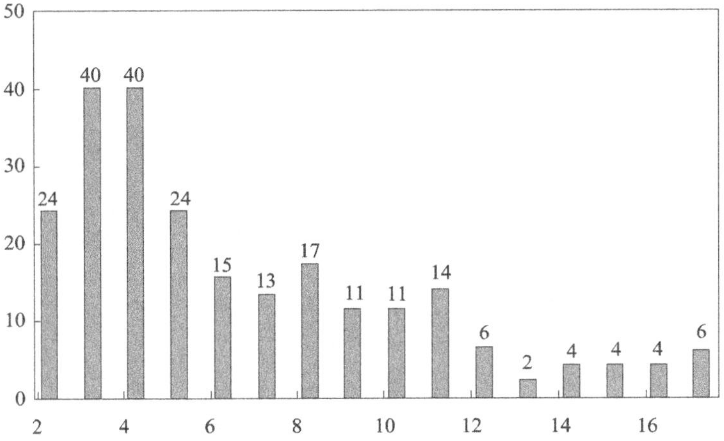

Figure 7 – 49 Histogram for managerial governance indicators total score in private listed companies

Table 7 – 94 Descriptive statistics of evaluation for managers of private listed companies

Variable	Mean	Median	Standard deviation	Skewness	Kurtosis
MS score	2. 22	1. 0	2. 39	1. 67	4. 17
SR score	4. 10	3. 00	2. 66	0. 85	2. 65
Managerial governance total score	6. 42	5. 00	3. 93	1. 01	3. 20

Table 7 – 95 Regression of corporate performance and manager governance index of private listed companies

Variable	EPS
Method	OLS (Non-linear)
Sample	PLCs in 2005
Variable	—
Managerial governance total score	0. 013428 ***
	(0. 0004447)
Constant	—
	—
R-squared	0. 006

Note: *** indicates significance level of 1%, ** indicates 5% and * indicates 10%; the values in the parentheses of the equation coefficients are the standard error. R-squared is reported, but it is not meaningful in the panel model. The Hausman and F statistic tests results in the panel model indicate that the fixed effect model is used. Since the Newey-West method is used in the OLS regression model to obtain the heteroscedasticity consistent estimate of the model, the control variables can be discarded in the OLS model.

4. Regional and industrial differences in the scores of managerial governance evaluation indicators

This part studies the governance of managers of the private listed companies and assess the regional and industrial differences to deepen our understanding of the evaluation. The sample we use is still that of 2005 in Shenzhen and Shanghai stock market of 235 private listed companies, including 85 of Shenzhen and 150 of Shanghai. In the sample selection process, we remove the ST and SME sector companies of Shenzhen. Weighted total numbers are used as the criteria of judgment. Horizontal axis for the score, vertical axis for the number of companies.

(1) Regional differences of evaluation for managerial governance.

We use dummy variables to represent regional differences, east 1, central 0 and western −1[①], where the specific meaning for eastern, central and western are shown in Table 7 −96.

After setting the dummy variable, regional differences in the managerial evaluation index are shown in Table 7 −97 and Figure 7 −50, from which we can see that the eastern gets the highest average score and the median value is the highest as well in line with China's economic development level of the region. Companies with sound managerial governance concentrate in the eastern. Scores of the western companies are the lowest, which indicates that the managerial governance index has a certain relationship with the regional development level and the market maturity degree.

Table 7 −96 Regional distribution of PLCs sample

Region	Number of Provincial District	Names of Provincial District
Eastern	8 provinces and 3 cities	Liaoning, Hebei, Tianjin, Beijing, Shandong, Jiangsu, Shanghai, Zhejiang, Fujian, Guandong, Hainan
Central	8 provinces	Heilongjiang, Jilin, Shanxi, Henan, Anhui, Hubei, Hunan, Jiangxi
Western	6 provinces, 1 city and 5 autonomous regions	Shaanxi, Gansu, Ningxia, Qinghai, Xinjiang, Sichuan, Chongqing, Yunnan, Guizhou, Tibet, Inner Mongolia, Guangxi

① This dummy variable setting does not affect the final measurement result, which is different from the general binary variable setting in the final measurement model scale, that is, the scale effect. See Intriligator: Econometric models, Techniques, and Applications.

Table 7 – 97 Regional scores of managerial governance in private listed companies

Region	Mean	Median	Max	Min	Standard deviation	Skewness	Kurtosis
Eastern	6. 76	6. 00	17. 00	2. 00	3. 98	0. 83	2. 78
Central	6. 32	4. 00	17. 00	2. 00	4. 08	1. 05	3. 13
Western	5. 64	5. 00	17. 00	2. 00	3. 63	1. 54	5. 21

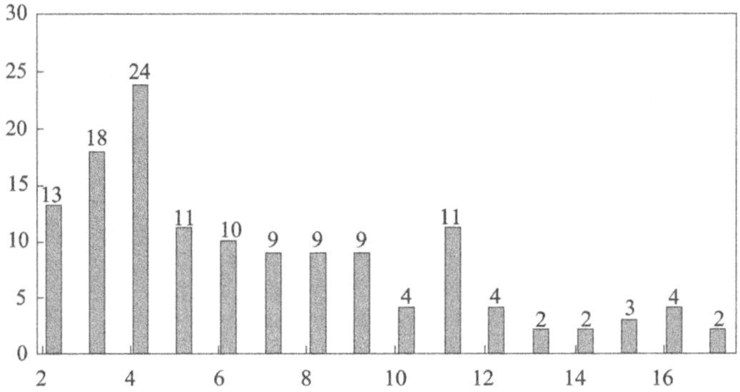

(a) Eastern

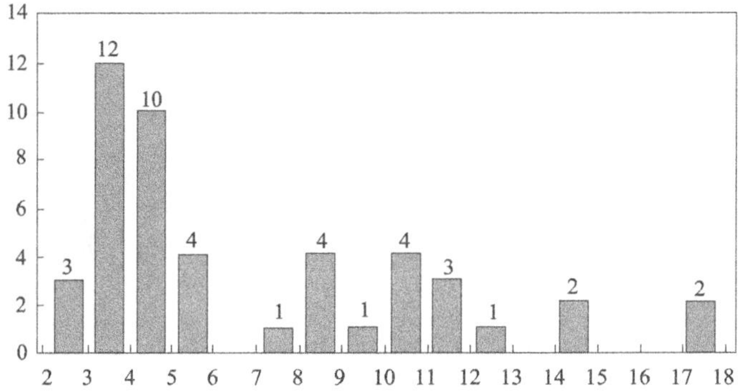

(b) Central

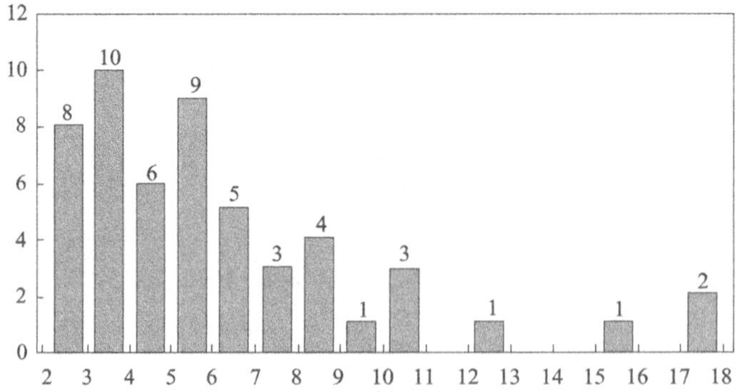

(c) Western

Figure 7 – 50 Histogram of regional managerial governance in private listed companies

(2) Industrial differences of evaluation for managerial governance.

According to the CSRC industry classification[①] standard on the private listed companies to industry division, dummy variables are used to represent the industry differences similarly, letters and numbers are corresponding to each other. For example, in the CSRC industry classification, the industry attributes of listed companies beginning with A are given 1, and the same dummy variables here will only bring about the difference in scale.

After setting the dummy variables for industry differences, we present the industry differences of scores of managers' management evaluation indicators in Table 7 – 98. Observing Table 7 – 98, we find that the managerial governance index scores higher in the construction and manufacturing sector, combined with China is currently the world's largest industrial base, construction and manufacturing industry has a history, relatively speaking in the industry chain of the company has developed to a stage, so the managerial incentive is also more perfect, so in the manufacturing sector management evaluation score is relatively high. At the same time, we also find that in the information technology industry, transportation services in the private listed companies have higher scores of managers, and in the social services sector and other departments of the evaluation index score lower.

Table 7 – 98 Industrial evaluation scores of managerial governance in private listed companies

Industry	Mean	Median	Max	Min	Standard deviation	Skewness	Kurtosis
Agriculture (7)	5.57	3.00	15.00	2.00	4.61	1.39	3.53
Manufacturing (143)	6.88	5.00	17.00	2.00	4.16	0.98	3.03
Construction (6)	7.17	7.50	14.00	2.00	4.26	0.31	2.14
IT (16)	6.87	6.00	14.00	3.00	3.56	0.58	2.16
Wholesales and Trade (12)	6.33	6.00	13.00	2.00	3.39	0.34	2.24
Real estate (14)	4.93	4.00	11.00	2.00	2.81	1.02	2.97
Social service (6)	4.50	4.00	9.00	3.00	2.26	1.60	3.88
Comprehensive (22)	4.91	4.00	12.00	2.00	3.34	0.97	2.53
Others (9)	5.89	4.00	12.00	3.00	3.72	0.74	1.80

Note: Others include industries of B, D, F, I and L. They are merged into one classification since number of the companies is small and they are of monopoly nature.

① CSRC industry classification description as a unified set.

7.6 Evaluation of Private Listed Company's Information Disclosure

7.6.1 Implication, domestic and overseas experiences of information disclosure mechanism

1. Theory of information disclosure

There are information asymmetry and moral hazard in corporate governance structure which would damage the interest of companies' owners. Information disclosure institution is the important method for solving these problems. Information disclosure institution can force managers to unveil the detailed situation about companies and let investors make effective decisions so that stock market come into a state of higher efficiency.

Information has the characteristics of externality, monopolist supplying and asymmetry, etcetera. As external corporate governance mechanism, information disclosure institution let information users obtain the needed information so as to improve the transparency and operating efficiency of market. Generally speaking, information disclosure institution is in favor of protecting investors, strengthening the encouragement and constraint of managers and promoting the development of market for corporate of control. The core of information disclosure quality should be reality, timeliness and integrity.

2. The mechanism design of information disclosure institution overseas

Since 1990s, the corporate governance reform has been intensified all over the world and a great deal of governance principles and guidelines have been issued. Meanwhile, the relevant accounting standards are updated constantly. With the development of capital market, content of information disclosure is expanded including disclosure of financial information and non-financial information which has already played a significant role in information disclosure.

In 2002, The Sox Act required the Securities and Exchange Commission (SEC) to take the following measures as soon as possible: (1) set rules, disclose all of important off-balance-sheet activities and relationship that have significant impact on corporate finance situations and formulate simulation financial information by a non-misleading way; (2) be responsible to study on disclosure of off-balance-sheet activities such as objects with special goals and come up with advices to report to congress; (3) enforce that internal control reports and its evaluations are included in annual reports of public companies, and reports about evaluation of companies' managers are issued by accounting firms; (4) enforce that there is one financial experts at least in corporate auditing committee who disclose the information. SEC made a set of rules and laws about strengthening information disclosure based on Sox Act's requirements.

According to listed companies' standards of NUSE, the corporates listed in NYSE must achieve that make sure that regular information disclosure has impacts on stocks' value and information of investing so as to protect the interests of shareholders, the public and stock exchange; publish financial reports conforming to the generally accepted accounting principles regularly on time as well. By the end of 2004, governance principles, directors and managers' behaviors and moral rules were required to be disclosed by corporate governance standards compiled by NYSE.

Corporate governance principles① of OECD require that corporate governance framework must make sure that companies could disclose relevant information about companies accurately and on time including financial information, firm performance, equity structure and governance mechanism. Information disclosed should contains financial and operating achievement, goals of companies, main shareholders, voting rights, directors and managers (including wages, standards of boards, selection process and if hold the position of director in other companies and its independency), internal trades, risks factors, employees, stakeholders and governance structure and principles (including the content of governance principles and executive processing) based on the governance principles and rules.

3. Relevant rules and regulations of LCs' information disclosure in China

The decade from 1990s to the beginning of 21th century was the important stage for the gradual establishment and promotion of security laws institution. The legitimacy of content and behaviors of information disclosure is guaranteed by a series of enforced laws and rules in information disclosure mechanism of security market in China. These laws and rules are classified into several levels: state laws, administrative laws,

---

① OECD Principles of Corporate Governance 2004.

corporate accounting institution and standards.

(1) State laws.

Corporation Law[①] is the basic law for all forms of companies to obey in China that constrains operating activities and financing behaviors of corporates. *Corporation Law* clearly regulates that companies limited by shares which trade stock publicly must make a public announcement of their financial accounting reports. *Security Law*[②] is the basic law of regulating security offering and trading which specifies the basic contents of LCs' information disclosure institution.

(2) Administrative laws.

To regulate the specific operating ways of information disclosure, SRC (Securities Regulatory Commission) and two Stock Exchanges separately issued many administrative laws about information disclosure. There are 22 series of laws that have a decisive impact on establishment of LCs' information disclosure in China such as *Standards of contents and formats for information disclosure of companies which stocks publicly issued.*

(3) Corporate accounting institution and standards.

Series of *Corporate accounting institution* and *corporate accounting standards* issued by the Ministry of Finance is the basic gist of all accounting activities in the whole domestic companies. LCs disclose their financial information and operating information by *Corporate accounting institution* and *corporate accounting standards.*

7.6.2 Study on the relationship between information disclosure and enterprise performance of private listed companies in China

1. Variables selection

(1) Firm performance.

In this part, EPS, NAPS and ROA of companies are selected to represent firm performance.

(2) Status of information disclosure.

Based on previous theory analysis, the core of information disclosure is supposed to be reality, timeliness and integrity. Given the difficulty and feasibility of collection

① "Company Law of the People's Republic of China", came into force on January 1, 2006.

② "Securities Law of the People's Republic of China", came into force on January 1, 2006. There are many provisions on the information disclosure system, the specific content here is no longer written.

of data, we choose two variables: the first is the time span between the actual time of issuing LCs' annual reports and deadline required by SRC in order to represent the timeliness of information disclosure; the second is the audit opinion brought up in companies' annual reports in order to the reality and integrity of information disclosure.

(3) Controlling variables.

To eliminate the interference from other factors which make an impact on relationship between information disclosure and firm performance and explore accurately the relationship between information disclosure and firm performance, we control other factors that affect firm performance probably, such as characteristics and other governance features. Specifically speaking, we control the ratio of shares of shareholders attendance at the annual general meeting, the times of board meeting in a year, the times of supervisory board meeting, the independency of board, the divergence between control rights in LC and cash flow right, the sum of salary from top three directors with best wages, the sum of salary from top three managers with best wages, auditing expenses, leverage and corporate size, etc.

There are variables, symbols of variables and their implication in this part (see Table 7 - 99).

Table 7 - 99 Variables and symbols of variables

Variables	Symbols	Implication
Dependent variables	EPS	Earnings Per Share (net profits)
	NAPS	Net Assets Per Share
	ROA	Return on Assets
Independent variables	Days	The time span between the actual time of issuing LCs' annual reports and deadline required by SRC
	Opinion_audit	Audit opinions, 1 = non-standard audit opinions; 0 = standard unqualified audit opinions
Controlling variables	Attendence	The ratio of shares of shareholders attendance at the annual general meeting
	Times_ds	The times of board meeting in a year
	Times_js	The times of supervisory board meeting
	Independence	The independency of board
	Diverge	The divergence between control rights in LC and cash flow right
	Lnpay_ds	The natural logarithm of the sum of salary from top three directors with best wages
	Lnpay_jl	The natural logarithm of the sum of salary from top three managers with best wages
	Lnfee	The natural logarithm of audit expenses
	LEV	Financial leverage
	LnTA	The natural logarithm of size of corporates

2. Data sources

CCER PLCs data base and general corporate financial data bases are basic data bases. The samples which information of variables are removed from our book. The samples with obvious wrong results (such as, the ratio of independent directors is more than 1) are corrected based on CNINF. We finally got panel data of 858 samples from 2002 – 2005, separately 126 companies in 2002, 186 companies in 2003, 245 companies in 2004, 301 companies in 2005. Therefore, we selected unbalanced panel date. On the one hand, deviation caused by unobservable heterogeneity which generally exists in regression of cross-sectional model can be avoided; on the other hand, the sample capacity of empirical analysis is enlarged to improve reliability of regression results.

3. Empirical analysis method and regression models

Since the panel data has two dimensions of section and time series, the regression model is more complicated than pure cross-sectional model. If observable independent variables control the whole relevant features of objects, there would not be relevant non-observable features. Under this circumstance, non-observable variables should be removed and pooled regression could be used to estimate this model reasonably. Meanwhile, observations of all the periods regarded as a single sample. If observable independent variables cannot control all the relevant characteristics of controlling units, non-observable effects would be correlated with any observable independent variables and regression estimation of dependent variables explained by observable variables would be affected by non-observable heterogeneity. The existence of non-observable effects could lead to inefficient estimation and invalid standard error of OLS, even though non-observable effects are uncorrelated with any observable variables. In this context, fixed effect or random effect regression method should be used to estimate based on the characteristics of data.

Hausman & Taylor (1981) indicates that fixed effect framework provide a general and unbiased method for controlling the influence of variables lacking provinces in panel data. In the following regression analysis, feasible regression method between fixed effect and random effect would be chosen by Durbin-Wu-Hausman test.

Based on analysis assumption and definition of variables mentioned above, regression model used in the below empirical analysis are as follows:

$\text{EPS} = b_0 + b_1 * \text{Day} + b_2 * \text{Attendence} + b_3 * \text{Times\_ds} + b_4 * \text{Times\_js}$

$$+b_5 * \text{Independence} + b_6 * \text{Diverge} + b_7 * \text{Lnpay\_ds} + b_8 * \text{Lnpay\_jl}$$
$$+b_9 * \text{Lnfee} + b_{10} * \text{LEV} + b_{11}\text{LNTA} + e$$

$$\text{NAPS} = b_0 + b_1 * \text{Day} + b_2 * \text{Attendence} + b_3 * \text{Times\_ds} + b_4 * \text{Times\_js}$$
$$+b_5 * \text{Independence} + b_6 * \text{Diverge} + b_7 * \text{Lnpay\_ds} + b_8 * \text{Lnpay\_jl}$$
$$+b_9 * \text{Lnfee} + b_{10} * \text{LEV} + b_{11}\text{LNTA} + e$$

$$\text{ROA} = b_0 + b_1 * \text{Day} + b_2 * \text{Attendence} + b_3 * \text{Times\_ds} + b_4 * \text{Times\_js}$$
$$+b_5 * \text{Independence} + b_6 * \text{Diverge} + b_7 * \text{Lnpay\_ds} + b_8 * \text{Lnpay\_jl}$$
$$+b_9 * \text{Lnfee} + b_{10} * \text{LEV} + b_{11}\text{LNTA} + e$$

$$\text{EPS} = b_0 + b_1 * \text{Opinion\_audit} + b_2 * \text{Attendence} + b_3 * \text{Times\_ds} + b_4 * \text{Times\_js}$$
$$+b_5 * \text{Independence} + b_6 * \text{Diverge} + b_7 * \text{Lnpay\_ds} + b_8 * \text{Lnpay\_jl}$$
$$+b_9 * \text{Lnfee} + b_{10} * \text{LEV} + b_{11} * \text{LNTA} + e$$

$$\text{NAPS} = b_0 + b_1 * \text{Opinion\_audit} + b_2 * \text{Attendence} + b_3 * \text{Times\_ds} + b_4 * \text{Times\_js}$$
$$+b_5 * \text{Independence} + b_6 * \text{Diverge} + b_7 * \text{Lnpay\_ds} + b_8 * \text{Lnpay\_jl}$$
$$+b_9 * \text{Lnfee} + b_{10} * \text{LEV} + b_{11} * \text{LNTA} + e$$

$$\text{ROA} = b_0 + b_1 * \text{Opinion\_audit} + b_2 * \text{Attendence} + b_3 * \text{Times\_ds} + b_4 * \text{Times\_js}$$
$$+b_5 * \text{Independence} + b_6 * \text{Diverge} + b_7 * \text{Lnpay\_ds} + b_8 * \text{Lnpay\_jl}$$
$$+b_9 * \text{Lnfee} + b_{10} * \text{LEV} + b_{11} * \text{LNTA} + e$$

The first three models are used to test the relationship between the number of days ahead of the disclosure of the annual report of the listed company and the performance of the firm. The latter three models are used to test the relationship between the audit opinion of the annual report of the listed company and the firm's performance.

4. Empirical results and analysis

(1) Descriptive statistical analysis and correlation analysis.

Table 7 -91 lists the results of descriptive statistical analysis of the variables used in this section for the period from 2002 to 2005.

Table 7 -92 lists descriptive statistical results for each year of the four years.

As can be seen from Table 7 - 91, the average earnings per share in the four years is negative, -0. 0275 yuan, in the past few years the income situation is poor. Of which the highest earnings per share is 1. 3637 yuan, the lowest is -14. 0837 yuan, and the standard deviation is 0. 7852, there is a large difference between sample companies.

From the annual earnings per share in Table 7 -101, the average of the earnings per share in 2002 and 2003 was positive at 0. 0449 and 0. 0665, respectively, and negative in 2004 and 2005, Respectively -0. 1086 yuan and -0. 05 yuan.

According to the results of Table 7 – 100, the average net assets per share in the four years is 2. 2981 yuan / share, the highest is 9. 2828 yuan / share, the lowest is – 12. 4813, and the standard deviation is 1. 8162. There is a big difference between the companies. In 2002, net assets per share is 2. 3573 yuan / share, then increased to 2. 5252 yuan / share, but in 2004 decreased to 2. 1753 yuan / share, then a slight increase, an increase of 2. 2329 yuan / share. The return on assets of the sample company averaged – 0. 0229 in four years. In the annual statistical analysis, the average return on assets in four years was negative, – 0. 0046, – 0. 0124, – 0. 0359 and – 0. 0266 respectively.

Table 7 – 100 2002—2005 4 – year total variables descriptive statistics

Variable	N	Min	Max	Mean	Standard deviation
Eps	858	– 14. 0837	1. 3637	– 0. 0275	0. 7852
Naps	858	– 12. 4813		2. 2981	1. 8162
Roa	858	– 1. 7874	0. 5102	– 0. 0229	0. 1846
Days	858	0	104	28. 8658	24. 4826
Opinion_ audit	858	0	1	0. 1760	0. 3810
Attendence_ gd	858	0. 22	1	0. 5553	0. 1711
Times_ ds	858	1	29	8. 2587	3. 5690
Times_ js	858	1	11	3. 6247	1. 7049
Independence	858	0. 125	1	0. 5250	0. 2064
Diverger	858	0	56. 5356	11. 3698	9. 5118
Lnpay_ ds	858	10. 0731	16. 7541	12. 5980	0. 9054
Lnpay_ jl	858	9. 9035	16. 7541	12. 6674	0. 8756
Lnfee	858	11. 0588	15. 5820	12. 9102	0. 4906
LEV	858	0. 0683	23. 7992	0. 7147	1. 4466
LnTA	858	16. 8843	23. 1867	20. 7535	0. 9268

Regarding the condition of deviation between actual date of PLCs' annual report disclosure and specified deadline, we can see statistical results from Table 7 – 100 and Table 7 – 101 that average days of advanced disclosure are 28. 8658 days during 4 years, the longest days of advanced disclosure are 104 days and the shortest is the last day of specific deadline. From the comparison in 4 years, there is less difference among different years. Average number of advanced disclosure days in 2003 is 30. 4140 which is highest, average number of advanced disclosure days in 2005 is 27. 4817 which is lowest, and 28. 4762 and 29. 5943 respectively in 2002 and 2004.

Regarding the condition of audit opinion of PLCs' annual reports, there is about 17. 6% of companies which are shown with non-standard unconditional audit opinions during 4 years. Except 2003, these companies are basically same which are shown with non-standard unconditional audit opinions given the changes among 3 years that proportion is between 19.05% and 19.93%, while the proportion is only 10.73% in 2003.

Table 7 – 101 Descriptive statistics of annual variables from 2002 to 2005

Year	Variable	N	Min	Max	Mean	Standard Deviation
2002	Eps	126	-1.4742	0.7021	0.0449	0.3263
	Naps	126	-1.3846	6.0216	2.3573	1.4138
	Roa	126	-0.9992	0.1517	-0.0046	0.1208
	Days	126	0	103	28.4762	24.0299
	Audit_opinion	126	0	1	0.1905	0.3942
	Attendence_gd	126	0.22	1	0.5524	0.1397
	Times_ds	126	1	16	6.5476	2.8750
	Times_js	126	2	8	3.4841	1.4240
	Independence	126	0.125	1	0.3721	0.2053
	Diverger	126	0	33.1485	10.3630	8.2013
	Lnpay_ds	126	10.3859	16.7541	12.1912	0.8718
	Lnpay_jl	126	10.5532	16.7541	12.2399	0.8276
	Lnfee	126	11.9184	15.0964	12.8658	0.5004
	Lev	126	0.1121	10.3751	0.6018	0.9058
	LnTA	126	17.5534	22.7588	20.6164	0.8919
2003	Eps	186	-3.3034	0.9713	0.0665	0.4794
	Naps	186	-2.7389	9.2828	2.5252	1.7257
	Roa	186	-1.4310	0.2193	-0.0124	0.1718
	Days	186	0	104	30.4140	25.0227
	Audit_opinion	186	0	1	0.1075	0.3106
	Attendence_gd	186	0.22	1	0.5420	0.1425
	Times_ds	186	2	23	9.3011	3.3362
	Times_js	186	2	9	4.1312	1.6815
	Independence	186	0.2	1	0.5149	0.1248
	Diverger	186	0	42.1035	11.1444	8.9579
	Lnpay_ds	186	10.1659	15.3841	12.4194	0.8335
	Lnpay_jl	186	9.9035	15.3841	12.4384	0.8657
	Lnfee	186	11.6953	15.2506	12.9512	0.4920
	Lev	186	0.0994	23.7992	0.7195	1.7604
	LnTA	186	16.8843	23.0414	20.7569	0.9177
2004	Eps	245	-14.0837	1.3637	-0.1086	1.1730
	Naps	245	-9.8556	7.9664	2.1753	1.8516
	Roa	245	-1.7874	0.5102	-0.0359	0.2416
	Days	244	0	102	29.5943	26.8766
	Audit_opinion	245	0	1	0.1918	0.3946
	Attendence_gd	245	0.2352	1	0.5451	0.1666
	Times_ds	245	3	27	8.5388	3.7389
	Times_js	245	1	11	3.6041	1.7863
	Independence	245	0.333	1	0.5523	0.1365

continued

Year	Variable	N	Min	Max	Mean	Standard Deviation
2004	Diverger	245	0	47. 87	12. 3696	9. 9064
	Lnpay_ ds	245	10. 0731	16. 0773	12. 6460	0. 8995
	Lnpay_ jl	245	10. 6194	15. 4016	12. 7340	0. 8470
	Lnfee	245	11. 6953	15. 5820	12. 9026	0. 4803
	Lev	245	0. 0683	19. 8671	0. 7890	1. 7952
	LnTA	245	17. 0612	23. 1535	20. 7581	0. 9388
2005	Eps	301	-5. 0098	1. 0454	-0. 0500	0. 6651
	Naps	301	-12. 4813	8. 0212	2. 2329	1. 9785
	Roa	301	-1. 5423	0. 1441	-0. 0266	0. 1587
	Days	301	1	96	27. 4817	22. 2388
	Audit_ opinion	301	0	1	0. 1993	0. 4002
	Attendence_ gd	301	0. 2709	1	0. 5730	0. 1197
	Times_ ds	301	3	29	8. 1030	3. 5664
	Times_ js	301	1	11	3. 3256	1. 6714
	Independence	301	0. 333	3	0. 5730	0. 2580
	Diverger	301	0	56. 5356	11. 1168	9. 9895
	Lnpay_ ds	301	10. 29031	15. 4903	12. 8397	0. 8882
	Lnpay_ jl	301	10. 5321	15. 4489	12. 9337	0. 8216
	Lnfee	301	11. 05879	14. 6432	12. 9095	0. 4944
	Lev	301	0. 0698	14. 4736	0. 6984	1. 0459
	LnTA	301	17. 12187	23. 1867	20. 8050	0. 9357

Regarding the basic condition of controlling variables, average proportion of shares belonging to shareholders who attend annual general meeting is 55. 53%. There is less changes from 2002 to 2005, the lowest average rate is 54. 10% in 2003 and the highest average rate is 57. 30% in 2005. The average proportions of 2002 and 2004 are respectively are 55. 24% and 54. 51%. And the highest rate is 100% in every year, while the lowest rate proportion is 22% averagely during 4 years. The average board meeting times in 4 years is 8. 2587, and highest times is 29 while lowest times is 1. From different years, the average times of board meeting in 2002 is lowest (6. 5476), the average times of 2003, 2004 and 2005 are relatively higher, respectively 9. 3011, 8. 5388 and 8. 1030. The times of board meeting in 2002 is relatively lower (16), while the times are higher in other three years, respectively 23 in 2003, 27 in 2004 and 29 in 2005.

The average times of board meetings of supervisors is 3. 6247 during 4 years. From different years, average times of 2003 is highest which is 4. 1312, while it is lower than 4 in other years. They are respectively 3. 4841, 3. 6041 and 3. 3256 in 2002, 2003 and 2004. The average proportion of independent directors is 52. 50%, and it is 37. 21% in 2002. After that, the rate grows rapidly to 51. 49 in 2003, 55. 23% in 2004 and 57. 30 in 2005. Between 2002 and 2005, average deviation between voting rights of shareholders and cash flow rights is 11. 3698. They are 10. 363 in 2002, 11. 1444 in 2003 and 11. 1168 in 2005, 12. 3696 in 2004 respectively that there is less difference among different years.

The results of correlation analysis among major variables are listed in Table 7 – 102 implying that the days of advanced disclosure of PLCs' annual reports are significantly positively correlated to EPS, NAPS and ROA at average significant level of 1%. Coefficients of Pearson correlation are 0. 275, 0. 252 and 0. 286 indicating that the inffs of disclosure of annual reports in PLCs are associated with firm performance significantly. The companies which have better firm performance would disclose their annual reports earlier, while others would do their information disclosure relatively late. The non-standard audit opinion shown by PLCs' annual reports are negatively correlated with PC at the 1% significant level. The coefficients of Spearman correlation between audit opinion and EPS, NAPS and ROA are respectively –0. 537, –0. 471 and –0. 514. It implies that the firm performance in PLCs which are shown non-standard audit opinions is relatively low. And more likely. It is because there are some mismanaged items in preparations of financial statements in companies with low performance. Meanwhile, the days of advanced disclosure of PLCs' annual reports has obviously negative correlation with possibility of being shown non-standard audit opinions indicating that companies shown with non-standard audit opinions would disclose annual reports relatively late.

Regarding the correlation between controlling variables and dependent variables, EPS is significantly negatively associated with and deviation between voting rights of shareholders and cash flow rights and leverage factor, and significantly positively correlated with proportion of share belonging to shareholders who attend annual board in PLCs, times of director board meeting in one year, the sum of salary from top three directors with best wages, the sum of salary from top three managers with best wages and total assets. The negative correlation between NAPS and deviation between voting rights of shareholders and cash flow rights is not significant statistically, while the correlations between NAPS and above-mentioned controlling variables are same. Correlation between ROA and controlling variables is same as the correlation between NAPS and controlling variables.

Table 7 - 102 **Results of correlation test among variables**

Variable	(1)	(2)	(3)	(4)	(5)	(6)	(7)	(8)
EPS(1)	1	0. 652 (**)	0. 933 (**)	0. 555 (**)	-0. 537 (**)	0. 303 (**)	-0. 076 (*)	-0. 055
NAPS (2)	0. 560 (**)	1	0. 499 (**)	0. 329 (**)	-0. 471 (**)	0. 280 (**)	-0. 127 (**)	-0. 086 (*)
ROA (3)	0. 734 (**)	0. 528 (**)	1	0. 569 (**)	-0. 514 (**)	0. 32A (**)	-0. 088 (**)	-0. 047
Days(4)	0. 275 (**)	0. 252 (**)	0. 286 (**)	1	-0. 392 (**)	0. 171 (**)	-0. 046	o. m
Opinion_ audit (5)	-0. 443 (**)	-0. 482 (**)	-0. 503 (**)	-0. 310 (**)	1	-0. 244 (**)	0. 032	0. 020
Attendence (6)	0. 193 (**)	0. 300 (**)	0. 198 (**)	0. 144 (**)	-0. 231 (**)	1	-0. 102 (**)	-0. 029
Times_ ds (7)	-0. 187 (**)	-0. 144 (**)	-0. 080 (*)	-0. 059	0. 032	-0. 129 (**)	1	0. 327 (**)
Timesjs (8)	-0. 012	-0. 062	0. 028	0. 011	0. 025	-0. 035	0. 311 (**)	1
Independence (9)	-0. 051	0. 040	-0. 018	-0. 015	-0. 026	0. 068 (*)	0. 079 (*)	-0. 034
Diverger (10)	-0. 122 (**)	-0. 021	-0. W4	-0. 032	0. 001	-0. 002	0. 002	0. 039
Lnpay_ ds (ll)	0. 119 (**)	0. 278 (**)	0. 096 (**)	0. 056	-0. 076 (*)	0. 072 (*)	-0. 047	-0. 106 (**)
Lnpayjl (12)	0. 108 (**)	0. 273 (**)	0. 107 (**)	0. 045	-0. 110 (**)	0. 072 (*)	0. 018	-0. 078 (*)
Infee (13)	0. 072 (*)	0. 193 (**)	0. 105 (**)	0. 023	-0. 064	-0. 109 (**)	0. 091 (**)	0. 043
LEV (14)	-0. 216 (**)	-0. 378 (**)	-0. 616 (**)	-0. 132 (**)	0. 298 (**)	-0. 125 (**)	0. 000	-0. 039
LnTA (15)	0. 237 (**)	0. 481 (**)	0. 389 (**)	0. 108 (**)	-0. 317 (**)	-0. 027	0. 025	-0 · (1) 1
Variable	(9)	(10)	(11)	(12)	(13)	(14)	(15)	
EPS(1)	0. 018	-0. 030	0. 236 (**)	0. 239 (**)	0. 152 (**)	-0. 400 (**)	0. 361 (**)	
NAPS (2)	0. 024	-0. 007	0. 309 (**)	0. 300 (**)	0. 215 (**)	-0. 563 (**)	0. 495 (**)	
ROA (3)	0. 007	-0. 037	0. 164 (**)	0. 168 (**)	0. 072 (*)	-0. 486 (**)	0. 203 (**)	
Days(4)	0. 009	-0. 035	0. 070 (*)	0. 066	0. 023	-0. 311 (**)	0. 131 (**)	
Opinion_ audit (5)	-0. 043	0. 005	-0. 095 (**)	-0. 112 (**)	-0. 083 (*)	0. 419 (**)	-0. 274 (**)	
Attendence (6)	0. 034	0. 002	0. 073 (*)	0. 068 (*)	-0. 081 (*)	-0. 316 (**)	-0. 031	
Times_ ds (7)	0. 132 (**)	0. 006	-0. 065	-0. 003	0. 077 (*)	0. 149 (**)	0. 024	
Timesjs (8)	0. 032	0. 030	-0. 107 (**)	-0. 093 (**)	0. 018	0. 066	-0. 003	
Independence (9)	1	-0. 006	0. 095 (**)	0. 144 (**)	0. 054	0. 033	0. 049	
Diverger (10)	-0. 031	1	-0. 015	0. 000	0. 126 (**)	0. (M9	0. 102 (**)	
Lnpay_ ds (ll)	0. 1 (M (**)	-0. 036	1	0. 864 (**)	0. 284 (**)	-0. 079 (*)	0. 407 (**)	
Lnpayjl (12)	0. 144 (**)	-0. 004	0. 858 (**)	1	0. 270 (**)	-0. 089 (**)	0. 388 (**)	
Infee (13)	0. 032	0. 095 (**)	0. 340 (**)	0. 327 (**)	1	0. 066	0. 593 (**)	
LEV (14)	-0. (M1	-0. 022	-0. 068 (*)	-0. 121 (**)	-0. 085 (*)	1	0. 020	
LnTA (15)	0. 030	0. 087 (*)	0. 417 (**)	0. 407 (**)	0. 591 (**)	-0. 364 (**)	1	

Note: the Pearson correlation is showed on the left down corner and the Spearman correlation is showed on the right up corner. * indicates the 95% significant level (two-tailed) and ** indicates the 99% significant level (two-tailed).

(2) Results of regression and analysis.

The regressions are respectively done based on the two above-listed models in this section, and fixed effect and random effect methods are applied in every model. The regression results are shown in the table. And results of fixed effect model are shown in the first column and results of random effect model are shown in the second column. Then Hausman test is applied to make sure the appropriate regression method. The results of regression between days of advanced disclosure in annual reports and firm performance are listed in the Table 7 – 103. Fixed effect method is supposed to be used based on Hausman text results of model (A) – (F) in Table 7 – 103.

According to the regression results of model (A), the days of advanced disclosure of annual reports is correlated positively with EPS at the 1% significant level. It implies that PLCs will disclose annual reports relatively earlier when these companies have higher EPS. The days of advanced disclosure of annual reports is significantly positively associated with NAPS and ROA at the significant level of 5% which further verifies the above-mentioned conclusions.

Table 7 – 103 Regression between days of advanced disclosure of annual reports and firm performance

MODEL	EPS		NAPS	
	A	B	C	D
Variable	Fixed effect	Random effects	Fixed effects	Random effects
Days	0.0034 ***	0.0058 ***	0.0039 **	0.0062 ***
	0.0014	0.0010	0.0017	0.0016
Attendence	0.6410	0.6743 ***	2.0479 ***	2.7844 ***
	0.3980	0.1612	0.5023	0.3216
Times_ds	−0.0279 **	−0.0396 ***	−0.0351 **	−0.0439 ***
	0.0113	0.0076	0.0142	0.0126
Times_js	0.0201	0.0253	0.0566 **	0.0380
	0.0216	0.0155	0.0273	0.0247
Independence	−0.2495	−0.2359 *	−0.2107	−0.1217
	0.2121	0.1231	0.2677	0.2125
Diverge	−0.0302 ***	−0.0138 ***	−0.0316 ***	−0.0220 ***
	0.0053	0.0028	0.0067	0.0053
Lnpay_ds	−0.1278	−0.0181	−0.1492	−0.0578
	0.0851	0.0561	0.1074	0.0935
Lnpay_jl	0.0228	0.0093	0.0106	0.0672
	0.0867	0.0576	0.1094	0.0957
Lnfee	−0.2890 **	−0.0602	0.0972	−0.0782
	0.1433	0.0701	0.1809	0.1351
LEV	0.0581 *	−0.0437 **	−0.0015	−0.0857 **
	0.0340	0.0197	0.0429	0.0336

continued

MODEL	EPS		NAPS	
	A	B	C	D
LnTA	0. 7054 ***	0. 2227 ***	1. 0070 ***	0. 9002 ***
	0. 1240	0. 0424	0. 1565	0. 0901
Constant	-9. 4780 ***	-3. 7633 ***	-18. 8071 ***	-16. 6240 ***
	2. 8762	0. 8384	3. 6299	1. 9041
R-sq	0. 1764	0. 2842	0. 2352	0. 3796
F_u_i	1. 78 (0. 0000)	—	6. 57 (0. 0000)	—
F	9. 42 (0. 0000)	—	13. 53 (0. 0000)	—
N/group	858 (363)	858 (363)	858 (363)	858 (363)
Wald chi^2	—	196. 07 (0. 0000)	—	350. 84 (0. 0000)
Hausman	44. 54 (0. 0000)		54. 88 (0. 0000)	

Note: *** indicates the 99% significant level, ** indicates the 95% significant level and * indicates the 90% significant level. The value in brackets under the coefficient is the standard error. F test and Hausman test results are present in the Table, t test is adopted in fixed effect model and z test in random effect model.

Meanwhile, we also found that the correlation between times of board meeting in one year and firm performance is significantly negative at the significant level of 5% in three valid regression models. It probably implies that excessive times of board meeting is negatively correlated with firm performance. Meanwhile, deviation between voting rights of shareholders and cash flow rights is negatively associated with firm performance at the significant level of 1% probably indicating that dominant shareholders in PLCs are likely to do tunnel behaviors causing harm to the benefits of other medium and small shareholders since deviation is increasing. And it would damage the firm performance.

Audit expense is significantly negatively correlated with EPS and ROA, while there is no significant association between audit expense and NAPS. There is significantly positive correlation between PLCs' asset size and firm performance in three - year valid regression model. The relationship between ratio of debt and asset and CP is still not clear. The ratio is significantly positively correlated with EPS at the 10% significant level, significantly negatively correlated with RAO at the significant level of 1% , and insignificantly correlated with NAPS.

The regression results between audit opinions and CP of annual reports are listed in Table 7 - 104 and Table 7 - 105. Based on the Hausman test results in model (G) - (J), fixed effect model method is supposed to be adopted. According to F test results of independent variables and error term, the random effect model (L) should be used to process the regression on the audit opinions and ROA in annual reports.

Table 7 - 104　Regression between advanced disclosure, audit opinions and FP

MODEL	ROA		EPS	
	E	F	G	H
Variable	Fixed effect	Random effect	Fixed effect	Random effect
Days	0. 0006 **	0. 0013 ***	—	—
	0. 0003	0. 0002	—	—
Opinion_ audit	—	—	-0. 6196 ***	-0. 7357 ***
	—	—	0. 0978	0. 0699
Attendence	0. 1634 **	0. 1158 ***	0. 3506	0. 4263 ***
	0. 0826	0. 0278	0. 3879	0. 1569
Times_ ds	-0. 0021	-0. 0036 ***	-0. 0266 **	-0. 0400 ***
	0. 0023	0. 0014	0. 0109	0. 0073
Times_ js	0. 0016	0. 0033	0. 0198	0. 0309 **
	0. 0045	0. 0028	0. 0209	0. 0149
Independence	-0. 0476	-0. 0357	-0. 2198	-0. 2386 **
	0. 0441	0. 0224	0. 2054	0. 1180
Diverge	-0. 0032 ***	-0. 0014 ***	-0. 0286 ***	-0. 0132 ***
	0. 0011	0. 0005	0. 0051	0. 0027
Lnpay_ ds	-0. 0134	-0. 0011	-0. 0815	0. 0250
	0. 0177	0. 0101	0. 0828	0. 0539
Lnpay_ jl	-0. 0154	-0. 0084	-0. 0061	-0. 0189
	0. 0180	0. 0103	0. 0834	0. 0552
Lnfee	-0. 0503 *	-0. 0201 *	-0. 2431 *	0. 0044
	0. 0298	0. 0120	0. 1387	0. 0673
LEV	-0. 0381 ***	-0. 0639 ***	0. 0457	-0. 0297
	0. 0070	0. 0035	0. 0329	0. 0189
LnTA	0. 1710 ***	0. 0489 ***	0. 5866 ***	0. 1220 ***
	0. 0257	0. 0070	0. 1210	0. 0418
Constant	-2. 5673 ***	-0. 6609 ***	-7. 4902 ***	-2. 2855 ***
	0. 5972	0. 1366	2. 7549	0. 8120
R-sq	0. 3477	0. 5906	0. 2311	—
F_u_i	1. 21 (0. 0000)	—	1. 71 (0. 0000)	—
F	23. 50 (0. 0000)	—	13. 22 (0. 0000)	0. 3494
N/group	859 (363)	859 (363)	858 (363)	858 (363)
Wald chi^2	—	773. 38 (0. 0000)	—	290. 67 (0. 0000)
Hausman	41. 05 (0. 0000)		38. 67 (0. 0000)	

Note: *** indicates the 99% significant level, ** indicates the 95% significant level and * indicates the 90% significant level. The value in brackets under the coefficient is the standard error. F test and Hausman test results are present in the Table, t test is adopted in fixed effect model and z test in random effect model.

Seen from the regression results in model (G) (I) and (L), EPS, the possibility of being given non-standard unconditional audit opinions to PLCs is negatively correlated to PC implying that CP of PLCs with the same conditions and non-standard unconditional audit opinions is relatively poor. It is probably because the companies with relatively poor CP are confronting the pressure from a great deal of investors and process some events loosely. The procession without abiding by relative rules and requirements leads to the circumstance that it is hard to be given standard unconditional audit opinion when relative firms audit the reports. The conclusions are same as those of previous models about the relationship between controlling variables and CP. These are not explained here.

Table 7 - 105 Regression results between audit opinions in annual reports and FP

MODEL	NAPS		ROA	
	I	J	K	L
Variable	Fixed effect	Random effect	Fixed effect	Random effect
Opinion_ audit	-0.6805 ***	-0.9371 ***	-0.1006 ***	-0.1473 ***
	0.1244	0.1124	0.0209	0.0129
Attendence	1.7063 ***	2.3894 ***	0.1319 *	0.0741 ***
	0.4931	0.3159	0.0826	0.0272
Times_ ds	-0.0339 **	-0.0434 ***	-0.0017	-0.0036 ***
	0.0139	0.0122	0.0023	0.0013
Times_ js	0.0563 **	0.0406 *	0.0018	0.0046 *
	0.0266	0.0240	0.0045	0.0027
Independence	-0.1817	-0.0930	-0.0414	-0.0389 *
	0.2611	0.2064	0.0438	0.0217
Diverge	-0.0299 ***	-0.0203 ***	-0.0030 ***	-0.0013 ***
	0.0065	0.0051	0.0011	0.000
Lnpay_ ds	-0.0968	0.0061	-0.0069	0.0079
	0.1053	0.0912	0.0177	0.0098
Lnpay_ jl	-0.0230	0.0268	-0.0199	-0.0142
	0.1061	0.0928	0.0178	0.0100
Lnfee	0.1428	-0.0114	-0.0380	-0.0058
	0.1763	0.1311	0.0296	0.0115
LEV	-0.0169	-0.0898 ***	-0.0393 ***	-0.0599 ***
	0.0418	0.0327	0.0070	0.0034
LnTA	0.8664 ***	0.7482 ***	0.1570 ***	0.0303 ***
	0.1539	0.0893	0.0258	0.0070
Constant	-16.3208 ***	-14.0931 ***	-2.4165 ***	-0.4213 ***
	3.5022	1.8520	0.5869	0.1325
R-sq	0.2748	0.4320	0.3713	0.6392
F_u_i	6.36 (0.0000)	—	1.11 (0.1397)	—
F	16.67 (0.0000)	—	26.04 (0.0000)	—
N/group	858 (363)	858 (363)	859 (363)	859 (363)
Wald chi^2	—	431.38 (0.0000)	—	916.76 (0.0000)
Hausman	54.49 (0.0000)		—	

Note: *** indicates the 99% significant level, ** indicates the 95% significant level and * indicates the 90% significant level. The value in brackets under the coefficient is the standard error. F test and Hausman test results are present in the Table, t test is adopted in fixed effect model and z test in random effect model.

5. The conclusions and index of information disclosure evaluation

The relationship between annual information disclosure and FIRM PERFORMANCE was empirically analyzed based on the data of Chinese PLCs from 2002 to 2005, we found:

First, the number of days that annual reports are disclosed in advance is positively correlated with EPS at the 1% significant level. It is indicating that the annual reports are disclosed relatively earlier when EPS is higher in PLCs. The number of days that annual reports are disclosed in advance has significantly positive correlation with EPS and ROA.

Secondly, the possibility of PLCs being given non-standard unconditional audit opinions is negatively correlated with firm performance implying that the firm performance of PLCs which are given non-standard unconditional audit opinions is relatively poor in the case that other conditions are same. It is probably because the companies with relatively poor firm performance are confronting the pressure from a great deal of investors and process some events loosely. The procession without abiding by relative rules and requirements leads to the circumstance that it is hard to be given standard unconditional audit opinion when relative firms audit the reports.

Meanwhile, we also found that the times of board meeting in one year is negatively associated with firm performance possibly indicating that overmuch times of board meeting is negatively correlated with firm performance. At the same time, the deviation between shareholders' voting rights and cash flowing rights has negative correlation with firm performance implying that the more deviation between two rights is, the more incentives for involving in the tunnel behaviors damaging other middle and small shareholders' benefit PLCs' shareholders have. And it weakens the firm performance.

The expenses has significant negative correlation with EPS and ROA, and has insignificant association with NAPS. The asset size of PLCs has significant positive correlation with firm performance at the 1% significant level. The relationship between debt-to-asset ratio and firm performance is uncertain. Debt-to-asset ratio has significant positive correlation with EPS at the 10% significant level and negative association with ROA at the 1% significant level. The correlation between debt-to-asset and NAPS is insignificant.

According to previous theory and empirical analysis, the evaluation indexes of PLCs' information disclosure contain two: the number of days disclosed in advance and audit opinions. Specifically speaking, the more the number of days disclosed in advance is, the higher timeliness of information disclosure is. And all the PLCs given non-standard unconditional audit opinions is poor at the authenticity and integrity of information disclosure.

7.6.3 Evaluation and current situation of private listed companies' information disclosure

1. Descriptive statistics of information disclosure evaluation index

(1) Enthusiasm of information disclosure (inffs).

As above-mentioned relevant specification, the deviation between the deadline of PLCs' issuing annual reports and actual date is adopted to the positivity in information disclosure. The more the number of days disclosed in advance is, the higher positivity in this PLC disclosing information is. The Figure 7 – 51 shows the column figure of information disclosure incentive and the graph of empirical cumulative distribution function. The descriptive statistics of positivity in information disclosure is listed in Table 7 – 106. The average value of information disclosure positivity evaluation is 29.05, the median value is 29, and standard error is 21.98. There is relative huge difference among different companies, and skewness is 0.51 and the distribution of evaluation results is skewed to left.

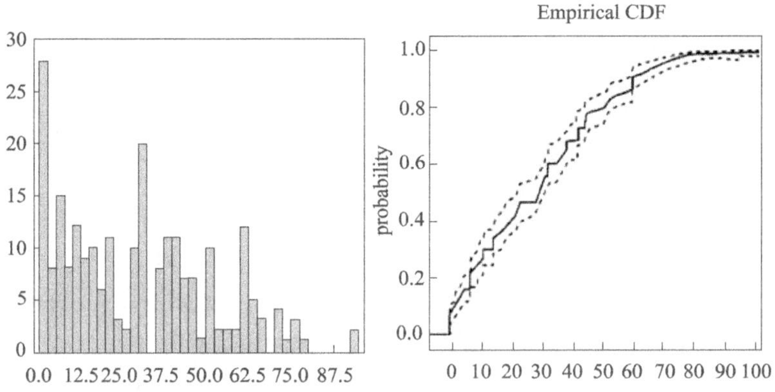

Figure 7 – 51 Column of inffs and empirical cumulative distribution function

(2) Audit opinions (audit).

Because there are only two types of literal statement about audit opinions in reports, that is standard unconditional opinions and explanatory unconditional opinions, it makes little sense to do descriptive statistics. We do a simple description here. The descriptive statistics of audit opinions is listed in Table 7 – 89. Based on this table, there are 215 listed companies given standard unconditional opinions, accounting for 91% of all companies. And there are 20 listed companies with explanatory unconditional opinions accounting for 9% of all firms.

Table 7 – 106 Descriptive statistics of timeliness and quality of information disclosure

Variable	Mean	Median	Max	Min	Standard deviation	Skewness	Kurtosis
Inffs	29.05	29.00	94.00	0.00	21.96	0.51	2.46
Audit	483 162	400 000	1 982 000	138 000	281 088	2.55	11.55

2. The principle of evaluation index score of information disclosure

(1) Inffs.

The stronger the motivation of PLCs' information disclosure, the better the governance condition is. The grading principles: the spacing between groups is 8 and is scored following the low to the high.

(2) Audit opinions.

Given the special circumstance of audit opinions. We make the following grading principles: the companies with standard unconditional opinions are scored at 10 scores, the companies with explanatory specialization and unconditional opinions are scored at 5 scores. The detailed standards and methods are shown in Table 7 – 107.

Table 7 – 107 Specifications of information disclosure timeliness and quality

Score	1	2	3	4	5	6	7	8	9	10
Inffs	0 – 8	9 – 16	17 – 24	25 – 32	33 – 40	41 – 48	49 – 56	57 – 64	65 – 72	73 –
Adfs	Explanatory specification unconditional opinions					Standard unconditional opinion				
Score	5					10				

3. Descriptive statistics of evaluation results of information disclosure

Two forms, column figure and sheet, are used respectively to describe reasonably the index grading. What need to be specified are horizontal axis represents grading and vertical axis represents the numbers of companies getting relative grades.

(1) Inffs.

Grading results of inffs are shown in column distribution Figure (see Figure 7 – 52), and the detailed distribution condition is shown in Table 7 – 108. Results of inffs evaluation are distributed relatively dispersedly in the graph and table. There are a few number of companies at different values. At first, the number of companies graded at 1 is the most (52), accounting for 22. 32% of total samples. Furthermore, the number of companies graded at 4 is 32, accounting for 13. 73%. The grade of 60% companies of total samples is less than 4. 14. 16% of companies has the grade of more than 7. Average grade (mean value) of PLCs' information disclosure is 4. 1, median value is 4, standard deviation is 2. 63, and skewness is 0. 49. The total distribution is skewed to left.

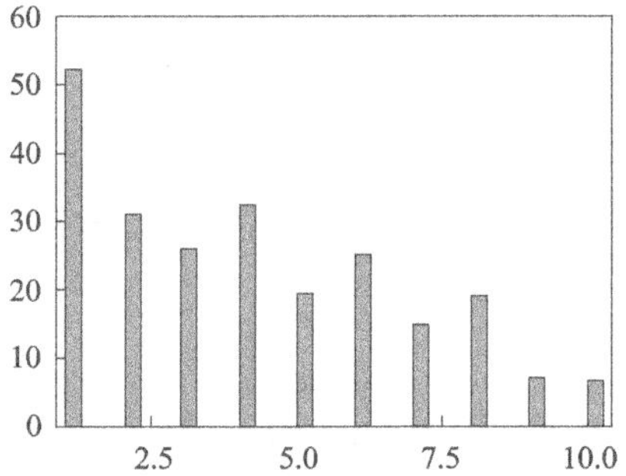

Figure 7 – 52 Column figure of grading inffs of information disclosure

Table 7 – 108 Distribution of information disclosure score

Value	Count	Percent	Cumulative count	Cumulative percent
1	52	22. 32	52	22. 32
2	31	13. 30	83	35. 62
3	26	11. 16	109	46. 78
4	32	13. 73	141	60. 52
5	19	8. 15	160	68. 67
6	25	10. 73	185	79. 40
7	15	6. 44	200	85. 84
8	19	8. 15	219	93. 99
9	7	3. 00	226	97. 00
10	7	3. 00	233	100. 00

(2) Auditfs.

The distribution of information disclosure's quality grading results is listed in Table 7 – 109. The number of companies graded at 5 is 20, accounting for 8. 55% of total samples. The other 214 companies are graded at 10 implying that most information disclosure's quality is higher relatively from the table. Based on evaluation results in Table 7 – 110, the mean grades of PLCs' information disclosure is 9. 57, median value is 10, standard deviation is 1. 4 and skewness is – 2. 96 and there is a notable right skew.

Table 7 - 109 **Distribution of quality grading results of information disclosure**

Value	Count	Percent	Cumulative count	Cumulative percent
5	20	8.55	20	8.55
10	214	91.45	234	100.00

(3) The total grades of information disclosure evaluation.

Figure 7-53 is the column distribution figure of information disclosure evaluation's total grades. Descriptive statistics of information disclosure's grades are listed in Table 7 - 110. PLCs in samples scored ab average if 13.67, the median value is 13, standard deviation is 2.91 and skewness is 0.03. There is a fairly large difference among different companies and an obvious left-skew.

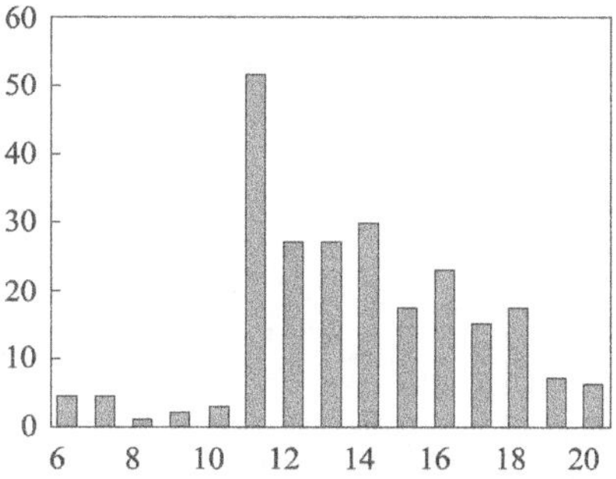

Figure 7 - 53 Column of evaluation scores of information disclosure

Table 7 - 110 **Descriptive statistics of information disclosure evaluation**

Variable	Mean	Median	Standard deviation	Skewness	Kurtosis
Inffs	4.1	4	2.63	0.49	2.16
Auditfs	9.57	10	1.4	-2.96	9.79
Infzf	13.67	13	2.91	0.03	2.8

4. Regional disparities and industrial differences in information disclosure evaluation results

(1) The analysis of information disclosure index of regional differences.

Statistical component index of information disclosure evaluation in different regions① are listed in Table 7 - 111. The average grade of information disclosure in eastern region is 13.52 which score is the lowest in three regions, average score of western region is the highest (13.96) which median value is the highest in three areas (14) according to Figure 7 - 54 that is the column figure of information disclosure in

① The regional division criteria are set as before.

eastern region and Figure 7 -55 that is the column figure of information disclosure in western region. The median values of other regions are both 13. The standard deviations in three regions are respectively 3. 03, 3. 05 and 2. 79. Relatively speaking, the disparity among different companies in previous companies is larger than it in western region.

The skew values of information disclosure in central and western regions respectively are 0. 12 and 0. 26 which is left-skewed. The skewness of information disclosure in western region is -0. 04 that is right-skewed.

Table 7 -111 Regional differences in information disclosure evaluation

Region	Number	Mean	Median	Max	Min	Standard deviation	Skewness	Kurtosis
Eastern	135	13. 52	13. 00	20. 00	6. 00	3. 03	-0. 04	2. 90
Central	47	13. 77	13. 00	20. 00	7. 00	3. 05	0. 12	2. 49
Western	53	13. 96	14. 00	20. 00	8. 00	2. 79	0. 26	2. 56

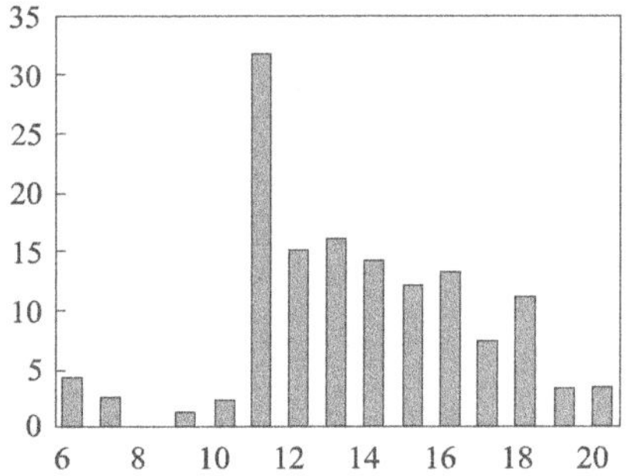

Figure 7 -54 Column of information disclosure quality of eastern regional difference

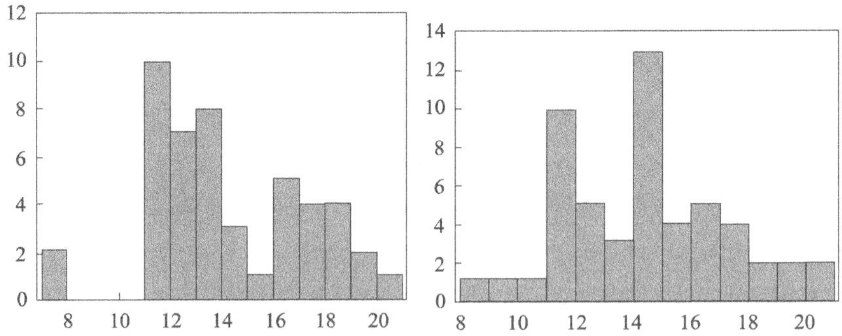

Table 7 -55 Column of information disclosure quality of regional difference

(2) The analysis of information disclosure index of industrial differences.

PLCs are categorized by ICB of CSRC. Group index is applied to represent regional differences. Letters correspond to numbers, for example, the industrial feature of LCs with A letter initially in CSRC category is evaluated at 1.

The basic conditions of information disclosure evaluation in different regions are listed in Table 7 – 112. According to general condition of information disclosure governance of construction industry is best scored at 14. 50 averagely among PLCs in 2005 from the perspective of single industry. The second is comprehensive industry scored at 14. 18. The lowest is social service with grade of 12. 67 averagely. The next is information technology industry with grade of 12. 81. PLCs' manufacturing information disclosure governance condition is shown in Figure 7 – 56 following a normal distribution.

Table 7 – 112 Industrial difference in information disclosure condition evaluation

Industry	Mean	Median	Max	Min	Standard deviation	Skewness	Kurtosis
Agriculture (7)	14. 14	14. 00	18. 00	10. 00	2. 85	-0. 25	1. 87
Manufacturing (143)	13. 66	13. 00	20. 00	6. 00	3. 02	0. 14	2. 60
Construction (6)	14. 50	14. 50	18. 00	12. 00	2. 07	0. 59	2. 52
IT (16)	12. 81	13. 00	18. 00	6. 00	3. 04	-0. 36	2. 89
Wholesales and trade (12)	14. 08	14. 00	18. 00	11. 00	1. 93	0. 43	2. 70
Real estate (14)	13. 79	13. 00	20. 00	7. 00	3. 70	0. 14	2. 21
Social service (6)	12. 67	13. 50	17. 00	6. 00	3. 67	-0. 93	3. 09
Comprehensive (22)	14. 18	14. 00	20. 00	11. 00	2. 63	0. 52	2. 49
Others (9)	13. 00	12. 00	18. 00	7. 00	3. 54	0. 07	2. 33

Note: Numbers in the brackets are the numbers of PLCs in the corresponding industry. Others include following industries of B, D, F, I, L. They are merged into one classification since number of the companies is small and they are of monopoly nature.

(3) The red shows that JB statistics is significant which follows normal distribution.

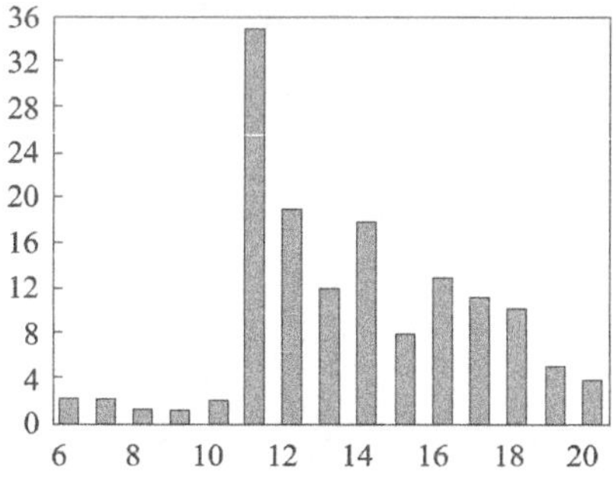

Figure 7 – 56 Column of PLCs manufacturing information disclosure governance

7.7 Analysis of private listed companies' governance index

7.7.1 The description of private listed companies' general governance

1. General governance

Chinese PLCs' governance index generally follows the normal distribution and there is a large difference among companies. Besides, the overall index is relatively lower (see Table 7 – 113), and average value is 58.66. The maximum is 73, while the minimum is 43.64 with a big gap from the max value. To further reflect the general governance condition of PLCs, samples are categorized into 10 groups with interval of 3 scores in this part (see Table 7 – 114). The first group with highest grades belongs to 70 – 73 scores which includes 3 listed companies. There are 117 companies concentrating in the fifth group and the sixth group (55 – 61 scores) that account for almost 50% of the whole samples. The tenth group contains 2 companies with the lowest scores (43 – 46 scores).

Table 7 – 113 Descriptive statistics of PLCs' governance general index

Variable	Mean	Min	Max	Median	Standard deviation	Skewness	Kurtosis
Totality	58.66	43.64	73	44.64	4.86	0.06	3.13

Table 7 – 114 Group distribution of PLCs' governance general index

Group number	Number	Interval
1	3	73 – 70
2	7	70 – 67
3	22	67 – 64
4	36	64 – 61
5	61	61 – 58
6	56	58 – 55
7	33	55 – 52
8	14	52 – 49
9	1	49 – 46
10	2	46 – 43

The major influencing factors on PLCs' governance index are analyzed by fractions of second-level index. The main factor causing lower PLCs' governance index is managers factor which average scores are only 32. 6 seen from Table 7 – 115. The second important factor is supervisory board which average scores are 33. 7. Shareholders' behavior evaluation gets highest scores that is 73. 69. The average scores of information disclosure is 65. 55 and the average scores of boards of directors are 61. 09. From the distribution of each group, the mean value of the first group is 71. 21, and the scores of shareholders' behavior, board of directors, board of supervisors, managers' evaluation, and information disclosure are respectively 83. 33, 74. 19, 57. 5, 43. 33 and 73. 33. The PLCs belonging to the first group have high-level shareholders' behavior regulation. However, the governance condition of board of supervisors and the condition of managers are supposed to be further improved. As the governance leading companies of PLCs, the first group includes only three listed firms. The most concentrated group is the fifth group which contains 61 PLCs averagely scored at 59. 65. Scores of the shareholders' behavior evaluation, board of directors, and board of supervisors, managers and information disclosure are respectively 72. 09, 59. 57, 35, 34. 67 and 72. 21.

Table 7 – 115 Descriptive statistics of second-level CG index in PLCs

Group number	Total scores index		Evaluation scores of shareholders' behaviors		Evaluation scores of board of directors	
	Mean	Standard	Mean	Standard	Mean	Standard
1 (3)	71. 21	1. 14	83. 33	2. 18	74. 19	2. 86
2 (7)	68. 57	0. 41	81. 63	4. 47	74. 08	7. 53
3 (22)	65. 52	0. 82	80. 39	7. 57	68. 90	6. 74
4 (36)	62. 34	0. 77	76. 75	6. 31	67. 14	5. 37
5 (61)	59. 65	0. 91	73. 28	6. 22	63. 65	5. 46
6 (56)	56. 38	0. 95	72. 09	6. 41	59. 57	6. 02
7 (33)	53. 50	0. 84	67. 27	8. 00	57. 71	7. 37
8 (14)	50. 75	0. 88	65. 00	6. 28	55. 51	5. 46
9 (1)	46. 82	0. 00	67. 14	0. 00	51. 43	0. 00
10 (2)	44. 09	0. 64	70. 00	2. 02	38. 57	12. 12
Mean	57. 88	—	73. 69	—	61. 09	—
1 (3)	57. 50	2. 50	43. 33	10. 41	73. 33	16. 07
2 (7)	43. 57	9. 67	50. 71	18. 35	71. 43	13. 45
3 (22)	37. 73	7. 56	50. 22	20. 09	72. 50	14. 45
4 (36)	37. 71	9. 53	35. 42	20. 82	71. 25	14. 11
5 (61)	35. 00	7. 96	34. 67	19. 66	72. 21	13. 43
6 (56)	33. 71	7. 04	25. 45	15. 29	66. 52	14. 29
7 (33)	32. 80	8. 79	23. 64	16. 78	61. 82	16. 19
8 (14)	26. 43	7. 38	22. 14	11. 39	61. 43	13. 79
9 (1)	10. 00	0	20. 00	0. 00	60. 00	0. 00
10 (2)	22. 50	3. 53	15. 00	0. 00	45. 00	21. 21

continued

Group number	Total scores index		Evaluation scores of shareholders' behaviors		Evaluation scores of board of directors	
	Mean	Standard	Mean	Standard	Mean	Standard
Mean	33.7	—	32.6	—	65.55	—

Note: Numbers in the brackets are the numbers of PLCs in the corresponding regions.

According to analysis of second-level index, the governance level of PLCs' managers is lower. In the tenth group with the lowest grades, the scores of managers are 15. Further verification from index analysis shows that there exist two problems about managers' governance in Chinese PLCs, as mentioned above: the first is the closure of people that PLCs have no faith in professional managers and lack of authorization, hence lacking of risk incentive; the second is family contract governance of managers, that is, managers belong to family members rely more on the constraints of family contract rather than adopting formal incentive contract system which causes agent problem due to "anti-altruism". These two factors would probably decrease the governance level of PLCs.

2. The industrial and regional differences in CG in PLCs

PLCs are categorized by ICB of CSRC①. Group index is applied to represent industrial differences. Letters correspond to numbers, for example, the industrial feature of LCs with A letter initially in CSRC category is evaluated at 1.

Seen from Table 7 – 116, the index of construction industry (E) is the highest including 6 PLCs and its average scores are 61.36. The second is others, containing B Excavation, D electric power gas and hydraulic production and supply industry, F transportation and storage industry, I finance and insurance industry, L media and cultural industry, which includes 9 PLCs totally scored averagely at 60.2. The industry with the lowest index is agriculture (A) evaluated averagely at 56.62. The industrial difference indicates that the CFR of different PLCs is decided by average rate of profit of different industries. Recently, the strong trend of real estate market brings high profit to construction industry, so CFR accounts for a large proportion in profit structure of UC in construction PLCs to encourage UC to improve the value of LCs in PLCs achieve the "incentive compatibility" with other medium and small shareholders and reduce the agent cost. The market condition with fierce competition in agriculture leads to lower industrial average rate of profit. Aggressive price competition strategy

① CSRC industry classification description as a unified set.

of PLCs in this industry leading to lower CFR would encourage UC to pursue controlling profits, such as "tunnel behaviors" et al. , and to cause higher agent cost between other stakeholders. The industries belonging to others have features of monopolization. Loose industrial environment will bring higher industrial rate of profit. This kind of firms are made by transferring to privatization of state-owned companies and has the advantage in the aspects of assets, resources and social capital. These factors are in favor of gaining higher CFR for PLCs, consequently to achieve incentive compatibility with other stakeholders and reduce the agent cost.

Table 7 – 116 Descriptive statistics of total CG evaluation of PLCs

Group	Mean	Median	Max	Min	Standard deviation
A (7)	9 – 56. 62	55. 90	62. 27	49. 09	4. 23
C (143)	4 – 58. 80	59. 09	72. 27	43. 64	4. 97
E (6)	1 – 61. 36	62. 05	66. 36	55. 00	4. 21
G (16)	3 – 58. 84	57. 05	70. 00	52. 27	6. 11
H (12)	5 – 58. 60	59. 09	63. 18	50. 00	3. 84
J (14)	8 – 57. 63	58. 82	65. 00	52. 73	3. 66
K (6)	6 – 58. 18	57. 35	65. 91	51. 36	5. 54
M (22)	7 – 57. 75	58. 18	65. 00	51. 36	4. 00
Others (9)	2 – 60. 30	60. 45	69. 09	53. 64	5. 96

Note: Numbers in the brackets are the numbers of PLCs in the corresponding industry. Others include following industries of B, D, F, I, L. They are merged into one classification since number of the companies is small and they are of monopoly nature.

According to the value of index, the mean value of information technology industry (G) is 58. 84, and manufacturing (C) has an average value of 58. 8. Wholesale, retail trade (H) and miscellaneous have the average value of 58. 6 and 57. 75 respectively. Real estate (J) ranked second lowest place in the penultimate with the average value of 57. 63.

There is no significant difference about the level of PLCs' governance among regions based on Table 7– 117. The significant disparities in the political and economic environment has no impact on the level of PLCs' governance among the eastern, central and western area in China. The factor that play an important role in PLCs; governance quality is industry indicating the unicity of the PLCs' ultimate controllers; goals which is different from the multiplicity of state-owned firms' operating targets.

Table 7 – 117 Regional differences of CG evaluation of PLCs

Region	Mean	Median	Max	Min	Standard deviation
Eastern (135)	58. 71	59. 00	71. 36	44. 55	4. 97
Central (47)	58. 59	58. 18	72. 27	43. 64	4. 77
Western (53)	58. 60	57. 73	68. 18	49. 09	4. 75

Note: Numbers in the brackets are the numbers of PLCs in the corresponding region.

However, there is a slight difference among eastern, western and central area according to the governance index distribution (see Figure 7 - 57). There is a bimodal distribution of governance index in eastern area and the kurtosiss are respectively at 53 scores and 62 scores implying that PLCs in eastern area are more sensitive to external environment factors. It leads to the reflection of complicated environment factors in governance condition. In this context, PLCs in eastern area has a strong "institutional isomorphism" and a significant marking-pole effect implying that PLCs in eastern area have a relatively strong ability of companies; governance institutional innovation. Comparatively speaking, the difference in index distribution is less than it in eastern and central area after abnormal values are eliminated indicating PLCs' governance structure in western area is less affected by external factors. It is mainly decided by firms' natural endowment. Eastern area has a typical normal distribution and its governance innovation ability is between the ability in western area and central area.

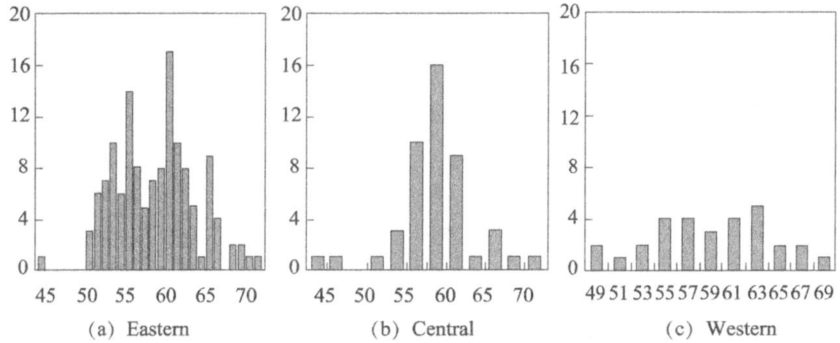

Figure 7 - 57 Column of CG evaluation of PLCs

7. 7. 2 Corporate governance index of private listed companies and enterprise performance

1. The regression between CP and CG index of PLCs

The relationship between CG index and CP would be validated in this part and EPS is the index to estimate the CP. The model used is $EPS_i = \beta \times scores_i + \xi_i$, and β is the coefficient. Heteroscedasticity in the cross-sectional model is amended in Newey-West, so there is no controlling variables in the model. Since standard deviation of all the governance index scores in the model is from the natural weighting according to the number of specific index in every section, there still exists pole effect.

The empirical results (see Table 7 – 118) indicate that the CG index of PLCs is significantly positively correlated with CP and the coefficient is 0. 001761 implying that EPS would be increased 0. 001761 for each unit of PLCs' CG improved. The second-level index is significantly positively associated with CP. And EPS would increase 0. 001414 for each unit of equity structure of shareholders' behavior increased. EPS would increase 0. 001664 for each unit of board of directors increased. EPS would increase 0. 002317 for each unit of board of supervisors increased. EPS would increase 0. 002658 for each unit of managers section increased. EPS would increase 0. 001501 for each unit of information disclosure index increased.

According to the regression results, there is still room for improvement for Chinese PLCs at the aspect of managers and board of supervisors. Meanwhile, the medium and small shareholders' right should be paid much attention by further improving the structure of CG and relationship between investors in order to further improve the value of firms. Reputation of Chinese PLCs in capital market is improved which not only increase the credibility value of the production market and CP, but also decline the trade cost.

Table 7 – 118　Regression results of EPS and governance index of PLCs

Method	WOLS					
Sample	PLCs in 2005					
Variable	—					
Governance index of PLCs	0. 001761 ***	—	—	—	—	—
	(0. 000409)	—	—	—	—	—
Equity structure and shareholders' behavior	—	0. 001414 ***	—	—	—	—
	—	(0. 000320)	—	—	—	—
Board of directors	—	—	0. 001664 ***	—	—	—
	—	—	(0. 000369)	—	—	—
Board of supervisors	—	—	—	0. 002317 ***	—	—
	—	—	—	(0. 000772)	—	—
Managers	—	—	—	—	0. 002685 ***	—
	—	—	—	—	(0. 000888)	—
Information disclosure	—	—	—	—	—	0. 001501 ***
	—	—	—	—	—	(0. 000345)
R-squard	0. 010	0. 010	0. 011	-0. 017	0. 006	0. 012

Note: *** indicates significance level of 1%, ** indicates 5% and * indicates 10%; the values in the parentheses of the equation coefficients are the standard error. R-squared is reported.

2. The analysis of influencing factors on governance index

We take the grouping-comparison method based on representative index to do further analysis of influencing factors.

(1) The impact of earning structure on governance index.

At first, we analyze the impact of cash flow rights on the governance index and divide the samples into 10 groups (see Table 7 – 119) ranked in the order of cash flow rights with the spacing of 5%. Generally there is increasing cash flow rights. Average of governance index increases from 58. 73 to 62. 31 and the trend is non-linear. The scores of the seventh group and the ninth group are respectively lower than the scores in the sixth and eighth group. To completely analyze the impact of equity structure of ultimate controllers in PLCs on governance index. We investigate the influence of deviation between controlling rights and cash flow rights on governance rights (see Table 7 – 120). Samples are divided into 10 groups based on the deviation to investigate the change of governance index as the deviation is declining. While the deviation is reducing, the governance index basically is increasing from 55 to 63 implying that the equity structure of ultimate controllers in PLCs is the important factors in affecting governance index.

Table 7 – 119 Grouping governance index based on score of cash flow rights

Group and number	Cash flow rights		Total scores manifestation				
	Interval (%)	Scores	Mean	Median	Max	Min	Standard deviation
1 (24)	0 – 5	1	58. 73	58. 18	66. 92	53. 18	3. 96
2 (31)	5 – 10	2	57. 18	55. 91	69. 09	44. 54	4. 91
3 (46)	10 – 15	3	57. 10	57. 27	68. 18	43. 64	4. 43
4 (33)	15 – 20	4	58. 32	58. 18	69. 09	50. 91	5. 00
5 (39)	20 – 25	5	59. 23	59. 55	72. 27	46. 82	5. 27
6 (23)	25 – 30	6	60. 58	60. 45	68. 64	51. 36	4. 45
7 (13)	30 – 35	7	59. 13	58. 64	65. 00	52. 27	4. 06
8 (6)	35 – 40	8	61. 44	61. 82	68. 64	51. 36	5. 87
9 (7)	40 – 45	9	57. 34	56. 82	70. 00	50. 45	6. 32
10 (13)	45 –	10	62. 31	62. 27	66. 36	55. 45	3. 38

Note: Numbers in the brackets are the numbers of PLCs in the corresponding industry.

Table 7 – 120 Grouping scores based on the score of deviation

Group and number	Deviation		Total scores manifestation				
	Interval (%)	Scores	Mean	Median	Max	Min	Standard deviation
1 (5)	≥45	1	56. 18	58. 18	60. 45	49. 09	4. 62

continued

Group and number	Deviation		Total scores manifestation				
	Interval (%)	Scores	Mean	Median	Max	Min	Standard deviation
2 (6)	40 - 45	2	55. 53	55. 68	60. 91	50. 00	4. 50
3 (5)	35 - 40	3	55. 27	55. 00	60. 45	51. 36	4. 06
4 (7)	30 - 35	4	55. 91	57. 73	61. 82	46. 82	5. 80
5 (8)	25 - 30	5	57. 67	58. 18	61. 82	50. 45	3. 94
6 (34)	20 - 25	6	56. 97	56. 82	65. 00	44. 55	4. 13
7 (33)	15 - 20	7	57. 66	57. 73	66. 82	43. 64	4. 85
8 (45)	10 - 15	8	58. 22	58. 18	68. 64	50. 91	4. 21
9 (39)	5 - 10	9	58. 74	59. 09	65. 91	51. 82	3. 84
10 (53)	0 - 5	10	62. 12	62. 27	72. 27	49. 55	4. 97

Note: Numbers in the brackets are the numbers of PLCs in the corresponding industry.

(2) The impact of equity structure on governance index.

The analysis on the impact of equity structure on governance index is followed. Herfindahl index is used to describe the features of equity structure in PLCs, which is the concentration condition and dispersion condition. According to the theory of equity balance, dispersive equity structure plays a balancing role in controlling shareholders' behaviors and reduce the agent cost among the shareholders. The samples are divided into 10 groups in the order of Herfindahl index with 5% spacing. Herfindahl index in the first group which includes 2 PLCs is more than 45% and its average is 57. 73. Herfindahl index in the tenth group including 16 PLCs is less than 5% with the average value of 60. 88. However, the changing trend of governance index from the first group to the tenth group is non-linear.

The Figure 7 - 58 is transferred from the data in Table 7 - 121, the horizontal axis shows the 10 groups from 1 to 10 and the vertical axis shows the index. Since there are only two companies in the first group and one company in the second companies, we remove these two groups to analyze the changing trend precisely. If the slightly declining trend from the sixth group to the eighth group is overlooked, the relationship between equity structure in PLCs and governance index is like "U" pattern after processing. The governance index in the third group is the highest which Herfindahl index ranges rrom 30% to 40% and governance index is 59. 55. As Herfindahl index is lower than the fifth group of 25% -30%, the lowest governance index is about 56. After that, with the decreasing of Herfindahl index, the governance index is gradually increasing to the highest in the tenth group which is 60. 88 and Herfindahl index is less than 5%.

Table 7 – 121 Grouping scores based on Herfindahl index

Group and number	Deviation		Total scores manifestation				
	Interval (%)	Scores	Mean	Median	Max	Min	Standard deviation
1 (2)	45 –	1	57.73	57.73	65.00	50.45	10.28
2 (1)	40 – 45	2	60.00	60.00	60.00	60.00	0.00
3 (8)	35 – 40	3	59.55	59.55	65.91	55.00	3.23
4 (9)	30 – 35	4	56.21	56.82	65.00	44.55	6.78
5 (20)	25 – 30	5	56.77	57.73	66.36	50.00	4.41
6 (15)	20 – 25	6	59.12	59.55	70.00	49.55	5.87
7 (32)	15 – 20	7	59.06	59.55	68.18	49.09	4.51
8 (71)	10 – 15	8	58.76	58.18	68.64	43.64	4.94
9 (61)	5 – 10	9	58.52	57.73	72.27	50.00	4.27
10 (16)	0 – 5	10	60.88	60.00	71.36	53.64	5.26

Note: Numbers in the brackets are the numbers of PLCs in the corresponding industry.

(3) The impact of board structure and managers incentive on governance index.

The analysis of impact of organization factors on governance index is following, including two aspects: the first is the controlling situation to board from major shareholders which can be described as holding positions by board members in the major shareholders' companies; the second is the incentive to managers described by the shareholding of managers.

The governance index of PLCs which are divided into 10 groups from the high to the low according their ratios of directors who hold position at the major shareholders' companies is shown in Table 7 – 122. Since there are fewer sample firms in the first 4 groups, we pay attention to the situation from the fifth group to the tenth group. The ratio of holding position of directors in the major shareholders' companies is decreasing from 0.42 to 0, while the governance index is increasing from 55.96 in the fifth group to 60.77 in the tenth group. These two variables are correlated with each other negatively. So the major shareholders have strong desire to control board in PLCs

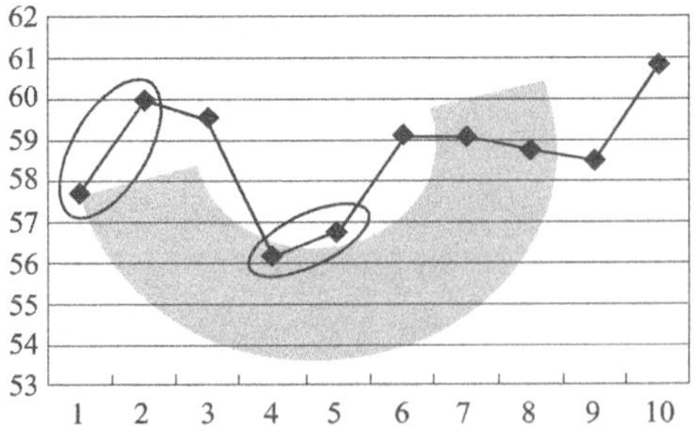

Figure 7 – 58 U-shape figure of shareholders structure and governance index

implying the board in PLCs play the important role in decision-making. On the other hand, there is the pan-family feature in the board.

Table 7 - 122 Grouping based on the holding position of directors in major shareholders' companies

Group number	Interval	Score	Mean	Median	Max	Min	Standard deviation
1 (1)	≥0.63	1	50.00	50.00	50.00	50.00	0.00
2 (2)	0.56 - 0.63	2	51.82	51.82	53.18	50.45	1.93
3 (4)	0.49 - 0.56	3	55.00	54.77	63.64	46.82	7.56
4 (1)	0.42 - 0.49	4	53.64	53.64	53.64	53.64	0.00
5 (19)	0.35 - 0.42	5	55.96	55.00	63.18	51.36	3.92
6 (27)	0.28 - 0.35	6	57.56	58.18	68.64	43.64	6.04
7 (40)	0.21 - 0.28	7	58.42	58.41	68.64	51.36	4.18
8 (50)	0.14 - 0.21	8	58.91	59.09	70.00	49.09	4.45
9 (52)	0.07 - 0.14	9	59.41	59.09	71.36	52.27	4.05
10 (39)	0.00 - 0.07	10	60.77	60.45	72.27	52.27	5.07

Note: Numbers in the brackets are the numbers of PLCs in the corresponding industry.

The governance index is, shown in the Table 7 - 123, according to the wages of managers from the low to the high, even though, overall, there is an unobvious increasing trend in governance index of PLCs. It is mainly because the managers in PLCs have already been involved in the family network leading to more complex targets. It is hard to completely solve the agent problems among complex groups only by salary mechanism. The overall increasing trend of governance index also indicates that salary mechanism still is the necessary method for PLCs.

Table 7 - 123 Grouping based on the high-Level managers' salary

Group number	Interval	Score	Mean	Median	Max	Min	Standard deviation
1 (27)	0 - 100 000	1	56.82	57.27	63.18	50.91	3.41
2 (49)	100 000 - 200 000	2	56.80	55.91	71.36	43.64	5.03
3 (46)	200 000 - 300 000	3	58.18	59.09	66.82	46.82	4.89
4 (31)	300 000 - 400 000	4	59.60	59.09	72.27	52.27	4.56
5 (20)	400 000 - 500 000	5	58.11	57.73	66.82	51.82	4.53
6 (13)	500 000 - 600 000	6	60.45	60.00	70.00	51.36	5.28
7 (13)	600 000 - 700 000	7	60.38	60.45	68.64	55.00	3.88
8 (10)	700 000 - 800 000	8	62.36	62.05	68.18	56.82	3.43
9 (9)	800 000 - 900 000	9	58.84	59.54	65.00	53.18	4.01
10 (17)	≥900 000	10	62.25	63.18	69.09	51.36	5.17

Note: Numbers in the brackets are the numbers of PLCs in the corresponding industry.

(4) The impact of information disclosure on governance index.

The companies with great governance would disclose the information of operating performance in time. The positivity in information disclosure has already been an important mark of investment evaluation for listed companies. The governance index is divided into 10 groups with the ranking of positivity in information disclosure from the low to the high into 10 (see Figure 7 – 124). There is only a difference of 0.04 scores between the least active group, the first group, and the most active group, the tenth group. The governance index in the fourth group to the ninth group is more than it in the tenth group. The relationship between positivity in information disclosure and governance index is non-linear implying that information disclosure in Chinese PLCs is affected by subjective factors.

Table 7 – 124 Grouping based on positivity in information disclosure

Group number	Interval	Score	Mean	Median	Max	Min	Standard deviation
1 (52)	0 – 8	1	58.07	57.95	72.27	43.64	5.13
2 (31)	9 – 16	2	58.18	58.18	69.09	44.55	5.28
3 (26)	17 – 24	3	56.80	56.36	65.91	49.09	3.86
4 (32)	25 – 32	4	59.39	60.23	71.36	50.00	4.51
5 (19)	33 – 40	5	59.21	59.09	65.00	52.27	3.78
6 (25)	41 – 48	6	59.78	60.00	68.64	46.82	5.72
7 (15)	49 – 56	7	60.61	60.45	66.82	51.36	4.16
8 (19)	57 – 64	8	59.26	58.18	70.00	50.00	5.92
9 (7)	65 – 72	9	58.51	60.00	63.18	53.64	3.89
10 (7)	≥73	10	58.11	59.09	62.27	53.64	3.55

Note: Numbers in the brackets are the numbers of PLCs in the corresponding industry.

7.7.3 Main conclusions

With the increasing number of PLCs, the associated benefits distribution, governance mechanisms and their agent problems are exposed gradually. Rating system of PLCs is came up with to evaluate the development of PLCs and Chinese PLCs' governance index is formed in this part. Based on the analysis of governance index, we found that behavior of the major shareholders of PLCs driven by benefits shows a strong negative external effect in the case that illegal benefits is higher than the costs. Particularly the UCSs adopt "tunneling effect" behavior and damaged the value of PCs in most cases by the formation of group control such as pyramid structure in the context of the severe deviation between ultimate control right and cash flow right leading to higher agent costs among medium and small shareholders. Complicated agent relation is formed based on the intertwining of institution factors and family factors in transformation period increasing the difficulty of governance in PLCs.

1. The main issues of governance in PLCs

The common rules of governance in Chinese PLCs in transformation period are unveiled in this part. It is difficult to touch the core of PLCs directly due to data availability. We take the way which is from outside to inside starting from the evaluation of governance in PLCs to find the problems, to explore the root causes and sum up the general rules.

(1) Group control is the main factor evoking behavior of encroachment effect of UC.

Due to the existence of group control that increases deviation of UC between control rights in LC and cash flow right declining the benefits of control right. What the UCs do to pursue the benefits of control right would damage the value of company. Ownership structure and extent and probability of others minority shareholders' interests being damaged would be increased that is the behaviors of UC show strong entrenchment effects. Ownership structure of PCs become the main factor of evoking the entrenchment effects behaviors in the context of further strengthening group control. Because of the existence of inner shareholders group, ownership structure did not develop into an effective counterweight. As persons acting in concert, the inner shareholders group's behavior completely embodies the will of the UC and becomes the tool of entrenchment effects behaviors acted by UCs.

(2) "Major shareholders control" characteristic presented on the board of directors.

Unlike the "operator control" of state-owned LCs, Chinese PLCs show apparently "major shareholders control". The vast majority of directors serve as other positions at the same time in PLCs which must have a significant impact on their fulfilling the duties of directors. Major shareholders control can solve the issue of "absence of owners". However, when the benefits of major shareholders and other small shareholders are not consistent, there would be agent problems between major shareholders and small shareholders which increase the private benefits of major shareholders in short term. On the contrary it would damage the long-term financing capacity of LCs which is detrimental to the LCs' long-term development.

(3) Low level of executive compensation and non-Linear correlation between proportion of shareholding and CP.

Although level of executive compensation equals to average level of industry market in China, executive compensation of PLCs in china is significantly correlated with index of CP which fully implies that on the one hand PLCs still spare no efforts to make executive compensation and CP tied closely, on the other hand "family contract" play important role of motivation and restriction in PLCs replacing "contract economy" to some extent. Another major finding is that relation between shareholding rate of senior executives and CP of PLCs is non-linear which reflects complicated agent relation in PLCs and the impacts of multi-purposes of senior executives on PLCs' behavior.

Although motivation of PLCs' independent directors' compensation is weak relatively, most of independent directors take part in almost all board conferences actively to lay the foundation for their fulfillment of responsibility and obligation.

(4) Further improvement of supervisory board's governance mechanism is needed.

We found that strong regional disparities and certain industrial differences are presented in PLCs' supervisory board governance and overall level is not high. Besides proportion of employee supervisors and motivation of members in supervisory board are low relatively. And it is common that supervisors are employed in the largest shareholders' companies.

(5) Enthusiasm of information disclosure in PLCs and independence of audit opinion are gradually improved.

The study found that the enthusiasm of private listed companies and the independence of the audit opinion is gradually improving the independence of the accounting firm's influence is improving. The independent director system has played an important role in improving the information disclosure of listed companies, which proves that the independent director system has played a positive role in the domestic securities market. But the research shows that the characteristics of listed companies themselves still largely affect the audit opinion. That is, the accounting firm has a tendency to condone a good or large-scale listed company, the risk of large companies are demanding. This shows to some extent, the reform of the domestic information disclosure mechanism there is still a long way to go, not through the improvement of the legal system can be achieved in the short term.

2. Policy suggestions on improving PLCs' governance

(1) Strengthen the supervision to group controlling phenomenon in PLC and improve related institution.

The rationality and legality of related party transaction in PLCs with grouping controlling should be strengthened. Encourage the private companies which shareholders are natural persons to be listed directly. Meanwhile constrain the hierarchy of grouping controlling by legislation from international experiences. The cost of controlling rights benefits is supposed to be controlled within a certain scale.

(2) Promote the independence and strategic involvement of the board of directors.

Recognize the impact of board of directors on PLCs' governance and promote positively the institution construction with the core of improving the independence of board of directors. Complete the internal mechanism of PLCs step by step and restrain and guide the ultimate controllers' behavior. Improve the governance level of board of supervisors in PLCs and enlarge the size of board of supervisors gradually. Increase the ratio of involvement of staff in the supervision properly and positivity of supervision. Commit the comprehensive incentive methods between supervisory secure incentive and risk incentive. Normalize the nomination of supervisors and promote the normalization of the meeting of board of supervisors.

(3) Establish complete information disclosure mechanism.

The fair and effective information disclosure mechanism would be the institutional guarantee for the long-term and stable development of security market in China. Recently, the law system of Chinese information disclosure has been gradually completed and form the law system focusing on the law, administration rules and accounting regulations. And relatively completed information disclosure mechanism would be formed by external auditing committed by account firms. As the major component of external companies' governance mechanism, the information disclosure is paid the more and more attention. However, the information disclosure evaluation index in PLCs indicates that information disclosure is supposed to be further strengthened, and the standards of information disclosure and the level of grouping controlling should be linked together. The disclosure of controlling situation of PLC should be strengthened. Besides, the situation of related party companies controlled by the same ultimate controller and the related directors' information are needed to be further refined and enriched. The hierarchical management should be done to the standards of information disclosure which are needed to be linked with the complexity of grouping controlling.

References

1. Agrawal A. , Knoeber C. Firm Performance and Mechanism to Control Agency

Problems between Managers and Shareholders. Journal of Finance and Quantitative Analysis, 1996, Vol. 31, (3): 377 –397.

2. Bai Chong'en, Liu Qiao, Luzhou. Empirical Study on China's Listed Companies Governance Structure. Economic Research Journal, 2005 (2): 81 –191.

3. Baysinger B., Butler H. Corporate Governance and the Board of Directors: Performance Effects of Changes in Board Composition. Journal of Law, Economics & Organization, 1985, Vol. 1, (1): 101 –124.

4. Berle A., Means G., The Modern Corporation and Private Property, Macmillan, New York. 1932.

5. Bhagat S., Black B. The Uncertain Relationship between Board Composition and Firm Performance. Business Lawyer, 1999 (54): 921 –963.

6. Chen Xiao, Jiang Dong. Equity Diversification, Corporate Performance and Industry Competitiveness. Economic Research Journal, 2000 (8): 28 –35.

7. Chen Xiaoyue, Xu Xiaodong. Ownership Structure, Corporate Performance and Investor Protection. Economic Research Journal, 2001 (11): 3 –2.

8. Chen Xinmin, Liu Shanmin. Listed Companies Operating Remuneration of Structural Differences in Empirical Research. Economic Research Journal, 2003 (8): 55 –63.

9. Cheng Hsiao. Panel Data Analysis (English version). Peking University Press, 2005.

10. DeAngelo L., Elizabeth. Auditor size and audit quality. Journal of Accounting and Economics, 1981, Vol. 3 (3): 83 –199.

11. Demsetz H. The structure of ownership and the theory of the firm. Journal of Law and Economics, 1983, Vol. 26, 2: 375 –390.

12. Determined Institution: A Survey of the Economic Literature (working paper 2000).

13. Final Rule. Strengthening the Commission's Requirements Regarding Auditor Independence, www. sec. gov.

14. Gu Qi, Yu Dongzhi. Corporate Governance, Board Behavior and Performance. Research on Financial and Economic Issues, 2001 (1): 58 –65.

15. Hall B., Liebman J. Are CEOs Really Paid Like Bureaucrats? Quarterly Journal of Economics, 1998, Vol. 113, 3: 653 –691.

16. Hanson R. C., Song M. H. Managerial Ownership, Board Structure, and the Division of Gains in Divestitures. Journal of Corporate Finance, 2000 (6): 55 –70.

17. Harold De Metsi. Enterprise Economics. China Social Sciences Press, 1999.

18. Harold de Msetz. Ownership, Control and Business. Economic Science Press, 1999.

19. He Jiacheng. Corporate Governance Comparison. Economic Science Press, 2003.

20. He Xiaoqun, Liu Wenqing. Application of Regression Analysis. China Renmin University Press, 2001.

21. HouGuangming, ZouRui. Private Enterprise Development Model Research. China Economist, 2003 (11): 8 – 10.

22. Huang Hai, Luo Youfeng, Chen Zhiying. Spss 10.0 for Windows Statistical Analysis. Post and Telecom Press, 2001.

23. Huang Mengfu. China's Private Economic Development Situation Analysis Will Theme Play, 2003.

24. JiaJunping, He Xiaoqun, Jin Yongjin. Statistics. China Renmin University Press, 2000.

25. Knapp M. C. Audit Conflict: An Empirical Study of the Perceived Ability of Auditors to Resist Management Pressure. The Accounting Review, Sarasota: 1985, Vol. 60, Iss. 2: 202 – 211.

26. Lang Xianping. Corporate Governance. Social Sciences Academic Press, 2004.

27. Li Dongping, Huang Dehua, Wang Zhenlin. Unaudited Audit Opinion, Earnings Management and Change of Accounting Firm. Accounting Research, 2001 (6): 51 – 57.

28. Li Minghui, He Hai, Ma Xikui. China's Listed Companies Internal Control Information Disclosure of the Situation. Auditing Research, 2003 (1): 38 – 43.

29. Li Wanli, Zhang Xiaolan. China's Listed Companies Annual Report Disclosure of the Situation. Journal of Financial Research, 2002 (3).

30. Li Wei'an, et al. Corporate Governance. Nankai University Press, 2001.

31. Li Wei'an, et al. China's Corporate Governance Principles and International Comparison. China Financial & Economic Publishing House, 2001.

32. Li Wei'an, et al. Modern Corporate Governance Research. China People's University Press, 2002.

33. Li Wei'an, Wu Lidong. Corporate Governance Course. Shanghai People's Publishing House, 2003.

34. Li Wei'an et al. China's Corporate Governance Evaluation System. Nankai Business Review, 2003 (3): 4 – 12.

35. Li Wei'an et al. Corporate Governance Evaluation and Index Research. Higher

Education Press, 2005.

36. Li Wei'an. Corporate Governance. Higher Education Press, 2005.

37. Liang Can. Corporate Governance Structure. China's Practice and Experience of the United States. China People's University Press, 2000.

38. Lin Junqing, Huang Zuhui, Sun Yongxiang. Executive Team Pay Gap, Corporate Performance and Governance Structure. Economic Research Journal, 2003 (4): 31 –40.

39. McConnell J. Servas H. Additional Evidence on Equity Ownership and Corporate Value, Journal of Financial Economics, 1990 (27): 595 –612.

40. Margaret M. Blair. Ownership and Control. Corporate Governance for the 21st Century Exploration. China Social Sciences Press, 1999.

41. National Bureau of Statistics Enterprise Investigation Corps Task Force. Private Economy Development and Private Enterprise Growth Research. Review of Economic Research, 2004 (22): 2 –12.

42. Oliver Hart. Business, Contract and Financial Structure, Fee Domain Translation. Shanghai Joint Publishing, Shanghai People's Publishing House, 1998.

43. Oswald S. L. Jahera. Jr J S. The Influence of Ownership on Performance: an Empirical Study. Strategy Management Journal, 1991 (12): 321 –326.

44. Ping Xinqiao, Li. Re-qualification of Listed Companies to Determine and False Information Disclosure. Economic Research Journal, 2003 (2): 55 –63.

45. Ping Xinqiao, Song Min, Zhang Junxi. China's Corporate Governance and Corporate Value. Governance Structure. Securities Market and Banking Reform, Peking University Press, 2003 Yearbook, 23 –42.

46. Ping Xinqiao, Song Min, Zhang Junxi. Governance Structure, Securities Market and Bank Reform. Peking University Press, 2003.

47. Rosenstein S., Wyatt J. G. Outside Directors, Board Independence, and Shareholder Wealth. Journal of Financial Economics, 1990 (26): 175 –191.

48. Shanghai Stock Exchange Research Center. China Corporate Governance Report (2004). Board Independence and Effectiveness. Fudan University Press, 2004.

49. Shanghai Stock Exchange Research Center. China Corporate Governance Report (2005). Private Listed Company Governance. Fudan University Press, 2005.

50. Shao Shaomin, Wu Canglan, Lin Wei. Independent Director and Board Sructure, Ownership Structure Research. The Journal of World Economy, 2004 (2): 66 –79.

51. Song Min, Zhang Junxi, Li Chuntao. Trap of Ownership Structure. Nankai

Business Review, 2004 (1).

52. Su Qilin, Zhu Wen. Family Control of Listed Companies and Corporate Value. Economic Research Journal, 2003 (8): 35 -45.

53. Su Qilin. Agency Issues, Corporate Governance and Corporate Value. China Industrial Economics, 2004 (4): 100 - 106.

54. Sun Yongxiang. Corporate Governance Structure. Theoretical and Empirical Research. Shanghai Joint Publishing, Shanghai People's Publishing House, 2002.

55. Sun Yongxiang, Huang Zuhui. Ownership Structure and Performance of Listed Companies. Economic Research Journal, 1999 (12): 23 -30.

56. Sun Yongxiang, Zhang Rong. Board Size, Corporate Governance and Performance. Enterprise Economy, 2000 (10): 13 - 15.

57. Walter J. Sammon et al. Corporate Governance. China Renmin University Press, 2001.

58. Wang Chengli, Xu Jiuping. Private Enterprises in the GEM Listed on the Risk of Comparative Research. Contemporary Finance & Economics, 2003 (3): 60 -63.

59. Wang Guocheng. Corporate Governance Structure and Entrepreneurial Choice. Economic & Management Publishing House, 2002.

60. Weisbach M. S. Outside Directors and CEO Turnover. Journal of Financial Economics, 1988 (20): 431 -460.

61. Wei Gang. Senior Management Incentives and Listed Companies Operating Performance. Economic Research Journal, 2000 (3): 32 -39.

62. Woodridge J. M. Introduction to Econometrics. Modern View. China Renmin University Press, 2003.

63. Wu Jinglian. Stock Option Incentive and Corporate Governance. Economy & Management, 2002 (6).

64. XieBaisan, XieShuguang. On China's Private Listed Companies Low-Performance Issues of Deep Thinking. Finance & Economics, 2003 (1): 32 -36.

65. Xu Xiaodong, Chen Xiaoyue. Largest Shareholder of Corporate Governance, Corporate Performance Analysis. Economic Research Journal, 2003 (2): 64 -74.

66. Xue Wei. Statistical Analysis and Application of SPSS. China Renmin University Press, 2001.

67. Ye Yinhua, Li Cunxiu, KeCheng'en. Corporate Governance and Rating System. China Financial & Economic Publishing House, 2004.

68. Yermack D. Higher Market Valuation of Companies with a Small Board of Directors. Journal of Financial Economics, 1996 (40): 185 -211.

69. Yu Dongzhi. Board of Directors and Corporate Governance. Tsinghua University Press, 2004.

70. Yu Dongzhi. Board of Directors, Corporate Governance and Performance-An Empirical Analysis of Chinese Listed Companies. Social Sciences in China, 2003 (3): 29 – 41.

71. Yu Dongzhi, Chi Guohua. Board Size, Stability and Corporate Performance. An Analysis of Theory and Experience. Economic Research Journal, 2004 (4): 70 – 79.

72. Yuan Hongqi, Li Haijian. Accounting Firm Organization Form, Size and Audit Quality. Auditing Research, 2003 (1): 32 – 37.

73. Zhang Junxi, Zhang Hua. Private Listed Companies Operating Performance and Governance Structure. Second Corporate Governance International Seminar Papers.

74. Zhang Limin, Qian Hua, Li Minyi. Status and Improvement of Internal Control Information Disclosure-from China ST Listed Companies Data Analysis. Auditing Research, 2003 (5): 10 – 15.

75. Zhang Weiying. Property Rights, Incentives and Corporate Governance. Economic Science Press, 2005.

76. Zhou Jianbo, Sun Jusheng. Managers of Equity Incentive Governance Effect. Economic Research Journal, 2003 (5): 74 – 82.

77. Zhou Qinye, Lu Zonghui, Jin Ying. Listed Companies Information Disclosure and Investor Information Access to the Cost-effectiveness of Questionnaire Survey. Accounting Research, 2003 (5): 3 – 10.

78. Zhou Xiuyun, Feng Junwen. China's Private Listed Companies Governance Model. Modern Economic Research, 2003 (12): 46 – 47.

79. Zhu Wuxiang, Song Yong. Ownership Structure and Corporate Value-Listed companies on Home Appliance Industry Empirical Analysis. Economic Research Journal, 2001 (12): 66 – 72.

Chapter 8

Policy Suggestions on Institution Innovation and Development of Private Economy

The purpose of the above chapters is to provide references for the practice of institutional innovation and development of private economy. Therefore, on the basis of summing up the above research results, this chapter puts forward the policy suggestions on the institutional innovation and development of private economy from the perspectives of legal institution construction, government policy, intermediary organization and other service support institutions, so as to promote the sustainable and healthy development of economy and companies in private sector.

8.1 Conclusions and policy suggestions of institutional change and organizational evolution in private economy development

Based on the review of the development of private economy and the history of organizational evolution in more than 20 years, this chapter analyzes the institutional changes in the development of private economy from the perspectives of ideological preference, local government behavior, historical path dependence, institution complementarity and productivity competition among economic organizations, institution complementarity and productivity competition among economic organizations. By comparing the characteristics of typical development model in different regions, this chapter generalized a universally significant evolution model in which the relationships among private economy, state-owned enterprise reform and foreign capital participation are interactive, penetrative, competitive and alternative, i. e. an institution complementary development model of "multi-interaction, up and down promotion".

8.1.1 Main Conclusions

1. Motive mechanism of the institutional innovation of private economy: productivity competition and institution complementarity

This study uses the historical data to describe and analyze the "historical logic starting point" of the reform of the state-owned economy and evolution of the non-state-owned economy, the nature of the public ownership economy, the "institution complementarity" and "mutual embedding" of state-owned economy and non-state-owned economy to "characterize" the evolution of private economy and institutional innovation trajectory in transition process and make an outlook into the development of private economy. The conclusion of the research shows that ideology preference of local government will determine its private economic policy and thus affect future expectation of the private enterprises. The productivity competition and institution complementarity between state-owned enterprises and private enterprises will jointly shape the "institution complementarity" in a particular region, resulting in different choices of governance structure for private enterprises in different regions. In addition, marginal efficiency of state-owned and private capital in different regions will lead to differences in "amendment rates of their traditional ideology preferences" among different local governments, and further lead to differences in their private economic policies and economic evolution trajectory bifurcation: different regions are subject to their respective historical conditions. Those who are more completely out of the traditional ideology of local government will encourage private enterprises to quickly get the organization's relative transaction efficiency advantage, so that private economy can go into a sustained innovation path, which is the origin of Wenzhou model; those who slowly get rid of the traditional ideology will participate in the process of corporate evolution in the form of grass-roots political regime, which developed township enterprises of fuzzy property rights structure, which is the origin of Southern Jiangsu model; those who adhere to traditional ideology and pay attention to the effect of state-owned enterprise reform on economic growth cannot provide a reasonable policy environment for the development of private economy, so that private enterprises lack stability expectations and clear comparative advantage of private economy in terms of efficiency does not appear, which is precisely the situation of development of private economy in the central and western region. Finally, productivity competition and complementarity institutions would inherently promote private economic evolution and formation of "dynamic mechanism" for the reform of state-owned economy, induce different types of organizations to continue to improve governance structure and pursue profit maximization. Under the influence of comparative efficiency, the evolution and institutional change trajectory of different regional economic organizations will converge, which makes the community ownership structure of Southern Jiangsu model change to the ownership structure of Wenzhou model.

We believe that it is the regional differences of the historical logic origin that result in different capital distributions and ownership structures of state-owned economy and private economy (including township enterprises), so there are significant differences in capital efficiency and organizational efficiency for these different types of economic organizations, which lead to productivity competition and "institution complementarity" among different types of economic organizations and jointly determine the "institution complementary features" differences of different regions. On the one hand, these differences have caused different evolutionary trajectories of private economy in different regions. For example, Zhejiang Wenzhou model, southern Jiangsu model and Guangdong's Pearl River Delta model have constructed their respective bifurcation evolution track at the beginning of the model formation. This kind of pluralistic private economic evolution will converge to the equilibrium points of different positions in their development processes, but under the pressure of productivity competition and complementarity of state-owned economy and private economy, these different evolution paths will eventually approach or converge to "optimal equilibrium point". On the other hand, the difference in "institution complementarity" makes different local governments have different "reactions" in revising their ideological preferences: the faster the reaction, the more local governments tend to "reform", the more active to choose to give priority to the development of private economy policy. On the contrary, the slow response of the local government will delay the timing of reform objectively and amendment of the ideological preferences will cause "time lag", so that its policy cannot always meet the need of private economic development. With further improvement of market economy, cross-regional flow of capital elements and human capital will prompt local government with lagging preference of ideology to make the policy of developing private economy. Private economy will get higher organizational efficiency in a relaxed economic environment and the marginal efficiency of private capital will also be improved, so as to promote local governments in the central provinces to achieve reversed ideological preferences and create incentives compatible institutional arrangements for the development of private economy. It is necessary to get rid of shackles of the development of private economy, adjust the local government's ideological preferences and improve the trading environment of private enterprises and marginal efficiency of private capital.

2. Important role of government behavior optimization in the development of private economy

Through the study of the development process of private economy, we can see the evolution mode of unique "pluralistic interaction, up and down promotion" in current institution of private economic organization: based on complex game among the central government, the local government and the market agent, they mutually promote the institution innovation from the level of legislation, collective action and operation. What's more, the central government is in the continuous absorption of results of independent innovation by local governments and market participants and puts forward laws and regulations to recognize and promote institutional innovation and create relatively independent competitive environment; local government acts as a "two-way agent" role and plays the role of message communication, protecting and promoting market independent innovation; private enterprises, intermediary organizations and other market players not only meet the needs of its institution, but also have made great development with dynamic game with the local and central government from their own reality. This reality reflects the current situation of China's gradual establishment and improvement of the market economy institution, the realization of the transformation of government functions, the existing interest requirement of different interest groups under current right structure and promote the rapid development of Chinese private economy organization since the 1990s objectively.

However, it is also necessary to see that an important prerequisite for this evolutionary model of multi-dimensional interaction to promote institutional change is that the central government, local governments and market players have their own independent interests and have the impulse to maximize their own interests through the choice of institutional innovation, which is a complex tripartite game process. In order to avoid a disorder game and achieve efficient institutional innovation, we must establish sound rules of the game and reasonable positioning of the institutional innovation agents to participate and effectively constrain their behavior, so that institutional innovation can go into a virtuous circle track. In fact, a new topic is put forward, that is, how to continuously promote the organizational changes of private economy under new power relations, role of positioning and pattern of interests. This is precisely the key for the future institutional innovation of private economy and the concept of government governance provide an important inspiration for us. With market and efficiency as the guide and emphasizing authorization and decentralization, the idea of multi-centered governance of social public affairs represents the trend of government public management, which is of great significance to the change of government governance in China's economic transition.

Under the background of changing government governance, the key to innovating the mode of private economic organization change is to implement the concept of governance in the behavior of the main body of institutional innovation and establish a set of rules system which effectively restrains and coordinates the behavior of all parties. The core issues include effectively defining the functions and limits of the government, straightening out the relationship between government and market and the relationship between government and civil society and its autonomous organizations.

8.1.2 Policy Suggestions

1. Promote the fundamental transformation of government functions as the core, and establish a limited, efficient, transparent government

There is no omniscient and omnipotent government under the conditions of uncertainty, incomplete information, and pursuit of maximizing utility, and the boundaries of government functions are determined by the range of public goods and services that can be effectively provided. Thus, it is necessary to proceed from the basic nature of public goods and services to analyze what should be provided by the government, which should not be provided by the government, which can be provided by the government but not efficient, so as to determine the optimal boundaries of government functions. Therefore, current transformation of the functions of our government, in essence, is to recognize the limitation of government functions and authorize power and right to enterprise, market and society. Under the framework of government governance, the basic goal of realizing the fundamental transformation of government functions can be summarized as follows:

First, limited government: the government should be limited in terms of authority, responsibility and size. First, the government should only provide pure public goods, quasi-public goods and public services that are related to the people's livelihood, social stability and sustainable development. Other public goods and services should be guided by the principles of marketization, provided by enterprises, markets and social organizations. Second, the government provides some kind of public goods and services, but it does not mean that the government must bear the responsibility of production, which can be achieved through market and social comparative advantage. The government must bear the responsibility of effective supervision and policy guidance, incentives and regulation. At the same time, the government's responsibility for citizens and society is limited and it cannot bear the full responsibility for the survival, enjoyment and development of citizens. Finally, the size of government should meet their powers and responsibilities on the basis of the minimization, in order to ensure the effective provision of public goods and services. Actually, the previous transformation of government functions in China is basically a reflection of the concept of limited government, "economic regulation, market regulation, social management, public services" is a good summary of the current stage of functional transformation objectives and contraction of the government should be further prompted and to improve the quality of public goods and services provided by the government, and the government should bear the due limited liability.

Second, efficient government: the ability to provide public goods and services at lower economic and social costs is the basic criterion for achieving good government governance. It can be considered from three aspects: first, introduce competition mechanism through the internal market and quasi-commercial way to improve the efficiency of providing public goods and services, which mainly relates to some of the general public but not suitable of fully market service functions, such as hospitals and post offices etc. Under the premise of state-owned assets, introduce competitive enterprise management model and the government sets up regulatory institution to ensure business efficiency and social equity balance through detailed regulatory measures. Second, reshape structure of the interests of government agencies and officials, achieve a substantial reduction of administrative approval projects and procedures and strictly control examination and approval fees. Standardize the approval process and should decouple approved fees with government officials bonuses to eliminate the internal impulse for examination of the project. Finally, streamline government agencies to control fiscal spending. The sustained expansion of government scale will inevitably bring about the rigid growth of fiscal expenditure, which will become the internal incentive of government administrative examination and approval fees and power rent seeking. Public goods and services are facing insufficient supply. China has carried out government reform for four times and government agencies and functional adjustment have been optimized since 2001. It has comprehensively promoted the reform of the administrative examination and approval institution to a certain extent and improved the efficiency of the government. The 2004 "Administrative Licensing Law" introduced more far-reaching reform, but the real establishment of efficient government needs the establishment of scientific achievements concept, improvement of the cadre performance appraisal institution, optimization of the government personnel management institution, improvement of the quality and capacity of civil servants and other aspects of work.

Third, rule of law government: rule of law is to ensure that the government behavior is normative, maintain good relations among government, business and market. Because government has the impetus of political coercion and internal expansion, the establishment of government governance mechanism can not only rely on government's own reform, but also need to be included in the government's behavior and interests within the universally recognized norms, in order to effectively restrain government behavior and fundamentally control and curb the government's behavior deviating from the maximization of social benefits, such as setting unreasonable market entry barriers, high tax burden, inefficient administrative examination and approval institution. China has made great progress in establishing the rule of law government, and the constitutional institution of socialism with Chinese characteristics has been initially formed. At the same time, judicial institution has also been improved and a series of reforms around presiding judge or prosecutor election, trial open, public affairs, judicial evasion, judicial relief institution and the national unified judicial examination have taken off. Establish a sound institution of laws and regulations, emphasize the transparency of justice, fairness and justice and ensure the independence of the judiciary will be the ultimate goal of government to achieve the rule of law.

Fourth, improve transparency of government behavior: to stress the transparency of government policy, information, budget and others is an important part of government governance. Through the openness of government information, it is conducive to ensure citizens' right to know and the effective supervision of government behavior. China's implementation of open government and to ensure transparency is in the continuous progress. The party and government departments has established a "two open one supervision" institution (that is, open service institution and results of public service institution and accept supervision of the masses) and press release institution. With the development of e-government, information dissemination in the use of network and online government is also a strong impetus to the transparency of the government. The key to further enhancing transparency of the government is to concentrate more and more public wisdom in the process of government decision-making, to listen to public opinion and to make decisions on major issues that are closely related to the interests of the masses with wide social impact. We should strengthen and improve publicity, hearing institution and interest coordination mechanism to promote the openness and transparency of the government with the full participation of citizens and social organizations.

2. Achieve effective local government governance and straighten out central local relations through a reasonable mandate and decentralization

Authorization and decentralization is an important concept of government governance reform. Through the transformation of government functions, the establishment of a limited government can realize government's authorization and decentralization of the market and society, and within the government organization, it is necessary to clear their respective rights, responsibilities and interests between the central and local governments and to achieve effective management of social affairs. As mentioned above, there is a fundamental conflict in the mode of change of the original private economic organization institution, that is, the vertical administrative decentralization has not solved the problem of rational allocation of power, and the decentralization reform only broke down the highly unified political economy into many decentralized political and economic integration, the result must be local protectionism and vassal economy. Based on the concept of government governance change, to achieve a reasonable authority and decentralization between the central and local governments and straighten out the central local relations need to start from the following points:

First, with the scope of public welfare to provide public goods and services to as standard, divide the central and local social affairs management responsibilities reasonably and improve the transfer payment institution as a breakthrough in the adjustment of central local relations. The Third Plenary Session of the 16th CPC Central Committee pointed out that in accordance with the principle of central reunification, give full play to the principle of local initiative and make clear the responsibility of the central and local economic and social affairs. According to the division of economic and social affairs, straighten out labor and responsibilities division of labor and finance, finance, investment and social security and other areas. The Sixth Plenary Session of the 16th CPC Central Committee also pointed out that it would further clarify the central and local rights and powers, improve the fiscal and taxation institution to match the financial and administrative rights, increase the financial transfer payments, promote the standardization and legalization of transfer payments. Enhance capabilities of the grassroots government to provide public service. In accordance with the above principles, in the central and local social affairs management division of powers and responsibilities, the central government should be mainly responsible for public welfare coverage of the nationwide, supply public goods and services to urban and rural areas and take regional public service as the focus, to strengthen the redistribution function. The local governments are mainly responsible for the supply of public goods and services in the region, should focus on the actual needs of residents, and strengthen the efficiency of supply. At the same time, in order to ensure that the central and local supply of public goods and services responsibilities and competencies, we must solve the problem of inadequate supply of public goods and services and regional imbalances through a sound transfer payment institution, so as to ease the central and local contradictions and promote the coordinated development of regional economy. It include the central government to increase subsidies to the local financial strength, the infrastructure construction and social development focus shifted to rural areas, to increase the transfer of horizontal payments and other measures.

Second, to effectively provide public goods and services as the guide, deepen the transformation of local government functions and administrative management institution reform, to establish public service-oriented government. The so-called "public service government" refers to the ability to correct the "market failure", and to effectively provide public goods and services including public infrastructure, democracy and the rule of law, fairness and justice, education, health care and social security to ensure the resources distribution efficiency under the market mechanism. Therefore, it is necessary to deepen the transformation of functions at all levels of government, to further promote the separation of government and enterprises, speed up the process of market-oriented reform, simplify the procedures of government agencies, improve the efficiency of the work, strengthen the internal checks and balances of government and public opinion supervision, improve the performance of public services and the cadre examination institution, and gradually establish the central to the local public service accountability institution to strengthen the local government's public service functions. It is noteworthy that in recent years, many local governments, construct a number of empirical models with local characteristics in the realization of functional transformation, such as Wenzhou model, Shenzhen model, Hainan model, which are the results of independent institutional innovation of local governments, providing valuable references for different places to construct their own governance models.

Third, with the improvement of laws and regulations, it is necessary to institutionalize, legalize and normalize the relationship of authority and decentralization between the central and the local. Since the reform and opening up, an important root cause of the central and local contradictions is the unestablished standardized and legalized distribution of benefits and coordination mechanisms, the lack of legal constraints on mode of central and local power operation, distribution of benefits, and liability and others. Conflict of interest and friction weakened the authority of the central government and increased the cost of policy implementation. Although the Third and Sixth Plenary sessions of the 16th CPC Central Committee have pointed out the principle of dividing the central and local powers, there is no standard in the legal form. To this end, we should first of all promote legislation on the relationship between the central and local in the form of legal clear central and local authority; secondly, we should establish laws and regulations on central and local shared tax sharing and financial transfer payment institution, clearly divide the central and local rights and obligations. Thirdly, we should clarify the control right of the central authorities on the local financial, fiscal, industrial and other aspects in the legal form, the scope, means, procedures and basic objectives of the regulation and the corresponding rights and obligations of the local government to ensure that the legal basis of the macro-control is normative and effective. Finally, strengthen the legislative institution of public services to improve the legal coordination and supervision of local government public service supply duties.

3. Improve the comprehensive quality of private economy and strengthen its consciousness and ability as a pole of social affairs governance

China's private economy development performance is unneglectable, but it is undeniable that many private companies obtain gray institution rent in the process of developing using the imperfection of the market institution and special historical opportunities under the extraordinary development also makes some private enterprises cover up their own deep-seated problems. For example, the industry development level is low, the governance structure is not perfect and the management institution and organizational structure are unreasonable. There is a lack of corporate credit culture, contradiction between labor and capital and even tax evasion exits. In the new economic environment, private economy shoulders the responsibility of development of national industry, enhancement the comprehensive national strength as the historical mission and the important functions of social and public affairs management, and thus we must prompt the continuous improvement of overall quality and competitiveness of enterprises, which is the inevitable choice of really mature private economy.

First, improve regulatory behavior and vigorously enhance the overall quality of private enterprises. We should guide and supervise the establishment of a modern enterprise institution and corporate governance structure, strengthen and improve the supervision of private enterprises, actively guide enterprises to change the mode of growth, promote product technology and institution innovation, improve corporate governance structure, standardize business behavior, strengthen staff skills training, build a harmonious labor relations and bear more social responsibility. Further improve the individual and private enterprise decision-making institution and increase transparency and social trust, so that enterprises can evolve from one-person-decision-making mode to scientific decision-making mode. Strengthen internal institution construction and organization construction in the individual and private enterprise, optimize the operation mechanism, achieve the combination of "family" management model and expert governance, strive to achieve the institutionalization of scientific decision-making and enhance the cohesion and competitiveness of enterprises.

Second, improve the industry access supporting policies to create a more equitable market environment. Further promote the relevant departments and industries to speed up the development of non-public economic market access policy, strive to eliminate the effects of interests of certain sectors, local interests and monopoly power interests and eliminate direct or indirect obstacles of market access on operational level. Speed up the formulation and improvement of all walks of life access policy, earnestly implement the principle of "equal access and fair treatment" put forward by the State Council, further break administrative monopoly based on administration, break the local blockade and promote industry access policy and management to be open, fair, procedural and standardized. Create a truly fair competition in the market environment for private economy.

Third, reform fiscal and financial management institution and build a more favorable development environment. Speed up the pace of reform of financial, fiscal and taxation institution, establish a credit policy institution suitable for and meet the needs of large, medium and small enterprises and actively develop small and medium-sized financial enterprises with various ownership, especially the development of regional banking institutions especially for small and medium-sized enterprises. Promote the establishment and improvement of multi-level capital market and unify all types of enterprises that are mainly foreign-funded enterprises in the tax institution as soon as possible. Implement tax support policies for entrepreneurship, employment, science and technology, service-oriented small and medium enterprises and regulate various administrative fees. Effectively create a more favorable development environment for the private sector.

Fourth, adhere to strengthen supervision and management according to law combined with rectification, standardize the order of the market economy and regulate individual business and private business operations. As for the sale of fake and shoddy goods by individuals and private enterprises, behaviors that result in harm to people's health, pollution of the environment, destruction of resources and other illegal acts, we must resolutely investigate and deal with it according to law. Strengthen tax publicity and education, improve individual and private owners according to law tax awareness. Strengthen tax collection and management, further improve methods and means of tax collection and management, gradually expand the individual private enterprises in the scope of collection and resolutely crack down on tax evasion.

Fifth, earnestly safeguard the rights and interests of workers. Strengthen the occupational safety and health supervision of individual and private enterprises, urge enterprises to strengthen labor protection, promote the establishment of safety production norms, effectively improve the working conditions and resolutely correct behaviors that violate workers' rights and interests, harm the safety and health of workers. Actively promote individual and private business owners and employees to participate in old-age insurance and basic medical insurance.

4. Encourage the development of civil society organizations such as chambers of commerce, trade associations and market intermediaries earnestly, and strengthen the self-discipline and normative development of private economic organizations

Due to historical factor and traditional institution, there are some problems such as lack of resources, lack of ability, lack of autonomy and lack of independence in the operation mechanism of the civil society organizations. There are barriers of high thresholds, restrictions, poor supervision and imperfect laws and regulations in the management institution. It lacks volunteer spirit, public spirit and social integrity in organizational culture, which requires more active and pragmatic support, guidance, supervision, nurture, to promote self-discipline and standard development of private economic organizations.

First, focus on promoting the transformation of government functions, speed up the separating pace of government and civil organizations, reform the trade association management institution and mode of operation thoroughly, and truly make it market-oriented, civilized and independent, entitle the private sector equal rights of normal survival and development in the market and gradually form the pattern of fair competition, mutual promotion and common development among industry associations and give full play of the important role of industry associations in the socialist market economy.

Second, improve and perfect functions of the Federation of Industry and Commerce at all levels. The Federation of Industry and Commerce should clarify the functions and institutionalize them. At the same time, it should promptly reflect to the government the problems existing in the development of non-public enterprises, create a relaxed and fair environment for enterprises, help non-public enterprises to strengthen communication with the government, provide information support, financing support and services, help enterprises improve their own quality and safeguard the legitimate rights and interests of enterprises. At the same time, strengthen the construction of the Federation of Industry and Commerce, especially the grassroots organizations, better play its various management and service functions and promote the rapid development of private economy.

Third, give full play to the role of trade associations and chambers of commerce. Encourage the bottom-up set-up of industry associations and chambers of commerce for the purpose of self-discipline and give full play to the role of intermediary organizations. Support industry associations and chambers of commerce to draw up industry development planning and industry service standards in accordance with the "self-management, self-service, self-coordination, self-restraint, self-education" approach; organize enterprises to accord with the law, self-discipline and get protected legally; Carry out industrial function carefully to make it truly become a bridge and link to promote the development of individual and private economy. Through publicity and education, guide individual and private business owners to carry out patriotism, dedication, integrity, law-abiding, ambitious to get rich and progress. Combine development of their own enterprises and development of the country together, combine individual wealth and common prosperity together and combine legal norms and moral norms together.

Fourth, improve the supervision institution of civil organizations. Change the existing "dual management model" of civil affairs departments and business departments. In order to promote the development of civil society organizations, including scientific research institutions, we should make fundamental change in the regulatory model on the basis of improving the legal institution, construct the regulatory institution combined by governmental supervision, juristic supervision, social supervision and industry self-discipline and focus on strengthening the supervision from the government, the judiciary and social forces.

8.2 Conclusions and policy suggestions of dynamic process of private economic system innovation

In this part, we mainly use the method of economic dynamic model to analyze the evolution of institutional innovation from the perspective of two key factors that restrict the development of private enterprises, that is, technological progress and information asymmetry, and draw some inspirational conclusions.

8.2.1 Main conclusions

In analyzing the dynamic process of private economic institutional innovation, we have come to the following conclusions: first, from the perspective of optimal technological progress rate, we find that the technological progress of private economy is not the faster the better. Second, through the analysis of the relationship between optimal patent system and dynamic efficiency of private economy, we find that both the optimal patent length and width are limited. Third, by constructing the model of endogenous economic growth to analyze the influence of asymmetry of quality information on the growth of knowledge and the development of private economy, we find that the asymmetry of quality information will not only lead to the shrinking of private economic products market, but also reduce the price of knowledge products and the investment of R & D, thus hindering the growth of knowledge.

1. Conclusion of the relationship between the rate of technological progress and the improvement of social welfare

This study builds an endogenous economic growth model to study a problem: that is, what is the optimal technological progress rate that the government should choose when pursuing maximized social welfare by choosing patent protection intensity. The results show that the higher the costs of inventions, the relatively lower for a country to maintain the rate of technological progress. When the invention costs are high, the effects of strengthening patent protection on social welfare will be weakened. Therefore, in order to maximize social welfare, the government should reduce patent protection intensity and the degree of distortions to the market. In addition, when the invention costs are high, the government should reduce patent protection intensity and make potential imitators threaten the inventor, forcing them to reduce the price of patented products, so that more end product manufacturers will enjoy the income brought by technological progress. Therefore, if the invention costs are high, this country should maintain a relatively lower rate of technological progress in order to pursue the maximization of social welfare.

2. Conclusion of the optimal patent length and optimal patent width

This study builds a dynamic general equilibrium model to study the optimal patent length and the optimal patent width to promote the development of private economy. The conclusion shows that both the optimal patent length and patent width are limited. Increasing patent length will increase the level of social welfare by promoting innovation; at the same time, it will also lead to distortions in the market, thereby reducing the level of social welfare. But with the continuous increase of the patent length, the latter effect will exceed the former effect. Therefore, the limited patent length is the best. The effective patent width should, on the one hand, make the quality of imitated products not too low to ensure that the imitation will pose a potential threat to patented products, therefore the price of patented products will be lower than monopoly price and market distortions will be reduced; on the other hand, make the quality of imitated products not too high to ensure that patented products will develop a higher monopoly price, therefore promoting innovation.

3. Conclusion of the relationship between information asymmetry and the development of private economy

This study constructs an endogenous economic growth model to analyze the impact of quality information asymmetry on knowledge growth and private economic development. The conclusion shows that the asymmetry of quality information will not only lead to the shrinking of private economy product market, but also reduce the price of knowledge products and the investment of R& D, thus hindering the growth of knowledge. As the growth rate of knowledge determines the long-term economic growth rate of a country, the asymmetry of quality information will hinder the innovation of knowledge and have far-reaching negative impacts on a country's private economy. At the same time, because the information asymmetry will reduce the level of social welfare, therefore, the community will give birth to some institutional arrangements to solve the problem of information asymmetry, so as to promote the development of a country's private economy.

8.2.2 Policy suggestions

1. Adjustment of patent protection level

China is a developing country with a large population but relatively scarce physical capital and human capital. As the invention and innovation requires relatively intensive investment of material capital and human capital, therefore, compared with developed countries, the costs of invention and innovation in China are relatively higher. This requires that our government should reduce the protection of patents: on the one hand, to reduce the degree of market distortions caused by patent rights granted to the inventors; on the other hand, to make potential imitators threaten the inventors, so as to reduce the price of patented products. In this way, more people will use the patented products and enjoy the benefits of technological inventions. At the same time, China's population is large; therefore, with the rapid economic development, China should gradually strengthen the protection of patents and enjoy the improvements of welfare. In other words, our policy should be: at this stage, we should reduce the protection of patents; later, with the rapid economic development, we should constantly strengthen the protection of patents. Since China's accession to the WTO, intellectual property protection have been increasingly strengthened under the pressure of developed countries. This may promote the inventions in our country. However, we must be clear that, from the stage of economic development in China, excessively harsh intellectual property protection may make it hard for our country to fully enjoy the benefits of technology, thereby reducing the welfare. Therefore, China should correctly handle the positive and negative effects of patent protection within the framework of the Agreement on Trade-Related Aspects of Intellectual Property Rights (TRIPS).

2. Establishment of product quality certification system

The asymmetry of quality information will allow low-quality products to expel high-quality products from the market. Therefore, in order to survive in the market, high-quality product manufacturers can often send signals. For example, investing huge advertising costs and participating in quality certification will distinguish their products from low-quality products, thereby solving the problem of information asymmetry. At the same time, because the information asymmetry will reduce the country's economic growth rate and social welfare level; therefore, a country has the incentive to develop appropriate institutions to solve the problem of information asymmetry. In addition, the development and implementation of corresponding institutions requires funds, so the government needs to impose a one-time cap tax on the firm (or personal income). Since the development and implementation of corresponding institutions will be beneficial to the whole society, the manufacturers (individuals) are willing to pay.

In reality, there are three main ways to solve the problem of quality information asymmetry: the government develops and implements the corresponding system; the enterprise sends the signal; the combination of government and enterprise. For manufacturers, through product quality certification, you can send a signal to the community and indicate that your products meet certain standards; for the country, product quality certification system is and important measure to solve the problem of quality information asymmetry. Therefore, this study believes that product quality certification system belongs to the third way. The government can formulate laws and regulations: if the company does not truthfully disclose information, it will be severely punished; in addition, certification marks will prevent corporate from fraud and shoddy, so as to solve the problem of quality information asymmetry. Enterprises can also create a brand to solve the problem of information asymmetry. With the economic development, China has more and more well-known brands. We will further study the other two ways to solve the problem of quality information asymmetry.

8.3 Conclusions and policy suggestions of entrepreneurial behavior of private enterprises and entrepreneurial environment

Since the reform and opening up, the rise of private economy has been considered an important driving force for China's economy to achieve sustained and rapid growth. Attaching great importance to civil power and encouraging private entrepreneurial activities are of great strategic significance to China in the 21st century. The development of private enterprises with innovative and entrepreneurial spirits has become the consensus of the government and the folk. Through empirical researches on entrepreneurial behavior, entrepreneurial activity and enterprise performance, we draw some enlightening conclusions and put forward some policy suggestions to improve the entrepreneurial environment.

8.3.1 Main conclusions

1. Entrepreneurship is the intertwined process between innovative, adventurous spirit and rational decision making

The rationality of entrepreneurial behavior is represented by the scientific nature of entrepreneur's access to entrepreneurial resources and response to environmental uncertainty, such as preferring partnership venture, focusing on service and emerging industries, valuing social capital, emphasizing innovative imitation and so on to control and reduce entrepreneurial risks. What's more, the intertwined process between innovative, adventurous spirit and rational decision making will finally determine the growth of new enterprises. This process is represented by a series of innovative behaviors that will promote and maintain the growth and development of new enterprises. Eventually, the rational elements of this kind of behavior will be integrated into the institution, culture, strategy and other parts of the enterprises.

2. Entrepreneurial environment has an important impact on corporate performance

Empirical analysis found that the internal entrepreneurial environment (IEE) was positively correlated with performance, while innovation and proactiveness were negatively correlated with performance. This conclusion is similar to that of other experts who studied Chinese issues.

Based on the study of 55 private enterprises in China and the interactive contingency model between entrepreneurial orientation (EO) and internal entrepreneurial environment (IEE), we find a significant positive correlation between entrepreneurial activity and firm performance. This conclusion is of great significance to the management of entrepreneurship: if we want long-term competitive advantage and extraordinary business performance, we should focus on two aspects, one is the senior management of entrepreneurial orientation; the other is the organization's internal entrepreneurial environment and institutional, cultural construction. However, most of our samples are traditional manufacturing enterprises, compared with high-tech enterprises, the environment they faced with is more confrontational and competitive, but lack of complexity and dynamism. We will use high-tech enterprises as sample in subsequent research for further verification. At the same time, it is also found that, compared with necessity entrepreneurship, opportunity entrepreneurship requires a higher match of entrepreneurial opportunity and entrepreneurial competency, and opportunity entrepreneurship is more dependent on favorable external circumstances. This means that the creation of entrepreneurial environment is the basic to encourage opportunity entrepreneurship, and entrepreneurial policy is an important way to enhance the number of opportunity entrepreneurship and to improve China's entrepreneurial structure.

3. Differences between opportunity and necessity entrepreneurship

Compared with the opportunity type, on the one hand, the necessity type is more reluctant to bear the risk of entrepreneurship; besides, the entrepreneurial purpose is to seek changes in the state of survival instead of the pursuit of self-realization. From the perspective of survey subjects, the MBA group is mainly concentrated in the opportunity type which is based on seizing opportunities, while the mass group is focused on necessity entrepreneurship which is based on getting out of poverty. In addition, the difference between opportunity and necessity entrepreneurship will influence the entrepreneurial process in terms of growth desire and choice of financing channels. On the other hand, by distinguishing the differences between opportunity and necessity entrepreneurship, it is helpful to identify policy recommendations for poverty-driven entrepreneurship, meet their unique policy needs and improve the level of necessity entrepreneurship, which is of great practical significance to address the problems facing vulnerable groups in China.

4. Differences between entrepreneurial policy and the policy of small and medium-sized enterprises

Firstly, unlike the policy of small and medium-sized enterprises, entrepreneurial policy is focused on 42 months after the start-up of entrepreneurial activities, while the SME policy is located from the start-up phase to stable expansion interval. Secondly, there is an organic link between these two. The 42-month from the start-up phase is the common focus for both of them, which will provide a relaxed environment for entrepreneurial activity and to increase its survival rate; finally, the focus of entrepreneurial policy is to build an entrepreneurial environment system, and to seek the match of entrepreneurial opportunities and entrepreneurial ability; the purpose is to enhance the overall level of entrepreneurial activities, and expand the scale of small and medium-sized enterprises. The focus of SME policy is to create a relaxed and favorable environment through a series of measures; the aim is to help new enterprises with growth potential and desire to achieve rapid expansion and growth. From this point, the entrepreneurial policy constitutes the basis of SME policy: without the support of business policy, SME policy will become a castle in the air.

The above conclusions are of great significance to enhance the overall innovation level of China's private enterprises. The public resources of our government are too focused on supporting the innovative activities of existing private enterprises, and neglect new private enterprises that have the potential for innovation. In other words, the existing policy measures mainly focus on the policy areas of small and medium-sized enterprises, but lack of effective support for entrepreneurial policies. This is why our government has invested a lot of public resources to improve the overall innovation level of private enterprises but has achieved little effects.

8.3.2 Policy suggestions

1. To use the policy of creating entrepreneurial opportunities to strengthen the construction of entrepreneurial environment

At present, our government should pay attention to the reduction of entrepreneurial cost, but cannot stay here. Policies which focus on the creation of entrepreneurial opportunities is the fundamental condition for the construction of business environment, and its foothold is to create favorable economic conditions and technical conditions. Specifically, for areas where the economy is relatively backward, the government should combine regional resource conditions to identify, expand, develop and even create local products and services markets to stimulate economic growth and create entrepreneurial opportunities for new market needs; for relatively developed areas, the government should enhance the investment in R & D funds to create new opportunities for entrepreneurship.

2. To distinguish the lack of entrepreneurial capacity and to develop flexible policy measures according to specific circumstances

To enhance the level of entrepreneurial ability and to seek the match between entrepreneurial ability and entrepreneurial opportunity should be the emphasis of current policy, whose focus is to create favorable social and cultural conditions, and an education and training system for entrepreneurship. Specifically, in areas where the willingness to start a business is low and the entrepreneurial capacity is relatively high, the government should improve the social and cultural environment through the formulation of relevant policies and the implementation of certain projects. Short-term interventions include: best entrepreneurship awards, trade fairs and other activities which will reward entrepreneurs; long-term policies involve education of entrepreneurial value. In areas where the willingness of entrepreneurship is high and entrepreneurial capacity is relatively low, the government should focus on policies that will enhance potential entrepreneurship and business skills. Effective interventions include: technical and vocational training, setting up short-term start-up courses and workshops. In areas where the willingness of entrepreneurship and entrepreneurial skills are low, financial assistance alone will not solve the problem. At the same time, we should adopt a policy of creating social and cultural conditions and establishing an education and training system in order to strengthen the entrepreneurial intention and improve the entrepreneurial capacity as a whole.

3. To pay attention to the differences between business policy and SME policy and to effectively link up the support policy and the innovation policy

Entrepreneurial policy and SME policy is an organic unity, these two are complementary and indispensable. The focus of entrepreneurial policy is to create a business environment and to seek the match of entrepreneurial opportunity and entrepreneurial ability. The effective integration of entrepreneurial policy and SME policy is the key to enhance the level of innovation. In practice, the government should focus on two aspects. First, to provide a more relaxed environment for potential entrepreneurs through the development of relevant policies, which include: the development of patent and intellectual property on legal norms, the improvement of government work procedures, the simplification of registration process, the contraction of registration time, and the reduction of operating costs. Second, to vigorously foster financial and non-financial support systems for new enterprises, improve access to capital, provide technical support, nurture industrial clusters, improve tax environment, enhance the level of entrepreneurial education, and fund entrepreneurs.

4. To use the operation mode of "working capital" and to extensively mobilize social forces to participate in the construction of entrepreneurial environment

Entrepreneurial environment construction is a complex system. It cannot fully rely on government power and must mobilize social forces to participate in. Experiences have shown that individuals and organizations can play a role in the construction of support services outside the policy area. There are two aspects for entrepreneurs to consider whether or not to accept external services, the effect of the service and the cost of the service. The mere provision of services by government agencies is often inefficient, while the private sector will give priority to profitability when providing services. Therefore, it is possible to use the "working capital" mode of operation, that is, the government provide partial capital as development funds to support research center or service agencies to provide "public goods and services" to the majority of small and medium-sized enterprises, such as free lectures, general consulting and information services, etc.; besides, the government should also stipulate that these research centers or service agencies must provide free services in order to expand the scope of services. At the same time, these research centers or service agencies cannot rely entirely on government funding. They should obtain income through the provision of special services in order to maintain normal operations. With the enhancement of viability and competitiveness of service agencies, the government can gradually reduce or even stop capital investment. On the one hand, it can ensure the guidance and supervision; on the other hand, it can make the service activities take into account the creation of business environment and growth environment.

5. To value both the construction and improvement measures to solve the problem of constructing entrepreneurial environment

China cannot be left behind in the global wave of entrepreneurship, and also need to cultivate outstanding private enterprises to promote the reconstruction of national economy and the upgrade of industrial structure, which requires both the construction and the improvement measures in the development of solving environmental issues; that is, on the one hand, to build entrepreneurial environment system, on the other hand, to improve the defects and deficiencies within the existing system. The GEM report shows that, on the whole, China can meet the needs of entrepreneurs in terms of government funds and policy support, entrepreneurial culture and tangible infrastructure and other historical and hardware aspects; while there are serious shortcomings in soft environments such as finance, service, business environment and government policy, which constitute the basic direction of improving the entrepreneurial environment.

8.4 Conclusions and policy suggestions of financing obstacles for private enterprises

In the context of transition economy, the development of private enterprise is subject to financial constraints. In this book, we systematically analyze the mechanism of endowment difference and institutional rent change on financing choice in private enterprises under the framework of a new theory, and study the financing and structural problems of private enterprise. We have come to some enlightening conclusions and put forward several policy recommendations to optimize financing channels.

8. 4. 1 Main conclusions

1. Institutional evolution determines the development mode of private economy

In the process of marketization, different combinations and synergistic evolution of state-owned economic influence, local government power and marketization level under specific endowment conditions lead to different institutional rent level and decreasing rate in different regions, which will determine the specific development mode and evolution path. The initial endowment determines the development mode in the beginning, which constitutes the historical starting point of the evolution of the private economy in a region. The reduction rate of institutional rent determines the concrete evolution path of the private economy. Different combinations of "historical starting point + dynamic evolution path" have led to a variety of private economic development model and the corresponding financing model. In a given area, the higher the reduction rate of institutional rent, the faster the development of private economy; the higher the institutional rent, the more serious the financing constraints faced by private enterprises.

2. Institutional rent determines the financing options of private enterprises

In the process of private economic development, the institutional rent level and its reduction rate will determine the development of private economy and its financing options. The higher the rent level, the more serious the financing constraints faced by private enterprises. The faster the reduction rate, the faster the development of private economy and the more financing options. In the case of rapid development of market mechanism, the market orientation of state-owned banks will also be stronger and the loans provided to private economy will increase. Of course, the rate of increase in loans will still be lower than the pace of development of private economy.

3. The structural contradictions of private enterprise financing is greater than the total contradiction

On the whole, private economy has received about 57.32% of the financial resources with its contribution accounts for 63% of GDP. Private enterprises are still faced with financing constraints. There are significant structural contradictions and regional differences. From the perspective of total amount, private finance has played an important role in the improvement of financing constraints for private enterprise. From the perspective of financing structure, due to the lag of formal private financial development and the limitations of the private finance itself, the funds obtained from private sector (including the developed regions) are mainly short-term. From the regional point of view, the more developed areas of private economy, the lower financing constraints faced by private enterprises, but structural problems still exist. In this sense, because of the non-standardized development of private finance, the financing channels are still poor and the financing structure is still unreasonable.

4. The more developed the private economy, the higher the contribution of private finance and the lower the contribution of state-owned finance

The role of private finance in different development stages of private economy is different. From the perspective of absolute value of the scale of private finance, the greater the scale of the private sector, the greater the scale of private finance; from the perspective of share of private finance in unit private economy output, the faster the development of private finance, the greater contributions to the financing of private enterprises. At the same time, the stronger the market orientation of state-owned financial institutions, the better the financing environment and the more financing channels. At this point, the proportion of corporate debt financing and corporate debt ratio in developed countries is basically the same (but lack of long-term capital). However, the less developed the private economy, the narrower the financing channels andthe higher the degree of dependence on private finance. This is because in primary stage of the development of private economy, the demand for funds is strong, their ability to accumulate is weak and the output value is low, and thus they will be more dependent on private finance. In the middle stage of private enterprises, their ability to accumulate is enhanced and private enterprises mainly rely on themselves to accumulate and develop.

The role of state-owned finance in different development stages of private economy is also different. The more developed private economy, the larger the scale of loans; the reduction rate of institutional rent will not only have a key impact on the development of private economy, but also will determine the financing options of private enterprise. The faster the reduction rate, the faster the development of the private economy and the more financing options. In the case of the rapid development of the market mechanism, the stronger the market orientation of the state-owned banks, the more loans provided to the private economy. This also shows that in the development of China's market, the process of market-oriented state-owned financial institutions is far behind the process of market-oriented private economy; the more developed the private economy, the lower the dependence on state-owned financial institutions.

8.4.2 Policy suggestions

1. To deepen the reform of banking system and to improve the indirect financing system of private enterprises

First, deepen the privatization reform of state-owned commercial banks and improve its corporate governance mechanism. Due to the lack of ownership and soft budget constraints of state-owned economy, it is difficult for state-owned commercial banks to establish a perfect corporate governance mechanism and inefficiently use resources. Therefore, it is an important way to solve the problem of low efficiency of state-owned commercial banks by promoting the privatization reform of financial institutions, promoting the improvement of corporate governance mechanism and increasing operational efficiency through the diversification of ownership structure. The introduction of private investors in financial reforms will be conducive not only to the optimization of state-owned commercial banks and the improvement of operational efficiency, but also to guide the positive role of private capital.

Through privatization reform, commercial banks will establish a market-oriented operation mechanism with the basic principle of "efficiency" theory rather than "composition" theory. Banks should promote fair credit between private and state-owned enterprises. For private enterprises with development potential, banks should also give credit support, especially for private enterprises with better qualifications. Banks should focus on helping them start and develop. For many small and medium-sized private enterprises, banks should innovate the credit system, explore flexible credit, provide credit support for private enterprises through "relationship financing" and other means, and share the fruits of private enterprise development.

Second, guide and standardize the development of private finance, vigorously develop local small and medium-sized financial institutions, and improve the multi-level indirect financing system. Under the premise of prudence, we should establish and improve the SME market access and exit standards, risk management system, competition rules and management practices as soon as possible, guide and standardize the development of private finance. Develop multi-level, multi-ownership, and multi-form of financial institutions, and create a financial service system which is complementary between state-owned commercial banks and private financial institutions. First of all, as mentioned above, through privatization reform, we can improve corporate governance mechanism of state-owned banks. Second, standardize the development of private finance. On the basis of existing civil financial institutions, we should guide and regulate its development to local small and medium-sized banks, such as urban cooperative banks, urban credit cooperatives, foundations, gold deposit and so on. The underlying factors that determine the development of financial services are information and credit which is based on information; local small and medium-sized financial institutions are able to make full use of local (community) information and are most likely to understand the operation status, project prospects and credit status of local SMEs at the lowest cost. Mastering this information can save a lot of research time and costs and reduce the cost of financial business. Private enterprises have the characteristics of large number, small size and wide geographical distribution. This determines that there should be appropriate financial institutions (small, local private institutions) to provide service for them. The neglect of grassroots financial institutions has made China's financial architecture lack of hierarchy and fail to meet the requirements of economic development. Therefore, the construction of small and medium-sized local private financial institutions can not only solve the financing difficulties, but also be conducive to long-term economic development. To this end, the local government should actively support the development of small and medium-sized financial institutions through various means, accelerate the construction of its modern facilities, and carry out risk supervision according to law. Local small and medium-sized banks also need to improve the level of financial services, innovate financial service tools, actively organize deposits, absorb customers, enhance financial strength, improve lending capacity, develop appropriate loan policy, guide the industry and promote industrial upgrading and structural adjustment of private enterprise.

Third, implement the reform of interest rate market and improve the enthusiasm and autonomy of bank lending. Private enterprise loans have two characteristics: First, the unit cost is relatively high. As the single financing amount of private enterprise is small and each loan must go through a certain audit procedure, so the fixed costs are roughly the same, which results in a higher cost of unit loans. Second, the risk is relatively large. The social credit system and the bank's credit record of private enterprises are not perfect, resulting in increased uncertainty and risks about the loans of private enterprises. Coupled with the imperfection and low transparency of private enterprise's own governance mechanism, commercial banks have to pay a higher unit loan cost and bear greater risks, it is bound to require additional risk premium to compensate. Therefore, we should further relax the restrictions on bank loan interest rates and transaction costs, so that the more flexible interest rates will give full play to the leverage of interest rates, and banks will have more profitability space and get access to real economic interests.

2. To improve the direct financing system and to develop multi-level, multi-species capital market

First, the establishment of multi-level capital market: the second board market, regional small capital market (i. e. the third board market), and venture capital market. In terms of its division of labor, the second board market mainly deals with the financing problems of small and medium-sized enterprises in the later stage of the venture; the regional small capital market mainly provides financing services for small and medium-sized private enterprises that cannot meet the qualification standards of the second board market; the venture capital market is specifically to provide private equity capital for small and medium enterprises in their early stage.

Second, the positive development of corporate bond market and long-term bill market, and the enrichment of capital market transactions types. From the long-term development trend, the position of bond financing will gradually increase within direct financing structure. From the experiences of mature market, bond financing has significant advantages: (1) bond financing is conducive to private enterprises to improve the sense of integrity and improve corporate governance mechanism. The biggest difference between corporate bonds and bank loans is liquidity. As many corporate bonds are traded on the exchange, the issuer must make detailed, complete and continuous information disclosure on its own financial condition, operation and risk control, which is conducive to enhancing the corporate governance level of the enterprise itself. (2) debt financing will improve the efficiency of the company's free cash flow. (3) debt financing will not change or transfer the company's total equity and structure, which can eliminate the concerns of corporate control for private enterprise owners. (4) the development of bond market is conducive for private enterprises to optimize financing structure and improve resource utilization efficiency.

3. To improve the government service system and to increase government support

First, improve the legal system. The basic law of small and medium-sized enterprises is often referred to as the constitution of small and medium-sized enterprises. It is the basis for government management and support and the basis for the legislature to formulate specific laws and regulations of small and medium-sized enterprises. It is also the basis for government departments to formulate specific policies.

Second, increase financial and tax support, and increase tax incentives for private enterprises. Such as the implementation of tax incentives for the newly opened individual industrial and commercial households; the implementation of tax incentives for private enterprises who have made great contributions to the community; to strengthen the management of fees and charges to prevent arbitrary charges and fines.

Third, improve the credit system and establish a multi-level, multi-channel credit guarantee system. The government should use the regulatory system to gradually create an atmosphere of honesty and trustworthiness in the whole society. The government should also use modern information tools to achieve the joint collection, professional assessment, authoritative release and multiple share of the social credit system. At the same time, it should build a multi level, multi-channel credit guarantee system: (1) the establishment of a credit guarantee system which views the government as the main body. (2) the establishment of commercial security system. (3) the establishment of mutual guarantee system. (4) to explore the core customers for a large number of "satellite" small and medium enterprises in order to provide a guarantee model and make full use of rich credit resources.

8.5 Conclusions and policy suggestions of institutional environment in the process of internationalization of private enterprises

In the context of the deepening of international division of labor and international market competition, it is necessary to study the way of private enterprises to enhance international competitiveness. This part of the study firstly follows the classical SCP paradigm in industrial organization theory, analyzes the relationship between the export behavior of private enterprises and their performance, and puts forward some corresponding policy suggestions. Secondly, from the perspective of international division of labor and value chain, we analyze the typical market "compartment" problem of private enterprise export and put forward some corresponding solutions. Finally, taking Zhejiang province as an example, this book studies the institutional barriers and supply problems in the development of private enterprises' foreign trade and exports, and clarifies the comparative benefits obtained from the international division of labor and trade in a country or region: it not only depends on the optimization of export product structure on the technical level, but also depends on the institutional innovation of foreign trade management on the organizational level.

8.5.1 Main conclusions

1. The degree of horizontal differentiation is low

First, the imitation competition and vicious price competition are quite common, the enterprise lack market forces. Most of our private enterprises are close to the atomic type and the horizontal differentiation is not significant. From the perspective of a single enterprise, the scale of private enterprises in China is generally small and the production of similar products is huge, so the behavior of one enterprise will have no significant impact on other manufacturers. Enterprises do not distinguish between limited horizontal differentiation and other companies. The lack of ability to transform this limited horizontal differentiation into "market forces", that is, the lack of ability to influence and control market prices, has led to the downward of price competition with other firms. Because the horizontal differentiation of product is not normally compensated, this has led to imitative competition. The imitative competition will further intensify horizontal homogenization and downward vicious price competition.

Second, the coexistence of horizontal differentiation and horizontal homogeneity. Private enterprises, which product similar products, usually gather in a specific geographical area and form external economies of scale and economy of scope on the basis of ultra-fine specialized division of labor; besides, they breakthrough "production possibility frontier" of horizontal differentiation and form a higher level of horizontal differentiation which is based on enterprise clusters. But at the same time, due to the fact that a large number of similar private enterprises find it difficult to form a "price collusion", a single enterprise cannot rely on enterprise clusters to obtain market power which is brought about by the external economy. The transfer of market power from cluster level to enterprise level is still a problem to be solved.

2. The degree of vertical differentiation is low

First, lack the incentives of upward vertical differentiation. Most of our private enterprises developed from the original "classical enterprise", which have the general characteristics of extensive, endogenous and expansive in the market competition, and focus on the production and sale of low-quality products for a long time. Besides, because the industrial organization of private economy is small and scattered, the development of high-end product has become a "luxury" consumption to a certain extent. The above two aspects have led to the huge costs of upward vertical differentiation in private enterprises. At the same time, due to the imperfection of market and institution environment, and the prevalent imitation competition, the upward product innovation income is difficult to be effectively protected and innovation income is likely to be dispersed in a short time. As a result, China's private enterprises lack the incentive of upward vertical differentiation.

Second, entry barriers have strengthened low-quality vertical differentiation. Production of high-quality products have some requirements for enterprise in equipment, capital, technology, management, scale and other aspects, which is unattainable for original private enterprises. In fact, even if most private enterprises are willing to carry out upward vertical differentiation, they will still find it difficult to go beyond entry barriers. In addition, the current foreign trade "separation" has strengthened this kind of entry barriers from another aspect, and made it difficult for private enterprises to grasp market demand, and made it less possible for them to sense product innovation, technology innovation, and institution innovation invoked by market opportunities, and finally led to the fact that these enterprises have become the workshop for low-quality products. As a result, China's private enterprises generally adopted the strategy of vertical differentiation for low-quality products. The problem is that the way to maximize the differentiation by reducing product quality will be narrower and narrower.

3. Low concentration of market structure led to the lack of market forces

There is a positive relationship between market concentration and market performance or profitability. China's private economy is led by core-free atom-oriented enterprises, and has "small and scattered" industrial organization. Low market concentration of industrial organization structure led to imitation competition, crowded phenomenon in the use of resources and the lack of power and capacity to change from family traditions to modern management; thus, it is difficult to obtain scale economy advantages in wholesale and distribution. So far, China's private economy has not yet formed a large-scale core or leading enterprise to internalize other "small and scattered" enterprises; due to the similar size of many small businesses, a certain degree of "price collusion" is difficult to form. The low concentration of similar market has led to Bertrand competition: the lack of market power, the sharp decline of market profits, and even vicious price competitions. These enterprises suffer from export losses and foreign anti-dumping litigation.

8.5.2 Policy suggestions

1. Policy suggestions on improving export performance of private enterprises

For the government, the focus is to promote the process of enterprise product differentiation, to help integrate the loose industrial organization, and to support enterprises to obtain market power.

First, to promote the reform of the Chamber of Commerce, to strengthen the intermediary organizations of industry norms and services, to reorganize the Chamber of Commerce and Industry Association, to cultivate the agency function of the Chamber of Commerce, to amend the "Anti-Unfair Competition Law" and "Anti-monopoly Law", and to give "monopoly" right to the Chamber of Commerce, associations and other organizations in export trade and other aspects.

Second, the construction of regional product innovation system is conducive to promoting the process of product differentiation. The government should support large enterprises to establish their own technology development institutions; strengthen the support of R&D; increase the investment in government research.

Third, to encourage and develop all kinds of higher education, especially vocational and technical education. The implementation of product differentiation strategy is highly relied on the support of talents. Higher education, especially vocational and technical education which is closely related to actual industry, can quickly and effectively reduce the entry barriers in the production of high-quality products.

Fourth, to combine the construction and development of various industrial parks with the promotion of product differentiation. The construction of industrial park should pay attention to the protection of cooperation system. The government should focus on the design and guide of system, mechanism and policy, support and encourage the implementation of product differentiation strategy. For example, to encourage the establishment of enterprise alliance and attract similar famous enterprises at home and abroad. To consider the brand, market power (rather than market share), economic density, technological innovation and internationalization as measuring indicators for the construction of industrial park.

2. The way to solve the "separation" problem of private enterprises' export market

First, correctly guide and encourage private export enterprises to set up various types of sales centers or research and development centers in foreign countries. In particular, to encourage and support private export enterprises with a certain scalefirstly set up management center or R & D center in foreign countries, and provide corresponding entry and exit, institutional settings and other policy support.

Second, change the differential treatment of enterprises practices, eliminate "ownership discrimination" and "scale discrimination" in foreign investment approval. The current management system and policies have set more obstacles for private enterprises and SMEs compared with state-owned enterprises and large enterprises. As a pilot reform, we can first give private enterprises with a certain scale the same treatment as state-owned large enterprises, and then gradually implement same treatment for all enterprises.

Third, the construction of knowledge and technical assistance projects aimed at OEM private export enterprises. First, help and strengthen the training and technical guidance of OEM private export enterprises practitioners, improve the technology absorptive capacity of enterprises; guide, encourage and help private enterprises to establish their own R&D institutions. Second, support "common technology research and development center" in specialized export base which product similar products.

Fourth, the establishment of domestic and foreign productivity promotion center. The task and function of this center is to overcome the "separation problem" in private sector, and to carry out the work of information consultation, knowledge and technology assistance.

3. To improve and promote the system of foreign trade export of private enterprises

First, the reform of foreign trade administration system. Responsible institutions at all levels should regulate in accordance with the requirements of open market economy, weaken administrative intervention on micro-economy, strengthen indirect macro-management, strengthen the guidance of foreign trade and economic planning, policy guidance, administrative services and supervision, change the government priority from approval and management of specific matters to planning and policies of foreign economic and trade development, so as to create a better institutional environment. The relevant policies, such as the quota for import and export commodities, should be standardized and published in the form of government announcements. In order to jointly create a better environment for the development of private enterprise, the government should strengthen the sense of service, strengthen the coordination and cooperation with customs, immigration inspection and quarantine, taxation and other departments, and implement unified and transparent policies and administrative rules.

Second, the establishment of foreign trade and economic promotion system. Specifically: first, to use tax rates, exchange rates, interest rates and other economic means to adjust foreign trade and economic activities, so that unnecessary administrative power will gradually withdraw from the market; to improve the export tax rebate mechanism to achieve full and timely tax rebates; to ensure that private enterprises and other enterprises are treated equally without discrimination. Second, to establish and improve the export credit system, to adjust the use of foreign trade development fund, to establish a synchronous growth mechanism for export growth and credit scale, and to provide necessary financial support for small and medium-sized private production enterprises to expand exports; to expand the scale and field of export credit insurance and to provide a comprehensive policy of investment and trade insurance business for private enterprises; to establish export enterprises financing guarantee fund to solve the problem of insufficient financing. Third, to provide quality service and policy support for enterprises in Zhejiang province in terms of foreign exchange management and foreign affairs management. Fourth, to take some financial support measures. Such as the implementation of export subsidies to optimize export structure and expand export scale; the foreign trade and financial sector should give some subsidies for enterprises to participate in overseas exhibition booths; to encourage brand competition.

4. To establish industry associations and commercial organizations and to improve foreign trade intermediary service system

We should learn from the experiences of Zhejiang, promote the reform of chambers of commerce and associations, modify the Anti-Unfair Competition Law and the Anti-monopoly Law, and give certain "monopoly" immunity to the chambers of commerce, associations and other organizations in export trade.

8.6 Conclusions and policy suggestions of evaluation on the governance of private listed companies

There is a prominent phenomenon inprivate listed companies: after being listed, the performance tends to decline and the return on investment tends to be low, the key issue lies in corporate governance barriers. In this regard, this chapter constructs four main dimensions of evaluation index of private listed company governance, including the board, ownership structure, executive incentive and restraint, and information disclosure. We found some problems in the management of private listed companies, and put forward the corresponding policy recommendations to improve the management of private listed companies.

8.6.1 Main conclusions

1. Group control is the main factor that evokes encroachment behavior

Due to the existence of group control that increases the deviation of ultimate controllers between control rights and cash flow right, the costs of control right benefit declined. What the UCs do to pursue the benefits of control right would damage the value of company. The extent and probability of other minority shareholders' interests being damaged would be increased due to strong entrenchment effects. Ownership structure of PCs becomes the main factor of evoking the entrenchment effects behaviors in the context of further strengthening group control. Because of the existence of inner shareholders group, ownership structure did not develop into an effective counterweight. As persons acting in concert, the inner shareholders group's behavior completely embodies the will of the UC and becomes the tool of entrenchment effects behaviors acted by UCs.

2. The board of directors presents the characteristics of "major shareholder control"

Unlike the "operator control" of state-owned LCs, Chinese PLCs show apparently "major shareholders control". The vast majority of directors serve as other positions at the same time in PLCs which must have a significant impact on their fulfilling the duties of directors. Major shareholders control can solve the issue of "absence of owners". However, when the benefits of major shareholders and other small shareholders are not consistent, there would be agent problems between major shareholders and small shareholders which increase the private benefits of major shareholders in short term. On the contrary it would damage the long-term financing capacity of LCs which is detrimental to the LCs' long-term development.

3. Executive compensation level is low and the correlation between executive shareholding ratio and company performance is nonlinear

Although the level of executive compensation equals to average level of industry market in China, executive compensation of PLCs in china is significantly correlated with index of CP which fully implies that on the one hand PLCs still spare no efforts to make executive compensation and CP tied closely, on the other hand "family contract" play important role of motivation and restriction in PLCs replacing "contract economy" to some extent. Another major finding is that relation between shareholding rate of senior executives and CP of PLCs is non-linear which reflects complicated agent relation in PLCs and the impacts of multi-purposes of senior executives on PLCs' behavior.

4. The governance mechanism of the board of supervisors needs to be further improved

Strong regional disparities and certain industrial differences are presented in PLCs' supervisory board governance and the overall level is not high. Besides proportion of employee supervisors and motivation of members in supervisory board are low relatively. And it is common that supervisors are employed in the largest shareholders' companies.

5. The enthusiasm of information disclosure and the independence of audit opinion are gradually improving

The study found that the enthusiasm of private listed companies and the independence of the audit opinion is gradually improving the independence of the accounting firm's influence is improving. The independent director system has played an important role in improving the information disclosure of listed companies, which proves that the independent director system has played a positive role in the domestic securities market. But the research shows that the characteristics of listed companies themselves still largely affect the audit opinion. That is, the accounting firm has a tendency to condone a good or large-scale listed company, the risk of large companies are demanding. This shows to some extent, the reform of the domestic information disclosure mechanism there is still a long way to go, not through the improvement of the legal system can be achieved in the short term.

8.6.2 Policy suggestions

1. Strengthen the supervision on group controlling phenomenon in PLC and improve related institutions. The rationality and legality of related party transaction in PLCs with grouping controlling should be strengthened.

2. Encourage private companies whose shareholders are natural persons to be listed directly. Meanwhile constrain the hierarchy of grouping controlling by legislation from international experiences. The cost of controlling rights benefits is supposed to be controlled within a certain scale.

3. Positively promote the institution construction with the core of improving the independence of board of directors. Complete the internal mechanism of PLCs step by step, restrain and guide the ultimate controllers' behavior.

4. Gradually improve the governance level of board of supervisors in PLCs. Enlarge the size of board of supervisors, and increase the ratio of staff involvement. Commit the comprehensive incentive methods between supervisory secure incentive and risk incentive. Normalize the nomination of supervisors and promote the normalization of the meeting of board of supervisors.

5. The fair and effective information disclosure mechanism would be the institutional guarantee for the long-term and stable development of security market in China. Recently, the law system of Chinese information disclosure has been gradually completed and form the law system focusing on the law, administration rules and accounting regulations. And relatively completed information disclosure mechanism would be formed by external auditing committed by account firms. The information disclosure evaluation index in PLCs indicates that information disclosure is supposed to be further strengthened, and the standards of information disclosure and the level of grouping controlling should be linked together. The disclosure of controlling situation of PLC should be strengthened. Besides, the situation of related party companies

controlled by the same ultimate controller and the related directors' information are needed to be further refined and enriched. The hierarchical management should be done to the standards of information disclosure which are needed to be linked with the complexity of grouping controlling.

This book is the result of a co-publication agreement between Economic Science Press (China) and Paths International Ltd (UK).

This book is published with the financial support of the Chinese Fund for the Humanities and Social Sciences

----

Title: China's Private Economy: Institution Innovations and Development
Author: Li Wei'an et al.
Translated by Liu Xingyun, Wang Yujin
ISBN: 978-1-84464-492-6
Ebook ISBN: 978-1-84464-493-3

Paths International Ltd

Published in the United Kingdom
www.pathsinternational.com

CPSIA information can be obtained
at www.ICGtesting.com
Printed in the USA
LVHW100238130419
614016LV00008B/44/P

9 781844 644926